The Mammoth Book of

INSIDE THE
ELITE FORCES

The Mammoth Book of

INSIDE THE ELITE FORCES

Training, Equipment and Endeavours of British and American Elite Combat Units

NIGEL CAWTHORNE

ROBINSON   RUNNING PRESS
PHILADELPHIA · LONDON

Constable & Robinson Ltd
3 The Lanchesters
162 Fulham Palace Road
London W6 9ER
www.constablerobinson.com

First published in the UK by Robinson,
an imprint of Constable & Robinson, 2008

A copy of the British Library Cataloguing in Publication
Data is available from the British Library

UK ISBN 978-1-84529-821-0
1 3 5 7 9 10 8 6 4 2

First published in the United States in 2008 by
Running Press Book Publishers

9 8 7 6 5 4 3 2 1
Digit on the right indicates the number of this printing

US Library of Congress number: 2008926178
US ISBN 978-0-7624-3382-7

Running Press Book Publishers
2300 Chestnut Street
Philadelphia, PA 19103-4371

Visit us on the web!

www.runningpress.com

Printed and bound in the EU

CONTENTS

Part Three – Equipment

Part Four – In Action

INTRODUCTION

The Special Forces are in action now. Units are deployed on covert actions in Iraq and Afghanistan, carrying out specialist actions that ordinary soldiers are not equipped or trained for. Others are on standby, waiting to counter the latest move by terrorists or insurgents, or undertaking special operations for friendly governments who have no elite forces of their own.

It takes a special kind of person to join the Special Forces and those who pass the stringent entrance requirements are subjected to the most rigorous training. They are trained to be super-fit, taught to survive in the most adverse conditions and turned into killing machines. Although they must be good team players, they must also be able to work on their own initiative. And they are trained to use a whole variety of specialist equipment.

Although Special Forces personnel are usually picked from serving soldiers and marines, few have the physical stamina to qualify for elite units. Many potential recruits who arrive at the SAS training centre in Hereford, England, cannot even complete the first week of endurance exercises. Only 10 per cent complete the induction course. The final exercise in the selection process is a 40-mile endurance march over rough terrain, carrying 80 lb of kit, usually in adverse weather conditions, navigating by map and compass and completed in just twenty hours. The US Delta Force has adopted the same test and finds that only one in four of the men they have pre-selected make it.

Of the thousands who apply to join the Green Berets, only a handful are picked for the Q (Qualification) Course. When they arrive at the training centre in North Carolina, they are required to run the mile-and-a-half to their makeshift barracks carrying their kit. Some fail the Q Course before they have even reached the barrack gates. Fifty per cent fail the physical part of the training. Another 25–40 per cent drop out during their specialist training, before they are even allowed on a simulated "unconventional warfare" exercise.

The US Navy SEALs go through "Hell Week", which is designed to drive recruits to the absolute limits of their physical endurance, so that in action they can overcome pain and fatigue by sheer willpower and concentrate thereby on completing the mission.

"Even if a guy is an absolute physical stud, it doesn't mean he's going to get through Hell Week," one instructor said.

Their UK equivalent, the SBS, are recruited from the Royal Marine Commandos, already an elite unit whose assault course even hardened US Marines on secondment are loath to attempt.

Once recruits have been selected they are taught basic first aid and survival. They get to use weapons they have never handled before and learn the combat procedures that separate the Special Forces from regular units. These include covert manoeuvres, reconnaissance techniques, insertion methods, signalling, encryption, communications, navigation and contact drills. They are taught demolition, the handling of various combat vehicles, patrol techniques, the use of camouflage, ambushing, hostage-rescue procedures and live-fire drills. Combat survival training takes recruits to the Arctic, the desert and the jungle, where they are taught how to find food and water, how to make fire and shelter, and how to survive natural disasters. These techniques are put to the test when recruits are abandoned, alone, in only the clothes they stand up in, in the most hostile environments.

Recruits are given parachute training, taught escape and evasion techniques, and subjected to realistic, even brutal, interrogations. If it appears a recruit is going to break at any point, he is sent back to his unit. Language and engineering skills are put to the test. Weapons training gives them the chance to familiarize themselves with foreign weapons – the kind they may be up against – as well as the specialist tools of the trade. In all, they will learn to handle thirty to fifty small arms. They are taught to abandon the regular soldier's "spray and pray" method of fighting and to make every bullet count. Alongside small arms, recruits are trained to handle large anti-personnel, anti-aircraft and anti-armour systems, including the Russian RPG7, now the most common anti-tank system in the world which, a recent edition of *Soldier* magazine said, could be picked up from street markets in the world's trouble spots for as little as $10. They are also taught unarmed combat.

Special Forces have access to very sophisticated vehicle-mounted weapons. They are taught how to call in artillery and air strikes, and targeting for laser-guided bombs. They practise how to throw grenades and lay mines. The recognition of planes, tanks, armoured vehicles and other military hardware has to be mastered; and they must learn how to use night-vision goggles, homing beacons, radio transmitters, surveillance equipment and a host of other kit.

US Navy SEALs and the SBS must learn to dive and handle a canoe, as well as landing craft and inflatables. They must be familiar with specialized scuba equipment that recycles the air to produce no bubbles, underwater escape and rescue, various types of submarine and underwater explosives. They are forced to run, even eat, waist deep in water.

Everything Special Forces recruits learn is put to the test in realistic combat situations before they are allowed to join their unit. Only then can they call themselves one of the elite.

This book tells you everything you need to know to become a member of one of the UK's or US's elite forces. It covers the origins of the various units and their role in modern warfare. It details their training and examines their equipment, and shows how these skills are being put to good use in Iraq, Afghanistan and other conflicts worldwide. With the growth of asymmetric wars around the world, the role of Special Forces is set only to increase.

PART ONE
THE UNITS

1

THE SAS

Second World War

Britain's Special Air Services Regiment – better known as the SAS – is the precursor of all other modern Special Forces units. The Green Berets, Delta Force and the US Navy SEALs all drew their inspiration directly from the SAS. The Regiment was founded in 1941, by a young lieutenant named David Stirling. Born in Keir, Stirlingshire, on 15 November 1915, he was the son of Brigadier-General Archibald Stirling of the Scots Guards. An unenthusiastic scholar, he dropped out of Cambridge with the intention of climbing Mount Everest. After initial training in Switzerland, he was in North America developing his climbing ability in the Rockies when war was declared in 1939.

Returning to Britain, Stirling joined the Scots Guards Supplementary Reserve as a subaltern, but volunteered for the commandos as soon as he had been commissioned. He became a member of Layforce – three specialist commando units under his friend Brigadier Robert Laycock – and was sent to the Middle East. By this time the war in North Africa had become a series of advances and retreats along the coast. The aim of the unit was to make amphibious raids down the coast behind enemy lines but, due to a shortage of naval craft, Layforce was disbanded by the time Stirling reached Egypt.

But Stirling believed that they idea of hitting the enemy in the rear was sound. Lacking the equipment needed to infiltrate by sea, he toyed with the idea of making airborne assaults or skirting the enemy's landward flank by sending raiding parties through the supposedly impassable sea of sand in the desert to the south to destroy targets far behind enemy lines. To put these plans into action, he joined forces with the Australian "Jock" Lewes, an officer with the Welsh Guards. They would become the nucleus of the Special Air Service Regiment.

Lewes scrounged fifty parachutes and he and Stirling started to make training jumps, but disaster struck when Stirling's parachute snagged on the tail of an aircraft. Injured in the fall, Stirling spent months in hospital, but it gave him time to do more detailed planning of his new unit. Until then, the operational thinking in the commandos was to make raids with anything up to 200 men. This had inherent logistical problems as a large proportion of the force had to be used just to secure the beachhead. Stirling's idea was that a smaller force operating behind enemy lines could do more damage, particularly to lightly guarded targets miles from the front. His plan was to insert small teams by parachute which would be collected by a second units in wheeled vehicles.

When he was released from hospital in July 1941, Stirling decided to take his plan to the Commander-in-Chief in the Middle East, General Sir Claude Auchinleck, but he was refused entry to Auchinleck's headquarters. Despite the fact he was on crutches, he clambered over the perimeter fence and barged into the office of Auchinleck's Chief-of-staff, Major-General Neil Ritchie. Ritchie was so impressed with the young man's audacity that he presented Stirling's plan to Auchinleck who quickly saw its virtue. Stirling was promoted to captain and ordered to raise a new unit of six officers and sixty men. It was to be called L Detachment of the non-existent Special Air Services Brigade.

There had been, however, a Special Air Service Battalion whose men had staged a daring raid on an aqueduct spanning the Tragino Gorge in southern Italy in November 1940 in what was known as Operation Colossus. It was formed from 500 men from No. 2 Commando who had been parachute trained, the object being primarily to see if the RAF could successfully deliver men accurately to an enemy target. This was to be a combined Army–Air Force–Navy operation and, after attacking their objective, the men were to be extracted by a submarine waiting off the coast of Salerno. The assault force was known as X Company of No. 2 Special Air Service Battalion, to differentiate it from the seaborne commandos.

As it was, five of the Whitley bombers used on the raid managed to drop their men near the target. But a sixth suffered navigational problems and dropped its men and much of the mission's explosives two hours late and two miles to the north. The aqueduct turned out to be made of concrete, not brick as intelligence had indicated, the explosives caused only minor damage and the men of X Company were captured. The remains of No. 2 Special Air Service Battalion formed the nucleus of the 1st Parachute Brigade. However, Lieutenant-Colonel Dudley Clark, founder of the commandos, wanted to give the impression that a large parachute force was stationed in North Africa, so Stirling's unit was christened the Special Air Services, and the SAS was born.

Within a week, Stirling had assembled his men at a camp near Kabrit in the Suez Canal Zone. All they had were a few old tents, so the SAS's first operation was a raid on a nearby New Zealanders' camp to get new ones. Training began, concentrating on desert navigation, physical fitness and familiarity with all types of weapons, including Italian and German ones. They began parachute training by jumping off the back of a Bedford 15-cwt truck travelling at 30 miles an hour, but this caused so many ankle injuries that a proper scaffolding training tower was built. The SAS then took to the air, but the first time up they went in a plane they lost two men due to faulty attachment rings. This shook morale so the next time they went up Stirling was the first man out of the plane.

After a week of planning, L Detachment of the Special Air Services Brigade set off on 16 November 1941 to make its first attack on five enemy airfields around Timimi and Gazala. The unit was to be dropped in teams of twelve, 20 miles from their targets, their mission to destroy as many planes as possible. To do this, they were armed with a special device – the Lewes bomb, the invention of Jock Lewes. He worked out that the easiest way to destroy a plane was to punch a hole in its wing and set fire to the fuel in the tanks inside. So what was required was a bomb that was both an explosive and an incendiary. A specialist sapper said that this was impossible, but after two weeks' experimentation Lewes came up with a solution. He took a little plastic explosive and rolled it in thermite from incendiary bombs, dousing the whole device with old engine oil to make sure the fire spread. The result weighed just 1 lb, so one man could carry enough to destroy a whole squadron of aircraft. For the SAS it became standard issue.

Once the mission was completed they would rendezvous with a Long Range Desert Group (LRDG) patrol in their trucks, who would take them back to Kabrit.

On the night of the raid, there was a storm, the planes were blown off course and after the drop, none of the teams found their target. On their way to the rendezvous point, they were lashed with rain, then scorched by the sun. Of the sixty-two men sent out, only twenty-two returned. The SAS's first mission had been a disaster.

Stirling went to Auchinleck to report his failure but managed to persuade the General that, despite the high losses, his unit was still viable. As the SAS were having little luck with aircraft, in future they would go into action – as well as come out of it – courtesy of the Long Range Desert Group. On 8 December 1941, the SAS set out for the LRDG patrol base at Jalo, far behind enemy lines. From there, they attacked enemy airfields at Tamit and Agedabia, destroying sixty-one aircraft before they disappeared back into the desert. A few days later they attacked the airfield at Tamit again, destroying another twenty-seven aircraft, but Jock Lewes was killed by a German plane that attacked the LRDG patrol returning from the mission.

The following month they staged another successful raid on the port facility at Bouerat. With Stirling promoted to major and the future of the SAS seemingly assured, he set about designing its famous badge. It was supposed to have been the sword of Damocles, but ended up looking more like a winged dagger, with the motto "Who dares wins" underneath. At the same time he began expanding his force with fifty Free French paratroopers, later known as the French Squadron SAS, the Greek Sacred Squadron, the Special Interrogation Group of anti-Nazi Germans and more commandos.

In July 1942, the SAS got Vickers "K" machine guns and American Willys jeeps with mounted heavy-calibre Brownings, and racks for extra jerry cans of petrol and water. These were fast and more manoeuvrable than LRDG trucks and Stirling developed the tactic of simply speeding down the lines of aircraft, guns blazing.

With this large force making lightning attacks, no enemy soldier, no matter how far behind the lines, felt safe, so special units were set up to pursue the raiders after an attack. In January 1943, one of these hunter units captured David Stirling who, after a number of daring escape attempts, ended in Colditz Castle, the German special prison for persistent escapers in Saxony. Command was passed to Irish rugby player "Paddy" Mayne, who had been in the SAS since its inception. By that time, numbers had swelled to regimental size with 750 officers and men. L Detachment of the SAS Brigade became 1 SAS and Lieutenant-Colonel William Stirling, David's brother, formed the 2nd SAS Regiment with men from 62 Commando in May 1943.

With the surrender of the Axis forces in North Africa, the SAS was reorganized. Number 1 SAS became the Special Raiding Squadron, or SRS. Its job was to attack German and Italian coastal installation in the central Mediterranean and the Balkans, while number 2 SAS was to be dropped behind the lines to support the landings on Sicily by attacking enemy supply lines. This were so successful that during the Italian campaign they were given a free hand to blow bridges, hit airfields and co-ordinate local partisan groups.

During the run-up to D-Day, 1 and 2 SAS returned to England to form a brigade as part of the 1st Airborne Division, along with 3 and 4 SAS, comprising French troops, and a Belgian squadron, which later became 5 SAS. In the four months after D-Day, some 2,000 SAS men operated in uniform from forty secret bases up to 250 miles behind enemy lines, disrupting communications, raiding supply depots, blowing up railway lines and gathering intelligence.

In February 1945, Brigadier Michael Calvert took over as brigade commander. A former Chindit, a long-range penetration group that worked deep behind the Japanese lines in Burma, he brought new expertise in unconventional warfare.

With the Western Allies closing in on Germany, the SAS worked as independent squadrons or with armoured units to protect the advancing army's flanks, or speeding up to 70 miles ahead of the front line to clear pockets of resistance. During the campaign in northwest Europe, they had killed or wounded 8,000 enemy soldiers, suffering just 350 casualties of their own – including twenty-four who were captured by the Germans and executed. At the end of the war, an SAS War Crimes Investigation Team, led by Major Eric Alistair "Bill" Barkworth Somerset, traced all the SS and Gestapo personnel responsible for these killings and handed them over to the Allied authorities for trial as war criminals.

After disarming the German Army in Norway, the SAS was broken up. The French and Belgian units returned to their own national armies, while 1 and 2 SAS were trained for operations against Japan. But the war ended before they could be put into operation and the SAS was finally disbanded on 30 November 1946.

Post-war

Malaya

On 1 May 1947, the SAS was reraised as a Territorial Unit, the 21st SAS, also known as the Artists Rifles after a famous volunteer unit formed in 1860. But the real heirs to the SAS's fighting tradition was the Malayan Scouts formed in 1950 under Major Michael Calvert to track down and eradicate Communist insurgents in Malaya. Alongside the hundred men of Calvert's A Squadron were B Squadron, who were recruited from 21 SAS in London, and C Squadron from Rhodesia (now Zimbabwe). In 1952, they were re-organized to become the present-day 22nd SAS Regiment.

By 1956, the height of the Malayan Emergency, the SAS had 560 officers and men. The Rhodesians had returned home, but were replaced by a New Zealand Squadron and a short-lived Para Squadron from the Parachute Regiment. Operating in four-man teams, penetrating deep into the jungle on assignments that could last up to three months, their services were much in demand.

One of the novel techniques they evolved in Malay was "tree-jumping". They would parachute into the jungle canopy from as low as 500 feet, breaking their fall by allowing the parachute lines to snag on the branches, then abseiling to the ground on a 250-foot rope. But this was dangerous and later patrols were inserted by foot or helicopter.

Carrying two-weeks' rations, they had to be resupplied by air. As the sight of parachutes would attract the insurgents, patrols would have to move on after a drop, setting up a fresh camp near running water. They learnt jungle techniques of making sharpened-bamboo booby-traps and laying trip flares to protect their bases. Deep in the jungle they had a routine: no smoking, no cooking, no talking, and they had to crawl 300 yards out of the camp to urinate or defecate. Their only communication with HQ was a nightly radio message.

In one operation thirty-seven men of D Squadron parachuted into the Telok Anson swamp in Selangor and, after an action that lasted fourteen weeks, forced the rebels to surrender. The Malayan Emergency came to an end after the SAS discovered that the insurgents were communicating with their leaders in Thailand via a radio transmitter in the Valley of No Return. To get there B Squadron were flown to Kota Bahru before being taken by boat down the Kelantan river to Tanah Merah, from where they climbed over the 600-foot Anak Reng ridge. It took twelve days to reach the summit in the steaming jungle heat, by which time the men had lost a considerable proportion of their body weight. The squadron commander, Johnny Cooper, knew that they had just fourteen days to put the transmitter out of action as a supply drop would alert the enemy, so they would move fast. On the thirteenth day, the patrol heard running water. Moving forward to reconnoitre, they found a waterwheel that turning the generators powering the radio. The subsequent attack destroyed the radio transmitter and ended insurgent activity in the border region.

Oman – Jebel Akhdar

The SAS then moved from the jungles of south-east Asia to the deserts and mountains of the Middle East. The ruler of Oman, Sultan Sa'id bin Taimur, found himself in the midst of a full-scale rebellion and requested assistance from the British. In November 1958, D Squadron of 22 SAS arrived. They initiated aggressive patrols on the rebel stronghold of Jebel Akhdar, regularly scaling the walls of the bare mountain at night. The rock there was so hard and metallic that regulation nail-shod boots made a great deal of noise and fell apart quickly. Deep ravines cut through the plateau, echoing loudly as the SAS men climbed their faces, made even more difficult as they had to carry all their food and water with them. The donkeys imported from Somalia to carry their equipment perished in the searing heat of the day and the freezing temperatures at night.

By Christmas it was clear that a full-scale assault was going to be needed to shift the rebels in vastly superior numbers from their well-entrenched positions on the Jebel. A Squadron were flown from Malaya, directly into the freezing Omani winter that had now closed in. They prepared their local donkey handlers for an attack from the village of Tanuf, instructing them, on pain of death, to tell no one – knowing that this was the quickest way to get a message to the rebels. They fell for it and within hours they were massing on the heights above Tanuf.

The SAS then attacked positions on twin peaks known as Sabrina, after a pneumatic 1950s movie star, some miles away. When rebel reinforcements began heading there, the SAS abandoned that position and moved swiftly in the rebel headquarters at Saiq. This involved a perilous climb, during which they abandoned much of their gear, but at the summit they seized an enemy Browning and were resupplied by air. Having lost their headquarters the rebel leaders fled across the border, leaving few pockets of resistance. The remaining tribesmen were easily disarmed and were given a display of SAS firepower, while SAS medics started a "hearts and minds" programme with free clinics. It was a classic SAS operation – swift and decisive.

Borneo

In 1959, a second territorial regiment was formed, 23 SAS, but the SAS was to see no further action until 1963 when they were sent to Borneo, where guerrillas from Indonesia were infiltrating across the border into the newly formed Federation of Malaysia. Their job there was to support a Malaysian, British and Commonwealth force of just five battalions to maintain security over 80,000 square miles. According to the British commander of the combined force, Major-General Walter Walker, the SAS's contribution was invaluable.

"I regard 70 troopers of the SAS as being as valuable to me as 700 infantry in the role of hearts and minds, border surveillance, early warning, stay behind, and eyes and ears with a sting," he said.

The task the SAS had been given was a daunting one. A squadron of not even a hundred men was asked to guard a frontier nearly a thousand miles long, and so wild and rugged in places that it was not even mapped. But their earlier time in Malaya had taught them valuable lessons. It also meant that many of the SAS men spoke Malay, so they could communicate easily with the local people.

Again the SAS sent four-man patrols out deep into the jungle for weeks on end. The patrol would be led by a local scout, followed by the patrol's commander, medic, signaller and another specialist – a linguist or an explosives expert – at spaced intervals. The last man usually carried a 7.62-mm general-purpose machine gun or a Bren gun, while the others carried the standard British Army SLR or the new American Armalite M-16.

At the time, military theorists were against these small patrols, believing them to be too vulnerable to enemy attack, but in Borneo they worked well. As the guerrillas had the advantage of knowing the jungle and the local tribesmen, the SAS had to adopt a "softly-softly" approach, key to which was the medic. While the commander chatted with the headman, the medic set up a clinic that would have to tackle everything from childbirth to gunshot wounds. Meanwhile there would be a small exchange of gifts. If the villagers had any urgent needs, these would be conveyed to base by the signaller and anything they requested sent. After a meal and more conversation, the patrol would withdraw, reappearing a few days later to continue this confidence-building exercise. SAS men would also help the villagers with planting, weeding and harvesting crops. In return, local people would alert them to telltale signs in the forests that revealed the presence of the enemy.

The SAS would also pay locals who would work for them and pay for their food, unlike the guerrillas who simply took whatever they needed from the villagers. There were, of course, more aggressive "Claret" cross-border incursions to attack enemy forward bases in Indonesia and ambush them on their infiltration routes. This had to be undertaken with the utmost care as Britain was not at war with Indonesia and risked being accused of escalating the conflict if detected. At one point they even attacked the Indonesia Army which was staging a build-up in the area and escape unscathed. Together these tactics were so effective that the guerrillas rarely penetrated much beyond the border and, after the Indonesian President Ahmed Sukarno was overthrown in 1966, Indonesia made peace.

Oman – Dhofar

Between 1970 and 1976, the SAS were back in Oman, this time in the Dhofar region, waging another counter-insurgency campaign. The guerrillas who fought in Dhofar were known as the *adoo* (enemy). They were members of the Dhofar Liberation Front, Arab nationalists who were supplied arms by the Communist government in South Yemen and were subsumed into the Marxist People's Front for the Liberation of the Occupied Arabian Gulf. Their arms originated in the Soviet Union, so the insurgents had considerable firepower in the form of Kalashnikov assault rifles, RPG-7 rocket-propelled grenades, 12.7-mm heavy machine guns and 122-mm Katyusha rocket launchers.

However, most of the Dhofaris were not Marxists and were more concerned with material progress than ideology. But the Dhofar rebellion had sparked a palace coup with the autocrat Sultan Sa'id bin Taimur, who had banned radios, spectacles, medicine and bicycles, being replaced by his son, the Sandhurst-trained Sultan Qaboos, who introduced cabinet government for the first time and was attempting to modernize the country. The SAS also formed a bodyguard for the new Sultan and put in what were officially known as British Army Training Teams (BATTs).

Again the SAS's main tactic was to win hearts and minds with medical and veterinary services. They also encouraged ex-guerrillas to join the *firqat*, a militia force trained by the SAS. Although it was rarely effective in combat, it provided considerable intelligence for the Sultan's regular forces.

The SAS's tactics were clearly working and the *adoo* knew that they had to do something in response. On 19 July 1972, they decided to attack Mirbat, a small town defended by a *firqat* unit under the command of a nine-man SAS team, who were at the end of their tour.

They chose to attack during the monsoon season when there was fog in the morning and low cloud base, so the defenders could not rely on air support. The *adoo* attacked with 250 men armed with AK-47s, heavy machine guns, mortars, 75-mm recoilless rifles and a 84-mm Carl Gustav rocket launcher. The *adoo* were highly professional soldiers and the previous day they had lured most of the *firqat* away into the hills. Taking the town should have been a walkover.

The nine SAS men from B Squadron, under 23-year-old Captain Mike Kealy, were lodged in the BATT house. Around 100 yards to the north-west on the shoreline was an old fort, inside which were thirty *firqat* warriors armed mostly with Lee Enfield .303 rifles. About 700 yards inland was another fort belonging to the Dhofar Gendarmerie with twenty-five gendarmes inside. Next to it was a gun pit with a vintage 25-pounder manned by an Omani gunner. Beyond it, the town's perimeter was ringed with barbed wire.

Some 800 yards north, outside the wire, was another DG outpost with eight gendarmes inside. At around five o'clock in the morning, an *adoo* scouting group attacked it, killing four gendarmes. The rest fled. Then six mortars, some 2,100 yards to the north, opened up. Meanwhile two other groups of *adoo* attacked the town from the east. Things were getting serious, but the SAS men, now manning the roof of the BATT house, did not open fire, not wishing to give their position away prematurely.

As explosions rocked the building Lance-Corporal Pete Wignall radioed for help, while Trooper Talaiasi Labalaba, a Fijian, raced to the gun pit to assist the Omani gunner. The DG fort then received a direct hit from a 75-mm recoilless rifle.

At about 0600 around forty *adoo* approached the DG fort. As they straddled the wire Pete Wignall with a .50 Browning and Roger Chapman with a 7.62-mm general-purpose machine gun started shooting. Bob Bradshaw in the command sangar calmly picked off the leader with a well-aimed shot with his SLR. Nevertheless *adoo* kept on coming ten at a time, pulling on the barbed wire with their bare hands – until the 25-pounder scored a direct hit at point-blank range.

Although the DG fort and the 25-pounder were the focus of the attack, other *adoo* penetrated the town. Then the firing rate of the gun slowed down. A message came over the walkie-talkie that Labalaba had been shot in the chin. Sek Saveseki, another Fijian, volunteered to race over to him with medical supplies. It was a 700-yard dash though a hail of bullets. Saveseki, a rugby player, made the run of a lifetime and got to the DG fort unscathed.

The Omani gunner, named Khalid, had been shot in the stomach. But together Labalaba and Saveseki kept the gun firing, though they had to crawl back and forth to load and shoot it due to the intense small-arms fire. When Saveseki was hit in the shoulder, head and back, he was only able to use his SLR. With an almost superhuman effort, the wounded Labalaba continued to load and fire the gun on his own.

At 0700 there was a lull in the shooting. Wignall radioed HQ at Salalah for helicopters to medevac the wounded and sent a request for air support. Meanwhile, they could make no radio contact with the gun pit, so Kealy and Tommy Tobin race over to the gun. They found the Omani gunner mortally wounded, but Labalaba was still firing the 25-pounder and Saveseki was covering the west side of the fort with his SLR. Just then there was a huge explosion and more *adoo* came rushing through the wire towards the gun pit. As Labalaba reached for another shell, he was shot in the neck and killed. Tobin, too, was hit and mortally wounded. As Kealy fired his SLR point-blank at the attackers, he called the BATT house for mortar support and machine-gun fire on each side of the fort. "Fuzz" Harris could not make the elevation with the mortar so he held the tube to his chest to adjust the firing range.

A grenade rolled into the gun pit, but it turned out to be a dud. In the nick of time, Strikemaster jets came in at a hundred feet, strafing and rocketing the *adoo*. As Kealy and Bradshaw directed the jets on to the important targets, twenty-three men from G Squadron SAS – formed in 1966 in Borneo – landed by helicopter on the beach south of the town. They had arrived in Oman just twenty-four hours before and were on their way for acclimatization training in the hills when they heard of the situation in Mirbat. They brought with them nine GPMGs and soon the *adoo* were forced back; with help of some local *firqat*, the town was cleared. By 1230 the battle was over.

The SAS lost two men in the action, Labalaba and Tobin; Saveseki was badly wounded. After the fight thirty-eight dead *adoo* were found on the battlefield. Other bodies were taken by the retreating *adoo* and it is thought that they lost eighty all told. The battle had been a close-run thing, but proved to be a turning point in the war, which ended in 1976.

Mike Kealy was awarded a DSO for his actions, after volunteering to go and lead the *firqat* patrol, which had been lured away, back to safety. Tobin and Bradshaw were awarded the Military Medal, and Labalaba got only a Mention in Despatches. His comrades thought he should have got the Victoria Cross for what he did but, at the time, Britain was keeping a low profile about its involvement in Oman.

Counter Revolutionary Warfare

The SAS's role change in the 1972 in response to a new threat – terrorism. At the 1972 Munich Olympics, eight Palestinians from the terrorist organization Black September stormed the Olympic village, killed two Israeli athletes and took nine more hostage. They demanded the release of some 200 Palestinians in Israeli jails, along with two well-known German terrorists. After a day of unsuccessful negotiations, the terrorists were allowed to take their hostages to the military airport in Munich for a flight back to the Middle East. But at the airport, German sharpshooters opened fire, killing three of the Arabs. A horrifying gun battle ensued, claiming the lives of all nine of the hostages, along with one policeman and two terrorists.

It was clear that the Germans did not have a specialist force who could deal with such a crisis – nor did anyone else. Plainly it was time that security forces worldwide put in place such provisions. In Britain the job fell to the SAS. Given their lack of previous experience in bodyguarding and close-quarter urban warfare, they had to prepare for such an eventuality. With no limit placed on it budget or resources, a special wing of the Regiment was formed called the Counter Revolutionary Warfare Department. It kept a low profile until the Iranian Embassy siege of May 1980. But they had not been idle. At Bradbury Lines, the SAS headquarters in Hereford, they had built a close-quarters battle house, where they practised the use of small arms in enclosed spaces. SAS men would sit in a room in the CQB house surrounded by straw "terrorist" dummies, while their colleagues burst in and, hopefully, only riddled the dummies with live rounds. This training is not for the faint-hearted.

The unit was already up and running by the time of London's Spaghetti House siege of 1975. Employees of a Spaghetti House restaurant in Knightsbridge were held hostage for five days by a Nigerian and two West Indians who claimed to be members of the Black Liberation Army, an offshoot of the American Black Panthers, though, in fact, they were just common thieves. The SAS were prepared. But in the event they were not called in and the siege ended peacefully when the gunmen surrendered. However, later that year, IRA men holding a couple hostage in their flat in Balcombe Street, Marylebone, surrendered when they heard on the radio that the SAS were in the vicinity. It was thought that this was because of the fearsome reputation the Regiment had built up fighting terrorists in Northern Ireland, where the SAS had been used for intelligence gathering and covert operations. Most of their activities there remain classified to this day.

In 1977, the two SAS men were on hand with stun grenades developed by the Regiment when Germany's new Grenz Schutz Gruppe 9 anti-terrorist unit freed the hostages being held on a hijacked Lufthansa passenger plane at Mogadishu Airport in Somalia. The stun-grenade – known as a "flash-bang" in the Regiment – had been specifically developed by the SAS for hostage situations. When detonated, the grenade creates an ear-deafening bang together with a blinding flash of light, causing disorientation for a few seconds. This allows the attacking force to enter and overwhelm the terrorists before they could regain their senses and react. There are several types – one, for example, causes a shockwave that blows out electric lights, plunging the terrorists into darkness and giving the advantage to Special Forces operatives equipped with night-vision goggles.

During the Mogadishu operation, the SAS got to see GSG9's Heckler & Koch MP-5 sub-machine gun in action. As the SAS are the only unit in the British Army who get to pick their own weapons, the CRW Department now carry German-made Heckler & Koch MP-5s. In the spirit of reciprocity, the founder and leader of GSG9, Ulrich Wegener, was invited to observe the SAS in action with their newly acquired H&K MP-5s at the Iranian Embassy Siege in London in 1980.

The siege began at 1132 hours on Wednesday, 30 April 1980, when six armed terrorists stormed into the Iranian Embassy at 16 Princes Gate in Kensington, West London. They were armed with two Polish versions of the Russian Scorpion machine-pistol, one Spanish .38 revolver, three Browning 9-mm pistols and a number of Russian RDG-5 fragmentation grenades. Inside the Embassy was Trevor Lock, a policeman on diplomatic guard duty, who managed to alert his superiors by radio before the terrorists had got the Embassy and the hostages locked down. Within minutes specialist police squads had arrived. They included the marksmen of D11, the C13 anti-terrorist squad, C7 technical support branch and the Special Patrol Group. Meanwhile a former SAS man, then a police dog handler, contacted the Regiment and at 1148 hours the beepers of the Blue and Red team of the SAS went off. Soon Special Forces operatives in plain clothes were on the scene.

Initially, it was not clear how many people had been taken hostage, but it turned out to be twenty-six: nineteen Iranians and seven non-Iranians, including two men from the BBC, who were visiting, and PC Trevor Lock.

The terrorist leader was named Oan, but he called himself Salim. It seemed that he was the only one would could speak English. He made the demands on behalf of an Arabic organization known as the Group of the Martyr. These included freedom for Khuzestan, an oil-rich part of Iran inhabited by Arabs who have traditionally suffered persecution at the hands of the non-Arabic majority, and the release of ninety-one Arab prisoners held by Iran who were to be flown to London. He also insisted that an Arab ambassador be brought in to mediate. If these demands were not met by noon the following day, the hostages would be killed and the Embassy would be blown up.

The police set up an incident room, Zulu Control, down the terrace and began negotiating with the terrorists. Meanwhile preparations were made for an armed assault. That night, police carpenters built a scale model of the Embassy. The next day, work began on a life-sized replica, built in timber and hessian, in Regents Park Barracks.

Technicians from C7 lowered microphones and surveillance devices down the chimney to monitor the movements of the terrorists. And when two hostages were freed – a pregnant woman and a man who had stomach pains – they were debriefed. It was then confirmed that there were six terrorists; previously there were thought to be only five.

As the siege progressed and deadlines passed, the negotiators began to make headway. Plainly the liberation of Khuzestan was not in their gift and the terrorists dropped their demand for freeing the ninety-one Arab prisoners. It turned out that the men concerned had already been executed. The terrorists then asked for a coach to Heathrow Airport and a plane to take them and their Iranian hostages to a Middle Eastern country.

Although it seemed as if the hostage crisis might be solved peacefully, the debacle of Munich was still on everyone's mind so the SAS continued making plans of their own. They were briefed by the embassy caretaker who knew every corner of the fifty rooms inside. From him they learnt that the windows and the front door were reinforced, so it would be impossible to burst in using sledgehammers. However, C7 men in the next-door building had removed part of the adjoining wall brick-by-brick, leaving only a thin layer of plaster. To cover the noise of removing the brickwork, an emergency crew from the gas board, armed with pneumatic drills, had been called in to repair a fictitious gas leak outside, while planes to Heathrow were diverted to fly low over the building. The SAS also discovered an unlocked skylight on the roof that gave access to a bathroom.

After five days, the terrorists were beginning to get desperate. They picked a political argument with the Iranian hostages and began to get suspicious about the noise they heard from outside.

The male hostages were moved together into the telex room and PC Lock appeared at the window to say that the terrorists were going to start shooting the hostages if there was no news of the long-waited Arab mediator.

At 1331 hours three shots were heard from inside the Embassy. At 1850 hours three more shots were heard and the body of the Embassy's press officer was pushed outside the front door. Ten minutes later the police handed over control to the military. The SAS were now going into action.

At 1923 hours, the negotiators got Oan back on the phone so that he, at least, could be located. Then the SAS's Red Team abseiled in pairs from the back roof down to the balcony and ground floor. Another group burst through plaster from the building next door. At the front, Blue Team used frame charges to break the windows. When a terrorist appeared a sniper killed him with a single shot. Stun grenades and CS grenades were thrown in, but the terrorists had put newspapers soaked with lighter fuel under the windows so a fire rapidly broke out.

The raiders were wearing black so that they were visible against smoke, their torsos protected with Nomex body armour. Their faces were covered with gas masks and flash hoods to protect them from fumes and blast – this was also to instil fear in their opponents and protect their identity for fear of reprisals.

Other things were not going so smoothly. Only one of the charges lowered by rope down a light well went off – and prematurely. At the back one trooper got entangled in his ropes so his colleagues could not use their frame charges. He had to be cut down later. Instead, a sledgehammer was used on the lock of the French windows. Nevertheless, front and back, the SAS were in.

When an SAS man appeared through the front window, Oan raised his gun to fire. But Trevor Lock sprang into action, grappling with the terrorist leader until the SAS man could shoot him.

In the telex room one of the terrorists started shooting into the hostages; one hostage died and another was wounded. When the SAS burst into the room, two terrorists hid among the hostages on the floor. When they were pointed out by the hostages, they were killed, but the terrorist guarding the women in another room was spared.

The last terrorist was by the stairs between the hostages when a SAS trooper saw a grenade in his hand. With the hostages at such close quarters it was not possible to shoot him, so the trooper hit him with the stock of his MP-5 on the neck. As he fell down the flight of stairs, he was hit by thirty-two bullets from four SAS weapons, killing him. Fortunately, the pin remained in the grenade.

But the action was not yet over. All the rooms had to be systematically cleared and checked for booby-traps. Locked doors were opened with a burst of 9-mm rounds. The SAS men could not be sure that they had accounted for all the terrorists, so the hostages were thrown down the stairs from trooper to trooper and bundled into the back garden. There, everybody was handcuffed and searched for weapons and proof of identity, just in case terrorists were hiding among them. Once the SAS were sure that everyone in the garden was a hostage and there were no more terrorists at large in the buildings, command was then handed back to the police.

The action was over in seventeen minutes. Of the twenty-six hostages, two died, five had been released and nineteen rescued. Five of the terrorists were dead; the one survivor was sentenced to life imprisonment. The SAS, who were expecting 40 per cent casualties, had three wounded – one suffered burns, one had a leg wound and one had an injured finger.

The Falklands War

Until the embassy siege, the SAS had been a shadowy, secretive organization. Now they were front-page news in their new anti-terrorist role. But just two years later, the SAS were back doing what David Stirling had first devised them for – blowing up enemy aircraft. Indeed, the Falklands War of 1982 gave them the opportunity to practise all the soldierly skills they had acquired in the Second World War. These would include the strategic ones of infiltration for surveillance and intelligence gathering, as well as the tactical ones concerned with diversionary attacks and seizing key features in front of the main force.

But their first task was reconnaissance of South Georgia, an island 1,000 miles to the east of the Falkland Isles, with the object of recapturing it. The Argentines had claimed sovereignty over the Falklands Islands – or the Islas Malvinas as they called them – which lie some 300 miles off their coast since the early nineteenth century. However, the islands had been occupied and administered by the British since 1833, so that the inhabitants were of British descent and owed their allegiance to the British Crown. At the beginning of 1982, the Argentine military junta under Lieutenant-General Leopoldo Galtieri gave up on long-running negotiations over the status of the islands and decided to invade, in the hope that the patriotic fervour engendered by the "recovery" of the Malvinas might help prop up his discredited regime. An invasion force trained in secret. Then when a dispute blew up between Argentine salvage workers and British scientists stationed on South Georgia, the government in Buenos Aires seized this as an excuse to move against the British possessions in the South Atlantic. On 2 April 1982, Argentine troops invaded the Falklands, quickly overcoming the small force of Royal Marines garrisoned in the capital Port Stanley. The following day, they took South Georgia. As the dispute in South Georgia had been the original excuse for the Argentine invasion of the Falklands, it was decide to retake that island first. The job was given to the SAS. On 21 April 1982, a helicopter inserted sixteen men of Mountain Troop – D Squadron, SAS – to establish an observation point at a place called Fortuna Glacier. The weather was horrendous. Weapons froze up and the men only managed to advance 500 yards before camping for the night. In severe danger of frostbite and hypothermia, they requested extraction the next day. But one of the Wessex extraction helicopters crashed just after picking up seven SAS men at around 1330 hours. One SAS soldier damaged his back.

A second helicopter also crashed. A third helicopter managed to extract some of the men, but when it returned to collect the rest of them, it was unable to land. Later that day, after five attempts, the pilot managed to set down and pick up the remaining men. Overloaded, and flying in appalling flying conditions, the pilot crash landed, but he managed to get the men safely on board a Royal Navy ship. He was awarded a Distinguished Flying Cross for his actions.

The next attempt to reach the island was by boat. Five

inflatables set out for Grass Island, South Georgia, but only three boats made it to the shoreline. Later, SBS troops were inserted by helicopter. The SBS, or Special Boat Squadron, are the Royal Marines' equivalent to the SAS and train with them.

There was not much enemy activity on South Georgia, which was garrisoned by only 150 poorly organized enemy troops. On 25 April, the patrol on the island itself directed naval gunfire on them, helicopters inserted another thirty SAS troops and the Argentineans surrendered. Just the threat of facing British Special Forces was enough for the young conscripts. South Georgia had been retaken without bloodshed. Next to come were the Falklands themselves.

From 1 May, G Squadron, SAS and SBS patrols were inserted on the Falklands to look for sites suitable for an amphibious landing. Eventually, the SBS found San Carlos Bay, which was almost undefended. Other four-man patrols located the enemy's position, and ascertained the weapons and equipment they were using, having been inserted up to 20 miles from their objectives. Heavily laden, carrying stores for up to fourteen days, the patrols moved by night and laid up during the day.

Observation posts were set up. As the ground was too hard to dig into, they made hides. A fold in the terrain would be covered with chicken wire and hessian netting. This was then covered with local vegetation to blend in. These hides worked well and the Argentines did not discover a single one of them, even though they almost stepped on them. However, for the SAS men, manning the hides was not a pleasant task. The hides were cold, wet and cramped, and trench foot became a problem. One man would remain on watch as the others tried to cook and get some sleep. It was only possible for them to stretch their legs at night and even then it was dangerous. Although they only had rations for fourteen days, one patrol lasted twenty-six days on Beagle Ridge overlooking Port Stanley. Another OP watching Bluff Cove held out for twenty-eight days.

Air reconnaissance discovered an airstrip and possibly a radar station on Pebble Island, just north of West Falkland. Argentine aircraft using this base could attack the amphibious force landing at San Carlos, so it had to be dealt with, but Falkland Islanders lived nearby so it could not be bombed from the air. On 11 May, two four-man SAS patrols approached the island in Klepper canoes and made a reconnaissance of the area. Eleven aircraft were discovered and a small garrison housing 114 Argentineans, but no radar station. There were problems establishing an OP as there was very little cover.

On 14 May, the rest of D Squadron – another forty-five men – were flown in from HMS *Hermes* Sea King helicopters, landing 4 miles from the target. They had just thirty minutes to reach it. After a bombardment by their 81-mm mortar and naval gun fire had started the action, the Mountain Troop attacked the bunkers on each side of the airstrip, neutralizing them. Two seven-man groups then destroyed the aircraft with explosives, machine guns and hand-grenades. All eleven aircraft were damaged beyond repair. There was only one SAS casualty when a landmine blew one British soldier backwards and injured him slightly with shrapnel. The job done, helicopters extracted all the SAS men safely. It was a classic success, but there were problems ahead.

On 19 May, during a night cross-decking operation from HMS *Hermes* to HMS *Intrepid*, disaster struck when a Sea King helicopter dropped from an altitude of 400 feet into the freezing water of the South Atlantic. It is thought that an albatross flew into the engine intake. Eighteen SAS men from D and G Squadrons were killed, though ten men survived the crash. It was a severe blow for the Regiment as experienced soldiers had lost their lives. However, the Commanding Officer of 22 SAS, Lieutenant-Colonel Michael Rose, said at the time: "The Regiment has taken it well and are getting on with the fighting." But he added that he would be happier when all his men were ashore and their lives were in their own hands.

Their next job was to stage a diversionary attack on East Falkland itself. D Squadron was inserted to simulate an attack on Darwin and Goose Green. After a twenty-hour approach they were to make a lot of noise by attacking the 1,200 Argentineans there with 81-mm mortars, machine guns and Milan missiles. The enemy returned sporadic fire but, thinking they were under fire from a much larger force, did not dare counter-attack. Their attention was also diverted from other areas and the main British ground forces landed at San Carlos on 21 May, untroubled by the enemy.

G Squadron put an observation post on Mount Kent, a key

strategic position overlooking the Falklands capital, Port Stanley. When they reported that the mountain was not manned by
the Argentines, D Squadron moved 36 miles across enemy-held
territory to seize it, holding the mountain against Argentine
attack for almost a week until the Royal Marines arrived there
in force.

To replace battle casualties, B Squadron was flown in from
Britain. After a twelve-hour flight from Ascension Island, they
joined the Royal Navy Task Force by parachuting into the
Atlantic to be picked up by HMS *Glamorgan*.

On the night of 13 June, 2 Para were attacking Wireless Ridge.
One of their companies was commanded by a former SAS
officer. As the attack was in danger of getting bogged down,
the SAS decided to help their old comrade out by launching an
attack on an ammunition dump between the eastern edge of the
ridge and Port Stanley. They planned to go in on board helicopters, but when the weather closed in this proved impossible.
Instead they requisitioned four Royal Marine Rigid Raider
assault craft, along with the coxswains, and launched an attack
on Stanley itself, accompanied by three SBS teams.

The town was defended by around 8,000 Argentine soldiers,
armed with armoured cars, anti-aircraft guns, and 155-mm and
105-mm artillery. The attacking force was just sixty men – three
SAS troops and a six-man SBS section. However, they were
supported by other SAS troops on the northern shore who
descended from their positions on Murrell Heights to lay down
machine-gun and Milan missile covering fire.

Thinking they were facing a full-scale amphibious assault the
Argentine defenders – including those on Wireless Ridge –
turned their fire on the raiders, who had to turn tail. Despite the
withering fire, only three men were slightly wounded, though
the Rigid Raiders were badly holed. Nevertheless, this took the
pressure off the Paras on Wireless Ridge who quickly overcame
the opposition.

This was the SAS's last action in the Falklands, but not their
last contribution. On 14 June, with a general ceasefire in place
around Port Stanley, it was the SAS Commanding Officer,
Lieutenant-Colonel Michael Rose, who helicoptered in to Port
Stanley with a Spanish-speaking officer to broker peace. The
Argentine commander, General Mario Menendez, offered to

surrender the forces under his control on East Falklands, but he said that he could not speak for the garrison on West Falklands. This would have been acceptable to the commanders of the British Task Force as the Army were now down to six rounds per gun and were suffering other shortages. But Rose would not have it. A partial surrender, he said, was no surrender at all. He insisted that Menendez instruct all forces on the Falklands to lay down their arms. After two hours, Menendez gave way.

The following day, when Menendez and the commander of the British Land Forces, Major-General Jeremy Moore RM, signed the instrument of surrender, the SAS hoisted the Union Jack on Government House alongside their own regimental flag. The SAS had made a huge contribution to the victory in the Falklands, at a cost of twenty of its men.

Peterhead Prison, Scotland

In October 1987, the SAS were called on to deal with a problem nearer to home. This time they would need no guns. Prisoners at Peterhead Prison in Scotland had taken over the prison and had taken a prison officer hostage. He had to be rescued and the prison retaken. The SAS was the only unit at the time with the means to carry out such a mission.

The team pumped a mixture of smoke and tear gas into the building before an assault team went in, entering the building through a hole in the ceiling that the prisoners had made. As they would not be facing armed terrorist, the SAS would not be carrying guns. Instead of packing MP-5s, the SAS men were armed with long staves or batons. As the team emerged through the hole, they were greeted by a prisoner. A flash-bang disorientated him and he was quickly subdued. Then the team found the officer who had been taken hostage by the prisoners. They hurried him out of the building into the arms of more SAS men and order was restored.

As well as being a successful action on the ground, this was an extraordinary PR coup. It showed that the SAS were not just a bunch of action men. They could also employ good judgment and they did not always need guns to achieve success.

Overseas the SAS would see action again in the Gulf War, the Balkans, Sierre Leone, Afghanistan and Iraq.

2

THE SBS

The Second World War

The SBS can claim that it predates the SAS. The idea for a special boat force came from Robert Courtney, a young subaltern who tried to convince the then commander of the commandos, Lieutenant-Colonel Robert Laycock, to form units that could assault the enemy using folding kayaks – initially with little success. In order to convince the British armed forces of the effectiveness of such an outfit, he staged a daring one-man raid on a British commando ship by kayaking up to it, climbing the anchor chain, stealing a gun casing and leaving the way he had come, undetected. He then presented the trophy to a group of high-ranking commando officers in a nearby pub. He was promoted to captain, and given command of twelve men, the first Special Boat Section (SBS).

The SBS was provided with 16-foot long collapsible sports canoes made by the Folbot Company. These were easy to assemble, consisting of a rubberized canvas skin over a wooden frame. When dismantled, the canoe folded into a pack 4½ foot x 1 foot and weighed about 48 lb. They could easily be stowed on board a submarine, which would be used to deploy and extract the raiders, and easily hidden on a beach. The joints between the wooden struts would usually be bound with heavy insulating tape during operations to prevent them coming apart.

The two-man crews were equipped with double-bladed paddles which dismantled into two parts and the craft was steered with lines running from the rudder to the coxswain. As the SBS evolved its raiding techniques, it became common practice for the crew to have specific tasks. Usually one would be the canoeist whose job was to look after the craft, while the other – the swimmer – attacked the target, usually attaching a mine to the hull of an enemy craft. Although the Folbot was fairly seaworthy and was described as being very fast and silent in official reports, it did have several weaknesses. Most worrying was that it was very fragile and prone to turning turtle in all but the calmest seas. The canoe was also too lightly built to survive being dragged across a beach when loaded with heavy equipment.

The fledgling SBS trained on the Scottish Island of Arran, their first action being demolition work on the Lofoten Islands off Norway. In another daring raid of 22 June 1941, they paddled ashore from a submarine and blew up a railway tunnel in Italy with a train in it.

Courtney's command had increased to fifteen when they were sent to the Middle East with Layforce as Z Section. There it was reinforced and transferred to the 1st Submarine Flotilla in April 1941. Usually working in two-man groups, paddling ashore on canoes launched from submarine motherships, the teams would seek out and sabotage high-value targets such as rail and communication lines. They made attacks on Greece, Crete and Rhodes. The fledging Special Operations Force also developed anti-shipping skills, using canoes to sneak into harbours and plant limpet mines on the hulls of enemy ships.

By the end of the year, Z Section and the Special Boat Section (Middle East) – a raiding unit formed in the spring of 1941 at Kabrit – had suffered heavy losses. They were therefore absorbed into D Squadron of Layforce's other offspring, the 1st Special Air Service Regiment, along with three groups of canoeists under the command of Earl Jellicoe. Jellicoe then set about reorganizing them into three Special Boat Sections in the autumn of 1942.

Operation Frankton

In November 1942, the SBS made its most famous raid of the
Second World War – the Cockleshell Heroes raid on Nazi-
occupied Bordeaux. Since the fall of France, merchant ships
had used the port at Bordeaux to supply the German military
stationed in that part of the country. The Royal Navy had
prevented merchant ships supplying the Germans use of the
channel, but plenty were willing to sail into the Bordeaux
harbour. With German U-boats using the Atlantic ports as a
base, there was little the British could do about it as a bombing
raid on the port facilities would have led to many French
civilian casualties, and was ruled out.

The only thing to do was mount a seaborne commando raid.
This was to be named Operation Frankton. Its aim was to
destroy as many ships in the port as was possible, blocking the
harbour with wreckage and rendering it unusable.

The raiders were to be Royal Marine Commandos serving
with the SBS. They got their new name from the nickname they
gave their canoes – "cockleshells". During their months of
training, the twelve-man team were not told what their target
was – this was only made known to them once the submarine
HMS *Tuna* had surfaced off the French coast. The plan was for
the six two-man teams to paddle across 5 miles of open sea to the
mouth of the River Gironde, then paddle another 70 miles up
the river and plant limpet mines on the ships in the harbour.
After that they were to abandon their canoes and make their
home by way of Spain, which had remained neutral. It was an
ambitious plan.

The raid started badly when one of the canoes was holed as it
was being made ready on the *Tuna*, which meant that two Royal
Marines – Fisher and Ellery – had to be left behind. Then, as
the canoes approached the mouth of the Gironde, they hit a
violent rip tide. The waves were 5 feet high and the canoe
"Conger" was lost, so that the crew – Corporal George Sheard
and Marine David Moffat – had to be towed along in the water
by the other canoes, slowing them down. Once near the shoreline they let go, leaving the men to swim to the shore, but
neither made it and they are assumed to have drowned.

The crew of the canoe "Coalfish" – Sergeant Samuel Wallace

and Marine Jock Ewart – were caught by the Germans and shot. The crew of the "Cuttlefish" – Lieutenant John Mackinnon and Marine James Conway – had to abandon their canoe after it was damaged. They, too, were caught by the Germans, handed over to the Gestapo and shot. This left the raiders with just two canoes. The leader of the raid, Major "Blondie" Hasler, and his shipmate, Marine Bill Sparks, were on board the canoe code-named "Catfish". The other canoe, "Crayfish", was crewed by Marine William Mills and Corporal Albert Laver.

By then, the Germans knew that something was up and had increased their patrols along the river. However, the two crews, hiding by day and paddling by night, managed to elude them. As the canoes reached the harbour they were spotted by a sentry who somehow failed to raise the alarm, possibly mistaking their canoes for driftwood as the crews had been trained to remain motionless as they drifted by. The crews then placed limpet mines on the merchant ships they found in the harbour. The mines were armed with an eight-minute fuse, giving the Marines time to get away.

They succeeded in sinking one ship and severely damaging four others, which did enough damage to greatly disrupt the use of the harbour for months. Such was the significance of the raid that Winston Churchill said that it helped to shorten the war by six months.

"Crayfish" and "Catfish" escaped on the tide. Once out of danger, they abandoned their canoes and travelled on foot. They assumed the Germans would think that they would head south to neutral Spain. Instead, they turned north. Along the way, Laver and Mills got separated from Sparks and Hasler, were caught by the Germans and shot.

Some one hundred miles north of Bordeaux – a journey that took them two months – the two survivors linked up with the French Resistance at the town of Ruffec. With the help of the Resistance, Hasler and Sparks reached Spain, then moved on to Gibraltar. But even there, their problems were not over. The Chief of Combined Operations, Lord Louis Mountbatten, had assumed all the raiders were dead, so anyone claiming to be them was treated with the utmost suspicion. Hasler used his rank to get transport back to Britain, but Sparks was arrested. However, ever resourceful, he managed to give his military

police escort the slip at Euston Station and, after visiting his
father, made his way to Combined Operations Headquarters.

In the spring of 1943, the SBS was amalgamated with the
SAS, now minus David Stirling. Continuing their raids on
Crete, they were trained on caiques, Greek sailing ships. How-
ever, they did not lose their identity for long. Jellicoe's Special
Boat Squadron was transferred to Brigadier D.J.T. Turnbull's
Raiding Forces Middle East and was renamed the Special Boat
Service. They set up a new specialist training base at Athlit in
northern Palestine and went on to conduct operations in the
Mediterranean, Adriatic and Aegean Seas.

In May 1943, when operations in North Africa were drawing
to a close, S Detachment under Captain Sutherland made a
daring raid on Crete, destroying three airfields. The SBS made
further attacks on Sicily in the run-up to Operation Husky, the
Allied landings there.

Following the Italian capitulation in November 1943, they
became involved in attempts to gain control of enemy-held
islands in the eastern Mediterranean. Although several islands
fell to small raiding parties, the Germans soon stiffened their
defences. In early November 1943, the Germans dropped
paratroopers on the island of Leros, just 15 miles from the
Turkish coast, to counter-attack. After five days of fighting the
British surrendered after losing, with 400 killed. Only a small
SBS team escaped.

But the SBS kept up raids on Leros, Kos and other Greek
islands, forcing the Germans to maintain large garrisons there
and tying up men who could have been used against the Red
Army or Allied forces on the mainland of Europe. Their last
major operation in the Aegean took place on Simi, when eighty-
one SBS men accompanied the Greek Sacred Squadron as they
fought their way back onto the island

Post-war

At the end of the Second World War, the Special Operations
Group in the Far East was returned to the UK. Many SBS men
stayed on in the armed forces, moving to non-amphibious units
as few commanders and politicians saw any use for Special
Forces in the post-war atomic age. However, while the other

Special Forces units were disbanded altogether, the War Office decided to raise and train shallow-penetration Special Forces under the Royal Marines.

Those sections of SOG that remained intact, including the Special Boat Section, were transferred to the Royal Marines. Now numbering less than sixty, they came under the command of "Blondie" Hasler, who produced a paper outlining his vision of the future, defining the role of modern amphibious Special Forces. Despite the fate of his Cockshell Hero comrades, Hasler maintained that the SBS and Special Forces groups were not about sending men on suicide missions. Inadequately trained men would face certain death and badly planned operations spelt disaster. If Special Forces operations were to succeed, training and planning were vital, he insisted. The Admiralty agreed. In early 1946, it gave its approval for the opening of the School of Combined Operations, Beach and Boat Section (SCOBBS), at Fremington, Devon.

SCOBBS would train a core of men for beach surveying, intelligence gathering and sabotage, and within a year was placed under the command of the Royal Marines. At the end of August the two units of thirty-nine men and their stores moved to the Royal Marines base at Eastney, Portsmouth. By the summer of 1948 the Combined Operations, Beach and Boat Section had been renamed the Small Raids Wing of the Royal Marines Amphibious School at Eastney. Their first mission was to remove limpet mines from ships in Haifa harbour.

A row ensued about the title of SBS, which the Royal Marines won, and they began to use SBS as a functional title for their Special Forces unit. At this point the guidelines for the SAS and SBS were laid down. From then on, the SAS were to be responsible for reconnaissance at divisional level, deep-penetration raids, behind-the-lines harassment and training partisans, while the SBS were responsible for operations against ships and coastal installations, shallow, waterborne, penetration raids, beach reconnaissance, landing preparation and ferrying agents into and out of hostile territory.

Either could harass coastal targets, undertake landward reconnaissance, capture prisoners and eliminate undesirable people. However, at this time, the SBS were regulars, while the SAS remained part of the Territorial Army.

The Cold War

When the Cold War began to threaten Western Germany and the Western-occupied sectors of Berlin, a detachment of the Small Raids Wing was formed as part of the Royal Navy Rhine Flotilla based at HMS *Royal Prince* at Krefeld on the Dutch border. This detachment was originally known as the Royal Marine Demolition Unit, shortly to be reformed as 2 SBS. In 1951, 3 SBS was formed and the Small Raids Wing at Eastney was renamed Special Boat Wing. In the event of war, the SBS at Krefeld would form stay-behind parties to gather intelligence and carry out harassment of Russian troops before they reached the Rhine. Both 2 SBS and 3 SBS were part of the Rhine Squadron, with the SBS taking part in major BAOR exercises each year, their numbers being bolstered by the temporary inclusion of 4 SBS and 5 SBS formed from the Royal Marine Force Volunteer Reserve.

During the Cold War, the SBS were responsible for inserting and extracting agents from Eastern Bloc coastlines and gathering intelligence on Soviet naval capabilities. A pair of SBS divers covertly examined and photographed the hull of a new Soviet battle-cruiser when it docked in the port of Gibraltar.

Along with the SAS, SBS would frequently play the role of the Soviet Spetznaz – the Red Army's Special Forces unit – in mock attacks on NATO installations. Some military analysts believe that this resulted in the West overestimating the Spetznaz's capabilities.

In the mid-1950s, 6 SBS was hurriedly formed to support NATO navies in the Mediterranean against any breakout of Russian submarines from the Black Sea. The SBS also undertook coastline reconnaissance. Beaches and harbours of potential hotspots around the world were clandestinely examined with the aim of preparing the way for amphibious landings. SBS training teams also passed on their expertise to Cold War allies and strategic friends. Among those they instructed were the US Navy Seals and the Shah of Iran's Naval Special Forces.

The Korean War

When the Korean War broke out in 1950, the SBS joined the specially formed 41 Independent Commando of the Royal

Marines and US troops to lead sabotage teams blowing up railways and vital installations along the North Korean coastline. The SBS teams and the Royal Marines were among the first British units into action, operating from the USS *Perch*, *Bass* and *Wontuck*. In attacks on coastal railways, lines, tunnels, bridges and general targets of opportunity were blown up by the raiding parties, damaging the North Koreans' lines of supply and communications. The 41 Independent Commando was reassigned to the US Marines when China entered the war, continuing with night-time raids against enemy coastal targets with US support. Further SBS reinforcements joined the combined force, with their headquarters in Japan.

This force operated from bases in the islands off Wonsan along the eastern coast of Korea some 60 miles behind enemy lines. They made mainland reconnaissance raids using two-man canoes, rubber inflatable boats and motor boats. However, in December 1951, 41 Independent Commando was formally stood down and returned to England to be disbanded.

Egypt

In 1952, the SBS carried out a reconnaissance of the harbour near King Farouk's palace near Alexandria, in preparation for an evacuation of British residents from Egypt. As usual the teams and their canoes were delivered by submarine. However, one swimmer failed to make the rendezvous. He was picked up by the Egyptians and was handed over to Naval Intelligence.

The SBS were also readied to send in a raiding party to rescue Farouk, if the nationalist leader Gamal Nasser had attempted a violent coup. As it was, Farouk was forced to abdicate and was exiled. Later, 6 SBS was alerted to be prepared to evacuate King Idris from Libya, but in the event, some gunboat diplomacy achieved the desired effect. The SBS were stood down, but they did not waste the journey to North Africa and conducted reconnaissance along the coast from Tobruk to Tripoli.

The Suez Crisis

During the Suez Crisis of 1956, 1 SBS were tasked with cutting cables laid across the Suez Canal that prevented passage to shipping. They were flown to Malta, but before the operation could get underway, it was cancelled and they returned to the UK. Six SBS were also mobilized to prepare a detailed reconnaissance of possible beach landing sites, but again the task was cancelled before they got underway. Instead, 6 SBS boarded HMS *Ocean* and were sent to Port Said with 3 Commando Brigade.

In 1958 a manual titled *The Organisation and Employment of the Special Boat Sections*, produced by the Commandant General's Office of the Royal Marines, spelt out the ground rules of their operation, distilling what the SBS had learnt so far. It says:

It is important that SBS of sub-units avoid being engaged by superior forces. Success depends on detailed planning and rehearsals. It is essential therefore that all intelligence is made available and that adequate time is allowed for preparation before an operation is launched . . .

In accordance with the Supreme Allied Commander's policy governing Special Operations . . . directives for Special Boat Sections will be broad so far as carrying out the operation is concerned but precise in defining its object and in imposing any limitations on the operation . . .

The success of a small-scale amphibious operation depends mainly upon a carefully prepared and feasible plan in which sufficient time must be allowed for delays and taking alternative action if a turn of event or deterioration of the weather makes this necessary. The plan must be simple yet flexible, with every possible contingency thought through at planning stage. This will ensure that alternative courses of action are decided upon at planning stage . . .

The detailed plan will contain specific information and timings that are of paramount importance to each individual man taking part and which in fact must be committed to memory . . .

Planning requirement: up-to-date intelligence reports, large-scale maps, all available charts, detailed interpretation report; tide tables and Atlas of Tidal Streams, the Nautical Almanac for obtaining bearing and timings of Sun, Moon, etc. Appropriate list of lights . . .

SB operations may be considered in progressive stages of planning, preparation and rehearsal: 1) approach in parent vessel or aircraft to operational area, 2) the final approach by raiding-craft or by swimming or a combination of both, 3) carrying out the task, 4) recovery and withdrawal, 5) debriefing, 6) report writing.

In execution of the above and especially where a reconnaissance raid is a prelude to a larger operation, the following measures are essential: a) time must be allowed for at least one alternative method of recovery, b) alternative swimmer recovery positions must be laid down, c) an alternative craft homing position must be arranged, d) a suitable lying-up position must be pre-located, e) recovery on a subsequent night at an emergency rendezvous, f) if all else fails, escape overland.

Little has changed.

Borneo

In the build-up to the confrontation in Borneo, a section of SBS was formed from the ranks of 3 Commando Brigade, specifically to find and capture a guerrilla leader. It also played a part in freeing hostages taken by Indonesian-backed guerrillas. As the situation grew more heated, 2 SBS joined 42 Commando in Singapore, where they were later reinforced by 1 SBS. They remained in the theatre until 1971. The SBS were used to provide reconnaissance in the most inhospitable terrain where the guerrillas were most active. They joined the SAS in the "hearts and minds" campaign, winning the support of villagers with medical care and supplies.

Teams of three or four men would also be sent into the jungle or swamps to scout for Indonesian army patrols. In the jungle they would build hides and stay for three to five days, radioing back with hourly reports. Generally avoiding firefights, the teams monitored guerrilla activity, providing information that the assault force would use to attack the guerrillas. However, in October 1964, 2 SBS were flown in to the Sarawak area of Borneo to create the Tawau Assault Group with 40 Commando RM. This force was equipped with cabin cruisers, dories and native craft powered by outboard motors, as well as SBS canoes.

The border between Indonesia and Sarawak was difficult to follow as it ran through thick jungle along the backwaters of the River Serudong. The Indonesia border with Sabah State runs across Sebatik Island. Just south-west of Sebatik Island, across a channel just 2 miles wide, was Nanukan Island, where the Indonesian Marines had bases, which they used to disrupt the vital timber trade in Sabah.

Intelligence reports indicated that the Indonesians were also planning operations along the coast of the Sibuk Bay coast, where mangrove swamps and tidal rivers made it a difficult area to patrol. Nearby was the district capital of Tawau, a small port with a population of 4,300 and to the north-west lay Cowie Harbour, an anchorage north of Sebatik Island. In it was Wallace Bay, which would be 2 SBS headquarters. From there they would patrol southwards down the coast in Gemini inflatable boats.

In addition to using an observation post high in a dead tree near the border, the Indonesians also manned a harbour launch which openly watched the passing coasters, junks and local boats. Meanwhile, Indonesian Marines kept watch from the south-west coast of Sebatik Island, with a clear westward view across the waters to other Indonesian bases on Nanukan Island.

While the observation post posed no threat to 40 Commando in the Tawau area, the destruction of the Indonesian post was an obvious target that would undermine their morale. But before an attack could be launched, a recce would have to be made to determine the state of the ground just beyond the beach and ascertain whether there were barbed-wire entanglements and mines hidden along the edge of the jungle. Two SBS swimmers were sent in on a moonless night. With their inflatables just out of view of the Indonesian watchtower, the two swimmers slipped over the side. Coming ashore at a beach a little way south east of the tower, they found no defences in the palms and scrub nearby. The beach was sandy and wide enough to land several inflatables.

They could make out a hut to their right, about 80 feet from the tower, where the lookouts off watch were sitting round a flickering fire. The swimmers did a detailed recce, estimating the distance from the tower to the hut and locating the impenetrable clumps of scrub and thorn that could be used as cover. Then they withdrew.

Their report was studied by 40 Commando who decided to mount a raid in force against the post by fifteen Marines led by a SBS lieutenant. They sailed down the coast in a small motor cruiser on the night of the raid, before launching three inflatables a short distance from the border. One stayed near the border to give covering fire from a general-purpose machine-gun to deter any patrol boats from pursuing the commandos as they withdrew.

The other two were paddled south for the 5 miles to the beach by the watchtower. But as the lead craft beached, it was plain that the observers in the tower had spotted them and somewhat inaccurate machine-gun fire rained down. The Lieutenant told his assault team to spread out and move forward as he ran towards the hut. His Sergeant, with a GPMG gunner to the right, waded waist deep along the shore guided by the gunfire. Meanwhile the Lieutenant crossed the open ground and raced towards the hut.

His shout of "Grenades!" sent the Sergeant and his GPMG gunner ducking for cover under the water, holding their weapons over their heads. The Lieutenant had lobbed two M26 grenades into the palm-leaf hut, followed by a burst from his sub-machine gun. The assault team came up and, having counted the bodies, prepared to leave as the patrol was under strict orders not to get involved in any prolonged fire-fight. The element of surprise had been lost early on in the raid and there was no alternative but to withdraw before the enemy could organize an effective counter-attack. Back aboard the Geminis, the raiders soon had enough water under them to open up the throttles of the outboards, making good their escape just as mortar bombs began falling close to the observation post.

The situation in Borneo also allowed SBS sections to practise landing by canoe from submarines. In early May 1965, they made a reconnaissance on moonless nights across the Strait of Malacca to Labuhanbilik. The submarine lay well clear of the island until nightfall, when she floated off a Gemini and four canoes 5 miles from the shore. The Gemini and canoes beached without mishap. There was no sign of any enemy activity and the Marines paddled back to rendezvous with the submarine. But a recce on a second dark night found Indonesian patrols on another island. Covered by a canoe a little way offshore, two teams scaled a rocky cliff to observe the movements of enemy personnel. On a third occasion they reconnoitred a small river estuary looking for the boats used to smuggle arms across to Borneo. Similar carefully co-ordinated recces and raids continued to help Headquarters Far East Land Forces in Singapore to plan cross-border operations. By the summer of 1965, there were signs that Indonesian incursions were decreasing in Borneo. Ambushes set up through the summer by the security forces found fewer Indonesian intruders than they had for several years. By 1966, the 70,000-strong security force was intercepting Indonesian forces as they crossed the border. The Royal Marines fought their last action of the confrontation in mid-March, pursuing Indonesian Commandos south of Biawak. A truce was finally agreed in August. The total number of casualties of the Commonwealth military forces in this undeclared war, which lasted over four years, was 114 killed and 181 wounded, a fifth of the Indonesian losses.

Training and Further Operations

In 1965, the SBS had set up courses in Singapore to train Malaysian troops, along with men from the South Vietnamese Army and, later, US Marines preparing to fight in Vietnam. Trials were also carried out with the 7th Submarine Squadron to see if it was possible to launch SBS teams from submarines while they were still submerged in order to help the raiders infiltrate undetected – and pick them up the same way. These were code-named the "Goldfish" experiments and involved the British politician Paddy Ashdown, the High Representative for Bosnia and Herzegovina from 27 September 2002 to 30 May 2006, who was a member of the SBS at the time.

One problem with these operations was that it was difficult to brief the SBS teams on the latest intelligence while underwater; in addition, men and their gear took up valuable space within the submarine, which was already cramped. One way around this was to airdrop the SBS team at a pre-arranged rendezvous where the submarine would pick them up for the last leg of their journey. The trials were all carried out successfully with rubber inflatable craft rather than rigid canoes.

Later, Royal Navy engineers adapted a Mark XXIII torpedo as an underwater tug. It was codenamed "Archimedes" and had extra batteries for sustained operation. Paddy Ashdown was one of the test drivers. But while Archimedes itself was not successful, similar craft remain in service today.

During the 1960s, the SBS were active in the Mediterranean making coastline surveys, gathering intelligence and conducting operations throughout the area. Based in Malta, 6 SBS sent a detachment to Bahrain. From there they would deploy to any trouble spot throughout the Gulf. Exercises were also conducted throughout the Middle East including amphibious landings, developing new procedures and formats for signals.

Before the revolution in Iran in 1979, the SBS provided training and advice to Iranian Special Forces and helped several other friendly countries in the region. When India and East Pakistan began to threaten each other in 1971, the SBS were sent on board HMS *Albion* to assist in the evacuation of British nationals, if necessary. In the event, they were not needed.

As the British Empire shrank, Gibraltar became the only remaining British bastion in the Mediterranean. At the time it was under blockade by Spain. Six SBS were deployed to conduct reconnaissance around the Rock to ensure Spain was not planning an assault. When that fear proved groundless, the SBS found itself with little active role outside training friendly forces.

In the early 1970s, the SBS began taking on a drug enforcement role in support of civilian police forces in the Caribbean. During the 1970s, 1980s and 1990s, the SBS were also deployed in Northern Ireland. Their main role was covert surveillance and, apart from its own operations, many SBS operators joined 14th Intelligence Company, or "the Det" – a branch of Military Intelligence specially created for surveillance operations in Ulster. The SBS were also used to monitor and interdict gun running along the coastline and on inland waterways and lakes.

In 1972 the SBS assumed a more high-profile role when blackmailers threatened to blow-up the cruise-liner *Queen Elizabeth 2* (QE2), which was then in the mid-Atlantic. Men of the Royal Marines' Special Boat Squadron, along with an SAS sergeant and a bomb-disposal expert, were parachuted into the Atlantic from a RAF Hercules a thousand miles from Britain. The bomb-disposal expert, Captain R. Hacon Williams, was not parachute trained and had to be given instruction en route. The team was not advised of the ship's location until after take-off and had to jump into a rough sea before being picked up by the liner's lifeboat. Once on board, they were rushed to the ship's captain, who briefed the team while their equipment was mustered. The suspect packages were two suitcases on the boat deck and four large containers in the car deck, all of which proved to be harmless. The ransom money was delivered but not collected and the FBI eventually picked up the hoaxers.

Every member of the jump team received the Queen's Commendation for Brave Conduct and the exercise provided valuable experience in inter-service co-operation, with a RAF Nimrod providing secure and instant communications between the team and its British base. After this operation, some bomb-disposal experts were parachute-trained and the SBS kept a team on standby for future operations of this type.

Later that year, the SBS were on board the *QE2* again, following the Black September terrorist attacks at the Munich Olympics. The liner was carrying a sizable Jewish contingent on a cruise to Israel and it was thought advisable to put them under SBS guard. Another *QE2* cruise to Israel in 1976 again required the protection of the SBS. This time members of the unit posed as tourists aboard the liner with their Browning 9-mm pistols concealed under their T-shirts. Some SBS men brought their wives to add to the mission's cover. As before, the cruise was completed without incident.

With the threat of terrorism coming to the fore, security forces began to foresee the danger of a terrorist group taking control of a North Sea oil rig. In 1979 the Admiralty and Chiefs of Staff approved the formation of a new counter-terrorist force of 300 Royal Marines called Comacchio Company, based at RM Condor in Arbroath, and charged with oil-rig and ship-protection duties at sea. It was also to provide a quick-reaction force to protect nuclear weapons both in transit and on site. The SBS deployed a counter-terrorism-dedicated team to Comacchio, which became 5 SBS. In 1987, 5 SBS and 1 SBS – now a counter-terrorism force based in Poole, Dorset – were merged to form M Squadron of the SBS, dedicated to maritime counter-terrorist operations. By 1990 it had three troops.

The Falklands War

The SBS were engaged in winter exercises in northern Norway when Argentina invaded the Falklands. Due for leave as soon as they returned from Scandinavia, their departure was blocked when they returned to Britain and were put on standby.

Within twenty-four hours of the signal ordering the SBS to stand to, the SBS were on the move. On 1 April 1982, 2 SBS set off with the command team by air to Ascension Island, from where they would sail south. They were soon joined by D Squadron of the SAS, giving the Special Forces a combined force of around fifty men. M Company of 42 Royal Marine Commando also arrived. The men were at sea on board RFA *Fort Austin* before they learned that South Georgia was their intended destination.

Six SBS joined HMS *Conqueror* at Faslane and set off for the South Atlantic. Three SBS was the last section to leave aboard RFA *Stromness*, with a further twelve men joining them at Ascension. One SBS remained in Poole to deal with any counter-terrorist emergency closer to home.

The assault on South Georgia was code-named Operation Paraquat. On the way the SBS and SAS tested their equipment and practised launching from the *Fort Austin*. The elderly outboard motors often failed and the men found themselves having to paddle back to the ship in these practices.

On 12 April, they sighted HMS *Endurance*, and over the next day the SBS and SAS men heading for South Georgia were cross-decked to the *Endurance* with their equipment and stores by two Wessex helicopters. The *Endurance* and *Fort Austin* were joined by HMS *Antrim*, HMS *Plymouth* and the RFA tanker *Tidespring*.

The reoccupation of South Georgia was planned aboard HMS *Antrim*. The *Endurance* would put the main body of the SBS ashore at Grytviken and King Edward Point, with the SAS landing at Fortuna Glacier to reconnoitre Leith Harbour, Stromness and Grass Island.

The retaking of South Georgia was delayed by an Argentine

submarine, the *Santa Fe*, which had to be sought out by helicopter and depth-charged. Damaged, she limped back to Grytviken where she was scuttled. There then followed the disastrous insertion of the SAS. Finally a 75-man-strong force made up of SBS, SAS and Royal Marines were landed from the *Antrim*, only half the strength of the Argentine garrison. However, when it reached Grytviken, the entire place was covered in white sheets and the Argentineans surrendered.

After the Argentinian surrender on South Georgia, 6 SBS moved to join 3 SBS in the advance fleet. The SBS would reconnoitre three separate areas of the Falklands and maintain patrols in advance of the main landings. Sea King Mk4 helicopters were used to fly the patrols in, although occasionally the Geminis were used to go ashore. Helicopter movements were only carried out at night, and once dropped off the SBS teams dug in to the bare hillsides and remained hidden for days at a time as the Argentine forces searched for them. The SBS were hampered by the fact that they had to send reports back using Morse code, far too simple a system to relay beach recce reports which essentially had to be accompanied by maps and charts. SBS personnel therefore had to make dangerous exfiltrations to deliver these in person.

As the conflict progressed, the SBS had teams scattered throughout the islands, with patrols deployed to various locations for up to a week at a time before withdrawing to report, and then being inserted to another location. The teams usually numbered four men who, once landed, would proceed on foot to their observation posts, lying up in temporary hides during the daylight hours. A trio of hides would be built, one for the men and the other two for the substantial supplies necessary for a seven-day recce.

Although the Argentine forces came close to discovering SBS patrols on numerous occasions, they never actually succeeded. However, on one occasion two SBS corporals went missing, causing SBS Control a great deal of worry. The two corporals were part of a team that had run into an Argentine patrol and although they avoided actual contact, they were split up. Following their standard evasion procedures, the two missing corporals went to ground. Eventually, seven days later, they were picked up and returned to the Task Force.

The SBS were also sent to take over an Argentine fish-factory-ship, but while 2 SBS were en route, the ship was attacked by two Harriers and was listing badly by the time they arrived and boarded her. When the SBS discovered charts and operational orders showing that she had been shadowing the British fleet, they took off the crew before setting charges and blowing up the vessel.

Immediately prior to the landing of the main British ground forces at San Carlos, an Argentine company moved into the area and the SBS were tasked with clearing them out. Using a thermal imager, the SBS located the Argentineans from a Wessex helicopter and HMS *Antrim* bombarded the position with 4.5-inch naval shellfire for two hours, while the Wessex landed the SBS nearby. The SBS then moved in, calling for the Argentines to surrender. Their answer was a volley of small-arms fire. The SBS men gave the Argentines one more chance to give up before moving forward. They killed twelve, wounded three, and took nine prisoners.

The Argentineans they had taken out had been on Fanning Head manning anti-tank guns and mortars which would have been able to inflict considerable damage on the British landings if they had not been put out of action. However, the rest of the Argentine company were hiding in houses in Port San Carlos and were not discovered until after the landings began. In the meantime they had shot down two Royal Marine Gazelles.

As the landings at San Carlos continued unopposed, 6 SBS from HMS *Fearless* were inserted on the north coast to establish a forward base on Green Island ahead of the Commandos' advance. The section carried out a recce of Port Louis and Green Patch before the Commandos arrived. Two SBS joined them and operated in the Teal area, guiding 3 Para into Teal, before moving on to observe an enemy company on Long Island Mountain. When the SBS set about removing an enemy observation post, during the operation the team leader strayed into the SAS operational zone and was sadly killed in a friendly fire incident. From then on there was closer co-operation between the two units.

The SBS continued its operations, scouting West Falkland for enemy bases and airstrips. Although the SAS had already destroyed the planes at Pebble Island, there was still a garrison there, so the SBS planned an attack with thirty-six men, supported by two Harriers. Although the raid never took place as the Argentine commander had surrendered at Port Stanley, an SBS major nevertheless took the surrender of Pebble Island and its 114-strong garrison.

The SBS had also been in on the final action as the main force advanced on Port Stanley. On 12 June, while 2 Para were attacking Wireless Ridge, 5 miles west of them a six-man team from 3 SBS formed a volunteer raiding party with D and G Squadrons SAS to divert enemy attention from the main thrust, by creating a diversionary assault from the sea. The task was unplanned and a spur-of-the-moment operation.

The SBS team spent a day in an observation post before moving across the Murrell River in Rigid Raiders with a troop from D Squadron of the SAS, who were ferried by men from the Royal Marines 1st Raiding Squadron. The raiders then hid off Kidney Island until they were ready for the assault.

On the night of 13 June, the men approached the target area, bypassing the berthed Argentinean hospital ship *Bahia Paraiso*. As they did so, the hospital ship turned on its searchlights. Spotting the raiders, the Argentines opened fire with everything they had, certain they faced a full-scale seaborne assault. The British force did not open fire on the hospital ship, but were not displeased when it was hit by Argentine artillery fire.

The raiders had no choice but to withdraw, with one of the craft badly damaged, an SBS corporal and two SAS troopers having been lightly wounded. Nevertheless the effort provided the much-needed diversion for 2 Para and saved lives by diverting Argentine attention from the Paras' assault.

There also seem to have been SBS operations on the mainland of Argentina but for the time being the details remain classified. The SBS have drawn up plans to counter any future attack or invasion of the Falklands by the Argentines. They also have plans to protect Belize from Guatemala, which claims the territory as its own.

Following the Falklands War, there was a new debate about the need for Special Forces. In 1987, the Special Forces Group was formed, taking the SAS, SBS and 14th Intelligence Company under the control of the Directorate of Special Forces. It was under this new command structure that the SBS would join

Operation Desert Storm, stage security exercises at British nuclear power stations, take part in UN peacekeeping operations in East Timor, stage a daring raid on a Mauritian cargo ship heading for a London port carrying "terrorist materials", and see more action in Sierra Leone, Afghanistan and Iraq.

3

US ARMY SPECIAL FORCES
– THE GREEN BERETS

Although the Green Berets are a relatively new outfit, Special Operations are nothing new to the American soldier. There were frontiersmen stalking the woods of New England during the French and Indian War of 1754–63. Known as Rogers' Rangers after their commander Major Robert Rogers, they were the first of America's unconventional forces.

Rogers' Rangers fought in terrain regular soldiers avoided. "Move fast and hit hard" was Rogers' motto. However, during the American Revolution, Rogers backed the British. But his tradition of guerrilla fighting was continued by the "Swamp Fox" Francis Marion, who led daring raids on British forces in South Carolina and Georgia. His irregulars harassed the enemy and, exploiting the element of surprise to its fullest, had success out of all proportion to their numbers.

In the Civil War, Colonel John Singleton Mosby of Virginia raised a band of Confederate raiders that became the terror of the Union. Operating from the outskirts of his enemy's capital, Mosby's 300 hand-picked volunteers wrecked railroads, raided headquarters behind enemy lines, and cut off communications and supplies. Well-trained and well-disciplined, Mosby's men set a model for guerrilla warfare. They aimed to weaken the enemy's infrastructure and his front line, and win the support of the populace. Mosby did this by protecting the local population from plundering Union soldiers and by sharing any booty they captured with those in need. Because of his stealth and almost uncanny ability to elude capture, Mosby came to be known as the "Gray Ghost".

The Second World War

In the Second World War special-operations units began to multiply, and the public found themselves regaled with the daring exploits of the Devil's Brigade, Darby's Rangers, Merrill's Marauders and the Alamo Scouts.

The Devil's Brigade was known formally as the 1st Special Service Force, the direct predecessor of the Green Berets. It was in fact a joint US-Canadian outfit created on 9 July 1942 at Fort William Henry Harrison, Montana. Parachute-trained, the Devil's Brigade saw most of its action in Italy, but it also fought in southern France. Its forte was close-quarter combat against numerically superior forces. It was disbanded on 5 December 1944 after capturing the village of Villeneuve-Loubet near Antibes. With the fighting in southern France coming to an end, its men were returned to Canadian and American airborne units.

Darby's Rangers were the 1st Ranger Battalion under the command of Major William O. Darby, the unit being activated on 19 June 1942 at Carrickfergus in Northern Ireland. Darby's Ranger fought throughout the campaign in Western Europe, but achieved their greatest fame when they scaled the cliffs of Pointe du Hoc as part of the D-Day landings in Normandy to take out the batteries there that overlooked both Omaha and Utah beaches.

Merrill's Marauders was the name given to Colonel Frank D. Merrill's 5307th Composite Unit (Provisional). The 3,000-man force fought the Japanese in the jungles of Burma, beating them in five major battles and seventeen smaller skirmishes. One of the Marauders' greatest feats was their march of miles through thick Burmese jungle to capture the airfield at Myitkyina. This would prove an inspiration to US soldiers when they returned to the jungles of Asia twenty years later.

In the Pacific, Lieutenant-General Walter Krueger, a native of San Antonio, set up a small elite volunteer force called the

Alamo Scouts. Famously, the Scouts led US Rangers and Filipino guerrillas in an attack on a Japanese prison camp at Cabantuan on Luzon, freeing all 511 of the Allied prisoners held there. Never numbering more than seventy men, the Alamo Scouts earned forty-four Silver Stars, thirty-three Bronze Stars and four Soldier's Medals. In just under eighty dangerous missions, they never lost a man in action.

Besides these official units, a number of US Army officers conducted their own guerrilla operations behind enemy lines in the Philippines. Colonel Russell Volckman, who later would play an important role in the birth of the Green Berets, escaped from the Japanese and formed a Filipino guerrilla band in northern Luzon. By 1945 he had five regiments under his command. Major Windell Fertig, a reservist, also raised his own guerrilla force, which eventually totalled around 20,000 men.

Another important forerunner of the Green Berets was the Office of Strategic Services. Established in June 1942 at the suggestion of British spymaster William Stephenson, it was put in the hands of his friend William J. Donovan, a winner of the Medal of Honor in the First World War, who had since become a wealthy Wall Street lawyer. His free-wheeling attitude had earned him the nickname "Wild Bill".

When America finally joined the Allies in the Second World War, Donovan was made a colonel and put in charge of an agency called the Coordinator of Intelligence. In Donovan's hands COI blossomed quickly, forming operational units in England, North Africa, India, Burma and China. At Stephenson's suggestion, the agency was vastly expanded and renamed the OSS; Donovan was promoted to major-general. Its job was to collect and analyze strategic information required by the Joint Chiefs of Staff and to conduct Special Operations not assigned to other agencies. But it did not have jurisdiction over all foreign intelligence activities – that remained the responsibility of the FBI, which it jealously guarded. Although the military also ran their own intelligence operations, the OSS helped arm, train and supply resistance movements in occupied countries during the Second World War.

In Nazi-occupied Europe, these operations were called Jedburgh missions. Three-man teams were dropped into Belgium, Holland and France, where they trained partisan resistance movements and conducted guerrilla operations against the Germans in the run-up to the D-Day landings. Other OSS operations took place in Asia, where they aided the Viet Minh in Indochina and Mao Tsetung's Red Army in China. In Burma, OSS Detachment 101 organized 11,000 Kachin tribesmen into a force that eventually killed 10,000 Japanese, at the cost of just 206 of its own men.

Post-war

When the war was over, President Harry S. Truman disbanded the OSS, but it left an important legacy. From its intelligence-gathering operations came the Central Intelligence Agency which was formed on 18 September 1947 – its first directors were veterans of the OSS. From its guerrilla and training operations behind enemy lines came the US Special Forces, formed in June 1952.

Ex-OSS operative Colonel Aaron Bank and Colonel Russell Volckmann, who both remained in the military after the war, tried to convince the US Army to establish its own unit dedicated to unconventional warfare. They had an ally in Brigadier-General Robert McClure, head of the Army's psychological warfare staff in the Pentagon. Eventually Bank and Volckmann convinced the Army chiefs that there were areas in the world not suitable for conventional warfare – notably Soviet-dominated Eastern Europe. There, the only way to attack the enemy was by the type of harassment and guerrilla actions that they had developed during the Second World War. Their men would operate as a force multiplier – that is, a small number of men who could create a disproportionately large amount of problems for the enemy. They would sow confusion in the enemy ranks and objectives would be accomplished on enemy territory with extreme economy of manpower. Such ideas went against traditional Army thinking, but in 1952 the Pentagon finally grasped the nettle of unconventional warfare.

Formation of the Special Forces

The new unit was to be called Special Forces. The name came directly from the OSS who called their operational teams in the field in 1944 "Special Forces". Its strength was to be 2,300 personnel and it was to be based in Fort Bragg, North Carolina. In the spring of 1952, Colonel Bank went to Fort Bragg to find a suitable location for a Psychological Warfare/Special Forces Center. He picked a remote area of the post known as Smoke Bomb Hill that, within ten years, would become one of the busiest areas on the base.

Bank then began to pick officers and NCOs to form the core of his new unit. He sought out former OSS operatives, airborne troops, ex-Rangers and combat veterans of the Second World War and Korea. The men he picked had at least a sergeant's rank and were trained in infantry and parachute skills. Virtually all spoke at least two languages. They were volunteers willing to work behind enemy lines, in civilian clothes if necessary. This would mean that, if captured, they would not be protected by the Geneva Conventions and were liable to be shot as spies. But the first volunteers were unconcerned about the risk. Many of them had fled the Communist takeover of Eastern Europe at the end of the Second World War and were willing to risk their lives to liberate their country from Soviet domination.

Finally, on 19 June 1952, Bank's new unit was activated. It was designated the 10th Special Forces Group. According to the Army, the main mission of 10 SFG was "to infiltrate by land, sea or air, deep into enemy-occupied territory and organize the resistance/guerrilla potential to conduct Special Forces operations, with emphasis on guerrilla warfare". But there were secondary missions. These included counter-insurgency operations, intelligence missions and deep-penetration raids.

On the day of activation, 10 SFG comprised just its commander Colonel Bank, one warrant officer and eight enlisted men, but that soon changed. Within months, volunteers were reporting to 10 SFG in their hundreds as they completed the induction phase of their Special Forces training. Then, once he had enough men on board, Bank began teaching his troops the advanced techniques of unconventional warfare. This came as a revelation to volunteers who had been Rangers in the Second World War or Korea. Rangers had been designed as light-infantry shock troops. Their mission had been to hit hard and fast, then get out so larger, more heavily armed units could follow through. By contrast, Special Forces were designed to spend months, even years, deep within hostile territory. They would have to speak the language of their target area and know how to survive without extensive resupply from outside.

They were soon to see action behind enemy lines in Korea, directing the United Nations Partisan Forces, Korea (UNPFK). These were anti-communist guerrillas with homes in North Korea, but with historical ties to Seoul. Known in Korean as "fighters of liberty", the UNPFK were called "donkeys" by the Americans as the Korean word for liberty is *dong-il*. From tiny islands off the Korean coast, the Donkeys rescued downed airmen, maintained electronic listening posts and staged raids on the mainland. Numbering eventually 22,000, UNPFK claimed 69,000 enemy casualties.

On 11 November 1953, after an abortive uprising in East Germany, the 10th Special Forces Group was deployed to Bad Tölz in West Germany. The cadre remaining at Fort Bragg became the 77th Special Forces Group.

Throughout the 1950s, Special Forces would continue to grow slowly and would soon see action. On 1 April 1956, sixteen men from the 77th were formed into the 14th Special Forces Operational Detachment (SFOD). In June they were sent to Hawaii, then on to Thailand, Taiwan and, ominously, South Vietnam, where they were sent to train a cadre of indigenous Vietnamese Special Forces teams. It was the beginning of a sixteen-year stay. On 21 October 1956, a member of the 14th Special Forces Detachment, Captain Harry G. Cramer Jr, became the first American soldier to die in Vietnam.

The 14th SFOD was followed shortly by three other operational detachments – the 12th, 13th and 16th – each designated for Asia and the Pacific. These were then combined to form the 8231st Army Special Operational Detachment. On 17 June 1957, the 14th and 8231st were reunited in the 1st Special Forces Group that was based in Okinawa, to cover the Far Eastern theatre of operations.

By 1958, the basic operational unit of Special Forces had become a twelve-man A-detachment or A-team, comprising two officers, two operations and intelligence sergeants, two communications sergeants, two weapons sergeants, two engineers and two medics. Each member was trained in unconventional warfare, spoke at least one foreign language and were cross-trained in each others' specialties. Each detachment could also operate, if needs be, as two six-man teams, known as "split A-teams".

On 6 June 1960, the 77th SFG was redesignated the 7th and, by the time John F. Kennedy was inaugurated as President in January 1961, the three Special Forces groups – the 1st, 7th and 10th – were considered the Army's elite. Later that year President Kennedy visited Fort Bragg, where he inspected the Special Forces. He liked what he saw. As a student of global politics, President Kennedy knew that, under the superpower nuclear stalemate, Communist guerrilla groups had sprung up around the world. In the Special Forces troops, he saw the perfect vehicle to carry out counter-insurgency operations to defeat these guerrilla movements.

Since 1953, Special Forces troops had been wearing the distinctive green beret when they went in to the field, although the Army refused to authorize its official use. It had been borrowed from the Royal Marines whose fighting spirit they tried to emulate. However, at Kennedy's request, they had worn their green berets for his inspection. Afterwards the President told the Pentagon that he considered the green beret to be "symbolic of one of the highest levels of courage and achievement of the United States military". It was to become the Special Forces' official headgear. Soon, the green beret became synonymous with Special Forces and the two terms became interchangeable. They took as their motto "*De Oppresso Liber*" – Latin for "To Free the Oppressed", which was a reference to one of their primary missions to train and assist foreign indigenous forces.

With President Kennedy's backing, new Special Forces groups sprang up. On 21 September 1961, the 5th Special Force Group was activated, followed in 1963 by the 8th Special Forces Group on 1 April, the 6th on 1 May and the 3rd on 5 December.

The Vietnam War

Throughout the late 1950s and early 1960s, the number of Special Forces military advisors in South Vietnam grew steadily. Vietnam had been divided along the seventeenth parallel after the French defeat at Dien Bien Phu in 1954, but the Saigon

government in the South faced an indigenous guerrilla movement, along with, increasingly, enemy soldiers infiltrating from
the Communist North. The Special Forces' job was to train
regular South Vietnamese soldiers in the art of counter-
insurgency and to mould various hill tribes into a coherent
anti-Communist force. They also took part in the fighting. On 5
July 1964, Special Forces' Captain Roger H.C. Donlon won the
war's first Medal of Honor for leading the successful defence of
Nam Dong against an attack by Viet Cong guerrillas, despite
suffering a mortar wound to the stomach.

"The sensation of pain can be masked by other emotions in a
situation like that," said Captain Donlon. "I was fighting mad
right from the start. I also felt fear from the start . . . fear that
anybody would feel. It got to the point where we were throwing
the enemy's grenades back at them. Just picking them up and
throwing those grenades back before they could blow."

In September 1964, Vietnam became the exclusive operational province of 5th Group which set up its provisional
headquarters at Nha Trang. In February 1965, as the war
escalated, Nha Trang became the 5th's permanent headquarters. It was to remain there until 5 March 1971 when the Group
returned to Fort Bragg, though some A-teams remained in
Thailand, launching secret missions into Vietnam. But by
the end of 1972, the Green Berets' war in Vietnam was over.

During their time in South-East Asia, the Green Berets set
up 254 outposts throughout South Vietnam, often defended by
a single A-Team and hundreds of ethnic tribesman who they
trained in the art of guerrilla warfare. They took the Montag-
nards, the Nungs, the Cao Dei and tribesmen and moulded
them into the 60,000-strong Civil Irregular Defense Group
(CIDG). CIDG troops became the Green Berets' most valuable
ally in battles fought in remote corners of Vietnam, out of reach
of conventional forces. The Green Berets also built schools and
hospitals, provided medical care to civilians, dredged canals and
undertook other "heart and minds" projects.

The Green Berets' most high-profile operation of the Vietnam war took place on the night of 20/21 November 1970 when
Colonel Arthur D. "Bull" Simons led a team of fifty-six Special
Forces soldiers in a daring raid on prison camp Son Tay just
23 miles from Hanoi in North Vietnam, over 300 miles behind

enemy lines. The aim of the operation was to recover some seventy American prisoners of war thought to be held at the camp. In the area that night were over 236,000 defending enemy soldiers and the most concentrated surface-to-air missile defences so far seen in the history of war.

On 18 November 1970, President Richard Nixon approved the execution of the mission. Fifty-six Special Forces troopers were selected to conduct the raid and were flown by C-130 to their helicopter staging base at Udon Royal Thai Air Force Base. The Green Berets were organized into three groups: a fourteen-man assault group, codenamed "Blueboy", would crash-land inside the prison compound; a 22-man command group, codenamed "Greenleaf", would blow a hole in the prison wall and provide immediate ground support for the assault group; and a twenty-man support group, codenamed "Redwine" would provide back-up support for the other two groups and defend the prison area against any counter-attack made by the North Vietnamese Army.

The Special Forces raiders would each carry a rescue radio and be heavily armed. Between them they would carry fifty-one personal sidearms, forty-eight CAR-15 carbines, two M16 rifles, four M60 machine guns, two shotguns and four M79 grenade launchers. They also carried fifteen Claymore mines, eleven demolition charges and 213 hand grenades, along with wire cutters, bolt cutters, chain saws, crowbars, axes, ropes, bullhorns and other equipment. There would be 106 aircraft – fifty-nine Navy and forty-seven Air Force – supporting the mission, with twenty-nine aircraft crewed by ninety-two airmen in direct combat roles.

At 1125 hours on 20 November, the helicopters carrying the Green Berets took off from their base in Thailand. Shortly after midnight the A-1 Skyraiders combat-support planes and Combat Talons providing airborne command and illumination lifted off from Nakhon Phanom Royal Thai Air Force Base. As the force approached from the west at 0123 hours, Navy aircraft took off from the carriers USS *Oriskany*, *Ranger* and *Hancock*. As they approached the North Vietnamese coast from the east, they set off the North Vietnamese air defences reaction at 0217 hours, providing a highly effective diversion for the raiders.

At 0218 hours, the Jolly Green HH-3 helicopter carrying the

Blueboy Special Forces assault team crash-landed into
the centre of Son Tay prison as planned. This gave the operation its only casualty – a crew member with a broken ankle.
Captain Richard J. Meadows then led his force on a violent
assault. The sixty guards were overwhelmed and the camp
taken in a matter of minutes and the Green Berets began a
cell-by-cell search. At 0221 hours, the Greenleaf command
group, led by Colonel Simons, landed 400 yards from its
objective outside a similar-looking structure previously thought
to be a secondary school. It turned out to be the administrative
barracks for the North Vietnamese guards. The team immediately attacked the location, detonating charges on its walls and
buildings, and set off a five-minute firefight in which Colonel
Simons estimated 100 to 200 North Vietnamese Army soldiers
were killed. At 0226 hours the command group reboarded its
helicopter and moved to the correct landing area outside the
prison to find the Redwine support group, led by Lieutenant-
Colonel Eliott P. "Bud" Sydnor, already there.

At the same time, other diversionary tactics were implemen-
ted. Flares and "firefight simulators" were dropped at other
locations. The North Vietnamese fought back. At least eighteen
surface-to-air missiles were fired at the raiding force. One
F-105 was severely damaged and its crew were forced to eject
over Laos, but were rescued by the two other HH-53s with the
task force. Another had a near-miss but made it back to base.

After a thorough search, Meadows radioed "negative items"
to the command group. They had found no prisoners there. At
0236 hours the first helicopter extraction was made. A second
followed nine minutes later. The raiding force had been on the
ground only twenty-seven minutes. Though at first it was
feared one raider had been left behind, all the troopers were
accounted for. By 0315 hours the force was out of North
Vietnam, and landed back at Udon in Thailand at 0428 hours,
five hours after launch.

The mission was deemed a "tactical success" because of its
execution, but was clearly an intelligence failure. The sixty-five
prisoners at Son Tay had been moved in July because of the
threat of flooding in the area. The day before the raid, the PoWs
had been moved back to a prison 15 miles away, but it was too
dangerous to switch targets at the last minute.

For their actions at Son Tay, members of the task force won six Distinguished Service Crosses, five Air Force Crosses and eighty-three Silver Stars. All members of the Green Beret ground force received a medal.

By the time they pulled out of Vietnam, 5 SFG had won 16 of the 17 Medals of Honor awarded to the Green Berets in Vietnam, plus one Distinguished Service Medal, 90 Distinguished Service Crosses, 46 Distinguished Flying Crosses, 235 Legions of Merit, 232 Soldier's Medals, 814 Silver Stars, 13,234 Bronze Stars, 4,891 Air Medals, 6,908 Army Commendation Medals and 2,658 Purple Hearts. Despite its failure to rescue any prisoners of war, the raid on Son Tay had demonstrated the Green Berets' capabilities and was partly responsible for the creation of the joint United States Special Operations Command in 1987.

Despite the Green Berets' best efforts, the Vietnam War ran its tragic course. In March 1965, President Lyndon B. Johnson had committed conventional forces to the war. By 1968, there were over 500,000 US soldiers in Vietnam. After President Richard M. Nixon took office in 1969, the United States began its withdrawal from Vietnam, which the American people had become to regard as a quagmire, although the Green Berets had already taken their place American mythology. In 1966 Barry Sadler's "The Ballad of the Green Beret" went to number one in the US charts, and in 1968 John Wayne starred in the movie *The Green Berets*. In the 1980s, the A-Team was celebrated in a long-running TV series of the same name, starring George Peppard.

Training and Further Operations

During the 1960s other Green Beret training teams were operating in Bolivia, Columbia, Venezuela, Guatemala and the Dominican Republic. Counter-insurgency forces of the 8th Special Forces Group carried out some 450 clandestine operations against guerrillas between 1965 and 1968. And in 1968, Green Berets were involved in tracking down the Argentine revolutionary Che Guevara in the wilds of Bolivia.

In the years following the Vietnam debacle, the 3rd, 6th and 8th Special Forces Groups were disbanded and special operations scaled down. However, the remaining Green Berets used their talents in a programme called SPARTAN (Special Proficiency at Rugged Training and Nation-building). Under the programme, the 5th and 7th Special Forces Groups worked with Native American tribes in Florida, Arizona and Montana, building hospitals and roads. And they provided free medical treatment to the impoverished citizens of Hoke and Anson counties in North Carolina.

Although the Green Berets were honing their "hearts and minds" skills, this was not exactly what they had been trained for. Meanwhile, they were involved in Operation Eagle Claw, the failed mission to rescue the fifty-two hostages held in the US Embassy in Tehran in 1980.

However, when President Ronald Reagan took office in 1981, Special Forces teams were once again deployed to dozens of countries around the globe. Missions varied from training local armies and running counter-insurgency programmes to providing humanitarian aid such medical care to remote villages of the Third World. Special Forces were particularly successful in Honduras, El Salvador and Honduras, where they prevented the civil war in neighbouring Nicaragua spreading beyond its borders.

To meet the needs of President Reagan's defence policy, the Army revitalized the Green Berets. The Special Forces qualification course was made longer and tougher, and only the highest-calibre soldiers were allowed to join the ranks of the Green Berets. Training at Fort Bragg's John F. Kennedy Special Warfare Center and School, where prospective Special Forces soldiers are put through their paces, became harder, with dangerous tasks like freefall parachuting, escape missions and maritime operations being added to the course.

In June 1983, the Army authorized a Special Forces uniform tab showing a dagger crossed by three lightning flashes on the left shoulder. That October they took part in Operation Urgent Fury, the invasion of Grenada after the Marxist Depute Prime Minister Bernard Coard staged a coup d'état.

In October 1984, the Army established a separate career field for Special Forces, adding the warrant officer career field soon after and a separate branch of the Army for Special Forces officers in 1987. But one thing remained the same – the

A-detachment. The only thing that had altered about it was that the team executive officer was no longer filled by a lieutenant but by a warrant officer with several years of experience with an A-team.

The A-team remains the fundamental building block for all Special Forces Groups. There are six A-detachments in each Special Forces company. A captain leads the twelve-man team; second in command is a warrant officer. Two non-commissioned officers trained in each of the five Special Force functional areas – weapons, engineering and demolitions, medicine, communications, and operations and intelligence – make up the rest of the team. All team members are Special Forces-qualified and cross-trained in different skills as well as being multi-lingual.

A-teams are trained to: plan and conduct Special Forces operations separately or as part of a larger force; infiltrate and exfiltrate specified operational areas by air, land or sea; conduct operations in remote areas and hostile environments for extended periods of time with a minimum of external direction and support; develop, organize, equip, train and advise or direct indigenous forces up to battalion size in special operations; train, advise and assist other US and allied forces and agencies; plan and conduct unilateral Special-Forces operations; and perform other Special Operations as directed by higher authority.

In the Special Forces company, one of the six A-teams is trained in combat diving and one is trained in military free-fall parachuting. Both are used as methods of infiltration.

The detachment can serve as a manpower pool from which commanders organize tailored Special Force teams to perform specific missions. In general, A-teams are equipped with high-powered communications systems such as tactical satellite communications, burst transmission devices, high-frequency radios and global positioning systems. Medical kits include, along with field surgical kits, laboratory and dental instruments and supplies, sterilizers, resuscitator-aspirators, water-testing kits and veterinary equipment for hearts-and-minds operations. Other key equipment includes individual and perimeter defence weapons as well as night-vision devices, and electric and non-electric demolitions. How this equipment is distributed throughout the team naturally depends on the specific mission.

For underwater or waterborne infiltration, Scuba teams are equipped with open-circuit twin-80s SCUBA tanks, closed-circuit rebreathers, Zodiac boat and Klepper kayaks. Military free-fall parachuting teams use ram-air parachutes and oxygen systems.

There are also B-teams, usually comprising eleven men, whose job is to support the A-teams in the company. Instead of a weapons and engineering NCO it has a supply NCO who works with battalion to supply the company, or a NBC (Nuclear, Biological and Chemical) NCO, usually a sergeant, who maintains and operates the company's NBC detection and contamination equipment, and assists in administering NBC defensive measures. There is one B-team per company.

Finally, there is the C-team, which is a pure command and control unit with operations, training, signals and logistical support responsibilities. They are rarely deployed in a tactical zone. Usually the C-team joins the headquarters of the commander of the conventional force it is supporting at the operational or strategic level.

In December 1989, Special Forces were to serve alongside conventional Army units in Operation Just Cause – the invasion of Panama. Designated Task Force Black, soldiers from the 7th Special Forces Group – many already stationed in Panama – supported the entire operation by implementing blocking tactics and conducting surveillance. At H-Hour Task Force Black secured a bridge over the Pacora River and engaged Panama Defence Forces in an intense firefight. Despite being outnumbered, they prevented the PDF from reaching the incoming US Rangers. During the action, Special Force suffered not a single casualty.

In June 1990, 3rd Special Forces Group was reactivated, bringing the number of Special Forces Groups on active-duty status to five. With responsibility for the Caribbean and West Africa, it was stationed at Fort Bragg with the 7th FSG, whose area of operation is Central and South America. The original 10th SFG, covering Europe and Western Asia, was stationed at Fort Carson, Colorado, with its 1st Battalion in Stuttgart, Germany. The 1st SFG, which covers the Pacific and Eastern Asia, was at Fort Lewis, Washington, with C Company of its 1st Battalion, stationed in Okinawa. The 5th SFG was at Fort

Campbell, Kentucky, covering south-west Asia and north-east Africa. The 19th and 20th SFGs are National Guard units. The 19th is headquartered in Draper, Utah, with detachments in Washington, West Virginia, Ohio, Rhode Island, Colorado, and California. It has responsibility over South-East Asia which it shares with 5th SFG, as well as the Pacific, shared with 1st SFG. The 20th is headquartered in Birmingham, Alabama, under Southern Command, with battalions from Alabama (1st Battalion), Mississippi (2nd Battalion), and Florida (3rd Battalion), with detachments in North Carolina, Chicago, Illinois, Louisville, Kentucky and Pittsburgh, Pennsylvania. The 20th has an area of responsibility covering thirty-two countries, including Latin America south of Mexico, the waters, territories, and nations in the Caribbean sea, the Gulf of Mexico, and the south-western Atlantic Ocean. The area is shared with 7th SFG.

Despite their nominal bases, their units were rarely home. Their 4,500 men are deployed around the world tasked with seven specific missions: unconventional warfare, foreign internal defence, special reconnaissance, direct action, combating terrorism, counter-proliferation and information-collecting operations. Other duties include coalition warfare and support, combat search and rescue, security assistance, peacekeeping, humanitarian assistance, de-mining and counter-drug operations.

They were on hand for Operations Desert Shield and Desert Storm in Kuwait in 1990, Operation Restore Hope in Somalia in 1993, fighting in the Battle of Mogadishu that October, Operation Enduring Freedom in Afghanistan and the ongoing Operation Iraqi Freedom.

4

US NAVY SEALS

The acronym SEALs stands for Sea, Air, Land. They are
supported by their Special Warfare Combatant-craft Crewmen
– SWCCs or Swicks. These two units can trace their origins
back to the Second World War Scouts and Raiders, the Naval
Combat Demolition Units, the Office of Strategic Services
Operational Swimmers, Underwater Demolition Teams and
the Motor Torpedo Boat Squadrons that operated in the
Pacific. While none of those earlier organizations have survived
to the present day, the expertise they developed in seaborne
unconventional warfare is still in use today.

The Second World War

Amphibious assault was a tactic frequently used in the Second
World War – in the Pacific, North Africa, Sicily, Italy and,
finally, in France. Vital to the success of such a dangerous
manoeuvre was good beach reconnaissance, so a force of selected Army and Navy personnel assembled at Amphibious
Training Base, Little Creek, Virginia on 15 August 1942 to
begin training. The Scouts' and Raiders' mission was to identify and reconnoitre any beach chosen by planners, maintain a
position on the beach before the landing and, finally, guide the
amphibious assault onto the landing beach.

The first group of Amphibious Scouts and Raiders included Phil H. Bucklew, who became known as the "Father of Naval Special Warfare". The US Naval Special Warfare Center building is named after him. His group was commissioned in October 1942 and first saw action in November 1942 during Operation Torch, the US landings on French North Africa. They also supported landings in Sicily, Salerno, Anzio, Normandy and southern France.

A second group of Scouts and Raiders, code-named Special Service Unit No. 1, was established on 7 July 1943, as a combined operations force. Its first mission took place in September 1943 at Finschafen on New Guinea. It later took part in operations at Gasmata, Arawe, Cape Gloucester, and along the south and east coast of New Britain – all achieved without any loss of personnel. However, there was a conflict between the US Army and Navy at the time over operational matters, and all non-Navy personnel were reassigned. The unit was then renamed the 7th Amphibious Scouts. Its new mission was to go ashore with the assault craft, blow up beach obstacles, take offshore soundings, erect markers for the incoming craft, handle casualties and maintain voice communications between the troops ashore, the incoming craft and the ships standing off. The 7th Amphibious Scouts conducted operations in the Pacific for the rest of the war and participated in more than forty landings.

A third Scout and Raiders organization operated in China, where an amphibious force was deployed to fight with the Sino-American Cooperation Organization, or SACO. To help bolster the work of SACO, Admiral Ernest J. King ordered that 120 officers and 900 men be trained for the "Amphibious Roger" force at the Scout and Ranger school at Fort Pierce in Florida. They formed the core of what was to be a "guerrilla amphibious organization of Americans and Chinese operating from coastal waters, lakes and rivers employing small steamers and sampans". While most Amphibious Roger forces remained at Camp Knox in Calcutta, three groups saw active service. They conducted a survey of the Upper Yangtze River in the spring of 1945 and, disguised as coolies, made a detailed three-month survey of the Chinese coast from Shanghai to Kitchioh Wan, near Hong Kong.

Naval Combat Demolition Units started in September 1942, when seventeen Navy salvage personnel arrived at the Amphibious Training Base at Little Creek, Virginia for a one-week course on demolitions, explosive cable cutting and commando raiding techniques. On 10 November 1942, this first Combat Demolition Unit succeeded in cutting a cable and net barrier across the mouth of the Sebou River in Morocco during Operation Torch. This allowed the USS *Dallas* to cross the river and land a force of US Rangers who captured Port Lyautey air field.

When planning began for a massive cross-Channel invasion of Europe, intelligence indicated that the Germans were placing extensive underwater obstacles on the beaches at Normandy, where the landings would be. On 7 May 1943, Lieutenant-Commander Draper L. Kauffman – "Father of Naval Combat Demolition" – was directed to set up a school to train people to eliminate obstacles on an enemy-held beach prior to an invasion. Within a month, he had established the Naval Combat Demolition Unit training school at Fort Pierce, Florida. By April 1944, a total of thirty-four Naval Combat Demolition Units were deployed in England in preparation for Operation Overlord, the amphibious landing at Normandy.

When D-Day – 6 June 1944 – came, in the face of great adversity, the Naval Combat Demolition Units at Omaha Beach managed to blow eight complete gaps and two partial gaps in the German defences. In the process, these units suffered thirty-one killed and sixty wounded, a casualty rate of 52 per cent. Meanwhile, the Naval Combat Demolition Units at Utah Beach met less intense enemy fire. They cleared 700 yards of beach in two hours, another 900 yards by the afternoon. Casualties at Utah Beach were significantly lighter at six killed and eleven wounded. All these losses were due to enemy action. During Overlord, not a single man was lost due the mishandling handling of explosives. In August 1944, the Naval Combat Demolition Units from Utah Beach participated in the landings in southern France in Operation Dragoon, the last amphibious operation in the European Theatre of Operations.

Naval Combat Demolition Units also operated in the Pacific theatre. Naval Combat Demolition Unit 2, under Lieutenant Frank Kaine – after whom the Naval Special Warfare Command building is named – and Naval Combat Demolition

Unit 3 under Lieutenant Lloyd Anderson, formed the nucleus of six Naval Combat Demolition Units that served with the 7th Amphibious Force and was tasked with clearing boat channels after the landings from Biak to Borneo.

Some of the earliest Second World War predecessors of SEALs' missions were assigned to the Operational Swimmers of the OSS. They were under the command of British Combined Operations veteran Lieutenant-Commander Wooley of the Royal Navy, who was placed in charge of the OSS Maritime Unit in June 1943. Their training started in November 1943 at Camp Pendleton, then moved to Catalina Island in January 1944, and finally to the warmer waters of the Bahamas in March 1944. Within the US military, they pioneered combat swimming, limpet mine attacks, flexible swim fins and facemasks, closed-circuit diving equipment and the use of swimmer-operated submersibles.

In May 1944, General Donovan, the head of the OSS, divided the unit into groups. He loaned Group 1, under Lieutenant Choate, to Admiral Chester Nimitz, as a way to introduce the OSS into the Pacific Theatre. They became part of the Navy's Underwater Demolition Team 10 in July 1944. Five OSS men participated in the very first UDT submarine operation with the USS *Burrfish* in the Caroline Islands in August 1944.

These Underwater Demolition Teams sprang out of Admiral Nimitz's "Granite Plan" for central Pacific operations, which called for numerous amphibious landings. However, many of the targeted islands were coral atolls with reefs that acted as natural obstacles to landings. During early November 1943, SeaBees – members of the US Naval Construction Battalion – engaged in experimental underwater blasting work were assembled at Waipio Amphibious Operating Base on Oahu, Hawaii, to begin training in underwater demolition.

On 23 November 1943, the US Marine landing on Tarawa Atoll reported the need for hydrographic reconnaissance and underwater demolition of obstacles before any amphibious landing. After Tarawa, 30 officers and 150 enlisted men were moved to Waimanalo Amphibious Training Base to form the nucleus of a demolition training programme. This group became Underwater Demolition Teams 1 and 2.

The Underwater Demolition Teams (UDTs) saw their first

combat on 31 January 1944, during Operation Flintlock in the Marshall Islands. Success there became the real catalyst for the UDT training programme in the Pacific Theatre. In February 1944, the Naval Combat Demolition Training and Experimental Base was established at Kihei, Maui, next to the Amphibious Base at Kamaole.

Eventually, thirty-four Underwater Demolition Teams were established. Wearing swimsuits, fins and facemasks on combat operations, these "Naked Warriors" saw action across the Pacific in every major amphibious landing including Eniwetok, Saipan, Guam, Tinian, Angaur, Ulithi, Pelelui, Leyte, Lingayen Gulf, Zambales, Iwo Jima, Okinawa, Labuan, Brunei Bay and, on 4 July 1945, at Balikpapan on Borneo, which was the last UDT demolition operation of the war.

Post-war

The rapid demobilization at the end of the war reduced the number of active-duty Underwater Demolition Teams to two on each coast with a complement of seven officers and forty-five enlisted men each.

The Korean War

When the Korean War began on 25 June 1950, a detachment of eleven men from UDT 3 was sent. Eventually UDT participation expanded to three teams with a combined strength of 300 men. But this time they did not confine their activities to under the waves. As part of the Special Operations Group, UDTs successfully conducted demolition raids on railroad tunnels and bridges along the Korean coast.

On 15 September 1950, UDTs crucially supported Operation Chromite, the amphibious landing at Inchon. UDTs 1 and 3 provided personnel who went in ahead of the landing craft, scouting mud flats, marking low points in the channel, clearing fouled propellers and searching for mines. Four UDT personnel acted as wave-guides for the Marine landing.

In October 1950, Underwater Demolition Teams supported mine-clearing operations in Wonsan Harbour where Navy frogmen located and marked mines for minesweepers. On 12

October 1950, two US minesweepers hit mines and sank, but
the UDTs were on hand to rescue twenty-five sailors. The next
day, William Giannotti conducted the first US combat operation using an "aqualung" when he dived on the USS *Pledge*.
For the rest of the war, UDTs conducted beach and river
reconnaissance, infiltrated guerrillas behind the lines from
sea, continued mine-sweeping operations, and participated in
Operation Fishnet, which severely curtailed the North Korean's fishing capability.

The Vietnam War

When President John F. Kennedy came to office he asked the
armed forces to develop their unconventional warfare capability. The US Navy responded by establishing SEAL Teams 1
and 2 in January of 1962. Formed entirely with personnel from
Underwater Demolition Teams, the SEALs' mission was to
conduct counter-guerrilla warfare and clandestine operations in
the sea and up rivers. SEAL involvement in Vietnam began
immediately. They were sent as advisors to the South Vietnamese Navy on clandestine maritime operations. SEALs also
began a UDT-style training course for South Vietnamese
Commandos in Danang.

In February 1966, a small detachment of SEAL Team 1
arrived in Vietnam to begin direct-action missions out of Nha
Be in the Rung Sat Special Zone area, Saigon's outlet to the sea.
Eventually there would be eight SEAL platoons permanently
stationed in country.

Initially they were used only for intelligence-gathering missions in the Mekong Delta. The SEAL recon teams would map
Viet Cong water and trail networks. Later they would go back
and destroy them. These initial operations proved so successful
that four more platoons were deployed to carry out similar
operations further from the main waterways.

These reconnaissance teams were usually of between three to
seven men, each a specialist in a specific area. These RTs
consisted of the "wheel" or leader, a couple of swimmer-scouts,
the "powder train" or demolitions specialist, the "rigger" or
escort and cover for the powder train, a radio operator and a
heavy-weapons man.

As the war escalated, SEAL Teams 1 and 2 deployed platoons throughout the riverine area, with insertions and extractions performed by craft of the so-called Brown Water Navy. By late 1966, the SEALs received further support, which included Helicopter Attack Squadron Light 3 – HAL-3, also known as the "Seawolves" – which were equipped with UH-1B armed helicopters, the Special Boat Squadron and its PCFs – Patrol Craft, Fast, or "Swift boats" – and a Mobile Support Team.

The SEALs carried out a number of Search and Destroy operations during their time in Vietnam. These included: Operation Charlestown in December 1966, which involved the location and destruction of Viet Cong cells in the Rung Sat Special Zone; Operation Crimson Tide in September 1967, where the SEALs acted as scouts for regular large units during major operations; and Operation Bold Dragon III of March 1968, when they destroyed a Viet Cong arms factory and bunkers on Tanh Dinh island. The SEALs also paid frequent visits to Haiphong Harbour, the main port of North Vietnam, on reconnaissance and sabotage missions.

SEALs took part in the Intelligence Coordination and Exploitation programme to neutralize the Viet Cong command structure, and later the CIA-sponsored Phoenix Counter-Terrorist Program, which target potential Viet Cong recruits. Working alongside the Provincial Reconnaissance Units – elite strike force units recruited from the local Mike Forces, with combined US Special Forces and indigenous soldiers, Viet Cong traitors and convicted criminals – they formed the direct action branch of this programme. Missions ranged from reconnaissance to ambush, kidnapping and assassination missions against Viet Cong political cadres, tax collectors and spies. Joint operations were also conducted with the Lien Doc Nguoi Nhia, the Vietnamese SEALs, including raids on Viet Cong POW camps in the Delta. The SEALs made use of the amphetamine dexedrine on such operations to be more alert and aware of their surroundings.

In Vietnam, SEALs also fought alongside the Republic of Korea's Marine Corps, most notably in Operation Van Buren and the Battle of Hoi An. There some thirteen soldiers wiped out an elite North Vietnamese Army regiment, after the initial gun battle had devolved into bloody hand-to-hand combat.

More than 400 North Vietnamese Army soldiers were killed at a cost of just two Korean casualties.

As well as operating as a self-contained force, SEALs served as advisors for Provincial Reconnaissance Units and the Lien Doc Nguoi Nhia. The last SEAL platoon withdrew from Vietnam on 7 December 1971 and the last SEAL advisor left in March 1973.

Alongside the SEALs, the Underwater Demolition Teams saw combat again in Vietnam while supporting the Amphibious Ready Groups. While attached to the riverine groups the Underwater Demolition Teams conducted operations with river patrol boats and, as well as patrolling the riverbanks and beaches, moved well into the hinterland to destroy obstacles and bunkers. UDT personnel also acted as advisors to the South Vietnamese.

Further Developments

After the Vietnam War, the SEALs undertook standard peace-time duties such was instructing friendly troops in Central America. It is thought that SEAL elements and their locally trained troops mined Nicaragua's main harbour under CIA authorization.

On 1 May 1983, all UDTs were redesignated as SEAL Teams or Swimmer Delivery Vehicle Teams. Since then SDVTs have been redesignated SEAL Delivery Vehicle Teams.

Another precursor of the SEALs were various Special Boat Units that can also trace their history back to the Second World War, appearing under various guises. Motor Torpedo Boat Squadron 3 rescued General Douglas MacArthur and the Filipino President Manuel Quezon from the Philippines after the Japanese invasion, and then participated in guerrilla actions until American resistance ended with the fall of Corregidor. Patrol Torpedo Boats subsequently participated in most of the campaigns in the south-west Pacific, conducting and support-ing reconnaissance missions, blockades, sabotages and raiding missions, as well as attacking Japanese shore facilities, shipping and combatants. PT Boats were used in the European Theatre, beginning in April 1944, to land OSS agents and French

Resistance personnel, and for diversionary attacks during amphibious landing. While there is no direct connection between the organizations, the Naval Special Warfare Command use similar craft and are trained for similar missions.

The development of a riverine warfare capability during the Vietnam War produced the forerunner of the modern Special Warfare Combatant-craft Crewman. Mobile Support Teams provided combat craft support for SEAL operations, as did Patrol Boat, Riverine (PBR) and Swift Boat crew. In February 1964, Boat Support Unit 1 was established under Naval Operations Support Group, Pacific to operate the newly reinstated Patrol Torpedo, Fast (PTF) programme and to operate high-speed craft in support of Naval Special Warfare forces. In late 1964 the first PTFs arrived in Danang, South Vietnam. In 1965, Boat Support Squadron 1 began training Patrol Craft Fast crews for Vietnamese coastal patrol and interdiction operations. As the Vietnam mission expanded into the rivers, new craft, tactics and training evolved for riverine patrol and SEAL support.

SEAL Delivery Vehicle Teams themselves had historical roots that began in the Second World War – but with Italian and British combat swimmers and wet submersibles. Naval Special Warfare began using submersible in the 1960s when the Coastal Systems Center developed the Mark 7, a free-flooding SEAL Delivery Vehicle of the type used today, and the first SDV to be used in the fleet. The Mk 8 and Mk 9 followed in the late 1970s. Today the Mk 8 Mod 1 is used and a dry submersible, the Advanced SEAL Delivery System, has now been developed.

In November 1980, after the reorganization of the US Counter-Terrorist Units under the Joint Special Operations Command, SEAL Team 6 was set up. Also known as "the Mob", it was a special counter-terrorist combat swimmer unit along the lines of the SBS's Comacchio Company, tasked with countering attacks on ships and oil rigs, as well as supporting Delta Force in conventional counter-terrorist operations.

The Invasion of Grenada

Elements of Teams 4 and 6 saw action during Operation Urgent Fury, the invasion of Grenada, in 1983. The first America troops to land on the island was SEAL Team 4, whose mission included pre-landing beach reconnaissance in support of the 24th Marine Amphibious Unit.

Team 6 was sent in to reconnoitre Point Salines airfield. Sixteen men were to arrive off the island's southern coast in two C-130 transports, parachute into the sea, climb aboard Boston Whalers rescue craft and rendezvous with the destroyer USS *Clifton Sprague*. Another SEAL squad, accompanied by USAF Combat Controllers, would join them after their own sea-jump. After that they would move to the airfield, check the runway's serviceability, remove any obstacles, place homing beacons and await the US Rangers. But the operation began to go wrong from the start.

Delays pushed back the Team 6 parachute jump, which was scheduled for dusk, by a full six hours. The already hazardous night-time jump was made even more dangerous by a wind gusting to 25 knots – well over the recommended 18-knot limit. Two teams of eight jumped, each carrying the maximum combat load of over 60 lb and without the benefit of a "dip test" to check for buoyancy. Only five of the first eight men surfaced. Even though the surviving members had released their equipment as soon as their chutes opened, they dived 60 feet when they hit the water. Then they could not find their Boston Whaler and had to bob in the sea with their life-jackets until they were recovered by a launch from the *Clifton Sprague*. The other eight-man did a little better, losing only one man, but found their Whaler.

After the rendezvous with the *Sprague*, they picked up the six-man SEAL-USAF team and set-off, undermanned, for the Point Salines airfield. Issued with inadequate maps, the SEALs were unable to reach the airfield and carry out their mission, despite two attempts.

Team 6's next operations were the raids on Radio Free Grenada, and the rescue of the British Governor-General and his staff. While SEALs successfully seized the radio station, they came under fire from Soviet weaponry and were forced to retreat into the surf a mile offshore, or be overrun. In the end, the radio station was destroyed in an air strike.

Meanwhile the two TF 160 MH-160Ks helicopters transporting SEALs on a mission to rescue government employees being held hostage in Government House failed to find the building, which was hidden by trees. While circling, the helicopters began to take hits. Ignoring the ground fire, they finally located the target, but as they approached, they found the ground sloped too steeply to land. The SEALs abseiled to the ground, but the helicopters were forced to retreat before dropping the SEALs' equipment, which included a satellite radio.

The twenty-two SEALs quickly disarmed the police guard and released the fourteen hostages, but they had to shelter with their rescuers as Grenadian troops and Soviet BTR-60 armed personnel carriers laid siege to Government House. Without their satellite radio the SEALs had trouble calling in back-up, but they finally managed to establish communication with HQ via a relay of short-range radios. After four hours, an AC-130 Spectre gunship arrived, relieved the SEALs and evacuated the fourteen staffers.

After Grenada, SEALs were also deployed on sabotage and raiding missions on Iranian ships and oil platforms in the Persian Gulf. SEAL Team 6 elements were used in the capture of the terrorist involved in the *Achille Lauro* hijacking in 1985.

The Invasion of Panama

The next large-scale SEAL deployment came with Operation Just Cause, the invasion of Panama in 1989. Seal Team 4 elements, as part of Task Force Bayonet, were ordered to cut off General Noriega's possible escape routes. SEALs aboard two Navy PBRs and two Army landing craft closed the harbour at Colon, firing across the bows of any craft trying to leave. At H-Hour minus one hour and fifteen minutes, four SEALs left Rodman Naval Air Station and swam towards the patrol boat *President Porras* tied up at Balboa Harbour. The SEALs attached satchel charges and at H-Hour – 0100 – there was a loud explosion and the craft sunk.

The SEALs next task was to assault of the airfield at Paitilla where Noriega's Learjet was housed. Swimmer scouts had already sent ashore to reconnoitre the bay end of the airfield. However, having been notified that H-Hour had been moved up by fifteen minutes, Lieutenant-Commander Toohey decided to

move his men without waiting for the scouts' report. At about
midnight, a USN patrol boat launched 15 Zodiacs, containing
three 16-man platoons and a USAF Combat Command team to
communicate with the AC-130 Spectre in air support. Meeting
with the scouts, the SEALs moved stealthily on their objective.

When Toohey received a report saying that a helicopter,
thought to be carrying Noriega, had left Colon en route to
the airfield, he decided to speed two platoons to their objective
to head off the helicopter. Running across the field, a detachment of SEALs encountered Panamians and ordered them to
surrender, thinking they were security guards they had read
about in the intelligence reports. In fact, they were soldiers
from the Panama Defence Force who had been dispatched to
guard the Learjet after news of the invasion had leaked. With
their first volley, the PDF brought down seven of the nine
SEALs, killing one. In the minute-long firefight that ensued,
more SEALs were wounded, three of whom subsequently died.
Three PDF troopers were killed and eight wounded were
carried off. It took nearly two hours to evacuate the SEALs
due to heavy air traffic following H-Hour. However, during the
action a 40-mm grenade blasted a hole through the Learjet,
rendering it useless.

The First Gulf War

In August 1990, SEALs went to the Persian Gulf for Operation
Desert Shield. SEALs were the first Western forces to arrive in
Kuwait, infiltrating the city within hours of the invasion. Their
mission was to provide intelligence reports and develop plans to
rescue US embassy personnel should they become hostages.
SEALs were also first to capture Iraqi prisoners of war after
assaulting nine occupied Kuwaiti oil platforms on 19 January
1991. It is said that a SEAL sniper team on a reconnaissance
mission, armed with M21 and M40A1 rifles, had Saddam
Hussein within their sights, but decided not to shoot as it fell
outside their mission parameters.

On 23 February 1991, a day before the ground war began, a
six-man SEAL Team, led by Lieutenant Tom Dietz, left their
Saudi coastal base at Ras al-Mishab in a pair of Fountain 33
speedboats. At 2200 hours, the six swimmer scouts deployed

their Zodiac raiding craft and set off along Kuwait's shoreline, as they had been doing for the past month. When within 500 yards from shore, the swimmers set off carrying marking buoys, H&K MP5K sub-machine-guns, night-vision equipment and 20 lb satchel charges. The explosives were laid and set to detonate at 0100 hours on 24 February, three hours before the Allied cross-border assault. As expected, the charges and marking buoys fooled the Iraqis into believing an amphibious assault was imminent, forcing troops to be diverted to the east, rather than reinforcing the actual front to the west.

With the end of the ground war and the liberation of Kuwait City, the SEALs captured the world's attention as they were caught on camera, prowling the city in their three-man Fast Attack Vehicles, heavily armed dune buggies capable of skimming across the desert sands at speeds of 60 miles an hour.

Naval Special Warfare units have also conducted missions in the Lebanon, Somalia, Bosnia, Haiti and Liberia. Four men from SEAL Team 6 were part of the assault team involved in the Battle of Mogadishu in 1993.

Afghanistan

After the attacks on America on 11 September 2001, Naval Special Warfare forces put operators on the ground in Afghanistan in October, even though the country is landlocked. Indeed, the first military flag officer to set foot in Afghanistan was a Navy SEAL who was in charge of all special operations for Central Command. A Navy SEAL captain commanded Combined Joint Special Operations Task Force South in Afghanistan. Commonly referred to as Task Force K-BAR, the task force included US Navy, Army, Air Force and Coalition Special Forces. During Operation Enduring Freedom, Naval Special Warfare forces carried out more than seventy-five special reconnaissance and direct action missions, destroying more than 500,000 lb of explosives and weapons. They identified enemy personnel and conducted Leadership Interdiction Operations in the search for terrorists trying to escape by seagoing vessels.

The Second Gulf War

Naval Special Warfare has also played a significant role in Operation Iraqi Freedom, deploying the largest number of SEALs and SWCCs in its history. Naval Special Warfare forces were instrumental in numerous special reconnaissance and direct action missions including the securing of the southern oil infrastructures of the Al Faw peninsula and the offshore gas and oil terminals. They helped clear the Khawr Abd Allah and Khawr Az Zubayr waterways that enabled humanitarian aid to be delivered to the vital port city of Umm Qasr. They also conducted reconnaissance up the Shat Al Arab waterway, capturing high-value targets, raiding suspected chemical, biological and radiological sites, and staging the first successful POW rescue since the Second World War.

During the war on terrorism, Naval Special Warfare has also been involved in fighting in other global hot spots including the Philippines and the Horn of Africa. They can operate from forward-deployed Navy ships, submarines and aviation mobility platforms as well as their own overseas bases with their own transport units.

Composition and Training

A SEAL Team comprises three 40-man task units. Each task unit is made up of a headquarters element consisting of a task unit commander, a task unit senior enlisted man, a targeting-operations officer and a targeting-operations leading or chief petty officer. Under the HQ element are two SEAL platoons of at least sixteen men – two officers and fourteen enlisted SEALS – and sometimes two enlisted Explosive Ordinance Demolition men operators making a platoon of eighteen, along with support staff. Each task unit can easily be split into four 8-man squads or eight 4-man fire teams for operational purposes. The size of each SEAL team, with its task units and support staff, is approximately 300 personnel.

As of 2006, there were eight Navy SEAL Teams, the current SEAL Teams being 1, 2, 3, 4, 5, 7, 8 and 10. In 1987, SEAL Team 6 was renamed the United States Navy Special Warfare Development Group, although members are still referred to informally as "SEAL Team 6". Since the Vietnam War the SEAL Teams split into two groups. Group 1 consists of Teams 1, 3, 5 and 7 and is based on the West Coast at Coronado and in California across the bay from San Diego. Group 2 is on the East Coast at the Naval Amphibious Base, Little Creek, a naval base in Virginia Beach, Virginia. This is home to SEAL Teams 2, 4, 8 and 10.

The SEAL insignia is a winged trident, crossed with a rifle and anchor. Their code reads: "Loyalty to country, team and team-mates. Serve with honor and integrity on and off the battlefield. Ready to lead. Ready to follow. Never quit. Take responsibility for your actions and the actions of your team-mates. Excel as warriors through discipline and innovation. Train for war. Fight to win. Defeat our nation's enemies. Earn your Trident everyday."

They also have a SEAL creed, which reads:

In times of war or uncertainty there is a special breed of warrior ready to answer our Nation's call. A common man with uncommon desire to succeed. Forged by adversity, he stands alongside America's finest special operations forces to serve his country, the American people, and protect their way of life. I am that man.

My Trident is a symbol of honor and heritage. Bestowed upon me by the heroes that have gone before, it embodies the trust of those I have sworn to protect. By wearing the Trident I accept the responsibility of my chosen profession and way of life. It is a privilege that I must earn every day.

My loyalty to Country and Team is beyond reproach. I humbly serve as a guardian to my fellow Americans always ready to defend those who are unable to defend themselves. I do not advertise the nature of my work, nor seek recognition for my actions. I voluntarily accept the inherent hazards of my profession, placing the welfare and security of others before my own.

I serve with honor on and off the battlefield. The ability to control my emotions and my actions, regardless of circumstance, sets me apart from other men. Uncompromising integrity is my standard. My character and honor are steadfast. My word is my bond.

We expect to lead and be led. In the absence of orders I will take charge, lead my team-mates and accomplish the mission. I lead by example in all situations.

I will never quit. I persevere and thrive on adversity. My Nation expects me to be physically harder and mentally stronger than my enemies. If knocked down, I will get back up, every time. I will draw on every remaining ounce of strength to protect my team-mates and to accomplish our mission. I am never out of the fight.

We demand discipline. We expect innovation. The lives of my team-mates and the success of our mission depend on me – my technical skill, tactical proficiency, and attention to detail. My training is never complete.

We train for war and fight to win. I stand ready to bring the full spectrum of combat power to bear in order to achieve my mission and the goals established by my country. The execution of my duties will be swift and violent when required yet guided by the very principles that I serve to defend.

Brave men have fought and died building the proud tradition and feared reputation that I am bound to uphold. In the worst of conditions, the legacy of my team-mates steadies my resolve and silently guides my every deed. I will not fail.

Despite their seagoing origins, SEALs are trained for operations in the desert using Humvees or Desert Patrol Vehicles. This is vital for their deployment in the current operations in Iraq and Afghanistan. They are also trained to operate in the Arctic, sleeping in snow caves; and they must be familiar with woodland and jungle survival, as well as mountain and rock climbing.

SEALs can deployed by air, using static-line and free-fall parachuting, fast-rope and rappel operations, or jumping out of a helicopter into the sea with a Zodiac. They are also extracted by air transportation on occasions. But what distinguishes the SEALs from other Special Forces is the variety of water craft they have at their disposal.

USMC Force Recon

Closely related to the US Navy SEALs is the US Marine Corps
Force Recon, not to be confused with the Marine Corps Reconnaissance Battalions. Like the SEALs, Force Recon Marines
missions include scout swimming, small-boat operations, close-
combat skills, helicopter and submarine insertion and extraction
techniques, assault climbing, demolitions, forward observer
procedures for supporting arms, initial terminal guidance operations for heliborne assaults, airborne insertion operations, various waterborne operations, communications, photography and
various types of amphibious reconnaissance operations.

The Second World War

The Marine Corps Force Recon came into being during the
Second World War in the South Pacific as the Amphibious
Reconnaissance Battalion. Before 1944 the Marine Reconnaissance comprised primarily scout and sniper units. But in April
1944, a two-company amphibious reconnaissance battalion was
formed. They started operating with Underwater Demolition
Teams to conduct beach reconnaissance and hydrographic
survey prior to landings.

The Amphibious Reconnaissance Battalion first saw action in
the Marianas. Three weeks into the battle for Saipan, when
there was no doubt about the outcome, V Amphibious Corps
commanders began turning their attention to the next objective
– the island of Tinian, clearly visible 3 miles off the south-west
coast of Saipan. Its garrison of 9,000 Japanese, many of them
veterans of the campaigns in Manchuria, had been bombarded
for seven weeks by air and from the sea armadas. These were
joined in late June by massed Marine Corps and Army artillery
battalions on Saipan's southern coast.

The 2nd and 4th Marine Divisions, both still in the thick of
the fighting on Saipan, had been selected for the assault, but the
crucial question of where they would land was still unresolved.
There was strong support among the planners for a landing on
two narrow sand strips – codenamed White 1 and White 2 – on
Tinian's north-west coast. One was just 60 yards wide, the other
160. However, Vice-Admiral Richmond K. Turner, overall

commander of the Marianas Expeditionary Force, preferred Yellow Beach, which was made up of several wide, sandy strips. On the downside, it was in front of Tinian Town, the island's heavily fortified administrative and commercial centre.

On 3 July, V Amphibious Corps Amphibious Reconnaissance Battalion, commanded by Captain James L. Jones, was put on alert for reconnaissance of the potential landing sites. On 9 July, the day Saipan was officially declared secured, Jones got his operational orders from Marine Lieutenant-General Holland M. Smith, commander of Expeditionary Troops. His men were to scout out the Tinian beaches and their fortifications, and determine their suitability to cope with the landing force, then keep it supplied. Naval Underwater Demolition Teams were to accompany them to do hydrographic work and locate underwater obstacles, either natural or man-made.

Captain Jones decided he would use both Company A, under the command of Captain Merwin H. Silverthorn Jr., the son of a Marine general and a veteran of the First World War, and Company B, commanded by First-Lieutenant Leo B. Shinn. The Navy assigned UDT 5, led by Lieutenant Commander Draper L. Kauffman, and UDT 7 under Lieutenant Richard F. Burke.

Together they rehearsed the operation on the night of 9 July off the beaches of Saipan's Magicienne Bay. Then on the evening of the 10th, the Marine and Navy units boarded the destroyer transports *Gilmer* and *Stringham* for the short trip into the channels separating the two islands. The teams left the mother ship in rubber boats at 2030 hours, paddled to within 500 yards of the beach and then swam the rest of the way. Fortunately, it was a dark night. Although the moon rose at 2230 hours, it was largely obscured by clouds.

The reconnaissance of Yellow Beach was assigned to Silverthorn's Company A. He led twenty Marines of the Amphibious Assault Team and eight UDT swimmers ashore. They found the beach flanked on each side by formidable cliffs. There were many floating mines and underwater boulders in the approaches, while the beach itself had been strung with barbed wire. Second-Lieutenant Donald F. Neff worked his way 30 yards inland to scout possible exit routes for vehicles. Nearby, he heard talkative Japanese work crews building pillboxes and

digging trenches with blasting charges. Neff spotted three
Japanese sentries on a cliff overlooking the beach and every
now and then searchlights scanned the beach approaches.
Silverthorn, Neff and their men then made their way safely
back to the *Gilmer*, their impression of Yellow Beach as a
landing site distinctly unfavourable.

To the north, the White Beaches were assigned to Company
B. Things there had not gone well as strong currents pushed the
rubber boats off course. The team headed for White 1 was
swept 800 yards north of its destination and never got ashore.
The team headed for White 2 wound up on White 1 and
reconnoitred that area instead. Both parties were then picked
up by the *Gilmer*. The next night ten swimmers from Company
A were sent back to reconnoitre White 2 and this time were
successful.

The reports both Shinn and Silverthorn made on the White
beaches were encouraging. Although the landing areas were
very restricted, they concluded that amphibian tractors and
other vehicles could negotiate the reefs and get ashore. The
troops would then have little difficulty clambering over the low
cliffs that flanked the beaches and Marines forced to disembark
from boats at the reef could safely wade ashore through the
shallow surf. Members of Kauffman's UDT party confirmed
the Amphibious Reconnaissance Battalion's findings and reported that no mines or man-made underwater obstructions had
been found.

A few hours after the reconnaissance team returned from
White 2, Admiral Turner's objections were withdrawn and a
command decision to use the northern beaches was made. On 20
July, a time and date for the landing were fixed – 0730 hours on
24 July. When two Marine Divisions from Saipan landed on the
beach on the 24th, they took the Japanese commander, Admiral
Kakuda, and his 9,000-man garrison by surprise. By the evening, the Marines had established a large beachhead and 1,200
Japanese had died when they tried to force them back into the
sea. The 4th Marines cleared the southern part of the island,
while the 2nd took the north; within a week the island was in
American hands. The Marines had lost 327 killed and 1,771
wounded all told; the Japanese had lost their garrison almost to
a man. From there, the Amphibious Reconnaissance Battalion

moved on to Iwo Jima. At the end of the war, the 1st Amphibious Reconnaissance Battalion returned to Camp Catlin on Hawaii where it was disbanded on 17 September 1945.

Post-war

In the 1950s, Amphibious Reconnaissance was reborn. Two Amphibious Reconnaissance units were formed: the 1st Amphibious Reconnaissance Company on the west coast and the 2nd Amphibious Reconnaissance Company on the east coast. These two companies would use the submarines, USS *Perch* on the west coast and *Sea Lion* on the east, to conduct training in amphibious reconnaissance and raids. During the war in Korea, Marine Reconnaissance and Underwater Demolitions did a series of raids on Korea's east coast, destroying railroad tunnels and bridges. At one time they operated 200 miles behind enemy lines, and in 1951 Marine Reconnaissance made the first helicopter assault in the Marine Corps history.

The Marine Corps Force Reconnaissance was first conceived in 1954. It was formed at Marine Base Camp Pendleton, outside San Diego, California, as an experimental reconnaissance team. Three years later, that team merged with an existing Amphibious Reconnaissance Company to form the 1st Force Reconnaissance Company.

In 1958, half the Marines in the 1st Force Reconnaissance Company were sent over to the Eastern seaboard to form the 2nd Force Reconnaissance Company at Camp Lejeune, North Carolina. The 1st Force Reconnaissance Company was attached to the Fleet Marine Force Pacific (FMFPac), while the 2nd was attached to the Fleet Marine Force Atlantic (FMFLant).

Force Reconnaissance received their baptism of fire in the Vietnam War, first arriving in-country in 1965 and staying for five years. Deployed during August–October 1965, they were assigned to the 3rd Marine Division, Fleet Marine Force. Reassigned 1st Marine Division, Fleet Marine Force in November 1966, they operated from Da Nang, Dong Ha, Hué, Phu Bai, Chu Lai and An Hoe.

In August 1970, they returned to Camp Pendleton, California, and were assigned to the 5th Marine Amphibious Brigade, Fleet Marine Force. Forty-four Marines of the 1st Force

Reconnaissance Company were killed or missing in action during the course of the Vietnam War.

After America's withdrawal from Vietnam, 1st and 2nd Force Reconnaissance Companies were both deactivated in 1974, and the existing Force Marines were rolled into the non-Force 2nd Reconnaissance Battalion to maintain Marine Corps deep reconnaissance capabilities. However, the 1st Force Reconnaissance was reactivated as an individual unit in 1986, and was later deployed during the Gulf War.

Many Force Recon Companies are in existence today, and have been deployed to both Iraq and Afghanistan. They are special-purpose units, widely recognized as the Special Operations Force of the United States Marine Corps. Marine Force Recon personnel are trained for highly specialized, small-scale, high-risk operations, such as amphibious and deep ground surveillance, and assisting in specialized technical missions that involve NBC hazards. They handle radio sensors and beacons, and designate targets for close air support, and artillery and naval gunfire. They are trained to conduct direct-action raids, such as gas and oil platform raids, and the capture of specific personnel or sensitive materials.

Like other Special Forces, they are trained for assaults behind enemy lines, deep reconnaissance, rescuing hostages and prisoners of war, unconventional warfare, and counter-terrorism.

Force Reconnaissance units have been recently integrated into the United States Special Operations Command (USSOCOM), and are now part of Marine Special Operation Battalions East and West. However, United States Marine Corps Forces Special Operations Command (MARSOC) will not be fully integrated into Special Operations Command until 2010.

Force Reconnaissance companies are deployed within a type of larger Marine Corps unit called a Marine Expeditionary Unit (Special Operations Capable) that are deployed onboard Amphibious Ready Groups, a group of United States Navy ships primed for action. These groups are usually centred around an amphibious assault helicopter carrier. There may be as many as three of these groups, with their attendant Force Reconnaissances, deployed around the world at any given time. The Marine Corps' stated goal is to be able to field a MEU(SOC) on any shore around the world within six hours of an order being given.

There are currently seven MEU(SOC)s in the Corps. In Marine Expeditionary Force I WestPac, there are three MEUs – the 11th, 13th and 15th – which are responsible for the Middle East and Persian Gulf region. In Marine Expeditionary Force II MedFloat, there are another three MEUs – the 22nd, 24th and 26th – their theatre is the countries around the Mediterranean. The last Marine Expeditionary Force, MEF III, has only one MEU(SOC), the 31st, based on Okinawa.

Since 2004, there have been four active Marine Force Reconnaissance companies: the 1st Force Reconnaissance is based at Camp Pendleton, California; the 2nd Force Reconnaissance is based at Camp Lejeune, North Carolina; the 3rd Force Reconnaissance Company is based in Mobile, Alabama; and the 4th Force Reconnaissance Company is based in Honolulu, Hawaii. The 5th Force Reconnaissance was folded into non-Force 3rd Reconnaissance Battalion as Deep Reconnaissance Company, and is based with 31st MEU(SOC) at Okinawa.

The structure of a Force Reconnaissance Company is similar to that of an infantry battalion rather than a standard company. The command element includes the Commanding Officer who is normally a lieutenant-colonel, the Executive Officer who is normally a major, a sergeant major and administrative, intelligence, operations and training, supply and communications officers. The bulk of the company is divided into six platoons, each under a platoon commander, usually a captain, and a platoon NCO, usually a sergeant, staff-sergeant or higher. One of the six platoons is a scout–sniper unit retained from the MEU's Battalion Landing Team. Force Recon units also include US Navy corpsmen as integrated combat medical personnel. Like corpsmen in other Marine Corps units, these medics receive exactly the same training as the members of the units they support.

5

DELTA FORCE

Organization and Training

Along with Naval Special Warfare Development Group, the US Army's 1st Special Forces Operational Detachment-Delta – SFOD-D, more commonly known as Delta Force – is one of two of the US government's principle Special Force units which undertake counter-terrorist operations outside the United States.

Delta Force was created by US Army Colonel Charles Beckwith in 1977 in direct response to the growing number of terrorist incidents that occurred in the 1970s. From its beginnings, Delta was heavily influenced by the British SAS as a result of Colonel Beckwith's year-long exchange tour with that unit in 1962–3. Like the SAS it is organized into three operating squadrons – A, B and C Squadron – each divided into three troops – assault, sniper and recce. As with the SAS, each troop specializes in Scuba, HALO (high altitude, low opening) parachute or other skills. These troops can be further divided into smaller units to fit the requirements of a particular mission. Usually the troop breaks down into four or five 4- or 5-man teams.

Alongside the three operational squadrons, Delta Force maintains support units which handle selection and training, logistics, finance and the unit's medical needs. There is also a signals squadron and an aviation platoon that uses aircraft painted in civilian colour schemes, and with fake identification numbers, different from the aircraft of the 160th Special Operations Aviation Regiment (Airborne) which sometimes supports Delta Force. This aviation platoon has twelve AH-6 and MH-6 Little Bird helicopters. Then there is what is termed the "Funny Platoon", the in-house Intelligence arm of Delta Force that grew out of a long-running dispute with the Army's Intelligence Support Activity. They will infiltrate a country ahead of a Delta Force intervention to gather intelligence and are the only US Special Operation Force to employ women in a combat role. The only other SOF that has employed women at all has been Army Special Forces, and then only in a training role. Delta Force also runs a clandestine technical unit which develops and maintains the covert eavesdropping equipment used to monitor terrorists in hostage rescues and other operational situations. The strength of Delta Force is around 2,500, though only around 250 are trained to conduct direct action and reconnaissance missions.

The unit is headquartered in a remote area of the US Army's sprawling Fort Bragg, North Carolina, which is also home to the XVIII Airborne Corps, the 82nd Airborne Division and the Green Berets. Their facilities there include an Olympic-sized swimming pool, dive tank, a three-storey climbing wall and numerous shooting ranges for both close-quarters battle and longer-range sniping. Their facility at Bragg is said to be the best special operations training facility in the world. The $90,000 CQB – close-quarters battle – indoor training range has earned the nickname "The House of Horrors". Training involves runs through CQB killing houses designed to teach teams and individuals how to assault buildings that have been captured by terrorists. Selective firing – deciding whether or not to shoot a target – as well as the double tap – shooting the target twice to make sure that the target does not get up again – are vital skills for the counter-terrorist specialist. The facility comes equipped with mock-ups of trains and buses for practice assaults, and there is an "aircraft room" containing a section of a wide-body jet.

To develop their skills the unit undertakes frequent exchange and training programmes with foreign counter-terrorist units, such as Britain's 22 SAS, France's GIGN, Germany's GSG-9, Israel's Sayeret Matkal/Unit 269 and Australia's Special Air Service Regiment. This close co-operation helps with the development of new tactics and equipment as well as building relations with allied forces that might prove useful in future operations.

Delta Force is equipped with the most advanced weaponry and equipment in the US special operations arsenal. Much of their gear is highly customized and cannot be found anywhere outside Delta's lockers. They have, for example, a specially constructed HAHO (high altitude, high opening) parachute rig that was adapted to get jumpers to keep their hands at their sides during the descent rather than above their heads. Keeping your arms above your head during a long descent can cause numbness and loss of vital function in the hands on landing, which could be fatal if you need to defend yourself with a weapon as soon as you hit the ground.

Delta Force troopers are usually recruited from elite US Ranger battalions and Special Forces groups, though some are drawn from all branches of the Army, including the Army Reserve and National Guard. Candidates are often selected on the basis of a personal recommendation from a source whose opinions are important to Delta screeners. Others are recruited by word of mouth or through advertisements posted at Army bases across America. Occasionally recruits are headhunted if they have some special skill – they speak an obscure language or have some rare technical ability that the unit is in need of. Selection for all of these units is rigorous, with more focus on mental abilities and toughness than physical.

The Pentagon tightly controls information about Delta Force and publicly refuses to comment on the secretive unit and its activities. However, it is known that Delta Force operators are granted an enormous amount of flexibility and autonomy, similar to their Navy counterparts in the Naval Special Warfare Development Group. They reportedly do not maintain any general uniformed presence and civilian clothing is the norm on or off duty while at Fort Bragg. Civilian styles in hair and facial hair are encouraged to help conceal their identities. Uniforms, when worn, have no markings, names or branch names on them. In action, they wear hockey helmets to protect them from bumps and scrapes while entering buildings, rather than from gunfire, and hiking boots rather than the standard-issue footwear.

Delta's unconventional nature also allows its members to carry highly customized weapons. Choice of small-arms depends on the mission at hand and personal preferences.

The Tehran Embassy Hostage Crisis

In July 1979, Delta Force deployed with the FBI at the Pan American Games in Puerto Rico as part of an anti-terrorist team set up to protect the event against a possible terrorist attack. The following year they got their first taste of action in the ill-fated Operation Eagle Claw.

On 4 November 1979 a mob in Iran had stormed the US Embassy in Tehran and took the staff and Marine Corps security guards hostage. In all, fifty-two Americans had been captured and were being held by the Iranian Revolutionary Guard. It was unclear whether they were being tortured or held for execution. Within hours, the US Army Special Forces Operational Detachment-Delta (Airborne) – Delta Force – who had passed its certification exercise just the month before, was on full alert and plans were being drawn up for their rescue.

The Delta's commander, Colonel Charles Beckwith, was intimately involved with planning the rescue attempt. It was a daunting task. Tehran is deep inside Iran and over 400 miles from any friendly country. The hostages were not held at an airport as had been the case when Israel commandos rescued the hostages from a hijacked plane at Entebbe in 1976. Iran was in the middle of a revolution and good intelligence about that was going on in the Embassy, or in Tehran generally, was hard to come by.

What was ultimately decided on was an audacious plan involving all four services. They would use eight helicopters – US Marine Corps Sikorsky RH-53D Sea Stallions – and twelve planes – four MC-130 Hercules cargo planes, three EC-130 tankers, three AC-130 gunships and two C-141 Starlifters. The plan, which was approved by President Jimmy Carter, was to infiltrate the operatives into the country the night before the assault, get them to Tehran, take over the Embassy, free the hostages, transport them to an airfield and fly them home.

On the first night, three MC-130s were to fly to a barren spot in the Iranian desert and offload the Delta force men, combat controllers to liaise with the aircraft and translators who would double as truck drivers. Three EC-130s following the Hercules would then land and prepare to refuel the Marine RH-53s flying in from the carrier USS *Nimitz*. Once the helicopters were refuelled, they would fly the task force to a spot near the outskirts of Tehran. There they would meet up with operatives already in-country who would lead the task force to a safe house where they would lie low until the assault the next night. The helicopters would fly to another remote site in-country where they would stay, hopefully undetected, until they were called for by the Delta Force operatives.

On the second night, the MC-130s and EC-130s would again fly into the country, this time carrying a hundred US Rangers, and head for Manzariyeh Airfield, 115 miles south-west of Tehran. The Rangers would assault the field and hold it so the two C-141s that would ferry the hostages back home could land. The three AC-130 gunships would be used to provide ground support for the Rangers at Manzariyeh, support Delta's assault on the Embassy and to suppress any attempts by the Iranian Air Force at nearby Mehrabad Airbase to interfere.

Once Delta Force had assaulted the Embassy and freed the hostages, they would rendezvous with the helicopters at a nearby football stadium. Then they and the hostages would be flown to Manzariyeh Airfield and the waiting C-141s, and flown out of the country to safety. All the fixed-wing aircraft would be flown out of the country, but the eight helicopters would be left after being disabled. Unfortunately, the operation would not go to plan.

Detailed planning and training went on in conditions of the strictest secrecy on dummy buildings in the Arizona desert. On the night of 30 March 1980, a CIA Twin Otter flew to the first landing area, a dirt road in the Kavir Desert east of Tehran, code-named Desert One. A US Air Force combat controller rode around the landing area on a light dirt bike, testing the ground and taking soil samples. Having ascertained that the ground was hard enough to take the weight of a fully-laden tanker plane, he laid out two runways, one on each side of the road, marking them with six radio-activated, infrared landing lights to help guide the force in. That insertion went well. In his ninety minutes on the ground, the combat controller had seen some trucks pass by, and had even seen the face of a man lighting a cigarette behind the wheel of one. Luckily he had not himself been seen and no contact had been made. The pilots also reported that, although their sensors had picked up some radar signals at 3,000 feet, there was nothing below that.

Even so, to be on the safe side, the helicopter pilots were told to fly at or below 200 feet to avoid any radar contact. However, on the night of the mission, when the helicopters went in at that level, they ran into a *haboob*, or dust storm, that they could not fly over without breaking the 200-foot limit. Down on the deck, visibility dropped to less that 100 feet.

"It was like flying in a bowl of milk," one pilot recalled.

In the choking dust, cockpit temperatures soared to 93 Fahrenheit and in one of the helicopters, the electrical systems overheated. With no artificial horizon – and no real horizon to be seen – no radio compass and no flight-control computer, there was no choice but to abort. It barely made it back to the *Nimitz*, almost running out of fuel. Another helicopter had malfunctioned and had put down along the way; its wingman had put down to pick up the crew.

Another two helicopters landed to reorientate themselves, but when they heard that the sky over Desert One was clear, they continued. It was a gruelling trip, flying low over mountain ranges that rose to 6,000 and even 9,000 feet. Finally they made it to Desert One fifty minutes late. The other helicopters came in over the next thirty-five minutes, but by they time they had refuelled, they were an hour and a half behind schedule and there was no chance that they would reach Tehran by dawn.

They were already down to six helicopters – the minimum required for the mission. Then the final blow struck. One of the remaining helicopters lost its primary hydraulic system and was unsafe to use fully loaded for the assault. With only five helicopters serviceable and six needed, the entire mission had to be aborted.

To put a cap on it, in the darkness amid the dust kicked up its rotors, one of the helicopters drifted into one of the parked

EC-130s. Both the EC-130 and the RH-53 burst into flames, lighting up the desert night. The order came to evacuate. There were wounded and dying men to be taken care of and the aircraft had to be moved to avoid having the burning debris start another fire. In the confusion, the remaining helicopters were left intact. When they fell into the hands of the Iranians the next day, top secret plans were found, endangering the agents in-country, waiting to help the Delta Force.

Five Air Force personnel and three Marines were killed, with dozens more injured. The Iranians scattered the hostages around the country afterwards, making any further rescue attempts impossible. Failure to resolve the hostage crisis cost President Carter the 1980 election and the US Embassy staff were only released after President Ronald Reagan was voted into office.

Further Operations

Things went better for Delta Force in March 1980 when they were called in to storm an Indonesian aircraft that had been hijacked by four terrorists at Bangkok airport. A Delta team was flown out and performed the rescue without a hitch, killing all four terrorists.

In May that year Delta Force were put on alert again after reconnaissance photos from SR-71 Blackbird strategic reconnaissance planes and spy satellites, identified a probable prisoner-of-war camp in central Laos, where it was believed that American servicemen held prisoner since the Vietnam War were being held. An operation was planned to rescue the PoWs if further intelligence proved that they were indeed there. Delta would take part in the operation, and would, this time, co-operate with the Intelligence Support Activity. When a private mission, headed by renegade former Green Beret Colonel Bo Gritz, went looking for Americans at the same camp and found none, the mission was called off.

In 1982, a six-man Delta intelligence squad was sent to Italy to aid in the search for Brigadier General James Dozier, the deputy chief of staff at NATO's South European headquarters in Verona, after he had been kidnapped by the Italian Red Brigade terrorist group. However, after forty-two days an

Italian anti-terrorist squad located the terrorist hideout in Padua and rescued the General.

A small contingent of Delta Force troopers was sent to Honduras to act as security guards for an intelligence gathering operation, code-named Queens Hunter, in neighbouring Nicaragua. The Delta Force troopers abandoned their uniforms, donned baseball caps and windcheaters, and carried Uzis.

During Operation Urgent Fury in 1983 Delta Force was deployed alongside SEAL Team 6 and other Special Forces units in Grenada. Their primary objectives were the liberation of civilians imprisoned at Richmond Hill prison, and rescuing senior advisors of General Austin from Fort Rupert. The rescue missions were aborted twice due to poor intelligence and inter-service rivalry, but in the case of the Fort Rupert mission, they met with success and assisted in the seizure of a key airfield.

Delta Force operatives were also stationed in Beirut that year. One died in the 1983 US Embassy bombing, when it was said that they were looking for American hostages and planning rescue attempts. Delta Force operatives also worked as intelligence gatherers and embassy guards, and were said to be involved in direct-action counter-narcotics operations in the jungles of South America.

In 1984, Delta Force deployed to the Middle East in response to the hijacking of a Kuwaiti Airlines airliner, during which two Americans were killed. However, due to logistics problems, the Delta team did not go into action. That year Delta Force is also said to have participated in Operation Manta in Libya, where they accompanied small teams of French Special Forces into the country to plant surveillance equipment around terrorist training camps. Delta Force were also believed to have been sent to Chad to teach government troops to use sophisticated weapons systems, such the Stinger, which could be used to shoot down Libyan aircraft. In 1984, elements of Delta Force provided security at the Olympic Games in Los Angeles.

When TWA Flight 847 from Athens to Rome was hijacked by Hezbollah terrorists in June 1985 and flown to Beirut, then Algiers, Delta Force were despatched. However, the Algerian government refused permission for them to mount a rescue operation in the country. A US Navy diver named Robert Stethem who was on board was killed as the plane flew back and forth between Algiers and Beirut. Gradually the hostages were released and the terrorists escaped.

That October, the Italian cruise-liner SS *Achille Lauro* was hijacked in the Mediterranean by four Palestine Liberation Front terrorists and some 400 hostages were taken. As a large portion of the hostages were American, Delta and SEAL Team 6 were placed on full alert, eventually being deployed to Sigonella Naval Air Station in Sicily. Although the terrorists murdered a hostage – wheelchair-bound Leon Klinghoffer – they negotiated safe passage with Egypt and boarded an Egyptian Boeing 737 at Port Said, escorted by Force 777, Egypt's counter-terrorist unit, to make sure that no other unit would interfere. However, the plane was intercepted by US fighters and forced to land at Sigonella. Awaiting them on the runway was a joint force of Delta and SEAL 6 operatives in full tactical gear. As General Stiner approached the aircraft to apprehend the terrorists, a Carabinieri unit showed up and demanded that the terrorists be turned over to the Italians. While Stiner and the Carabinieri commander yelled at each other, the Italians and Americans had an armed stand-off, and the terrorists were eventually turned over to the Italians, arrested and tried. Three were given long sentences, but the leader Abu Abbas somehow escaped.

In 1986, it fell to Delta Force to provide security at the Statue of Liberty Centennial celebration. The following year, they were sent to Greece to protect US Army Colonel James "Nick" Rowe, one of the few prisoners of war to escape during the Vietnam War, in response to threats to assassinate him. Two years later he was shot dead in the Philippines. Later, in 1987, Delta Force was called to assist the FBI putting down a prison riot in the Federal penitentiary in Atlanta, Georgia – the first time a Special Forces unit was allowed on any aggressive domestic operation. It was said that when the prisoners got word that Delta Force were on their way, they surrendered.

During Operation Just Cause in 1989, a Delta Force team and SEAL 6 were deployed together again in Panama. Their main task was the apprehension of General Manuel Noriega, who was wanted in the US on drug-trafficking charges. The Delta Force operatives, in civilian clothes but sporting Heckler & Koch MP5 9-mm machine pistols under their jackets, searched the city and harbour for Noriega. On one occasion an eight-man Delta Force team burst into a brothel, where Noriega was purportedly hiding. Dashing upstairs, they caught a whiff of his characteristic cigars and the bed was still warm – they were informed that he had left less than an hour earlier.

However, as a counter-terrorist group, Delta's main function is in hostage rescue and during Operation Just Cause, Delta got their chance to do just that. Kurt Muse, an American business-man who operating an underground radio station, had been jailed in the city of Modelo. A 160th Special Operations Avia-tion Regiment MH-6 Little Bird helicopter transported a Delta Force team to the rooftop of the jail. The team fought its way down to the second floor and blew the door to Muse's cell, freeing him without injury. As the team and Muse made their way to the roof and the waiting MH-6, Kurt Muse counted at least five bodies, though not all had been killed. One terrified guard had been handcuffed to a staircase railing. As it lifted off, the helicopter was hit by small-arms fire and fell to the street below. The pilot slid the helicopter along the ground to a parking lot and attempted to take off again, but it was hit by ground fire again and crash-landed, this time permanently. A passing UH-60 Sikorsky Black Hawk spotted the infra-red spotlight held up by a Delta Force trooper and soldiers from the 6th Infantry Regiment came to the rescue. Four Delta operatives were wounded, but they had successfully rescued Kurt Muse and probably saved his life.

In 1990, Delta Force were deployed to Iraq as part of Operation Desert Shield. Along with the 22nd SAS Regiment, they were responsible for destroying mobile Scud missile launchers in the Iraqi desert. Delta operatives also served as Coalition Comman-der General Norman Schwarzkopf's bodyguards.

After doing their bit in the First Gulf War, they moved on to Somalia as part of Task Force Ranger, taking part in various operations to apprehend warlord Mohamad Farah Aidid in Mogadishu. In 1993, three Delta Force men were sent to Waco, Texas to help the FBI plan their assault on the Branch Davidian compound where they claimed a number of "hostages" – in fact, followers of the cult leader David Koresh – were being held. After a 51-day stand-off, the FBI attacked, the building caught fire and eight members of the group, including Koresh, died.

In October 1993, Delta Force were in Somalia just before the US contingent pulled out, when a joint Delta-SEAL-Ranger-Nightstalkers Task Force made another attempt to capture the warlord Aidid. The operation went wrong from the beginning. As one of the Ranger teams was fast-roping from a Blackhawk, a soldier fell and was critically injured. Within minutes, the Rangers and Delta Force men found themselves in a vicious firefight with Somali militia. Although the Delta Force team captured twenty of Aidid's top lieutenants, as the support convoy of Hummers and trucks that was to take them back to base neared, gunfire erupted from all sides. At the same time, the 160th SOAR MH-60 Black Hawk co-ordinating the attack from the air was hit by a rocket-propelled grenade and crashed. The Hummvee convoy sent to rescue the crew got lost on their way. For the next five hours the Task Force found itself fighting for their lives in what was said to have been "the largest firefight since Vietnam". Meanwhile, driving around the city hopelessly lost, the convoy was badly mauled by RPG and small-arms fire. Finally, with the help of Malaysian and Pakistani peacekeepers, the Task Force was evacuated and its dead and wounded flown back to base. The final death toll was eighteen Rangers and Delta Force troopers dead, with more Rangers wounded. The story is told in the movie *Black Hawk Down*.

The following year, Delta Force took part in Operation Uphold Democracy in Haiti. Delta operators served as bodyguards for visiting UN officials and diplomats, working together with the Polish counter-terrorist unit, "Grom". Some Delta operatives were also sent in to Bosnia to act as bodyguards for visiting state officials. In the mid to late 1990s, Delta Force and SEAL Team 6 contingents were deployed again together in Bosnia to plan the apprehension of the accused war criminal Radovan Karadzic. Although they carried out vital surveillance, the actual assault never went ahead.

In 1996, in conjunction with the Hostage Rescue Team, Secret Service, Bureau of Alcohol, Tobacco and Firearms and other law-enforcement agencies, Delta Force stood by in case of terrorist attack at the Olympic Games in Atlanta. Together with a large number of local SWAT (Special Weapons Assault Team) Teams and unarmed National Guard troops, they formed the largest peacetime security force in history.

In January the following year a small advance team of Delta Force troopers, along with six members of the British SAS, was sent to Lima, Peru immediately following the takeover of the Japanese Ambassador's residence,.

The following spring, Delta Force, the SAS and other NATO Special Operations units were deployed to Kosovo in support of Operation Allied Force. They were supposedly there to gather intelligence, target Serbian tanks and buildings, and rescue downed NATO pilots. It is possible that they also co-operated with the Kosovo Liberation Army to follow Serbian troop and armour movements. Then in June 1997, US officials acknowledged that UK and US special operations units, including Delta Force, were being trained for "snatch" operations in preparation for a possible mission to apprehend Serb President and war criminal Slobodan Milosevic.

Delta Force were also on hand for Operation Enduring Freedom in Afghanistan in 2001 and Operation Anaconda in 2002, as well as Operation Iraqi Freedom in 2003 and Operation Vigilant Resolve in 2004.

6

US AIR FORCE SPECIAL FORCES

Air Force Special Operations Command was established on 22 May 1990 with headquarters at Hurlburt Field, Florida. AF-SOC is the Air Force component of US Special Operations Command whose command centre is at MacDill Air Force Base, Florida. Like other special operations units, it has a distinguished heritage.

Second World War

In the European theatre of operations during the Second World War, regular Army Air Force units were used to conduct special operations in high-threat areas under the direction of the Office of Strategic Services and the British Intelligence Service. The US Air Force was only established as an independent command in September 1947. Until then, it had been part of the Army – during the second World War as the US Army Air Force and before June 1941 as the Army Air Corps.

The earliest USAAF special operations involved the Special Flight Section of the 12th Air Force's 5th Bombardment Wing in North Africa. In October of 1943, this small ad hoc unit flew highly modified and mission-specific B-17 Flying Fortressed, B-24 Liberators and B-25 twin-engined Mitchell bombers from North Africa over France and other parts of occupied Europe.

The Special Flight Section later became known as the 885th Bombardment Squadron and flew Liberators out of Brindisi on the heel of Italy, once the Allies had occupied the south.

Along with conventional AAF troop-carrier units, the special operations transports and bombers flew 3,769 successful sorties into the Balkans, largely into the area that became Yugoslavia. They dropped 7,149 tons of supplies to resistance groups, while the unit's C-47 Douglas Dakotas landed 989 times behind enemy lines, delivering another 1,972 tons. These special operations units also assisted in the evacuation of thousands of Allied airmen and wounded partisans in 1944 and 1945.

The largest USAAF special operations effort in Europe was conducted by the 801st Bombardment Group. Nicknamed the "Carpetbaggers", they were based in England. They specialized in the delivery of supplies, agents and propaganda leaflets behind enemy lines using B-24s specifically modified for their particular mission, and painted black.

Immediately before D-Day and during Operation Overlord itself, the 801st Bombardment Group and African-based units dropped specially trained three-man Jedburgh teams behind enemy lines in France. Once in place, the Jedburgh teams coordinated Free French and partisan Maquis operations. Special operations crews became proficient in night, low-level, long-range navigation and flying, often conducted in poor weather and over mountainous terrain.

During early June 1944, the Carpetbaggers dropped six teams into strategic locations in Brittany, France from where they relayed vital intelligence data critical to the success of the invasion of Normandy. Later, Carpetbaggers airlifted fuel vital to keep up the momentum of General George S. Patton's armoured drive out of France and into Germany.

There were separate developments in special operations flying in the Pacific theatre. These began in August 1943, when General Henry H. "Hap" Arnold met with British Admiral, Lord Louis Mountbatten, then Supreme Allied Commander South-East Asia, to discuss plans for American air support of British commando expeditions in China and Burma. At those meetings, General Arnold coined the term "air commando".

After reaching an accord with Mountbatten, General Arnold directed veteran fighter pilots Lieutenant-Colonels Philip G.

Cochran and John R. Alison to build a self-reliant, composite fighting force to support British Brigadier General Orde C. Wingate and his "Chindits" – British, Ghurkha, West African and Burmese guerrillas – on long-range penetrations into the Burma jungle to harass the Japanese. By March 1944, this force was designated the 1st Air Commando Group.

The air commandos flew over hazardous mountains and jungles to find and resupply the highly mobile British ground forces in hostile territory. From these missions, the 1st Air Commando Group earned its motto of "Any Place, Any Time, Any Where", a variation of which is still used today. The 1st Air Commando Group's success in these operations eventually led to the creation of two more air commando groups, the 2nd and 3rd Air Commando Groups.

Air commandos in the Pacific performed a variety of conventional and unconventional combat and support missions deep behind enemy lines. They used an array of aircraft including C-47 Dakota transports, P-47 Thunderbolt and P-51 Mustang fighters, B-25 Mitchell bombers, UC-64 utility aircraft, and a glider force of G-5s and CG-4As Waco cargo carriers, augmented by R-4 Sikorsky Hoverfly helicopters. Air commandos are credited with the first combat aircrew rescue by helicopter, and the first combat use of air-to-ground rockets. They destroyed multiple ground targets and shot down a number of enemy aircraft.

Enlisted pilots were an essential part of the 550-man force, flying resupply and medical evacuation missions with L-1 and L-5 Sentinel light liaison aircraft. The medical evacuation flights were extremely successful and proved to be critical to the morale of the Chindits.

Post-war Reorganizations and Operations

Like other special operations capabilities, the air commandos were mothballed after the Second World War, although their capabilities were resurrected in the late 1940s to combat the Hukbalahap, or Huk, Rebellion in the Philippines, when Communist-led guerrillas who had fought the Japanese threatened to unseat the government in Manila.

The airpower used to defeat the *Hukbo ng Bayan sa Hapon* –

or "People's Anti-Japanese Army" – was organized along unconventional lines. US assistance was provided by Lieutenant-Colonel Edward G. Lansdale, who employed the Special Forces' "Foreign Internal Defense" tactics as outlined by the Pentagon. Under his guidance, the Philippine Air Force flew C-47s, P-51s, L-5s, AT-6 armed trainers and a mixture of liaison aircraft against the Huks. Lansdale also began a successful psychological warfare campaign using air-dropped leaflets and airborne speaker operations. Psychological warfare, combined with air and ground attacks, kept the Huks on the defensive and led to their defeat in 1954.

At the same time, there were developments in Korea. Early in the Korean War, which broke out in 1950, US Army Intelligence and the fledgling Central Intelligence Agency, the OSS's successor, needed to deploy intelligence teams and supplies on short- and long-range low-level penetration into North and occupied South Korea. Initially, the US Air Force provided this special air support ad hoc, using C-47 and C-119 Fairchild Boxcar transports, B-26 Douglas Invader medium bombers and Air Rescue Service crash boats.

The Air Force then activated, equipped and trained dedicated units – the 580th, 581st and 582nd Air Resupply and Communication Wings – specifically for unconventional warfare and counter-insurgency operations. These wings possessed tremendous capabilities using a variety of aircraft such as C-47, C-54 Douglas Skymaster, C-118 Douglas DC-6, C-119 transports, B-29 bombers, SA-16 Albatros seaplanes, and H-19 Sikorsky Chicksaw transport helicopters. This revitalized special operations force now had the means to run the full spectrum of covert air operations and added the capability to recover downed airmen. However, while three wings were activated, only one saw action in Korea. After the war, all three were mothballed by late 1953.

Throughout the rest of the 1950s, air resupply and covert communications were taken over by four Air National Guard units in Maryland, Rhode Island, West Virginia and California. Meanwhile, the US used other active and reserve air assets in secret operations in Tibet, Iran, French Indo-China, behind the Iron Curtain and in the Caribbean during the abortive Bay of Pigs invasion of Cuba. Things changed radically the 1960s when Air Force duty special operations units were created to counter Soviet support of guerrilla movements in the Third World. General Curtis E. LeMay, Air Force Chief of Staff, established the 4400th Combat Crew Training Squadron in April 1961. Nicknamed "Jungle Jim", the CCTS was based at Hurlburt Field, Florida. Its two-fold mission was counter-insurgency training and combat operations. Aircraft such as U-10 Speaker Bird lightweight psychological warfare planes, C-46 Curtiss Commando transport planes, C-47s, B-26s and AT-28 Trojan Trainers soon showed up on the Hurlburt flight line.

The CCTS devised Foreign Internal Defense tactics and techniques for building a counter-insurgency capability throughout the Third World – Latin America, Africa, the Middle East and South-East Asia. The first Jungle Jim operation, code-named Sandy Beach One, involved training paratroopers in Mali. Then, in November 1961, the 4400th CCTS deployed a detachment to Bien Hoa, Republic of Vietnam, on Operation Farmgate, where the Air Force special operations forces flew some of the first US combat missions in Vietnam.

The Vietnam War

As the Vietnam War expanded, the Air Force increased its counter-insurgency capability. The 4400th CCTS became a group in March 1962, and the next month became part of the newly activated US Air Force Special Air Warfare Center (USAF SAWC) at Eglin Air Force Base, Florida.

The Special Air Warfare Center acquired new aircraft in the mid-1960s, including: O-1 Cessna Bird Dog and O-2 Armed Porter observation planes; A-1 Skyraider, A-26 Invader and A-37 Dragonfly attack fighters; C-123 Fairchild Provider, and later C-130 Hercules cargo planes; along with several types of helicopters. As well as being used as a short-field tactical transport, the C-123s were also modified as aerial sprayers for Ranch Hand missions in Vietnam, spraying the defoliant Agent Orange to deny the enemy the cover of the jungle.

In 1964, air commandos deployed to Laos and Thailand on Operation Waterpump. This was similar to a Foreign Internal Defense operation and involved training Laotian and Thai pilots, and supporting the Royal Lao Army against insurgents. Also in late 1964, the Air Force introduced the first gunships into combat with the deployment of AC-47 Magic Dragons or "Spookies" to Vietnam.

By 1966, the high-water mark for US Air Force special operations forces in Vietnam, the total contingent comprised 10,000 people and 550 aircraft in nineteen squadrons. At the same time air commandos were also deployed in other countries, including Malaysia, Greece, Saudi Arabia, Ethiopia, Iran and the Republic of the Congo. The following year AC-119 Shadow and Stinger gunships arrived in Vietnam, and by 1968 the first AC-130 Hercules gunships joined the war.

In the summer of 1968, the US Air Force renamed the Special Air Warfare Center as the USAF Special Operations Force (USAFSOF) which became the equivalent of a numbered air force unit. Subordinate units were redesignated as special operations wings and squadrons, eliminating all reference to air commandos which were now considered passé. By this time, the Vietnam War was at its peak and Bien Hoa consumed virtually all of the Air Force's special operations efforts.

One of the most notable missions supported by US Air Force special operations was the Son Tay prisoner-of-war camp raid in 1970. The Son Tay raiders trained at Hurlburt and Duke Fields, near Eglin Air Force Base, Florida. Although no prisoners were in the North Vietnamese compound, the tactical success of the mission boosted morale and treatment of American prisoners of war in enemy hands improved, making the mission strategically worthwhile.

As the Vietnam War began winding down, Special Forces capability gradually declined as well. In June 1974, the USAF Special Operations Force became the 834th Tactical Composite Wing, effectively bringing to a close the most aggressive effort by the USAF to support unconventional warfare.

In April 1975, Special Operations were involved in Operation Eagle Pull, when the last US Embassy staff were evacuated from Phnom Penh, as Cambodia fell to Pol Pot and the Khmer Rouge. This was followed by Operation Frequent Wind, where Special Operations once again helped in the evacuation from an American embassy, this time in Saigon. On 12 May, the Khmer

Rouge captured the US freighter *Mayaguez* in the Gulf of Siam. Two days later, the freighter was recaptured, but in the operation one helicopter crashed and two more were lost when they landed on Kong Tang Island, and came under small-arms fire from Khmer Rouge stationed there. Forty-one men were lost and over fifty wounded. Despite this precipitative action, the Cambodians decided to release the forty-man crew of the *Mayaguez*.

Post-Vietnam Operations

In July 1975, the USAF renamed the 834th Tactical Composite Wing the 1st Special Operations Wing, and by 1979 it was the only special operations wing in the Air Force. The wing was armed with AC-130H Spectre gunships, MC-130E Combat Talons and CH-3E Jolly Green and UH-1N Huey helicopters. Two MC-130 Combat Talon squadrons remained overseas and the Air Force Reserve maintained an AC-130A gunship group and one HH-3E Jolly Green squadron.

After the failure of the attempt to rescue the hostages from the United States Embassy in Iran, the Holloway Commission was convened to analyse why the mission failed and what could be done about it. This led to the gradual reorganization and rebirth of United States special operations forces.

Meanwhile, in December 1982, the Air Force transferred responsibility for Air Force special operations from Tactical Air Command to Military Airlift Command. Consequently, in March 1983, MAC activated the 23rd Air Force at Scott Air Force Base, Illinois. This newly numbered Air Force unit's responsibilities included special operations missions worldwide, combat rescue, weather reconnaissance and aerial sampling, security support for intercontinental ballistic missile sites, the training of USAF helicopter and HC-130 crewmen, para-rescue training and medical evacuation.

In October 1983, the 23rd Air Force participated in Operation Urgent Fury, the invasion of Grenada. During the seven-day operation, it took over Grenada's Point Salines International Airport, where it stationed MC-130s, AC-130s, aircrews, maintenance and support people. An EC-130 from the 193rd Special Operations Group of the Air National Guard also played a significant psychological-warfare role. During this crucial combat test of emerging Special Forces capability, a 1st Special Operations Wing Combat Talon crew earned the Mackay Trophy, instituted in 1911, for the "most meritorious flight of the year" and a Spectre crew earned the Lieutenant-General William H. Tunner Award, an Air Force prize for the most outstanding airlift crew.

That same year Special Operations staged Operation Big Pine, which landed 60,000 troops in Honduras just north of the Nicaraguan border, and began Operation Bild Kirk in El Salvador. The following year, they lent a hand in the rescue of President Jose Napoleon Duarte's daughter, when she had been kidnapped.

In 1986, they were also involved in Operation El Dorado Canyon – the bombing of Libya – and were on hand when Pan Am Flight 73 was hijacked at Karachi Airport. When the hijackers began massacring the passengers, Pakistani commandos stormed the plane. At least twenty passengers died. Others survived by forcing the doors and jumping from the wings.

In May 1986, new legislation led to the formation of the US Special Operations Command. Senators William Cohen and Sam Nunn introduced the Senate Bill, and the following month Congressman Dan Daniel introduced a like measure in the House of Representatives. The key provisions of the legislation formed the basis to amend the 1986 Defense Authorizations Bill. Signed into law in October 1986, the Bill in part directed the formation of a unified command responsible for special operations, and in April 1987 the Department of Defense established the United States Special Operations Command (USSOCOM) at MacDill Air Force Base, Florida, under the command of Army General James J. Lindsay. Four months later, the 23rd Air Force moved to Hurlburt Field, Florida.

In 1987, Air Force Special Operations deployed in the Persian Gulf with the US Navy SEALS, Special Boat Units and the US Army to ensure the safe transit of oil tankers and other neutral shipping during the height of the Iran-Iraq War. The following year, they deployed with other US troops in Operation Golden Pheasant which aimed to protect Honduras incursions by the Sandinista government in Nicaragua chasing US-backed Contra guerrillas across the border.

In August 1989, General Duane H. Cassidy, Commander-in-Chief of Military Airlift Command, divested the 23rd Air Force of its non-special operations units. However, this still left the 23rd Air Force with a dual role – reporting to MAC while functioning as the air component of USSOCOM. That year a team was sent to Afghanistan in Operation Safe Passage to assist the Mujahadeen deal with the huge number of landmines left by the Soviets. Others were deployed to El Salvador and to the Philippines where there was an attempted coup against President Aquino.

From late December 1989 to early January 1990, the 23rd Air Force participated in Operation Just Cause, the invasion of Panama. The special operations aircraft in use included AC-130 Spectre gunships from active service units as well as the Air Force Reserve, EC-130 Volant Solo psychological operations aircraft from the Air National Guard, HC-130P/N Combat Shadow tankers, MC-130E Combat Talons, and MH-53J Pave Low and MH-60G Pave Hawk helicopters. Special tactics combat controllers and medics from the unit were also on hand to support combat units during this operation.

Spectre gunship crews of the 1st Special Operations Wing earned the Mackay Trophy and Tunner Award for their efforts, while their maintenance crew won a Daedalian Award. A 919th Special Operations Group Spectre crew earned the President's Award, while a 1st SOW Combat Talon crew got the greatest honour of all – ferrying the captured Panamanian President, Manuel Noriega, to prison in the United States.

On 22 May 1990, General Larry D. Welch, Air Force Chief of Staff, renamed the 23rd Air Force as Air Force Special Operations Command. This new major command consisted of three wings – the 1st, 39th and 353rd Special Operations Wings – as well as the 1720th Special Tactics Group, the US Air Force Special Operations School and the Special Missions Operational Test and Evaluation Center. The Air Force Reserve components included the 919th Special Operations Group at Duke Field, Florida, and the 193rd Special Operations Group of the Air National Guard at Harrisburg International Airport, Pennsylvania.

Currently, after major redesignations and reorganizations, Air Force Special Operations Command direct-reporting units include the 16th Special Operations Wing, the 352nd Special Operations Group, the 353rd Special Operations Group, the 720th Special Tactics Group, the USAF Special Operations School and the 18th Flight Test Squadron.

In January 1991, Air Force Special Operations Command participated in Operation Eastern Exit in Somalia, along with a nine-man team of US Navy SEALs and the 4th Marine Expeditionary Brigade, to evacuate 281 American and other foreign non-combatants from the US Embassy in Mogadishu. This was conducted at night by waves of CH-46s helicopters flying at night into and out of the darkened Embassy compound using night-vision goggles. All 281 people, from thirty nations, were rescued. As the last wave of CH-46s left with the security force, armed looters could be seen scaling the walls of the compound. That year they were also involved in Operation Sea Angel to take humanitarian aid to Bangladesh after tropical cyclone Marian killed 140,000 people and left over five million homeless.

The First Gulf War

From early August 1990 to late February 1991, Air Force Special Operations Command participated in Operations Desert Shield and Desert Storm, protecting Saudi Arabia and liberating Kuwait. Active duty, Air Force Reserve and Air National Guard components of Air Force Special Operations Command deployed to Saudi Arabia and Turkey. The 1st Special Operations Wing with its AC-130s, HC-130s, MC-130s, MH-53s and MH-60s, the 193rd Special Operations Group with its EC-130s, and the 919th Special Operations Group with its AC-130s – along with the 71st Special Operations Squadron's HH-3s – were all deployed south of Kuwait. Meanwhile the 39th Special Operations Wing deployed north of Iraq with its HC-130s, MC-130s and MH-53s. And special tactics personnel operated throughout the theatre on multiple combat-control and combat-rescue missions.

Special operations forces performed direct-action missions, combat search and rescue, infiltration, exfiltration, air base ground defence, air interdiction, special reconnaissance, close air support, psychological operations and helicopter air refuellings. Pave Low crews led the helicopter assault on radars to blind Iraq at the onset of hostilities, and they also accomplished the deepest rescue for which they received the Mackay Trophy.

Combat Talons dropped the largest conventional bombs of the war and, along with Combat Shadows, dropped the most psychological-warfare leaflets. The AC-130s provided valuable fire support and armed reconnaissance, but they also suffered the single greatest combat loss of Coalition air forces when Spirit 03, an AC-130H Spectre gunship, was shot down near the Kuwaiti border while supporting the Marines during the first Iraq offensive on 13 January 1991. All on board were killed. Fourteen of the twenty US Air Force personnel lost during the First Gulf War were from Spirit 03.

Further Reorganizations and Operations

Following the Gulf War, Air Force Special Operations Command came up with a new version of the old Air Commando motto of "Any Place, Any Time, Any Where". Now it was "All The Time, Everywhere". Air Force Special Operations Command aircraft stood by for personnel recovery and various other missions in support of Operation Provide Comfort to defend the Kurds fleeing Iraq after the First Gulf War, and Operation Southern Watch, the enforcing of the "no-fly" zone over Iraq. During July 1992, Air Force Special Operations Command units began participation in Operations Provide Promise and Deny Flight, the humanitarian relief effort and policing of the no-fly zone in the Balkans from 1992 to 1996.

In December 1992, Air Force Special Operations Command special tactics and intelligence personnel were employed in Operation Restore Hope in Somalia. Then Air Force Special Operations Command's AC-130H Spectre gunships went into Somalia on Operations Continue Hope and United Shield in the spring of 1993. In late 1994, Air Force Special Operations Command units spearheaded Operation Uphold Democracy to restore order in Haiti, and in 1995 Operation Deliberate Force in the Balkans, bombing Bosnia and Herzegovina.

These deployments were accompanied by a number of organizational changes. The most significant one took place under Operation Fiery Vigil, when the 353rd Special Operations

Wing relocated from Clark Air Base in the Philippines to Kadena Air Base, Japan, in June 1991 due to the volcanic eruption of Mount Pinatubo. The unit was supported by temporary duty personnel under Operation Scimitar Sweep in Iraq for more than a year.

In January 1992, the 39th Special Operations Wing moved from Rhein-Main Air Base in Germany to RAF Alconbury in the UK. Later that year the 39th Special Operations Wing was dissolved, and its personnel and equipment were reconstituted as the 352nd Special Operations Wing. In December 1992, Air Force Special Operations Command redesignated both overseas wings as groups.

More reorganization occurred on Hurlburt Field with the 1720th Special Tactics Group becoming the 720th Special Tactics Group in March 1992, and in October 1992 the ownership of Hurlburt Field was transferred from Air Mobility Command (formerly the MAC) to Air Force Special Operations Command. This was followed by the merger of the 834th Air Base Wing into the 1st Special Operations Wing, which assumed host unit responsibilities. A year later the 1st Special Operations Wing became the 16th Special Operations Wing in an effort to preserve Air Force heritage.

Meanwhile, the Special Missions Operational Test and Evaluation Center (SMOTEC), which filled the unique role of developing new heavy lift capabilities for special operations, was also reorganized. In April 1994, the Air Force, in an effort to standardize these types of organizations, redesignated SMOTEC as the 18th Flight Test Squadron.

In March 1994, a 16th Special Operations Squadron AC-130H gunship, call sign Jockey 14, was deployed in Operation Continue Hope II in Somalia, when it suffered an in-flight explosion that forced it to ditch off the coast of Kenya. Eight crew members were killed, six survived.

Air Force Special Forces were in action again when a pair of US Army UH-60 Black Hawk helicopters were shot down in a friendly-fire incident during Operation Provide Comfort III in Iraq. The 9th Special Operations Squadron, the 55th Special Operations Squadron and the 23rd Special Tactics Squadron played significant roles in the search, support and recovery operations.

In the autumn of 1994, the US decided to send forces into Haiti. The 16th Special Operations Wing, the 919th Special Operations Wing and the 193rd Special Operations Wing led the formations of fixed and rotary winged aircraft to complete Operation Uphold Democracy. Air Force Special Operations helicopters flew from US Navy aircraft carriers during this massed deployment.

During this operation, most of the Air Force Special Operations Command aircraft operated out of Guantanamo Bay, the now-notorious US Naval base, on the island of Cuba. This deployment also included the largest gathering of MH-53 Pave Lows to participate in one action, and the last time the 919th Special Operations Wing's AC-130As would see action before retirement.

Following the genocide in Rwanda in 1994, the Air Force Special Operations Command's 352nd Special Operations Group becoming involved in the humanitarian relief effort known as Operation Support Hope, also referred to as Quiet Resolve or Provide Relief.

In early 1995, the Air Force Special Operations Command was tasked to support a number of peacekeeping and humanitarian missions. These included Operation Provide Comfort III, taking aid to Kurds in Turkey and Iraq, and Operation Provide Promise/Deny Flight, which evolved into Operation Deliberation Force and Operation Joint Endeavour into Bosnia Herzegovina-Croatia, out of Italy. Pave Low helicopter crewmen received combat wounds while flying as part of a force trying to rescue two French aviators who had been shot down near Sarajevo during Operation Deliberate Force. The efforts of the Pave Low flight crew during this attempted rescue effort resulted in their receiving the 1995 Air Force Cheney Award, presented each year to an airman for valour on a humanitarian mission. Air Force Special Operations Command also supported Operation Continue Hope III in Somalia which evolved into Operation United Shield – the evacuation of the remaining peacekeeping force from the war-torn region.

In 1996, Air Force Special Operations Command aircraft were the first on the scene when the CT-43 aircraft carrying US Commerce Secretary Ron Brown crashed near Dubrovnik, Croatia, killing everyone on board. The 352nd Special

Operations Group sent two MH-53J Pave Low medium-lift helicopters and one MC-130P Combat Shadow aeroplane for mid-air refuelling as part of the search and rescue effort. Crews of the 16th Special Operations Wing and the 20th Special Operations Squadron also participated. These crew members were awarded the Air Force Cheney Award for 1996.

The crews involved in this mission soon found themselves in Africa for Operation Assured Response, which provided support to the emergency Non-combatant Evacuation Operation of more than 2,100 US and foreign citizens from Monrovia, Liberia. Operating under a hostile fire environment, Special Operations personnel conducted dozens of helicopter evacuation flights using MH-53J Pave Lows and overhead fire-support sorties in AC-130H Spectres, often guiding friendly aircraft through small-arms and rocket-propelled grenade fire. For their efforts the Pave Low crews were presented the Tunner Award as the outstanding strategic airlift crew of the year.

Following the break-up of the Soviet Union, Air Force Special Operations Command found its forces in constant demand for co-operative engagements and peace enforcement activities, though it was still, technically, organized to counter the Soviet threat. But something had to give. As part of Commando Vision, which started in 1994, the 919th Special Operations Wing would not receive the AC-130Hs from the 16th Special Operations Wing as planned. Instead, the 919th Special Operations Wing at Duke Field, Florida, retired its AC-130A gunships and was given support planes in the shape of MC-130P Combat Shadows, to be flown by the newly activated 5th Special Operations Squadron, and MC-130E Combat Talons, to be flown by the 711th Special Operations Squadron. While these changes were being made the 919th Special Operations Wing reservists deployed to Brindisi Air Base in Italy in December 1995 to support Operation Joint Endeavor, the deployment of an international peacekeeping force in Bosnia Herzegovina to enforce the Dayton Agreement. The 919th Special Operations Wing completed the conversion to a support role by 1997.

Air Force Special Operations Command were being kept so busy that, in February 1997, they captured the "triple crown" of Air Force Safety Awards for 1996, a feat accomplished only once before by a major command. They took the Secretary of the Air Force Safety Award for the best overall mishap prevention programme, the Major-General Benjamin D. Foulois Award for best flight safety programme, and the Colonel Will L. Tubbs Memorial award for the top ground safety programme. Later in that year, the 16th Special Operations Wing received the Colombian Trophy for military flight safety achievements in 1996. This marked the first time in the 62-year history of the award that it was presented to a non-fighter unit.

In April 1997, Air Force Special Operations Command units on temporary duty in Brindisi in support of the NATO missions in Bosnia took on a key support role in the evacuation of Americans trapped in Albania by the civil war there. Supporting Operation Silver Wake, they assisted State Department officials in the rescue of more than a thousand evacuees, including some 450 Americans removed from the warring nation.

In June 1997, when the civil war in the Republic of Congo threatened to engulf the nation's capital, an Air Force Special Operations Command MC-130H Talon II from the 352nd Special Operations Group flew an American military assessment team into Brazzaville, then evacuated fifty-six people. The crew earned the Mackay Trophy for its endeavour.

September 1997 saw three EC-130E Commando Solo psychological-operations aircraft from the 193rd Special Operations Wing deploy in support of Operation Joint Guard, the renewed effort to stabilize Bosnia Herzegovina. The stabilization force commander requested the deployment of the aircraft to Brindisi to serve as a NATO broadcast centre to counter Serb radio and television transmissions misrepresenting the Dayton Peace Accords.

Two 4th Special Operations Squadron AC-130U Spectre gunships flew to Taegu Air Base in South Korea on 24 October 1997, on a 36-hour non-stop flight from Hurlburt Field, Florida. The flight brought members of the 4th Special Operations Squadron to participate in Foal Eagle, an annual counterfiltration exercise held throughout South Korea. Members of the 6th Special Operations Squadron also joined in the exercise.

Throughout 1998 Air Force Special Operations Command maintained a constant combat search and rescue alert posture as part of Operation Joint Guard, with aircraft and personnel rotating from the 16th Special Operations Wing and 352nd Special Operations Group to San Vito, Italy, on a routine basis. This role increased significantly in March 1999 during the crisis in Kosovo and Operation Allied Force, the NATO air strikes against Serbian military targets in Kosovo. During the air campaign, special operators conducted two successful "combat search and rescue" operations to rescue American pilots from one F-117 and one F-16 downed in the area of conflict.

During Operation Allied Force, EC-130E Commando Solo aircraft from the 193rd Special Operations Wing were used once again to counter Serb radio and television broadcasts. The unit's MC-130Hs conducted extensive leaflet drops over Serbia, and its AC-130Us provided armed reconnaissance. These operations played a significant role in bringing the conflict in Kosovo to an end.

Following the conclusion of Operation Allied Force, special operations units entered a period of reconstitution, while also supporting humanitarian operations such as Operation Atlas Response, the relief effort following the flooding in Mozambique and South Africa in February 2000. That year, members of the 6th Special Operations Squadron were given qualification training on several foreign aircraft, including Russian-made MI-17 helicopters, AFN-26 and AN-32 aircraft.

Following the attacks on the World Trade Center in New York City and the Pentagon on 11 September 2001, the Air Force Special Operations Command changed roles again, returning to the forefront of the war against terrorism.

By the end of September 2001, Air Force Special Operations Command had deployed its forces to south-west Asia for Operation Enduring Freedom to confront and remove the Taliban regime in Afghanistan, along with the Taliban-supported al Qaida terrorist organization headed by Osama bin Laden. Air Force Special Operations Command airpower delivered special tactics forces to the battle ground, supporting Afghanistan's pro-Western Northern Alliance ground forces as they pushed the Taliban and al Qaida out of the country. At the same time, Air Force Special Operations Command personnel were sent to the Philippines to help aid that country's efforts against Islamic fundamentalist terrorists. Throughout 2002 and continuing into 2003, Special Forces continued to lead the war against terrorism.

In March 2003, Air Force Special Operations Command again deployed its forces to south-west Asia, this time in support of what would become Operation Iraqi Freedom – the removal of Saddam Hussein and the destruction of his ruthless Ba'athist regime. The Air Force Special Operations Command's personnel and aircraft teamed with other special and conventional forces to bring down Saddam Hussein's government quickly by May 2003. Air Force Special Operations Command forces continued to conduct operations against insurgents and terrorists well into 2005 in support of the new Iraqi government.

From 1 October 2003, the US Air Force's rescue forces based on the continental United States were moved from Air Combat Command, and Air Force Special Operations Command inherited the 347th Rescue Wing and 563rd Rescue Group, and was given oversight responsibilities for the 920th Rescue Wing of the Air Force Reserve Command, and the 106th and 129th Rescue Wings of the Air National Guard.

On 1 September 2005, the Air Force Special Operations Command opened its new War-Fighting Headquarters as part of an Air Force-wide initiative to improve America's warfighting capabilities and support attempts to achieve the nation's strategic objectives across the full range of military operations. On 13 December 2005, the command at Hurlburt Field was redesignated the Air Force Special Operations Forces. It was to give worldwide Air Force special operations command and control support to combatant commanders, and to be the air component of US Special Operations Command. It was also to provide a special operations liaison element to regional air operations centres, and a forward command and control team to be the air component to a joint special operations task force commander. Its units are designed for global special operations missions ranging from precision application of firepower, to infiltration, exfiltration, resupply and refuelling of Special Forces operational elements, combat support, airborne foreign internal defence, air mobility, intelligence, surveillance and reconnaissance. Its unique capabilities include airborne radio and television broadcast for psychological operations. The command's special tactics squadrons combine combat controllers, special operations weathermen and para-rescuemen to form versatile joint special operations teams.

It has approximately 12,900 active-duty, Air Force Reserve, Air National Guard and civilian personnel. The Command's active-duty and reserve component flying units operate fixed and rotary-wing aircraft, including the CV-22, AC-130H/U, C-130, EC-130, MC-130E/H/W, MC-130P and MH-53. The command's forces are organized under one active-duty wing, two reserve wings and three ANG wings, two overseas groups and several direct reporting units.

The 1st Special Operations Wing, also at Hurlburt Field, is the Air Force's only active-duty special operations wing. The 352nd Special Operations Group, based at RAF Mildenhall in England, is the Air Force component for Special Operations Command Europe. The 353rd Special Operations Group, at Kadena Air Base, Japan, is the Air Force component for Special Operations Command Pacific. And the 720th Special Tactics Group at Hurlburt Field trains, organizes and equips more than 800 combat controllers, special operations weathermen, and para-rescuemen for assignment to special tactics squadrons

Hurlburt Field, Florida, is also home to the US Air Force Special Operations School, which provides special operations-related education to Department of Defense personnel, government agencies and allied nations. The 18th Flight Test Squadron, at Hurlburt Field and Edwards Air Force Base, California, conducts operational and maintenance suitability tests and evaluations for aircraft, equipment, concepts, tactics and procedures for employment of special operations forces.

Based at Duke Field, Florida, the 919th Special Operations Wing is the command's reserve special operations wing. It provides MC-130E and MC-130P aircraft that support helicopter refuelling requirements to USSOCOM. The 193rd Special Operations Wing, at Harrisburg International Airport, Pennsylvania, provides the only airborne psychological operations platform in the Department of Defense with the EC-130 Commando Solo. The 123rd Special Tactics Squadron at Standiford Field, Kentucky, provides combat controllers and para-rescuemen for worldwide operational needs. The 209th Civil Engineer Squadron at Gulfport, Mississippi, is the Command's civil engineering squadron. The 227th Special Operations Flight at McGuire Air Force Base, New Jersey, provides modified C-32B aircraft to support airlift operations worldwide. The 280th Combat Communications Squadron at Dothan, Alabama, is the Command's communications squadron. And the 107th Weather Flight at Selfridge Air National Guard Base, Michigan, the 146th Weather Flight at Greater Pittsburgh Air Guard Station, Pennsylvania and the 181st Weather Flight at Dallas Naval Air Station, Texas are the Command's three National Guard weather units.

7

US ARMY RANGERS

History of the Rangers

The history of the US Rangers began before Major Robert Rogers raised his unconventional force in the 1750s. Units specifically designated as Rangers and using Ranger tactics were employed on the American frontier as early as 1670. A band of Rangers under Captain Benjamin Church brought the Indian conflict known as "King Phillip's War" to a conclusion in 1676 at the cost of the lives of some 600 settlers and 3,000 Indians. While more than half the ninety settlements in New England were attacked and a dozen destroyed, whole Indian villages had been massacred. Those Indians who survived fled northwards and westwards, leaving the New England settlers to expand south without fear.

In 1756, Major Robert Rogers, a native of New Hampshire, recruited nine companies of Rangers from among the American colonists to fight alongside British regulars during the French and Indian War of 1754–63. The techniques and methods of operation of this irregular force were those that came naturally to the American frontiersmen. However, Major Rogers was the first to utilize them and incorporate them into the fighting doctrine of a permanently organized fighting force.

Articulate and persuasive, Rogers developed the Ranger

concept to an extent never known before. A soldier from boyhood, he personally recruited his men and published a list of twenty-eight common-sense rules and a set of standing orders that stressed operational readiness, security and tactics. He also published an account of his service in the French and Indian War called *A Concise Account of North America*, in London in 1765.

In 1759, Rogers took part in General James Wolfe's expedition to take Quebec and the successful Montreal campaign the following year. He was in the West in 1763 and, during Pontiac's War of 1763–64, he participated in the Battle of Bloody Bridge. However, during the American Revolution he sided with the British, commanding the Queen's Rangers, which saw service around New York, and, later, the King's Rangers, though command passed to his brother James Rogers when Robert returned to England.

But the American colonists had learnt Rogers' lessons well. When the British attempt to tax the colonists to help pay for the French and Indian War, they rebelled and on 14 June 1775, the Continental Congress resolved that "six companies of expert riflemen be immediately raised in Pennsylvania, two in Maryland, and two in Virginia".

In 1777, this force of hardy frontiersmen was formed into an elite unit George Washington called the "Corps of Rangers" – also known as the Continental Rifles – under the command of Colonel Dan Morgan, who had been with the Virginia Rangers during the French and Indian War. According to the victor at Saratoga, British General John Burgoyne, Morgan's men who he met there were "the most famous corps of the Continental Army, all of them crack shots".

During the Revolutionary War Thomas Knowlton led another unit of Rangers. Knowlton distinguished himself at Bunker Hill and was promoted major by Congress. Then in 1776, Washington made him a lieutenant colonel and asked him to organize an elite force of less than 150 hand-picked men from Connecticut, Rhode Island and Massachusetts, known as "Knowlton's Rangers". This force of was used primarily for reconnaissance, though some of their actions were analogous to the modern Special Forces. Knowlton was killed leading his men in action at the Battle of Harlem Heights.

The best-known Rangers of the Civil War were commanded by the Confederate Colonel John Singleton Mosby. Mosby's Rangers operated behind Union lines south of the Potomac. From a three-man scout unit in 1862, Mosby's force had grown to eight companies of Rangers by 1865. He believed that, by bold actions and surprise attacks, he would force the Union forces to guard a hundred points at any one time. Then, with good reconnaissance, he would locate the enemy's weakest point and attack it, confident of victory. On his raids, Mosby employed small units, comprising usually only twenty to fifty men. Once he attacked and routed an entire Union regiment in its bivouac with just nine men. Famously, Mosby carried out a daring raid far inside Union lines at the Fairfax County courthouse in March 1863, where his men captured three high-ranking Union officers, including Brigadier-General Edwin H. Stoughton. After the Confederate surrender, Mosby simply disbanded his Rangers, refusing to surrender formally.

Equally resourceful were the Rangers under the command of Colonel Turner Ashby, a Virginian widely known for his daring. Ashby's vigorous reconnaissance and screening were strong factors in the success of Jackson's legendary Valley Campaign in the Shenandoah Valley in 1862. Jackson said of him: "As a partisan officer I never knew his superior; his daring was proverbial; his powers of endurance almost incredible; his tone of character heroic, and his sagacity almost intuitive in divining the purposes and movements of the enemy."

The Rangers of Ashby and Mosby did great service for the Confederacy. Specialists in scouting, harassing and raiding, they were a constant threat and kept large numbers of Union troops occupied. But there were Rangers on the Union side too. Organized by disaffected Virginians at Waterford in Loudoun Country, the Loudoun Rangers were commanded by Captain Samuel C. Means. They moved across the Potomac and set up camps in Maryland from where they staged guerrilla raids into their home state. On one occasion they managed to capture Confederate General Longstreet's ammunition train, and even succeeded in engaging and capturing a portion of Colonel Mosby's force.

The Second World War

The Rangers were resurrected in the Second World War when, on 26 May 1942, Major-General Lucian K. Truscott, US Army Liaison Officer with the British General Staff, submitted proposals to General George Marshall that "we undertake immediately an American unit along the lines of the British Commandos". The British had developed the commando concept early in the Second World War as a way of hitting back at the enemy when the German and British forces were separated by the English Channel. Commandos were basically amphibious raiders, who went ashore in small groups, hit an enemy installation and then swiftly departed as they had arrived, by sea.

Following Truscott's proposal, a cable was sent from the War Department to Major-General Russell P. Hartle, commander of US Army Forces in Northern Ireland, authorizing the activation of the First US Army Ranger Battalion. The name Ranger had been selected by General Truscott because:

the name Commandos rightfully belonged to the British, and we sought a name more typically American. It was therefore fit that the organization that was destined to be the first of the American Ground Forces to battle Germans on the European continent should be called Rangers in compliment to those in American history who exemplified the high standards of courage, initiative, determination and ruggedness, fighting ability and achievement.

General Hartle appointed his own aide-de-camp, Captain William Orlando Darby, a graduate of West Point with amphibious training, its commander. Truscott approved, saying that Darby was "outstanding in appearance, possessed of a most attractive personality . . . and filled with enthusiasm".

Promoted to major, the energetic Darby organized the new unit within weeks of receiving the assignment. Thousands of applicants from the 1st Armored Division, the 34th Infantry Division and other units in Northern Ireland were interviewed by his hand-picked officers, and after a strenuous weeding-out programme, the 1st Ranger Battalion was officially activated at Carrickfergus, Northern Ireland, on 19 June 1942.

The Rangers were then sent to the Commando Training
Centre at Achnacarry in Scotland where they were given rugged
training with live ammunition. Coached, prodded and challenged by the battle-hardened Commando instructors under
Colonel Charles Vaughan, the Rangers learned the rudiments of
Commando warfare. Five hundred of the 600 volunteers who
Darby brought with him to Achnacarry passed the Commando
training with flying colours, although one Ranger was killed and
several wounded by live fire.

In August 1942, five officers and forty-four enlisted men took
part in the disastrous Dieppe Raid alongside the Canadians and
the British Commandos. They were first American ground
soldiers to see action against the Germans in occupied Europe.
Three Rangers were killed and several captured. All won the
commendation and esteem of the Commandos. Darby was
promoted to lieutenant colonel and the 1st Ranger Battalion
was sent to North Africa to spearhead Operation Torch, the
American landings in French North Africa. At the Port of
Arzew, Algeria they made a silent night landing, silenced
two gun batteries and opened the way for the 1st Infantry
Division to capture Oran.

Later, in Tunisia, the 1st Battalion made their behind-the-
lines night raid at Sened, killing a large number of defenders
and taking ten prisoners at the cost of only one Ranger killed
and ten wounded.

On 31 March 1943, the 1st Ranger Battalion led General
Patton's drive to capture the heights of El Guettar with a
12-mile night march across mountainous terrain, surprising
the enemy with an attack from the rear. At dawn the Rangers
swooped down on the Italian positions and cleared the El
Guettar Pass, capturing 200 prisoners. For this action the
Battalion won its first Presidential Citation and Darby won
his first Distinguished Service Cross.

However, senior American commanders failed to grasp what
commando operations were all about. The British concept was
to put them up against a target regular infantry could not
handle, getting them in and out again fast. Instead, commanders tended to use Rangers as elite infantry. The British
practice was to take only what was needed on a mission.
Usually, British Commandos carried just small-arms and light

machine guns. Consequently the Commandos were raiders who were not being sent to slug it out in a sustained infantry fight. But American commanders missed the point and loaded up the Rangers with heavier weapons. Instead of 20 lb Browning automatic rifles, the Rangers were equipped with 45 lb M1919 machine guns; instead of 60-mm mortars, the Rangers had to lug around 81-mm mortars. The Rangers were also equipped with bazookas, even though they kept their obsolete and heavy British anti-tank rifles.

After Tunisia, the 3rd and 4th Ranger Battalions were formed from volunteers in North Africa with the 1st Battalion as their cadre. The Rangers adopted the British form of organization, which was shaped by the amphibious landing craft the Commandos used on their raids. Because an assault landing craft – or LCA – could hold thirty-five troops (or 800 lb of equipment), the Commando and, consequently, the Ranger platoon contained thirty-two men. Two platoons made up a company, with a headquarters of four men, and six companies made up the battalion. The battalion headquarters and support troops added another 108 men, giving a total strength of twenty-seven officers and 489 men. With this form of organization, a battalion of Commandos or Rangers could be sent ashore in twelve to fifteen LCAs.

Darby trained the new battalions for the invasion of Sicily at Nemours, Algeria in April 1943. Major Herman Dammer assumed command of the 3rd, Major Roy Murray the 4th, while Darby remained in command of the 1st. In effect, though, he was in charge of the entire unit which became known as Darby's Rangers.

The three Ranger Battalions spearheaded the Seventh Army landing at Gela and Licata in southern Sicily, and played a key role in the Sicilian campaign that culminated in the capture of Messina. The three battalions were then the first Fifth Army troops ashore during the invasion of Italy, landing near Salerno. They quickly seized the strategic heights on both sides of the Chinuzi Pass and fought off eight German counter-attacks, winning two Distinguished Unit Citations. At this point Colonel Darby was commanding a force of over 10,000 troops, including elements of the 36th Division, several companies of the 82nd Airborne Division and artillery. It was from there that the Fifth Army advance against Naples was launched with the British X Corps.

All three Ranger battalions joined the bitter winter mountain fighting near San Pietro, Venafro and Cassino, after which they were allowed a short period of rest and reorganization, recruiting new volunteers as replacements. However, they had now grown so large, and had suffered so many casualties, that it was hard to fill their ranks with men of the same calibre.

Nevertheless the three Ranger battalions, reinforced by the 509th Parachute Battalion, the 83rd Chemical Warfare, 42nd Mortar Battalion and 36th Combat Engineers, were designated the 6615th Ranger Force under the command of Darby, who was then promoted to Colonel. The Force spearheaded the surprise night landings at the port of Anzio, captured two gun batteries, seized the city and struck out to enlarge the beachhead before dawn in a classic Ranger operation.

On the night of 30 January 1944, the 1st and 3rd Battalions infiltrated 5 miles behind the German lines, while the 4th Battalion fought to clear the road toward Cisterna, a key Fifth Army objective. But preparing for a massive counter-attack, the Germans had reinforced their lines the night before, so that both the 1st and 3rd were surrounded and greatly outnumbered. The beleaguered Rangers fought bravely, inflicting many casualties, but ammunition was soon running low. Time was also running out when supporting troops could not break out of the beachhead through the strong German positions. Among those killed in action was the 3rd Battalion Commanding Officer, Major Alvah Miller, while the Commanding Officer of the 1st Battalion, Major John Dobson, was wounded. Along with the loss of the 1st and 3rd Battalions, the 4th Battalion sustained heavy casualties. But at least this was not entirely in vain. Later intelligence revealed that the Ranger-led attack on Cisterna had helped spike the planned German counter-attack and thwarted Hitler's order to "push the Allies into the sea".

Although all three battalions had been virtually destroyed and were subsequently disbanded, two more had been formed in the US. The 2nd Ranger Battalion was activated on 1 April 1943 at Camp Forrest, Tennessee. Trained and led by Lieutenant Colonel James Earl Rudder, it carried out the most desperate and dangerous mission of the entire Omaha Beach landings on Normandy on 6 June 1944. General Bradley said of Colonel Rudder, "Never has any commander been given a more desperate mission."

Three companies, D, E and F, assaulted the perpendicular cliffs of Pointe du Hoc under intense machine-gun, mortar and artillery fire and destroyed a large gun battery that would have wreaked havoc on the Allied landing fleets offshore. For two days and nights they fought without relief until the other new Ranger Battalion, the 5th, linked up with them.

The 5th Ranger Battalion had been activated on 1 September 1943 at Camp Forrest, under Lieutenant Colonel Max Schneider, former executive officer of the 4th Ranger Battalion. As part of the provisional Ranger Assault Force commanded by Colonel Rudder, it landed on Omaha Beach with three companies of the 2nd Battalion, A, B and C, at the point where elements of the 116th Regiment of the 29th Infantry Division were pinned down by murderous crossfire and mortars from the heights above. The situation there was so critical that General Omar Bradley was seriously considering redirecting reinforcements to other areas of the beachhead. It was there that General Norman D. Cota, Assistant Divisional Commander of the 29th Division, gave the now famous order that has become the motto of the 75th Ranger Regiment: "Rangers, Lead the Way!"

The 5th Ranger Battalion broke across the sea wall and barbed-wire entanglements, and up the pillbox-rimmed heights under intense enemy machine-gun and mortar fire, with A and B Companies of the 2nd Battalion and some elements of the 116th Infantry Regiment. They advanced four miles to the key town of Vierville, thus opening the breach for supporting troops to follow-up and expand the beachhead. Meanwhile C Company of the 2nd Battalion, due to rough seas, landed west of the Vierville draw. They suffered 50 per cent casualties during the landing, but still scaled a 90-foot cliff using ropes and bayonets, to knock out a formidable enemy position that was sweeping the beach with deadly fire.

After that, the 5th Battalion, with elements of the 116th Regiment, finally linked up with the beleaguered 2nd Battalion on D-Day plus three, although Lieutenant Charles Parker of A Company, 5th Battalion, had penetrated deep behind enemy lines on D-Day itself and reached the 2nd Battalion with twenty prisoners. Later, with the 2nd Battalion, the unit distinguished itself in the hard-fought battle of Brest, taking the German fortifications along the La Coquet Peninsular.

The 2nd Ranger Battalion fought through the bitter central Europe campaign and won commendations for its heroic actions in the battle of Hill 400. The Battalion earned the Distinguished Unit Citation and the French Croix de Guerre, and was inactivated at Camp Patrick Henry on 23 October 1945.

Under the leadership of Lieutenant-Colonel Richard Sullivan, the 5th Ranger Battalion took part in the Battle of the Bulge, Hürtgen Forest and other tough battles, winning two Distinguished Unit Citations and the Croix de Guerre. It was deactivated on 2 October 1945 at Camp Miles Standish, Massachusetts.

In early 1944, the 6th Ranger Battalion was formed in the Pacific and activated at Port Moresby, New Guinea in September 1944. Under Colonel Henry "Hank" Mucci, it was the first American force to return to the Philippines. This, its first mission, was to destroy the coastal defence guns, radio and radar stations on the islands of Dinegat and Suluan off Leyte. Landing three days before the main Sixth Army invasion force, they swiftly killed and captured some of the Japanese defenders and destroyed all enemy communications.

The unit took part in the US landings on Luzon, making several behind-the-lines patrols, penetrations and small-unit raids. These served to hone the Rangers for what became one of the most daring raids in American military history. On 30 January 1944, C Company, supported by a platoon from F Company, struck 30 miles behind enemy lines and rescued some 500 emaciated and ailing prisoners of war, who had been survivors of the Bataan Death March thirty months before. Carrying many of the prisoners on their backs, the Rangers, aided by Filipino guerrillas, killed over 200 of the garrison and evaded two Japanese regiments to reach the safety of American lines the following day. Intelligence reports had indicated the Japanese were planning to kill the prisoners as they withdrew towards Manila.

Later, the unit, then commanded by Colonel Robert Garrett, played an important role in the capture of Manila and Aparri, and was preparing to spearhead the invasion of Japan when the news came that the war had ended. It received the Presidential Unit Citation and the Philippine Presidential Citation, and was deactivated on 30 December 1945 in the Philippines.

Merrill's Marauders

Merrill's Marauders were another antecedent of the modern Rangers to come into existence in the Second World War. At the Quebec Conference of August 1943, Winston Churchill, Franklin D. Roosevelt and other Allied leaders conceived the idea of having an American ground unit spearhead the Chinese Army, another ally, with a Long Range Penetration Mission behind enemy lines in Burma. Its goal would be the destruction of Japanese communications and supply lines and generally to play havoc with enemy forces while an attempt was made to reopen the Burma Road, the Allied supply route into China.

A Presidential call for volunteers for "a dangerous and hazardous mission" was issued, and some 2,900 American soldiers responded. Officially designated as the 5307th Composite Unit (Provisional) and code-named "Galahad", the unit later became popularly known as Merrill's Marauders, after its leader, Brigadier-General Frank Merrill. Marauder volunteers came from a variety of theatres of operation. Some came from stateside cadres; some from the jungles of Panama and Trinidad; and the remainder were battle-scarred veterans of Guadalcanal, the Solomon Islands and New Guinea campaigns. In India some Signal Corps and Air Corps personnel were added, along with pack troops with mules. They were organized into six 400-man combat teams, two to each battalion, colour-coded Red, White, Blue, Green, Orange and Khaki.

After preliminary training in great secrecy in the jungles of India, about 600 men were detached as a rear-echelon headquarters to remain in India to organize the vital air-drop link between the Air Transport Command and the six Marauder combat teams. The other 2,400 Marauders then began their march up the Ledo Road that led from India over the outlying ranges of the Himalayan Mountains into Burma. The Marauders walked over 1,000 miles through dense jungle, fighting five major and thirty minor engagements along the way. With no tanks or heavy artillery to support them, and vastly outnumbered, they defeated the veteran soldiers of the Japanese 18th Division, who had conquered Singapore and Malaya. Always moving to the rear of the Japanese main forces, the Marauders completely disrupted enemy supply and communication lines. The pinnacle of their behind-the-lines campaign was the capture of Myitkyina Airfield, the only all-weather airfield in Burma, in August 1944. For their accomplishments in Burma, the Marauders were awarded the Distinguished Unit Citation in 1944.

The unit was consolidated with the 475th Infantry Regiment on 10 August 1944. On 21 June 1954, the 475th was redesignated the 75th Infantry Regiment. It is from this redesignation that the modern-day 75th Ranger Regiment traces its current unit designation.

Post-war

Korea

With the outbreak of hostilities in Korea in June 1950, there was a need for Rangers once again and Colonel John Gibson Van Houten was chosen to head the Ranger training programme at Fort Benning, Georgia. On 15 September 1950, he was ordered to report to the Chief of Staff, Office of the Chief of Army Field Forces, Fort Monroe, Virginia, where he was told that training of Ranger-type units was to begin at Fort Benning at the earliest possible date. The target start date was 1 October 1950 with a tentative training period of six weeks. Four airborne infantry companies were to be formed, along with a headquarters detachment.

When the request for volunteers willing to accept "extremely hazardous" duty in the combat zone in the Far East went out, the response was astounding. Among the 82nd Airborne Division alone it is estimated that as many as 5,000 men, all experienced Regular Army paratroopers, volunteered. A ruthless selection process began. Wherever possible, the selection was done by the officers who would command the companies – a throwback to colonial days when Robert Rogers did his own recruiting.

Orders were issued and those selected were shipped to Fort

Benning. The first group arrived on 20 September 1950 and training began on 9 October. In 1950, the US Army was still segregated and, alongside three companies of qualified airborne white personnel, the 4th Ranger Company, an all-black unit formed by former members of the 505th Airborne Infantry Regiment and the 80th Anti-aircraft Artillery Battalion of the 82nd Airborne Division, went into training. They were the 2nd Ranger Infantry Company (Airborne) and the only all-black Ranger unit authorized by the Department of the Army in the history of the United States.

All volunteers were professional soldiers with diverse skills that they taught each other. Some of the men had fought with the original Ranger battalions, the 1st Special Service Force, or the Office of Strategic Services during the Second World War. Many of the instructors were drawn from this same group. Although they were young, these men were highly trained and many battle-hardened from the Second World War.

The training was extremely rigorous. It included amphibious and airborne operations (with low-level night jumps), demolition, sabotage, close combat and the use of foreign maps. They trained on all American small arms, as well as those used by the enemy. Communications were a vital skill, as was the control of artillery, naval gunfire and air-strikes. Much of the field training took place at night.

The 1st Ranger Infantry Company (Airborne) left Fort Benning on 15 November 1950, arriving in Korea on 17 December 1950, where it was attached to the 2nd Infantry Division. It was soon followed by the 2nd and 4th Ranger Companies, who arrived in Korea on 29 December 1950. The 2nd Ranger Company was attached to the 7th Infantry Division, While the 4th Ranger Company served both Headquarters, 8th US Army and the 1st Cavalry Division.

Throughout the winter of 1950 and the spring of 1951, the Rangers went into battle by air, land and water. They were nomadic warriors, attached first to one regiment and then another. They performed their duties beyond the front line – scouting, patrolling, raiding, ambushing, spearheading assaults and counter-attacking to regain lost positions – attached on the basis of one 112-man company per 18,000-man infantry division. The Rangers combat record was second to none, partially because they were four-fold volunteers – they had volunteered for the Army, volunteered for airborne training, volunteered for the Rangers and volunteered for combat.

The 1st Ranger Infantry Company (Airborne) began their operations with a daring night raid nine miles behind enemy lines, destroying an enemy complex. The enemy installation was later identified by a prisoner as the Headquarters of the 12th North Korean Division. Caught by surprise and unaware of the size of the American force, two North Korean Regiments hastily withdrew from the area.

The 1st Company was in the middle of the major battle of Chipyong-Ni, the first mass assault by the Chinese Communist forces, and the "May Massacre", where Chinese forces tried to wipe out four UN battalions before their spring offensive. In the ensuing bloodbath, the Chinese suffered 10,000 casualties. As a result of these actions the 1st Company was awarded two Distinguished Unit Citations.

The 2nd and 4th Ranger Companies made a combat jump at Munsan-Ni, behind enemy lines and north of the 38th Parallel. The 2nd Ranger Company plugged a critical gap left by a retreating allied force. The 3rd Ranger Company was attached to the 3rd Infantry Division and earned the motto "Die Bastard, Die!" while the 4th Ranger Company executed a daring amphibious assault on the Hwachon Dam.

The Rangers had then expanded to six companies committed in Korea. The 5th Ranger Company, fighting as an attachment to the 25th Infantry Division, proved their worth during the Chinese "Fifth Phase Offensive", where the UN forces absorbed the onslaught of four Chinese armies, or 125,000 men. Gathering up every soldier he could find, the Ranger company commander held the line with Ranger sergeants commanding line infantry units. In the eastern sector, the Rangers were the first unit to cross the 38th Parallel on the second drive north.

The 8th Ranger Infantry Company (Airborne) was attached to the 24th Infantry Division and were known as the "Devils". A 33-man platoon from the 8th Ranger Company fought a between-the-lines battle with two Chinese reconnaissance companies. Seventy Chinese were killed. The Rangers suffered two dead and three wounded, all of whom were brought back to friendly lines.

Vietnam

The present-day 75th Ranger Regiment is linked directly and historically to the thirty Infantry Companies of the 75th that were active in Vietnam from 1 February 1969 until 15 August 1972. It has the longest sustained combat history for an American Ranger unit in the more than 300-year career of US Army Rangers.

The 75th Infantry Regiment was activated in Okinawa during 1954 and traced its lineage to the 475th Infantry Regiment, then to the 5307th Composite Unit (Provisional), or Merrill's Marauders. During the Vietnam War, Company I (Ranger), 75th Infantry, 1st Infantry Division, and Company G (Ranger), 75th Infantry, 23rd Infantry Division, produced the first two US Army Rangers to be awarded the Medal of Honor while serving as a member of a combat Ranger company. Specialist Four Robert D. Law of I/75, a Texan, was awarded the first Medal of Honor while on long-range patrol in Tinh Phoc Province, South Vietnam. Staff Sergeant Robert J. Pruden, from Minnesota, with G/75 was awarded the second Medal of Honor while on a reconnaissance mission in Quang Ni Province, South Vietnam. In addition, Staff Sergeant Lazlo Rabel was awarded the Medal of Honor while serving with the 74th Infantry Detachment (LRP), an antecedent of Company N (Ranger), 75th Infantry, 173rd Airborne Brigade, while on a long-range patrol in Binh Dinh Province, South Vietnam. He was from Pennsylvania.

Conversion of the Long Range Patrol Companies of the 20th, 50th, 51st, 52nd, 58th, 71st, 78th and 79th Infantry Detachments, and Company D of the 151st Infantry Long Range Patrol of the Indiana National Guard, into Ranger companies of the 75th Infantry began on 1 February 1969. Only Company D, 151st retained its unit identity. It became a Ranger company, but did not join the 75th.

Companies C, D, E, F, G, H, I, K, L, M, N, O and P (Ranger) 75th Infantry conducted Ranger missions for three years and seven months while in Vietnam, and were deployed every day of the year. Like the old Marauders, the men of the 75th Rangers in Vietnam were drawn from the infantry, artillery, engineers, signals, medical units, military police, logistics, parachute riggers and other Army units. They were joined by former adversaries – defecting Viet Cong and North Vietnamese Army soldiers who became "Kit Carson Scouts" and fought alongside the Rangers against their former units and comrades. Unlike Rangers earlier in the twentieth century who trained in the United States or in friendly nations overseas, the Long Range Patrols and Rangers in Vietnam were activated and trained in theatre in South-East Asia.

At the outset of the war, many of the men were graduates of the US Army Ranger School. Later, there were volunteers, some of whom were graduates of the in-country Ranger School or the Recondo School at Nha Trang. Others had been line company cadres, paratroopers and Special Forces-trained men. But the bulk of the Ranger volunteers came from the soldiers who had no chance to attend the schools. Their selection and basic training was essentially done on combat missions. Volunteers were assigned to various Ranger companies. But they were not accepted into the unit until they had completed a series of patrols and passed the acid test of a Ranger – combat. After that, once a man was accepted by his peers, he was allowed to wear the black beret and wear the Red, White and Black scroll shoulder-sleeve insignia of his Ranger company. All Long Range Patrol Companies and 75th Ranger Companies were given parachute pay, even if their feet never left the ground.

In Vietnam, helicopter deployment was the primary means for insertion and exfiltration behind enemy rear areas. They were also inserted by foot, wheeled and tracked vehicle, airboats, Navy Swift Boats and left on stay-behind missions where the Rangers remained in place when a larger tactical unit withdrew. False insertions by helicopter were also used to fool the ever-present enemy trail watchers.

General missions consisted of locating the enemy bases and lines of communication. Special missions included wiretaps, prisoner snatches, platoon-and company-size raids and bomb-damage assessments following B-52 missions. These Ranger units undertook some of the most difficult patrolling actions in US Army history, and frequently fought much larger enemy forces when compromised on their reconnaissance missions.

Further Reorganization and Operations

With the outbreak of the 1973 Middle East War, the Department of the Army saw the need for a light mobile force that could be moved quickly to any trouble spot in the world. In the autumn of 1973, the Army Chief of Staff, General Creighton Abrams, came up with the idea of the reformation of the first battalion-sized Ranger units since the Second World War. As Commander of US Forces in Vietnam, Creighton Abrams had seen the 75th Rangers in operation there and he selected them as the role model for the first US Army Ranger units to be formed during peacetime.

In January 1974, he ordered the formation of a Ranger battalion, selecting its missions and picking its first officers. He felt a tough, disciplined and elite Ranger unit would set a standard for the rest of the US Army, and that, as Rangers moved on from Ranger units to Regular Army units, their influence would improve the entire Army. He summed up what he required from the force in what became "Abram's Charter":

> The Ranger battalion is to be an elite, light, and most proficient infantry battalion in the world; a battalion that can do things with its hands and weapons better than anyone. The battalion will not contain any "hoodlums" or "brigands" and if the battalion is formed of such persons, it will be disbanded. Wherever the battalion goes, it will be apparent that it is the best.

On 25 January 1974, Headquarters, United States Army Forces Command, published General Order 127, directing the activation of the 1st Battalion, 75th Infantry (Ranger), with effective from 31 January 1974. In February, the worldwide selection was begun and personnel were assembled at Fort Benning, Georgia to undergo the cadre training from March to June 1974. On 1 July 1974, the 1st Battalion, 75th Infantry (Ranger), parachuted in to Fort Stewart, Georgia.

The 2nd Battalion, 75th Infantry (Ranger) soon followed when it was activated on 1 October 1974. These elite units eventually established headquarters at Hunter Army Airfield, Georgia and Fort Lewis, Washington, respectively.

"Abrams' Own" first went into action in 1980 when elements of 1st Battalion, 75th Infantry (Ranger) were called on to help in the Iranian hostage rescue attempt. The groundwork for the Ranger's Special Operations capability was laid during training and preparation for this operation. Rangers and other Special Operations Forces from throughout the Department of Defense developed tactics, techniques and equipment from scratch as there had been no experience of this kind of operation anywhere in the world.

The combat effectiveness of the Abrams' Ranger battalions was demonstrated during the United States' invasion of Grenada in October 1983. The mission of the Rangers was to protect the lives of American citizens on the island and restore the legitimate democratic government. During Operation Urgent Fury, the 1st and 2nd Ranger Battalions conducted a daring low-level parachute assault from 500 feet and seized the airfield at Point Salinas. They rescued American students at the True Blue Medical Campus and conducted air-assault operations to eliminate pockets of resistance.

The Ranger Battalions were so impressive in action, the Department of the Army announced in 1984 that it was activating another Ranger Battalion and a Ranger Regimental Headquarters, increasing the size of the active-duty Ranger force to its highest level in forty years. These new units – the 3rd Battalion, 75th Infantry (Ranger) and Headquarters and Headquarters Company, 75th Infantry (Ranger) – received their colours on 3 October 1984 at Fort Benning, Georgia. Not only did these colour ceremonies establish the Ranger Regiment as a force for the future, it also made an important link with the past as it took place at the same time as the first reunion of the Korean War-era Rangers, some of whom were still on active duty. Rangers, both current and retired, took their place alongside distinguished visitors to witness the inauguration of the new 75th Ranger Regiment. On 3 February 1986, Second World War Battalions and Korean War lineage and honours were consolidated and assigned by tradition to the 75th Ranger Regiment. It was the first time that an organization of that size had been officially recognized as the parent headquarters of the Ranger Battalions. Not since the Second World War and Colonel Darby's Ranger Force Headquarters had the US Army had such a large Ranger force with over 2,000 soldiers assigned to Ranger units.

The entire Ranger Regiment participated in Operation Just Cause, in which US forces invaded Panama. Rangers spearheaded the action by conducting two important operations. The 1st Battalion, reinforced by Company C, 3rd Battalion, and a Regimental Command and Control Team, conducted an early morning parachute assault onto Omar Torrijos International Airport and Tocumen Military Airfield, to neutralize the Panamanian Defence Forces 2nd Rifle Company and secure airfields for the arrival of the American 82nd Airborne Division. The 2nd and 3rd Ranger Battalions, with a Regimental Command and Control Team, conducted a parachute assault onto the airfield at Rio Hato, to neutralize the Panamanian 6th and 10th Rifle Companies and seize General Manuel Noriega's beach house. Following the successful completion of these assaults, Rangers conducted follow-on operations in support of Joint Task Force South. The Rangers captured 1,014 enemy prisoners of war and over 18,000 arms of various types. In the action the Rangers suffered five killed and forty-two wounded.

Elements of Company B and 1st Platoon, Company A, 1st Battalion, 75th Ranger Regiment deployed to Saudi Arabia from 12 February 1991 to 15 April 1991 in support of Operation Desert Storm. The Rangers conducted raids and provided a quick reaction force in co-operation with Coalition forces. They contributed to the overall success of the operation and sustained no Ranger casualties.

From early 1993, to 21 October 1993, Company B and a Command and Control Element of 3rd Battalion, 75th Ranger Regiment were deployed to Somalia to assist United Nations forces there. Their mission was to capture key leaders in order to end clan fighting in and around the capital Mogadishu. On 3 October 1993, the Rangers conducted a daring daylight raid in which several special operations helicopters were shot down. For nearly eighteen hours, the Rangers delivered devastating firepower, killing an estimated 300 Somalis in what many have called the fiercest ground combat since Vietnam. Six Rangers were killed during the mission.

Present Organization

Currently the 75th Ranger Regiment is part of the United States Special Operations Command (USSOCOM). Its regimental headquarters remain at Fort Benning, Georgia, along with the 3rd Battalion. The 1st Battalion is at Hunter Army Airfield, Georgia and the 2nd Battalion is at Fort Lewis, Washington. Each of these Ranger battalions is made up of three combat companies and a battalion headquarters and headquarters company. Each battalion is authorized a full complement 580 Rangers. However, the battalions may be up to 15 per cent over-manned to make allowances for training, school programmes and temporary duties.

Regimental Headquarters consists of a command group, a communications detachment, a fire support element, a reconnaissance detachment of three six-man teams, a cadre for the Ranger training detachment and a company headquarters. Also, the Regiment has the capability of deploying a planning team consisting of experienced Ranger operations, intelligence, fire support, communications and logistics planners. The team can deploy at short notice, with USSOCOM approval, two theatre Special Operations Commands to plan Ranger operations during crisis action planning or contingency operations.

In addition, there are the training battalions. The 4th Ranger Training Battalion is at Fort Benning, Georgia; the 5th Ranger Training Battalion is at Dahlonega, Georgia; the 6th Ranger Training Battalion is at Eglin Air Force Base, Florida; and the 7th Ranger Training Battalion is at Fort Bliss, Texas. Personnel there are sworn to uphold the Ranger Creed, which states:

Recognizing that I volunteered as a Ranger, fully knowing the hazards of my chosen profession, I will always endeavour to uphold the prestige, honour and high esprit de corps of the Rangers.

Acknowledging the fact that a Ranger is a more elite soldier who arrives at the cutting edge of battle by land, sea or air, I accept the fact that as a Ranger my country expects me to move further, faster and fight harder than any other soldier.

Never shall I fail my comrades. I will always keep myself mentally alert, physically strong and morally straight and I will shoulder more than my share of the task whatever it may be, 100 per cent and then some.

Gallantly will I show the world that I am a specially selected and well trained soldier. My courtesy to superior officers, neatness of dress and care of equipment shall set the example for others to follow.

Energetically will I meet the enemies of my country. I shall defeat them on the field of battle for I am better trained and will fight with all my might. Surrender is not a Ranger word. I will never leave a fallen comrade to fall into the hands of the enemy and under no circumstances will I ever embarrass my country.

Readily will I display the intestinal fortitude required to fight on to the Ranger objective and complete the mission, though I be the lone survivor.

The premier light-infantry unit of the United States Army, the Ranger mission is to plan and conduct special military operations in support of US policy and objectives. Its specially organized, equipped and trained soldiers provide the National Command Authority the capability to deploy a credible military force rapidly to any region of the world. In addition, Rangers are often called upon to perform missions in support of regular forces.

The cornerstone of Ranger missions is direct action. They are the premiere airfield seizure and raid unit in the Army. Proficient in all light-infantry skills, Ranger units master the essential tasks of movement to contact, ambush, reconnaissance, airborne and air assaults, and hasty defence.

A typical Ranger Battalion or Regimental mission would involve seizing an airfield for use by follow-on general purpose forces and conducting raids on key targets of operational or strategic importance. Once secured, follow-on forces are introduced into theatre to relieve the Rangers so they can plan future Special Operations. Rangers rely heavily on external fire support. Ranger fire-support personnel train extensively on the employment of close-air support, attack helicopters, naval gunfire, AC-130 gunship and artillery. They establish close working relationships with units that habitually support the Ranger Force.

The flexibility of the Ranger Force requires it to perform under various command structures. The Force can work unilaterally under a corps, as part of a Joint Special Operations Task Force, as an Army Special Operations Task Force, or as an Army component in a regular Joint Task Force. Historically, it is common for the Ranger Force to conduct forced-entry operations as part of a Joint Special Operations Task Force, then become Operational Control to a Joint Task Force, giving them the capability to conduct special operations or direct-action missions.

The Army maintains the Rangers at a high level of readiness. Each battalion can deploy anywhere in the world at eighteen hours' notice. The Army places responsibility on the 75th Ranger Regiment to possess a number of capabilities which include: infiltrating and exfiltrating by land, sea and air; conducting direct-action operations; conducting raids; the recovery of personnel and special equipment; and conducting conventional or special light-infantry operations.

Each Ranger battalion possesses twelve Ranger Special Operations Vehicles (RSOVs) for its airfield seizure mission. The vehicle is a modified Land Rover. Each vehicle carriers a six- or seven-man crew. Normally, each vehicle mounts a M240G machine gun and either a MK-19 grenade launcher or a M2 .50 cal machine gun. One of the passengers mans an anti-armour weapon – a RAAWS, AT-4, LAW or Javelin. The main purpose of the vehicle is to provide the operation force with a mobile, lethal defensive capability. They are not assault vehicles, but useful in establishing battle positions that provide the force some stand-off capability for a short duration. Each battalion also possesses ten 250-cc motorcycles that assist in providing security and mobility during airfield seizures. Most commonly used as listening or observation posts, or as an economy of force screen for early warning, the motorcycles offer the commander tactical mobility.

But the Rangers have their limitations. Ranger battalions have a limited anti-armour capability – only sixteen 84-mm Carl Gustav Ranger Anti-Armour Weapons and nine Javelins. They also lack organic indirect fire support, apart form six 60-mm mortars. Their only air defence artillery (ADA) system is the Stinger. Otherwise they carry twenty-seven M240G machine guns, fifty-four M249 squad automatic weapons, twelve MK-19 grenade launchers and twelve .50-cal machine guns.

Ranger units have no organic combat support or combat service support units, and deploy with only five days of supplies. Consequently, Ranger units require logistical and mission support from other units or agencies. As light infantry, Ranger units have only a few vehicles and require transportation from other units to deploy.

On any given day, one Ranger battalion is on standby as Ready Reaction Force 1 that will be required to be "wheels up" within eighteen hours of notification. And one rifle company with battalion command and control can deploy within nine hours. RRF1 rotates between the three battalions normally every thirteen weeks. While on RRF1, the battalion cannot conduct any off-post training or other duties that might slow down their reaction time. Regimental Headquarters remains on RRF1 status at all times.

The Ranger Regiment can deploy in any number of ways. The force can deploy directly from home station to the area of operations. More often, the force deploys to an intermediate staging base within or outside the continental United States to link-up with attachments, plan, rehearse or undertake specialist training before conducting operations.

Each Ranger battalion has a Ranger Support Element that supports home station training. This unit – comprising riggers, truck drivers, maintenance and the like – is not organic, but belongs to the individual posts and provides the battalion with the help needed during training. However, while it is responsible for supporting the Ranger Force when they are going out to combat, it does not deploy with the unit. The logistical and support arrangements for extended deployment have to be provided by outside units.

Each combat company consists of 152 Rangers. It has a headquarters and headquarters company, three rifle platoons and a weapons platoon. The weapons platoon has a mortar section of two 60-mm mortars – a third is available for special operations – and an anti-tank section of three three-man teams firing the 84-mm Carl Gustav Ranger Anti-Armour Weapon

Systems. This weapon is unique to Ranger units and not currently under any testing for other infantry units. A versatile weapon, it can fire high explosive, high explosive anti-tank, illumination, smoke and, in the future, a flechette round. Finally, the weapons platoon has a sniper section consisting of two-man, M24 7.62-mm sniper teams. The third team in this section employs the .50 cal Barrett Sniper System. The Barrett is a Special Forces-specific weapon, though it has undergone testing for possible use by other Army units.

PART TWO

TRAINING

8

QUALIFICATION

SAS

To join the SAS you must already be in a British Armed forces. Even then it is reckoned that only 10 out of every 125 who apply get in. However, there is another way in. If you join the UK Special Forces Reserve, it is sometimes possible to transfer across into the Regular Army unit if you have some particular skill they are looking for.

The reserve component of the UK Special Forces group comprises 21 SAS (R) set up in 1947 and 23 SAS (R) formed in 1959, along with the SBS (R) and 63 (SAS) Signals Squadron. The aim of UKSF (R) is to deliver a second-tier Special Forces capability, both as augmentation to the regular component of UKSF and as standalone elements up to task group, or regimental, level. According to the Ministry of Defence:

SF (R) operations require the skill sets and equipment to operate beyond the range and capability of conventional forces. The conduct of SF (R) operations predominantly focuses on Support and Influence and the provision of ground truth to achieve effect in conflict resolution. They require sufficient endurance, field craft, surveillance, communications, mobility and "life skills" to work in isolation, whilst remaining in sync with multi agency effect across the spectrum of conflict.

They do not comment on the specifics of Special Forces operations, however, they will say that the SAS Reserve "have made a significant contribution to recent operational deployments".

The SAS (R) accepts male volunteers aged up to thirty-four from any part of the Regular or Reserve Armed Forces – the Royal Navy, the Royal Marines, the Army and the RAF. However, applicants with no previous military experience can apply, but must be aged thirty-two or under and may be required to attend the Combat Infantry Course before to going on to selection. Under the current Ministry of Defence policy regarding the employment of women in the Armed Services, service with the SAS (R) is restricted to men. Recruits need to be healthy with near-perfect eyesight, physically and mentally robust, and a good swimmer. They must also be mature, intelligent and flexible of mind.

It takes at least twelve months to get into the SAS (R). There are two intakes a year, one in February and one September. Recruits must commit to training every other weekend and about twenty-one days of continuous training every year. They must also be able to deploy overseas for several months at a time in an emergency.

During the induction period, a candidates' physical and mental endurance are tested, as well as their ability to navigate by day and night over arduous terrain. This culminates with "Endurance" – a 40-mile over the Brecon Beacons carrying over 60 lb. In all, the recruit has to undergo nine weekends of endurance training, one week of endurance training in the Brecon Beacons and a one-week assessment in the Brecon Beacons, known as "test week".

At the same time, candidates have to learn UKSF's Standard Operational Procedure and tactic. The training comprises nine weekends of patrol SOPs including surveillance and reconnaissance, one week live-firing including patrol contact drills and troop offensive action, and one nine-day battle camp. There the recruit undergoes a live-firing assessment, a field-training exercise to test the skills learned so far and a course on conduct after capture.

On successful completion of this training, ranks are given an SAS (R) badge. They then enter a period of probation. But before they are fit for mobilization, they must undergo a basic parachute course, a Special Forces communications course and further training which often takes place overseas. Recruits are also encouraged to get additional qualifications as patrol medics or in advanced surveillance and reconnaissance, languages, emergency close-air support, support weapons and close protection.

According to the Ministry of Defence:

SAS (R) provides an opportunity for soldiers to work within a unique, independent organization which takes pride in its heritage, role and professionalism. Service is physically and intellectually challenging, but the rewards are significant. In addition to a strong sense of purpose in embracing the challenges of a complex world, SAS (R) provides challenge and adventure with the additional benefit of Special Forces pay rates. While the Regiment contributes to UKSF operational capability in its own right, it also provides an excellent grounding for those who aspire to serve with the Regular UKSF.

SBS

Although the SBS is now officially tri-service it traditionally recruits directly from the Royal Marines. Volunteers from the other services are considered, but the vacancies are few and competition intense. It too has a Reserve but only candidates with military experience are eligible. Although SBS (R) units are located throughout the UK, the training is carried out in the South of England. It is not possible to enter the SBS direct from civilian life.

Over a four-day initial selection course, the candidate must cover 8 miles carrying 55 lb within 1 hour and 50 minutes, and swim 600 yards using any stroke, in uniform and with a weapon and belt, and swim 25 yards underwater without diving equipment. As the course goes on, he must walk 10 miles carrying 55 lb, then 15 miles carrying 66 lb. The Ministry of Defence recommends a twelve-week training programme just to get up to this standard. A high degree of commitment is therefore required. The candidate must also take a one-week diving course, where he must complete a number of dives, demonstrate all drills taught to the instructor's satisfaction, and show the confidence and willingness to dive.

Continuation training is carried out alongside regular forces, but the reservist will not be eligible to transfer in the active-duty SBS, though he may have the opportunity to serve overseas alongside regular counterparts.

Green Berets

Recently the US Army has been recruiting civilians to join the Green Berets. This means that a candidate can enlist on a Special Forces contract, which puts him in the pipeline for the Special Forces training programme – once he has jumped all the hurdles on the way.

Recruiters stress that, to become part of the US Army's Special Forces, the candidate needs to be mentally and physically tough, endure difficult training and face challenges head-on. Also he must be male (Special Forces positions are not open to women), aged between twenty and thirty, a US citizen, have a high-school diploma, and achieve a General Technical score of 110 or higher and a combat operation score of 98 on the Armed Services Vocational Aptitude Battery.

The Armed Services Vocational Aptitude Battery is given at over 14,000 schools and Military Entrance Processing Stations. It covers arithmetic reasoning, mathematical knowledge, word knowledge and paragraph comprehension. However, as joining an elite team like the Green Berets is competitive, a high score is needed. Entry qualifications for other branches of the Services are in the low to mid thirties. The candidate's score also makes a difference to his enlistment bonuses.

The candidate must also qualify for a secret level security clearance, qualify and volunteer for airborne training, take a defence language proficiency test and achieve an overall minimum score of 229 on the Army Physical Fitness Test.

If the candidate reaches the standard required to join the Green Berets he gets an enlistment bonus of up to $20,000 and over $70,000 to further his education.

Like others soldiers, Special Forces recruits begin their career with nine weeks of Boot Camp. Upon completion of Basic Combat Training they move on to Advanced Individual Training. To join Special Forces, recruits go to Infantry School to learn to use small arms, anti-armour weapons, howitzers and heavy mortars. This AIT lasts four weeks and takes place at Fort Benning, Georgia.

After graduating from AIT, Special Forces recruits go on to the Army Airborne School for airborne training. The three-week Basic Airborne Training course teaches them the techniques involved in parachuting from aircraft and landing safely. The first week is "ground week", where recruits start with an intensive programme of instruction to build individual airborne skills, preparing them to make a parachute jump and land safely. They train on the mock door, a 34-foot tower and a lateral drift apparatus.

The following week is "tower week". This completes their individual skills training and builds team skills. On the final week, they must qualify on the Swing Lander Trainer, master the mass exit procedures from the 34-foot tower and pass all physical training requirements.

The final week is "jump week", where recruits must successfully complete five jumps at 1,250 feet from a C-130 Hercules or C-141 Starlifter aircraft. The final test includes a non-assisted jump. After that, recruits can wear the coveted "silver wing" on their uniforms.

Once Special Forces recruits graduate from the Army Airborne School they are sent to the thirty-day Special Operations Preparation Course taught at Fort Bragg, North Carolina. Here they are prepared for the Special Forces Assessment and Selection course. The preliminary course focuses on physical training and – one of the most important skills a Special Forces soldier can have – land navigation. However, even if a recruit has got this far, it does not mean that he is guaranteed to pass the Special Forces Assessment/Assignment and Selection that is coming next.

US Navy SEALs

The US Department of Defense point out that there is no easy way to become a SEAL. However, there are several ways to become a SEAL candidate. A civilian can request to join the SEALs prior to enlisting in the US Navy through the SEAL Challenge Contract, also known as the Seaman to SEAL programme. The SEAL Challenge Contract guarantees the recruit the opportunity to become a SEAL candidate and entitles him to certain bonuses and benefits when he enlists.

If a recruit does not get a SEAL Challenge Contract before enlisting, he can still volunteer to take the Physical Screening Test during the first week at Boot Bamp. If he passes the PST a Naval Special Operation Motivator will interview the recruit. The motivator will then submit a request for him to enter the Naval Special Warfare – or Basic Underwater Demolition/ SEAL – training pipeline. However, recruits who volunteer this way, after they have joined the service, do not qualify for the same benefits as applicants who have the SEAL Challenge Contract.

All SEAL candidates must be between eighteen and twenty-eight years old, though seventeen year olds can join with parental permission. They must also be a US citizen and a high-school graduate, or meet High Performance Predictor Profile (HP3) criteria. In any case, they must be proficient in reading, speaking, writing and understanding the English language.

Furthermore, they must have clean record. They must not be under civil restraint, a substance abuser, have a pattern of minor convictions or any non-minor, misdemeanour or felony convictions – though waivers are granted depending on the number and severity of the convictions. The Special Assistant for Legal Affairs is constrained not to enlist applicants with lawsuits pending against them without prior approval.

The applicant must also sit the ASVAB test. The minimum requirement to become a SEAL is a composite score of 165 in general science, mechanical comprehension and electronics information, or a composite score of 220 in word knowledge, paragraph comprehension, knowledge of mathematics, mechanical comprehension and, until 2002, coding speed. Since then the coding speed and numerical operations tests have been replaced with a test called "assemble object". Again these scores are much higher than those required to enter any other branch of the service.

The eyesight requirements are that the uncorrected vision in the better eye is no worse than 20/70, and in the worse eye no more than 20/100. Both eyes must be correctable to 20/20. Any form of colour blindness requires specific approval.

If these qualifications are met, a Navy Special Operations Motivator administers the Physical Screening Test once the applicant arrives at Boot Camp. SEAL training is extremely demanding and is not designed to get the recruit into shape. The applicant must be in excellent physical condition and pass the PST before he can be considered a SEAL candidate.

To pass the SEAL PST the applicant must swim 500-yards using breast or sidestroke in less than 12 minutes and 30 seconds. After a ten-minute rest, he must perform a minimum of forty-two push-ups in two minutes. After two minutes' rest, he must perform a minimum of fifty sit-ups in two minutes. After another two minutes' rest, he must perform a minimum of six pull-ups, though there is no time limit on this. After another ten minutes' rest, he must run 1½ miles wearing shorts and trainers in under eleven minutes. While at Recruit Training Center, SEAL recruits will have to pass the PST again, this time performing the running section in long trousers and boots. To stay in the SEAL training pipeline, the SEAL recruit must perform the 1½-mile run portion of the PST in long trousers and boots in 11 minutes 30 seconds or less.

If the recruit has passed all these tests, once they have finished Boot Camp, they will be sent on a two-week course Apprenticeship Training Division School. Then they will be assigned immediately to the Basic Underwater Demolition/SEAL programme.

Currently there is no direct enlistment route into Marine Force Recon. Recruits must join the Marine Corps first, then apply for selection as a Reconnaissance Marine. To be eligible for Marine Force Recon, the recruit must be a US citizen, eligible for secret security clearance and score 105 or higher on the general technical portion of the ASVAB, covering arithmetic reasoning, word knowledge and paragraph comprehension. Again a high score is reflected in the recruit's enlistment bonus.

The recruit must have a first-class swimming qualification and obtain a first-class score on the physical fitness test. He must have 20/200 near visual acuity or visual acuity not to exceed 20/400 with a completed Photorefractive Keratectomy corrective eye surgery. Normal colour vision is preferred, but not required provided the Marine can complete a vivid red and vivid green recognition test.

He must also have completed a Marine Rifleman Course and be assigned to a primary Military Occupational Specialty like other entry-level Marines, then obtain approval for a lateral move from his commander. After graduating from the Basic Reconnaissance Course, volunteers from any MOS may be certified for additional awarded MOS only by Recon unit commanders after attending the Surveillance and Reconnaissance Center, or through on-the-job at a Basic Reconnaissance Course-endorsed unit-training programme that includes months in a reconnaissance man's billet.

Delta Force

Again, there is no direct route into Delta Force. First, anyone with the ambition to become a member of the elite 1st Special Forces Operational Detachment-Delta must join the US Army with an entry-level Military Occupational Specialty. If possible, the recruit should go into the Army with a Ranger contract as the Ranger Battalion is a Special Operations unit that a would-be Delta operative can enter as a low-ranking soldier. This will also help the recruit for the trials that he will face on the long road to becoming a member of Delta Force.

The would-be recruit must perform well and stay out of trouble. Adverse actions on a recruits' records can exclude them from consideration. Again they must be male and a US citizen, eighteen years old or over. However, some women are recruited for the "Funny Platoon" for their special skills, but they are handled separately on a case-by-case basis. Recruits must have a general technical score of 110 or higher on the ASVAB and be a non-commissioned officer, at least a sergeant or sergeant first class. Additionally, they must pass the Defense Language Aptitude Battery or Defense Language Proficiency Test.

The recruit must be airborne qualified or agree to volunteer for airborne training and qualify for an interim secret clearance.

He must be able to pass the standard Army Physical Fitness Test and pass very thorough psychological and physical examinations.

Next comes the hard part. The applicant must talk to a Delta Force recruiter – which is difficult as Delta Force, officially, does not exist. But if a man is eligible he will be contacted.

Although Delta Force are always on the lookout for men who are in excellent shape, a Delta Force operative does not have to be a world-class athlete. What Delta Forces trainers are looking for is consistency. They do not want recruits who are motivated one day and demotivated the next. The men they pick show themselves consistently to be above their peers in all areas.

Land-navigation skills are vital to Delta Force, so recruits have to know how to use a compass and map. They should also practise walking for very long distances – 20 miles or more – carrying a 70-lb rucksack. The recruit should aim to cover each mile in fifteen minutes, though they will be expected to travel at a much faster pace during selection.

There are dire warnings about joining Delta Force – being an operative is a difficult and dangerous profession. Delta Force conducts a wide variety of direct action and covert operations around the globe, protecting American interests. As a Delta Force operative is working in a unit that does not officially exist, its operatives do not get the same operational support that the regular Army gets. In other words, when they go on operations in plain clothes, if they are caught they face criminal prosecution or, worse, may be shot. Delta Force operatives have to rely on their own resourcefulness and determination to stay out of trouble. It is not a job for the fainthearted.

It is not advisable to join the Army with the sole intention of making it into Delta Force. The recruit is looking at a commitment of at least four years before he will even be considered. Realistically it will take much longer than that. Even if a recruit completes the selection phase, there is still no guarantee that he will be accepted into the ranks of the elite unit. In that case, he will be returned to his previous Military Occupational Specialty and will have to wait some time before he can try again. It takes a great deal of patience and dedication to get into Delta Force. However, occasionally opportunities do come up. Recently, Personnel Command of the US Army did advertise around Army posts for officers who wanted to be assigned to Delta Force. The ad read:

Officer Assignment Opportunities in Delta Force
The US Army's 1st Special Forces Operational Detachment-Delta (1st SFOD-D) plans and conducts a broad range of special operations across the operational continuum. Delta is organized for the conduct of missions requiring rapid response with surgical applications of a wide variety of unique skills, while maintaining the lowest possible profile of US involvement. Assignment to 1st SFOD-D involves an extensive pre-screening process, successful completion of a three- to four-week mentally and physically demanding Assessment and Selection Course, and a six-month operator Training Course. Upon successful completion of these courses officers are assigned to an operational position within the unit. As an officer in 1st SFOD-D, you will have added opportunities to command at the CPT, MAJ, and LTC levels. You may also serve as an Operations Officer. After service with 1st SFOD-D there are a wide variety of staff positions available to you at DOD, JCS, DA, USASOC, USSOCOM, and other joint headquarters because of your training and experience. In addition, there are interagency positions available to you as well.

The prerequisites for an officer are:

- Male.
- Volunteer.
- US Citizen.
- Pass a modified Class II Flight Physical.
- Airborne qualified or volunteer for airborne training.
- Pass a background security investigation and have at least a secret clearance.
- Pass the Army Physical Fitness Test (APFT), FM 21-20, 75 points each event in the 22–26 age group (55 push-ups in two minutes, 62 sit-ups in two minutes, and a 2-mile run in 15 minutes and six seconds or less), wearing your unit PT uniform.

- Minimum of two years active service remaining upon selection to the unit.
- Captain or Major (Branch Immaterial).
- Advance Course graduate.
- College graduate (BA or BS).
- Minimum of 12 months successful command (as a Captain).
- 1st SFOD-D conducts worldwide recruiting twice a year to process potential candidates for the Assessment and Selection Course. Processing for the March Course is from October through January. Processing for the September Course takes place April through July.
- Assignments with 1st SFOD-D provide realistic training and experiences that are both personally and professionally rewarding.

This indicates something of the standard of recruit they are looking for.

As we have seen, one way into Delta Force is to join the Army Rangers first. As a civilian it is possible to contact an Army Recruiter and ask about enlisting on the Army Ranger Contract. The contract ensures the candidate's place at Airborne School and assignment to the 75th Ranger Regiment to attend the Ranger Indoctrination Program.

US Air Force Special Forces

Before an applicant can join the USAF Special Forces he has to join the Air Force. Then to become a Special Forces candidate – a combat controller, a para-rescuemen or a special operations weatherman – he must meet the following basic requirements. The applicant must be a male high-school graduate and score at least 43 on the Armed Services Vocational Aptitude Battery test. Again his score affects his enlistment bonus. Vision in his best eye must be 20/70, in the worst eye 20/100, correctable to 20/20 without radial keratotomy. He must have normal colour vision, be a good swimmer and physically fit, passing an Initial Flying Class III physical qualification of aircrew, parachute and maritime diving duty. He must be able to obtain a secret security clearance.

Next the candidate must be able to complete the Physical Ability and Stamina Test successfully. To do that, he must swim 500 yards in fifteen minutes or less using any freestyle or side stroke, without using flippers or fins. Then he must do six chin-ups in one minute, fifty sit-ups in two minutes, forty-two push-ups in two minutes and run 1.5 miles non-stop in 11 minutes 30 seconds.

US Army Rangers

Generally, to be a Ranger, an applicant has to be a US citizen or permanent resident alien. The candidate must have a High School Diploma or equivalent, and be eighteen years old or more. Naturally the recruit must be able to pass the Army Physical Fitness Test and be eligible for a secret-level security clearance. He must score 50 or more on the Armed Force Qualification Test and have a general technical score of 110 or more on the Armed Services Vocational Aptitude Battery test.

Once qualified to become a Ranger, the trainee is, officially, inside the Special Forces.

9

SELECTION

Once a candidate has qualified to join Special Forces and been picked by the unit he wants to join, then the hard work really starts. By any standard, those chosen to go on the selection course are mentally and physically fit. Now they will be pushed to the limits.

SAS

Candidates for the British Special Air Service are selected from the British armed forces. Most enter from the Army or Marines but a few from the Royal Air Force make it onto selection. Although the average soldier, Marine or airman is in pretty good condition, out of an average intake of 125 candidates, only ten will pass the gruelling selection course.

The SAS run two selection courses a year, one in winter and one in summer. To be accepted onto the selection course, candidates must have served three years with a regular unit and must have at least three years left to serve after they have completed selection and training. They must have been declared fit by their regiment's medical officer and they must be able to complete the standard Battle Fitness Test in the time permitted for infantry soldiers.

The selection process for the SAS is divided into six stages: endurance, test week, continuation training, escape and evasion, jungle training and static-line parachute training. The endurance phase lasts for one month and is run by the Training Wing of the Special Air Service, and throughout it candidates who do not reach the required standard are either ejected or leave voluntarily.

During the first week the SAS try to let the candidates ease into the rigours ahead by pairing them up and putting them through a series of road runs that get steadily longer as the week progresses. After this, they move to the Black Mountains and Brecon Beacons in South Wales, where the weather is cold and wet, and the terrain bleak, barren and featureless. Initially, they remain paired off but they are soon left to operate on their own as a greater emphasis is placed on the candidate's ability to navigate in the bleak terrain alone.

As there are no regular landmarks, to get a bearing candidates must rely on the compass and distance method of navigating, especially when the weather closes in and the visibility is reduced to only a few yards. Navigating featureless terrain is probably the single most important skill an SAS man will acquire. The SAS are frequently being dropped in the jungle or the desert and will need this skill to orientate them and find their way to the objective, then find their way back to safety, often with the enemy snapping at their heels.

Candidates start the day with a rucksack and the grid reference of a rendezvous point which they have to get to in a certain time. They are not told how long they have got. Only the SAS Directing Staff (DS), all fully-badged members of the Regiment, know this, but if the candidate does not make it within that time he is "binned". At the rendezvous point, the candidate gets no encouragement or chastisement, in marked contrast to what they would have experienced in their parent units. All they are given is the grid reference of the next rendezvous point. They are not told how many legs they are going to cover that day. At the end of the day, when the trooper is on his last legs, he might be sent off to yet another rendezvous to see if they quit there and then. If not, they are called back after 100 yards or so. Another trick used by the DS is to tell a candidate, when he has got to a rendezvous point, to take his shoes off and rest, or take a breather in the back of the truck. If the candidate falls for that one, he fails.

Candidates are put through a number of other psychological tests on the candidates, such as being questioned about the terrain they have just covered, or being asked to remember a long series of numbers.

This hill stage of the selection training lasts for three weeks. Each day, the distances get longer and the weights in the bergen rucksacks get heavier. Then comes test week. This is a series of night and day timed marches through the Brecon Beacons which culminates with the "Long Drag" or "Fan Dance" – a 40-mile trek with a 55 lb bergen over some of the highest peaks of the Brecon Beacons. This must be completed in twenty hours regardless of injury or weather conditions. Though this is punishing, most candidates manage it, as those not tough enough to make it have already been weeded out by the DS.

Successful candidates will be given a week's leave to recuperate, then go on to continuation training. This is a series of specially designed courses that last fourteen weeks. The trooper will learn the basic SAS skills, including how to survive behind enemy lines. Many of the recruits come from infantry regiments so have most of the fieldcraft skills required. However, those who come from other regiments and corps in the Army will be given a special course on infantry tactics. During continuation training the SBS candidates join the SAS at Hereford to be put through their paces.

They learn the standard operating procedures for the SAS four-man unit – how to move through hostile territory, the arcs of fire of each patrol member and how to conduct contact drills, and weapon training including the use of pistols and foreign weapons. They are also taught basic field medicine, camouflage, how to set up and survive in an observation post, escape and evasion, anti-interrogation techniques and signalling. Every SAS man is trained to the British Army Regimental Signaller standard. Recruits then go on to combat survival training, where they learn all aspects of living in hostile environments – building shelters, finding food and water, laying traps and lighting fires.

The combat survival phase ends in an escape and evasion exercise. Like many SAS exercises the premise is simple:

survive in the wild while being pursued by a hunter force. First, candidates are given brief instructions on appropriate techniques. This may include talks from former POWs or Special Forces soldiers who have been in escape and evasion situations in the real world. Then candidates are let loose in the countryside, wearing civilian clothing with instructions to make their way to a series of rendezvous points without being captured by the hunter force of other soldiers.

With no kit, they must use the skills learnt on the combat survival course to survive and avoid being caught by the hunters. The candidate must cover his tracks, only move at night and lay-up during the day. He has to find a way to eat and drink and eat, and formulate plans and courses of action to cope with as many eventualities as possible.

The biggest test of the exercise is mental. If a soldier can keep his focus and remember what he has been taught, he has a good chance of making it to the last day. But when sleep deprivation, cold and hunger seep in, a candidate's mental ability is tested to the limit.

The most common reason for a candidate to be captured is when he takes the shortest and easiest route to a rendezvous point. Candidates are taught not to follow roads or paths, to avoid populated areas and to stick to concealed areas that offer good camouflage such as dense woodland and shrubbery.

This phase lasts for three days after which, captured or not, all candidates report for tactical questioning to test their ability to resist interrogation. They are treated roughly by their interrogators, often made to stand in "stress positions" for hours at a time, while disorientating white noise is blasted at them. When their turn for questioning comes, they must only answer with the so-called "big four" – name, rank, serial number and date of birth. All other questions must be answered with a tactful "I'm sorry but I cannot answer that question". Otherwise the candidate fails the course.

Interrogators use all sorts of tricks to try and get a reaction from the candidates. They may act friendly and try to get their subjects chatting, or they stand inches away from their subjects and scream unfavourable remarks about the sexual habits of their mothers. Female interrogators may mock the size of their subject's manhood. Of course, a real interrogation would be a lot harsher and the subject would not know whether he gets to leave alive when it's all over. However, days of interrogations and enduring the stress positions and white noise warp a man's sense of time and reality. The SAS are looking for men who can withstand such treatment long enough so that the effects of revealing any operational information they might have can be mitigated.

The interrogators are highly trained, and masters at reading people and taking advantage of situations. Even a simple yes or no answer from a candidate can result in failure of the exercise because a yes or no recorded on tape can easily be manipulated by the enemy so a question as harmless as "Are you OK?" must be ignored, or answered "I'm OK." Failure to resist interrogation is the downfall of many candidates. The sleep deprivation and hunger sustained over the previous week means they are physically and mentally weak, and many struggle under the psychological abuse of the interrogator. The best approach is to be the "grey man" – don't give away any information but just sit there and look pathetic, appear exhausted, make the most of any injury and, if the going gets tough, faint. Should a candidate successfully hold out, a previously identified person (usually a doctor or officer) will reveal themselves and tell the candidate that the exercise is over. But SAS selection is not.

If the candidate has made it this far through the selection process and the DS have decided that they want him for the Regiment, the candidate is flown to Brunei or Borneo for six weeks of jungle training. Here the survival and patrol skills they have learnt so far are adapted for jungle survival. They learn how to build shelter, find water and food, cross rivers and navigate under the thick jungle canopy. Many candidates fail at this point, unable to stand the claustrophobia that the heat and denseness of the jungle bring on.

Jungle training culminates in a final exercise that will test all the skills they have learnt as candidates are split into four-man patrols and live as they would if they were behind enemy lines. A typical training exercise would be to locate an enemy strongpoint, set up an observation post and plan, then execute, an assault on the enemy position. As with all Special Air Service selection exercises, failure means you are denied entry into the Special Air Service at least for the time being. Then, unless the candidate already has his Para wings, he must take a static-line parachuting course. All SAS personnel must be airborne trained.

The course lasts four weeks and takes place at No. 1 Parachute Training School at RAF Brize Norton, Oxfordshire. The candidates must make a total of eight jumps including one from a balloon, one at night and an operational descent. At the end of the course candidates who pass are awarded their Sabre wings before they return to Credenhill in Herefordshire where they are given the coveted SAS badge.

Although the candidates are now in the 22nd Special Air Service, they have not finished their training. Any candidate unable to drive or swim undergoes further training in those areas. Once added to a squadron, the SAS man must also continue honing his patrol skills, including signalling, demolition, languages and medical. An SAS four-man-patrol is a self-contained unit and must have all of these skills. They must also learn their specialist troop skill – mountaineering, mobility, anti-terrorism, advanced parachuting. SAS soldiers pride themselves on being one of the highest-trained troopers in the world.

SBS

The initial stages of SBS selection are much like those for the SAS. Candidates begin by taking a two-day Special Forces briefing course. In a series of lectures and tests, they are shown what to expect as a Special Forces soldier, and basic skills such as swimming, map reading and basic fitness are tested. Kicking off the four-week endurance phase is a battle fitness test that weeds out anyone not up to scrach.

SBS candidates then join with SAS colleagues for three weeks among the barren hills of the Brecon Beacons in Wales, doing the same marches. Wearing heavy bergens, candidates must navigate themselves over the steep hills along a series of way points. Endurance not only tests stamina, but also the ability to keep going while suffering inevitable blisters, cramps and the unusually harsh climate. Over the three weeks, the marches get progressively longer, and the bergens get heavier, culminating in the "long drag" – the 25-mile march that must be completed in less that twenty hours.

The next four weeks are devoted to the basic SF skills of weapon handling, patrolling and explosives. Candidates who cannot absorb and apply these skills are returned to their unit. Next comes jungle training in the thick rainforests of Belize. Candidates are taught the skills of navigating, patrolling, fighting and surviving in dense jungle. A series of exercises tests the candidates' ability to apply what they have learned as they are pushed to the limits of their endurance.

Four weeks of combat survival follow. This begins with a series of lectures on escape-and-evasion techniques, followed by exercises in which the candidates are hunted down by other troops, usually Royal Marines or Paras. When captured, candidates are subjected to intense interrogation. While waiting for "tactical questioning", they are placed in stress positions, deprived of food, water and sleep, and subjected to white noise. They are then interrogated and must only give their name, serial number, date of birth and rank. All other questions must be answered with a stock reply: "I cannot answer that question."

Whereas at this point, having made it through the first five stages of selection, SAS candidates are given their beige beret, regimental badge and are assigned to a squadron and troop, SBS candidates go on to more selection phases before they qualify. This tests their ability in the water.

SBS candidates are sent on a swimmer canoeist, SC3, training course that involves training in diving in all conditions, canoeing over long distances, underwater demolition, beach reconnaissance and surveying techniques. Although a man who has reached this stage of selection is technically in the SBS, he is considered under probation and can still be returned to his unit if he fails to measure up. However, the Royal Marines literature says that the course is:

within the capability of most marines, particularly those with the mental commitment and determination to succeed. Training is demanding, but that's the way it has to be. The rewards are most definitely worth the effort and include: a structured career; job satisfaction; realistic and challenging exercises; extra skills training work with other SF units at home and abroad; operational employment and extra pay . . . but you earn it.

The Green Berets

Candidates for the US Special Forces – the Green Berets –
begin with the Special Operations Preparation Course. This
thirty-day course at Fort Bragg is designed to help soldiers
prepare for the Special Forces Assessment and Selection
course. It focuses on physical training and one of the most
important skills a SF soldier can have – land navigation.
Completing the course does not guarantee that the candidate
will pass the Special Forces Assessment/Assignment and Selection. Indeed, many fail on the first day.

Candidates turn up by bus in groups of 200. When they have
lined up in formation they are forced to run to the school
compound about a mile-and-a-half away, carrying all their
gear. Some cannot make it and fail the course before they have
even entered the school gates.

From the off, recruits begin a seventeen-hour-day routine.
There are plenty of push-ups and running. The accommodation
is rudimentary – tar-paper huts that belong in the Third World.
Rations are standard-issue MREs – Meals Ready to Eat, said to
taste of Styrofoam. The showers are cold.

The day begins with a six-mile route marche carrying a heavy
pack. At the start of the course, which is designed to test the
recruit to the limit, the pack weighs 45 lb; by the end it weights
65 lb. At the beginning, the recruit has to cover each mile in
fifteen minutes; by the end, the pace has been increased so that
every mile has to be covered in eight minutes or faster. The rest
of each day is given over to instruction on patrolling, survival in
hostile territory or living off the land.

As good land navigation is essential in Special Forces
operations, so the recruit's ability is under constant review.
In one test, he has to find four survey stakes that have been
planted about a mile apart in a heavily wooded area. The
candidate has five hours to find all four. If not, he fails the
selection, though he can opt to be recycled and begin again
with the next intake.

Although recruits must be airborne qualified before they can
apply to join Special Forces, they are given training on specialist and advanced tactical parachute systems. They are also
trained in rappelling from a tower.

Recruits must also be able to survive in the wild. In one test, they are sent out to the Uwarrie National Forest in North Carolina with a poncho, a knife, a book of matches and a live rabbit, and left there for three days. Traditionally, the instructor grimly reminds the recruit: "Remember to kill the rabbit before you eat it."

There follows a SERE – Survival, Evasion, Resistance and Escape – test where, armed only with a knife, recruits must survive off the land while being pursued by man-hunters. If they pass this, they are permitted to move on to the Special Forces Qualification Course, the first thirteen weeks of which are devoted to individual skills. Recruits must learn small-unit tactics, Special Forces tactics, survival skills and live-fire training.

During the next phase, recruits will be assessed for their Military Occupational Specialities – that is, the individual specialty they will bring to a Special Forces unit, if selected. Special Forces have six enlisted Military Occupational Specialties: 18B – Special Forces Weapons Sergeant; 18C – Special Forces Engineer Sergeant; 18D – Special Forces Medical Sergeant; 18E – Special Forces Communications Sergeant; 18F – Special Forces Assistant Operations and Intelligence Sergeant; and 18Z – Special Forces Operations Sergeant.

Weapons sergeants must be familiar with over eighty different types of modern small arms. Particular emphasis is placed on marksmanship, and proficiency in the building and use of less conventional weapons, such as crossbows. Specialists are also taught the tactical deployment of their weapons at squad, platoon and company levels.

Engineering specialists go on an eight-week course where they are taught the finer points of construction and destruction. As with other specialist courses, a lot of the time is devoted to putting classroom theory into practice. Most days are spent on the range making explosives out of various substances and trying them out. Prospective demolition experts have to familiarize themselves with potential targets, working out their weakest points. As well as blowing things up, they have to know how to construct things, and candidates are taught how to build bridges, dams and stockades.

Recruits chosen for the medical specialist courses undergo the long and most difficult training, which lasts up to fifty weeks, during which they are trained to deal with all types of combat wounds. As Special Forces are also involved in "hearts and minds" programmes, they must also be able to cope with all of the most common conditions they are likely to come across in their area of operation. They are also likely to need some veterinary skills and are assigned an animal to practise on during the course. If it dies, the recruit is thrown out of Special Forces.

Communication sergeants must be familiar with all kinds of communications equipment, and how to use, maintain and repair them. In the Special Forces, recruits must also learn how to disrupt enemy communications – an invaluable skill.

Intelligence sergeants will need to know about intelligence gathering and assessment, interrogation techniques and the establishment of intelligence networks, while operations sergeants need to know how to set up and run an indigenous guerrilla force.

Language training is a key phase of the qualification course. Proficiency in at least one foreign language is part of being a Green Beret. Arabic, Spanish, Chinese and Russian are just some of the languages learned, along with the culture, customs, habits and traditions of those nations. At the same time combat and unconventional warfare skills are honed.

Following the completion of the second phase, recruits are brought together to learn the operational procedures of the Special Forces. After an initial period of theoretical training at Camp Mackall, they are formed into teams and dropped back into Uwarrie Forest, where they will have to evade the enemy in the form of an aggressor force drawn from the 82nd Airborne Division. They also have to create a "guerrilla force" from "untrained natives" drawn from other parts of the army. The Special Forces recruits are supposed to knock them into shape as a guerrilla army within a month.

Capture by the 82nd Airborne, or failure to organize an effective guerrilla force, marks the end of the line for a recruit. However, if he is successful, he finally gets to wear the famous green beret.

US Navy SEALs

The selection programme for the US Navy Seals is the most gruelling. The Basic Underwater Demolition/SEAL – or BUD/ S – selection course is some seven months long, beginning with three weeks of Indoctrination where the recruit learns the expectations and ways of Navy SEALS. Time is also spent preparing physically and mentally for what is ahead.

Next comes the seven weeks of Basic Conditioning at the Naval Amphibious Base at Coronado, California. The First Phase trains, develops, and assesses SEAL recruits in physical conditioning, water competency, teamwork and mental tenacity. Training begins at 0530 hours and recruits are put through their paces until late afternoon.

Divided into "boat crews" of six to eight men, they undertake exercises such as "log PT", where the boat crews exercise with logs that weigh 150 lb each, and they must make "surf passage", where they must navigate the Pacific surf in inflatable boats. Each team must carry its IBS – Inflatable Boat, Small – just about everywhere. Some recruits find that they develop a bald spot from the chaffing of the hull on their head.

Meanwhile they are undergoing continuous physical conditioning with running, swimming and callisthenics that grows harder and harder as the weeks progress. Recruits participate in weekly 4-mile timed runs in boots, timed obstacle courses, swim distances up to 2 miles wearing fins in the ocean, and learn small-boat seamanship. At each stage, a recruit's time and performance must improve continuously.

An important part of basic conditioning is "drown-proofing". Recruits must learn to swim with both their hands and their feet bound. To pass drown-proofing, recruits enter a 9-foot-deep pool with their hands and feet tied and bob for five minutes, float for five minutes, swim a hundred yards, bob for another two minutes, do some forward and backward flips, swim to the bottom of the pool and retrieve an object with their teeth, return to the surface and bob five more times.

Another endurance test is "cold water conditioning", also know as "surf torture". Recruits are deluged with water the temperature of which usually hovers around 65° Fahrenheit, and never goes above 68° Fahrenheit. After that, they are

ordered to do some callisthenics, or run a mile and a half down
the beach in their wet clothes and boots, before being ordered
back into the surf. Many drills also require that teams carry
their rubber boats over their heads as they run from one task to
another. This phase produces the most "drops on request"
where recruits return voluntarily to their units.

The instructors know the human machine is capable of
amazing endurance even in the harshest of conditions and
environments, but they also know the mind must be made to
ignore the pleading of the body. After three-weeks' preparation,
the remaining recruits are just about to go through the most
gruelling phase – five and a half days of physical torment during
which they are allowed to sleep for a maximum of four hours. It
is called, appropriately enough, Hell Week.

During Hell Week, recruits are constantly in motion and
always cold, wet and hungry. Mud gets everywhere. It covers
their hands, faces and uniforms. Sand and salt burns their eyes
and chafes their skin raw. Medical personnel monitor the
recruits and are on constant standby for emergencies. The
recruits eat up to 7,000 calories a day and still lose weight.

Even their meagre allowance of sleep – a mere three to four
hours depending on how sadistic the instructor is – is only
granted near the end of the week. And their sleep deprivation
presents the instructors with another chance to psychologically
torment them. An instructor paces along the line of waterlogged
men with his bullhorn, shouting: "If you quit now you could go
get a room at one of those luxury hotels down the beach and do
nothing but sleep for an entire day."

In this condition, recruits are forced to spend hours doing
inflatable boat drills, landing on rocky beaches, crawling under
barbed wire and clearing obstacle courses. While these drills are
going on there are bullet and grenade simulators going off all
around them. But for the would-be Navy SEAL, there is a
reminder of why they are going through this. Over the main
doorway to the Phil H. Bucklew Center for Naval Special
Warfare at Coronado is an inscription: "The more you sweat
in peace, the less you bleed in war."

Throughout Hell Week, BUD/S instructors continually
remind candidates that they can "drop on request" any time.
If they feel they cannot go on all they have to do is ring a

shiny brass bell that hangs prominently in the camp for all to see.

"Whaddaya think? All you have to do is get up and go smack the hell out of that shiny, brass bell," yell the instructors. "You *know* you want to."

Beside the bell is a line of white helmets bearing the names of the recruits who decided that they could take no more.

Although that BUD/S requires a certain amount of physical strength, BUD/S instructors maintain that it is 90 per cent about mental strength and only 10 per cent about physical strength. When recruits decide that they are too cold, too sandy, too sore or too wet to go on, it is their minds that give up on them, not their bodies. Indeed it is not the physical trials of Hell Week that are difficult to cope with so much as the duration. Recruits must endure 132 hours of continuous physical labour.

"Even if a guy is an absolute physical stud, it doesn't mean that he's going to get through Hell Week," said one instructor.

Hell Week is so gruelling that even the instructors get exhausted and after eight hours they are replaced by the next shift. There are no replacements for the recruits.

Through the Week, there are whistle drills. At the sound of whistle, the recruit must throw himself to the ground, cover the back of his head with his hands, cross his legs and open his mouth. This is the standard position to adopt if there is incoming artillery fire. Two blasts and he must crawl towards the instructor and three he must stand. These whistle-drills go on all the time.

Recruits spend time in the mud pits, which are 100-feet long, 25-feet deep and filled at regular intervals by seawater from a hose which maintains a thick layer of mud at the bottom. The mud pits are surrounded by barbed wire that recruits must slither under to reach them.

In the pits, recruits take part in wheelbarrow races, where the face of the man who is the wheelbarrow's nose is barely above the mud. There are also caterpillar races where the entire boat crew sit on each other's laps, interlock their arms and slither backwards through the mud. Whistle drills also occur in the mud pits. One blast and the recruits have to bury their faces in the muck. Sometimes recruits are served lunch while standing in the mud pits with water and mud up to their hips, and grenade and shell simulators going off over their heads, showering them with debris.

But Hell Week helps build team spirit. Throughout the long days and nights of Hell Week, recruits learn to rely on one another to keep awake and stay motivated. They tap one another on the shoulder or thigh periodically and wait for a reassuring pat in response that says, "I'm still hanging in there, how about you?" They cheer loudly when they notice a mate struggling to complete his mission, calling on the same reserves as when they themselves feel drained. And they learn to silence that inner voice urging them to give in and ring that hideous, beautiful bell.

Recruits get to the point where they cannot remember what day it is, or when they last slept. But they remember that sleep felt good, while nothing about Hell Week felt good. They have been cold and wet for days on end. Sores open along their inner thighs from being constantly soaked. And every time they move, the coarse, wet camouflage clothing rakes over the wounds, sending lightening bolts of pain through their bodies. The result is the "Hell Week shuffle", a way of walking that attempts to keep salt-stained clothing away from chafed skin.

The last day of Hell Week is known as "So Sorry Day" where recruits spend practically the whole day crawling around the, by now, particularly unsavoury mud pits as automatic weapons fire blank rounds over their heads and artillery simulators explode around them.

Although SEAL training and duty is voluntary, many BUD/S students find that they do not have the desire to continue to endure the physical and mental strain of training, and drop on request. Classes typically lose between 70 and 80 per cent of their intake – either due to DORs or injuries sustained during training, but it is not always easy to predict which of the recruits will DOR during BUD/S. Winter class dropout rates are usually higher due to the cold. SEAL instructors say that in every class, around 10 per cent of the students simply do not have the physical ability to complete the training. Another 10 to 15 per cent will definitely make it through unless they sustain a serious physical injury. The other 75 to 80 per cent can make it, depending on their motivation.

Most recruits are eliminated prior to completion of Hell Week, but they continue to leave voluntarily in the next phase of training, or are forced to leave because of injuries, or by failing either the diving tests or the timed runs and swims. In fact, the instructors tell the recruits at the very start of BUD/S that the vast majority of them will not successfully complete the course and that they are free at any time to drop out if they do not believe they can make it. There has been at least one BUD/S class where no one has completed the course.

A recruit who DORs from first-phase of training before the completion of Hell Week, and reapplies to the BUD/S programme, must start again from the beginning of indoctrination – if they are accepted again. Any BUD/S recruit who drops on request after Hell Week is treated the same as those who quit before. However, if they reapply to BUD/S they would stand a very good chance of being accepted – but they do have to go through Hell Week all over again.

Those who have completed Hell Week but cannot continue training due to injury are usually rolled back into the next BUD/S class after Hell Week, or the one before they were forced to drop out. There are many SEALs who have attempted Basic Conditioning two or even three or more times before successfully completing selection.

Once through the First Phase of Basic Conditioning, recruits begin the eight-week Second Phase of diving training, to teach them to become competent combat swimmers. The physical training begun in the First Phase continues and becomes even more intensive. They are taught to use two types of scuba: open circuit, which uses compressed air, and closed circuit, which uses 100 per cent oxygen. Emphasis is placed on long-distance underwater dives which teaches the recruit to use swimming and diving techniques as a means of transportation from their launch point to their combat objective. This is what separates SEALs from all other Special Forces.

The nine-week Third (Land Warfare) Phase trains and qualifies SEAL recruits in basic weapons, demolition and small-unit tactics. Physical training continues to become more strenuous as the run distance increases and the minimum passing times are lowered for the runs, swims and obstacle course. The Third Phase concentrates on teaching land navigation, patrolling techniques, rappelling, marksmanship and military explosives. All recruits must qualify on the M-4 rifle as Marksman and most – some 60 per cent – as Expert. Recruits also spend hours on special reconnaissance, a key SEAL mission area.

The final three and a half weeks of the Third Phase are spent on San Clemente Island, where recruits apply all the techniques they have acquired during training, including increased rehearsals with Immediate Action Drills (IADs), Over-The-Beach (OTB) scenarios and ambush techniques. There is also a live-firing Field Training Exercise, which provides the most realistic scenario possible without entering a real-world combat situation.

Recruits must then attend Military Free-Fall School at Tactical Air Operations (TACAIROPS) school in Otay, outside San Diego, for one week of static-line parachute training, and three weeks of free-fall parachute training. Until 2003, the Army trained Navy Special Warfare teams to free fall, but this new school allows more SEALs and Special Warfare Combatant Crewmen (SWCC) to become free fall and HALO – High Altitude Low Opening – qualified than ever before.

Recruits must now go through SEAL Qualification Training, or SQT, a fifteen-week course of advanced training which builds on the skills developed during BUD/S. This culminates in a final three weeks of Extreme Cold-Weather Survival in the freezing, mountainous environment of Kodiak, Alaska. There they plunge into the coastal waters from small boats, wearing bulky dry-suits to protect them from the chill of the water as they make their way to shore carrying everything they need to climb cliffs, traverse gorges, rappel mountain faces and sleep in the snow.

One of the first candidates to complete the Extreme Cold-Weather Survival course was from Louisiana and had never seen snow before. He dreaded the training that included submerging himself in ice water and spending several nights exposed to Kodiak's extreme elements. But during the experience, he found he and his team-mates relied more on their perseverance than their equipment.

"It was one of the roughest parts of training for me," he said. "Even though we were issued cold-weather gear, nothing kept me warm. It was just above a freezing rain, really miserable weather and everyone was sick. But, I knew there was no way I was going to let it get to me after coming so far."

Candidates must break through ice-encrusted waters, jump in without the protection of their dry-suit, tread water for three to four minutes, pull themselves out of the water, then dry their clothes and gear off.

While some might question the necessity of being inducted into this "Polar Bear Club", SEAL candidates once again silence inner doubts and follow instructions as given. Even in the later phases of SQT, candidates call upon their mental determination. But usually the mental determination they developed during Hell Week pulls them through.

After the completion of Cold-Weather Survival Training, they are awarded their trident badge and Navy Enlisted Classification code at Naval Special Warfare Center, Coronado, California. Finally, they are assigned to their teams on a probationary basis for an additional six- to twelve-months' on-the-job training.

Marine Force Recon

Candidates for Marine Force Recon will have passed regular US Marine Corps training. They have to attend the Basic Reconnaissance Course at either Expeditionary Warfare Training Group Pacific or Atlantic. Next they will have to undergo Survival, Evasion, Resistance and Escape (SERE) Training at either the National Army School in North Island, California, or in Brunswick, Maine and take a parachute course at the Army Airborne School in Fort Benning, Georgia. Also candidates are required to complete several distance learning courses including land navigation, operations against guerrilla units, terrorism awareness, infantry patrolling and communications. Advanced training opportunities include courses in combatant diving, scout sniper training, military free fall, or how to become a jumpmaster or dive supervisor.

Delta Force

Delta Force selection is an arduous six-month process. It is both extremely mentally and physically stressful. Candidates are supposed to show their potential and trainability under stress. Like all special operations units, Delta operatives must be experts in both day and night land navigation. What makes Delta's land navigation so difficult is that points can be miles apart. They are asked to complete very long road marches but, like the SAS, they are given no indication of what passing times are. Recruits are simply required to give 110 per cent effort and never quit. To add mental stress, evaluators will come upon the Delta candidates during their training, ask the candidate's name, make a note on a clipboard and move on, giving no indication to the student of his performance, good or bad.

Other tests given to candidates include having them read a series of books in eighteen hours and then write a report on each of them to test mental agility and alertness. The next and final step in the selection process is an interview with senior Delta commanders. There are no correct answers to these questions. The commander and his staff are simply conducting one final test to see how an applicant stands up under pressure.

If the candidate is accepted, his selection and assessment records are sealed forever. Neither he nor anyone in Delta Force is ever allowed to see the scores or what the minimum standards were for passing. It is all part of Delta Forces well-deserved reputation for secrecy.

US Air Force Special Forces

Air Force Special Tactics units recruit in three separate disciplines – combat controllers, pararescue and special ops weathermen – each involving a separate selection procedure.

Combat Controllers

Combat controllers are among the most highly trained personnel in the US military. They must maintain a Federal Aviation Administration air traffic control qualification throughout their careers in addition to other special operations skills. Their thirty-five-week training and unique mission earns them the right to wear the scarlet beret.

It begins with an Indoctrination Course at Lackland Air Force Base in Texas. This is a one-week orientation to focus on sports physiology, nutrition, basic exercises, and the history and fundamentals of combat control.

There follows a fifteen-and-a-half-week Combat Control Operator Course at Keesler Air Force Base in Mississippi. This teaches aircraft recognition and performance, air navigation aids, weather, airport traffic control, flight assistance service, communication procedures, conventional approach control, radar procedures and air traffic rules. This is the same course that all other air traffic controllers attend and is the heart of a combat controller's job.

Next the trainee goes to the US Army Airborne School at Fort Benning in Georgia for a three-week course teaching the basic parachuting skills needed to infiltrate an objective area by static line airdrop.

As combat controllers are liable to operate in a forward area, they are sent to the US Air Force Basic Survival School at Fairchild Air Force Base in Washington State. This two-and-a-half-week course teaches basic survival techniques for remote areas that should enable an individual to survive, regardless of climatic conditions or unfriendly environments.

After the survival phase, the trainee is sent to the Combat Control School at Pope Air Force Base in North Carolina. This course provides final combat control qualifications. Training includes physical training, small-unit tactics, land navigation, communications, assault zones, demolitions, fire support and field operations including parachuting. At the completion of this course, each trainee gets their scarlet beret and CCT flash.

Although the trainee is now qualified, he must go on for Special Tactics Advanced Skills Training with the unit at Hurlburt Field in Florida. This is a twelve-month programme for newly assigned special tactic operatives. It produces mission-ready operators for the Air Force and United States Special Operations Command. The course is broken down into four phases: water, ground, employment and full mission profile. It is designed to test the trainee's personal limits through demanding mental and physical training.

Combat controllers also have to attend US Army Military Free Fall Parachutist School at Fort Bragg in North Carolina and Yuma Proving Grounds in Arizona, where they are instructed in free fall parachuting procedures. The five-week course provides wind-tunnel training, in-air instruction focusing on student stability, aerial manoeuvres, air sense and parachute-opening procedures.

From there it's on to the US Army Special Forces Combat Divers School at Key West in Florida. Here trainees become combat divers, learning to use scuba to covertly infiltrate denied areas. The four-week course provides training to depths of 130 feet and stresses the development of maximum underwater mobility under various operating conditions.

Finally there is the US Navy Underwater Egress Training course at Pensacola Naval Air Station in Florida, which teaches the trainee how to escape from an aircraft safely once it has ditched in the water. The one-day course includes principles, procedures and techniques necessary to get out of a sinking aircraft.

Pararescuemen

USAF Special Forces pararescuemen endure some of the toughest training in the US armed forces. Their training, as well as their unique mission, earns them the right to wear the maroon beret. They complete the same technical training as Emergency Medical Treatment Paramedics, along with specialist training. This begins with a ten-week Indoctrination Course at Lackland Air Force Base in Texas, which recruits, selects and trains future operatives through extensive physical conditioning. Training accomplished at this course includes physiological training, assault courses, marches with heavy rucksacks, the physics of diving, dive tables, metric manipulations, medical terminology, cardiopulmonary resuscitation, weapons qualifications, parajump history and leadership reaction course.

From there they go to the US Army Airborne School at Fort Benning in Georgia, where recruits learn the basic parachuting skills required to infiltrate an objective area by static-line airdrop on a three-week course. At the US Army Combat Divers School at Key West in Florida, trainees become combat divers, learning to use scuba to covertly infiltrate denied areas. The four-week course provides training to depths of 130 feet, stressing development of maximum underwater mobility under various operating conditions. Again, it is on to the US Navy Underwater Egress Training at Pensacola Naval Air Station in

Florida for a one-day course on how to escape from a ditched aircraft. The US Air Force Basic Survival School at Fairchild Air Force Base, Washington gives them a two-and-a-half-week course on basic survival in remote areas and the US Army Military Free Fall Parachutist School at Fort Bragg, North Carolina and Yuma Proving Grounds, Arizona teach them free-fall parachuting.

Next comes a specialist Paramedic Course at Kirtland Air Force Base in New Mexico. This twenty-four-week course teaches trainees how to manage trauma patients prior to evacuation and provide emergency medical treatment. Upon graduation, an EMT-Paramedic certification is awarded through the National Registry. But the USAF Special Forces operative moves on to the Pararescue Recovery Specialist Course also at Kirtland Air Force Base. The twenty-week training includes field tactics, mountaineering, combat tactics, advanced parachuting and helicopter insertion and extraction. Graduating from this course qualifies airmen as pararescue recovery specialists for assignment to any American pararescue unit worldwide.

Weathermen

Special Operations Weathermen conduct the same technical training as all US Air Force weathermen. Unlike other special operations forces, special operations weather only recruits from airmen already within the unit. Their training includes the Air Force Operation Command's Advanced Skills Training conducted at Hurlburt Field, Florida, which produces combat-ready Special Forces operators through an "intensive mentoring training philosophy".

They do the basic three-week static-line training programme at the US Army Airborne School at Fort Benning, Georgia, and the two-and-a-half-week basic survival in remote areas course at US Air Force Basic Survival School at Fairchild Air Force Base, Washington. Basic water survival skills are taught on the one-week course at the US Air Force Water Survival School, Pensacola Naval Air Station, Florida.

The six-week Initial Skills Training course at Hurlburt Field provides newly assigned weathermen those skills necessary to deploy and operate in various environments. Training includes basic communication, navigation and employment techniques, weapons training and small-unit tactics. Finally, they go on to Air Force Special Operations Command's Advanced Skills Training for six months. The training there includes advanced communication, navigation techniques, employment techniques, weapons training and small-unit tactics. Advanced Skills Training employs a "warrior-training-warrior" philosophy to teach the skills necessary for successful service in a Special Factics unit.

US Army Rangers

Ranger candidates, like all recruits into the US Army, begin with nine weeks of Boot Camp. Once the recruit completes Basic Training, he moves on to Advanced Individual Training to earn their Military Occupational Specialty. This training varies in length depending on the specialty.

After graduating from Advanced Individual Training, the would-be Ranger's training continues at US Army Airborne School at Fort Benning, Georgia. There the recruit undergoes the three-week Basic Airborne Training course that teaches him the techniques involved in parachuting from aircraft and landing safely.

The first week is Ground Week, where recruits begin an intensive programme of instruction to build individual airborne skills. They train on the mock door, the 34-foot tower and the lateral drift apparatus.

The second week is Tower Week. This completes their individual skill training and builds team skills. To go forward to Jump Week, recruits must qualify on the Swing Lander Trainer, master the mass exit procedures from the 34-foot tower and pass all physical training requirements.

The third week is Jump Week where recruits must successfully complete five jumps at 1,250 feet from a C-130 or C-141 aircraft. If they successfully meet all the course requirements they will be allowed to wear the coveted "Silver Wing" on their uniform before being assigned to the 75th Ranger Regiment to attend the Ranger Indoctrination Program.

This begins when the Ranger Liaison picks up the Ranger trainees at the Airborne School immediately after graduation.

The four-week programme, run by the 4th Battalion of the Ranger Training Brigade, is designed to determine if the trainee is suitable for service in the 75th Ranger Regiment. It continues physical training and preparation for service in the Regiment, teaching the trainee the operational procedures, equipment and the standards of the Regiment prior to their assignment.

The programme begins with a Ranger Assessment Phase. There is daily physical training, a Ranger history test, a map-reading course, courses on airborne operations and Ranger standards, day and night land navigation tests, combat training, a course on knots, driver training leading to a Defensive Driving Course card, fast-rope training and paramedics course resulting in a Combat Lifesaver Certificate.

To qualify for the 75th Ranger Regiment the recruit must score 60 per cent on the Army Physical Fitness Test in the seventeen to twenty-one age group, and complete a 5-mile run in less than eight minutes per mile. The recruit must also pass the Combat Water Survival Test, swimming 15 metres in full uniform, with boots and equipment belt, and carrying an M-16. The recruit must complete a number of road marches, one of which must cover 10 miles and they must score at least 70 per cent on all exams.

If the recruit has successfully completed the Ranger Induction Program, they will be assigned to either the 75th Ranger Regiment Headquarters or one of the three Ranger battalions.

Once a recruit has proved himself at his Ranger battalion, he will be sent to Ranger School, a requirement for becoming a Non-Commissioned Officer in the Rangers. Ranger School is one of the toughest training schools a soldier can volunteer for. Army Ranger NCOs lead soldiers on difficult and dangerous missions. To do this they need rigorous training. For over two months, Ranger students train to exhaustion, pushing the limits of their minds and bodies.

There are three distinct phases of Ranger School that require soldiers to make quick decisions in adverse situations. The first is the Darby or Crawl Phase. It lasts twenty days and is designed to assess and develop the necessary physical and mental skills to complete combat missions and the remainder of Ranger School successfully. If a Ranger is not in top physical condition when he reports to the Ranger School, he will have extreme difficulty keeping up with the fast pace of Ranger training, especially during this first phase.

The second is the Mountain or Walk Phase and lasts twenty-one days. During this phase, the Ranger will receive instruction on military mountaineering tasks as well as techniques for employing squads and platoons for continuous combat patrol operations in a mountainous environment. They will further develop their ability to command and control a platoon-sized patrol through planning, preparing and executing a variety of combat patrol missions.

Finally, there is the Swamp or Run Phase, which continues to develop the Ranger's combat arms functional skills and tests their ability to operate effectively under conditions of extreme mental and physical stress. This is accomplished through exercises in extended platoon-level patrol operations in a swamp environment. Swamp Phase training further develops the Ranger's ability to lead small units on airborne, air assault, small-boat, ship-to-shore and dismounted combat patrol operations in a low-intensity combat environment against a well-trained, sophisticated enemy.

10

FITNESS TRAINING

Members of the Special Forces have a rare level of fitness. There are sprinters who can run faster, weightlifters who can lift greater weights, mountaineers who can climb faster, and stronger swimmers. However, there are few who can match Special Forces men as all-rounders. This is because the Special Forces aim for what they call "Total Body Fitness".

To have Total Body Fitness a soldier needs the right height-to-weight ratio. Today this is measured by the Body Mass Index, which divides the weight in pounds by the height in yards squared. For a short man with a small frame this should be between twenty and twenty-three; with a larger frame between twenty-three and twenty-five. For a taller man with small frame it should be between twenty and twenty-one; with a larger frame between twenty-one and twenty-four.

Although no serviceman should be obese, the Special Forces recruit should tend to be towards the higher end of the scale. Endurance and survival trading requires extra fat as fuel. If the body does not have the necessary reserves of fat, it begins to break down other types of body tissue, which can cause health problems. The elite soldier aims to maintain his fat intake at around 10 per cent of his total dietary intake – which should be nearly twice that of an average individual. The average man needs around 2,500 calories a day, while the Special Forces operative needs 4,000–5,000 calories a day to sustain his energy requirements.

The real indicator as to how fit you are is your heart rate when you are exercising and when you are at rest. The faster the heart rate, the more oxygenated blood is pumped to the muscles. However, in normal circumstances, the slower your heart rate is, the better, as this indicates that the heart is fit and is working to full capacity as a pump.

To measure your at rest heart rate, perform this simple test sitting in a chair just after you have woken up in the morning. Make sure that you have not had breakfast first as your heart will be pumping faster to aid digestion. Place your watch in front of you where you can see it easily, then place the fingers of one hand on the other wrist, about one centimetre below the base of the thumb and locate the pulse. You should never try to take a pulse with your thumb as it has a pulse of its own. Then count off now many beats you can feel in sixty seconds. If it is between thirty and sixty you are very fit. Between sixty and seventy-five is good. Between seventy-five and eighty-five means you have some work to do. Any higher than eighty-five means you have a long way to go.

Next, dress in light training gear and step up and down from a training bench, or step 6–10 inches high for exactly three minutes. Wait for thirty seconds. After that, count how many beats you can feel in the next thirty seconds. Between thirty-three and thirty-six is excellent. From thirty-seven to forty is OK. Forty-one to forty-three is average. Forty-four to forty-seven means you have some work to do. And higher than forty-eight is very poor indeed.

If your heart rate is not below seventy-five at rest and forty after exercise, you have a great deal of work to do to qualify to be in the Special Forces.

US military training puts a lot of emphasis on push-ups, squat-thrusts and weightlifting to develop upper-body strength. The SAS and SBS are not so interested in muscle development. However, strengthening all the body's muscle groups is impor-tant for Total Body Fitness. British Special Forces men have to carry kit weighing over 80 lb on long marches. This puts a formidable stress on the physique and can distort the human frame, causing breathing problems if the musculature is not built up. The knees and back can suffer if the muscles of the abdomen and legs are not properly toned.

The muscles also need to be flexible. Tight, shortened muscles and ligaments can tear easily. Stretching exercises are necessary if a Special Forces operative is going to endure a long mission. The SAS mountain-running in the Brecon Beacons is designed to promote muscle condition and stamina, as well as lung capacity. Applicants are advised to develop muscle flexibility and endurance through cross-training – mixing swimming, running, cycling, racket sports, circuit training, etc.

Many completely fit people are rejected during Special Forces selection due to injury. If a recruit is injured during selection, he is advised to seek a thorough examination by his own doctor before trying again. He might be suffering a predisposition to injury or, once injured, may never fully heal.

Some smokers have passed the SAS selection course, but it is discouraged as inhibiting the performance of the lungs is bound to affect performance in the long run. Servicemen tend to drink and a beer can provide some much-needed energy after a long and draining day. However, drinking to excess can cause weight problems as alcohol has a high calorie content. It can also impair your judgment and cause other psychological problems, including indiscipline, that are not tolerated in the Special Forces. Of course, the consumption of illegal drugs – even marijuana – is out of the question and Special Forces units have stringent drugs tests.

In the armed forces, servicemen eat pretty much what they are given. However, those intending to join Special Forces should take care with their diet. They should cut out junk food and eat plenty of vegetables and fruit. Five servings a day is recommended. They should also avoid sugary snacks. Although these give an initial rush of energy, sugar is easily burnt off leaving you more drained than ever. A better source of long-term energy is the carbohydrates you find in pasta, potatoes and other starchy vegetables, bread, fruit and pulses.

Large meals should be avoided as they overload the system. Instead you should eat little and often. However, it is good to have a substantial breakfast, though not a greasy one. Eggs should be scrambled or poached, and bacon and sausages should be grilled rather than fried. This should be supplemented with grilled tomatoes, cereal and fruit juice. A solid breakfast will give you energy all day.

When training it is important to keep your water intake high. You need at least three to five litres of water a day. When running, drink half a pint of water half an hour before you begin and another half a pint for every twenty minutes you are on the road. Dehydration drains energy and impairs your mental facilities. If your urine is dark yellow in colour, then you are not getting enough water. When the urine is clear, the person is properly hydrated.

SAS fitness trainers recommend that any applicant working on muscle development or flexibility training should put themselves in the hands of a qualified instructor. Performing complex exercises incorrectly can cause injury and it is inadvisable to build in bad habits that may be difficult to shed during selection. Overtraining is also discouraged. Once on the selection programme or in a Special Forces unit, the amount of training is strictly regulated, even if it often feels excessive. But SAS trainers recommend that potential recruits take one day off a week from their training programme. Fitness develops by the structure of the muscles breaking down, then building themselves up again. They cannot do that if they are always in use or in a constant state of fatigue.

Before taking any sort of exercise, it is necessary to warm up. This increases the heart rate slightly so that it is ready for any exertion. Warming up will also make the muscles looser and more flexible. When they are cold, they are taut and any sudden exertion can cause a torn muscle or ligament.

A brisk five-minute walk is a good way to increase the heart rate and raise the body temperature. To warm the arms and loosen the shoulders, swing your arms forward in large circles several times. Then do the same thing backwards. Twist the head from shoulder to shoulder to warm the neck, then rotate your head in a circle in either direction.

Stand with your legs apart, stretch your arms up, then twist from the waist side to side until you can see behind you. Put your hands on your hips and rotate your pelvis as if you had an imaginary hula-hoop. Do this in both directions.

Your legs should be warmed from the brisk walk. Now it is

time for some serious stretching. Put your hands behind you and, standing on one leg, raise the other foot behind you. Grab the ankle and pull it until the heel touches the thigh. Repeat with the other leg. Then reach down in front of you, grab one leg by the knee and bring it up to your chest. Repeat with the other leg. This routine should save you from muscle problems while you are exercising, so do it religiously.

Once you have warmed up, you can begin on muscle development. This must be done slowly and systematically. To develop muscle tone, it is necessary to exercise a muscle to the point where some of the muscle fibre breaks down. When it grows back, it will be stronger. But if you over-exert a muscle, you can break too much fibre, causing a painful injury and possibly damaging the joints.

For Total Body Fitness, every muscle group must be developed. Many muscles are interconnected and if you develop one without exercising those related to it, you can cause severe problems. Many people work on their abdomen as well developed abs look good. However, if they also strengthen the *latissimus dorsi* in the middle back and the erectors in the lower back, they may suffer severe back pain.

The truth is, while Special Forces soldiers are wiry and well-honed, they do not look like body builders. An overdeveloped body can be a serious hindrance in many combat situations and overdeveloped muscles often contain a lot of scar tissue from over-exercising. This does not have any real strength.

The basic unit of any military training programme is the push-up, which promotes strength and stamina. The body should be kept straight and rigid while going from the upper position, with the arms locked to the lower position with the nose against the floor and back again. It is no good rushing these. No drill sergeant will let you get away with it. The true, slow, gently executed push-up is much more exhausting. To get maximum benefit to the muscles of your arms and shoulders, vary the position of your hands. Sometimes have them widely separated; at others have them close beside one another. A Special Forces soldier should be able to do at least forty-two full push-ups in two minutes.

Chin-ups also need to be performed properly for the maximum benefit. You should take a good wide grip and pull up to the bar at throat level, while crossing your feet at the ankles. This should be done without jerking and the descent should be done at the same rate as the ascent.

Standard SAS fitness training, the SEALs' Physical Screening Test and Delta Force's induction, all include sit-ups. However, crunches are a much better way to develop abdominal strength. This is because you can use your back muscles to power you into position in a sit-up, while crunches isolate the abdomen. Lie flat on the floor with you hands behind your head, then curl up, raising your back from the floor and bringing your knees towards your chest. Do not pull the neck with your hands. Keep the small of the back on the floor and be careful not to put the back into too much tension. Uncurl and lie back ready to start again. This develops the front abdominals only. Those to the side can be developed by adding a twisting motion, aiming your shoulder at the opposite knee.

Parallel dips are best done between two parallel bars, but two solid pieces of furniture will do. Take your weight on your straight arms, lower yourself until they are parallel to the ground, then raise yourself up again. This strengthens the shoulders, biceps and triceps.

Lunges are useful to strengthen the upper leg and thigh. Stand up straight and take one long step forward with one leg, bending the knee until the thigh is parallel with the ground. Then step back and repeat with the other leg. Make sure you keep your body upright as bending from the waist reduces the effectiveness of the exercise.

When it comes to weight training, you should not use heavy weights. This will only increase muscle mass and will often make muscles slow on the move. It is best to bench-press lighter weights with more repetitions. This will train the muscles to respond speedily – something you will be needing both in training and in combat.

Squats are a good way to develop the strength in the legs, back and shoulders. Make sure you use a weight you can handle comfortably. Begin by standing up straight with your legs a shoulder-width apart and the bar of the weight across your shoulders. Then bend your knees slowly as low as you can go without toppling forward. The weight should be kept over the legs, not the back. Straighten the legs slowly, moving back into the starting position. This exercise needs considerable concentration.

Lifting dumb-bells builds up the strength of the shoulders, arms and upper back. You should sit down with your legs spread. Hold the weights out to the side with your lower arms raised and your upper arms parallel to the floor, then push them up until the dumb-bells touch above your head. Lower them again and repeat.

You can also press with dumb-bells to strengthen the pectorals, deltoids and biceps. Lie on the bench facing upwards, holding the dumb-bells with your arms extended out to the side, but keeping the elbows bent. Lift them until they meet over your chest. Lower them slowly to the starting position and repeat.

You should always divide your training sessions between the four main areas of the body: the legs, the abdominals, the arms and back, and the shoulders and chest. That way you will not run the risk of ending with a structural imbalance in your musculature.

It is necessary to build up slowly when you are using weights. You should exercise for no more than an hour and take a day off between each session to let your muscles recover. If you feel any intense pain, dizziness or nausea you should stop and, if it persists, consult a doctor.

As with developing your strength, it is best to go into flexibility training slowly. Stretch only the point where you can feel the strain, then stop and relax before taking it a little further. SAS fitness trainers recommend yoga to extend the muscles millimetre by millimetre in a process that may take months. You must also concentrate on your breathing throughout as it is vital to all kinds of exercise. You should also concentrate on the flexibility of your hips as this comes in useful in running, swimming, marching and tackling assault courses.

Each week a potential recruit should practise short fast runs, distance runs and runs carrying a heavy rucksack, preferably over a hill course and different surfaces – grass, sand, gravel. The endurance run with a heavy pack should cover as much ground as possible. To avoid exhaustion, switch between running and speed walking. But remember that the walking is not a rest period. Take long fast steps with your arms swinging. Always bear in mind that the "Long Drag" awaits you.

When running you should let your body fall into a natural rhythm, rather than a forced pace. Keep your arms and shoulders as loose as possible and do not clench your fists, but hold them in a loose claw. Your arms should be held close to the body, with the elbows making a right angle and the arm should move diagonally, swinging smoothly in time with your legs. Your right arm and your left leg should move in the same direction at the same time. Your hand should not move above chest height on the upswing, and should not pass your hip on the backswing. This will help your speed and endurance.

You should lean slightly forward with your head in line with your spine. To do this, look at the ground 10 to 15 yards in front of you.

Keep your feet near to the ground. This reduces the impact on your feet and ankles, a vital consideration when you are carrying a heavy weight. Athletic coaches disagree about the best way to let your foot hit the ground – whether the heel should hit the ground first or the ball of your foot. Olympic runners use both styles. However, landing on the ball of the foot seems to favour sprinters, while long-distance runners land on their heels then roll through onto the toe. This is the technique you should adopt.

Your knees should be slightly flexed, which cushions the impact on the rest of your body and lowers your centre of gravity, stabilizing the motion. And do not force your legs into an unnatural stride. Longer strides take more energy so, especially as a beginner, take shorter strides to improve your endurance.

Breathe slowly and evenly – don't be tempted to gasp. Gradually you get your breathing into the rhythm of your running and, for maximum exchange of oxygen, concentrate on exhaling rather than inhaling.

Circuit training also improves strength and endurance, as does cycling and swimming. And as swimming is usually part of any selection course, it is best to practise it. You should also practise jumping in off high diving boards and learn to swimming in combat gear, though make sure you have someone with you when you try this.

Both in training and combat, you need to be prepared mentally as well as physically. Try solving problems when you are in an exhausted state. Devising your own programme for this develops self-reliance and an independent attitude. Try and solve a problem at the end of a long run and up against a deadline. In combat, Special Forces men often need to make decisions with lightning speed. It is a facility that can be developed by practice.

One approach is the US Marine Corps' "rule of three". When faced with a problem, leathernecks are taught to come up with three alternative solutions – no more, no less – then pick one and stick to it. The course of action they have chosen might not be the perfect one, but it is likely that taking some positive action is going to be better than sitting around in a state of indecision. You can practise this, to good effect, in everyday life.

SAS trainers also advise recruits to practice mental arithmetic as it is not unknown for the Directing Staff to given them a maths problem when they arrive exhausted at a rendezvous point. Recruits are also advise to socialize. The SAS are looking for people who can work with others in teams and get on in the most stressful conditions, not a reclusive, obsessive loner.

The US Army's John F. Kennedy Special Warfare Center and School set out a five-week fitness programme to get Special Forces candidates into the appropriate shape before they arriveat Fort Bragg. It warns that soldiers attending the Special Forces programme will perform physical tasks that will require them to climb obstacles 20 to 30 feet high using a rope, swim while in uniform and travel great distances cross-country while carrying a rucksack with a minimum of 50 lb. The Special Forces programme requires upper- and lower-body strength and physical endurance to accomplish daily physical-oriented goals on a continuous basis for twenty-four days. Although their physical training programme is set out over five weeks, they recommend that candidates work out for more than five weeks prior to arrival if at all possible.

The programmes also lays out the stages of physical fitness, as follows:

Attaining physical fitness is not an overnight process; the body must go through three stages:

1. The first is the toughening stage, which lasts about two weeks. During this time the body goes through a soreness and recovery period. When a muscle with poor blood supply (such as a weak muscle) is exercised, the waste products produced by the exercise collect faster than the blood can remove them. This acid waste builds up in the muscle tissue and irritates the nerve in the muscle fibre causing soreness. As the exercise continues, the body is able to circulate the blood more rapidly through the muscles and remove the waste material, which causes soreness to disappear.

2. The slow improvement stage is the second stage in attaining physical fitness. As the body passes through the toughening stage and continues into the slow improvement stage, the volume of blood circulating in the muscle increases and the body functions more efficiently. In the first few weeks the improvement is rapid, but as a higher level of skill and conditioning is reached, the improvement becomes less noticeable. The body reaches its maximum level of performance between six and ten weeks. The intensity of the program and individual differences account for the variance in time.

3. The sustaining stage is the third stage during which physical fitness is maintained. It is necessary to continue exercising at approximately the same intensity to retain the condition developed.

The preparatory course says that physical workouts should be conducted a minimum of four days a week; work out hard one day, ease off the next. A hard and easy workout concept will allow maximum effort for overloading both the muscle groups and cardio-respiratory system; it will also prevent injury and stagnation in the programme. For example: on Mondays, Wednesdays and Fridays the trainee should undertake hard workouts, overloading the muscles. On Sundays, Tuesdays and Thursdays he should do easy workouts. And on Saturdays he should do extra long workouts. Trainees should also practise swimming and work on overall fitness with sprints, pull-ups, push-ups and especially stretching.

Prior to each workout, ten to fifteen minutes should be devoted to performing stretching exercises. The Special

Warfare School surgeon recommends a well-balanced diet alongside this recommended physical programme and that daily fluid – that is, water – intake should be increased. This is the programme:

Week 1:
(Only hard workout days are listed here. Make up your own workouts on your "easy" days.)

Day 1: See what you can do. Do the best you can do.
(a) APFT (Army Physical Fitness Test) (maximum performance in all events, see what you can do).
(b) 100-yard swim (non-stop, any stroke, do not touch the side or bottom of the pool).
(c) Force march with a 30-lb rucksack, 3 miles in 45 minutes (along road) or 1 hour if cross-country (wear well broken-in boots with thick socks).

Day 2:
(a) Three sets of push-ups (maximum repetitions in one-half-minute period).
(b) 3-mile run (moderate 8- to 9-minute mile pace).
(c) Rope climb or three sets of pull-ups (as many as you can do).
(d) Forced march with a 30-lb rucksack, 5 miles in 1 hour and 15 minutes (along a road) or 1 hour and 40 minutes (cross-country).

Day 3: Forced march with a 30-lb rucksack, 5 miles in 1 hour and 15 minutes (along the road) or 1 hour and 40 minutes (cross-country).

Week 2:
Day 1: Repeat of Day 3, Week 1 (forced march), extend distance to 8 miles with a 35-lb rucksack in 2 hours (along a road) or 2 hours and 40 minutes (cross-country).

Day 2:
(a) Three sets of push-ups, pull-ups, sit-ups (maximum repetitions in 35-second period three times).

(b) Run 5 miles (moderate 8- to 9-minute mile pace).
(c) Three sets of squats with a 35 lb-rucksack (50 each set).
Go down only to the point where the upper and lower leg
forms a 90 bend at knee.

Day 3: Forced march with a 35-lb rucksack, 10 miles in 3
hours (along a road) or 4 hours (cross-country).

Week 3:
Day 1:
(a) Four sets of push-ups, pull-ups and sit-ups (maximum
repetitions in 40-second period).
(b) Run 4 miles (fast to moderate 7- to 8-minute mile pace.)
(c) Four sets of squats with a 40-lb rucksack.

Day 2: Forced march 12 miles with a 40-lb rucksack in 4
hours (along a road) or 4 hours and 40 minutes (cross-
country).

Day 3:
(a) Four sets of push-ups, sit-ups, pull-ups (maximum
repetitions in 45-second period.)
(b) Run 6 miles (fast to moderate 7- to 8-minute pace).
(c) Four sets of squats with a 40lb-rucksack.

Week 4:
Day 1: Forced march 14 miles with a 50-lb rucksack in 4
hours (along a road) or 4 hours and 40 minutes (cross-
country).

Day 2:
(a) Four sets of push-ups, sit-ups and pull-ups (maximum
repetitions in one-minute period).
(b) Run 6 miles (fast to moderate 7- to 8-minute mile pace).
(c) Four sets of squats with a 50-lb rucksack.

Day 3: Forced march 18 miles with a 50-lb rucksack in 4
hours and 45 minutes (along a road) or 6 hours (cross-
country).

Week 5:
Day 1:
(a) Run 3 miles (fast 6- to 7-minute mile pace).
(b) 500-metre swim (non-stop, any stroke, but not on your back).

Day 2: APFT. You should be able to achieve a score of at least 240 (minimum of 70 points in any one event) in the 17- to 21-year age limit. If not, work out harder.

Day 3: Forced march 18 miles with 50 lb rucksack in 4 hours and 30 minutes (along a road) or 6 hours (cross-country).

The APFT, or Army Physical Fitness Test, mentioned here is the standard procedure is designed to test the muscular strength and endurance, and the cardiovascular–respiratory fitness of soldiers in the US Army. Soldiers are given a score based on performance consisting of three events – sit-ups, push-ups and a two-mile run. Scores can range from zero to 300. A passing score is 180 or higher with a minimum score of 60 in each event. The procedure is laid out in Army Field Manual FM 21-20, which covers the administering of the APFT, as well as ways to conduct personal, squad and unit level physical training sessions.

Every soldier in the US Army is required to take an APFT once every six months for the official record. If, due to a diagnosed medical condition, a soldier is temporarily unable to conduct one or more of the events in the record APFT, they can be granted an extension to allow them to overcome their injury and return to an acceptable level of physical fitness. If a soldier has a permanent medical condition that keeps him from conducting the two-mile run, he can undertake an alternative event, such as a two-and-a-half-mile walk, an 800-yard swim or a 6.2-mile bike ride. There are no alternate events for the push-ups or sit-ups.

According to Army Field Manual FM 21-20:

The Sit-Up: The sit-up event measures the endurance of the abdominal and hip-flexor muscles. On the command

"get set," assume the starting position by lying on your
back with your knees bent at a 90-degree angle. Your feet
may be together or up to 12 inches apart. Another person
will hold your ankles with the hands only. No other
method of bracing or holding the feet is authorized.
The heel is the only part of your foot that must stay in
contact with the ground. Your fingers must be interlocked
behind your head and the backs of your hands must touch
the ground. Your arms and elbows need not touch the
ground. On the command "go", begin raising your upper
body forward to, or beyond, the vertical position. The
vertical position means that the base of your neck is above
the base of your spine. After you have reached or sur-
passed the vertical position, lower your body until the
bottom of your shoulder blades touch the ground. Your
head, hands, arms, or elbows do not have to touch the
ground. At the end of each repetition, the scorer will state
the number of sit-ups you have correctly completed. A
repetition will not count if you fail to reach the vertical
position, fail to keep your fingers interlocked behind your
head, arch or bow your back and raise your buttocks off
the ground to raise your upper body, or let your knees
exceed a 90-degree angle. If a repetition does not count,
the scorer will repeat the number of your last correctly
performed sit-up. The up position is the only authorized
rest position. If you stop and rest in the down (starting)
position, the event will be terminated. As long as you make
a continuous physical effort to sit up, the event will not be
terminated. You may not use your hands or any other
means to pull or push yourself up to the up (resting)
position or to hold yourself in the rest position. If you
do so, your performance in the event will be terminated.
Correct performance is important. You will have two
minutes to perform as many sit-ups as you can.

The Push-Up: The push-up event measures the endurance of the chest, shoulder, and triceps muscles. On the
command "get set", assume the front-leaning rest position
by placing your hands where they are comfortable for you.
Your feet may be together or up to 12 inches apart. When

viewed from the side, your body should form a generally straight line from your shoulders to your ankles. On the command "go", begin the push-up by bending your elbows and lowering your entire body as a single unit until your upper arms are at least parallel to the ground. Then, return to the starting position by raising your entire body until your arms are fully extended. Your body must remain rigid in a generally straight line and move as a unit while performing each repetition. At the end of each repetition, the scorer will state the number of repetitions you have completed correctly. If you fail to keep your body generally straight, to lower your whole body until your upper arms are at least parallel to the ground, or to extend your arms completely, that repetition will not count, and the scorer will repeat the number of the last correctly performed repetition. If you fail to perform the first ten push-ups correctly, the scorer will tell you to go to your knees and will explain to you what your mistakes are. You will then be sent to the end of the line to be retested. After the first ten push-ups have been performed and counted, however, no restarts are allowed. The test will continue, and any incorrectly performed push-ups will not be counted. An altered, front-leaning rest position is the only authorized rest position. That is, you may sag in the middle or flex your back. When flexing your back, you may bend your knees, but not to such an extent that you are supporting most of your body weight with your legs. If this occurs, your performance will be terminated. You must return to, and pause in, the correct starting position before continuing. If you rest on the ground or raise either hand or foot from the ground, your performance will be terminated. You may reposition your hands and/or feet during the event as long as they remain in contact with the ground at all times. Correct performance is important. You will have two minutes in which to do as many push-ups as you can.

Two Mile Run: The two-mile run is used to assess your aerobic fitness and your leg muscles' endurance. You must complete the run without any physical help. At the start, all soldiers will line up behind the starting line. On the command "go," the clock will start. You will begin running at your own pace. You are being tested on your ability to complete the two-mile course in the shortest time possible. Although walking is authorized, it is strongly discouraged. If you are physically helped in any way (for example, pulled, pushed, picked up, and/or carried) or leave the designated running course for any reason, you will be disqualified. (It is legal to pace a soldier during the two-mile run. As long as there is no physical contact with the paced soldier and it does not physically hinder other soldiers taking the test, the practice of running ahead of, along side of, or behind the tested soldier, while serving as a pacer, is permitted. Cheering or calling out the elapsed time is also permitted.) The number on your chest is for identification. You must make sure it is visible at all times. Turn in your number when you finish the run. Then, go to the area designated for the cool-down and stretch.

Scoring on the APFT is based on age, sex and repetitions, and run time. For example, a 26-year-old male who does seventy push-ups, seventy-seven sit-ups and runs 2 miles in 14 minutes 40 seconds would be given a total score of 271; 94 points for the push-ups, 96 points for the sit-ups and 81 points for the run. There are score cards on the Internet if you want to check your APFT.

If a soldier is unable to take the two-mile run and is given an alternate event, this will have a pass time based on the age and sex of the individual. Provided he passes that, his score for the event is computed by taking the average of that for the push-ups and sit-ups. Then the total scores is computed as before.

Failure to pass consecutive record APFTs means that the soldier is put into a remedial programme – in other words he gets a second daily session of PT. It also makes him ineligible for promotion and attendance to a military school or specialist training. However he cannot be denied an award or decoration, which is a common misconception otherwise.

Soldiers who score 270 or above, with a minimum score of 90 in each event, are awarded the Physical Fitness Badge, which can be worn on their PT uniform. The APFT score also converts to promotion points which are used to determine the eligibility of a soldier for promotion to the ranks of sergeant and staff-sergeant.

The Special Warfare School's programme continues with some recommendations:

a. For forced marches, select boots that are comfortable and well broken-in (not worn out). Wear lightweight fatigues and thick socks (not newly issued socks). Army issue boots are excellent if fitted properly.

b. Utilize map and compass techniques whenever possible during forced march cross-country workouts.

c. Insoles specifically designed to absorb shock will reduce injuries.

d. Practice proper rucksack marching and walking techniques:

(1) Weight of body must be kept directly over feet, and sole of shoe must be flat on ground taking small steps at a steady pace.

(2) Knees must be locked on every step in order to rest muscles of the legs (especially when going uphill).

(3) When walking cross-country, step over and around obstacles; never step on them.

(4) When travelling up steep slopes, always traverse them; climb in zigzag pattern rather than straight up.

(5) When descending steep slopes, keep the back straight and knees bent to take up shock of each step. Dig in with heels on each step.

(6) Practice walking as fast as you can with rucksack. Do not run with a rucksack.

When testing, you may have to trot to maintain time, but try not to do this during training, it may injure you.

(7) A good rucksack pace is accomplished by continuous movement with short breaks (five minutes) every 6 to 8 miles.

(8) If you cannot ruckmarch, then do squats with your rucksack. (One hundred repetitions, five times or until muscle fatigues.)

e. On each day (not listed in training program) conduct less strenuous workouts such as biking and short or slow runs. To compliment push-up workouts, weight lifting exercises should be included (for development of upper body strength) in easy day workout schedule. Swim as often as you can (500 meters or more).

f. Once a high level of physical fitness is attained, a maintenance workout program should be applied using the hard and easy workout concept. Once in shape, stay in shape. Do not stop this five-week program. If you have met all the goals, then modify program by increasing distance and weight and decreasing times. Be smart, don't injure yourself.

Finally it warns recruits:

a. Do not expect to get "free" time from your unit to work out so you can come to SFAS (Special Forces Assessment and Selection). The responsibility to get in shape is yours and yours alone. Work out in your own time if that is all you have. If you go to the field, work on strengthening drills: Push-ups, sit-ups, pull-ups, squats (with extra weight) when you can, as often as you can. The mission is to get in shape.

b. Eat things that are good for you and stay away from junk food and fat foods.

c. You need to be in very good shape and able to carry a rucksack day after day for the entire time you are at SFAS. This is an assessment of you. We do not teach or coach you to get through SFAS. You will be challenged.

d. The Army Research Institute (ARI) has been able to closely correlate performance on the APFT and a four-mile rucksack march with success in SFAS. During fiscal year (FY) 89 and FY 90 ARI evaluated the cumulative APFT score (17 to 21 age group standard) with the per cent of candidates who started SFAS and who passed the course. The average PT score for SFAS graduates is 250. The average PT results are depicted below:

APFT Score Per cent Passing Course
206–225 – 31%
226–250 – 42%
251–275 – 57%
276 or higher – 78%

The higher the APFT score, the better the per cent that passed the course. You need to be in top physical condition and you should do well in SFAS.

e. ARI evaluated the ability of SFAS students to perform a four-mile rucksack march in battle dress uniform (BDU), boots, M-16, load bearing equipment, and a 45-lb rucksack. The overall average 4-mile rucksack march time for graduates is 61 minutes. The average PT results are depicted below:

Ruckmarch Time (Min) Per cent Passing Course

54 and less – 81%

55–64 – 63%

65–74 – 34%

75–84 – 10%

The less time to complete a four-mile rucksack march, the better the per cent who passed the course. The Soldiers who prepare for SFAS through PT should succeed at SFAS.

This all goes to show, just how hard you have to work if you want to be inside Special Forces.

11

WEAPON TRAINING

SAS and SBS

Special Forces operatives have to be experts with all kinds of weapons. The British SAS and SBS will naturally be familiar with the standard issue SA80 assault rifle from their infantry training as well as the basics of throwing a hand grenade. They will also be familiar with platoon support weapons such as the Milan, LAW-80 or the GMPG – general-purpose machine gun. But after selection they are introduced to a wide variety of other weapons, learning their strengths and weaknesses, how to strip, clean and reassemble them in the dark, and how to get the best from them. Many of them will be foreign weapons. In extremis, the Special Forces man may have to seize an enemy's weapon and use it as easily as he uses his own. And during weapon training he will learn the one vital lesson that every small-unit fighter needs to know – how to make every bullet count.

Men of the SAS and SBS are allowed to use any weapon they choose. The American M-16 Armalite assault rifle has long been a favourite. The Regiment first used it during the Borneo Campaign in 1963–6, when it was fitted with an M203 grenade launcher. Now as the M-16A2 it has been adapted to accept standard NATO 5.56-mm ammunition, the same as the standard SA80, and to fire three-round bursts. New sights have been added and the non-metallic parts such as the stock, butt and pistol grip have been strengthened. The M203 grenade launcher is attached beneath the stock extending beneath the M-16's barrel and is fired by a separate trigger. It can fire a range of 40-mm high-explosive and anti-personnel grenades nearly 400 yards and was used to great effect using fragmentation grenades against the Pucaras and other Argentinian attack aircraft on Pebble Island in the Falklands.

The M-16 has always had a reputation for being unreliable, especially in harsh conditions, and is gradually being dropped in favour of the Austrian Steyr AUS 5.56-mm assault rifle, first adopted by the Australian SAS in 1985. Capable of putting down automatic as well as semi-automatic fire, the AUG is accurate, durable and dependable. It also has a three-round burst option. But there is a lot to learn. By swapping parts, the trained operator can turn it into anything from a sub-machine gun to a light support weapon. Light and easy to maintain, it has a transparent magazine so you can see at a glance how many rounds are remaining. It too can be modified to carry the M203 grenade launcher.

However, as well as the American M-16 and the Steyr AUG, SAS men are taught to use the various AK-47s that most of their enemies are likely to carry. The AK-47 assault rifle, designed in 1947 by Mikhail Timofeyevich Kalashnikov, was produced in the former Soviet Union, Albania, Bulgaria, China, East Germany, Egypt, Finland, Hungary, India, Iraq, Morocco, North Korea, Pakistan, Poland, Romania and the former Yugoslavia. Most are manufactured without a proper licence and it is estimated that one million are manufactured illegally every year. Costing between $30 and $125, they are the weapon of choice of terrorists and insurgents, so all Special Forces men are thoroughly trained on them.

All Special Forces recruits must be proficient with a rifle before they are even assigned. It is the basic infantry weapon. However, a variety of stances are used with the modern automatic and semi-automatic assault rifle as they can be used to spray a burst of bullets at the enemy.

In line with the Special Forces need to make every bullet count, the elite force recruit will be drilled in the four classic firing positions, and when each should be used. The most common and effective is the prone position. Not only does this position give you the most stable platform to fire from – the ground – it reduces your silhouette and allows you to use even very low cover for protection. You should be lying face down with your spine and your right leg directly in line. Your left leg should be spread out to the side. You should support the weight of your upper body on your elbows. Your right hand should pull the rifle stock firmly against you while your left hand should support the front hand-guard with the elbow directly under the receiver. Your arms and elbows should be comfortable before you start firing and your body should be directly behind the stock to absorb the recoil.

In a combat zone, the ground can be strewn with debris and it is often impossible to adopt this stance, so it may be more appropriate to fire from the kneeling position, especially if you have the cover of a low wall, a parked car or a tree trunk. The kneeling position is also very effective if you are dashing between cover. To keep up the momentum of an attack, you can kneel down, loose off a few rounds, then move on.

In the kneeling position, your left knee should be raised to support your left elbow, while your right elbow is pushed outwards, parallel to the rifle. The weight of your body should rest on your right foot. However, although the kneeling position lets you fire fairly accurately for a short period, your muscles will soon begin to ache and your shooting will suffer.

You can also fire from a sitting position, but again if you are doing this from the ground, it gets uncomfortable quite quickly. In the sitting position your body should be turned at forty-five degrees to the line of fire. Your knees should be raised and your feet spread. Your left elbow should rest on your left leg just below the knee with your forearm extended to carry the weight of the rifle. Some marksmen prefer to shoot with their legs crossed, while others like to cross their ankles.

A rifle can also be fired from the standing position, but the rifle gets very little support and you will not be able to fire more than a few rounds before the stance becomes unstable. However, you have the advantage of greater mobility in this position and can move between various targets with greater speed, though you will be more vulnerable if the enemy are shooting back.

Riflemen are taught, when standing, to make their body as stable a platform as possible. Your left foot should be in front of the right, with your weight on your left leg. This will help you absorb the recoil as it rocks you back onto the right foot. The weight of the rifle should be carried by your left hand and forearm, with your right elbow jutting out horizontally.

The Special Forces trooper, especially, should regard his weapon as a physical and mental extension of his body. When he sees a target, his rifle should swing towards it by reflex action. This is achieved by pivoting on the balls of the feet. The chest and hips twist towards the target as you push your weapon slightly forward and squeeze the trigger.

In an ambush, quick reactions are vital and against a hidden enemy who has the drop on you, using the assault rifle's automatic fire is appropriate. Elite forces are taught, in an ambush, to loose off a burst as they drop down into a squat with their feet parallel. As the back of their thighs hit their calves, they fire a second burst, then bounce back upwards, firing again. They are also taught how to fire and move. Making a tactical retreat is an essential skill in Special Forces as their small units are not suited to fight a prolonged action against a much larger foe.

In an all-out assault, troopers are taught to fire on the run. The stock should be pulled into the side, just above the hip bone. Then a burst of fire can be rained down on the enemy as they charge towards him.

These techniques are taught on the range and honed in exercises. The key is flexibility, to assess the combat situation and pick the appropriate response. But the basic firing positions are the tools of the rifleman's trade.

While all Special Forces men are taught the use of weapons and their maintenance to a high degree, they still train snipers whose standards are far higher. Sniper rifles are typically less robust than other small arms and must be meticulously maintained to avoid problems. However, a sniper rifle can be too clean. The sun glinting off the barrel can give a sniper's position away, as can a little too much oil in the barrel which will produce a telltale puff of smoke when the gun is fired.

The SAS sniper's weapon of choice is the Accuracy International PM, designated the L96A1. It fires 7.62-mm

ammunition fed singly through the ejection port from a detachable ten-round magazine and is accurate up to 1,000 yards. The
stock and butt are made of high-impact green plastic and it is
fitted with an adjustable rubber butt-pad, which is vital for the
sniper who may have to lie motionless for a long period before
firing. The barrel is fitted with a Parker Hale bipod as standard
and there is a spike on the rear of the butt so the weapons can
rest comfortably on the ground while the sniper awaits his
opportunity. The L96A1 is fitted with a Schmidt & Bender
PM6x42 telescopic sight, which is rugged and has 93 per cent
light transmission, so it can be used in low-light conditions.
Accuracy International has also produced a silenced version
that is accurate to 300 yards.

The SAS train with handguns for counter-terrorist and
hostage-rescue operations, but they are carried on other missions as back-up as well. The Browning High Power, made by
Fabrique National of Belgium to an American design, remains
the favoured weapon, even though it has been in service since
1935 and was used by both sides during the Second World War.
It is a 9-mm semi-automatic pistol with a magazine that will
hold fourteen rounds, but is usually loaded with less than that to
prevent jamming. It has an effective range of 50 yards but is
exceptional at close quarters. Its short barrel makes it easy to
draw and SAS men are taught to use it with either hand and
to draw, aim and fire within three seconds. They are also taught
the "double tap" – fire two shots in quick succession. This is
usually enough to stop a determined terrorist using his own
weapon or detonating explosives.

It is drilled into SAS men that sustained and accurate fire will
keep a terrorist's hands away from his body and make it
impossible for him to reach for a gun or push a button. Unless
the gunman is at close range, shots are aimed that the torso.
While a single shot to the head can be fatal, the trunk is a bigger
target and contains most of the vital organs. A shot to the head
follows to make sure the target is finished off.

The effect of such training was seen on 6 March 1988, when
the SAS took out an IRA Active Service Unit who planned to
detonate a bomb outside the Governor's residence on Gibraltar.
Thinking that the three terrorists – Mairead Farrell, Daniel
McCann and Sean Savage – were about to activate a remote

control device to detonate the bomb, the SAS fired. Within seconds, Farrell had been hit by five rounds – three in the torso and two in the head. McCann was hit nine times and Savage fifteen. At the inquest, Soldier "A" said: "I thought she was going for the button and I shot Farrell in the back. I then engaged McCann. His hands were away from his body."

A British court found that the three had been killed lawfully, though a European court later found that the soldiers had used excessive force.

Since 1977, the SAS have used Heckler & Koch MP5 9-mm machine pistols, which are now favoured by the US Navy SEALs, Delta Force and other American Special Forces units. Even Scotland Yard's SO19 uses the MP5. The gun is a closed-bolt, delayed roller-locked, blowback firearm, derived from the Heckler & Koch G3 battle rifle. The majority of modern self-loading rifles operate their mechanism with gas tapped from the barrel; the G3 and MP5 use straight recoil as an impelling force, with a clever arrangement of rollers which hold the chamber shut until the gas pressure has fallen within safe limits. As with other H&K products, the MP5 is "modular" – the various basic components of the weapon can be interchanged. There are versions with retracting stocks, no stocks at all, short-barrelled compact versions – the MP5K – favoured by the US Navy SEALs – a version with an integral silencer – the MP5SD – even a version that can be concealed and fired from within a special briefcase.

As the standard operation unit in the SAS is a four-man patrol, they need what are known as "force multipliers" – grenade launchers, anti-tank weapons and the like – to give them the firepower to take on a larger force. Fortunately modern weaponry of this type is light enough to carry when the patrol is on foot. One of the most effective force multipliers is a machine gun. Traditionally, the Regiment's favoured machine gun is the L7A2 GPMG – known as the Gimpy or General – made by the Belgian Fabrique Nationale Mitrailleuse d'Appui Generale. Until recently this was the principal section support weapon of the British Army. It is accurate and reliable, though a little heavy. With the bipod fitted as standard, it is accurate to 800 yards, but when mounted on a tripod it is accurate to 1,400 yards at a firing rate of 800 rounds a minute.

In recent years, the Belgian Fabrique Nationale de Herstal Minimi – the name is a contraction of *mini-mitrailleuse*, French for "mini-machine gun" – has come into favour. For the SAS man on foot patrols the advantages are obvious. It is lighter – 15 lb compared to the 24.25 lb of the GPMG, and its 5.56-mm round is also much lighter than the GPMG's 7.62-mm ammunition. It also has a second feed slot. When belts are not available, this will take a standard M-16 magazine. Such flexibility is vital for teams operating behind enemy lines.

Unlike conventional infantrymen who operate machine guns in teams of two, SAS men are taught to use them solo so they do not tie up another member of the team. As well as learning to use them in the standard positions with the bipod or tripod on the ground, SAS men are taught how to shoot them from the hip using a sling, or from the shoulder with the belt running over the left arm. Considerable strength is needed simply to lift the GPMG into this position, let alone hold it there like a rifle. Only short bursts of up to four rounds can be fired in this position. After that the gun becomes difficult to control. However, using the machine gun this way can be devastating at short range.

While a machine gun provides heavy accurate fire over long distances, its usefulness in the urban environment or in the jungle is limited. Early in the Malayan campaign the SAS began carrying shotguns. These have now become standard training weapons. Loaded with buckshot and carried by the patrol's lead scout, they can be a very effective weapon against a potential ambush. But SAS soldiers must learn the limitations of various ammunition. Small buckshot – AA or BB – works best at short range, while large buckshot – SSG, SG or LG – has less of a spread, but is effective up to 40 yards and can stop a man at 30. A SSG cartridge contains eight 9-mm balls. These have a spread of around 25 mm per metre and, at close range, have the effect of a tight eight-round group fired from a machine gun.

The M203 grenade launcher on the M-16 is used to fire shotgun-style anti-personnel rounds on strictly military operations, but in practice the shotgun itself is more useful in a counter-terrorist role. It is particularly good for blowing the hinges off doors during an assault. The civilian pump-action shotgun has now been superseded by purpose-built paramilitary models, such as the police-issue Remington 870, Mossberg 590A1 and Franchi special-purpose automatic shotguns.

A version of the Remington 870 has been officially adopted by the US Marine Corps as its combat shotgun and was used by British close-observation platoons in Northern Ireland. It can be used as an "entry gun" and can be mounted under an M-16. Both the Remington and Mossberg use aluminium in their construction, cutting down on weight.

The Italian-made Luigi Franchi SPAS 11 and 12 were designed specifically for the military. They operate in both pump-action and semi-automatic mode, which knock out four rounds a second. SAS men are taught to use the SPAS 12 one-handed. It also fires tear-gas rounds and a launcher attachment can project a grenade 150 yards.

With SPASs loaded with SSG rounds, SAS men are trained to put four shots per second into a target at 40 yards. They also train on the SPASs fitted with a shot-diverter, which increases the spread of the shot, and practice loading the SPAS with a British-made Hatton round that is specially designed for taking door-hinges off. They load them with a tungsten-carbide, sabot-discarding "penetrator" round that, at close range, will go through the side of light armoured vehicles.

Although anti-tank warfare is not the SAS's primary role, men are taught to used the tried-and-tested Swedish Carl Gustav recoilless 84-mm anti-tank gun (also used by the US Rangers who call it the "Goose"), the newer lightweight American shoulder-fired M72 66-mm Light Anti-armour Weapon and the heaver 94-mm LAW 80, so they can knock out armour in an ambush. These LAWs are one-shot weapons, discarded after use, and the LAW 80 can fire a fin-stabilized warhead capable of penetrating an armour vehicle or a bunker at 500 yards and comes with a built-in spotting rifle and a low-light sight.

Another medium-range anti-tank weapon an SAS man must be intimate with is the Franco-German Milan, which can be fitted with a thermal-imaging device for use at night. It can be used at ranges up to 1,500 yards, but weighing 50.7 lb means it is little used to a foot patrol, though it can be carried on a Land Rover in true David-Stirling style. The SAS operator must also be trained to steer the wire-guided missile.

An SAS man must also know how to use an American-made FIM-92A Stinger anti-aircraft missile that British Special Forces first deployed during the Falklands campaign. The first time it was used, it shot down an Argentine Pucara, but was ineffective after that as the British operators were unfamiliar with its recharging system. However, it proved its worth when the CIA supplied them to the Mujahedeen in Afghanistan who used them to shoot down Soviet helicopters. The Stinger fires a heat-seeking missile with a range of five miles and the SAS operator must know how to use the IFF (Identification Friend or Foe) system as they often work with friendly air forces. It is light to carry and can be fired from the shoulder by a single operator.

All SAS men must be proficient with mortars, which the Regiment uses for indirect fire support and providing illumination or smoke. The 51-mm mortar they carry can be used by one man. Firing a HE round 750 yards, it can dramatically increase a patrol's fire power. The trained operator can fire eight rounds a minute. SAS men must also know how to use the heavier and more powerful 81-mm mortar, used with great effect at Pebble Island. Usually, though, this has to be carried on a vehicle.

These days, Special Forces are called on to handle hostage-taking and other terrorist action, so a great deal of their training goes into close-quarters combat. Units have built special facilities to train CQB – close-quarters battle. Delta Force's famous "House of Horrors" at Fort Bragg, where US Special Forces train is based on the SAS "Killing House" at Stirling Lines in Hereford, the SAS's UK base. It is a long windowless building with a corridor running down the centre. On one side of the corridor there are a variety of different-sized rooms, while on the other side there are two large rooms. There are also video cameras and screens to allow interaction between different rooms and to record the action, the footage of which can later be used in debriefs. Each day the building is filled with SAS soldiers shooting off thousands of rounds of ammunition as they refine their weapons skills and reaction times. This is where the Regiment's men perfect their weapons and hostage-rescue skills.

At any one time there is a SAS Sabre Squadron on 24-hour standby for anti-terrorist and hostage-rescue operations. The squadron is divided up into operational troops called Special Projects Teams. Each team consists of a captain and fifteen soldiers, but for the purposes of an actual assault to free hostages it will be divided further into four-man assault teams. The amount of time a squadron will spend on hostage-rescue duties will depend entirely on the Regiment's commitments, but every six months is the norm. If the Regiment is stretched, though, then a squadron may face an interval of eighteen months before assuming anti-terrorist duties again.

Like everything in the Regiment, the course in the Killing House starts with basics. Each man will learn how to enter a room and take out targets to his front – nothing complicated at this stage. Once he has mastered this, the drills get more difficult. Multiple entries will be practised, where two or four men will burst into a room and clear it of targets. Once an individual has mastered working in a team, the team itself will practise clearing several rooms at a time, and then a whole floor.

As the men become more proficient, the number of targets in each room will increase. This sharpens reaction times – something that is vital to the success of a real operation. At first there will be just one room, but then the instructors will put three or more in one room. In another, the terrorists and hostages will be mixed together. The SAS team will, in a split second, have to identify the terrorists and take them out, though making sure they do not hit any hostages. One favourite trick is to have three or more figures in a room with their backs to the assault team as it enters. Suddenly, all the figures move but only one will be armed. The SAS troopers have no time at all to shoot the armed target. As the course continues complications are added.

The weapons used in the Killing House are 9-mm pistols and Heckler & Koch MP5 sub-machine guns – the guns that are used by SAS teams during real hostage-rescue operations. The targets the men shoot at are old diving suits stuffed with rags – crude but sufficient to look like real people. The Regiment also uses the Killing House to experiment with new types of ammunition. Hostage-rescues invariably take place within confined spaces, such as inside rooms and aircraft cabins. In such areas there is a real danger of hostages being killed by a ricochet. New weapons and ammunition are continually being tested in the House. Among the latest introductions is a new fragmentation round. It explodes on impact, so if a team has to storm a boat it will hit the bulk-heads and burst without ricocheting, unlike ball rounds.

When a squadron takes over the anti-terrorist role it has a four-week handover period, during which time it has a chance to put its men through the four-week course and introduce those new members to hostage-rescue training. Initially SAS men find this training good fun, but the novelty soon wears off. The fumes and the heavy protective gear they wear quickly reduce the enjoyment factor – with all the rounds being fired and the special sound effects it is very noisy inside the building. The training is exacting.

One experienced instructor says:

> We are never satisfied with times – one second to draw and fire is too long in SAS reckoning. But it's not just about being able to fire quickly. Guys must be able to identify the bad guys and also prioritize threats. So, when you go into a room you have to clear the doorway – you don't want to get silhouetted – and take the point of dominance so you can sweep the room. You shoot whoever shows intent first. Speed with accuracy, that's what it's all about.

The staff of the training wing that run the courses make sure that everything is as realistic as possible. By moving partitions and chairs about, the Killing House can be turned into the cabin of an aircraft, a railway carriage or cinema. Often the scenario is of a series of corridors and small rooms, each of which has to be cleared. This exercise takes place in the dark as it is standard operating procedure in anti-terrorist raids to take the power out before storming the building. The rooms are fairly stark, but they can be laid out to resemble any potential target.

Terrorist scenarios are projected onto the walls to hone reaction times. When the terrorist appears he must be shot. Then the film is stopped and the screen is examined to see if the shot would have taken the terrorist out.

As well as altering the lighting conditions, smoke can be added. And there are other distractions. Tapes are played simulating the cries of hostages, the yelling of terrorists or simply loud rock music – anything to put the SAS raiders off.

The layout of the Killing House is changed every day, so those practicing there never know what to expect. This keeps everyone on their toes. Another ploy is for the instructors to tell the team leaders to stand down moments before the exercise, so that junior members of the team have to run the raid on their own.

In the Killing House, men wear full combat gear, just as they would in a real terrorist situation. The outfit consists of a Nomex flame-proof assault suit, assault vest, ballistic helmet, respirator, ceramic armour plates, a medical kit, spare ammunition, a radio, some "flash-bangs", a pistol and the Heckler & Koch MP5. Usually two magazines are carried. They are held together by magnetic clips, rather than taped together as GIs do. Although it is rare to need more than one magazine, the extra weight helps stop the weapon pulling into the air when firing.

Together all the SAS assault kit weighs 80 lb. Worse, it is cumbersome. The ceramic plates are rigid so the assault team cannot bend as they try and squeeze though a window or climb a staircase.

The Killing House is in constant use and at any one time there may be ten or twenty men training there. Although they are using live ammunition this is not as dangerous as it may seem. The walls of each room are covered in thick, absorbent rubber to cushion the bullet. Behind the rubber are brick, metal and wooden railway sleepers, so there is no possibility of a bullet passing through the wall.

There are dangers in the Killing House. Because they use live ammunition, the place fills up with toxic fumes that have a dangerously high lead contents. Despite a costly extraction system, the men of the squadron on anti-terrorist duty have monthly blood tests to check for levels of toxicity. Although they wear respirators during training, toxins are absorbed through the skin. Consequently, training is conducted outside the building wherever possible.

This is always the attendant dangers of training with live ammunition, especially as the men are psyched up as they would be in a real hostage-taking situation. There are "negligent discharges" – guns go off when they are not supposed to. One SAS man has been killed and others shot in the foot during training exercises in the Killing House. Although using live rounds is dangerous, firing blanks would be counter-productive. Live rounds increase the danger, making the situation more like that which an SAS man is going to face on a live operation. The danger focuses everyone's mind. Instructors believe that using live ammunition boosts confidence. It is not unusual for a man to fire over 5,000 live rounds during his training.

The drills are repeated and honed until they are perfect as, in a real terrorist situation, this could make the difference between life and death. For example, if a man has a problem with his primary weapon – usually the Heckler & Koch MP5 – he will hold it to his left, drop down on one knee and draw his handgun. The man behind him will stand over him to protect him until the problem with the weapon is sorted out. The kneeling man will then tap the other man's weapon or shout "close" to indicate that he is ready to continue.

The SAS's Killing House and Delta Force's House of Horrors have done their work. They have produced teams of men who can identify a target and empty the entire magazine of sub-machine gun or pistol into it within three seconds. And so far, in hostage-taking situations, the actions of neither the SAS nor Delta Force have resulted in the large-scale loss of life among the hostages.

US Special Forces

The US Department of Defense has detailed plans on just how much weapons training each member of the Special Forces, both active service and reserve, must receive. For training purposes Special Forces are divided in two. Category I consists of operational detachments (OD)A and (OD)B, Support Operational Team A (SOTA), Chemical Reconnaissance Detachments (CRD) and Tactical Air Control Party (TACP). Category II consists of group headquarters, headquarters and headquarters company, and battalion support assets. All personnel in Category I have to participate in at least three live-fire exercises a year if they are on active service, or three in three years if they are in the reserve. In these, they have to fire TOW and Dragon anti-tank missiles, 106-mm recoilless rifles, Bofors AT-4 anti-tank weapons, light anti-tank weapons, M2 heavy-barrelled machine guns, M60 machine guns, M249 Squad Automatic Weapons (Minimis), the shortened M-16A2 Rifle/M4 Carbine, the M203, hand grenades and .38, .45 and 9-mm pistols. Category II personnel also have to practise on the M60 machine gun, M249, M-16, M203, hand grenades, and .38, .45 and 9-mm pistols. Designated snipers have to fire over a thousand rounds with the M24 sniper rifle a year. All personnel must be familiar with the MK19 grenade launcher and assigned gunners must practice on it annually if they are on active service, or every three years if they are in the reserve.

Both Category I and Category II personnel have to know how to arm and disarm a Claymore mine. Category I must know how to load, fire, clear and practise on such non-standard handguns as the Smith & Wesson M10 revolver, Walther P38, Colt M1911A1, Browning High Power, Glock 17, Heckler & Koch P7M13, Sig Sauer P226 and the standard semi-automatic Russian Makarova (PM). They must also know how to load, fire, clear and practise on such non-standard rifles such as Nato's FNFAL, Heckler & Koch's G3A4 and 21A1, the old M14, Austria's Steyr STG-77 ARG, the French Famas, the AK-47 and newer AKM, M1200, Springfield M1903A4, PSG sniper rifle, Israeli Galil, the Russian SKS and the old M1 Garand and M2 Carbine; sub-machine guns such as the Uzi, M3A1 "grease gun", Sterling 9-mm L2A3, Beretta M12, Swedish M45B, Reising M50, Heckler & Koch MP5A3, Czech VZ23 and Model 61 Skorpion, British MkIII Sten gun, Polish WZ63 and American MAC11; and machine guns such as the German MG3, DSHK M1938 anti-aircraft gun, DP38, Belgian MAG 58, Kalashnikov RPK-74, Browning 1919A6, Soviet DP/DTM and SGM, and the RPD series and PK series.

ODA personnel are trained with mines and demolition charges. They have to know how to construct various demolition firing systems and booby traps, and be able to calculate charges to cut through wood or steel. They must know how to use delayed percussion detonators and delayed firing devices with time pencils. As well as knowing military ordnance, they must also know how to used civilian explosives. Training is conducted on how to neutralize obstacles, calculate and place breaching and cratering charges, prepare and employ a demolition ambush, make improvised explosive devices, install and remove various types of mine, install and remove anti-handling devices, and lay and remove a minefield. They also need to know how to fire a 84-mm and 90-mm recoilless rifle, a Stinger missile and a 107-mm mortar.

The 160th Special Operations Aviation Regiment (Airborne) uses full-calibre live-firing exercises to develop and maintain weapon proficiency. All personnel joining the Regiment must qualify with the M-16A2, 9-mm pistol and the MP5 sub-machine gun before being assigned to one of the operational battalions. They then have to be trained in firing the M-16 while wearing protective clothing and firing at night. Those assigned a 9-mm pistol take a combat pistol qualification course. Additional training is given on the MP5 such as practising various approaches to a target and how to take on two targets at the same time. Assigned M2 and M60 machine gunners and assistant gunners must qualify on the range in both day and night fighting. M2 gunners get 1,308 rounds a year for practice, M60 gunners get 2,072, while those training on the M249 SAW get just 684. Those issued with M203 grenade launchers get ten explosive grenades a year and forty-four "training projectiles".

Two personnel per company qualify to use the light anti-tank weapon by successfully engaging five out of ten targets with the M73 sub-calibre rocket, while the rest of the company get to observe the LAW working with a 66-mm HEAT – High Explosive Anti-Tank – round. Those who qualify fire forty sub-calibre practice rounds a year, please two HEAT rounds. Ninety per cent of all company personnel will successfully negotiate any grenade practice exercise – they get twenty to practise with – and 90 per cent of all company members will observe a live fragmentation hand grenade practice within twelve months.

Ninety per cent of assigned company personnel are taught to place, arm and disarm an inert Claymore mine within twelve months, and 90 per cent of assigned company personnel will observe a live Claymore mine detonation in that time. All flyers have to pass an aerial gunnery course before they become basic mission qualified, then they must continue to practise once a month. Each aircrew get one AGM-114 Hellfire tank-buster missile to fire a year.

Qualified Little Bird gunners get to train monthly. Qualified crew-chief door M134 minigunners must be able to fire from the door gunnery position in various aerial approaches, at ranges of up to 500 yards as various angles to the target. Then they get to practice on a monthly basis and are assigned thousands of rounds to do so.

The 1/245th Aviation Battalion (SO) of the Oklahoma National Guard, which is under the command of the 160th Special Operations Aviation Regiment get similar, if less intensive, training. Ninety per cent have to qualify on the M-16A1/A2 rifle within twelve months on the range and firing at night, with an allocation of 178 rounds a year, plus twenty of tracer. All personnel assigned to the Battalion must familiarize themselves with the pistol and its uses under different conditions, and all soldiers assigned a pistol must qualify within twelve months, with an allocation of fifty rounds.

Ninety per cent of the assigned M2 HB machine gunners and assistant gunners must qualify within twelve months in day and night firing. Each gun is allocated 527 rounds. All M60 machine gunners and assistant gunners must qualify within twelve months. As well as firing at night, they must be able to handle the gun while wearing protective clothing. They get 1,016 rounds a year, per weapon. All personnel assigned a M249 SAW will qualify within twelve months. The allocation is 697 rounds a year, per weapon.

Again, all personnel issued with a M203 grenade launcher must qualify within twelve months. Each soldier gets eight high-explosive grenades and eighteen training projectiles. Two personnel per company will qualify with a light anti-tank weapon by successfully engaging five of ten targets with the M73 sub-calibre rocket. Ninety per cent of each company must observe a 66-mm HEAT M72 LAW fired within the first months. Each gunner gets twenty sub-calibre M73 rockets and one HEAT M72 to practise with.

Ninety per cent of all company personnel have to negotiate successfully any grenade practice exercise within twelve months and 90 per cent of all company personnel will observe one live fragmentation hand grenade within twelve months. They get ten M228 practice grenades and two M67 fragmentation grenades per company. Ninety per cent of assigned company personnel must also learn how to place, arm and disarm a Claymore mine within twelve months, and 90 per cent of assigned company personnel must observe a live Claymore mine detonation within that same period.

Ninety per cent of the assigned M60D door gunners get twenty-four months to quality. And each gunner must have sustainment training within twenty-four months. Each helicopter is assigned 924 rounds. Meanwhile all crew chiefs must fully qualify with the M134 minigun within twelve months. To do so, they must be fully proficient in a number of angles of attack. They get 2,500 rounds to achieve this.

Members of the 75th Ranger Regiment get to train in dry-fire exercises, blank-fire exercises, sub-calibre exercises and full-calibre live-fire exercises. Again, when it comes to weapons training the Rangers are divided into two categories. Category I applies to all Rangers assigned to the 75th Ranger Regiment, except if they are in Category II which includes those assigned to the regimental or battalion headquarters, the medical platoon, the company headquarters section, the food service section, the support platoon, the supply section and the Ranger Training Detachment.

All Rangers in both Category I and II assigned an M-16A2 or M4A1 must qualify every six months. They have to qualify in night firing and firing in protective clothing. They are also assessed in various exercises. In all, Category I soldiers get an allocation of 2,900 rounds, 200 tracer and 1,530 blanks, while those in Catergory II get 356 rounds, 40 tracer and 320 blanks.

All Rangers assigned a 9-mm pistol must qualify every six months. This includes firing the combat pistol in fully protective gear and training for fighting in an urban terrain. They are assigned 219 rounds. All Rangers assigned a 12-gauge shotgun also have to qualify every six months. For this, and exercises, they get 272 rounds.

Designated snipers have to qualify with the M24 Sniper Rifle every three months. Iron sights and scopes have to be zeroed monthly. They get 1,416 round of 7.62-mm ammunition and eighty .50 cal.

Rangers assigned a M203 grenade launcher must qualify every six months. They get 18 high-explosive grenades, 294 orange-dye practice cartridges and 53 white star parachute illumination rounds. Rangers assigned a M249 SAW also have qualify every six months. For this and exercises, they get 10,419 rounds, plus 9,400 blanks.

All Rangers must throw one live, fragmentation hand grenade a year and either negotiate a grenade practice exercise every six months or practice throw a grenade in conjunction with squad or platoon external evaluations, live-fire exercise or field training exercise every six months. They get 12 fragmentation grenades, 21 fused practice grenades and six concussion grenades.

Two Rangers per rifle or weapon squad must qualify with the Bofors AT-4 anti-tank system every six months. Qualification consists of firing 9-mm sub-calibre ammunition. They get 92 rounds, plus 25 L367 simulator rounds and 16 rounds of HEAT.

All M240B machine gunners and assistant gunners must qualify every six months, including night firing. For that and exercises they get 28,280 rounds of live ammunition and 10,000 blanks. All M2 machine gunners and assistant gunners must also qualify every six months, including night firing. They get 7,997 live rounds and 2,233 blanks. Ranger Mk19 grenade machine gunners and assistant gunners also have to qualify every six months. They get 1,135 training projectiles and 498 high-explosive cartridges.

All squad leaders, gunners and assistant gunners must pass the mortar gunner's exam on the 60-mm mortar every six months, and all mortar sections must receive a satisfactory rating under Army Training and Evaluation Program standards every six months. And each unit must take part in a live-fire exercise every two months. They get 237 high-explosive, 45 white-phosphor, 49 short range and 69 illumination rounds.

Ranger forward observer teams have their training within the regimental schedule so they take part in three missions every six months, covering such things as the immediate suppression of the enemy, maintaining and building a smoke screen and coordinating the illumination of the battlefield. All Rangers must lay, arm and disarm one inert Claymore Mine every six months, and each rifle or weapon squad must incorporate three live Claymore Mines in their live-fire exercises. Thirty-six mines are allocated per squad, 1,188 per battalion.

All Ranger squad members must perform the individual anti-tank mine warfare tasks every six months. These include installing and removing the M15, M19 and M21 Anti-tank mines and the standard US Anti-handling Devices. Also, all Ranger squads and platoons must perform the unit mine warfare tasks every six months using inert devices. These tasks include installing, recovering or transfering a hasty protective minefield, conducting routine minesweeping operations, laying a non-standard pattern minefield and clearing a vehicle lane through a minefield.

Each Ranger rifle squad has to have a demolition team that performs the basic demolition and explosive breaching charge tasks live every six months. These include constructing and detonating a non-electric initiation demolition charge, an electric initiation demolition charge and a shock tube initiation demolition charge. They must also construct an electric firing circuit – common series and leapfrog series – to detonate two or more demolition charges, construct and detonate explosives using detonating cord, construct and detonate a detonating cordline main system and ring-main system, breach a wire obstacle with a Bangalore torpedo, prepare and detonate an expedient platter charge, prepare and detonate an expedient grapeshot charge, construct and detonate a field-expedient Bangalore torpedo using the Claymore, picket or pole method, construct a non-electric dual-firing system, construct and detonate an earmuff charge, construct and detonate three or more M18A1 Claymore mines simultaneously, and construct and detonate a saddle charge.

The explosive breaching charge tasks include constructing an AT&T charge, a flexible linear charge, a flexible linear window charge, a silhouette charge, a rubber strip charge, a general charge, a chain-link ladder charge, a doughnut charge, a wall-breach charge, a shooting-hole charge, and constructing and detonating a "Brashier Breach", as the Ranger's have nick-named their version of the Bangalore Torpedo.

Each Ranger rifle platoon must also have an advanced demolition team that performs the advanced demolition tasks every 12 months. These include: computing and detonating a TNT charge using the standard formula for an untamped external charge; laying and detonating a 40 lb cratering charge using detonation cord and dual priming below ground, electrically and non-electrically; laying two shaped charges, one 15 lb bore holing to insert a cratering charge and one 40 lb as a command-detonated anti-tank mine; computing and detonating a charge for a structural steel-beam target; installing a M147 time-delayed firing device on standard military explosives; constructing and employing a fireball; preparing and detonating a linear shaped charge; and preparing and detonating a field expedient-shaped charge.

The Regiment is required to qualify every six months to maintain readiness. Each Ranger battalion has to conduct a live-fire exercise every six weeks and participate in a minimum of two combined arms live-fire exercises a year. These CALFEXs are extensive live-fire exercises that integrate all weapon systems into the operation. Each Ranger battalion must also participate in one major exercise annually and in one Joint Operations Training Centre, Joint Readiness Training Centre or National Training Centre rotation at least every other year.

Joint Readiness Exercises are conducted four times a year. They involve one or more Ranger battalion and aviation assets from Special Operations Aviation Regiment and 16th Special Operations Wing. Bilateral Training is conducted at a smaller scale eight times a year, with one battalion conducting four, and two battalions conducting two each. They are used to enhance the special operations skills of both Rangers and the supporting air unit. Each Ranger battalion must also undergo an intensive period of military operations on urban terrain training period twice a year. This training is conducted by each rifle company.

All this training must not get in the way of their stand-by duties as the Ranger Ready Force. RRF-1 duties are rotated four times a year. One Ranger battalion will become RRF-1 twice, while the other two battalions will become RRF-1 once each. The Regimental emergency deployment readiness exercise programme requires at least one RRF-1 rifle company be evaluated per RRF-1 cycle.

12

COMBAT TRAINING

When David Stirling first began the SAS, he envisaged that the basic unit would be a five-man patrol. However, that has been fined down into the standard four-man patrol. After a recruit has been assigned to the Regiment, he will join a four-man unit and do his combat training with them.

The Army opposed the SAS's use of the four-man patrol at first, because it was thought that a smaller patrol was too vulnerable. It would not have the specialists required for the kind of behind the lines missions the SAS would be called on to perform. It would have limited carrying capacity and fire power, and if one man got killed or wounded the unit would no longer be viable.

However, a larger group is harder to conceal and harder to command in the covert activities in which the SAS get involved. So the five-man team got dropped in favour of the four-man unit because soldiers are inculcated into the "oppo" system from the earliest days of training. Men naturally pair up in dangerous situations to provide each other with physical and psychological support. Not only will they perform the majority of tactical operations together, the two buddies will be happy sharing the mundane domestic side of a patrol – cooking meals, brewing up tea and making a "basha" (what the SAS call their bivouacs). With five men you can't do that.

Soldiers who train and operate together for long periods get to know each other's weaknesses and strengths. They can compensate for the weaknesses and learn to depend on the strengths. The two men form a bond, knowing they can trust each other implicitly in the most hazardous of situations. This confidence in one another's abilities is vital to the success of a Special Forces mission.

The patrol is usually made up of a demolitions expert, a medic, a linguist and a navigator. Each has his own 90 "arc". The man on point covers the front. The two men following cover the sides and the "trailer" covers the rear.

Although each patrol has a specialist navigator, each man is taught to navigate using the minimum of natural and artificial aids. SAS troopers are trained such basic map-reading skills as the use of a prismatic compass, setting a map by inspection and using a compass bearing and the distance marched method – by counting paces – to reach a given destination during the hours of daylight or in darkness. In Continuation Training they are taught how to make a rudimentary compass from a needle or razor blade.

Urban Warfare

Of course, not all Special Forces operations take place in the desert or the jungle. A trooper must be equally well trained to fight in the city. Urban warfare is taught in ranges where rifles, machine guns, grenades and light anti-tank weapons are deployed. In the urban environment, the defender always has the advantage. They can always remain concealed and have the tactical advantage of prepared firing positions. For the attacking force, speed of movement and lightning decision-making are the key to survival.

During an assault, the first rule is to maintain the momentum of the attack and to keep moving. At the same time, you must protect yourself as best you can from machine gunners who can lay down crossfire from ground-floor loopholes and anti-tank crews in concealed bunkers, as well as from snipers in tower blocks. You should avoid open areas such as parks, squares and wide streets and never silhouette yourself against the sky or a flat wall. Walls should be crossed by rolling over the top of them, after checking what is on the other side.

When moving forward, keep an eye out for the best cover available – a low wall, a parked car, a pile of rubble. As you advance, always select the next cover before you make your dash and be careful not to mask your covering fire.

Certain features of the urban environment make movement very hazardous and demand extreme caution when approaching. The blind spots at corners, for example, are extremely dangerous. Special Forces troopers are warned not to make the common mistake of allowing the barrel of their assault rifle to protrude as they approach, giving their position away to the enemy. You should approach the corner as low as possible, then lie flat on the ground. With your helmet firmly secured, quickly poke your head out just long enough to see what is going on. An enemy watching for troops coming around the corner would normally be watching for a head to appear at normal standing height. Even if he does spot your head at ground level, it is unlikely that he will have time to get a fix on you, aim and shoot.

Passing ground-floor windows is particularly dangerous. Crouch down below the level of the sill in case there is a gunman inside. Basement windows are equally dangerous and should be cleared with a running jump. Doorways are potentially a hidey-hole for an enemy, although they provide cover if unoccupied. Entering a door, you should always use standard operating room-clearance procedures. You never know who is in there. Coming out is just as bad. For a moment at least you will be silhouetted in the doorframe. And you should never leave a door unless you have a clear idea of where you intend to go and where the next piece of cover is.

Although open spaces are natural killing zones, many of the risks of crossing them can be avoided. Never cross open ground diagonally. If you can, stick to the perimeter where you are more likely to find cover – from one direction at least. Formulate a clear plan before you set off. Use smoke grenades to cover your movements and make sure that you have arranged for enough covering fire to ensure that the enemy keeps his head down.

A patrol clearing an area building by building should move as a group, not one by one. The men should spread out with four or five yards between them. Keep as low as possible and stick to the plan of movement where you can. As soon as you reach your new position, get ready to give the rest of the team immediate fire support.

When taking an urban objective, Special Forces teams are often sent in first to identify enemy positions. These are then isolated to prevent them being reinforced and their weapons are neutralized by direct fire. After that, the area can be cleared by ordinary soldiers moving house by house.

Special Forces troops are trained to be masters of the dangerous art of house clearing. A well-defended building is always a tough nut to crack. Reconnaissance from outside is difficult and the defenders have the advantage of knowing the layout of the rooms, corridors and stairways. On the other hand, when it comes to close-quarters fighting, the SAS have the advantage of training in their Killing House, while American Special Forces visit Delta Force's House of Horrors.

The attacking force has one advantage – surprise – and they should make the most of it. The defenders never know when the attack might come and that is bound to put them on edge.

The first consideration when planning an assault is the selection of your point and method of entry. Wherever possible, a building should be cleared from the top downwards, finally forcing the enemy out into the open outside while the assault force now holding the house seize the advantage. If, on the other hand, an enemy is cornered on an upper floor, he might well put up a last-ditch defence that would prove costly in both time and lives.

This means, if possible, you have to get to the top of the building. If you are in the thick of a running street battle this can be extremely hazardous. Trying to cross to the rooftop of the building you are assaulting, climbing a drainpipe or a rope, or abseiling from a helicopter, leaves you particularly vulnerable, so it is vital to mask your movements with smoke or set up some diversionary tactic. Even if you reach the roof, it may be difficult to break into the house from there.

Doors and windows should be avoided. It is sometimes possible to get into a house from the sewers or a cellar, but you would need to watch out for booby traps and this method of entry has the disadvantage of forcing you to fight up the house, rather than down. Special Forces teams always have a demolitions expert with it who has been specially trained in blowing holes in walls. This compounds the element of surprise.

Special Forces teams are drilled endlessly to get in quickly when making an attack. Inside, the sub-machine gun is the weapon of choice for close-quarters fighting. Troopers are trained to watch their ammunition. In an enemy-held house, an empty magazine can spell death, though the Special Forces always carry a pistol as a second line of defence if their sub-machine gun jams. If there are no hostages or civilians involved, the quickest way to dispatch the enemy is with hand grenades. Grenades are also a useful way to break into a house from the roof, though it requires extensive drilling to avoid injuring friendly forces.

Once inside the house it is important to move as quickly as possible from room to room. Any explosive entry will have alerted the enemy and he will know from which way you are coming. Teams are taught to take cover behind the door jambs while one man kicks or shoots the door down. Then a grenade is thrown in. Directly it has detonated the assault team rushes in. If the defender has not been killed or wounded, he is likely to be stunned and you must seize your moment of advantage.

If you have to enter by the door, there is a very clear drill. Once the door had been kicked or shot open, the first man must rush in as fast as possible, take up a position to one side of the entrance, then finish off any enemy with a burst of sub-machine gun fire. The second man should then enter, search the room and check it is secure. The rest of the team should remain outside in the passageway to provide security against attack from the rear.

As corridors in an enemy-held house present a clear and present danger, Special Forces troops are trained to move from room to room by cutting or blowing "mouseholes" in internal walls. Then a grenade is thrown in before the next room is cleared.

Stairways are equally dangerous. When you approach a stair-way, you should move to one side and toss a grenade to the head or foot of the stairs. If you are working up the house, you must be careful not to throw it too hard. Otherwise it might bounce off the far wall and come bumping down the stairs towards you. Once it has detonated, move quickly to the next floor and take up a defensive position, ready for the next move.

Every assault is different. Drills must be meticulously practised so that, once the attacking force are inside the building, they are ready for every eventuality.

Camouflage and Concealment

Working behind the lines, the Special Forces trooper must be an expert in camouflage and concealment. These skills are fundamental to survival especially in clandestine forward reconnaissance operations or deep-penetration combat patrols. In theatre, troops are issued with uniforms that blend in with the background. In North-West Europe, combat gear is full of browns and greens; in the desert, khaki, beige and yellows. In mountain and arctic warfare troops wear white to help them blend in with snowfields. DPM – disruptive pattern material – also helps break up the obvious shapes of an arm or a leg. And at night, or in a hostage-rescue when troops are going to operate indoors, black is used.

In the field, one of the most obvious shapes is that of the helmet. While the standard-issue helmet cover will help conceal it, the addition of a little extra mud and some local twigs and leaves will make it even more difficult for the enemy to spot. Camouflage material should always be drawn from the immediate surroundings and held in place with strips of hessian material, rubber bands or string. It should be changed regularly to stay in keeping with the immediate surroundings and because picked foliage quickly discolours. The trooper needs to be careful not to overdo it. A walking bush attracts attention.

The face also needs camouflage, especially when operating at night. Whether you have light or dark skin, the natural oil reflects light, so applying a matt covering is important. Camouflage cream needs to be applied in colours – a light colour for the shadow areas under your nose, eyes and chin; and a dark colour for the raised areas of your nose, forehead, cheeks and chin. The neck, forearms and hands should also be covered. If there is no ready-made camouflage cream to hand, mud, lamp black or charcoal will do. It is important to make the patterns as irregular as possible to break up the shape of your face. It is best to get your oppo to apply your war paint. You can reciprocate afterwards.

Remember your enemy cannot only see and hear, he can smell. Avoid the use of soap or insect repellent. In Malaya the SAS discovered that the guerrillas could detect the aroma from a considerable distance. American Long Range Patrols in Vietnam found the same. And cigarette smoke can be detected from a quarter of a mile away.

A gun has a pretty familiar shape, especially to an enemy. It should be camouflaged by wrapping it in hessian material or netting around it, though you must be careful that this does not foul the moving parts. Care must be taken not to carry any shiny material, such as glass or polished metal. A glint of sunlight or even the full moon on a night operation can be seen over a long distance. Buckles, belts, dog-tags, watches, compasses and the blades of knives or bayonets must be kept concealed, especially when moving.

Much modern equipment comes with a "subdued" finish in dark-green or non-reflective black plastic to minimize reflective flash. But where this is not the case, reflective surfaces should be smeared with camouflage cream, mud or boot polish. Of course, it is not possible with the lenses of sniper sights and binoculars. Great care must be taken with their use and they should be kept in deep shadow if possible. The sniper's Starlight Scope night-vision sight must be kept pressed close to the eye to prevent its light illuminating the face, giving his position away to the enemy.

In all likelihood, the enemy will also have sophisticated surveillance equipment such as night-vision goggles, so Special Forces operatives have specialized training in building concealed observation posts where they can lie for days on end watching the enemy's movements. These must be constructed with the minimum possible disruption of the soil, which is difficult to dispose of, or the surrounding vegetation. Such changes can easily be spotted from the air. The careless use of a lighter, match or torch can give the position away and troops on reconnaissance missions are trained to keep movement and noise to a minimum. Their lives depend on it.

Night Fighting

The Special Forces trooper must learn to be an effective night fighter. Darkness breeds confusion – not just in the enemy – so it is important to be extremely well organized. It is important for the trooper to be able to lay his hands on any piece of equipment he may need without having to search around for it. This boosts confidence. They are taught always to pack their kit in exactly the same way.

Strong leadership is also important, so the patrol leader must be sure that everyone knows exactly what he is supposed to be doing at any one time. The men must be trained to work together closely to the point where they can anticipate each other's moves. The patrol leader must always act decisively and keep his men well informed.

Confidence is crucial to night fighting so the relevant skills must be practised until they become second nature. The first of these to learn is how to use your eyes in the dark. In broad daylight, you look straight at an object in order to observe it as clearly as possible. This does not work at night. Because of the uneven distribution of cells in the retina that sense colour and those that sense black-and-white, in darkness it is better to direct your gaze slightly away from the object you are trying to observe and look at it out of the corner of your eye. That way you use the light around the edge of the retina where the rods that are prevalent in nocturnal animal are in the majority. The cones that give more detailed colour vision are predominant in the centre.

It takes about thirty minutes for your eyes to adjust fully to functioning in darkness, so you need to make sure that they are fully acclimatized before going into action at night. When preparing for a night mission, it is best to wear sunglasses the preceding day. Exposure to bright sunlight inhibits night vision for as long as 36 hours.

As vision is restricted at night, an enemy sentry will be relying a great deal on his sense of hearing to detect anyone approaching his position. Stealth and the ability to move silently over unfamiliar terrain are vital. Remember that sounds carry further at night because the air is colder. Special Forces troopers are taught to take very short steps when moving forward. You should lift one foot high in the air then put it down carefully, feeling for any dry twigs or loose rocks as you do so. Then slowly move your weight onto it. Pause for moment, then repeat the action with the other foot. If you are stalking an enemy, you should crouch down as you move in. Every few paces you should stop completely, listen and look around you, then move on a few more paces before doing the same again. Such stealth takes a great deal of discipline and self-control.

Sometimes outside noise – a plane flying over, a train going by, distant thunder – can be used to mask any sound you may make while moving. You should stay away from woods and scrub if possible, as leaves and twigs underfoot can give your presence away. But do not venture too far out into open ground where an enemy illumination flare may catch you. Never run, except in cases of extreme danger or in a combat assault.

Limited vision at night makes it difficult to use a rifle unless you have a night-vision scope. Otherwise Special Forces operatives are taught to use the "pointing" technique employed by wildfowlers. To shoot, you should raise your gun to your shoulder with your normal sighting eye two inches above the top of the backsight. Concentrate on the base of the target. If you aim at the centre your shot will go high. Then fire with a sharp pull of the trigger. Mastering this firing technique requires a great deal of practice, but with the necessary training troopers can hit targets up to range of 50 yards with a fair amount of consistency.

Muzzle flashes are highly visible at night and one shot could result in the area being saturated with return fire. Troopers are taught that the grenade is the weapon of preference at night. It spreads confusion as the enemy cannot identify where it came from. And for close combat there is always the knife.

In modern warfare, there is a great deal of equipment to help the night fighter – infra-red equipment, image intensifiers, night-vision goggles and night-sights. There are also a variety of flares and illumination rounds the trooper must be familiar with. When a patrol is digging in for the night, tripflares can be places along the likely avenues of an enemy's approach. Any incoming troops attempting to probe the perimeter will be floodlit in the harsh glare of the flare when they set off the trip mechanism. However, this may not be appropriate if the patrol is surrounded by a greater force as the flare, in the ensuing firefight, will give away your position to the enemy.

If you see a flare going up, conceal yourself as best you can before it bursts. Then do not move. Flares last a relatively short time and the enemy, whose eyes will be adjusting to the light, will be looking for anything that is moving.

Ambushes

Special Forces men must also learn how to conduct an effective ambush. It is one of the oldest stratagems in battle, but it works as well today as it ever did. And for the Special Forces patrol with its limited firepower, it is the perfect opportunity to inflict considerable damage on a much larger force. Using the hit-and-run tactic of ambush followed by a quick withdrawal, it is possible to keep the enemy on the back foot, deny him reinforcements and supplies, generally harass him and gradually grind him down.

More commonly, Special Forces use the ambush as a counter-insurgency tactic to play the guerrilla at this own game. Usually it is a fruitless task to try and lure an elusive enemy out into open battle. But if a Special Forces patrol can find out where the enemy eats, where he finds fresh water and the trails he uses, it is possible to hit him hard.

The details of how exactly you set up an ambush depends on the circumstances, but Special Forces are taught two main approaches. The first is the area ambush. This depends on having sufficient force to cover more than one trail. Thorough reconnaissance is used to ascertain the likely routes a guerrilla force is likely to use and which way they will run once the ambush is sprung. Once these lines of movement have been established, a killing ground should be selected. This should have plenty of cover around it so that the element of surprise can be used to the maximum effect. But the real key to the success of an area ambush is deployment in depth. Once the ambushers open up, the enemy will scatter in an attempt to break out of the killing ground as quickly as possible. All the likely escape routes should be covered so that the fleeing enemy are caught in secondary ambushes. As no one can be absolutely sure what the enemy will do once the trap is sprung, all possible angles should be covered.

With a smaller force, only a limited ambush is possible. Its effectiveness demands scrupulous reconnaissance, which depends on knowing for certain which trail the enemy will use.

The ambushers, naturally, should be deployed down one side of the trail to prevent them being hit by friendly fire.

As the ambush depends on surprise for its effectiveness, it requires great discipline. Any noise, telltale sign of your presence, or any early shot can scupper it. Every member of the team needs to be thoroughly drilled and briefed. They need to know precisely when to open fire and which part of the enemy force they should engage in the ensuing fire-fight.

The danger of lying in ambush too long is that concentration may easily lapse. Men on observation duty may fall asleep or get careless, perhaps making a noise that would give your position away. Duties should be rotated regularly and part of the party should always be resting up. Those on guard should adopt a kneel position to prevent them dozing off, while noisy sleepers should have their mouths covered with cloth.

Special Forces troopers are taught to use their weapons to maximum effect, so positioning is crucial. No action should open with a single shot. That would only take one man out. The best weapon for springing an ambush is the Claymore anti-personnel mine. When triggered, the Claymore blasts out a hail of 700 solid-steel ball bearings in a 60-degree fan, two yards high. They are most effective at a range of 50 yards, where the arc of fire is a 100 yards wide, so Claymores need to be concealed 50 yards from the trail, if possible, at 100-metre intervals along the killing ground, with the ambushers concealed behind them. From there, they will tear anyone walking along the path to shreds. To create maximum confusion, all the Claymores should be set off together.

If the aim of the ambush is to take prisoners who might yield valuable intelligence, a gap should be left in the middle of the killing ground so that a snatch team can rush in and seize anyone who has not been killed by the mines. It is essential that troops are briefed about the positioning of this gap as, in the confusion of close-quarters combat, it is easy to mistake your own men for the enemy.

Once the Claymores have gone off, the patrol must open fire immediately. Well-sighted machine-gun positions should cover the vanguard and the rear of the enemy column to cut off any escape, and troops alongside the trail should aim to prevent any survivors dispersing outwards.

Once the action is over, the area should be searched for any stragglers. Enemy weapons should be taken if needed, or destroyed. The dead should be searched for maps and other documents that might provide useful intelligence. During the Second World War, letters and diaries were regularly captured and translated, providing invaluable information about enemy movements and morale. Then the patrol should withdraw taking any prisoners, and regroup at a predesignated rendezvous point.

Close Target Recce

The bread and butter of the SAS and other Special Forces is the Close Target Recce (CTR), which provides main-force units with essential intelligence on enemy positions, strengths and supply routes. They begin with detailed planning and discussion so that every member of the patrol knows exactly what they are doing and what the objectives are. That will determine the equipment required. A pencil and notebook is vital. You may also need a camera and night-vision equipment, and booby traps and explosives in case a landing zone has to be cleared prior to extraction.

During training various methods of getting to the target should be practiced. Troops will get helicoptered in near to the target before walking to it, parachute to it or even canoe to it. Once in the target area, they will establish an Emergency Rendezvous Point. This should provide a lot of cover, be easy to conceal from the enemy and defend if necessary. It is also where the patrol will plan the specifics of the recce, and it will meet should the teams be compromised.

If the CTR is only expected to last a couple of nights they will probably stop at the ERV until nightfall and eat as much as they can – probably cold rations as they don't want the enemy to spot a fire. Then in the morning they will leave their bergens behind, totally camouflaged, and make their way to their target.

The way in which the patrol breaks up varies totally on the situation, but training covers all eventualities. If there is an eight-man patrol, it may well break in half, four men on guard duty and four men working as dedicated observers. So there will be two men guarding the ERV, two covering the observation posts, with two men observing the front of the target and two observing the rear. Depending on the length of the CTR – which could be anywhere up to ten days normally, or even thirty in the Arctic – the paired teams may well swap over. This should be done at night.

Once the patrol is in place, the two men in the OP – also called the "hide" – will begin what is known as "hard routine". They will take it in turns to monitor the enemy using binoculars and infra-red cameras. They will probably swap over every hour so they can take it in turn to get a rest. But it is inadvisable for any one man to sleep longer than forty minutes. Forty minutes is long enough to restore the vision, but if you sleep much longer you enter REM sleep which will leave you much drowsier when you wake.

The OP will be very well camouflaged but provide the best view of the target possible. From there, the patrol will make a detailed record of everything they see. The key points of interest are the enemy's troop numbers and type of weaponry they have, along with any defences that the target has – gun towers, gun pits, minefields, patrols, lights – and the general layout of the target. In some situations, this may mean them entering the target under cover of darkness. The observers must also map the surrounding area, making note of natural and man-made features with an eye on how best to attack the target. Intelligence must be detailed, accurate and easily understood by the strike team, who are unlikely to be the same men who made the reconnaissance.

They may well leave bugging devices, either in the actual base or along trails leading to it. Or they may install remotely controlled hidden cameras around the base. Otherwise they may be called on to "laze" the target so an air-strike can be called in using laser-guided bombs.

The CTR will continue until the necessary intelligence has been gathered and the mission is completed. Then the team will move back to the ERV during the night, and move on either to the next target or to the extraction point.

Back at base, the patrol will go over the intelligence they have gathered, and construct a map of the area and a map of the target. They build a model of the area out of mud using string, coloured ribbons and flags to scale that will be used to communicate the

information to other personnel who are drawing up the plan of
attack. One of the patrol is designated the job of destroying the
plan in case the base is attacked. Although the Special Forces are
seen abseiling from rooftops, blowing enemy airfields, freeing
hostages and making daring attacks behind enemy lines, more of
their active service is spent lying on their bellies in the dirt
silently writing down everything the enemy is doing.

Patrolling

But there are, occasionally, combat patrols behind enemy lines
to take out vital installations, disrupt supplies and throw the
enemy into confusion. Or the aim may be a direct counter-
insurgency attack on a guerrilla force. Combat patrols tend to be
larger than reconnaissance patrols, and may comprise two four-
man patrols or even a whole troop.

The SAS plan these raids in what is a "Chinese parliament"
where they talk through the various attack and defence options.
Everyone has a chance to air their views and point out problems
or hazards of the various different courses of action using maps
and the latest aerial reconnaissance photographs and intelligence. The team leader may even supplement this by overflying
the objective. By the end of the discussion, everyone has a good
idea of what lies ahead. This way there are no surprises and
everyone has a clear idea of what is expected of him.

Patrolling is broken into three phases – rehearsal, execution
and debriefing. Once the team have been briefed they carry out
a full-scale rehearsal. When a detailed plan has been drawn up,
the supply company will have a clear idea of how much rations
and water the patrol will require. The patrol will know what
weapons to take. The specialist equipment needed – such as
explosives, ropes and wire-cutters – should be assembled. As
everything has to be carried, only those things essential to the
mission are included. The patrol commander will make sure
that everything has been tested thoroughly. Radios and batteries will be checked, weapons and ammunition cleaned and
test-fired, and grenades primed. Each man is responsible for his
own bergen, weapon and belt kit. He will carry emergency
rations, water, spare ammunition and an escape tin on his belt in
case, during a firefight, he has to abandon his bergen. The

patrol commander will carry a spare radio, navigational equipment, night-vision goggles if needed and a detailed map which
he will take care not to mark in case it falls into enemy hands.
Then a final briefing is given and a final inspection made before
the patrol moves out.

Again, methods of insertion to or extraction from the target
area depend on the mission. All are meticulously practiced. The
slightest foul-up on the way in can ruin the mission completely.
Once on the ground the patrol formation depends on the terrain
and the enemy strength in the area. In open country, Special
Forces are trained to move in an extended formation. In the
jungle or over rugged terrain, a close or file formation is used.
But at all times a patrol must be flexible, so that it can
manoeuvre easily to meet new and unforeseen situations.

Special Forces troops are taught to avoid routes that other
patrols have used. They are also trained to be on the lookout for
ambushes. The crucial task of watching for ambushes falls to
the man walking point (or leading scout), who should move well
ahead of the others, checking out the area to the left and right,
investigating any unusual sounds or suspicious movements.
The point must be ever alert for booby traps, tripwires or
anti-personnel mines, and he must remain in visual contact
with the rest of the patrol so that he can alert the patrol leader of
any potential hazard. In danger areas, the patrol should make
regular security halts. At the point's signal, everyone should
freeze in their tracks and look and listen for any enemy movement. Listen out for any sudden cessation of the sound of
wildlife. It could mean that the enemy are around. The point
is responsible for maintaining momentum. In addition to his
personal equipment, he will carry wire-cutters, night-vision
aids and, perhaps, an M203 grenade launcher. Walking point,
especially in the jungle, is particularly nerve-racking and on
lengthy patrols the assignment is rotated around the men.

Behind the point comes the commander and signaller, with
the second in command – 2IC – bringing up the rear. In the
jungle they will proceed in single file. Where the undergrowth
thins, they may open out into a diamond formation. Each man
must be in sight of the next man, but far enough away so that he
does not get caught in the same burst of gunfire, or blast from a
mine or booby trap. In contact with the enemy, each man must

be guided by the actions of the man in front of him, or what happens to him. Usually, it is important to remain as quiet as possible so the men communicate through a series of hand signals. If the patrol is attacked, after an initial return of fire, the patrol will break off and disperse, each member returning independently to a pre-arranged rendezvous point, where they regroup before, if possible, continuing the mission.

As a Special Forces' patrol is likely to come up against a larger force, they need polished drills to survive. Once the point has made contact, the rest of the patrol break left and right so they can fire on the enemy without risking hitting their own men. If this action leads to the destruction of the enemy, the patrol may wish to continue. But if the enemy force is too large to overcome in a short firefight, the patrol will withdrawal – holding ground is no part of the Special Forces' remit. In the four-man patrol, two men will lay down covering fire, while the other two withdraw some distance. They will then lay down covering fire while the other two withdraw.

When on reconnaissance missions or raids behind enemy lines, patrols are often confronted by barbed-wire defences and minefields. Special Forces troops are taught to cross them with the minimum of equipment – and at night.

Another Special Forces' tactic is "shoot and scoot" as a way to minimize casualties. When a patrol comes under fire, it returns as much fire as possible. Then in the general confusion, the patrol breaks off and heads back to the emergency rendezvous with each trooper taking a different route to further puzzle the enemy. In this case any wounded man has to make his own way back to the rendezvous.

In Vietnam, the Australian SAS abandoned the four-man patrol in favour of a five-man configuration. This was because they did not like leaving their wounded behind who were often tortured and died horribly, their screams filling the jungle as the rest of the patrol made it back to the rendezvous point. Fighting the lightly armed and fast-moving Viet Cong, it was sometimes difficult to break contact. If a four-man patrol has to continue fighting as a unit and one man gets injured, another is going to have to carry him. That leaves only two men wielding weapons. In those circumstances, another man with a gun improves the odds significantly.

Obstacle Crossing

Crossing an enemy minefield is an extremely dangerous business. The first rule is to remain absolutely calm and approach the task methodically. Anti-personnel mines are usually triggered either by direct pressure from the foot or by a tripwire. Troopers must remain alert for both types. To minimize the possibility of casualties a path three-feet wide must be cleared and carefully marked. But first the mines need to be located.

Special Forces teams rarely have the luxury of carrying an electronic mine detector, so they have to locate the mines by probing. The best implement for this is a strong wooden stick, sharpened at one end. The lead trooper should then divest himself of all extraneous gear, particularly loose equipment that could fall on a pressure mine or snag on a trip wire. Lying face down on the ground, he should probe the ground in front of him with the stick, while feeling gingerly for tripwires with his free hand. If there is nothing ahead, he should edge his way forward and repeat the operation. As soon as the probe meets with a solid object, he should remove it and start scraping the earth from around the suspected mine with his fingers. Once he has confirmed that it is a mine, he should indicate its position to those behind him and mark it.

He then has to check either side for other mines. If he does not find one, he can begin moving around the first mine. This way he can slowly move across the field leaving a marked path behind him. The area on the other side of the minefield must be checked out as being secure as men following are at their most vulnerable when traversing a minefield.

Coils of barbed wire are another defence that have to be breached. In an all-out assault this is usually done by crashing an armoured vehicle through it or blowing it up with a Bangalore torpedo. This is a long pipe full of explosives that can put pushed under the defences and detonated.

But breaching wire obstacles during a clandestine operation requires a different approach as a Bangalore torpedo is bound to alert the enemy. In that case the trooper must crawl through the wire, snipping the strands as he goes. To reduce the sharp sound of the wire snapping, Special Forces operatives are taught to wrap cloth around the strand they are going to snip, then apply a steady pressure on the cutters. If no cutters are available, it is possible to cut the wire between a bayonet and its scabbard.

You should start work at the bottom of the wire and cut only enough strands to make a breach wide enough to get through. The soldier should then wiggle through the wire on his back. This way his hands are free to push the wire upwards so that it does not snag on clothing.

As crossing both a minefield and wire defences requires a steady hand and nerves of steel, neither can be tackled hurriedly. The Special Forces trooper must be so well drilled in these skills that they become second nature when he has to use them under pressure.

Defensive Positions

In enemy territory it might be necessary to build a hastily constructed defensive position. A gully, ditch or fold in the ground works perfectly, even though it may be wet and miserable if it rains. Otherwise there is no choice but to dig in. The position should have a clear field of fire, as well as affording protection from shrapnel and small-arms fire.

The soil take from the position should be built up in front of it to give extra cover. The mound of earth should be camouflaged with leaves or grass. A pile of freshly dug earth would give your position away too easily. Fallen trees, rock and rubble – any natural material to hand – can provide extra cover. If possible it should be built near to trees or a clump of bushes to conceal it from low-level reconnaissance aircraft. Even a position 20 inches deep will afford protection.

The best defence is given by a two-man fighting position. This not only doubles your firepower, it also gives one man the chance to rest or eat while the other keeps watch. The position should be as narrow as possible. Even though a larger hole would give you more chance to move around, it increases the chance of grenades, bullets and airburst fragments penetrating the position.

A rectangular hole is easiest to construct, but this can be extended into a curve if an attack from both the front and flanks is expected. Ideally, it should be about chest-deep. Once you, your oppo and your gear are in it, you should shape the floor into a gently sloping inverted "V". At either end, dig a small ditch 12-inches deep. These are "grenade sumps". If the enemy gets close enough to lobe a grenade into the position, you can roll it down the bottom of the "V" into the sump. When it explodes, most of the blast will be absorbed by the earth with the minimum of lateral deflection. These sumps also provide a rudimentary form of drainage. If the soil is soft, to prevent the walls collapsing, you may have to improvise revetments made from wood and wire or anything else to hand.

A depth of 18 inches of cover along the front will be enough to stop small-arms fire. There should enough space between the cover and the edge of the trench to rest your elbows when firing and, if you have an automatic rifle, dig a small slit to stabilize its bipod legs. It should also be high enough and long enough to protect your head when firing your rifle, and disguise the muzzle blast. If time permits, you should built a partial roof over the middle or one of the flanks of the position using branches. This will help protect against shells bursting over-head and friendly small-arms fire or discarding-sabot tank rounds from the rear. It can be constructed with any wood to hand. Slinging a ground sheet over logs or branches will keep rain out. The whole thing would them need to be camouflaged with dirt and earth sods. In flat terrain, this might protrude too much. In that case, the supports must be sunk into the sides. If the overhead cover is placed at the flank, you will need to dig another grenade sump along the back wall of the trench.

Once the enemy has discovered your position, he is unlikely to use just a single line of advance. You should make provision to protect it to the rear and the flanks. If the rest of the unit is also digging in, you should make sure that your primary sectors of fire interlock. These should be marked with stakes, if pos-sible, to prevent firing on friendly positions. Other stakes should be hammered in at routes of likely attack as aiming posts.

It may be necessary to clear away some of the undergrowth if it obscures your field of fire, but leave a thin, natural screen of vegetation to hide your position. Use what you have cut down as additional camouflage on your position and be careful not to leave scattered brush, branches or uprooted vegetation around that might draw attention to your position.

When you have a prepared defensive system, you must make sure that you make maximum use of every weapon at your disposal. To do this you must draw what is known as a "range card" for every emplaced weapon, from automatic machine guns to anti-tank systems such as TOW or Milan.

The range card is basically a rudimentary sketch of the surrounding terrain. On it are delineated your primary sectors of fire, the main geographical features and the ranges at which your defensive weapons are at their most effective.

To begin with, allot each of your weapons a primary and secondary sector of fire. The secondary sector is the one you turn to when there are no targets left in your primary one. Reading the terrain you should fix a final protective line. This is the line where suppressive fire can be laid down to the greatest effect. In battle, this will become the primary sector limit closest to your position. When not firing at specific targets, your men should aim their guns along the final protective line.

While plotting your final protective line, you may find that there are large areas of "dead ground" – behind hills, trees or houses, for example. These offer the enemy a refuge from your fire. If this is the case, you must plot what is known as the principal direction of fire. This should point towards a ditch or a gully that leads into your position. Patrol members should be ready to fire directly down this should the enemy approach. It may also be necessary to designate locations within your sector of fire where targets are most likely to appear. Mark these on the range card along with any natural or man-made features that can be used as target reference points. These are invaluable when sighting anti-armour weapons for direct fire.

The final element on the range card is the maximum engagement line, beyond which the enemy is out of range. This does not just depend on the range of your weapons, but also the lie of the land.

The range card should be drawn up as soon as your men are in position. You should note down the map co-ordinates of your position and, with a compass, note the angle of the reference points. This will be vital if you call in an air-strike.

In the case of a General Purpose Machine Gun, for example, lock the traversing slide to the extreme left or right of the bar and align the barrel on the final protective line by moving the tripod legs. Then traverse the slide to the other side and move the tripod to align the barrel on the other limit of your primary sector. Align on the principal direction of fire by traversing the slide until your gun is aimed at the centre of the target.

Each time this procedure is done, read off the direction and the elevation from the traversing slide and the elevating hand-wheel, and make a note of them. Now the gun can be laid easily whichever way the target is coming.

Similar cards should be drawn up by those with anti-armour weapons and copies should be sent to the unit leader so that he will know exactly where his principal weapons are sited and will be able to plug in any weak spots in the overall defensive position.

Special Forces deployments are rarely big enough to make such paperwork necessary. However, analyzing the battlefield in front of you in such detail is a good discipline and, with enough training, a Special Forces trooper will get to know his, and others, zones of fire instinctually.

Demolitions

When advancing or withdrawing though a built-up urban area, a Special Forces soldiers will often find it necessary to use explosives to breach masonry or destroy buildings. Offensive demolitions involve clearing lines of fire, opening avenues of approach and destroying enemy firing positions. Defensive demolitions creating obstacles in the path of an enemy advance, destroying their cover and clearing sheltered routes of with-drawal within buildings.

The setting of demolition charges is usually performed by a specialist engineer. But Special Forces teams are cross-trained, so that each man knows the basics of setting an explosive. The training is rigorous as, without proper care, explosives that can punch a hole through a reinforced concrete wall can inflict terrible casualties if they goes off at the wrong time, and a device designed to kill the enemy can just as easily kill you.

The basic demolitions kit contains a reel of firing wire or coils of time fuse, electric or non-electric blasting caps, a "Hell Box" blasting or firing machine for electrical detonation, adhesive tape or paste, pliers and blasting-cap crimpers, a galvanometer and the explosive charges themselves. Explosive charges should never, under any circumstances, be carried in the same bag as the detonators.

The most commonly used explosives are TNT – trinitro-toluene – which is usually moulded into rectangular blocks, and the plastic explosive compound known as C4, which looks and feels like putty. Both are very stable under normal temperatures and conditions, although TNT becomes more sensitive if exposed to the light for long periods, and at high temperatures it exudes a liquid that is very easily ignited when absorbed by other materials. For obvious reasons, no flame or spark should ever be allowed near explosives.

TNT presents another health hazard. It is very poisonous and is easily absorbed through the skin, so gloves of a non-absorbent material should be worn when handling it – or you should wash your hands thoroughly after laying a charge.

While demolitions equipment should be divided up and the bag that holds the blocks of explosive should never be carried by the same man who is carrying the other equipment, when it comes to laying the charges, only one man should be involved. That way the correct procedures will be carried out in the correct order.

The most difficult demolitions job is to blow your way into a building through the external masonry or reinforced concrete walls. The amount of explosive required will vary according to the thickness of the wall, which may not be easy to judge. It also depends on where you place the charge and whether you can tamp it – that is, pack material such as sandbags or rubble around it. You need double the quantity of explosive for an untamped charge placed at the bottom of a wall than the amount required if the charge is secured above ground level.

If you have the opportunity to set a charge against an outside wall without interference from the enemy and can place it between waist-height and chest-height, about 10 lb of C4 secured to the wall by adhesive tape will be enough to blow a hole large enough for a man to get through. If enemy fire prevents you approaching the wall, it may be possible to mousehole it by placing an untamped charge at the foot of the wall by means of a pole. However, the detonator must be fitted and the firing wire attached first. You cannot set off C4 or TNT by firing small arms at it.

Since internal walls are not usually load-bearing they are flimsier and much easier to blast through. A 2½-lb block of C4 divided into three and placed at knee-, waist- and neck-height should blow a large enough mousehole to let you through into the next room.

While electrical methods of detonating explosive charges are the most efficient and safest, it is sometimes simpler to use a time fuse. This consists of a core of black powder sealed in a waterproof sheath which burns slowly but steadily when ignited. Soldiers are taught always to cut off the first 6 inches of the free end of the fuse in case it has absorbed moisture. Time fuses usually burn at a rate of between 36 and 47 seconds a foot. If possible, you should cut a test length of at least two feet from the coil you are going to use and time how long it takes to burn. This will allow you to calculate how long a fuse you need to give you enough time to get to safety.

Then you slide the fuse into the blasting cap, making sure that the end is in contact with the flash charge in the cap and, holding it away from your body, crimp the end carefully with pliers to secure it. If you do not have an automatic fuse lighter, do not try and light it directly with a match. Instead, split the end of the fuse, insert a matchhead and light this.

In the event that the charge does not go off, leave it alone for thirty minutes after the time you have calculated the fuse would burn.

When using the electrical method detonation, always lay out the firing wire from the charge to the firing position first. As these may be out of sight of each other, always carry the firing device or blasting machine with you while placing the charges. This is the golden rule for laying explosives as it ensures that no-one can accidentally – or even deliberately – detonate the charge while you are setting it. Also, make sure that no radio transmitters are in use in the immediate area, since the signal picked up in the fuse wire might be enough to detonate the electrical blasting cape and consequently the charge. For the same reason, do not use electrical detonation during a thunderstorm.

Check the firing wire for breaks or short circuits. This is done by attaching the two strands at one end of the fuse wire to the galvanometer, while holding the other pair apart. If the galvanometer registers, you have a short circuit. Repeat the operation with the two wires at the far end touching. If the galvanometer shows no reaction, there is a break in the wire. In either case, replace the wire completely.

Once the wires have been attached to the electrical blasting cap and this is set in the explosive, retire to the firing position. Only then attach the wire to the firing machine. Before firing, check that all friendly forces are at a safe distance. If there is little cover in the area, all personnel should be more than 300 yards away.

Should a misfiring occur, first check the contacts at your end and, if they are all right, check the wire for breaks along its length and for disconnections at the charge end. Again, remember the golden rule: disconnect the firing machine first and carry it with you. Even if the circuit appears complete, on no account attempt to move the explosive or disconnect the blasting cap. Set a smaller charge next to it whose explosion should set off the first one.

Anti-tank Tactics

Although Special Forces are not expected to enter into sustained combat with larger forces, on some occasions it may be necessary to take on a tank. Special Forces are trained to you TOW, Milan, Carl Gustav and anti-armour RPGs. However, more often than not, anti-tank weapons will not be at hand. Obviously a Special Forces team will not be expected to take on a squadron of tanks or armoured personnel carriers, but there is a possibility that they might be able to take out one, or perhaps even two, enemy armoured vehicles by using what are known as "field expedient devices".

Modern tanks with their composite armour are pretty well invulnerable to a direct frontal assault on the hull. But tanks do have their weak points. Special Forces troopers are taught to attack the fuel tanks which, on most Russian designs, are located forward of the engine compartment with two large secondary tanks that can be jettisoned mounted to the rear. The Russian T-72, which saw action in the Iraqi Army in both Gulf Wars, has a slightly different layout. All its integral fuel tanks are located behind the engine. Like other old Soviet designs, the ammunition is stored inside a steel sleeve that actually goes into the fuel cells. Although the diesel fuel has a high flash point, photographs of burnt-out hulks scattered across the desert testify to their vulnerability. Consequently, when attacking a tank, the first thing a Special Forces soldier has to do is check out what type it is so he knows where its fuel tanks are.

Another target worth aiming for is the ammunition storage compartment. Not every one followed the old Soviet design of putting them in the fuel cells, though it is usually located towards the rear. And it is worth attacking the engine itself. This is because the engine compartment is not so heavily armoured and the engine and transmission systems of Soviet-designed tanks were notoriously unreliable. So if you can hit them, there is a good chance you can at least immobilize the vehicle. Lastly, the suspension system is vulnerable to attack, although the armoured skirting plates that are fitted to most tanks are there to protect them from HEAT warheads and fragmentation shells.

Special Forces are trained to begin their attack on a tank by firing their rifles or machine guns as the vision blocks. They should take out any optical systems, such as the laser range-finder or passive night-vision device, and, if operating at night, dowse the tank's searchlight. You have a fighting chance attacking a tank that is blind. If the tank is all buttoned up against attack, these measures will inflict only minor damage, but they may significantly affect its ability to fight.

The most simple of these field expedient devices is the Molotov cocktail. This is simple incendiary device comprising a breakable container filled with a flammable liquid with a simple fuse – a bottle filled with petrol with a cloth stuck in the end and lit. Sugar can be added to the petrol to make it stick. When hurled at a tank the bottle breaks, engulfing it in burning petrol. With a decent shot and a bit of luck, it is possible to blind the vehicle's driver and if enough burning petrol gets inside the tank the crew have the choice between staying inside and being asphyxiated, burning to death or abandoning ship.

More sophisticated and far more destructive is the "Eagle

Fireball". This can be made by filling a metal ammunition box with a mixture of petrol and oil. A white phosphorous grenade wrapped in detonating cord and covered in tape should be dropped in. One end of the detonating cord should be attached to a non-electrical fuse that protrudes out of a slit cut in the rim. A rope with bent nails pushed through it should be tied around the outside. Once the tank is within range, light the fuse and hurl the device at the target. The nails or grapnel should hook onto the outside of the vehicle. Then, when it goes off, flames should engulf the vehicle. A similar device can be made using smoke thermite grenades to ignite the contents.

There are three types of explosive devices that can be used against a tank, in the absence of dedicated anti-tank missiles. One is a towed charge. Tie a long length of rope to a stake on one side of the road and connect a series of anti-tank mines to it. Make sure that the other end of the rope is far enough away from the mines that you can detonate them safely and run the free end across the road. Attach an electrical firing system to each of the mines and connect it to the main detonator. A thorough circuit check should be made before connecting the firing wire to the blasting machine.

When a tank or APC appears along the road, wait until the last possible moment before pulling the rope, which will tow the mines in front of the approaching vehicle. Then when the tank is directly over the mines, fire the charge.

Another successful way to knock out a tank is using an explosive device known as a pole charge. What you need is some TNT or C4 explosives, non-electrical blasting caps, time fuse, detonating cord, fuse igniters, a long pole and some tape or string to attach the device to it. Once you have primed the explosives with the blasting caps, attach them to a small board and tie this board to the pole. The fuse will only need to be about 6 inches long as the men in the tank will know what you are up to the moment they see the pole. The areas to aim for are under the turret, over the engine compartment, in the suspension system or down the main gun barrel.

A third device, known as a satchel charge, was used very effectively against American armoured vehicles by the Viet

Cong during the Vietnam War. The arrangement is exactly the same as the pole charge, but it is in a satchel rather than on the end of a pole. The fuse and fuse igniter hang outside the bag. All you have to do is fire the igniter and hurl the satchel at the tank. Crude but effective.

13

SURVIVAL TRAINING

Both in behind-the-lines operations and in counter-insurgency there is a growing tactical need for greater individual and unit dispersal. This requirement inevitably increases your chances of becoming isolated from friendly forces. Indeed Special Forces are, by their very nature, out there on their own. The unit may be cut off from its extraction point by a sudden movement of the enemy forces and enemy action, or tactical considerations might mean that an individual finds himself alone in hostile country.

Escape and Evasion

The first priority of the Special Forces trooper is to carry out the original assignment. Only when this has been achieved does his objective become extraction and his return to friendly forces. Survival in these circumstances depends on three things – a soldier's ability to live off the land with only limited resources, his ability to move across the land without being spotted and his ability to make an early escape should he fall into the hands of the enemy.

If a Special Forces man is captured, he is trained to focus his mind on planning his escape at the earliest possible moment. His chances are greatly reduced the longer he waits. A prisoner's rations are unlikely to be sufficient to sustain his health, let alone give him the chance to build up reserves of energy. Mistreatment and lack of medical care may also take its toll. In the early days of capture, the prisoner's powers of reasoning and morale are at their highest. They soon begin to ebb.

Usually a Special Forces man will not have been captured without a fight. The enemy are liable to be confused and disorientated. For the first few hours, he will be held by front-line soldiers rather than prison guards. His captors are likely to be concerned with the firefight that has just occurred or maybe is still continuing. Good soldiers often make bad guards as they have so many other things on their minds. There may be wounded men to attend to and reports to make. Indeed, the fighting may still be going on and the enemy may be seeking to capture others of the team.

When you are first captured, you are reasonably well acquainted with the surrounding terrain, the relative position of your extraction point and the approximate deployment of any friendly forces. You know the location of nearby water sources, inhabited areas and suitable lying-up positions. The Special Forces trooper is trained to keep an eye on his captors, watching for any momentary lapse of scrutiny that may present the opportunity to bolt. Once you have been transported to prison – possibly by several days of hard trekking – the surrounding country is likely to be unfamiliar, you will be weaker and a prison, by its very nature, is harder to escape from.

An escape from a prison or prison camp requires a great deal of organization. It should be approached like planning a military operation, thinking through all the possibilities and narrowing the margins for error. Circumstances of captivity are so varied that there are no cardinal rules here.

Once out of the enemy's hands, the first requirement is to get as far away as possible. Pinpoint your position as accurately as possible using the sun, stars or any known landmarks. In the northern hemisphere the sun will be due south at midday. If you have an analogue watch, hold it horizontally with the hour hand pointing at the sun. True south will lie halfway between the hour hand and the twelve. Remember your watch should be set to Zulu time, that is, time in that time zone, with no adjustment for daylight saving time. The same procedure will indicate true north in the southern hemisphere. Special Forces are taught to navigate at night by the stars, locating the North Star from the Plough in the northern hemisphere and the Southern Cross in the southern hemisphere. Knowing the cardinal points will help stop you becoming disorientated in unfamiliar terrain.

Most of your movements should be at night. But do not become overconfident just because you cannot see the enemy. One sniper with an infra-red sight and it will all be over. Avoid roads, crossing them after a vehicle has passed and only after you have a fix on sentry positions. The headlights will have temporarily dazzled any enemy soldiers in the vicinity.

Rivers are another useful method of escape, but avoid large ones as they are often guarded and inevitably lead to towns and cities.

In hilly or mountainous terrain, avoid crossing ridges where you will be silhouetted. Run along the ridge some way below the crest, taking care to travel on the far side from any known enemy position. If you have to cross a ridge, change direction on the downward slope after crossing the skyline and check regularly that you are not being followed.

Enemy cordons should be relatively easy to breach under cover of darkness, provided you locate the position of the nearest sentry. Silence and careful observation are the keys here. Listen for the routine sounds of the sentry being relieved, then pass as near to the guards as is safe.

If you can, make your silhouette as similar as possible to that of the local inhabitants, or those of enemy sentries and soldiers. The headgear here is particularly important. It is possible that an individual guard will not be expecting an enemy presence in the vicinity and, if one spots you, he may have a moment of uncertainty before he decides to fire. This gives you an opportunity to throw him off-guard. Special Forces men are trained linguists. Knowing a phrase such as "Don't shoot" in the enemy's language might just save your life. It may sound simplistic, but this technique has been used to great effect by Special Forces teams around the world.

During the day you should lie up. Any lying-up position you establish must be well concealed from the ground and air, with access to fresh water if you intend to stay there for more than a day. The site should only have one good approach route, which should be guarded by a sentry if you are in a group of more than two. Cover your tracks when moving on, burying all refuse and removing every trace of your presence. The extraction point or friendly forces may be days away and you cannot afford to give the enemy any idea of which way you are travelling.

The secret of successful escape and evasion lies in your determination to avoid capture, to resist intimidation if captured and to seize every opportunity to reach friendly forces. In addition to the techniques of navigation, stealth and survival in the field, you will need to draw on all your resources as a combat soldier to evade the enemy. Cover, concealment, the passing of obstacles, the use of silent weapons, health precautions and cautious patrolling – these are all basic to the survival of Special Forces behind enemy lines.

Survival in the Field

The three essential prerequisites for survival in the field are food, water and warmth. Special Forces are trained to seek them out so that they can survive behind enemy lines even if they are separated from their unit and short of supplies.

In many areas the most readily accessible source of food is meat. The secret of successful hunting is to see your quarry before it sees you. Early in the morning and at dusk when the light is dim are the best times to concentrate your efforts. Tracks, trails, trampled undergrowth and droppings are good indications that animals pass that way and, having chosen your killing ground, apply the principles of military movement and concealment.

Stand downwind of your quarry so that it does not detect your scent, and freeze if it looks your way. Take careful aim. Chest, head or neck shots are best in the case of large animals. Then whistle sharply to encourage your quarry to stop. Once you have felled it, bleed the animal immediately by cutting its throat and hanging by its rear legs from a tree. Wait for the body temperature to drop before you clean and skin the carcass – fleas and other parasites leave their host soon after death and are looking for another warm body to inhabit.

The most basic snare is a wire noose with a slip knot held

open on a trail or at the entrance to a hole. The free end should be attached to a branch or heavy stone. When the quarry puts its head through the opening, the noose closes and as it struggles to get away it tightens.

A simple variation is to make a baited spring snare. Tie the end of the noose to a bend sapling and secure the wire to twig pushed into the ground that will release at the slightest jerk. Make sure that the loop is not wide enough from the quarry to get through. Then, when it gets its head stuck, the sapling will spring upright giving the animal a quick and painless death.

Fish are another good source of food. Hooks can be improvised from the pins on insignia and line from thread from clothing. Bait, such as worms or insects, is easy to find. You could of course try shooting fish, but you must take account of parallax. Aim slightly under the fish if it is in less than three feet of water. Never shoot with the end of the barrel underwater. The water will seal the barrel of the weapon causing a potentially lethal backward blast. If you spot a school of fish explode a hand grenade in the middle of them. You will have food for days.

Many wild plants are edible – wild onions, blackberries, dandelions and certain parts of bracken for example. Avoid mature bracken, however, as chemicals in it destroy the Vitamin B in the body and produce a fatal blood condition. You should eat only the tightly coiled "fiddle heads". You can, in fact, eat all 250 species of fern found in northern temperate zones when they are still young. Some have abrasive hairs that have to be removed before you can eat them, others are too bitter to be palatable. Break then off as long as they remain tender, then pull them through your closed hands to removed the irritating wool they are covered with.

Roots, tubers, shoots, stems, leaves, nuts, seeds, fruit and bark are all potential sources of food. Plants can also be a vital source of water, but never drink milky or coloured sap unless it comes from a coconut or cactus. Special Forces troopers are trained to get acquainted with the flora and fauna of the area they are to operate in. But if in doubt over which plants to eat, observe the eating habits of the animals around you. What does not kill them is unlikely to kill you. If in doubt, cook the plant in question. Most food poisons are removed by cooking.

There are some general rules here that Special Forces troopers are taught. Avoid laurel-like leaves. If unsure, crush the leaf and sniff it. If it smells of bitter almonds or peaches, discard it. The plant contains prussic acid which is poisonous. Another poison is oxalic acid which is found in the leaves of rhubarb and wood sorrel. You can recognize it by the dry, sharp, burning or stinging sensation it produces when you rub it on your skin or apply it to your tongue.

Avoid old and wilted leaves. The leaves of peach, plum, cherry, blackberry and raspberry plants can be eaten when they are young, but as they wilt they produce hydrocyanic – or prussic – acid. Do not eat fruit that divides into five segments, unless you know for certain that it is not poisonous.

Do not eat red plants, particularly in the tropics, unless you know they are safe. The streaky red stalk of the wild rhubarb is edible, though its leaves are not. Do not eat grass and other plants that have tiny barbs on their leaves and stems. These will tear the flesh of your mouth and digestive tract.

Even more important than food is water. Assuming no physical activity, a man can survive without drinking water for up to 109 days in temperatures of 50° Fahrenheit, seven days at 90° and two days at 120°. Beyond these limits the body becomes incapacitated by dehydration and death would become inevitable. However, your degree of thirst is not always an accurate indication of your need for water. If you are involved in strenuous work in a cold climate, you may not feel thirsty when you are actually in danger of becoming dehydrated.

On no account drink water that has not been treated against disease or hostile organisms. Use water-treatment tablets if they are available, or boil the water for at least one minute. If you suspect you have caught dysentery from untreated water, try boiling some bark and drinking the juice.

If necessity forces you to drink water from a muddy or stagnant pool, pour some through a cloth that contains sand or fine gravel to filter it, boil it and add charcoal from the fire to remove the pungent odour. Then leave the water to stand for forty-five minutes before you drink it.

If no surface water is available, you will have to tap into the area's water table. Look at the contour of the land. If you are in mountainous terrain, try digging into dry stream beds. The presence of patches of rocky soil should indicate that there are springs or seepages in the area. Alternatively look for water along valley floors. Find a relatively green area under a steep slope and dig down to a depth of about two feet – the water table should be close to the surface and very little digging usually yields a good supply. Along a seashore, look in hollows between the sand dunes for moist patches and dig down. Never drink seawater. Its salt content is so high your kidneys will cease functioning.

Look for places where animals have recently scratched the earth, or where flies hover. These are signs that there has recently been surface water and there may be some if you dig down. If you find moist earth under the surface you can make a solar still (see Chapter 17) or collect dew in the morning with a cloth. If it is heavy, you should be able to collect a pint in an hour. Ready distilled, this too will be drinkable.

To keep warm, boil water and cook food, you need fire. If you have no matches, empty the powder from a cartridge. Place a small pile under a sheltered pile of kindling and wood. Take two rocks and sprinkle a little more power on one of them. Then grind the two rocks together immediately above the powder at the base of the pile. It will ignite. If you have no cartridges try concentrating the sun's rays using the convex lens from binoculars or a telescopic sight onto dry leaves. In desperation, you can always try the old Boy Scout's method of rubbing two sticks together.

Once you have got a fire going, scavenge around for more dry, dead branches for fuel and bank the fire with green logs to ensure that it burns slowly – though be careful as green logs give off a lot of smoke that may give your position away. In an Arctic environment, use blubber or other animal fat as a source of fuel.

Medical

Simple health care is also vital to survival behind enemy lines. All Special Forces men are taught basic first aid – how to cope with bullet wounds, broken bones, fractures, cuts and burns. The nearest field hospital is likely to be miles away and enemy action, the need for concealment and the absence of any communications equipment could mean a long delay before any injured person can be medevacced out of the combat zone. Even with just their basic training, Special Forces troopers should be able to save lives and prevent permanent disabilities and long periods of hospitalization.

Normally, a Special Forces man will be carrying the basic first-aid kit of field dressings, syringes of morphine and various ointments, and he will be trained in the recognized rules for the treatment of wounds and injuries. The first is to staunch any bleeding. With a bullet wound you must check both the entry and exit points – a bullet usually makes a larger wound when it exits than when it enters due to hydrodynamic shock. Cut and lift any clothing away from the wound. A bullet itself is quite sterile. It is scalded by hot gases in the barrel of the gun and heated due to friction during its passage through the air, killing any bacteria. Wounds get infected from the unsterile clothing blasted into them.

Once the wound is exposed, do not attempt to touch or clean the area. Take one of the sterilized dressings and tie it around the wound with a square knot. If the bleeding continues despite the pressure being applied to the wound by the dressing, raise the injured limb above the level of the heart. But first look for any swelling or discolouration of the skin. This usually indicates that the bone below is fractured or broken. In that case the limb must be splinted before it is moved. Splints can be improvised by a stick tied on with strips of cloth and should extend for one foot either side of the break.

If blood is spurting from the wound, the nearest main artery must be located. Pressure must be applied to staunch the blood flow. A tourniquet can be applied, but only as a last resort. Cutting off the blood supply can lead to gangrene, which could mean that the limb would have to be amputated. Tie the tourniquet between the wound and the place where the limb joins the trunk. Tighten it with a stick. Never loosen or remove it unless in the presences of qualified medical personnel. If possible, mark a "T" on the injured man's forehead to make sure that he is dealt with promptly when he reaches a field hospital.

If the victim is experiencing difficulty with his breathing, clear the mouth and any obstructions with a sharp blow between the shoulder blades. Then lie him on his back with his chin tilted upwards and his head back, and begin mouth-to-mouth resuscitation. If breathing stops altogether, it may be necessary to restart the heart. Locate the tip of the breastbone and begin external heart massage by squeezing the heart between the breastbone and the backbone. This will provide artificial circulation, forcing blood into the lungs, brain and body. You must begin this procedure the moment you cannot feel a pulse. After four to six minutes without oxygen, the brain is likely to suffer terminal damage.

In the case of a chest wound, it should be noted that the injury may not be dangerous in itself. However the air entering the chest cavity will be as this can collapse the lungs. Seal the wound and make it airtight by covering it with the plastic or metal-foil side of the first-aid dressing. The victim should then be laid face down.

For an abdominal wound, dress the injury like any other but do not attempt to push any protruding organs back into place. The casualty should be laid on his side with his head turned to one side. He should be given nothing to eat or drink. Anyone with a belly wound should be given the highest priority when evacuation becomes possible because excreta leaking from the intestine can cause blood poisoning.

Shock is one of the most subtle killers on the battlefield and you must be able to recognize the symptoms as early as possible. A pale face, cold clammy skin, a rapid but weak pulse and shallow breathing are the warning signs. But as shock occurs some time after an injury, it is always advisable to begin treatment before the symptoms become evident. Lay the man on his back, lowering the head and elevating the feet. Loosen his clothing wherever it restricts circulation and quench his thirst with a hot drink, if possible. It is important that you appear calm and confident when treating a victim of shock. He will need all the reassurance you can give that help is on its way.

Minor burns where the skin has not erupted into blisters should be covered with a sterile dressing or, if none is available, left uncovered. When there are severe burns, the victim should be treated for shock and every attempt should be made to prevent infection setting in. If no sterile dressings are available, cover the area with any clean cloth to hand. Do not try to clean the wound or remove the clothing as this will only aggravate the injury. Put the victim in the shock position and replace the bodily fluids by giving him salt water.

However, a Special Forces soldier might find himself without a first-aid kit. If he is being held as a prisoner of war, say, or has escaped and is evading recapture, he may easily find himself in a position where he only has the clothes on his back to defend against disease and disability. Consequently, a Special Forces soldier is taught the basic precepts of primitive medicine so that he can still save lives and stay alive himself.

Dysentery becomes a severe problem behind enemy lines, especially if the sufferer has no iodine tablets. The condition is caused by drinking contaminated water or tainted food. Once it sets in, the victim will begin losing water which must be replaced. He must drink boiled water if possible, but in any case he must drink. Charcoal can alleviate the condition. Find a partially burnt piece of wood, scrape off the blackened portions and get the victim to swallow them. Ground chalk and bones will also help. Boiled bark can cure the condition. It contains tannic acid which makes a vile and evil-smelling brew. Nevertheless, the cure is better than the condition.

Worms are an ever-present danger in unhygienic conditions. As one doctor in Korea said: "Although there are other symptoms, proof positive that you are infested with worms is when a worm crawls out of your nose. That will undoubtedly shake you up a bit." It always does. In the absence of any medicine, try swallowing a couple of tablespoons of kerosene or petrol. It will make you sick, but the worms will be a lot sicker.

Under extreme conditions, there are three treatments for a wound. The first is to clean it and sterilize it. As you are unlikely to have hot water to hand, use your own urine. This was often the only method of sterilizing a wound open to downed pilots in the Vietnam War held in prisoner-of-war camps in North Vietnam and it worked quite well. Urine is quite sterile – so much so it is possible to drink it without doing yourself any great harm.

Another treatment for wounds available in the wild is maggots. They eat only dead tissue and will clean out a wound if surgery is not available. In most extreme conditions all you have to do is expose the wound. Flies will find it and lay their eggs in it. It will not be long before maggots appear. For internal bleeding and bruises leeches can be used. Again this may seem distasteful, but modern doctors use this to reduce swelling after plastic surgery.

Survival at Sea

Although the SBS and the US Navy SEALs are the sea-borne specialists, other Special Forces troops often find themselves in the drink. The SAS paddled ashore in the Falklands. Delta Force were scrambled for the hijacking of the *Achille Lauro* and were ashore with the Green Berets and the US Rangers on Grenada. So all Special Forces units get a course on how to survive at sea.

While the sea is a hostile environment, SAS instructors emphasise that it is possible to survive at sea by following a few basic rules. The first is never give up hope. The Special Forces trooper is resourceful and resourcefulness often brings with it its own luck. So there is no reason why a trooper who finds himself lost at sea should not survive.

The second rule troopers are taught, is to be prepared. Warm clothing, a towel around the neck, a flashlight and a pocket full of sweets and chocolates can significantly improve your chances of surviving. If abandoned at sea, always try and throw in something wooden, or something else that will float first. Then jump in close to it to save precious energy.

Once in the water it is important to stay calm. If you are relaxed, it is much easier to stay afloat. You should swim on your back, which is less fatiguing than swimming face down. It is also easier to breath on your back, especially in rough water. If the water is cold, it is important to get out of it quick. If there is a raft around, the survivor should make for it and climb aboard. Once safe, he should take a look around for other survivors. Rafts themselves need attention and need to be topped up with air if it is cold or at night, when the air inside contracts. And in hot weather, when the air expands, a little needs to be bled off to prevent the raft bursting.

Again the key to raft survival is to relax. Reassure yourself that sooner or later someone is going to come and rescue you. If there is a group of people on board, each can be assigned one of the different tasks there is so do with the meagre equipment at hand. It is important to keep the mind active and ready for rescue.

If there is a group in the water, they should try and reduce the loss of bodily warmth by huddling together with other survivors. Survivors should cross their legs and press the stomach onto the other to conserve heat.

In tropical waters where sharks are around, the SAS recommend that survivors bunch together facing outwards and stay as quiet as possible. It is best to float if you can, but if you have to swim, use a slow regular stroke. If you make frantic irregular movements, a shark might mistake you for an injured fish. If threatened you should move towards the shark, not away. People have warded off sharks by hitting them on the nose with a hard object or kicking them.

Jellyfish are also dangerous. If stung remove the tentacle from the wound straight away, but do not try to suck the poison out or rub the wound with anything abrasive. If you have them to hand, apply lemon juice, baking powder or soap. If not, urine will have to do.

Again for survival you need fresh water. Preserve whatever you have. It may be possible to collect rain. Or if you are on board a vessel that is adrift, you might be able to improvise a simple solar still to desalinate seawater. In any case, fluid intake must be controlled. It is recommended that you drink nothing at all for the first day, then no more than a pint and a half per day. Alcohol should be avoided as it dehydrates the body. To conserve fluid, eat little; rest and sleep as much as possible. To reduce your thirst, suck on a button – this will keep the saliva flowing.

If you have enough water to survive, food is plentiful. Rig a makeshift net under the raft. Fish and turtles often shelter in the shade there. A torch can be used to attract fish at night. With a little ingenuity you can fashion a hook out of a piece of metal. A shiny buckle can be used as bait. Once you have caught one fish, you can use its guts as bait for the next, but do not use such quantities that you attract sharks.

Sea birds are also edible, if you can attract them with off-cuts of fish. Seaweed can be eaten but if raw, it can be a violent laxative which will hardly help you conserve fluid. It should not be eaten if drinking water is scarce.

The dangers, as any mariner knows, multiply when you approach shore. Landing in a raft is a skilled business which, fortunately, most Special Forces troops are taught. Avoid places where the surf is high. The raft may capsize. Look for a sandy beach on a lee shore where the slope is gentle and the waves low. You are going to need your wits about you, so avoid landing where the sun is shining in your eyes.

Do not attempt to land on coral reefs or at the bottom of rocky cliffs. You might find yourself in more trouble than when you were adrift. In northern climes, icebergs should be avoided and you should only attempt to land on ice floes if they are large and stable. Ironically, many lives are lost when safety is in sight.

14

JUNGLE TRAINING

Beginning with the selection process, SAS men are given jungle training. It is also a staple of the training of American Special Forces, who have long experience in fighting jungle wars from the Second World War through to Vietnam.

After being taught the basic jungle survival skills, SAS men undertake a four- to six-week jungle training course in the Far East, usually Brunei. The SAS call the jungle "*ulu*" after the Malay word for jungle. There they are taught patrol skills and the standard operating procedures. The course, inevitably, ends in an exercise. The men are split into four-man patrols and given a detailed task that is designed to test all their newly acquired skills. Jungle patrols can go on for up to two months. Every day the men are on the move and 0500 hours with breaks for a brew at 0630 and 1300. They stop at 1600 hours to make camp and the one meal of the day. Each man will be carrying up to 80 lb, enough to sustain him for a fortnight in the forest. For hours on end they will be wading though swamps carrying their weapons above their heads in a test of physical endurance. The SAS, particularly, prides itself on its jungle training, hard won from the campaigns in Malaya and Borneo. So even at this stage, if a man fails, he can be RTUd – returned to unit. As one jungle instructor said: "You're wet all the time from the humidity, and the jungle is full of creepy-crawlies. As a result, a lot of people can't hack it."

Special Forces are keen on jungle training, not just because of their history – the jungle has been the home of conflict in recent times. The SAS have been deployed in Sierra Leone, America's Special Forces in central America. Africa and Latin America are seen as powder kegs where Special Forces may well be called on to serve again. And for training purposes, a man is put on his mettle in the hostile environment of the jungle.

The Jungle Environment

It is a great testing ground for Special Forces soldiers because it is unlike any environment with which they would be familiar at home. Men have to cope with high temperatures and heavy rainfall. Even when the rain is not falling the high humidity means that everything is damp and men sweat a great deal. Special Forces jungle training begins with men being told that they need two sets of clothing – one wet, one dry. They should wear the wet ones during the day. The dry ones should be kept in a plastic bag and brought out only to sleep in at night.

The jungle itself contains two distinct environments. Primary jungle is formed by tall trees that grow to over 200 feet. High up the foliage forms one, two or even three canopies. Little light can penetrate a triple canopy so very little vegetation can grow at ground level to hamper movement. On the other hand it is dark and the gloom – and the tree trunks – reduce visibility to 50 yards, often less. Firefights in the jungle usually involve small groups and normally take place at a range of 15 feet.

Along rivers banks, in clearings and where the canopy is thinner, sunlight penetrates. In these places there is lush under-growth. Shrubs, grasses, ferns and vines grow up to 10 foot tall. Again visibility is restricted and the thick vegetation makes movement arduous and slow. Although water is plentiful it is rarely clean. The jungle is full of disease and parasites, so that remaining healthy there is a constant battle.

There are other dangers – snakes, insects and other wild animals. When not hacking their way though thick under-growth men are likely to be wading through swamps or fording rivers and will usually emerge covered with leeches. And all the time they have to be on the lookout for the enemy. However, if a man is taught how to find food and water, and build a basic shelter, he should have little difficulty remaining fit enough to fight.

Recruits are taught how to make a rudimentary A-frame shelter to sleep in. You need to sleep under a mosquito net if possible. Otherwise you need to keep covered up. Use a bamboo pole or a sapling to support a little tent of clothes and cover your top half with large leaves. It is important to keep your face and hands covered too. A smoky fire helps keep insects away, but it might give your position away as well. Oil, fat or mud smeared on your hands and face may give some protection against mosquitoes. Insect repellent is usually eschewed as guerrillas native to the forest can smell it at a distance. It is, of course, vital to take Paludrin anti-malaria tablets.

Clothing and Footwear

You should wear a net over your head, or cover it with a T-shirt or singlet, especially at dusk and dawn. When moving you should tie a strip of cloth around your head. This will stop sweat running down into your eyes. It should be about 18 inches deep and cut vertically to make a long fringe that will help keep mosquitoes off your face. Another strip of cotton is worn around the neck to stop sweat running down your torso.

It is important to keep your feet, ankles and legs well protected as they are the part of the body most exposed to sapling spikes, poisonous centipedes, snakes, leeches and chigoe – known better as chiggers, the larva of a flea that likes to feed on skin and spread disease. Special Forces generally wear light rubber or canvas boots, usually with a metal plate in the sole to protect against sharp – and indeed sharpened – sticks. They wrap cloth or bark around the legs to make puttees and stop frequently to remove parasites. Chiggers left for more than an hour or so will cause infection.

Even though it is hot in the jungle, Special Forces never wear shorts. To protect their legs they wear long cotton camouflage trousers. These are loose and baggy to allow air to circulate and are fitted with a draw string around the waist to allow for the weight loss that inevitably results from a long patrol. They wear baggy cotton shirts, also in camouflage disruptive pattern material, with long sleeves to protect the arms. SAS men favour a floppy hat in DPM attached by a cord so that it is easy to retrieve if knocked off by branches.

Insects, Parasites and Snakes

Slashing your way though secondary jungle is likely to disturb bees, wasps and hornets. Hornets, especially, may attack. Any part of your body left uncovered is vulnerable to painful stings. Run, but do not drop anything. You will not want to go back for it. Goggles can afford some eye protection.

As you work up a sweat, certain insects, desperate for salt, will attack the sweatiest parts of your body – the armpits and groin. They also sting, so keep these parts well covered.

At night keep footwear and clothing off the ground. Snakes, scorpions and other insects like to take up residence, so shake out clothing and check inside your boots before putting them on. Also, take care when putting your hands in your pockets as centipedes like to curl up in your more intimate body parts for warmth.

Leeches do not just inhabit the water. In the humidity of the jungle they lie around on the damp earth or on moist vegetation, waiting to attach themselves to any warm-blooded creature that walks by. Their bite is not painful, but to feed on your blood they pump in anti-coagulant. When they have had their fill they drop off, leaving you bleeding profusely. If you are covered with them, you have to do something about it. Don't pull them off. With their jaws locked in the flesh, you are liable to pull their head off, which will then turn septic. The classic method it to remove them with a lighted cigarette, but as Special Forces troops are now encouraged to stay fit and not to smoke, you can get rid of them with a dab of alcohol, salt, an ember or flame.

Watch out for hairy caterpillars. Take care to brush them off in the direction they are travelling or small irritant hair may stay in your skin and cause a rash that may fester in the heat. And be even more careful of the candiru, a small, Amazonian, translucent, eel-like catfish that lives on blood and can swim into the urethra of anyone in the water. They have not got reverse gear and the spines of their gill covers dig into the sides, making them impossible to get out and causing inflammation, haemorrhaging and even death.

Other parasites and diseases to watch out for include hookworm whose larvae penetrate the skin, malaria transmitted by mosquitoes and other insects, typhus that comes from fleas and body lice, amoebic dysentery from uncooked food or contaminated water and bilharzia, a disease of the bowel or liver caused by the flatworm.

There are plenty of snakes in the jungle. Normally a snake bite is not fatal if the victim can reach hospital within an hour or two. If the type of snake is known, the appropriate anti-venom can be prepared. However, for the Special Forces trooper in the jungle behind enemy lines, a medical evacuation may not be possible, so it is best to know the drill.

Fortunately, only a small proportion of snakes are poisonous. However, all snake bites should be treated as venomous unless you are certain that the snake is harmless. The aim of any treatment is to prevent the poison from spreading throughout the body. Reassure the victim and get them to relax. Get them to rest while keeping the bite lower than the heart. Wash away any venom left on the skin, with soap if possible as it is an antiseptic. Put a restricting bandage, not a tourniquet, above the bite and bandage down towards the wound. This will impeded the toxin spread and being taken up by the lymphatic system. Immobilize the limb in the horizontal position, using a splint, and keep the area cool with water or, if possible, with ice. The victim should be treated for shock and their breathing should be checked regularly. They may need artificial respiration. Despite what you see in the movies, it is best not to cut into the wound and suck the venom out.

Spider bites should be treated the same as snake bites. Use a cold compress to take away the pain. The sting of a scorpion and those of bees, wasps and hornets should be treated likewise. Some people have a severe reaction to such stings and multiple stings are particularly dangerous. Bee stings left in a man's flesh should be removed by stroking gently with the side of a needle. Do not squeeze the end of the sting or you will inject more venom.

Moving through Jungle

In dense secondary jungle, you may have to hack your way through the undergrowth if there is no way of going around it.

Chop downwards as low as possible, cutting the stem on both sides so that the plant falls sideways away from the path rather than across it. Take care not to leave spikes. Bamboo points can be lethal if someone falls on them. Some vines and creepers can simply be cut and walked over. It is best to travel slowly as some jungle vegetation has thorns and hooks that will attach themselves to you, tangling you in vegetation. In Malaysia, rattan and other climbing palms are known as *nanti sikit*, which means "wait-a-while". If you travel fast through a patch of them, they will tear your clothes off. In any case you need to be careful. Bacteria live in abundance in the humidity of the forest and even a tiny scratch can turn septic quickly.

Hacking your way through the jungle should be avoided if possible. It makes a noise that the enemy might hear and leaves a very obvious trail that they can follow. In dense jungle, SAS patrols aim to travel no faster than a hundred yards an hour, stopping every twenty minutes to listen.

Jungle Hygiene

Because of the dangers of disease in the jungle, recruits are immunized before they are sent and instructors emphasis the importance of hygiene in the tropics. Cuts and scratches must be cleaned and covered at the first opportunity. The groin area, particularly, must be kept as clean and dry as possible to guard against fungal infections. Recruits are taught to defecate in rivers like the locals do. That way the fish dispose of the results. Otherwise, they are told to scrape away an area of earth, then cover the faeces over with earth and smooth the surface down. No clue should be left that anyone has even been there. It is important to keep your backside clean too. As toilet paper is bulky to carry around and a sure sign that people other than the local people of the forest have been around, soldiers wipe their rears with the rags they have used for cleaning their weapons.

Jungle Navigation

Special Forces men are taught how to navigate in the jungle as this is essential to jungle warfare. This is done by a method called cross-graining. Avoiding tracks that are fraught with the dangers of booby traps and ambushes, you follow a compass and pace out the distance you have travelled, working out your position by dead reckoning. Then you can match your calculated position with features on the map. These days, on an operation, Special Forces use GPS to tell them their position, but it is best to learn the old-fashioned way in case the Sat Nav breaks down or runs out of batteries.

Food and Water

There is no shortage of food in the jungle and, as in all circumstances, the Special Forces are taught how to live off the land. Training staff set up survival camps as part of the squadron's two-week acclimatization course. The instructors collect all the edible plants, animals and fish from the area and lay them out so that recruits can see what is safe to eat. Recruits also learn the taste test to find out if a plant or animal is edible. First you rub it on your skin to see if there is any reaction. If nothing has happened after two hours, then rub it on your lips. Again if there is no reaction, lick it. Things that are not good for you usually taste bad. If, once more, there is no reaction, you should eat a little of it. If nothing happens then, eat some more, and so on. Generally it is inadvisable to eat anything that is brightly coloured as this is often a warning that it is poisonous. Flowers are usually inedible and the jungle's colourful tree frogs are lethal.

In the jungle a large variety of fruit and edible roots and leaves are available. Even civilians would have little trouble recognizing bananas, figs, mangoes and papaya, which is one of the few plants with milky white sap you can eat. In the jungles of Malaysia, southern Thailand, Indonesia and the Philippines you will find the durian, the large, thorny fruit of the Durian tree, part of the Malvaceae (Bombacaceae) family, which resembles an elm with oblong leaves and yellowish green flowers. It has a spherical husk covered with coarse spines and is one of the few fruits with five segments that you can eat. They are filled with a cream-coloured custard-like pulp that you can eat and chestnut-sized seeds that are edible when roasted. Unfortunately, while it has a mild, sweet taste, it smells like limburger cheese.

Palm shoots are edible and manioc, also known as cassava, produces large tubers that are a staple in many parts of world, but it must be cooked before you can eat it. Certain yams, wild potatoes and taro are poisonous raw, but are edible if you cook them. This means that you will have to light a fire in the jungle where everything is damp, a new skill that the recruit has to learn. You need to take standing dead wood and shave off the outsides to get it started. Dead bamboo makes good tinder, as does a termites' nest. Anything you do not recognize should be tested and cooked thoroughly.

Few Special Forces men are vegetarians and there is plenty of game in the jungle. Wild pigs, deer, monkeys and other animals can been hunted and trapped. Birds are plentiful and can been lured from the jungle canopy with fruit. Parrots abound and advertise their presence with their screeching, but they are clever. You will have to get them used to taking the bait before you set the trap. Near rivers traps can be baited with fish or offal for fish eagles and other birds that fly up and down looking for prey. Other birds, such as the Asian hornbill, prefer snakes and lizards – though these too are edible and easier to catch. All you need is a forked stick. SAS men are taught how to kill and eat snakes, how to make a spear and how to build traps to catch wild pigs and deer.

Rivers are full of fish – indeed many jungle people depend on them for nourishment. They are full of protein and easy to digest. If you have no fishing tackle, dam a small pool and bail it dry. You will find a surprising number of fish and, sometimes, turtles left high and dry in the mud at the bottom. It is also relatively easy to make a fish trap out of twigs and creeper, and certain vines and roots stun fish.

In the tropics fish spoil quickly, so gut them quickly and cook them thoroughly. Fish in slow-moving water are infested with parasites and where humans have no other sanitation they carry tapeworms. Boil any fish you catch for at least twenty minutes.

While fishing, you must keep your wits about you. Rivers are dangerous places. Piranhas live in the rivers of South America and a similar carnivorous fish inhabits the waterways of Burma. Electric eels can discharge as much as 650 volts. Some species of catfish can also deliver a powerful jolt and their dorsal fins and gills are covered with sharp spikes. The rivers of West Africa and South America are inhabited by stingrays. Water snakes, though foul smelling, are non-venomous. But crocodiles and alligators can kill.

In tropical climates you need to drink up to twelve pints of water a day, supplemented by salt tablets. Water is found in abundance in the jungle, but it is rarely clean and needs to be treated with water purification tablets or boiled before it is drunk – or you can use a Milbank filtration bag, which has been standard issue to the SAS since the campaign in Malaya.

Shelter

Although men are issued with a poncho, a groundsheet and a sleeping bag, they are taught how to make a shelter out of local materials. They are advised not to sleep on the ground, which is home to insects, snakes and other wild animals. In the jungle, you should always sleep on a raised platform if possible. Again, there are plentiful building materials in the jungle – wood, vines, large leaves, bamboo and elephant grass. Instructors teach the recruits how to make their shelters waterproof with a thatching of palm, banana or other large leaves. Leaves from the atap vine can be used to make effective waterproof panels for walls and roofs by weaving them into frames made from straight twigs. Bamboo is a particularly versatile building material. Thicker poles can be used for support and if you split bamboo vertically and lay them alternately to interlock with each other you can make waterproof pantiles. Bamboo can also be split down one side, then flattened or used as smooth walls, floors and shelves.

However, you need to take great care when collecting bamboo. It grows in tangled clumps and some of the stems are under tension. When cut they can spring up or shatter into a shower of razor-sharp slivers. The husks at the base of bamboo stems carry small stinging hairs that can cause severe skin irritation.

When collecting building material, you are also in danger from falling dead wood that can come crashing down from a great height. This may also dislodge a wasps' or hornets' nest. Even falling coconuts can kill.

Weapon Handling

During jungle training, men practice contact drills. As jungle patrols progress in single file. The point usually makes contact first. The other men quickly move up either side of him. Sustained fighting is no part of Special Forces standard operating procedure, so the patrol is always looking for ways to break contact, aiming to shoot and scoot.

The SAS picked the American M-16 Armalite to use in the jungle. It has the advantage of being short – just 39 inches– which helps when there is not much room to swing a weapon. It is light to carry and has little recoil, making it comfortable to raise and fire.

When on patrol in the jungle, the SAS do not shoot from the hip. Instead they keep the butt against their shoulder. Dispensing with the rifle sling, the gun is supported in the hands with the trigger-finger on the trigger guard. This is so that, at the first sign of trouble, the trooper can turn and raise the gun, leaning into the weapon to make firing easier.

Instructors teach the men to pivot as they move onto a target. If you swing, you will miss, they are told. You must keep both eyes open and only fire then the target is visible. Wild shooting wastes ammunition and attracts unnecessary attention. Once they see the target Special Forces men fire two shots in quick succession.

Every weapon must work first time, every time. This is particularly difficult with the M-16, which is notoriously unreliable. Although the Armalite is supposed to be self-cleaning, in the humidity of the jungle metal parts quickly rust, so troopers are trained to clean and oil their weapons every day. SAS men are also taught to "dry-clean" the barrel. Guns are stripped. The working parts are cleaned first, then the barrel pulled through to remove excess oil, otherwise oil in the barrel will make the first bullet tight in the barrel, which means that it will go high. And when the oil burns off, it will create a tell-tale puff of smoke, which could prove fatal in an ambush.

Although all weapons are cleaned every day, they are not all cleaned at the same time. On patrol, there must always be at least one weapon that this loaded and ready to fire. Standard operating procedures demand that a man's personal weapon must be within reach at all times.

M-16 magazines also present a problem. They must be cleaned and changed regularly, otherwise their spring can fail in operation. Every five days the magazine is changed and, although the M-16's magazine is designed to take 30 bullets, SAS men only ever load them with 29 so that spring is not fully compressed. A magazine left loaded with 30 rounds over a long period is liable to fail at a critical moment, possibly with fatal results.

In a hostage-taking situation, SAS men carry a Browning High Power as a back-up. But on patrol in the jungle, they do not carry a pistol as well as an Armalite. This is because the M-16 takes 5.56-mm rounds, the Browning 9-mm. That would mean every man would have to carry two types of ammunition and every pound counts when you are on a foot patrol in hostile conditions.

At the end of their course, SAS men will be able to survive and fight in the jungle. And because of their long experience of jungle fighting, the SAS are renowned worldwide as the masters of the tropical environment. Both the Australians and the Americans send their men to learned jungle fighting and survival in the SAS jungle training schools in the Far East and Belize.

15

MOUNTAIN TRAINING

The US Rangers, the Green Berets and the US Navy SEALs all have specialist mountain training and each SAS "Sabre" Squadron has a specialist Mountain Troop that specializes in fighting in rugged terrain.

Washington Army National Guard's 1st Battalion, 19th Special Forces (Airborne) also has a mountain specialty detachment which runs a "sustainment" mountaineering training course. Special Forces Guardsmen from Washington and Utah are trained on basic and intermediate military mountaineering tasks in the hills of the Tonto National Forest, Arizona. The soldiers hit the ground on the first day in an airborne operation, dropping into Coolidge Drop Zone, near Tucson. They begin the course on an indoor rock wall to assess an individual's level of proficiency. The training then progresses to real rock faces in the hills nearby, where they are taught advanced rope work, movement in a mountain environment and even climbing at night using night-vision goggles. According to one of the instructors: "We're not here to do sport climbing; we're here to learn military mountaineering. While some of the skills are similar, the focus is on tactical applicability."

Some students have been assigned to active-duty Special Forces mountain detachments in the past, but most have only learnt these skills in Ranger School, sports climbing or civilian alpine mountain climbing. The biggest challenge for the instructors is standardizing the techniques that each student uses to the accepted Army standards, and then demonstrating how a Special Forces detachment would use the skills in a tactical environment.

Military Mountaineering

"Military mountaineering is a key skill for both the Utah and Washington Guard, where these skills lend themselves to mountain rescue, downed pilot recovery and disaster relief. Perhaps more than any other specialty, the SF mountain teams have relevance to the states in which they serve," says the Battalion Commander, Lieutenant-Colonel Telleson.

All SAS troopers are taught the skill of mountain walking. These may seem basic enough, but one of the things they are taught to do is to step over certain obstacles, rather than stand on top of them. This minimizes the possibility of injury which always causes problems in the mountains and cuts own the amount of noise a patrol makes – in the mountains sound travel miles.

Troopers must also learn the basic techniques of rock climbing, abseiling, belaying and negotiating seemingly impossible obstacles. And they need to know the dangers of rock falls and avalanches. To hone their skills, SAS men attend courses run by the Royal Marines, who train their own Special Forces group, the SBS, as well as the Special Forces of several NATO allies. They attend the German Army Mountain and Winter Warfare School at Luttensee near Mittenwald in the Bavarian Alps. Men are put through five weeks intensive rock-climbing training at Oberreintal on the Wendelstein. Living high up in the Bavarian Alps, they spend up to ten hours a day climbing.

Next they are taught the techniques of ice-climbing in Chamonix, finishing the course with an exercise on Mont Blanc. Then they are taught skiing. No concession is made to lack of experience. Even those who have never skied before must pass the German Ski Association Instructor's Test within six weeks. Graduates then have three or four weeks on the high alpine course in Italy's Gran Paradiso region, before returning to Luttensee for a final exam.

SAS men going into the Mountain Troop also join 3 Commando Brigade of the Royal Marines on exercises in Norway. Everyone attending has to pass the three-week Arctic Warfare Training Course, where they are taught the techniques of fighting and surviving in Arctic conditions, and more skiing instruction is given by Military Ski Instructors (MSIs). Norwegian skiing is different from Alpine skiing – Norwegian is characterized by cross-country skiing on the flat while Alpine skiing is also known as downhill skiing. In addition, MSIs teach cold-weather survival, constructing snow-holes and four- and ten-man shelters. After that students spend eleven days – including four nights – in the field. The three-months of training in Norway includes camouflage and concealment, anti-ambush drills, patrolling and battle drills. At the end there is a contact drill with personnel from the course playing both sides.

Further training is given by Mountain Leaders from the Mountain and Artic Warfare Cadre. They run a course for would-be SAS mountain warfare specialists that lasts over eight months, beginning with a strenuous seven-day selection period in Devon and Cornwall. This section is so gruelling that the drop-out rate is often 60 per cent. Those remaining move on to the Black Mountains in Wales, then via Plymouth to Rjukan in Norway. There they undertake the Military Ski Instructor course. This entails living six days a week in the field when they are taught how to surviving in sub-zero temperatures and are given the ultimate off-piste training. The course ends with an eleven-day combat exercise.

Graduates of this course do further training with Italy's mountain troops, the Alpini, and the US Marine Corps who have their own Mountain Warfare Training Center at Picket Meadows in the Sierra Nevada, Northern California. Established in 1951 to provided cold-weather training for American troops bound for Korea, it comprises 46,000 acres of the Toniyabe National Forest. The centre is at 6,762 feet, but peaks in the training area climb to nearly 12,000 feet. During the winter snow accumulates to a depth of six to eight feet, with severe storms depositing as much as another four feet in twelve hours. Annual temperatures range from − 20° to + 90° Fahrenheit. There the SAS and American Special Forces units undertake the 28-day course to teach them how to survive at over 10,000 feet in sub-zero temperatures. Along with ski instruction, students are taken on forced marches the mountains – five miles carrying 29 to 40 lb and nine miles carrying 49 to 70 lb.

Avalanches

Along with all the other dangers of the mountains, Special Forces troops are trained to survive avalanches. First, they are taught to look out for the likely sites of avalanches. They usually occur in winter on the side of the mountain away from the wind on a slope of 30–45 degrees, usually within twenty-four hours of a snowfall, when the snow is still unstable. After a heavy snowfall of several hours' duration, it is best to wait a day before you set out so that the snow can stabilize. You should also avoid deep snow-filled gullies, valleys with steep side walls and convex slopes where the snow will be under tension.

Rain or a rise in temperature after a snowfall also raises the risk. Water under the snow from the melting process helps lubricate the snow as it slides. Steep rocks at the top of a slope are also a danger sign as falling rocks, icicles and snow can set the whole slope in motion. If possible look for irregular or wooded slopes where the snow is prevented from slipping by rocks and trees.

The heat of the sun on the snow can make it more prone to avalanche so stay in shaded areas in the morning and avoid those exposed to the sun. In the afternoon, keep to those that have already been out in the sun and avoid those being exposed to sunlight for the first time. Special Forces mountain specialists are taught to watch out for signs of earlier avalanches. Try and assess how long ago they took place, their size and direction. That will give you a guide to the avalanche activity in the area and will give you a clue to where fresh avalanches are likely to take place. If possible stick to ridges and high ground above the likely paths of avalanches. You are more likely to trigger an avalanche that way, but have a better chance of surviving as you will be on top of the snow and ice rather than under it.

If troops are caught in an avalanche, they are taught to discard their skis and backpacks, and try to work their way to the side of the cascading mass of snow and ice. They should keep their backs to the flow, their heads up and their mouths closed to avoid swallowing snow. Most of all, they should conserve their strength until the avalanche has slowed to a halt, then try to dig themselves out, survey the area and make for a valley where there is a likelihood of finding food and shelter. This is the drill for the so-called point-release avalanche, where the weight of the snowpack exceeds the sheer strength within it. These are most common on steeper terrain. In fresh, loose snow the release is usually at a point and the avalanche then gradually widens down the slope as more snow is entrained, usually forming a teardrop shape when viewed from a distance.

It is also appropriate for slab avalanches which account for around 90 per cent of avalanche-related deaths. They occur when there is a strong, stiff layer of snow known as a slab, which is usually formed when snow is deposited by the wind on a lee slope. When the slab fails, the fracture in a weak layer very rapidly propagates so that a large area, that can be hundreds of yards in extent and several yards thick, starts moving almost instantaneously.

However, the drill is rather different in a third starting type called a slush avalanche, which occurs when the snow pack becomes saturated by water. These also tend to start and spread out from a point. They normally occur at the spring thaw or when the temperature rises rapidly after a snowfall. They move slowly picking up rocks and trees on the way, creating great snow boulders. When the avalanche stops, the flow freezes solid immediately, making escape or rescue almost impossible.

The drill here is to lay flat and swim using the crawl stroke to try and stay on top of the slide. The wet snow coming down the mountain can get very deep. Again discard skis and packs and any other encumbrances. Cover your mouth and nose to avoid swallowing snow. When the avalanche comes to a halt, quickly make as big cavity around you as you can before the snow freezes. Get rid of any other equipment that may hamper your rescue. Then save your energy to shout when you hear rescuers nearby.

There is one other type of avalanche that occurs when new snow falls over old snow that has already formed a crust, or in cold, dry conditions. This may begin like a slab avalanche, but soon begins to kick up a cloud of powdered snow. Powdered-snow avalanches are the largest type. They can contain tens of millions tons of snow and their speed can exceed 200 miles an hour. They can flow for long distances along flat valley bottoms and even uphill for short distances. To stand any chance of survival you must cover your nose and mouth, otherwise you will inhale the snow and die by drowning.

Night Movement

Moving across mountains at night or in periods of poor visibility is dangerous – you should find shelter from the wind until visibility improves. Above the snowline you can dig yourself a snow-hole to give some sort of protection as the snow provides insulation. Below the snowline you must cover yourself with anything to hand to prevent exposure. Even a large plastic sack can make an improvised sleeping bag. Do not pull your clothes too tightly around you as air between the layers helps stop heat escaping. Sleep with your head uphill; on rocky ground it is more comfortable to sleep on your stomach. If possible, light a fire. This will provide warmth and psychological comfort.

Glaciers

Glaciers should be avoided as they are riven with hidden crevasses. These usually occur where the glacier starts at the valley wall, spreads out into a widening valley or changes direction. If men do find themselves on a glacier, as the SAS did on South Georgia, they should proceed slowly probing the ground and watching out for any slight depression that might indicate a crack in the ice. They must rope themselves together with at least 30 feet between them; that way, if one man does fall down a crevasse, there will be others to pull him out. A rope with a loop on the end should be belayed to him so that he can put his foot in it as a rope tightening around the chest can cause asphyxiation. It is very cold down crevasses so speed is of the essence. If the victim is unconscious, it might take three people to rescue him – they will need to harness themselves together to do this. Snow and ice bridges should also be avoided. But if they have to be crossed, men should go across one at a time, with the lightest going first. It is also best to go across on your belly to spread your weight.

Climbing Techniques

When climbing a slope, soldiers are taught to take a zig-zag route as it is less tiring than trying to go straight up. The lead person will get tired more quickly than the rest and should be changed often. All equipment must be secured at all times. Falling items are a danger to those below and are likely to be lost forever. Plan your route at the bottom of the mountain and keep an experienced man at the rear to check the route. Do not assume that the lead man cannot get lost. If possible travel early in the morning. After a cold night snow and ice are going to be frozen solid and more stable. Once the intense sunlight at high altitudes warms them, climbing becomes more difficult and more dangerous.

To conserve energy, men are taught to keep their centre of gravity over their feet while rock climbing. This is so that the strain is kept on the legs rather than the arms. For the same reason the hands should go not higher than shoulder level. Avoid overstretching by using small intermediate holds and avoid becoming spreadeagled. Keep your body away from the rock and look up. And always keep your feet as flat as possible so that you make the maximum contact with the rock.

You should maintain three points of contact with the rock at all time, moving only one hand or foot at a time and watching carefully where your feet are placed. Test holds for stability before you put your weight on them and try and move slowly but rhythmically, thinking ahead for your next hold as you go.

It is always safer to climb around an obstacle rather than over it, especially if you do not know where you are going. You could find yourself stuck above a feature with no way back.

To ascend a fissure, keep your back against one side and your feet braced against the other, then slowly move yourself up. Plan your ascent first. If the chimney opens out, you may have a problem turning from one side to the other and find that you have to come down before you can climb it again the other way round.

It is far more difficult to climb down a cliff than to climb up it. On the steepest cliffs, where is it necessary to descend facing inwards, it is difficult to see the footholds below. If a colleague can find a vantage point, he can help by giving directions. Once you are down, you can direct him from below.

On rock faces that are less steep and have deeper ledges, turn sideways, using the inner hand for support. For those with an even shallower slope, descend facing outwards with the body bent and taking your weight on the palms of your hands.

Even the most fearless climber should not attempt descending a high cliff without a rope. With a rope it is possible to abseil or rappel down the steepest slope. To do this you can use a special sling with a karabiner or snap ring for the rope to pass through. However, you can abseil simply using a double rope. First you must find a suitable anchor at the top of the cliff – a rock or a tree – to loop the rope around. You should test this to see that it can carry your full body weight. There must be no sharp ends that might cut the rope. Pass both ends of the rope between your legs from the front, around your body and across your back. Hold the rope in front with your left hand and at the back with the right.

Now comes the moment of truth, even for the hardened Special Forces trooper. You have to step over the edge of the cliff, leaning back with your feet about 18 inches apart. You should not try and support yourself with your left hand. Instead your weight should be borne by the rope across your back. You may have to move a few steps down to get into a good position.

To descend, pay the rope out one hand at a time, while you walk backwards down the slope. It is not comfortable, even with your body at the correct angle and friction can damage your clothing and your skin, but it is still the safest way to descent a steep or slippery slope. If there are a series of ledges with similar anchor points, you can descend the slope in stages, though if there is more than one of you there must be room for all of you at each staging point. If there is someone left at the top who can untie the rope, you can descend on a single rope, twice as far. Otherwise, you can simply pull the rope around, but first you must make sure you are in a safe position. As the rope comes free it is easy to lose balance. And make sure you have planned your next move – once the rope has come away it will be difficult to climb back up again.

On vertical slopes, men are taught to make a cradle with a knot called a bowline-on-the-bight. With a doubled rope you make two loops that will not tighten or jam. One goes round the chest, the other round the buttocks, making a rudimentary bosun's chair. A man can be lowered down or hauled up using this simple device.

You can also use ropes to ascend, but first someone must climb up carrying a light line which he can use to haul the heavy rope up after him. Again, if ascending in stages, there must be room for the entire party at each stage.

The rope should then be anchored to a spike of rock, a tree or a thread – that is, a hole in a rock or a crevice with a stone or small boulder firmly wedged into it. The man at the top must tie himself on with another rope so that he is in no danger of being pulled over the edge. He then passes the rope over his head, seating it around his back with a twist around the arm nearest the anchor. Below, the next climber ties the other end of the rope around his waist with a bowline.

The upper man then takes up the slack as the man below starts his ascent. The belayer above keeps the rope taut by pushing with the hand nearest the anchor and pulling with the other one So that the rope slips around his body. If the rope is anchored around a spike, it should be above the belayer's head. If necessary, the belayer should be sitting down.

The anchor, belayer and climber should be in a straight line. If the climber slips, the belayer should arrest the rope by bringing his hands together. The rope should tighten around his body, while he leans back to take the weight. It is possible to belay without an anchor, but the man above needs to be strong. In this case he should not pass the rope around his back in case he is pulled over the edge by the climber.

There is another danger here. The rope can easily dislodge loose rocks that could kill or injure those below. The first man up should check the rocks as he goes.

Climbing on ice generally requires sophisticated equipment. Mountain troops are trained with crampons and ice axes which can be driven into the snow when climbing to give a stable handhold. They can also be used to cut steps or footholds, or be driven in horizontally on steep slopes. With crampons, you should dig your heels in using the ice axe as a walking stick to steady you on gentle slopes, or driving it in to make a handhold on steeper ones.

If you slip or are descending, dig in your heels and use the ice axe as an additional brake. Although sliding down a slope can be fun, it is also dangerous. There could be a precipice ahead that you have not spotted and it is an easy way to start an avalanche.

When crossing an ice field, it is best to tie a line once the first man has crossed. This can be used as a handhold, or a man can be secured to it with a slip knot that moves freely along the line, but tightens if he falls.

If there is no firm tree or rock for belaying, an anchor can be cut from the ice. Chip out a mushroom shape at least six inches high and 18 inches in diameter. Test it first and if there is the slightest crack in it, cut another one. You can make a similar bollard in snow. It must be a least one foot deep in and 40 inches in diameter in hard snow and 10 feet in diameter in soft.

Survival in the Mountains

As there is snow on high mountains, there is an abundance of water, but food is scarcer. However, mountain goats are to be found high up and sheep inhabit lower slopes. All the stealth of the Special Forces trooper must be used to catch one. To stand any chance at all, you have to move around downwind, then surprise the animal when it has its head lowered to eat. However, even the hardiest trooper is warned not to chase after them if they get away. He is unlikely to be as surefooted as his prey and a badly twisted or broken ankle on a remote peak can be a death sentence.

Another danger is lightning which is attracted to peaks and pinnacles. Avoid summits and the tops of ridges, lone trees, and exposed plateaus and gullies filled with water. Metal equipment and wet ropes attract lightning and even recesses in cliffs and overhangs offer little protection. Those caught out in the mountains during a thunderstorm are advised to sit with their knees drawn up to the chest. This affords the best protection against earthing currents.

The best advise for those exposed in the mountains when the weather turns nasty is to get out of there as quickly as possible – just as the SAS men on the Fortuna Glacier on South Georgia did.

16

ARCTIC TRAINING

Special Forces troopers also undergo specialist Arctic training. Although fighting has yet to break out in the polar regions, SAS and SBS men found what they had learned on Arctic warfare courses in Norway, Bavaria and the French Alps came in extremely useful in the Falklands.

Arctic Survival

Before you can even think of fighting in Arctic conditions you must learn how to survive. The human body is only designed to operate at certain temperatures and the human brain quickly numbs with cold, so you must make your plans while you are still warm. Even a simple task can take a long time once you are cold. The wind can freeze exposed flesh in minutes or even seconds. Touching metal can burn the skin off and immersion in cold water, even if well protected, will cause death in a matter of minutes. Even at relatively normal temperatures, wind chill – a combination of the ambient cold, humidity and the cooling effect of the wind – can prove fatal. A wind of 20 miles an hour takes a temperature of +7° Fahrenheit down to –30° Fahrenheit. At that temperature, exposed flesh will freeze in thirty seconds. Wind speeds of 40 miles an hour take the temperature down to –34° Fahrenheit and winds of 110 miles an hour have been recorded in the Antarctic. These can whip fallen snow up to a height of 100 feet, giving the impression of a blizzard even when it is not snowing.

In the Arctic, temperatures fall as low as −81° Fahrenheit, though in summer, with 24 hours of sunlight, they can rise to +65° Fahrenheit, except on glaciers and frozen seas. Even in forested areas away from the Pole, the altitude can push the temperature even further down. A temperature of −94° Fahrenheit has been recorded at Yerkhoyansk in Eastern Siberia, while in the northern forests the summer temperature can soar to +100° Fahrenheit. Temperatures in Antarctica are worse. At Vostok Station, a record low temperature of −129° Fahrenheit has been recorded.

Personal Hygiene

Soldiers are instructed in the specialized equipment they are going to need to carry with them, the construction of a shelter to protect them from the elements and the types of food they must eat to maintain their strength. To survive in Arctic conditions they must be extremely fit and pay attention to personal hygiene, though they are discouraged from shaving. Not only does shaving remove an insulating layer of hair, it also removes the natural oils from the skin that protect the face from frostbite.

Men are taught the vital importance to keeping their whole body, especially their hands and feet, covered when operating in the extreme cold. Proper clothing is vital. The material must be tough and light, as well as waterproof and windproof, and multiple layers are worn rather than items that are heavy and thick. Clothing is worn loose to allow blood to circulate easily. This helps protect against frostbite as warm blood reaches exposed areas. The key to keeping warm, the Special Forces are taught, is in the acronym C.O.L.D. – keep Clean as dirt and grease block air spaces and reduce circulation; avoid Over-exertion as sweat freezes more quickly than it can evaporate; wear clothes Loose to allow air and blood to circulate; and keep Dry by avoiding moisture on the outside of your clothes and within. Socks made wet by perspiration can lead to the debilitating condition called trench foot.

Clothing and Equipment

Thermal-knit cotton long johns are a must. These are tight from the ankle to the knee to prevent drafts blowing up from the foot, then baggy from the knee to the waist to trap an insulating layer of air. A high-necked cotton vest with long sleeves and elasticated wrists traps the warm air over the upper part of the body. Some SAS men favour silk long johns and vests, which they buy privately.

It is vital to keep the feet warm and dry. Generally Arctic warfare soldiers wear two pairs of mountaineering socks. These are made of wool rather than cotton as sweat builds up inside waterproof boots and cotton absorbs moisture better than wool, making the foot colder. Cotton acts like a wick, absorbing moisture and, when wet, it can lose heat 240 times faster than when dry. Over the woollen socks, a pair of Gore-tex socks are worn. Gore-tex is an expensive breathable synthetic material which prevents water from the outside getting in, but allows water in the form of sweat to get out. Over these the soldier wears a pair of boots, usually of the Berghaus mountain variety which have an outside cleat where you can attach Gore-tex gaiters. They are also equipped to take cross-country skis and snowshoes, although many men in the SAS prefer German *Bundeswehr* (Army) ski boots.

The snowshoes issued to Special Forces are small and only used in close-quarter fighting or routine tasks around the camp. Some troopers prefer to retain downhill or Alpine-tourer-type skis with ski-mountaineering bindings.

SAS troopers wear Royal Marine DPM trousers with a Velcroed slash from the knee to the ankle so that they can be changed quickly. They also have pockets closed with Velcro and large buttons which can be handled easily with gloved fingers. A Gore-tex jacket is worn on the top half with a hood to keep the head warm. Under these windproof items, quilt thermal liners comprising an inner jacket and trouser are sometimes worn. White trousers, hooded smock and pack cover are worn over everything for camouflage against the snow.

Inner mittens are usually worn beneath windproof and waterproof outer gloves, which may be replaced for short periods by thinner water-resistant gloves when working in wet conditions.

Some men wear commercial ski gloves, though the thickness of the finger makes it difficult to pull a trigger. Others wear several pairs of thin cotton gloves under their white outer nylon gloves. Another solution is to wear mittens over the gloves that can be pulled off hastily when going into action. These mittens are attached by tape so they do not get left behind.

Special Forces Arctic troops wear woolly hats or balaclavas under their hoods. The balaclava is warmer but has the disadvantage of muffling the wearer's hearing which can be a danger in war. Face masks are also worn, especially during the night. They have silk next to the skin and white cotton outside to camouflage the face. Some soldiers wear tinted goggles to help prevent snowblindness; these are similar to the type worn in the desert but camouflaged with white tape. Otherwise tie a strip of cloth or bark with a narrow slit in it across their eyes. As a great deal of sunlight is reflected from the snow, soldiers apply a thick layer of sunblock to the eyelids, nose, lips and any other area that is liable to become exposed.

In the Arctic, the SAS abandon their standard bergen for the so-called "arctic bergen". This has a light tubular aluminium H-frame that carries the pack high on the back – a better position when skiing or mountaineering.

Although much of their Arctic training is done on skis, Special Forces men are familiarized with Snow Cats and practise deploying in the snow from helicopters. But Arctic weather and poor visibility often keep helicopters grounded for days on end. Even surface traffic is restricted and in extreme conditions oil and lubricants can thicken and freeze.

Care of Weapons and Ammunition

Particular care has to be taken of weapons which have to be stripped and cleaned of excess lubricants. Snow must be kept out of the barrel, sights and other working parts otherwise they will rust. In a warm shelter, condensation will form on a weapon brought in from the cold. This must be thoroughly cleaned off before the weapon is taken outside again as it will freeze, jamming the gun. The SAS men lashed by winds and snow on the Fortuna Glacier on South Georgia found ice forming in the feed trays of the GPMGs, making them unusable.

Ammunition must be stored off the frozen ground and left covered in its boxes, protected from the elements. Before it is used it, too, must be cleansed of all ice, snow, oil and condensation. Communications equipment is also vulnerable in the extreme cold as certain electronic components get brittle and break down.

Movement and Navigation

During their two-week Arctic warfare and four-week Arctic survival courses, SAS men are taught snow-shoeing, rapid military skiing and trail-breaking, and how to make improvised snowshoes from willow or other soft wood. As well as travelling in the snow, they are taught how to cross the thawing bog that some polar regions become in summer. Tundra turns into swamp and sea-ice turns into slush underfoot.

Although even in the worst whiteout when the clouds merge with the land causing total disorientation, GPS still works. However, as electronics are never 100 per cent reliable, especially in extreme conditions, troops are taught the old methods of navigation needed when the proximity of the magnetic poles makes a compass next to useless, and landmarks change with each snowfall. Unless you are at the Pole itself, you can find out which direction is north by using a stick if the sun appears over the horizon. On a patch of flat ground or snow, stick a three-foot stick upright. Mark where the shadow of the end of the stick falls. Wait at least a quarter of an hour, then make a second mark where the shadow of the end of the stick has moved to. Draw a straight line through the two points. This points east-west, so the north-south line runs at right-angles to it. If you have a piece of string and more time you can use a more accurate method. Again push the stick into the ground or snow and mark where the shadow of the tip falls some time in the morning. Tie one end of the string to the bottom of the stick and describe an arc through the point you have marked. As it approaches midday, the shadow of the stick will retreat from this line. In the afternoon, it will advance again. Mark the exact spot where it touches the arc again. A straight line from one mark to the other will run exactly east-west. In both cases you can tell which is east and which is west by the way the sun is moving –

the tip of the shadow, of course, moves west-east. The second method takes a good deal longer than the first, which is usually used to double-check your direction while on the move. However, both methods preclude travelling in a blizzard or in the thick fogs you get near the sea in polar regions.

The movements of birds can also help you navigate. During the summer thaw, birds migrate towards land; most seabirds fly out to sea during the day and back to land at night. You can also get some idea of what is happening in the distance by looking at the reflection on the upside of clouds. Over open water, forest or snow-free land, they appear dark underneath; over snow-fields or sea ice they appear white. New ice gives a greyish reflection, drifted snow or pack ice gives a mottled effect.

When travelling on ice floes, soldiers are warned not to use icebergs or distant landmarks to fix their position. Floes are moving constantly and the relative position changes with it. When an ice floe breaks up, jump from piece to piece, staying at least two feet from the edge. In Arctic waters, avoid ice cliffs which often collapse, suddenly dropping thousands of tons of ice into the sea. You should also steer clear of icebergs. As they melt from the bottom they often turn over without warning as the centre of gravity clears the surface. This is especially likely to happen if you clamber on, adding your weight to the top half.

In deep loose snow, abandon your skis and use snowshoes. To walk wearing them, keep the foot parallel to the ground when lifting them and avoid angling the foot as you would when you walk normally. You can make snowshoes by bending a long green sapling back on itself and tie the ends together. Tie twigs from side to side as crosspieces and lace string to make a diamond pattern. Then add some more twigs in the middle to make a strong platform for your foot, but avoid making them too heavy as that will make walking tiring.

During their time in the SAS, members of the Regiment will be given regular refresher courses on Arctic survival. Soldiers are taught to follow rivers as the fish in the water and the plant-life on their banks are good sources of food. Remember, though, if you are in Siberia, rivers flow north. However, making a raft to sail down the river is discouraged. Melt-water rivers are fast and dangerous. A raft can easily turn over, dumping its passengers in the water which is very cold. Large chunks of ice float down most rivers within the Arctic Circle, even at the height of summer, causing another hazard to navigation.

When following a frozen river, stick to the smoother ice near the bank and on the outside of a bend. Where two rivers meet, follow the outer edge or mount the outer bank. And if a river bends a lot, travel over the ridges in between. It will save time.

Arctic Survival

Special Forces men are taught how to stave off frostbite by keeping the body well covered at all times by changing clothes inside their sleeping bag and wrinkling the face to stop stiff patches forming. Exercise your hands and feet, and watch for patches of waxy, reddening or blackening skin especially on your fingers, toes, ears and the exposed parts of your face. Never go out without sufficient clothing, even for a moment. Snow must be brushed off clothing before entering a shelter. It will melt giving you the problem of drying the clothes again. Always wear gloves. Keep them dry and never touch metal with your bare hands. Be careful not to spill petrol on bare flesh. In sub-zero temperatures it will freeze almost immediately and do more damage than water because of its lower melting point.

Fluids

In Arctic climes, dehydration is another danger, so the fluid intact – especially hot fluid – must be maintained at a high level. Even when it is cold, you need about at least two pints of water a day to replace losses. In the summer, melt water is abundant. Pond water in the tundra may look brown and taste brackish, but the vegetation growing in it keeps it fresh. However, it should be boiled or purified before it is drunk. Soldiers are taught not to eat snow or ice if they are thirsty as this will lower the temperature of their body, possibly catastrophically. Crushed ice can injure your mouth and lips, and cause further dehydration. Ice and snow must be melted and possibly warmed first before you drink it. Frozen sea water should be avoided too, unless it is old, or is bluish or blackish and shatters easily – then it is free of salt.

Hypothermia

Another real danger is hypothermia – when the body temperature drops due to prolonged exposure to the cold and the metabolism slows, eventually, to a standstill. Its onset is how to recognize it in oneself. At the very least, troopers must travel in pairs. In another form, hypothermia manifests itself in violent shivering, loss of purpose, irrationality, unconsciousness and, ultimately, death.

If you fall in icy water you are in imminent danger. The shock of the cold knocks the breath out of you, violent shivers run through you and, as you lose control of your muscles, your body curls up. Exposed parts freeze in around four minutes. After seven minutes your consciousness begins to cloud. Death will follow in 15 to 20 minutes. So the moment you hit the water you must take strenuous action to get out; as soon as you reach land, roll in the snow. This will act like a towel, absorbing water. Then get under shelter and dry your kit immediately.

Food

Finding food in polar regions is problematic. In the Antarctic, edible mosses and lichens live on dark, heat-absorbing rocks. But they are the only plants. However, the seas are full of krill which grow up to two inches long and are the staple of most species living there. They are bioluminescent, so they can be caught at night if you have any sort of net. Penguins make good eating, although they usually take to the sea at the first sign of danger, unless hatching their eggs. Whales can be caught off-shore if you are armed with anything sufficiently powerful, while seabirds and seal can be trapped on land. Newborn seals cannot swim and are easy to catch. You can simply walk out on to the ice and club them. The easiest way to catch the adult is to wait by one of the breathing holes they make in the ice. These have a characteristic cone shape which is wider on the under-side. When they pop up to take a breath, club them, then open up the ice to recover the carcass. Do not eat the liver as it contains dangerous concentrations of Vitamin A.

The large mammals that inhabit the Arctic – walrus, bears and musk ox – are dangerous and can inflict fatal injuries. Polar bear meat must be well cooked as it is full of the trichinosis worm; again its liver contains dangerous levels of Vitamin A. Arctic foxes, which turn white in winter, follow polar bears out onto the sea ice to scavenge their kills. Leave walruses alone unless you are armed. They may looked cumbersome on land, but they can kill. Fish are often plentiful in deep water under ice, if you can cut a hole in it and drop a baited line through. Elk and moose stalk the islands of the Canadian archipelago, while reindeer and caribou inhabit Alaska, Canada, western Greenland, Scandinavia and Siberia. Bark and greenery stripped from trees is an indication that they are in the vicinity. Reindeer are notoriously nosey and can sometimes be attracted by waving a cloth and moving on all fours. However, this may also attract the wolves that inhabit Canada, Alaska and Siberia, who might think you are prey. Foxes prowl the tundra in summer and confine themselves to the woodlands in winter. They prey on mountain hares, squirrel and rodents that burrow under the snow looking for seeds. Weasels, mink, beaver and wolverine all inhabit low Arctic latitudes, and lemming make runs under the snow. Ground squirrels and marmots sometimes run into you if you place yourself between their burrows. Kissing the back of your hand can attract some carnivores – apparently they think it sounds like the cries of a wounded bird or rodent. Squirrels and other rodents carry ticks infected with tularemia, a type of plague. Wear gloves when you are skinning them and boil the meat.

Ptarmigans, owls and ravens can be approached if you move slowly and do not make any sudden movements. Many Arctic birds moult in the summer, for two or three weeks are rendered flightless and can be caught readily on the ground. Eggs are also a safe form of foodstuff that can be eaten at any time during the development of the embryo.

Once you have killed your prey, gut it quickly while it is still warm to prevent contamination. Bleed it and skin it before it freezes. Cut the meat into usable potions. Surplus meat can easily be frozen for future use, but hide it well as other Arctic animals will be searching for a meal. Once the meat is cooked do not reheat it. Eat the leftovers cold. Leave the fat of all animals except seals, whose blubber quickly turns rancid but can be used as fuel. Fat is essential for energy in the cold but, if you eat a lot, you will need to drink more.

Plants and animals can be found in the tundra, winter and summer, and northern forest teem with flora and fauna. Again there is edible lichen and mosses – reindeer moss is particularly nutritious. Low, spreading willow, birch, juniper and other berry-bearing plants are rich in vitamins. While most Arctic plants are edible, you must learn to avoid the poisonous water hemlock, the Arctic buttercup and the purple berries of the neckleweed baneberry, whose irritant resin has a cathartic effect and induces vomiting. Unless you have a good knowledge of fungi, avoid them. Some are poisonous. Learn to distinguish edible lichen from them. Poisonous species from temperate zones are also found in the far north, notably larkspur, vetch, lupine and give-away death camas, which is hard to distinguish from the onion or edible camas, false hellibore and wolfbane or monkshood which was once administered to criminals.

Shelter

But the most urgent necessity in Arctic regions is shelter to get out of the biting wind. Special Forces troops are taught how to build rudimentary shelters from whatever is to hand. In forested areas, a simple bivouac can be made with branches, remembering that the central pole must be the strongest as everything else rests on it. More branches, grass or other insulating material should be placed on the ground on the inside to sleep on. Avoid making shelter near to water. The larvae of mosquitoes, midges, black fly and deer fly live in water and the adults appear in clouds in the summer. Keep your collar up, your sleeves rolled down and wear netting over your head. Burning green wood and leaves on the fire helps keep them at bay, but may also give away your position.

Above the tree line, men are taught how to make igloos. Each block should be 18 x 20 inches and four to eight inches thick. Blocks should be cut from vertical surfaces to avoid internal strains. The entrance should be kept as small at possible to minimize heat loss, but be careful not to seal it completely as the occupants, though warm, are liable to asphyxiate. Inside you should be able to see your breath – if not, the temperature is too high. There will be condensation and the inner surface will start melting. If possible you should dig a tunnel to a snow cave to use as a lavatory so you will not have to go outside. Do not delay defecation no matter how unpleasant the process might be in the cold. Constipation can be brought on this way. If you have no snow hole to go in, do it in the shelter shortly before you are going to go out and take your faeces with you.

Although you need shelter to stay out of the wind, avoid building it on the lee side of cliffs where snow could drift, burying it. Of course, you should also avoid anywhere there is liable to be an avalanche. You should also avoid snow-laden trees as the weight of snow could bring down frozen branches. Lower boughs that touch the snow make ready-made shelters, however, any heat you produce – from your body or a fire you may light – could melt enough of the snow on the underside to loosen the load and produced a snowfall.

Lighting a Fire

Finding fuel to build a fire is a problem at high latitudes. Bird fat and seal blubber burns well, while along the coast you may find driftwood. Pieces of wood that have been carried down Siberian rivers find themselves as far away as Greenland, where they are used to build houses. The ground-spreading willow that grows in the tundra also burns. Beyond the forest line you also find juniper and birch, the bark of which makes good kindling. Feather a branch and the oily wood will burn even when it is wet. Eskimos use a spreading evergreen heather with white bell-shaped flowers called *Cassiope hypnoides* as fuel. It is so full of resin that it burns even when wet.

Remember that a hood pulled tight around your face detaches you from reality. As the cold gets to your brain, your mind gets sluggish and it is easy to overlook the obvious. Try and keep alert and active, though be careful not to wear yourself out on unnecessary tasks. You will need all the energy you can get when the bullets start flying. Do not let the cold get you down. Always be thinking about how you can make your living conditions better. Exercise your fingers and your toes, and sleep as much as possible. Unless you are completely exhausted and your body cannot generate enough heat to compensate for that lost to the air, the cold and involuntary shivering will wake you before you freeze to death. However, you should be especially careful if you have been working hard and are tired. If you are ill, rest.

17

DESERT TRAINING

The desert is the spiritual home of the Special Forces. The SAS, the inspiration behind the other Special Force units, began life there. More recently, both British and American Special Forces have been deployed in Iraq and Afghanistan – countries that are largely desert.

Desert training has a particular appeal for the Special Forces as it is physically demanding. Men suffer the extremes of temperature and the dangers of dehydration, sunburn and sunstroke. During the Second World War, the SAS developed ways not only to survive in these severe conditions, but to fight in them. These have been passed on to the other Special Forces units that have drawn inspiration from them.

Desert Survival

Survival in the desert depends on good water discipline, personal hygiene, physical fitness and stamina. Eating and drinking properly is essential as appetite and thirst are knocked off balance by the heat. In the desert, it is not unusual for a trooper to drink three gallons of water a day. This means that extra salt must been added to food to maintain a healthy balance in the body.

There are other dangers from animals that inhabit the desert. There are flesh-eating spiders, packs of rabid wild dogs, venomous snakes and scorpions that can cause paralysis with a single flick of their tail. Snakes seek warmth and are keen to slither into a sleeping bag to curl up for the night with a sleeping soldier, while scorpions prefer the refuge of a boot, which should be shaken out before being donned in the morning. In the eyes of many soldiers fighting in the Gulf, the worst of the lot is the camel spider that is unique to the Arabian desert. The SAS first encountered these eight-legged carnivores in Oman years earlier. The palm-sized arachnid injects its prey with anaesthetic before feasting on its numb – often sleeping but still living – victim. However, camel spiders, like most of the other nasties in the desert, will usually only bite you if you go out of your way to upset them, although there are cases of spiders eating lumps out of soldiers' faces while they slept.

Troopers are taught to be more wary of a far more familiar pest – the common fly. In the heat of the Gulf, flies breed quickly and a lapse in the standards of hygiene and poor field skills can quickly put a unit out of action. Flies can go from being eggs to egg-laying in a week, so a camp can quickly became infested if rubbish, waste water and the like are not disposed of properly. Flies are directly linked with the spread of gastric illnesses such as diarrhoea and vomiting. Once an epidemic begins it can be difficult to snuff out. Particular attention has to be paid to cleaning cooking utensils and the proper disposal of waste, no matter how tiring a patrol has been. Lice and mites also carry dysentery and scrub typhus.

Another danger is the extremely venomous horned vipers that hide under the sand in the heat of the day. Other venomous snakes hide in rock crevices that should be avoided. Most bites occur on the hand or forearm, or below the knee.

Scorpions lurk in the sand and can inflict a lethal sting – more than 5,000 people a year die from scorpion stings. There is no effective cure and the effect is immediate, but those who have been bitten are advised to stay calm. Only twenty-five species produce venom capable of killing people. The other 1,200 are not deadly, though they inject haemotoxins that cause swelling, discolouration and pain, though it is usually less painful than the sting of a bee. Victims recover fully in minutes or, sometimes, a matter of days.

There are sandflies that suck blood and cause the disease leishmaniasis, which can be fatal if not treated. Sandflies and poisonous snakes are endemic to both Iraq and Afghanistan. In both countries, there is also the ever-present danger of industrial pollutions, not to mention NBC alerts, and the constant danger of snipers, suicide bombers and ambushes.

Mobility

In the desert, the SAS have abandoned standard British Army combat boots in favour of desert boots with suede uppers, rubber soles and ankle support. These keep the feet cooler, which is essential if you are going on long foot patrols behind enemy lines, while puttees help keep the sand out. For mobility the SAS and Rangers still use the tried and tested Land Rover and cross-country motorcycles, although men need special training on how to handle these machines in the desert. When traversing a sand dune, one man must climb it on foot first to check that the sand is not too soft or the slope on the other side too steep, otherwise it is easy to get the vehicle stuck on the top. They are also taught to drive with partially deflated tyres to get better traction, Which, on return to harder surfaces, must be pumped up again as running with soft tyres can lead to overheating.

Desert Survival

The SAS do their desert training in Saudi Arabia, Oman, the United Arab Emirates and the Namib Desert in south-west Africa. US Special Forces use the Desert Training Range near Fort Bliss, Texas and the Dugway Proving Grounds in Utah, and sometimes train with the French Marines at their Desert Training School at Camp Lemonier in Djibouti, East Africa.

A key element of desert training is the effect of sun and sand on weapons. Weapons must be kept covered when not in use as sand blown into the barrel can clog it, resulting in a dangerous malfunction. Condoms have traditionally been used to prevent sand going down the barrel, but kitchen plastic wrap or cling-film is now more commonly used. After cleaning a weapon, all excess oil must be wiped off the working parts, otherwise sand sticks to them making an abrasive paste that will damage them.

The heat of the desert also affects radios, softening the solder and making the connections loose. Batteries run down quicker and need frequent recharging. But heat is not the only problem in the desert. At night, under a clear sky, men suffer the extremes of cold. Temperatures in the Gobi Desert in Mongolia can go down as low as -50° Fahrenheit – compare that to the top Sahara temperature of +136° Fahrenheit. During the 1991 Gulf War, SAS men put in behind the Iraqi lines in January and February found themselves lashed by rain and sleet, complaining that it was "worse than the Falklands". Two men on Andy McNab's Bravo Two Zero patrol – Sergeant Vince Phillips and Lance-Corporal "Legs" Lane – died of hypothermia as they tried to escape from Iraqi troops. Others improvised with Arctic and mountain kit and were pictured wearing woolly hats, Arctic smocks, Gore-tex⒯⒨ jackets, jumpers, gloves and swathed with blankets.

In a flat and featureless desert, camouflage is vital. Camouflage netting should have hessian patches sown onto it to generate some shade. This is vital if you are using binoculars or other optical equipment which, if exposed to direct sunlight, might give off a tell-tale glint.

Special Forces troopers are taught to seek out caves and other natural hiding places, which also afford some protection from the elements, but they should avoid deep wadis. In the desert there are sometime sudden downpours that result in flash floods. Usually, though, it is a shortage of water that is the problem, not its abundance. Without water, even the strongest man will die in less than sixty hours in the heat of the Sahara, even when resting in the shade, compared to twelve days at a temperate 70° Fahrenheit. He would be able to walk no further than five miles without collapsing in 120° Fahrenheit, though resting up during the day and travelling only at night he might cover 25 miles. With just four pints of water, he might last three days and cover 35 miles.

Maps have oases, wells and waterholes marked on them. However, smaller waterholes in the bottom of wadis are seasonal and are often covered with brushwood or a large stone, and are therefore hard to find unless you know the area.

In the desert, water often runs underground, beneath the creeks, canyons and wadis created by flash flooding. Troopers are taught to locate the lowest point of a dry lake or river bed and dig there. Once the sand appears wet, they should stop digging and wait for the water to collect. Surface vegetation is often an indication that there is water below. Palm trees only grow where the water table is two or three feet below the surface. Sage and cacti are not indicators of water below, although cactus flesh can be a useful source of water itself. The leaf stems of pigweed and other desert plants also render a limited supply of water and will also provide much-needed nutrition.

In some deserts, any water in the air condenses in the cold of the night and the dew can be collected. In the Namib Desert, fog coming in from the sea provides usable amounts of water.

Special Forces troopers are taught to make a large desert still that will provide enough water to sustain life, with a hole dug about six feet wide and three feet deep in a place that water might reasonably be expected to collect. With any luck, once you are three feet down, the earth will become a little damp. Fill the pit with waste water, urine, vegetation and anything else that might contain water. Put a container in the centre, then cover the whole with plastic sheeting, held in place with stone around the edge. Put one or two stones in the middle, over the container. Heat from the sun will evaporate the water from whatever is in the pit. This will condense on the plastic sheet. Droplets will run down the sheet to the point where it is weighed down by the centre stone. Then they will drop off into the container. You can make about two pints of drinkable water this way. To preserve water, SAS men are told to stay fully clothed and move as slowly as possible. If you strip off your clothes – apart from risking sunburn – you will lose the sweat on your skin through evaporation, requiring you to sweat more to stay cool. In periods of extreme shortage, you should give up washing and only drink sips to prevent wastage and stomach cramps.

In high temperatures and low humidity, sweating may not always be apparent, however dehydration is a major danger in the desert. Activity should be kept to a minimum and you should stay wrapped up. This will help prevent sweat evaporating and once the outside temperature is higher than your body temperature, an insulating layer of clothing helps keep the heat out. Heat exhaustion is caused by the excessive loss of water and salt, through sweating. It can be fatal if not treated. One symptom is heat cramps. Where possible the victim should be given a great deal of salt water to drink, though any fluid is useful. He should lie down in the shade with his legs raised and be massaged to return the blood to his heart. Men should take care to avoid heat exhaustion in the first place by a gradual build-up in exposure to the sun and activities in hot climates so that the body can acclimatize.

Heatstroke occurs when the body can no longer cool itself by sweating, and is potentially fatal. Early symptoms are dizziness, headache, nausea, restlessness, weakness, mental confusion, a rapid pulse and hot, dry, flushed skin. If the body temperature rises to 106–110° Fahrenheit, there will be damage to the central nervous system, the victim will collapse and go into a coma. The pulse will weaken and the victim will die if not treated immediately. He must be placed in the shade, his clothes removed and his body sprinkled with water from head to foot. If possible, he should be given an ice bath and massage to promote circulation. The cooling should stop when his temperature has come back down to 102° Fahrenheit, though begun again if his temperature begins to rise. Professional medical attention should be sought to treat possible brain damage or circulatory disorders that could ensue.

Other disorders occur in the desert that, while not life threatening, still affect the performance of troops. Heavy sweating and the chaffing of clothes can block the pores leading to an irritating condition known as prickly heat. Troops often suffer from constipation, experience pain when passing water and a deficiency of salt can cause cramps. Micro-organisms thrive on sweat particularly in the armpits, the groin and between the toes. These areas should be kept clean and dry.

Men are instructed to eat only when strictly necessary for survival if water is short. And then they should avoid protein-rich food as it requires water to digest it. Dates and figs grow around oases and dry lakes. You can also eat prickly pears, wild gourds and carrion flowers – though, as elsewhere, flowers with milky or coloured sap should be avoided as they are poisonous. The desert gourd is a member of the squash family, whose vine can run over the ground for up to 15 feet. It has fruit the size of oranges and its flowers and water-filled shoots are also edible – as are its seeds if boiled or roasted.

Some desert grasses are edible, but not those found in the Sahara or Gobi. The acacia tree found in the scrub on the fringes of the Sahara yields an edible bean and its flowers, fruit, seeds, bark and young shoots are all edible. The desert is also home to members of the agave family of plants. The species that lives in the Mexican desert is mescal, used in the production of tequila, but the central stalk is good to eat, especially if boiled and mashed. It is also full of water. You can cut the ends off and suck the water out. However, you need to be careful as many desert plants are protected by thorns and sharp spikes that can cause intense skin irritation if they scratch you. Even the most trivial wound in the desert quickly becomes infected if not dealt with straight away. Thorns should be pulled out and any open wound bandaged straight away.

Food

Food spoils quickly in the desert. Once rations are opened, eat them as quickly as possible. Anything left out should be covered and shaded, otherwise flies will appear from nowhere and settle on uncovered food.

Animals are few and far between in the desert, though in some places birds can be trapped or rabbits smoked from their burrows. Jack rabbits with large ears for cooling purposes live in the deserts of North America, along with kangaroo rats, coyotes and the Arizona road runner whose feathers provide good insulation. Tortoises and amphibians survive in deserts from the time when they once ran with water. Gerbils, gerboas, hyenas and caracals all inhabit the deserts of Africa and Asia, along with lizards and geckoes. Gazelles live on the fringes, living off the sap in the leaves they eat. In the Kalahari there is a species of squirrel that uses its tail for shade. Lions roam the deserts of Namibia and the presence of larger mammals usually indicates that there is a water supply within a day's walk of their hunting grounds.

Snakes are edible, but usually venomous. In a survival situation, men are instructed to turn to insects for sustenance. These can be found by turning over stones during the day, or attracting them at night with a small light.

You can boil your prey by digging a pit in hard ground, lining it with leaves, adding stones heated in the fire and filling it with water, if you have any to spare. SAS men are taught how to make a rather more sophisticated "Dutch oven". Again dig a hole and place hot stones in the bottom with the meat on top of them. This should be covered with a damp cloth. The hole should then be filled in and left for several hours. This method of cooking not only produces a nutritious and sometimes tasty meal, it also protects your food from predators.

Desert Navigation

Although deserts are generally empty places, they are criss-crossed these days by roads, railways and pipelines; elsewhere there are the traces of trails used by nomadic tribesmen on their migrations. Despite these signs of human life, travelling in the desert can be extremely dangerous. Special Forces troops are taught never to underestimate the ferocity of the climate or the harshness of the terrain. Even though civilization can be seen on the horizon, distances in the desert are much greater than they appear to the untrained eye. The low levels of moisture in the air increase the brightness of the sun offering amazing visibility. The hot air plays tricks, magnifying faraway objects or creating mirages. Non-existent seas, lakes, mountains and hills can be seen in the distance. These should be ignored at all times as they have often led unsuspecting travellers to venture further into the desert and get hopelessly lost.

Men are taught to avoid the midday sun, travelling as much as possible in the evening or at night. They should avoid travelling on foot across soft sand or rough surfaces as this is very tiring. Extra care must be taken when crossing rocky or mountainous terrain as a badly twisted ankle in the desert can be a death sentence. And in a sandstorm, seek shelter in the lee of a hill and do not attempt to move on until it has blown over.

At night the sky is usually clear, so it is easy to navigate by the stars. During the day, you should navigate by compass. How-ever, in some deserts there are piles of magnetic rock that can cause considerable inaccuracy in compass readings, so it is important to fix your position relative to landmarks to prevent walking in circles. However, sandstorms can alter the features in the desert considerably. If a sandstorm seems imminent, troopers are told to fix a course and stick to it.

Clothing and Equipment

During desert training, instructors make sure that the trooper's entire body, especially the head, is covered to protect it against sunburn, sunstroke, insects and sand. Desert camouflage is worn at all times, with the sleeves rolled down and the legs covered. Clothing should be as loose as possible so it traps a layer of insulating air. This way sweating cools you more efficiently.

Instructors insist that the neck is covered at all time. SAS men wear the *keffiyeh* or *shemagh* – the traditional Arab headdress – which they picked up in the Second World War as the best way to protect your head and neck from the sun. Exposed areas of the face are covered with camouflage cream, and sunglasses or goggles should be worn to protect your eyes from the glare. If none are available, tie a strip of clothe or bark with a narrow slit cut in it across your eyes, and smear soot beneath the eye to protect them from the sun reflecting from your cheek bones. Troopers are also told only to remove their boots and socks in the shade. Burnt feet can put you out of action for some time and leave you in a potentially life-threatening situation.

Shelter

The importance of shelter is impressed on all troopers during desert training. Pile up rocks to make a windbreak and exploit any other natural feature that might provide some useful shade. If making a shelter out of fabric, leave the bottom raised during the day to allow air to circulate; at night weigh it down with stones. Avoid lying directly on the hot ground. If you can construct some sort raised platform, the air will circulate under you.

At night, you may need a fire for warmth and for boiling water. Be careful as smoke can be seen a long way away across the desert, though it can be used for signalling. Desert scrub burns easily, so do sun-dried donkey and camel droppings. Otherwise, mix petrol, oil and sand in a container and set fire to it. With the same mixture and a string to use as a wick, you can make a primitive lamp.

When making a shelter, it should be done in the early morning, late evening or at night if the moon is bright enough. Working in the cooler air then will help conserve energy. Despite the dangers of the desert, at the end of the Desert Survival course, all Special Forces troopers will be equipped to survive there, no matter how difficult the going gets.

18

INSERTION AND EXTRACTION

Unlike conventional soldiers, the Special Forces are not concerned with taking or holding land. Their job is to get in and out as quickly and efficiently as possible, inflicting the maximum damage to the enemy along the way. A variety of methods are used.

In the run-up to the First Gulf War, a joint UK–US Special Forces task force was formed to capture an Iraqi SAM missile and its launcher so that its capabilities could be assessed. The Coalition planners needed to know how much of a threat it posed to our planes. For maximum surprise, they took Egyptian helicopters of Soviet design and painted them in Iraqi colours. These were used to fly in the Special Forces, who were dropped almost on top of their objective, seized the SAM and its launcher, and flew it back to Coalition lines. The ruse was so successful that the rumour spread that that an Iraqi helicopter squadron had defected.

Vehicles – UK

Types of Vehicle

During the Second World War, the SAS perfected the art of fast land-vehicle insertion, using the US-made Willys jeeps made available under the Lend-Lease Act. Today the Mobility

Troop attached to each Sabre squadron uses a variety of vehicles, the SAS "Pink Panther" or "Pinkie" being the best known. This is a Land Rover, painted pink as desert camouflage, after an old aircraft, shot down during the Second World War and burnished pink by the sand, was found in the middle of the desert.

The Land Rover has been in use by the SAS since it first came into being in 1948. It is a tough and reliable vehicle, which can carry a good payload and is adaptable to most terrain, though in reality is most likely to be used in the desert or on open grassland. In the First Gulf War, the Regiment used the standard Land Rover 110, modified with extra stowage and weapons mounts, including smoke dischargers mounted on the front and rear bumpers. Carrying a crew of three, they were armed with GPMGs, heavy machine guns, Stinger surface-to-air missiles and Milan anti-tank missiles. Some did not have the fixture to mount Milans, but the crews improvised one using wood and rope tied to the roll bar.

Land Rover now produce a Special Operations Vehicle (SOV), based on the 110 used by the SAS, and retaining many of its special features and modifications. This is a special version of the standard army Land Rover with an extended wheel base and greater load-carrying capacity. These SOVs are usually festooned with machine guns and other weapons, including the M2 machine gun, a .50 cal heavy machine gun which will penetrate soft-skinned vehicles and even light armour, and a Mark 19 Grenade Launcher that fires a 40-mm grenade at a high rate and has a devastating effect on enemy troops. A 7.62-mm General Purpose Machine Gun fitted to the vehicle commander's station on the passenger side can be quickly removed for dismounted use and a Milan anti-tank missile launcher has the capability to take out everything from tanks to bunkers. The Milan uses an infra-red sensor unit which can be detached and used for surveillance.

Aside from mounted weapons, the SOV also carries BAR anti-tank mines, used to secure routes into laying up positions (LUPs), LAW anti-tank rockets, 81-mm mortars and Stinger anti-aircraft weapons. They usually have their head and brake lights disconnected to avoid accidental illumination at night. Smoke canister launchers fitted to the front and rear of the wagons can be fired to obscure the vehicle in the event of a contact. The SAS Land Rover 110s can be transported into combat two at a time by Chinook helicopters and four at a time by C130 Hercules transport planes.

Also in use is the four-by-four Cobra Light Strike Vehicle (LSV). A three-man dune buggy, the LSV is designed for recce and air-drop situations. To save weight, the Cobra is made up of a high-tensile tubular steel frame and is powered by a 1.9-litre diesel engine. Two separate radiators keep the engine cool in the most extreme of climates. The full roll-over cage can mount a .30- and .50-cal pair of machine guns, 40-mm grenade launcher, a 30-mm ASP-30 cannon or six Milan anti-tank missiles. Though a simple design, it has a low thermal signature and can be air-dropped by nearly any aircraft, including helicopters, so it is perfect for rapid airborne insertion. Longline LSVs were taken to Iraq in 1991, although the SAS found they were unsuitable for the rough terrain in Western Iraq. They could not carry a large enough payload for long-range operations, so were relegated to reconnaissance along border areas. However, the tried-and-tested long-wheelbase Land Rover soldiered on. Despite its lack of sophistication, the Land Rover has shown that it is one of the few vehicles that can cope with the vast distances involved and carry all the kit needed. It can also be relied upon to keep going and is easily maintained in even the harshest conditions.

Other vehicles used by the SAS Mobility Troops include KTM 350 and Honda 250 motorcycles. Although the KTM is a purpose-build cross-country bike, the Honda is preferred as it is very quiet. They also use the Mercedes-Benz Unimog U1100, a cut-down army truck that acts as a mothership on operations, carrying extra fuel, water and ammunition. Unimogs are often armed with GPMGs, M2 .50-cal machine guns or Mk-19 grenade launchers, although they are not generally used in offensive operations. For greater protection, Unimogs will tend to travel in the middle of SAS columns.

Vehicle Courses and Tactics

At their headquarters in Hereford the SAS run courses on vehicle insertion which include crossing rivers, tackling inclines, winching vehicles out of soft ground or over obstacles, and getting a heavily laden vehicles over all kinds of terrain. Modern-day SAS troopers have access to electronic navigation aaids such as GPS, but they are taught more basic skills such as map reading and navigating by the stars over a featureless terrain to fall back on.

Courses for members of Mobility Troop include several weeks with the Royal Electrical and Mechanical Engineers (REME) learning basic mechanical fault finding and training in cross-country conditions, so they can keep their vehicles working even deep behind enemy lines. Logistics is another important consideration. On long missions behind enemy lines and away from supply, SAS men must master the rationing of fuel, ammunitions and other stores. Patrol leaders become adept at assessing their fuel requirements and payload priorities, along with mission planning and communications.

Contact drills, scouting and other vehicle tactics are taught, as well as the use of heavy support weapons. An SAS fighting column of eight vehicles can, when properly deployed, attack with the firepower and effect of a much larger unit. Heavy weapons such as mortars, anti-tank missiles, heavy machine guns and grenade launchers can be brought to bear on the enemy while other elements push forward. They are taught to fire heavy weapons from the vehicles or dismounted.

Vehicles – US

Because of the Green Berets' experience in Vietnam they were used to airborne insertion by helicopter, while the US Navy SEALs naturally specialized in insertion by sea. However, after the catastrophic failure of Operation Eagle Claw, the US Special Forces had a rethink about insertion. They began to accept that it needed a dedicated covert-operations road vehicle and the Fast Attack Vehicle, or FAV was born. Now redesignated as the Desert Patrol Vehicle, or DPV, it is a high-speed, lightly-armoured vehicle something like the dune buggy that first saw combat during the First Gulf War in 1991. Due to their speed and off-road mobility, the DPVs were used extensively during Operation Desert Storm. The first American forces to enter Kuwait City were US Navy SEALs in DPVs.

However, the DPV is currently operated only by SEAL Team 3, the unit assigned to the Middle East.

The Desert Patrol Vehicle was built by Chenowth Racing Products of El Cajon, California. Powered by a 200 hp VW engine and carrying a payload of 1,500 lb, it is capable of accelerating from nought to 30 miles an hour in just four seconds. The DPV can travel at speeds up to 80 miles an hour. With its standard 21-gallon fuel tank, it has a range of some 210 miles and with an optional fuel bladder its range can be extended to over 1,000 miles.

The original tests used Chenowth commercial dune buggies modified to carry weapons such as TOW missiles and recoilless rifles. However, the recoilless rifles still had enough recoil to overturn the light dune buggies. The TOW missile launchers worked better, but DPVs could not carry the three men the US Army insists are needed to fire a TOW. Nevertheless, Chenowth delivered 120 two-man FAVs to the Army in 1981, along with light off-road motorbikes.

The basic weapons on a DPV consist of a heavy .50-cal M2 Browning machine gun, two lighter 7.62-mm M60 machine guns, and two AT4 anti-armour rocket launchers. In some cases, the driver's M60 or the gunner's M2 is replaced with a 40-mm Mk-19 grenade launcher.

When FAVs were replaced by High Mobility Multipurpose Wheeled Vehicles – HMMWVs or Humvees – in general military use, the remaining FAVs were transferred to Special Forces. However, they have now been largely replaced by the Light Strike Vehicle. The Special Operation Groups adopted the LSV for its small size and high mobility. It is used for fast hit-and-run style raids, scouting missions, Special Forces support and low-intensity guerrilla warfare. The current generation model is the ALSV, with the "A" standing for "advanced".

Like the DPV, the LSV looks like a dune buggy with a low bonnet, giving the crew little protection from small-arms fire; the engine is also uncovered. However, it can be air transported inside CH-47 or CH-53 transport helicopters. A 7.62-mm machine gun, usually an M60E3, is mounted on the back with a gunner's seat that can spin around 360 over the driver and passenger seat in front below. Two AT4s are sometimes fitted forward-facing on rollover cage bars, one on each side, above the driver. If TOW is mounted, it replaces the passenger seat and rollover cage.

Until the First Gulf War, the US Rangers were the only American Special Forces unit to make use of infiltration by land. In Arctic areas they used Snowcats, motorized sledges, skis and snowshoes. Elsewhere, until recently they have been using Ford M151 Military Utility Tactical Truck, the successor to the Korean War M38 and M38A1 jeeps. The MUTT was developed with guidance from the US Army's Ordnance Truck Automotive Command. Although it looks much like its predecessors, has the same basic layout and roughly the same dimensions, and provides space for four men, including the driver and some equipment, the M151 was actually a completely new design, using a monocoque instead of a steel frame. This gives better ground clearance, while lowering the centre of gravity, making it more stable. Also it is a little longer, wider and roomier than previous jeeps while keeping the same light weight.

Another new departure was the independent suspension with coil springs all around, making the M151 capable of high-speed, cross-country travel. And as the M151 did not need to be designed in such a hurry as the wartime original, technicians took their time to engineer it so that all maintenance and basic repairs could be done with a minimal tool kit under field conditions. It was said that you could fix anything on the MUTT with a Phillips and a straight screwdriver, a half-inch wrench and some wire.

First put into service in Vietnam, the MUTT played an active part in American military operations well into the late 1999s, when it began to be phased out in favour of the Humvee. Nevertheless the M151 had some distinct advantages over its much larger and heavier successor, which made it attractive to Special Forces. It was small enough to fit inside a C-130 cargo plane or CH-53 heavy transport helicopter.

Various models of the M151 have seen successful military service with fifteen NATO countries and M151s were sold to many countries, including Canada, Denmark, Lebanon, Israel, the Philippines and the UK. However, they were not sold for to civilians as the US Department of Defense deemed the M151 series unsafe for public highway use. Retired vehicles have been rendered unusable by destroying the body of the vehicle and selling off the parts.

The M998 Humvee that replaced the FAV and the MUTT is a military four-wheel-drive vehicle designed by AM General. It has also largely supplanted the M561 "Gama Goat", the M718A1 and M792 ambulance versions, the CUCV – Commercial Utility Cargo Vehicle – and other light trucks with the United States military. Humvees were originally also referred to as Hummers, though that term was later reserved for a civilian SUV – sports utility vehicle – based on the Humvee.

There are at least seventeen versions of the HMMWV in service with the US armed forces. They serve as cargo and troop carriers, automatic weapons platforms, ambulances, M220 TOW missile carriers, M119 howitzer movers, M1097 Avenger Pedestal Mounted Stinger platforms, MRQ-12 direct air support vehicles and S250 shelter carriers. The M1025 and M1043/ M1044 armament carriers provide mounting and firing capabilities for the Mk 19 grenade launcher, the M2 heavy machine gun, the M240G/B machine gun and M249 SAW. The new M1114 features a similar weapons mount but has more armour. In addition, some M1114, up-armoured M1116 and M1117 Armored Security Vehicle models feature a CROWS (common remotely operated weapon station), which allows the gunner to operate the weapon from inside the vehicle. Its excellent ground clearance makes the standard model capable of fording 2.5 feet, or 5 feet with a deep-water fording kit installed. Optional equipment includes a winch with a maximum load capacity of 6,000 lb.

AM General got the contract to deliver 55,000 Humvees in 1985, the first seeing combat in the invasion of Panama in 1989. They also saw service in the 2003 invasion of Iraq.

The Humvee was designed primarily for personnel and light-cargo transport behind front lines. Like the jeep, the basic Humvee has no armour or protection against NBC threats, but even so, losses were relatively low in conventional operations, such as Desert Storm. Vehicles and crews suffered considerable damage and losses during the battle for Mogadishu due to the nature of the urban engagement. Nevertheless, the majority of the crews returned safely, though Humvees were never designed to offer protection against intense small-arms fire, much less machine guns and rocket-propelled grenades.

After Somalia, the military recognized a need for a more protected Humvee and developed the M1114, an armoured Humvee to withstand small-arms fire. The M1114 has been in limited production since 1996 and had seen restricted use in the Balkans before deployment to the Middle East. This design is superior to the M998 with a larger, more powerful turbo-charged engine, air conditioning and a strengthened suspension system. It boasts a fully armoured passenger area protected by hardened steel and bullet-proof glass. With the increase in direct attacks and guerrilla warfare in Iraq, AM General has diverted the majority of its manufacturing power to producing these vehicles.

Thanks to the changing situation in Iraq, "up-armour" kits were designed and installed on the old M998 Humvees. These kits include armoured doors with bullet-proof glass, side and rear armour plates, and a ballistic windshield, all of which offer greater protection from ballistic threats and simple improvised explosive devices, or IEDs. American forces in Iraq also improvised their own "hillbilly armour" in an attempt to improve the protection offered by the Humvee.

Land Insertion

During the First Gulf War the UK and US methods of land insertion were put to the test. The SAS road-watch patrols, keeping an eye on the main thoroughfares, failed and had to be withdrawn. However their fighting columns of 12 or more vehicles were more successful. The heavily armed Land Rovers carried 1.5 tons of supplies and were accompanied by motor-cycle scouts. They patrolled an area from Karbala, 50 miles south-west of Baghdad to Iraq's border with Jordan and Syria. Although they stayed as far from Iraqi units as possible, they had the strength to defend themselves without the need to call in Coalition air strikes. However, frequent contact left them low on ammunition and fuel, and they had to be resupplied by a convoy of ten 4-ton trucks, escorted by armed Land Rovers from B Squadron. This convoy penetrated 90 miles inside the borders of Iraq to establish a supply base. The SAS's prime objective was to locate the surface-to-surface missile sites that were raining down Scud missiles on Israel, in an attempt to draw her into the war. They then called in air strikes to destroy them. The SAS patrols also destroyed targets of opportunity including microwave repeater stations, observation towers and fibre-optic cables.

The US Delta Force were tasked with a similar mission to the north of the SAS. However the short range of the FAVs – just 250 miles – meant they were restricted to short, penetrating raids rather than long-range operations. Both missions were successful, but Delta had to rely on resupply from the air and the operations would have been severely comprised if the Coalition had not establish total air superiority early on.

The SAS are now replacing the Land Rover Defender 110 series with Supacat HMT 400 or MWMIK – Mobility Weapons Mounted Installation Kit – for its main patrol and strike vehicle. The HMT 400 is made by Devonport, a subsidiary of the UK defence contractor Babcock. The Supacat has a chassis and wheelbase closer to a truck, and has better armour, better off-road mobility and greater load-carrying ability than the Land Rover 110. Its ability to carry more stores enables SAS long-range patrols to operate for longer with fewer, risky resupply operations. Despite its greater bulk, the Supacat is as agile as the Land Rover with a top speed of 80 miles an hour.

Like the Land Rover 110s, the SAS Supacat can carry combinations of M2 .50-cal machine guns, Mk-19 or HK Grenade Machine Gun 40-mm grenade launchers, GPMGs and Javelin anti-tank missiles. There are smoke-grenade dispensers on the front and rear of the Supacat that can be fired to create a smoke screen. For deployment by air, Supacat HMT 400 can also be transported in RAF Chinooks and C130 Hercules cargo planes.

Alongside the new MWMIK is the HMT 600, a six-wheeled truck which has many common parts to the HMT 400. The HMT 600 fulfils the role of a "mother" vehicle, a role previous performed by cut-down army trucks such as the Unimog. The HMT 600 would be loaded with spare ammo, fuel and water, and travel with a fighting column of SAS HMT 400s. Sharing common parts would simplify the logistics of such operations.

Water-borne Insertion

UK Craft and Methods

The SAS have used canoes for water-borne insertion since their inception and often work alongside the Royal Marines Special Boat Service that also does some of its training at the SAS headquarters in Hereford. The SAS also has a specialized Boat Troop whose training concentrates on all water insertion methods. These include diving, swimming, canoeing and even padding ashore on a surf board. Several operations have been jointly carried out using the SBS using water insertion.

As well as crossing-training with the SBS, the SAS Boat Troop also train alongside the US Navy SEALs, practising the retaking of an ocean oil platform, planting explosives on a ship, underwater insertion via submarine, patrolling inland canals or the capture of a ship or tanker.

When using water-borne insertion, the SAS usually use Rigid Raider assault boats, piloted by the members of the Royal Marines 539 Assault Squadron. These boats are the same boats used by the SBS. They come in 5.2-, 6.5- and 8-metre versions. Their hulls are made out of tough glass-reinforced plastic that make them ideal for beach assaults. Usually, each sixteen-man Boat Troop will be carried in three Rigid Raiders with one standing offshore to provided covering fire if the landing teams run into enemy resistance.

Powered by single or twin 140-horsepower outboard motors or, in the latest version, an inboard diesel, Rigid Raiders have a top speed of 35 knots. Their low profile and quiet engines make them perfect for raids on hostile shores. They were used in the raid on Port Stanley in the Falklands War and, despite being damaged by heavy fire, managed to stay afloat and reach safety. They also use Gemini inflatables as a Special Forces raiding craft, which can have up to a twin 250-horsepower diesel inboard.

Wooden-frame Klepper folding kayaks have been with the SAS since the 1950s and have been used when the noise of a motorboat might give the raiders away. The two-man canoe was used for Special Forces reconnaissance of Pebble Island on the Falklands, before the raid. A reconnaissance team from D

Squadron's Boat Troop was dropped by Sea King helicopter on 10 May 1982, then crossed the headland carrying their bergens and canoes before paddling over to the island under the cover of darkness.

UK Special Forces also have a submersible recovery craft. This is an inflatable that can submerge and insert a diving team under the waves. It can then be left concealed on the bottom ready for the team's exfiltration after the mission is completed.

US Craft and Methods

The US Naval Special Warfare Command has fourteen Patrol Coastal Cylone-class ships. These are primarily used for coastal patrols and interdiction of enemy vessels, but they are also used for Special Warfare support and their crews are trained to carry out escort duties, monitoring and detection operations, non-combatant evacuation and foreign internal defence. Their missions also include intelligence collection, drug interceptions, tactical swimmer operations and SEAL insertions and extractions. Their armament includes a Mark 25 rapid-fire gun, a Mark 96 25-mm rapid-fire gun, a Stinger station and four pintles carrying a combination of .50-cal machine guns, M60 machine guns and Mark 19 grenade launchers. They carry a Mark 52 Mod 0 chaff decoy launching system.

A number of these PC vessels have had a 9-foot hull extension added to allow them to launch 11-metre Rigid Inflatable Boats and SEAL Delivery vehicles. PCs usually operate as a two-boat detachment, backed up by a Mobile Support Team.

While the PC is a fully functioning ship displacing 328.5 tons with a range of 3,000 nautical miles, American Special Forces also use fast 81-foot Mark V Special Operations Craft that displace just 57 tons. Propelled by two 2,285 horsepower diesels and two Kamewa waterjets, they have a top speed of 57 knots – almost twice that of a PC. Their primary task is the medium-range insertion and extraction of SEAL teams. They also have a Stinger station and five pintles carrying a combination of .50-cal machine guns, M60 machine guns and Mark 19 grenade launchers. There is also provision for a GAU-17 mini-gun, Mark 95 twin .50-cal machine gun and a Mark 38 chain gun.

Mk-V SOCs usually operate in a two-craft detachment with a Mobile Support Team to provide technical assistance and maintenance during the mission. The typical mission has a twelve-hour turnaround, but they are essentially tasked for twenty-four. They are deployed by USAF C-5s and crews are trained to be in theatre within forty-eight hours of notification.

SEALs are also trained to operate from 32-foot River Patrol Boats, first used for insertion and extraction in Vietnam. Heavily armed and armoured, they draw just two feet and can operated in shallow, debris-filled water. For river and harbour work, Special Forces have the Mini-Armoured Troop Carrier. A 36-foot flat-bottomed boat and powered by two 283 horsepower diesels and two Jacuzzi water jet pumps, it has a top speed of 25 knots and beaches easily. It has a large well for transporting troops and a hydraulic bow ramp to make insertion and extraction easy. The craft is very quiet, particularly when idling and has a low silhouette which makes it difficult to detect at speed.

SEALs also deploy from Light Patrol Boats of the Boston Whaler type, with no armour. They are powered by duel outboard motors and are highly manoeuvrable, can run at a cruise speed of 25 knots for eight hours carrying .50-cal heavy machine guns or 7.62-mm machine guns, and draw just 18 inches. They can be transported under a helicopter or in a Hercules. These large boats are under the command of the Special Boat Units, which are manned by specially trained naval personal for the specific task of providing small-craft support for the Special Forces.

Rigid Inflatable Boats are high-buoyancy, high-speed craft designed for the insertion and extraction of SEALs on enemy beaches even in extreme weather conditions. The hull is made of glass-reinforced plastic with an inflatable gunwale made of reinforced nylon fabric. The 24-foot version carries a crew of three- and a four-man SEAL team. The 30-foot RIB carries an eight-man squad, along with the three-man crew. Lightly loaded it can work in sea state six – that is, with waves up to 18 feet high – and winds of 45 knots. For other than heavy weather coxswain training, however, operations are limited to sea state five with waves below 12 feet and winds of 34 knots or less. It can travel 200 nautical miles at 32 knots and can be transported by a C-130.

A new Naval Special Warfare RIB has now been deployed with a 36-foot Kevlar deep-vee hull with inflatable sponsons. They are designed for infiltration, extraction, night-time surveillance and resupplying Special Forces. With twin Kamewa WaterJets, it can reach speeds of over 40 knots in sea state three, where the waves are under 1.25 yards. The fuel capacity of 180 gallons gives it a round-trip endurance of more than 300 nautical miles at 30 knots.

For clandestine operations involving a lightly armed force, Combat Rubber Raiding Craft are used to land or recover Special Forces from over the horizon. Carrying a maximum of eight people, it is 15 feet 5 inches long, 6 feet 3 inches in the beam and draw two feet of water. The 35 to 55 horsepower engine gives it a top speed of 18 knots.

CRRCs can be dropped from an aircraft or helicopter, or launched from a ship or landing craft. It can also be deck-launched from a submarine on the surface, or "locked-out" from one while submerged. The low visual and electronic signature makes it ideal for covert operations and it can easily be hidden by its crew once ashore.

SEALs also use an inflatable and a speed boat for a technique of rapid insertion for beach reconnaissance. It has traditionally been part of the SEALs' role to check out beaches before the landings of a large amphibious force. The speed boat travels at about 18 knots parallel to the shoreline with an inflatable alongside, on the opposite side from the beach. Each man then roles in rapid succession from the speedboat into the inflatable, then on into the water. This way a six-man team can be dropped at 25-yard intervals in just twenty seconds. The men tread water and at a pre-arranged signal from their leaders swim towards the beach, taking care not to break the surface with their fins. They count their kicks as a measure of distance. Along the way, they take note of the depth of the water, details of the bottom, the current, how violent the surf pounds the beach and any potential hazards.

Near the beach, each man swims 10 or 12 yards along the shore, noting what he can see inland, before turning out to sea again, counting his kicks. When he has kick as many times as he did on the way in, he will stop. The speedboat returns at around 15 knots, the SEAL in the water raises his arms and kicks hard to lift himself high in the water. Another SEAL on board the inflatable lassoes him with a rubber hoop before hauling him on board. This technique is only used for beach reconnaissance. If the team has other tasks, other methods of insertion are used as the rapid roll-off spreads the men dangerously thin, making mutual defence difficult if they are discovered.

The SEAL Delivery Vehicle is a "wet" submersible designed to carry combat swimmers and their equipment to their targets. Crew and passengers wear wetsuits and breathing apparatus. It is powered by an electric motor connected to silver-zinc batteries and steered with planes and rudder. The electronics displaying speed, distance, heading and depth provided by a Doppler navigation sonar are kept in dry watertight compartments.

The SDV and or CRRC can be launched from a submerged submarine using a Dry Deck Shelter (DDS). This is 40 feet long and has three separate compartments. The first is the hangar where the craft is stowed. The second is a sealed transfer trunk to allow the crew and passengers to move between the submarine to the SDV or CRRC. The third is a hyperbaric decompression chamber. While the mission is being prepared the hangar is kept dry; when everything is ready, the chamber is flooded. Once the water pressure reaches that of the water outside, the door is opened for the vehicle to launch. On its return, the craft enters the hangar, the door is closed, the water is pumped out and the occupants make their way to the decompression chamber for the bodies to acclimatize to the pressure inside the submarine itself. The DDS weighs 65,000 lb and has to be delivered by transport plane.

There is now an Advanced SEAL Delivery System that can take a SEAL squad from a ship or submarine to its objective in the dry. This permits insertion from a longer range and allows the SEALs to carry more equipment. The submersible displaces 60 long (Imperial) tons with a beam of 6.75 feet, a height of 8.25 feet and an overall length of 65.2 feet; it is driven by a 62-horsepower electric motor.

The captain is a submariner, but has a SEAL co-pilot who is responsible for the co-ordination of the mission, planning and the deployment of the Special Operations unit. While the submariner is in charge of controlling the craft, the ballast and trim, and the navigations and steering, the co-pilot's responsibilities include life support, the lock-in and lock-out systems, and the sensor systems, as well as communications.

Airborne Insertion

Parachute

All Special Forces troops are trained parachutists as using airborne insertion is the easiest way to get men behind enemy lines. Britain's SAS have recently begun to train in the US as the Regiment found that RAF pilots at Brize Norton in Oxford-shire had little operational experience. In a leaked email the SAS said that they "had had enough of asking for the course to be updated to prepare troopers more realistically for the hard business of jumping from 25,000 feet at night, with large operational loads, onto dark and unmarked drop zones".

In the US, standard "static line" airborne training takes three weeks. During the first week men are taught parachute landings. Learning to land properly is, of course, the most vital part of airborne insertion – it is no good getting a man to the drop zone only to have him injured once he hits the ground. The men are taught the proper position for landing – elbows tucked in, chin on chest, legs together, feet flat on the floor and knees bent. They practise the parachute roll on mats, rolling to the left, right and forward. This is leavened by lectures on the theory of parachute aerodynamics, flight techniques and the types of aircraft from which the men are going to jump.

Next they are taught flight drills. After leaving the plane, the men are trained to look upwards to check that their parachute has opened and the canopy is fully deployed. They learn the procedure to untangle twisted rig lines.

In the second week they are introduced to mock-ups of the Hercules transport aircraft they are going to jump from and practise checking their equipment, hooking up their chutes and exit drills. Then they progress to the exit trainer which is 75-foot tower. The men wear a harness that is attached to a wire, which allows them to descend as if making a real jump. This gives the men the feel of what it would be like to make a jump and gives the instructors a chance to iron out any problems the students have in landing.

The men are also introduced to their equipment – the Irwin PX1 main chute and the PR1 reserve which are strapped to the man's chest. The man's bergen is strapped below the reserve chute. During the descent it is released and hangs on a 40-foot line that is secured to the man's webbing by two hooks. As, in action, the packed bergen will weigh at least 40 lb, and is not carried on the back during the descent as the extra weight would greatly increase the chances of being injured on landing. At the end of a line, the bergen hits the ground first, harmlessly, and helps anchor the parachutist if there is a strong side-wind. The parachutist is also relieved of the weight of his weapon which is carried in a sleeve at the side of the bergen. The men also familiarize themselves with the lifejacket which they will wear if they are jumping into or near a stretch of water.

The men make their first jump in the third week by which time they are fully familiar with the procedure. Some twenty minutes into the flight, they are given the order to check their kit. They stand up and check their own reserve parachute, then check the main parachute of the man in front.

The next command is "action stations". The men file down towards the two doors – one on either side – at the back of the plane and hook the ripcord from their main parachute to a line. When the plane is over the drop zone, the light above each door changes from red to green and the instructors yell: "Go! Go! Go!" and the men throw themselves out of the door one after another, forming two "sticks" in the air. The static line should pull out the parachute which opens above the man's head. He looks up, as he has been trained, and checks the canopy. If any of the lines are twisted, he untangles them as he has been taught. If that fails, he jettisons his main chute and pulls the ripcord on the reserve manually.

The first jumps are made from the safe height of 1,000 feet, so there is plenty of time to adopt the emergency procedure if needs be. In operations, Special Forces soldiers will jump from as low as 400 feet. The second jump is with the bergen.

During training, the men make seven more jumps, each one more like the experience they are going to have in action. They are briefed on the height of the jump, wind speed and direction, visibility, weather conditions, the exact time they are going to leave the plane and rallying points after they are on the ground.

The last training jump is done in full kit at night, which is the one the men fear most – when you can't see, you might land in power lines or in water. The bigger men fear this most as their landing is a lot heavier. Sprained ankles, broken legs and damaged knees and backs are common. Broken bones usually occur when the parachutist lands with his legs apart; other leg injuries occur when rookies get their rig lines twisted and attempt to untangle them by flailing their legs around.

Problems in the air are rare these days. Canopies used to be made of silk and when they got wet they would not open, leaving the parachutist to "Roman candle" to a certain death. These days there is still a danger of men colliding in the air and getting their parachutes tangled, which usually means certain death for both of them. And when one parachutist gets under another, his canopy "steals" the air from the top one, making the upper canopy collapse. However, the SAS has only had one fatality in parachute training. Even so, big men get the jitters, but in the end they go through with it. Their fear of what their mates are going to think of them if they bottle out overcomes any fear of making the jump itself.

And that is only the initial training for the SAS. When they are deployed to units they are trained to jump from heights of over 36,000 feet in what is called a HALO – high altitude, low opening – insertion. This was developed in 1963 by James W. Hauck who was part of a joint US Army–US Air Force programme developing specialist techniques for use by the US Special Forces. The programme was known as TAC TEST 63-18 and involved fourteen parachutists – nine Army, five USAF – and various support personnel at the Tatu Drop Zone, El Centro Naval Air Station, El Centro, California. During the programme sixteen jumps were made from a USAF Hercules C-130-B at altitudes of from 20,000 feet to 43,500 feet, establishing a world record. Previously, the world record had been held by nine men from the Soviet Union who had jumped from 38,000 feet.

On 16 December 1963 sealed barographs supplied by technicians from Edwards Air Force Base were carried aloft by the aircraft and individual jumpers. After the jump the barographs were read and averaged together to establish the exit altitude of 43,500 feet. These jumps were not without their dangers. An hour before take-off, the 14 jumpers and flight crew started breathing oxygen to rid their bodies of nitrogen. Even with this precaution several jumpers suffered the bends. Frostbite affected several people as the outside air temperature with windchill was close to 125 degrees below zero. All the participants in these jumps were awarded the Distinguished Flying Cross.

HALO is favoured by the Special Forces. Men jump from the back ramp of a C-130 Hercules, flying at a height where it is almost invisible to the naked eye and out of range to hand-held SAM systems. The team free-fall, sticking close together, which gives a considerable advantage especially when jumping at night. They descend to the chute height relatively fast. Parachutes are normally deployed automatically at 2,500 feet, giving the paratrooper a chance to use his reserve parachute should his main parachute fail.

There are other dangers. Parachutists can suffer barometric trauma caused by the low pressure at great heights or stress-induced hyperventilation. Plummeting at 120 miles an hour, they suffer the effects of wind-chill; ice forms on their altimeters and goggles. When they pull in a hand to try and rub it off, they can lose their free-fall symmetry and go into an uncontrollable spin, which can prove fatal. The free-fall lasts just two minutes with the parachutist falling about 200 feet per second. To minimize the speed, the parachutist lies flat, maximizing the area of resistance. The legs are bent slightly to give stability and subtle movements of the hands allow the parachutist to steer by adjusting the airflow. To move laterally, the parachutist moves one hand in towards his head, moving the leg on the same side in towards the centreline of the body. Decreasing the drag on that side of the body moves it in that direction.

However, any violent break from symmetry – if the jumper tries to wipe ice from his goggles, say – will send him into a spin. It is possible to recover, but only if there is enough height above the ground. The jumper must pull his arms into his sides as the drag on his feet will turn him head down. This will stop the spin, he can put out his arms and resume the flat free-fall position. However, this head-down will also greatly increase his speed, which could prove fatal if he is too near the ground.

Special Forces also use another form of parachute insertion known as HAHO – high altitude, high opening. Men are dropped from a transport aircraft at 32,000 feet or above. After free-falling for eight to ten seconds, they open their parachutes at around 28,000 feet. Instead of using a standard PX1 parachute, they carry a GQ 360, nine-cell flat ramair canopy that has the aerodynamic properties of an aircraft wing. Usually, when dropped from around 32,000 feet, a parachutist would spend about ten minutes in the air and land around three miles from the release point. With a HAHO jump using a GQ 360, the paratrooper would be in the air up to eighty minutes and land as much as fifteen miles from the release point. This has obvious advantages. The transport aircraft does not have to overfly a hostile country – instead it can drop a Special Forces team outside its borders and allow them to paraglide into enemy territory. The GQ 360 is fully steerable, allowing the team to stay together; for shorter distances, the parachutist steers in a circle so he spirals down his glide-path. The GQ 360 can also be made to stall, making landings safer.

To make a turn, the parachutist simply pulls down on the steering toggle on the side which he wants to turn. This pulls the back of the canopy on that side down, increasing air resistance. Pulling the toggle all the way down to the waist makes the tightest possible turn. But for the best possible glide ratio – that is, the distance travelled for the height lost – he must leave the toggles in their uppermost position, allowing the air to flow unhindered under the canopy.

Then, as with a static-line jump, the parachutist drops his equipment on a line when he is several hundred feet from the ground. As he nears the ground, he pulls down hard on both steering toggles. This impedes the airflow and slows the forward motion. A skilled parachutist can reduce this to walking speed for a smooth landing. However, as with an aircraft, if you cut forward speed, you also lose lift, so if the parachutist applies the brakes too soon, the rate at which he drops will increase and he will suffer a hard landing.

As with HALO jumpers, the parachutist must wear oxygen equipment to breathe at high altitudes and a helmet with an altimeter built into the headset. However, parachutes, by their very nature, are vulnerable to wind and can drift off-course, so the parachutist has a GPS strapped to his chest so that he can compensate by adjusting his glide-path.

Men are also in danger of frostbite. At 32,000 feet the temperature can be as low as –50° Fahrenheit.

Getting the team to stick together in close formation has its own attendant dangers – men can easily collide, which may prove fatal to both parties. Some parachutes have panels covered in luminous material to increase their visibility, particularly at night. Nevertheless, mid-air collisions are a constant danger.

Helicopters

However, the most common method of insertion used by the Special Forces these days is by helicopter. Even the SAS finally succumbed and has its own dedicated flight of the Army Air Corps flying Chinooks fitted with airborne refuelling probes for long-range insertion.

In Vietnam, American Special Forces developed a number of techniques for heliborne insertion and extraction from jungle clearings too small for a helicopter to set down in. Two were particularly successful and are now used as standard methods of insertion and extraction in places where a helicopter cannot put down, such as the side of a mountain, a treetop, a small boat or a narrow city street. In both, the trooper wears a harness similar to the ones used with a parachute. This is either worn into action or carried in a rucksack – or, in extremis, one can be improvised using rope.

The Green Berets developed STABO – Stabilized, Tactical, Airborne Body Operations. Men are winched out of or up to the helicopter. Each man has his own rope and, when dropped as a team, they link arms and hook their ankles around one another. For additional control a safety rope links them around the waist to stop them drifting apart if they lose their grip with their arms and legs – it would be very dangerous if they swung about independently, crashing into one another. Once they are all line up, there is a tendency for the bunch to spin, But this can be countered by the end man in the line putting his arm out.

The Navy SEALs have developed a similar method called SPIE – Special Procedures Insertion/Extraction – which uses a single rope with the men hooked one above another down it. A harness clip simply attaches to a metal ring spliced into the rope. It makes the helicopter more difficult to control, but it has other advantages. There is no danger of the men getting separated or colliding, the men's arms are free so they can fire their weapons and an injured or unconscious man can be hooked to a SPIE line and snatched to safety.

In both cases the helicopter pilot must be sure that the men on the end of the line are clear of the jungle or other obstruction before moving forward.

A Chinook can also be used to deliver an inflatable within range of its objective. The inflatable is widely used as a method of insertion if water is involved because, with an outboard motor muffled by rubber insulation, it is fairly quiet and can reach speeds of up to 20 knots. However, inflatables tend to have a range limited to no more that 25 to 35 nautical miles – that is, 29 to 40 land miles. A Chinook is used to move the inflatable forward because it is powerful enough not to be troubled by shipping a little water. If it dips into the water it can take on a thousand gallons and still take off. What's more, the cockpit area is raised so there is no danger of it flooding.

There is plenty of room inside to carry the boat fully inflated. As the Chinook hovers over the drop point, the Special Forces team clamber aboard the inflatable, the rear ramp is lowered and the helicopter crew pushes the inflatable out. At this point, the men on the inflatable get very wet and the rotor whips up spray. But in no time they have the outdoor going and are on their way to the shore while the Chinook makes off back to base.

At a prearranged time, the Special Forces team on board the inflatable and the Chinook return for the extraction. The helicopter descends up wind of the dingy. The rear ramp is lowered and the aircrew throw out the end of the winch cable which the dingy team attach to the bow of the inflatable. The winch then hauls the dingy up the ramp into the belly of the Chinook. With the ramp closed, the Special Forces men grab for any handhold as the Chinook raises its tail to give it forward speed, while water cascades through drainage holes in the fuselage.

The Skyhook or Fulton STAR

The most dangerous method of extraction is the Skyhook or
Fulton STAR – the Surface to Air Recovery system developed
by Robert Edison Fulton Jr in the 1950s which was designed to
pick up operatives behind enemy lines in areas too remote for
even STOL aircraft. First the recovery aircraft airdrops a
package weighing 400 lb to the man on the ground waiting
to be extracted. It contains a balloon, a helium tank to inflate it,
a suit-cum-harness and a 500-foot rope. The whole thing is in a
buoyant container in case it has to be dropped at sea. The agent
awaiting extraction dons the suit, inflates the balloon, attaches
one end of the line to the suit, the other to the balloon, and lets it
go. He then waits for the pick-up aircraft to return with the line
tethered to the balloon rising 500 feet above him.

On the nose of the recovery aircraft there are two booms in a
forward-facing V-shape, which aim to catch the rope below the
balloon. There are also wires running from the nose to the wing
tips to keep the rope away from the propellers and leading edge
of the wing should they miss. The rope is marked by coloured
ribbon to make it more visible; at night a rope with a string of
flashing lights along its length is used. If the rope is caught, it
slides down to the point of the V, where it is locked.

The man on the ground is jolted into the air with tremendous
force. For the first hundred feet he travels vertically reducing
the danger of hitting trees or other obstacles, while the balloon,
connected to the line by breakaway cords, is snapped free by the
stress. The first part of the lift, though rapid, is smooth and a lot
of the force is taken up in the stretch of the rope. When that is
exhausted, the man being recovered feels a tremendous jolt. As
the plane speeds up the line runs back below the belly of the
aircraft and a grapple is dropped from the back of the plane to
pick up the rope. This is hauled in and attached to a winch,
which drags the man into the fuselage. The whole process takes
about four minutes.

The idea of the Skyhook developed during the Second World
War, when agents often had to be rescued from behind enemy
lines. Experiments were made using a modified version of a mail
pick-up system invented by Lytle S. Brown during the 1920s
and perfected before Pearl Harbor by All American Aviation.

The All American system used two steel poles, set 54 feet apart, with a line slung between them attached to a mail pouch. An aircraft approached the ground station in a gentle glide of 90 mph, while a flight mechanic paid out a 50-foot steel cable. As the aircraft pulled up, a four-finger grapple at the end of the cable grabbed the transfer line;shock absorbers cushioned the impact. Finally, the flight mechanic winched the mail pouch onto the plane.

In July 1943, the need to rescue airmen from difficult terrain led to tests of this system by the US Army Air Force, but initial results, using containers full of instruments, were not promising. The acceleration of over Gs following the pick-up was far more than the human body could tolerate, but modifications to the transfer line and parachute harness brought this down to a more acceptable seven Gs. The first live test, using a sheep, failed when the harness twisted and strangled the animal; on subsequent tests other sheep fared better.

Lieutenant Alex Doster, a paratrooper, volunteered to be the first human pick-up on 5 September 1943. A Stinson aircraft engaged the transfer rope at 125 mph, Doster was yanked vertically off the ground, soared off behind the aircraft and it took less than three minutes to retrieve him.

The USAAF continued to improve the system, even developing a package containing telescoping poles, transfer line and harness that could be dropped by air. The first operational use of the system was in February 1944, when a C-47 snagged a glider in a remote location in Burma and returned it to India. However, whereas the USAAF never used the system to pick up individuals, the British did use it to retrieve agents.

During the Korean war, the CIA took another look at the All American system in the spring and summer of 1952, when they were trying to establish a resistance network in Manchuria. It was easy enough to drop parachutists into Manchuria and it seemed that the All American system was the way to bring them out. In the autumn of 1952, Civil Aviation Transport pilots in Japan made a number of static pick-ups, then successfully retrieved mechanic Ronald E. Lewis.

On the evening of 29 November 1952, a CAT C-47 with CIA officers Richard G. Fecteau and John T. Downey left Seoul for Manchuria, intending to extract members of a team that had been inserted the previous July using the All American system, but a double agent had betrayed the team. The Chinese shot down the C-47 as it came in for the pick-up, killing the pilots and capturing the CIA officers. Fecteau was not released until December 1971; Downey was freed in March 1973.

However, adventurer and amateur inventor, Robert Edison Fulton Jr had seen a demonstration of the All American system in England after the Second World War and believed he could do better. He had achieved some measure of fame in the 1930s by travelling from London to New York by motorcycle, visiting 32 countries and covering 40,000 miles in 17 months. After Fulton, in 1939, had developed an aerial gunnery trainer that used film to simulate aerial combat, in May 1942, Commander Luis de Florez of the Special Devices Division of the Navy ordered 500 trainers at a cost of $6 million and they became the Navy's primary method of teaching air-to-air marksmanship.

Meanwhile, at same the time as Fulton saw the All American system, he was busy trying to develop a flying automobile. He built and tested eight versions of the Airphibian, but he ran out of money before he could go into production.

While flight-testing the Airphibian, Fulton had often wondered what might happen if he had been forced down in inaccessible terrain as helicopters had only a limited range and he began work on the All American system.

In 1950, he began experimenting using a weather balloon, nylon line and 10- to 15-lb weights. After making a successful pick-up at last, he got his son to film the operation and took it to his old friend, now Admiral de Florez, who had become the first director of technical research at the CIA. Believing that the project could best be handled by the military, de Florez put Fulton in touch with the Office of Naval Research. Thanks to de Florez's recommendation, Fulton received a development contract from ONR's Air Programs Division.

Based at El Centro, California, Fulton conducted numerous flights over the desert, using a US Navy Lockheed P2V Neptune to make the pick-ups. He gradually increased the weight of the object he was picking up until the line began to break. In the end, a braided nylon line with a test strength of 4,000 lb solved the problem, but more trials had to go into perfecting the locking device, or sky anchor, that secured the line to the aircraft.

By 1958, the Fulton aerial retrieval system, or Skyhook, had taken its final shape. A package that could easily be dropped from an aircraft contained the necessary ground equipment for a pick-up. It featured a harness for the person or cargo attached to a 500-foot, high-strength, braided nylon line, with a portable helium bottle to inflate the dirigible-shaped balloon, which raised the line to its full height.

The pick-up aircraft sported two tubular steel "horns" protruding from its nose, 30-feet long and spread at a 70-degree angle. The aircraft would fly into the line, aiming at a bright plastic marker placed 425 feet from the bottom of the rope. As the line was caught between the forks on the nose of the aircraft, the balloon was released at the same time as the spring-loaded trigger mechanism – or sky anchor – secured the line to the aircraft. As the line streamlined under the fuselage, it was snared by the pick-up crew, using a J-hook. It was then attached to a powered winch and pulled on board.

Fulton first tested his invention on dummies filled with instruments. He next used a pig, as pigs have nervous systems close to humans. Lifted off the ground, the pig began to spin as it flew through the air at 125 mph. It arrived on board un-damaged but in a disoriented state, and once recovered, it attacked the crew.

The first human pick-up using Fulton's STAR took place on 12 August 1958, when Staff Sergeant Levi W. Woods of the US Marine Corps was winched on board the P2V. Because of the geometry involved, the person being picked up experienced less of a shock than during a parachute opening. After the initial contact, which was described by one individual as similar to "a kick in the pants", the person rose vertically at a slow rate to about 100 feet, then began to streamline behind the aircraft. Extension of arms and legs prevented the oscillation that plagued the pig as the individual was winched on board. The process took about six minutes.

The US government considered using the Skyhook to rescue the Dali Lama from Chinese-occupied Tibet in 1959, but he was extracted by yak instead.

In August 1960, Captain Edward A. Rodgers, commander of

the Naval Air Development Unit, flew a Skyhook-equipped P2V to Point Barrow, Alaska, to conduct pick-up tests under the direction of Dr Max Brewer, head of the Navy's Arctic Research Laboratory. With Fulton on board to monitor the equipment, the P2V picked up mail from Floating Ice Island T-3, retrieved artefacts, including mastodon tusks, from an archaeological party on the tundra and secured geological samples from Peters Lake Camp. The high point of the trials came when the P2V dropped a rescue package near the icebreaker USS *Burton Island*. Retrieved by a ship's boat, the package was brought on deck, the balloon inflated, and the pick-up accomplished.

In 1961 a CIA plane was fitted with the Skyhook to rescue downed Air America pilot Allen L. Pope from Indonesia, but the mission was scrubbed. Then in 1962 came Project Coldfeet – reconnaissance of an abandoned Soviet ice station on the polar icecap, which would be the first use of Skyhook to pick up a man in a real operation. In May 1961, a US Navy plane flying an aeromagnetic survey over the Arctic Ocean reported sighting an abandoned Soviet drift station. A few days later, the Soviets announced they had been forced to leave Station NP 9 when the ice runway used to supply it had cracked.

The prospect of examining an abandoned Soviet ice station attracted ONR's interest. Having set up an acoustical surveillance network on a US drift station the year before, which they used to monitor Soviet submarines, ONR wanted to know whether the Soviets had a similar system to keep track of American submarines as they moved through the polar ice pack.

The problem was how to get to NP 9 as it was far too deep into the ice pack to be reached by an icebreaker and it was out of helicopter range. Captain John Cadwalader, who would command Operation Coldfeet, saw that this was "a wonderful opportunity" to make use of Fulton's pick-up system. The idea was to drop a team of investigators by parachute then extract then by Skyhook. The mission was scheduled for September, a time of good weather and with ample daylight. NP 9 would be within 600 miles of the US Air Force base at Thule, Greenland, the planned launching point for the operation.

ONR selected two highly qualified investigators for the job: Major James Smith, of the US Air Force, an experienced parachutist and Russian linguist who had served on US Drift

Stations Alpha and Charlie, and Lieutenant Leonard A. LeSchack, of the US Navy Reserve, a former Antarctic geophysicist, who had set up the surveillance system on T-3 in 1960. Although not jump qualified, LeShack quickly went through the course at Lakehurst Naval Air Station. During the summer, the two men trained on the Fulton retrieval system, working in Maryland with an experienced P2V crew at the Naval Air Test Center, Patuxent River.

Meanwhile, ONR's scheme was running into difficulty at the highest levels of the Navy, where sceptics argued that the plan would never work and would probably cost the lives of the investigators. When it was eventually approved, it was late September when the darkness of the Arctic winter was already closing in.

There was also trouble with the equipment which was sent to Eglin Air Force Base for testing in the cold chamber and problems developed with the gear at very low temperature. These took several weeks to correct. All the while, NP 9 kept moving farther away from Thule.

Then in March 1962, the mission planners received the unexpected news that the Soviets had also abandoned ice Station NP 8 in haste after a pressure ridge destroyed its ice runway. was Apart from being a more up-to-date facility than NP 9, at 83N 135W, it also was in a more accessible position, and after the Canadian government agreed to the American use of the Royal Canadian Air Force base at Resolute Bay, 600 miles from NP 8, Project Coldfeet got under way.

In mid-April, the P2V and a C-130 support aircraft from Squadron VX-6 left Patuxent River for Resolute Bay via Fort Churchill. Captain Cadwalader, the project's commander, had hoped that the Hydrographic Office's monthly ice reconnaissance flight that flew between Thule and Point Barrow would provide an up-to-date position on NP 8. However, due to bad weather and a navigational error there was no sighting. With the last known position only a month old and given the general dependability of the Hydrographic Office's drift predictions, Cadwalader expected no difficulty in finding the target. A C-130 carrying the drop party would be sent to locate NP 8, while the P2V would be standing by in case an immediate extraction was necessary.

The hunt for NP 8 began in perfect weather. The C-130

flew to the station's last known position and began a box search at 10-mile intervals, but they saw nothing except ice. The next day, the C-130 started searching at five-mile intervals and spotted the abandoned US Ice Station Charlie but not NP 8. Four more searches failed to reveal the elusive, drifting Soviet station. With the flight time available for the C-130 running out and the weather deteriorating, Cadwalader called off the operation.

The expedition had no sooner returned to the US when the monthly ice reconnaissance flight on 4 May spotted NP 8 well to the east of its predicted position. ONR remained convinced that Coldfeet could work, but its funding for the project had run out, so they turned to the Intelligence Community in the hope that they might be persuaded to support the operation.

By coincidence, Fulton had been working with the CIA on the further development of Skyhook since the autumn of 1961. Intermountain Aviation, a CIA front at Marana, Arizona, that specialized in aerial-delivery techniques, had equipped a B-17 with Fulton's gear in October. Over the next six months, Intermountain's veteran CIA-contract pilots Connie W. Seigrist and Douglas Price flew numerous practice missions to perfect the equipment needed to infiltrate and extract agents. They conducted demonstrations for the Forest Service and Air Force while training for the covert operation to extract fellow CIA-contract pilot Allen Pope from an Indonesian prison that was later aborted.

Fulton then approached Intermountain about participating in Coldfeet. Garfield M. Thorsrud, head of the outfit, liked the idea. After $30,000 was made available by the Defense Intelligence Agency, Coldfeet was ready to resume, with Intermountain furnishing the Skyhook-equipped B-17 and a C-46 support aircraft for the project.

On 26 May, the B-17 and C-46 flew to Point Barrow in Alaska which had been selected to replace Resolute Bay to avoid any delays caused by obtaining the necessary diplomatic clearance from the Canadian Government. Carrying William Jordan, an experienced Pan American Airways polar navigator who had been hired by Intermountain, the B-17 began the search for NP 8 the following day.

Seigrist and Price flew a northerly heading at 8,000 feet for almost four hours until they reached the ice station's predicted position. They then descended to 1,500 feet and initiated a square search pattern. The visibility was poor.

"A forbidding dusky grey," Siegrist reported. "It was the most desolate, inhospitable looking and uninviting place I had ever seen."

NP 8 never appeared, and the B-17 returned to Point Barrow after more than thirteen hours in the air.

On 28 May, assisted by a P2V from Patrol Squadron One at Kodiak, the B-17 located NP 8. Seigrist circled the station while Major Smith and pick-up co-ordinator John D. Wall selected a drop point. Drift streamers were drop to determine the wind, then Smith left the aircraft through a "Joe hole", followed by LeSchack. After dropping supplies to the men and receiving a favourable report from Smith over his UHF hand-held radio, the B-17 departed.

Smith and LeSchack were to have seventy-two hours to explore the Soviet base. Meanwhile, Intermountain mechanics Leo Turk and Carson Gerken installed the pick-up booms on the nose of the B-17, and Seigrist and Price tested the equipment on 30 May by making a practice pick-up in front of the Arctic Research Laboratory at Point Barrow.

The next day the mission to retrieve Smith and LeSchack got under way. In addition to pilots Seigrist and Price, the B-17 carried navigator Jordan, co-ordinator Wall, jumpmaster Miles L. Johnson, winch operator Jerrold B. Daniels, nose-trigger operator Randolph Scott, and tail-position operator Robert H. Nicol. Cadwalader, Fulton and Thorsrud also climbed aboard to observe the operation.

The weather, Seigrist and Price soon learned, had deteriorated since their last trip over the frozen sea – warmer temperatures had heated the ice mass, causing dense fog. The B-17 could not find the weather station once more and again returned to Point Barrow.

After a second fruitless search on 1 June, Thorsrud asked Cadwalader to call out the P2V. The next morning, it took off from Point Barrow two and a half hours before the B-17. Using its more sophisticated navigational equipment, it quickly located NP 8, then guided the B-17 in using UHF/DF steers. Conditions for the pick-up were marginal at best. The ice had a grey hue, it was difficult to make out a horizon and the surface wind was blowing at 30 knots, nearing the limits of Skyhook's capability. Nevertheless they decided to have a go. The first pick-up was to be 150 lb of exposed film, documents and equipment samples. However, once the balloon was inflated Smith and LeSchack had a hard job keeping hold of the canvas bag containing the cargo, to stop it blowing away.

As Seigrist lined up for the pick-up, the horizon disappeared. It was, he said, like "flying in a void". The pick-up line and its bright orange mylar marker, however, provided sufficient visual clues to enable Seigrist to keep his wings level. He flew into the line, made a good contact, then immediately went over to instrument flying to avoid vertigo. Winch-operator Daniels brought the cargo on board without difficulty.

As prearranged, Price, a former Navy pilot, now took over the left seat to make the pick-up of LeSchack. The wind was blowing stronger and Smith had to struggle to hold LeSchack from being blown away. As the rising balloon caught the wind, LeSchack slipped from Smith's grasp, pitched forward on his stomach and began to drag across the ice. After 300 feet, his progress was stopped by an ice block. As he lay on the ice and tried to catch his breath, the B-17 hooked into the line and he was away.

Smith watched as LeSchack rose slowly into the air, then disappeared into the low cloud. Although LeSchack rode through the air facing forward, he managed to turn around and assume the correct position before being hauled, successfully, on board the B-17. Price and Seigrist again changed seats so that Seigrist could make the final pick-up.

Smith held on to a tractor as he inflated his balloon. Even so, he started to be dragged across the ice until he managed to catch a crack with his heels. He lay on his back as Seigrist approached the line.

"The line made contact on the outer portion of the left horn," Seigrist said. "It just hung there for what to me was an eternity."

Slowly, the line slid down the horn and into the catching mechanism. As the line streamed along the bottom of fuselage, assistant jumpmaster Johnson reached down through the "Joe hole" and placed a clamp on it. He then signalled nose-trigger operator Scott to release the line. Next, tail-position operator Nicol secured the line, Johnson released his clamp, and winch-operator Daniels quickly brought Smith on board. Inside he received a warm welcome from Fulton, Cadwalader, and Thorsrud – and a medicinal dose of Scotch.

Operation Coldfeet produced intelligence "of very great value", Cadwalader reported. ONR learned that the Soviet station was configured to permit extended periods of silent operation, confirming the importance that the Soviets attached to acoustical work. In addition, equipment and documents obtained from NP 8 showed that Soviet research in polar meteorology and oceanography was superior to US efforts.

Beyond that, Cadwalader wrote, perhaps the greatest accomplishment of Coldfeet "was to prove the practicality of paradrop and aerotriever recovery to conduct investigations in otherwise inaccessible areas". Certainly, Coldfeet had been an outstanding operational success; the recovery of Smith and LeSchack had been especially challenging. As Admiral Coates wrote to Thorsrud, the pick-up had been conducted "under stronger winds and lower visibility than had previously been attempted; nonetheless, through the exceptional skill of pilots and the coordination and efficiency of the crew, all pickups were made without a hitch, and in the best time (6½ minutes) yet achieved".

While the Skyhook system provided an important asset for all manner of intelligence operations, its utility as a long-range pick-up system was somewhat undermined during the 1960s by the development of an aerial refuelling capability for helicopters. Still, it appears likely that Fulton's Skyhook did find employment in a number of specialized clandestine operations following Coldfeet, although its subsequent use by the CIA and the Special Forces remains shrouded in secrecy.

However, the Skyhook itself became unclassified and became the subject of articles in *Popular Mechanics*, *Time* and other magazines. A set of public demonstrations took place at Fort Bragg in 1964 in which no less than thirty-five soldiers were carried aloft over the span of a day, including at least two generals. Many report that it was an enjoyable ride. It was later seen in action in the films the *Green Berets* and the James Bond movie *Thunderball*.

The Army experimented with the contraption on the CV-2 Caribou aircraft and the US Navy tested the system on modified S-2A Tracker aircraft in the 1960s for use in pilot recovery at sea. It was used by the US Air Force on at least fifty modified HC/MC-130 aircraft from 1965. Although it was deployed in Vietnam it was never successfully used to recover downed pilots.

When a practice recovery during a 1982 exercise in West Germany ended in death, a chest-mounted parachute was added to the rig so in an emergency the person being recovered could parachute to the ground. But it is generally considered so dangerous that it is only to be used in an emergency, training taking place using practice weights instead of actual personnel.

19

SABOTAGE AND DEMOLITION

Special Forces troops are the masters of sabotage and demolitions. When the SAS was started by David Stirling, its first missions were the sabotage of enemy airfields, supply routes, and fuel and ammunition dumps in North Africa. On 21 December 1941, a five-man patrol under the command of Lieutenant Bill Fraser was dropped off by a Long Range Desert Group unit 10 miles south of the Italian airbase at Agedabia. They marched through the night, each man carrying a revolver, a water bottle, eight Lewes bombs, a compass and rations comprising a tin of chocolate, cheese, raisins and broken biscuits. By dawn they had reached a lying-up position where they could observe the airfield throughout the following day. It was surrounded by wire and heavily guard. Nevertheless, when night fell, Fraser and his men succeeded in infiltrating the airfield, placed the Lewes bombs with delayed-action fuses high up on the wings of the aircraft there and withdrew unseen. When the bombs went off, they destroyed thirty-seven Italian CR42 fighter-bombers. In the confusion, the patrol made their way back to the pick-up point without loss, but sadly two men were killed by friendly fire when two Blenheims strafed the LRDG vehicle carrying them back to their base at Jab Oasis.

As the war moved on to Italy and France, the SAS perfected the art of infiltrating enemy installations, setting explosives to go off some time after they had left, before escaping unmolested. Often a number of explosives in different locations were set to go off at the same time to cause maximum confusion.

During the Borneo campaign, SAS patrols made covert infiltrations into Indonesia to sabotage enemy camps and supply routes there, but both sides suppressed news about them, fearing the adverse effect on international opinion. There were plans to infiltrate men into Argentina from Chile during the Falklands War to attack the airbases there, but these were abandoned for fear of drawing other South American nations into war.

Special Forces are trained to sabotage major strategic targets, such as the enemy's means of delivering nuclear missiles. They also aim to attack command, control, intelligence and communications centres, along with major supply routes by blowing up raid junctions, bridges and dams. However, Special Forces are only deployed when the same job cannot be done from the air because of the presence of civilians, the small size of the target or heavy air defences.

Operational Procedures

Once infiltrated, teams are often given multiple missions. The "Bravo Two Zero" SAS mission during the First Gulf War was expected to gather intelligence as well. Along with two other Special Forces teams, they were to report on traffic along main supply routes and the movements of Scud-missile launchers, as well as destroying the telephone lines between Saddam Hussein's command centre in Baghdad and his Scud launch teams in western Iraq that were threatening Israel. Overland telephone lines and radio masts had already been taken out by Coalition aircraft. Saddam's only remaining means of communication with the Scuds were underground landlines, which "Bravo Two Zero" were supposed to find and cut. Simply blowing up the landline in one place would not be effective as a single break could be mended easily. So the SAS men laid a series of charges alongside the cable primed to go off at different times over a couple of days. Each was protected by a booby trap in case an Iraqi soldier discovered it.

Special Forces troops are taught that simply making a big bang is not enough – a smaller charge can cause more damage if placed in a vulnerable place. Enemy aircraft, for example, can be effectively put out of action by relatively small charges placed in their engines, in their air intakes or under their nose cones. The SAS in North Africa discovered that, while a slab of explosive might destroy a single aircraft, an entire squadron could be knocked out by placing smaller charges in the cockpit, or on the wing or undercarriage.

There are other considerations. SAS men in Iraq were to take out Scud missile launchers as a target of opportunity. The "Bravo Two Zero" team pored over detailed plans of Scud missiles and their launchers. They had to be careful not to blow up the missile's warhead that could be filled with lethal biological, chemical or nuclear agents. Instead, they decided to use explosives to destroy the control centre at the heart of the Scud-missile launcher.

In the run-up to a war, sabotage teams are sometimes sent into a country in plain clothes and unarmed, singly or in small groups. They then gather at a safe house where they are armed and equipped ready to undertake acts of sabotage once the war starts. Special Forces sometimes familiarize themselves with potential targets prior to a war. During the Cold War, the *Spetsnaz* – Soviet Special Forces – regularly toured the West as sports teams or other seemingly innocent organizations. Then, on their way between fixtures, they would detour via sensitive installations, building up a comprehensive picture of the enemy's defences and other vulnerable points should war ever break out.

Use of Explosives

Special Forces troopers are trained to use explosives not just for sabotage. Jungle units use them to blow holes in the jungle canopy so that injured men can be winched to safety by a helicopter or, where the forest is not so thick, used them to clear a landing zone. One of the things SAS men learn early on in their Continuation Training is placing a charge to make a tree fall in a certain direction.

While all Special Forces soldiers are taught the use of explosives, a number will go on to be trained as specialists. As well as being taught by their own Regimental experts, SAS men are also trained by instructors from Royal Engineers EOD (Explosive Ordnance Device) Teams and the Royal Logistics Corps. They are taught to use both military ordnance as well as improvised devices.

First they are taught the proper handling of explosive materials. This is not difficult as most commercially manufactured explosives are practically inert in normal conditions. PE4, the explosives carried by the SAS during the First Gulf War, is so inert that, even if you set it alight, it will simply burn like a candle. You can mould it with your hands, jump up and down on it, and hit it with a hammer – it will still not explode without a detonator.

The detonator or blasting cap embedded in the explosive causes a shock wave that sets off the primary charge. Sometimes even this is not enough to cause an explosion. To set off the main charge you have to make a hole in it and fill it with a more volatile explosive called a primer. When the detonator goes off, it sets off the primer which, in turn, sets off the main charge.

The blasting cap itself is a thin aluminium tube closed at one end and pushed into the main charge. It is packed with a main output explosive that sets off the main charge. Behind that is an initiator explosive which is trigger by an electric current or a pyrotechnic fuse.

The simplest form of pyrotechnic fuse available is the safety fuse which is a flexible fibre cord encasing a core of gunpowder. The whole thing is then wrapped in a waterproof casing. Once lit is burns at a rate of about a foot a minute. It is usually coloured black to distinguish it from detonating cord which is brightly coloured or transparent. This has a high-explosive core wrapped in six layers of material which explodes rather than burns with a speed of around 25,000 feet a second. This speed allows several charges to be set off more or less simultaneously, even though they are at a distance. As the detonating cord is an explosive, it too must be set off by a blasting cap initiated by a safety fuse or an electric current.

Alternatively, electric wires can be run directly to an electric blasting cap in the main charge. When an electric charge is applied to the wires, a current passes through a thin piece of wire joining them in the detonator. This heats up and ignites the initiator explosive, setting off a chain reaction.

The SAS have always preferred setting charges with a pre-set timing device, which started with Jock Lewes' invention of the Lewes bomb, set off by a pencil detonator, back in 1941. With the same dimensions as a pencil, the pencil timer was a tube of aluminium – or brass in early versions – with a copper section at one end containing a glass phial of a green corrosive liquid called cupric chloride which corrodes iron at a relatively steady rate. Underneath the vial is a spring-loaded striker under tension, held back by a thin steel wire.

To set the device the copper tube is crushed, breaking the vial inside. As the liquid begins to attack the steel wire, the safety pin holding back the striker is removed. The other end of the pencil is then attached to the end of the detonator or safety fuse by a spring snout And the saboteur beats a hasty retreat.

When the cupric chloride has eaten through the steel wire, the striker is released. The spring fires it down the inside of the pencil until it hits a percussion cap at the end which sets off the detonator, or lights the safety fuse. Unfortunately, Lewes bombs were notoriously unreliable and terrorists have recently improved on the concept with the "condom fuse". A condom filled with acid and the open end tied off is surrounded with volatile material and placed next to the explosive. When the acid has slowly burnt its way through the rubber of the condom, it ignites the volatile material and sets off the explosive.

Special Forces have traditionally avoided electrical fuses because it is difficult to keep them dry and unscathed in the adverse conditions SF troops are expected to work under. Any break in a wire or short circuit renders them useless. At the very least there has to be a back-up and on Special Forces missions men are usually concerned about how much weight they are going to be carrying. Electrical detonation circuits are also susceptible to so-called "random frequency hazard", when radio transmissions picked up in the wires detonate the charge prematurely. However, a new generation of electronic fuses have now proved themselves in use. Timers can be set accurately for up to nine-ninety years and can also be activated at a distance by a radio signal. Terrorists have recently perfected this by linking a detonator to a mobile phone, then ringing the number.

Troopers are taught various formulas for working out how much explosive is needed. They are also taught methods of placing and shaping the charge so that the force of the explosion is channelled into the target, rather than away. A rectangular slab of explosive, for example, may not have much effect on a flat wall of reinforced concrete or steel. But if it is stretched out into a long line known as a "ribbon charge" it might easily crack the concrete or cut through a steel beam.

Shaping charges different ways directs the shockwaves, producing different effects. A "saddle charge" produces a cross fracture , while a "diamond charge" cuts at right angles to the explosive. Indeed, a properly shaped diamond charge will deliver the same explosive effect as a solid slab of explosive five times more massive. One of the most effective shapes is when the explosive it fashioned into a "beehive". The shock waves are then focused and punch a deep hole in the material against which it is placed. Counter-forces can be harnesses by placing one charge on either side of an object and detonating them both together with devastating effect on its internal structure.

A two-to-one charge – that is, one twice as thick as it is wide – will send the shock waves down into the target for their maximum destructive effect. It is also important where the detonator is placed as the explosion starts at the detonator and spreads out through the material, producing different patterns of shockwaves. If the detonator is placed at the end of a flat slab of explosive, a lot of the force of the explosion will be lost sideways, but if the detonator is placed on top of the charge, again the shock waves go down into it.

Another especially destructive technique Special Forces troops are taught is to place two charges inside a building, with the larger main charge set to go off just before the smaller second one. The main charge should then be covered in petrol, coal dust or wheat flour. When the main charge goes off the air inside the building will be filled with an explosive mixture of petrol vapour, dust or powder that will be ignited by the secondary explosion.

Intelligence

Good intelligence is needed before a sabotage mission. On an airfield, it may be more effective to blow up a control tower or a fuel dump as attacking the planes themselves. Blowing out a section of railway track is rarely effective, unless a train is on it at the time. Rails can quickly be replaced by a track-laying crew.

Bridges are always a prime target. Again good intelligence is needed so that the structure of the bridge can be studied for weak points. However, if a bridge is on a main supply route, it may not be necessary to destroy it completely to be effective. If the structure is weakened sufficiently that it can no longer bear the weight of armoured vehicles or loaded trucks, the job is done.

It would be hard for a Special Forces demolition expert to carry enough explosives to cut through a bridge's load-bearing piers, but placing relatively small charges at the end of the central beam could easily do enough damage to collapse the roadway. The cables of a suspension bridge are vulnerable, as are the pylons, particularly near the top. The destruction of a couple of girders of a truss bridge is likely to weaken it sufficiently that it would collapse under a heavy load. Older masonry arch bridges are harder to knock down. Their massive piers and solid roadway are hard to destroy unless you can drill in the stone or brick-work to lay the charges – a procedure that would make too much noise to be envisaged on a covert operation.

Demolition experts are trained to study stereoscopic photographs to work out the weak points. They can then calculate how much explosive they are going to need to bar the enemy using the bridge. As apart of SAS training in demolition and sabotage, men make dummy attacks on power stations and nuclear facilities in the UK, and factories across Europe. These exercises also help those in charge of these installations to plan their defence.

Mines and Booby Traps

As part of their explosives trainings, Special Forces troopers must learn how to lay mines and set booby traps. They must also learn to do this with discrimination as civilians are just as vulnerable to being blown up by remote devices as enemy soldiers, and mines and booby traps often remain in place and dangerous long after the front has moved on or the fighting is over.

Still pressure mines such as the Russian PMN are buried along the route taken by regular patrols or are planted around the perimeter of the enemy's base. They detonate when someone steps on them, relying on the blast itself, along with bits of mine casing and earth carried with it to do the damage. Second World War blast mines became easily detectible due to their metal casing which could be picked up by a magnetic detector, so a plastic casing has now been substituted. Again it is detonated by pressure on a plate on the top surface of the mine. The mine contains a shaped charge designed to direct the shock wave directly upwards, straight through the victim's foot.

During the First Gulf War, the SAS carried Elsies – C3A Canadian minimum-metal anti-personnel mines – which can be laid with an easily detachable aluminium detector ring. Unlike other anti-personnel mines, the Elsie is designed primarily to injure its victims, rather than kill them. In situations where medical facilities are not readily available, a wounded man is more of a liability than a dead one. Whereas a fatality can easily be disposed of by burying the body, an injured man can knock out an entire unit as they try and take care of him, and carry him to seek medical help.

The American Claymore mine is a fragmentation device that fires shrapnel, in the form of steel balls, out to about a hundred yards, across a 60-degree arc in front of the device. It is used primarily in ambushes and as an anti-infiltration device against enemy infantry, but it is also of some use against soft-skinned vehicles. The Claymore can be detonated remotely, by a tripwire stretched out across a trail or by a timer fuse.

Bounding mines that are buried like normal blast mines, but are fitted with a lifting charge that throws the body of the mine out of the ground. When it reaches the optimal height – about three feet off the ground – the main charge blows, sending out steel balls over $360°$. Bounding mines may be triggered by direct pressure, a tripwire or remotely.

Special Forces are also taught the use of low – as opposed to high – explosives. These are incendiary devices that can be used against fuel depots, ammunition dumps and buildings that store flammable materials. They contain a chemical mixture that is easily ignited and hard to put out. Burning with an intense heat, they set fire to anything around them.

SAS troopers are issued with percussion detonators that can be used to fashion booby traps when screwed into an explosive charge. When a spring-loaded striker is tripped, it hits a percussion cap, the primer explodes and the resulting heat and pressure wave is used to detonate the main charge. Men are taught to fashion explosives in innocent-looking objects, such as a piece of wood, and lay multiple traps. An inexperience soldier, finding a booby trap, will get so intent on not setting it off and finding a way to disarm it that he will not be on the lookout for a second or third device.

A simpler booby trap can be made by attaching a tripwire to a standard-issue grenade. The SAS in Borneo and the Green Berets in Vietnam used punji pits – concealed holes lined with sharpened stakes. When an enemy fell into them, they would suffer a severe wound to the feet and legs. The stakes were usually smeared with excrement to ensure that the victim suffered blood poisoning. Again the aim was to injure a man rather than kill him, making him a burden to his unit. In Vietnam, the Viet Cong got wise to this ploy and dug punji pits of their own.

Other booby traps can be made from bamboo spikes attached to a frame that is set to spring from the foliage when released by a trip wire. Even a sharpened stake pointing backwards down a trail can impale a pursuing enemy.

PART THREE
EQUIPMENT

20

RIFLES AND SHOTGUNS

Introduction

Special Forces troopers must not only be trained to use the weapons of their own country and its allies, they must also train on the weapons of any enemy or potential enemy. Due to the constraints of weight, Special Forces troops often carry a very limited supply of ammunition. In a firefight, they might easily have to abandon their own weapon and grab that of the opposition.

Accuracy International 7.62-mm PM Sniper Rifle System

The Accuracy International PM – Precision Marksman – bolt-action sniper rifle replaced the L42 Enfield sniper rifle used by the British Army in the 1980s and was designated the L96A1. It is almost unique in being a purpose-designed sniper rifle, rather than an improved version of a general purpose gun.

Later, the Swedish Army were looking for a new rifle and took an upgraded version of the PM, now known as the AW or Arctic Warfare. This had special de-icing features allowing it to work at temperatures as low as –104° Fahrenheit. The stock, bolt, magazine release and trigger guard on the AW are large enough to be used with heavy Arctic mittens. In 1988, the

Swedes accepted the AW as the Psg 90. The rifle's reliability in adverse weather and the easy interchangeability of its parts has led to it being adopted by a number of other countries, including Australia, Belgium, Germany, Ireland, The Netherlands and Singapore. It is known for its accuracy, shooting less than 2-inch groups at arrange of up to 600 yards, using boat-tail match ammunition. Its maximum effective range with a Schmidt & Bender 6 x 42 scope is around 800 yards.

Instead of a wooden or polymer rifle stock, the AW has an aluminium chassis that runs the entire length of the stock. All other components are bolted directly to it, creating a sturdy yet comparatively light weapon. This modular design almost means that it can be serviced and repaired easily under field and combat conditions. The AW is usually equipped with an integrated bipod and has a monopod mounted on the butt stock.

Most Arctic Warfare rifles are chambered for the 7.62 x 51 mm NATO cartridge, but can also be fitted for other cartridges. In 1998, the German Army also adopted the folding-stock AW Super Magnum rifle chambered in .300 Winchester magnum (7.62 x 67 mm) with German-made Zeiss optics as the *Scharfschutzengewehre* – "sniper rifle" – G22. Super Magnum can also be chambered in .338 Lapua Magnum and 7-mm Remington Magnum.

Other models are Police (AWP), Folding (AWF) and Suppressed (AWS). There is also the AWS Covert, which is essentially an AWS with a folding stock. It comes in a small suitcase which houses the rifle with the stock folded and the barrel/suppressor combination detached. This is considerably smaller than any competing system, though its special barrel and integral suppressor keep the weapon's overall length within normal limits when deployed. It is notably used by the US 1st SOCOM Delta Force and British SAS.

Armalite 7.62-mm AR-10B Rifles

In 1995, former Army Ordnance officer Mark Westrom purchased Armalite and introduced a modern version of the AR-10, the assault rifle that had been superseded by the AR-15, better known by its US military designation, M-16. The new Armalite AR-10B was scaled up to take the 7.62 x 51-mm NATO round and various design improvements were made to strengthen the rifle. Individual sub-components of AR-10B were tested on a special lower receiver made of two slabs of aluminium fitted to a Knights Armament Company SR-25 upper receiver assembly. The AR-10B now comes in several versions including a carbine with collapsible stock, a target model, and one version chambered for a .300 Remington Short Action Ultra Magnum.

Armalon PR Series

The Armalon PR is a high-precision, magazine-fed, bolt-action rifle and is essentially a reworking of a Remington 700 series rifle. First produced in 1988 using 7.62-mm/.308-cal ammunition, the PR has been modified to use 5.56-mm/.223-cal and other ammunition.

The barrel is fluted, making the rifle lighter, better balanced and easier to carry and use. However, stiffness and the shot to shot consistency associated with the heavier profile barrels are maintained. The increased surface area produced by the deep flutes improves heat dissipation from the barrel, which allows performance to be maintained at higher rates of fire.

Light, easily detachable fabric bands are used to minimize mirage distortion by deflecting the heat rising from the barrel. They also reduce problems caused by steam from the barrel misting the optics when it is wet.

A muzzle brake reduces the recoil and muzzle deflection so the image of target through the scope is not lost between shots and the fall of shot remains visible. Since its launch, the Armalon PR has been consistently successful in competition.

Arms Tech Compak-16 5.56-mm Compact Assault Rifle

Arms Tech aimed to produce a compact version of the M-16 while avoiding the muzzle blast and firing signature that usually ensues. They took a standard M-16 lower receiver and added a modified upper receiver with a specially designed barrel shroud muzzle brake, reducing the firing rate to 600 rounds per minute. The standard stock was replaced by a sliding wire stock, and the carrying handle was replaced with a MIL-STD-1913 rail usually carrying an Occluded Eye Sight of South African design. The Compak-16 comes with either an integral or detachable silencer.

BAe Systems 5.56-mm
L85A1/L85A2 Individual Weapon

In the 1960s, the British Army began looking for a replacement for the old L1 SLR, a British-made version of the Belgian FN FAL. They came up with the SA80 – Small Arms for 1980s – which was adopted by the British Army as the L85A1.

Its bullpup design decreased the rifle's length compared with other ordinary automatic rifles, so it could be used when there was limited space areas such as in armoured personnel carriers.

The weapon is fed from the standard NATO (STANAG) 30-round magazines similar to that of an M-16, and fires at a rate of 650 rounds per minute. It is fitted with a multipurpose knife-bayonet.

The L85A1 has a main SUSAT – Sight Unit, Small Arms, Trilux – L9A1 optical sight, designed especially for 5.56 x 45 mm chambered firearms, which gives accurate fire at single shot out to 400 to 500 yards. It has 4x magnification and 10° sighting angle, and is mounted on a quickly-detachable mount. It acquitted itself well during Operation Desert Storm. However, troops found problems with maintenance and reliability in the field. In response the improved L85A2, which can carry a 40-mm under-barrel grenade launcher, was introduced in 1997. During 2000 to 2002, around 200,000 of existing 320,000 L85A1 were upgraded, but there are now plans to replace it with the Heckler & Koch G36 Automatic Rifle.

Barratt M82A1 Light Fifty

The Barrett M82A1 Light Fifty was the first large-calibre sniper rifle, and after a short time it gained worldwide popularity. It was the idea of 26-year-old American entrepreneur Ronnie Barrett who designed a semi-automatic rifle for the powerful .50 BMG ammunition originally developed for Browning M2HB heavy machine guns. His first working rifles were available in 1982, hence the designation M82. The .50 and the rifle's light weight, compared to the Browning, gave it its nickname, Light Fifty.

At first, no one saw the need for such a large-calibre rifle, until Barrett explained that, using a one-dollar round, his gun could destroy a million-dollar jet, helicopter or vehicle. In 1989, the Swedish Army bought a hundred M82A1s. Then the US Army, Air Force and Marine Corps began buying them for Operation Desert Shield and Desert Storm. They called it the SASR – "Special Applications Scoped Rifle". The long effective range – accurate to 1,000 yards – and high energy made it highly effective against tracks, parked aircraft and radar cabins. It was also used as an EOD (explosive ordnance disposal) tool. Potentially, the M82 can also be used against snipers or terrorists from stand-off range, or when targets are behind the cover.

The M82A2 bullpup version, designed to be fired from the shoulder as an anti-helicopter weapon, was developed in 1987, but was soon dropped from production. The latest in the M82 family is the M82A1M rifle, which has a full-length Picatinny rail allowing a huge variety of scopes and sighting devices to be mounted on the rifle. It has a rear monopod, lightened mechanism and a detachable bipod and muzzle brake, that reduces the recoil to that of a 12-gauge shotgun.

Beta Company C-MAG 5.56-mm 100-round Magazine

The C-MAG is a twin-drum, high-capacity ammunition magazine for rifles, light support weapons, firing port and other specialized weapons in 5.56-mm calibre. It can be used on almost any modern 5.56-mm combat rifle or other weapon without any modification to the weapon. The C-MAG loads and functions just like standard magazines, and can be reloaded and reused repeatedly without special tools or disassembly.

Colt 40-mm M203 Grenade Launcher

Colt's M203 Grenade Launcher is a lightweight, single-shot, breech-loaded 40-mm device to be attached under the barrel of the M4 Carbine and the M-16A2 Rifle. This creates a combination weapon system capable of firing both 5.56-mm rifle ammunition as well as the complete range of 40-mm high explosive and special-purpose ammunition – most commonly the M406 anti-personnel round, which has a lethal radius of five yards, and the M433 multi-purpose round which can also penetrate up to three inches of armour plate. Other types of ammunition available include buckshot, tear gas and various signal rounds.

A self-cocking firing mechanism, that includes barrel latch, trigger and safety lever, allows the M203 to be operated as a completely independent weapon. The barrel simply slides forward in the receiver to accept a round of ammunition and slides back to lock automatically in the closed position, ready to fire.

Diemaco C7 5.56-mm Light Support Weapon

The Canadians developed their own version of the M-16 assault rifle. Designated the C7, it was manufactured by Diemaco/Colt Canada, a subsidiary of Colt Firearms and became one of the weapons of choice of the UK Special Forces. Like earlier M-16s, it can be fired in either single-shot or automatic mode, instead of the burst function selected for the M-16A2. The C7 also has the structural strengthening, improved hand-guards and longer stock developed for the M-16A2.

A carbine version, the C8, was also developed along with the Light Support Weapon (LSW). It can only be fired on fully-automatic and features a heavy barrel suitable for sustained fire. The British SFW model, designated the L119A1, has a shorter 15.8-inch (401-mm) barrel, instead of the standard 20-inch version.

FAMAS G2 5.56-mm Assault Rifle

FAMAS stands for *Fusil d'Assaut de la Manufacture d'Armes de Saint-Étienne* or "Saint-Étienne arms factory assault rifle". Since 1978, it had been the standard assault rifle of the French Army; some 400,000 of the F1 version were produced. The manufacturers then replaced the F1 with the G1 that included several minor improvements such as redesigned grips and an enlarged trigger guard. This was updated to the G2 and was adopted by the French Navy in 1995, but the French Army has continued with the F1, which is now to be produced in a Félin version that integrates a video camera into its sights.

The FAMAS assault rifle has a bullpup configuration and fires in single-shot, three-shot-bursts or fully automatic mode. The original versions were designed to use the French-made 25-round magazines with the 5.56 x 45 mm NATO cartridge. These magazines were incompatible with standard NATO weaponry, and the G2 uses the STANAG magazine as used by most other NATO rifles, such as the M-16 and SA80. The FAMAS G2 weighs 8.38 lb. The G1 and G2 have a large, grip-length trigger guard like a Steyr AUG for ease of use when wearing gloves.

The FAMAS has seen action in Operation Desert Storm and various peacekeeping missions, and the French have found it reliable under combat conditions.

FN FAL

The *Fusil Automatique Léger* – Light Automatic Rifle – or FAL, was the standard 7.62 x 51 NATO self-loading, selective fire, magazine-fed rifle issued during the Cold War. It was produced by the Belgian armaments manufacturer Fabrique Nationale de Herstal (FN) and adopted by many NATO countries. It was also produced under licence in many of the adopting countries, who each gave it their own designation. Those produced in the UK, Canada and Australia were built to imperial measurements, while other versions were metric and sometimes the magazines are not interchangeable. The only countries still producing them are the US and Brazil.

While the FAL was produced in many versions with different barrel lengths, sights and furniture, there are four basic configurations: the simple FAL with a standard barrel and fixed butt stock; the FAL "Para" with a short barrel and folding skeleton butt; a second "Para" version with a standard-length barrel and a folding skeleton butt; and the FAL Hbar or FALO, a heavy barrelled model intended primarily as a light support weapon.

The barrel is equipped with a long flash hider which also serves as a rifle grenade launcher, though the design of the flash hider may differ slightly from country to country. The furniture can be made of metal, wood or plastic of various colours. Some models, such as the Brazilian LAR and Austrian Stg.58 were fitted with light bipods as standard. Almost all heavy barrel versions were also were fitted with bipods. Sights usually have a hooded front post and adjustable diopter at the rear. Almost all FAL rifles are equipped with sling swivels and fitted with bayonet lugs.

FNC 5.56-mm Assault Rifle

The Belgian company Fabrique Nationale began to develop the new assault rifle using the 5.56-mm NATO cartridge in the early 1970s. Its gas drive and rotating bolt resembles the AK-47, though other features have been borrowed from the M-16.

The FNC has of a four-position mode selector switch on the left side giving a safety mode, single shot, three-rounds bursts and full automatic fire. The barrel is equipped with a flash hider which also serves as a rifle grenade launcher. It also has a flip-up, "L"-shaped rear diopter sight with two settings, for 250 and 400 yards range. Maximum range is 450 yards. It fires 700 rounds a minute from a 30-round NATO standard magazine.

The FNC has a side-folding butt stock, made of steel and covered by plastic. A solid, non-folding plastic butt is also available. The pistol handle and the fore end are made from plastic. It can be fitted with a special bayonet or an adapter for the US M7 knife-bayonet. It can also be fitted with 4x telescope sight, or various infra-red or night-vision sights.

Harris M-89 Multi-barrel Combo Sniper Rifle

The Harris M-89 is a popular replacement for the M24 in the hands of US snipers. It comes in a kit containing the weapon, a telescopic sight, a set of five barrels and bolts for use with the different calibres the M-89 may fire, and a set of magazines for each calibre, along with a set of tools appropriate to the task. Changing calibre can be accomplished in around two minutes.

Haskins M500 Sniper Rifle

The .50-cal Model 500 rifle was originally designed by the team lead by D. Haskins, then working at Research Armaments

Prototypes, a small company located in Jacksonville, Arkansas. Developed at the request of the US Armed forces during 1981–2, along with smaller Model 300 rifle, Model 500 was purchased by the US military around 1983 in small numbers. Some 125 rifles were initially delivered and saw service in Beirut, Grenada, Panama and Iraq. The Model 500 paved the way into military service for numerous other .50-cal anti-materiel rifles, such as various Barrett models. It can fire a .50-cal round as far as 1.2 miles and still hit a target the size of a garbage bin.

Heckler & Koch 5.56-mm G36 Assault Rifle

In the early 1990s, Heckler & Koch designed a new assault rifle for the German Army and for export. It came up with the G36 5.56-mm assault rifle, which was adopted by the *Bundeswehr* in 1995. The Spanish adopted the export version, the G36E, as their standard infantry rifle in 1999. The G36 was also taken up by various law-enforcement agencies worldwide, including the British police and some US police departments, and was incorporated into the US military Objective Individual Combat Weapon programme.

The G36 is a conventional gas-operated, selective-fire rifle, using an operating system similar to the older American Armalite AR-18 rifle. But the receiver and most of the external parts of the G36 are made from reinforced polymers, with steel inserts where necessary. A wide variety of firing mode combinations can be produced by installing the appropriate trigger unit. Standard options are single-shot, fully automatic fire, two- or three-round bursts in any combination.

The rifle is fed by 30-round box magazines, though a 100-round US Beta-C dual drum magazine can be used. A folding, skeleton butt stock is standard. It also comes with two scopes – a 3.5x telescope sight for accurate shooting at long range with, above it, a second 1x red-dot sight for fast target acquisition at short ranges. Both are built into the plastic carrying handle. The export versions are available with the single 1.5x telescope sight with open sights moulded into the top of the carrying handle. The sub-compact G36K Commando version has as integral Picatinny-type scope and accessory rail. The standard

G36s can be fitted with the HK AG36 40-mm under-barrel grenade launcher and a bayonet.

Heckler & Koch 5.56-mm HK53 Short Assault Rifle

The Heckler & Koch 53 is a scaled-down version of the HK33 assault rifle which fires the standard 5.56-mm NATO round. However, many consider it to be a sub-machine gun as it is virtually identical to the MP5 sub-machine gun. The two weapons' dimensions are so similar that many parts are interchangeable. The gun combines the power of an assault rifle, including the ability to penetrate body armour, with the handling characteristics of a sub-machine gun. The GR2 – German Rifle 2 – version is favoured by NATO Special Operations troops.

Heckler & Koch G3

The G3 is a 7.62-mm automatic rifle developed in the 1950s by Heckler & Koch with the Spanish state-owned agency Centro de Estudios Técnicos de Materiales Especiales (CETME). Based on CETME's 7.92-mm LV-50, it was engineered to take the NATO 7.62-mm round. H&K further modified it to fire in both semi-automatic and automatic firing modes. The West German Army adopted it as the Automatisches Gewehr G3. The weapon can be fitted with an optional four-position safety/fire selector that enables a three-round burst mode of fire. The sight is mechanically adjustable for both wind and elevation. It has a notch used to fire up to 100 yards and three apertures used for 200, 300 and 400 yards. It can also mount day or night optics.

The rifled barrel ends with a slotted flash suppressor, which can be used to attach a bayonet or as a base for launching rifle grenades. The rifle comes with a detachable bipod, bayonet, sling, cleaning kit and a speed-loading device. It can also mount a 40-mm HK79 under-barrel grenade launcher.

The G3 served as a basis for many other weapons, among them: the PSG-1 and MSG-90 precision rifles, the HK11 and HK21 family of light machine guns, a single-fire version and the MC51 sub-carbine.

Heckler & Koch PSG-1 Sniper Rifle

The PSG-1 – *PrazisionsSchutzenGewehr*, or "high-precision marksman"'s rifle" – was developed by the German company Heckler & Koch in the 1980s as a police and counter-terrorist weapon in collaboration with German elite law-enforcement groups. It has since been adopted by various police forces in Europe and America. Alongside it H&K developed two more sniper weapons – the G3-SG1, a custom-made version of the G3, and the MSG-90, for export military sales. However, H&K still produce the PSG-1 as one of the most expensive factory-made sniper rifles at $10,000 for the basic package.

Technically, the PSG-1 itself is no more than a heavily modified G3 rifle. The barrel is precision made using the cold-hammer forging process with polygonal rifling for improved accuracy and longer life. The adjustable trigger has a pull of about 3 lb. The pistol grip and plastic butt stock are adjustable for height and for length of pull. The PSG-1 also has a "silent bolt closing device", similar to the "forward assist" found on M-16 rifles. This allows the sniper to maintain complete silence until the shot is fired.

The weapon is fed using a standard twenty-round G3 magazine or a specialist five-round magazine. It is fitted with the Hendsoldt 6x42 fixed-power telescope sight with illuminated reticle and built-in range adjuster. The maximum effective range is 600 yards. Strangely for a sniper rifle, it has no integral bipod. It is often used with a separate rest, mounted on the compact tripod.

Imbel MD-97 5.56-mm Rifles

The Imbel MD-97 family of assault rifles was developed for the Brazilian Special Forces and are fed from standard M-16 rifle magazines. There is the MD-97L, where the "L" stands for "*Leve*" or "Light". This assault rifle is designed to fire standard NATO 5.56 x 45-mm rounds in single, burst and fully automatic modes. Its bullets can penetrate 3.5-mm of ballistic plate at a distance of 600 yards and it can be fitted with an under-barrel grenade launcher. The MD-97LM has a Picatinny rail for various sights and accessories, and fires in single-shot and fully automatic modes.

The Imbel MD-97LC carbine is a shortened version of the MD-97L – the "LC" stands for "*Leve/Curto*" or "Light/ Short" – and can fire single shots only. With its reduced weight and dimensions, its bullets can penetrate 3.5 mm ballistic plate at a distance of 300 yards.

They come with fixed or folding butt stocks and can be equipped with accessories, such as sound suppressors and optical sights.

However, MD-97 rifles have a short barrel life of only about 6,000 shots and Brazilian Special Forces are planning to adopt the HK G-36C carbine instead.

IMI Galil Assault Rifle

During the 1967 Six-Day War, the Israeli Army found that the standard NATO FN FAL did not work well in a desert environment. So Israel Galili, chief weapons designer for Israeli Military Industries, developed a new weapon based on the AK-47 used by the Arabs. It was designed to perform under arid conditions and was officially adopted by the Israeli Defence Forces in 1972. It was later developed to work with standard 7.62-mm NATO-ammunition as well as the 5.56-mm M193 ball ammunition used by the IDF.

The SAR and AR versions have 35-round magazine; the ARM version a 50-round magazine or a 12-round magazine for blanks used to launch rifle grenades. The barrel has a ported flash hider used to launch rifle grenades, and a bayonet lug. It has a folding metal skeleton stock and a flip-up sight with apertures set for firing at 0–328 yards and 328–546 yards. Some versions have a receiver-mounted adapter to mount optical sights and a sound suppressor. The light machine-gun version has a carrying handle and a folding bipod stowed.

The MAR sub-carbine, also called the Micro Galil, is a reduced version of the Galil SAR and is one of the most compact and lightweight weapons of its kind. It has a shortened barrel, receiver, piston, gas tube and fore grip. The fire selector allows automatic fire, a three-round burst and semi-automatic fire. It can be equipped with a night-vision device, a daytime optical sight, iron sights with illuminated dots, a vertical forward grip with integrated laser pointer, silencer and a nylon sling.

Iron Brigade Armory Chandler
M40 Series Sniper Rifle

The Chandler M40 is designed to be accurate to one minute of arc out to 1,000 yards, consistently, even in the worse field conditions. It is a custom-made rifle built to better the USMC specifications.

The rifle uses a Remington 700 Action, McMillan stock, Hart barrel, high-quality Leupold tactical scope with Mil-dot reticle, Iron Brigade Armory one-piece scope mount and Badger Ordnance M5 steel one-piece steel trigger guard. It is chambered as a standard for .308 Winchester for the Sierra 168 or 175 grain Matchking bullet, though other calibres – such as 300 Win-Mag, 30-06 and .223/5.56 – are available.

Kalashnikov 7.62-mm AK-47 Assault Rifle

Developed in the aftermath of the Second World War by Soviet engineer Mikhail Kalashnikov, the AK-47 has remained the basic infantry weapon for the armies of the former Communist bloc and insurgents for over fifty years. The AK stands for *Avtomat Kalashnikov* – "automatic Kalashnikov" – and 1947 was the year the first model was produced.

It comes in two main variants: AK-47 with a fixed wooden stock, and AKS-47 with folding metal stock, intended for airborne and armoured troops. This version has no field tool-kit which is carried inside the stock of the standard version. Otherwise the design is identical. Using standard 7.62-mm ammunition, the AK-47 fires on single or automatic at a rate of 600 rounds a minute from its distinctive curved 30-round magazine.

The Kalashnikov has become the weapon of choice for guerrilla movements because it is reliable and seldom misfires even after being immersed in mud or water. The chromed barrel allows it to be used even in extremely low temperatures. It can be stripped down in a minute. A knife-bayonet or 40-mm under-barrel grenade launcher can be mounted. It has a range of up to 800 yards, but is most effective at 400 yards.

In 1959, the lighter, more accurate, modernized AKM version was developed. In 1974, the AKM was rebuilt to use 5.45 x

39-mm calibre ammunition to produce the AK-74. Nowadays the most modern is the Russian AK-100 series with a wide range of characteristics.

Kalashnikov also developed the RPK machine gun (later modified as the RPK-74) and the PK machine gun (later PKM) with a similar automatic mechanism. These weapons have the same reliability as AK assault rifles.

Versions of the AK-47 have been produced in Albania, Bulgaria, Romania, Hungary, Germany, China, the Czech Republic, Egypt, Finland, Iraq, Indonesia, Israel, North Korea, Poland, Yugoslavia and even the US. A version of the AKM, the AKMS, is used by the Green Berets. It is thought that some 70 million AK-47s have been made.

M1 Garand and M2 Carbine

The M1 Garand was the first semi-automatic to be on general issue to the infantry. It was the standard rifle of the US military from 1936 to 1957, when it was replaced by the M14. The M1 Carbine lightweight semi-automatic became a standard firearm in the US military during the Second World War. Because of the large-scale production of these weapons during and after the Second World War, Special Forces troops are expected to master their use. The M2 Carbine was a selective-fire version that gave fully automatic fire. Some 600,000 were produced.

M14 Rifle

The M14 rifle is the standard US general-issue rifle, largely superseded by the M-16 rifle. Using 7.62 x 51-mm NATO ammunition, variants are still in use by various Special Operations Forces, notably the US Navy SEALs, who have used the M14 as an infantry, marksman and sniper rifle. SEALs also use the Mk 14 Mod 0 EBR (Enhanced Battle Rifle) for close-quarters battle and in a designated marksman role. The M14 provides the basis for the M21 sniper rifle, which added a Leatherwood 4–9x Adjustable Ranging Telescopic. That remained the US Army's official sniper's rifle until 1988, when it was replaced by the bolt-action M24 Sniper Weapons System –

which itself was superseded by an upgraded version of the M21 known as the XM25.

M-16 Assault Rifle

The 5.56-mm M-16 is the US military designation for a family of rifles derived from the Armalite AR-15, further developed by Colt. It is also made in the US by at least a dozen companies including Bushmaster, FN Manufacturing, Hesse, Les Baer, Olympic, Wilson Combat and a number of smaller companies. In Canada, it is made by the Diemaco Company. It has been the general issue rifle for the US military since 1964 and is in use with fifteen NATO countries, making it the most produced firearm in its calibre. It is favoured by the SAS over the standard-issue British SA80.

Such the initial flaws of the M-16 have been ironed out, it now is considered among the best assault rifles in the world. However, in harsh conditions it cannot match reliability of its main rival, the Kalashnikov AK-47.

It can be used in both semi-automatic and fully automatic modes. Weighing less than 8 lb, it is 39 inches long. It fires standard 5.56-mm ammunition and is fed from a 20-or 30-round magazine at between 700 and 950 rounds a minute.

M4A1 Close Quarters Battle Weapon

The Colt company developed various carbine versions of the basic M-16 rifle. In the 1970s and 1980s, the US Military adopted the Colt CAR-15 Commando and XM-177 carbines. In 1994, the US Army adopted the Colt Model 720 selective-fire carbine – which was basically a shortened version of the M-16A2 rifle – as the US M4 Carbine.

The new weapon was much more handy and comfortable to carry than the long M-16A2 rifle and the US Special Operations Command suggested adopting a modified version of the M4 as a possible universal weapon for all Special Forces. The M4A1 was given an integral Picatinny-type accessory rail instead of its former M-16A2-style carrying handle and the trigger unit was modified to fire fully automatic instead of three-shot bursts.

The US Naval Surface Warfare Center then developed the SOPMOD (Special Operations Peculiar Modifications) M4 kit – a M4A1 carbine equipped with the Knight's Armament Company's Rail Interface System (RIS) instead of the standard hand guards, ACOG 4x telescopic sights, ACOG Reflex red-dot sights, detachable back-up open sights, visible and infra-red laser pointers, a detachable silencer, a modified M203 40-mm grenade launcher with a shortened barrel and improved sights, and a detachable front grip and tactical light.

At first, the resulting SOPMOD modular weapons system was thought to be the ideal Special Operations weapon, but its use in Afghanistan has reveal flaws. The shorter barrel gives a lower muzzle velocity, significantly decreasing its range, and the M4 barrel quickly overheats. It is now considered less than ideal for Special Forces.

Norinco 5.8-mm QBZ Type 95 Assault Rifle

China's Norinco QBZ-95 Assault Rifle was first see publicly shown in 1997 when Britain formally handed Hong Kong over to the People's Republic. It is a new generation Chinese assault rifle. QBZ means "*Qing Buqiang Zu*" or "light rifle family" and it has now become the standard infantry assault rifle of the People's Liberation Army. A bullpup design like the British SA80 and Steyr AUG, it has the firing mechanism behind the trigger, allowing for a longer barrel, improving aim and trajectory. The internal design is thought to resemble that of the AK-47. However, it does not use standard ammunition, but rather a 5.8 x 42-mm round designed specifically for the new generation of Chinese small arms.

It is made from high tinsel aluminium and polymer materials, making it lighter than its predecessor, and it is fed from a thirty-round magazine.

The opened sight is built-in to the rifle's carrying handle, which can itself carry various optical or night-vision sights. The QBZ-95 can also be fitted with an under-barrel grenade launch-er and a knife-bayonet. It comes in two main variants: the main assault rifle and the CAR-95 carbine intended for law enforce-ment and the Special Forces. This has no fore grip but a larger additional pistol handle.

The QBB-95 Light Machine Gun resembles the QBZ-95 with a longer and heavier barrel and bipod. It is fed from a 75-round drum magazine, though it also accommodates the standard thirty-round magazines. The QBZ-97 now takes standard NATO 5.56 x 45-mm (.223 Rem) cartridges and is intended for export.

SIG 5.56-mm SG550 (Stgw 90), SG551 and SG552

The SIG SG550 assault rifle was developed for the Swiss Army in the late 1970s and adopted as a Stgw 90 in 1983. It remains the standard Swiss service rifle but is also available for export.

It uses an AK-47-style action and fires in semi-automatic and fully automatic modes, though a modified trigger mechanism gives three-round bursts. Rear sights are drum-type like those found on Heckler & Koch rifles. The NATO-standard diameter flash hider allows rifle grenades to be launched from the muzzle. It can also be fitted with a bayonet. It has a side-folding, skeleton polymer butt stock and a folding bipod under-the-hand guard. The Swiss-Army issue Stgw 90 is usually seen with 4x fixed power scope, while export versions carry commercial telescope sights, ACOG or "red dot" sights.

The SS551 is a carbine version of the SS550 with a shorter barrel that cannot fire rifle grenades. The SS551 SWAT is equipped with accessory rails and comes with a Trijicon ACOG optical sight and cheek pad on the stock. Another version, the compact SS552 is similar to the SS551 with an even shorter barrel and hand guard. All are equipped with semi-translucent plastic magazines that can be clamped together for quicker reloading.

SKS Semi-Automatic Carbine

The Russian SKS – or *Samozaryadniy Karabin sistemi Simonova* – was designed by Sergei Gavrilovish Simonov and is sometimes known as the Simonov SKS. It is a simple self-loading, gas-operated rifle, the first Soviet weapon to fire 7.62 x 39-mm M1943 rifle rounds, also referred to as an "intermediate" cartridge.

The SKS is robust, easy to operate and can be field-stripped quickly. It can be hand-fed single rounds or box-fed from a standard ten-round magazine. A modified 30-round magazine is also available. An integral bayonet system is folded underneath the barrel.

Produced in large numbers in the Soviet Union, the SKS was made in Yugoslavia as the M59, in China as the Type 56, in North Korea as the Type 63 and in the former East Germany as the Karabiner. It has recently become a popular sports weapon in the US.

SOPS Assault-Rifle Suppressor

The SOPS Assault Rifle Suppressor was developed for use on standard 7.62-mm and 5.56-mm assault rifles. The idea is to suppress the sound so the rifle can be operated without damaging the human ear, and to eliminate muzzle flash. The Vortex muzzle-flash hider allows the quick and secure mounting of the suppressor, while the semi-Vortex flash hider will allow the attachment of a rifle-grenade launcher and all other accessories.

Steyr 5.56-mm AUG Rifle

The AUG is an Austrian 5.56-mm assault rifle, designed in the early 1970s by Steyr Mannlicher GmbH & Co KG. The *Armee Universal Gewehr* – "Universal Army Rifle" – was adopted by the Austrian Army in 1977 to replace the aging 7.62-mm licence-built FN FAL. A version was made by Australian Defence Industries in Lithgow and in 2007 an American version, the MSAR STG-556 made by Microtech Small Arms Research Inc, was introduced.

The gun has a two-stage trigger. Pulling the trigger halfway produces semi-automatic fire, while pulling the trigger all the way back produces fully automatic fire. The magazine carries thirty rounds of standard NATO 5.56-mm ammunition. There is also a light machine gun version of the AUG, which uses an extended 42-round magazine. An M203 grenade launcher can also be fitted. The fixed carrying handle contains a 1.5x Swarovski telescopic sight. The optic is permanently set to firing at 328 yards.

Steyr 9-mm Para

A 9-mm version of the AUG assault rifle, with a new barrel, bolt and magazine well adapter is also available. Any AUG can be easily converted to this configuration using a special parts kit, a conversion that takes ten minutes and requires little training. The long barrel increases the muzzle velocity and gives it the range of a carbine. The 9-mm version cannot mount or use combat rifle grenades, though a bayonet attachment point may be fitted if necessary and an added muzzle device allows the AUG Para to fire riot-control grenades. The barrel is threaded to accept a silencer or suppressor.

Tsniitochmash 5.66-mm
APS Underwater Assault Rifle

The *Avtomat Podvodnyy Spetsialnyy* – "Special Underwater Automatic rifle" – is a version of the AK-47, designed in the Soviet Union in the early 1970s for use by combat swimmers and frogmen. Underwater, ordinary bullets have a limited range and are inaccurate. Instead the APS fires special 5.66-calibre steel bolts that are 4.75 in long. The magazine holds 26 rounds.

The barrel is not rifled and the projectile is kept straight by hydrodynamics. Consequently, the APS is rather inaccurate when fired out of water. Its range and firing rate decrease with depth. However, the underwater rifle has a greater range and more penetrating power than a spear gun. Its round can penetrate reinforced dry-suits, protective helmets, breathing apparatus, and the plastic casings and covers of small underwater vehicles. Russian "SEALs", however, prefer to used a pistol which is more compact and easier to stow. The APS is more powerful but is bulkier and takes longer to aim as its long barrel and large flat magazine cannot easily be moved sideways through water.

Tsniitochmash 9-mm AS Special Assault Rifle

The 9-mm AS "Val" *Avtomat Spetsialnij* – "special assault rifle" – was developed by Tsniitochmash in the late 1980s as a part of a family of silenced weapons for Soviet Special Forces.

Its design is similar to that of the VSS "Vintorez" sniper rifle, but with a different butt stock and pistol grip. The AS is widely used by Russian Army recon units as well as Special Forces. It fires 800 rounds a minute and has an effective range of about 300 yards.

Tsniitochmash 9-mm VSS Silent Sniper Rifle

The "Vintorez" *Vinovka Snaiperskaja Spetsialnaya* – "special sniper rifle – was designed for Soviet Special Forces in 1987 for silent attack, with no tell-tale muzzle flash. It is like the AS "Val", but has a wooden butt stock fitted with a rubber shoulder buffer. The magazine is also smaller, allowing the sniper to aim better when lying on the ground.

The VSS Sniper Rifle uses special cartridges with lowered muzzle velocity to make the silencer more effective, but the heavy bullet makes it lethal. At 200 yards, the bullet's core – a hardened-steel penetrator – would pass through 6 mm of steel plate. At 400 yards, it would penetrate most military body armour or unarmoured vehicles. Even at 500 yards distance, it would pass through 2-mm of steel plate and kill anyone it hit.

Every working part is engineered for silent operation. The integral suppressor covers the entire barrel making the gun noiseless in normal conditions. The sniper rifle can also be dismantled into three parts – barrel with suppressor, mechanism and butt-stock – that will fit in a case just 14.5 x 10.6 x 1.7 inches

An optical or night sight is fitted to a multi-purpose hard point. The Russian Army use a PSO-1 optical sight or the later PSO-1M1 with 4x magnification and 6 sighting angle. The NSPUM-3 night sight can also be fitted. This has 3.5x magnification with 9.5 sighting angle. The effective range at night is 300 yards.

Tsniitochmash KS-23/KS-23M
Drozd "Special Carbine"

While the Russians refer to the KS-23 as a "special carbine", the KS-23 is essentially a very heavy-gauge, pump-action shotgun or light grenade launcher, though the shells it fires are more shotgun-like than grenade-like. The barrel is cut from rejected or shot-out 23-mm aircraft cannon. In Western terms it is approximately four-gauge.

The receiver is made of light alloy, with steel operating parts, and a tubular alloy under-barrel magazine. The polymer stock has a thick rubber recoil pad to absorb recoil. Several different shells are available for the KS-23, while a muzzle adapter allows it to fire rifle grenades.

The KS-23M version has a chopped barrel and a pistol grip instead of a stock, though a skeleton tubular metal stock can be attached. A KS-23SM version has also been seen with a side-folding wire stock, a box magazine and a slide that completely surrounds the barrel.

US Marine Corps 7.62-mm Designated Marksman Rifle

The Designated Marksman Rifle is a semi-automatic, gas-operated rifle chambered for the standard 7.62 51-mm NATO cartridge. It is a modified and more accurate version of the old M14 rifle, used solely by the US Marine Corps. All DMRs are built at the USMC Precision Weapons Shop at Quantico, Virginia.

Unlike the basic M14, the DMR has 22-inch stainless-steel, match-grade barrel made by Krieger Barrels, Inc or Rock Creek Barrels, Inc. It has a McMillan Tactical M2A fibreglass stock with a pistol grip and an adjustable saddle cheek piece. The MIL-STD-1913 Picatinny rail allows a wide variety of military scopes and imaging devices to be fitted. Most DMRs use the traditional M14 muzzle device, although since 2001, some DMRs are now equipped with a two-port muzzle brake, which is threaded and collared to accept an OPS-Inc sound suppressor. The basic DMR without secondary sight, magazine, sling, suppressor and bipod, weighs less than 11 lb.

It has a range of 650 to 875 yards using match-grade M118LR 175-grain long-range ammunition. The DMR design allows the sight mount, barrel, bolt, and other key assemblies to be repaired or replaced easily. It is used primarily by designated marksmen, though it is also issued by Marine Scout Snipers when a mission requires rapid accurate fire, spotters in sniper teams and Marine Corps Explosive Ordnance Disposal teams.

Winchester Model 1200 Shot Gun

The Winchester Model 1200 is a pump-action twelve-gauge shotgun. It has five rounds capacity, one in the chamber and four in its tubular magazine. A large number were bought by the US military in the 1960s, ostensibly for riot control. The gun also has a fixing for an M1917 bayonet.

XM25 "Spotter Rifle"

The XM25 – also officially known as the M25 – was originally developed by the 10th Special Forces Group at Fort Devens for the Green Berets and the Navy SEALs. SOCOM called it a "Light Sniper Rifle", but it's also known as the "Sniper Security System" and "Product Improved M21", itself an improvement on the M14.

Like the M21 in many regards, it has a BPT (Brookfield Precision Tool) Advanced Scope Mounting System. Most carry the B&L 10x tactical scope. Although designated the M25, it was not designed directly as a replacement for the M24, but rather was requested by the USSOCOM to fill a specific need. However, it proved its worth in the Persian Gulf.

21

MACHINE GUNS, SUB-MACHINE GUNS AND LIGHT SUPPORT WEAPONS

AT-4 Anti-Tank Weapon

The AT-4 is a portable one-shot anti-tank weapon built in Sweden by Saab Bofors Dynamics. In the US and NATO inventory it replaces the M72 LAW and is now one of the most common light anti-tank weapons in the world. It was designed to give infantry units a means to disable armoured vehicles and destroy fortifications, though it is not powerful enough to take out a modern main battle tank. The launcher and projectile come as a single unit of ammunition and the launcher is discarded after it is fired.

When the US Army first tested the AT-4 they saw room for improvement. The sights and slings were redesigned and the modified AT-4 was adopted by the US Army as the M136 anti-tank grenade launcher.

The AT-4 is a recoilless weapon. The force of the projectile coming out of the front of the barrel is balanced by the propellant gases coming out of the rear. This means a relatively large projectile can be fired and, as the barrel does not have to cope with the pressures of a traditional gun, it can be light-weight. The disadvantage of this design is back-blast, which can cause severe burns to friendly forces behind the user, or the user

himself if the weapon is fired in a confined space. This problem
has recently been overcome with the AT4-CS (Confined
Space), which uses a salt-water counter-mass to neutralize
the back-blast.

With the older version, the firer must check that no-one is
within 50 feet behind him. If he is firing in the prone position,
he must spread his legs well out to the side to avoid burning
himself. The weapon is aimed with range-adjustable plastic
sights, which are kept under sliding covers when transported, or
through an optical night-sight carried on a removable mount.
After disengaging two safeties, the firer cocks a mechanical
firing pin and presses a trigger button. Little training is needed
to fire the AT-4, which is as well as the rounds are prohibitively
expensive.

The AT-4 is 40 inches long and weighs 14.75 lb. Its maximum effective range is 984.3 feet, although the projectile has
been known to cover over 1,640 feet. With a muzzle velocity of
950 feet per second, the fin-stabilized projectile with shaped
charge warhead takes less than a second to reach 820 feet.

The AT-4 HEAT round can penetrate up to 16 inches of
armour, while a HP – High Penetration – round can penetrate
20 – 24 inches of armour. The weapon also comes armed with a
HEDP – High Explosive Dual Purpose – round to take out
bunkers and buildings. The projectile can be set to detonate on
impact or with a delayed detonation.

Beretta M12S

The Italian arms company Beretta has manufactured sub-
machine guns since the end of the First World War. In
1958, it developed the Model 12, which was adopted by the
Italian Army. It was also widely exported, and manufacturing
licences were sold to Brazil and Indonesia. In the early 1980s,
the basic design was improved with the introduction of the
Model 12S sub-machine gun, which was also known as the PM
12S – *Pistola Mitralligica*, or machine pistol – and is widely
used by European police and security forces.

The Model 12S uses a 32-round box magazine, and is chambered for the 9 x 19-mm NATO cartridge. Capable of either
semi- or full-automatic fire, it was billed as the "ultimate sub-

machine gun". Its unique feature is the grip safety which, if not held firmly, locks the trigger and the bolt in the closed position. This safeguards against accidental firing if the gun is dropped.

Browning .30-calibre M1919 Machine Gun

The Browning M1919 was a .30-cal light machine gun family widely used during the twentieth century. Developed from the M1917, the standard US machine gun of the First World War, it was used as a light infantry, aircraft and anti-aircraft machine gun during the Second World War, the Korean War and the Vietnam War. Although it was superseded by newer designs, notably the M60, many M1919s were rechambered for the new standard 7.62 x 51-mm NATO round and served into the 1990s in the US. In some countries, they are still in use today.

Browning M2 HB .50-calibre Heavy Machine Gun

The M2 Machine Gun, or Browning .50-calibre Machine Gun, is a heavy machine gun designed towards the end of the First World War by John Browning. It was very similar in design to the smaller Browning M1919 machine gun.

The .50-calibre was found to be effective against infantry, lightly armoured vehicles, light fortifications and low-flying aircraft. It has been used extensively as a vehicle weapon and for aircraft armament by the United States from the 1920s to the present day. Used throughout the Second World War, the Korean and Vietnam Wars, it was still in service in Iraq during Operation Desert Storm and Operation Iraqi Freedom. Still in use today, it remains the principal heavy machine gun of the NATO countries.

Carl Gustav M45B

The M45 sub-machine gun was developed in Sweden in 1945. It is sometimes known as the "Swedish K" – the K stands for "*Kulsprutepistole*" which translates roughly as "bullet squirting pistol".

It fires 9-mm Parabellum rounds at a rate of 600 rounds a minute from a single 71-round magazine or a double-column box magazine of thirty-six or fifty rounds. In the 1960s, Swedish Ks with a distinctive turquoise finish were used on various US Special Forces operations in Vietnam, often fitted with a silencer made by Sionics in Alpharetta, Georgia. However, in protest against the war in Vietnam the Swedish government stopped the export of the M45 to America. Consequently Smith and Wesson developed a similar design called the Model 76. The design has since been superseded by the Heckler & Koch MP5.

Colt 9-mm Sub-Machine Gun

The Colt 9-mm Sub-machine Gun is a lightweight sub-machine gun based on the M-16 assault rifle. Its straight line construction, coupled with the low-recoil from the 9-mm ammunition, provides accurate fire with less muzzle climb, especially in full automatic fire. Like the M4 Carbine and Commando models, the Colt 9-mm sub-machine gun is equipped with a four-position sliding butt stock and can be field stripped without special tools. Operation and training are similar to that of the M4 Carbine and M-16 Rifle, cutting out the need for special training.

Degtyaryov DP Light Machine Gun

The *Degtyarev Pechotnyi*, or Degtyarev Infantry light machine gun was one of the first small arms of Soviet design. It was adopted as a standard LMG of the Red Army in 1928. A rugged and reliable weapon, its flaws were ironed out in 1944 with the introduction of the DP Modernized, or DPM.

In 1946, its heavy flat-pan magazine was replaced by a belt feed in the *Rotnyj Pulemet* – "company machine gun" – or RP-46. It was used as a front-line weapon until the 1960s, when it was gradually replaced by the Kalashnikov PK. All versions of these guns were used widely in the Soviet bloc and the RP-46 was also manufactured in China as a Type 58 machine gun.

Dragunov KEDR 9-mm Machine Pistol

Dragunov KEDRs are a family of small sub-machine guns designed by Evgeni Dragunov, the designer of the SVD

Dragunov sniper rifle. They are described as machine pistols by the Russians and fire the 9-mm Makarov cartridge.

The standard KEDR uses a short barrel, just 4.7 inches long. Its tip is threaded for screw-on silencers and it has a ring lip for clamp-on type silencers. It is simple to build and operate. Variants of the KEDR were developed, including the PP-91-01, which has a noise and flash suppressor that is not as efficient as a true silencer, and the KEDR-B, which has an integral silencer.

The best-known version of the KEDR is the Klin, which has a stronger construction to permit the use of 9-mm Makarov Hi-Impulse ammunition and designed to carry night-vision scopes, tactical lights and laser-aiming units. A variant of the Klin was chambered for 9-mm Parabellum ammunition and made for export.

DShK M1938 Anti-Aircraft Gun

The DShK M1938 is a Second World War-vintage Soviet heavy anti-aircraft machine gun firing 12.7 x 108-mm rounds. It was also used as a heavy infantry machine gun with armour-plated gun shield and a two-wheeled mounting. It took its name from the weapons designers Vasily Degtyaryov, who designed the original weapon, and Georgi Shpagin, who improved the feed mechanism. The K comes from *Krupnokaliberniy*, which means "large calibre". It is sometimes nicknamed *Dushka*, which means "dear" or "sweetie" in Russian.

Enfield Sten Gun

The Sten gun gets its name from its designers – Shepard and Turpin – and the Enfield arsenal where they worked. Between 1941 and 1945, nearly four million were made.

Some 100,0000 of the first – the 9-mm STEN Machine Carbine, Mk I – were produced. This was replaced by the smaller and lighter Mk II. About two million of those came out of the factory, though there were problems with the magazine and its housing. This problem was overcome in the Mk III, which was introduced in 1943.

The Mk IV, designed for airborne troops, only appeared as a

prototype. The Mk V was introduced in 1944 and remained in service until the 1960s, when it was replaced by Sterling sub-machine guns.

FIM-92 Stinger Shoulder-Fired Anti-Aircraft Missile

The FIM-92 Stinger is a portable infra-red homing surface-to-air missile that entered service with the US military in 1981. It is also used by twenty-nine other countries and around 70,000 missiles have been produced.

It is light and can be fired from the shoulder by a single operator, although officially it requires two. It can attack air-craft at heights of between 600 and 12,500 feet and at a range of up to three miles. It can also been mounted on a vehicle or a helicopter, though it is small enough to be used by paratroopers. A helicopter-launched version exists called the ATAS or Air-to-Air Stinger.

The launcher weighs just 33.5 lb and the missile weighs 22 lb. It is 5 feet long and 2.75 inches in diameter. It is launched by a small ejection motor that pushes it a safe distance from the operator before the main two-stage solid-fuel engine is fired. This accelerates it to a speed of Mach 2.2 (820 yards a second). The 6.6 lb warhead is armed with an impact fuse and has a self-destruct timer in case it misses its target.

Newer versions have reprogrammable microprocessors to combat enemy countermeasures, a dual-detector seeker and uses both the infra-red and ultra-violet parts of the spectrum.

FN 5.7 x 28-mm P90 Sub-Machine Gun

The FN P90 is designed for use in close-quarter battles. It is built around FN's unique 5.7 x 28-mm ammunition that easily penetrates soft body armour. A 50-round magazine runs hor-izontally across the top of the P90 in keeping with the compact bullpup design. The empty casings are ejected downward, allowing ambidextrous use. It gives outstanding accuracy and is easy to keep on target. The FN P90 sub-machine gun is used as a handy personal defence weapon for armoured vehicles or helicopter crews.

FN Herstal 5.56-mm Minimi Light Machine Gun

The Minimi is a Belgian 5.56-mm light machine gun developed by the Fabrique Nationale (FN) company in Herstal. It was originally designed for the 7.62 x 51-mm NATO round, and later redesigned around the 5.56 mm cartridge. However, at the behest of USSOCOM, Herstal has recently revived the more powerful 7.62-mm version in several different configurations.

The 5.56-mm version was first introduced in 1974. The M249 SAW version of the Minimi was adopted by the US military in February 1982, and, since 1984, production is carried out entirely in the US by FN Manufacturing LLC. The Minimi is configured in several variants: the standard model as a platoon or squad support weapon; the Para model for use by armoured vehicle crews, helicopter pilots and parachute infantry; and the vehicle model as secondary armament for fighting vehicles. A lightweight variant of the Para with a Picatinny top-cover rail adapter is known as the SPW – Special Purpose Weapon. It has the magazine feed port removed to reduce weight. Another variant of the SPW requested by the US Special Operations Forces is the Mk 46 Mod 0 that incorporates a lightweight fluted barrel but lacks the magazine feed system, vehicle mounting lugs and carry handle.

FN Herstal 7.62-mm MAG General-Purpose Machine Gun

The FN MAG was developed in Belgium by Fabrique Nationale and was adopted as the 7.62-mm NATO machine gun, used by more than twenty countries. MAG stands for *Mitrailleuse d'Appui General*, or "general-purpose machine gun".

Based on earlier Browning designs, the FN MAG is extremely reliable under all conditions. In a US Army test, it was found it could fire an average of 26,000 rounds before failure. The barrel is supposed to be changed after every second 220 rounds to prevent overheating, which can be done in three seconds, though it is often skipped. During the assault on Goose Green in the Falklands War, British paratroopers were forced to fire over 8,000 rounds without significant pause to change the barrels. The muzzles were glowing red hot, but the weapons went on working.

There are, of course, dangers. When the belt is changed, the operator is supposed to lift the feed tray to inspect the breach block. If there is a round in the chamber, it can easily cook off. If this is likely, the best course of action is to slam the feed cover shut, put the weapon to fire and squeeze the trigger to fire off the round.

Even under normal conditions the barrels can become hot enough to inflict second-degree burns and they can easily be seen glowing brightly by anyone using any sort of night-vision device. In Arctic conditions, care must also be taken not to lay the removed barrel on the snow as it will melt its way through and the barrel can easily be lost.

There are three different settings for the rate of fire – 750, 850 and 950 rounds a minute. These settings are changed by turning the gas regulator using the C-tool provided and generally performed before missions, as changing the setting is awkward under field or combat conditions.

It was adopted by the US military as the M240 and by the British as the L7A2.

Gorjunov SGM Machine Gun

When the Soviet Union entered the the Second World War, its army was armed with the obsolete Maxim M1910 machine gun. Soon a team led by P.M. Goryunov at the Kovrov machine-gun plant began developing a new heavy machine gun using ammunition ofstandard 7.62-mm rifle calibre. This became the SG-43.

After the end of the Second World War, the SG-43 was modernized to become the SGM, which was replaced by the PK in the mid-1960s. Meanwhile, the SGM was widely exported to the Soviet bloc and manufactured in other friendly countries such as China.

The SG-43 and SGM machine guns used a belt feed with non-desintegrating links. Both can be mounted on the universal wheeled mount, designed by the Degtyarev, allowing for both ground and anti-aircraft roles. SGM machine guns have also been seen on more modern tripod mountings.

Harrington & Richardson Reising M50

The Reising sub-machine gun was designed by Eugene Reising in 1940. The following year it went into production at the Harrington & Richardson arms factory and by the end of the Second World War tens of thousands of Reising M50 sub-machine guns had been delivered to the US Marine Corps.

Other versions were sold to various US agencies and a model with a folding stock, known as the Reising M55, was designed for USMC paratroopers and tank crews. H&R also produced semi-automatic versions for training and guard purposes. Generally the Reising was found to be unreliable, especially in conditions were it could not easily be cleaned.

Heckler & Koch 9-mm
MP5 Sub-Machine Gun

The *Maschinenpistole* 5 – "Machine Pistol 5" – is a 9-mm sub-machine gun developed in the 1960s by a group of engineers at Heckler & Koch, based on its G3 design and chambered for the 9 x 19-mm Parabellum pistol cartridge. Work began on the MP5 in 1964; two years later it was adopted by the German Federal Police and army special forces. Since then it has been adopted by the US Navy Seals and the British SAS, SBS and CO19, the Special Firearms Command of London's Metropolitan Police.

It comes in various configurations that allow automatic, semi-automatic and single-shot fire, as well a two- or three-round bursts. Most Special Forces favour the compact MP5A3 which has a retractable metal stock.

In 1974 Hecker & Koch began work on a sliced version called the MP5SD – *Schalldämpfer* or "silencer". Reducing the length of the barrel and bleeding exhaust gases through ports kept the muzzle velocity below the speed of sound. Two years later a shortened version known as the MP5K – *Kurz* or "short" – was introduce for use by Special Forces in close-quarters battle.

Heckler & Koch HK11A1 Light Machine Gun

The HK11 is a light-machine-gun version of the Heckler &

Koch G3 battle rifle that fires 900 rounds a minute. The HK11A1 is an improved version whose barrel can be changed quickly and simply. It can use three kinds of ammunition: the NATO 5.56-mm round, the NATO 7.62-mm round and the Soviet 7.62-mm round.

The weapon can be field-stripped and completely disassembled into its components without tools. A lightweight bipod gives increased stability to the weapon for prone fire. It has a maximum effective range of 1,200 yards.

Heckler & Koch HK21A1
General-Purpose Machine Gun

The HK21 is another version of the G3 rifle and the HK21A1 is an updated version of it. It is a belt-fed general-purpose machine gun or squad automatic weapon using the 7.62 x 51-mm NATO rounds usually carried on disintegrating link belts. By changing the barrel, the belt feed plate and the bolt, the gun can be converted to firing the 5.56 x 45 mm NATO or the 7.62 x 39-mm ammunition.

By inserting a magazine adaptor in place of the feed mechanism it can take the 7.62 mm box magazines designed for the G3 rifle or the HK11 automatic rifle. It can be fired single-shot or fully automatic. Heckler & Koch now manufacture two improved models: the HK21E, chambered for 7.62 x 51-mm NATO ammunition, and the HK23E, chambered for 5.56 x 45-mm NATO ammunition. The HK23E is similar to the HK21E in every respect except for the chambering and barrel length. They fire in semi-automatic and three-round bursts, as well as fully automatic.

IMI 5.56-mm Negev Light Machine Gun

The Negev light machine gun was adopted by the Israeli Defence Forces in 1995 and put into service on helicopters, patrol ships and armoured vehicles, as a replacement for the NATO-standard MAG machine-gun. Still using NATO-standard 5.56-mm ammunition, the Negev has a distinct weight advantage over its rival. It weighs just 16.5lb, 9.6lb with a 150-round soft assault drum, or 22.5lb with a 200-round soft assault drum. It is also designed for use in harsh desert conditions.

The weapon can be used as a traditional squad assault weapon or, with a quick change of barrel, as a compact machine gun. The weapon is available with a standard or short barrel, with folding stock or without one, allowing it to be used in close-quarters battle.

The Negev Commando is a shortened variant of the Negev LMG with a 330-mm barrel and a forward handgrip instead of a bipod. It can be used as an assault rifle as well as a light machine gun.

IMI 9-mm Mini-Uzi Sub-Machine Gun

In the mid-1980s IMI came up with the Mini Uzi. It was designed for use by men crammed into armoured personnel carriers or aircraft by reducing the bulk and length without sacrificing the old fixed butt stock which was found to be superior to the folding stock.

The Mini Uzi also has a front sight that uses a spring-detent and ratchet assembly to allow adjustment instead of the threaded post with lock-ring prevalent on the standard model. The adjustable rear sight is also adjustable with the same improved adjustment tool. This produces better results when fired from the shoulder.

IMI 9-mm Uzi Sub-Machine Gun

The Uzi sub-machine gun was designed in Israel by Uziel Gal, an officer in the Israeli Army in 1949. It has since been adopted by police and military of more than ninety countries, and is produced under licence in Belgium by FN Herstal, and without licence in Croatia.

The Uzi's compact size and firepower proved themselves in clearing Syrian bunkers and Jordanian positions during the 1967 Six-Day War. The Uzi sub-machine gun is used as a personal defence weapon by rear-echelon troops, as well as a front-line weapon by elite infantry forces. The sales of Uzi sub-machine guns has netted IMI over $2 billion. It has also found its way into the hands of gangsters and terrorists.

Javelin Anti-Tank Weapon

The Javelin is the medium-range anti-tank guided weapon used by US armed forces and has proven itself on operations in Iraq and Afghanistan. Although designed primarily to destroy tanks and light-armoured vehicles, Javelin is also effective against fixed defences, such as bunkers and buildings.

The integrated sight allows the firer to acquire the target, lock-on, then "fire and forget". This means that as soon as the missile is launched, the firer can acquire another target, or move position. Javelin has a maximum range of 2,500 yards. It can be used in "direct attack mode" or "Overfly Top Attack" (OTA) mode.

In 2005, the British bought the Javelin to replace the Franco-Germany Milan portable anti-tank weapon that was capable of destroying enemy armour out to 2,132 yards. In the first Gulf War, British Special Forces used the Milan to destroy Scud missiles. In the Falklands War, it was used to destroy bunkers and, in Afghanistan, it was used against caves in the mountains. Milan sights also provided a useful night surveillance asset.

Kalashnikov RPK-74

The Kalashnikov RPK-74 light machine gun was developed in the 1970s alongside the AK-74 assault rifle as the standard squad automatic weapon of the Soviet, then Russian, Army. It uses 5.45-mm RPK-74 ammunition from 45-round box magazines, though it is also compatible with thirty-round AK-74 magazines. Various large-capacity magazines (drums and flat pans, holding up to 100 rounds and made of plastic) were experimentally developed for RPK-74, but never achieved production status. The most recent version is the RPK-74M with black polymer furniture, a side-folding butt and rail for sighting equipment.

Kovrov Mechanical Plant 7.62-mm PK Machine-Gun Family

Kovrov PKs were the standard GPMG in Russian service and can be found in the armies of almost every country that is or was once a Russian or Soviet client state, or did business with

China. It uses the same action as Kalashnikov AK assault rifles, turned upside down and enlarged. This is added to the trigger group of the DP, the belt-feed mechanism of the VZ-59, and the cartridge feed and quick-change barrel of the Goryunov, though the barrel is shorter at 25.9 inches. This Kalashnikov-Goryunov combination makes the PK a very reliable and robust weapon, despite its light weight.

Introduced in 1964, the PK was designed to be used from a bipod or tripod, or pintle and vehicular mounts. The barrel is heavy and fluted for most of its length, with a conical flash hider at the end. It can be fed by several different lengths of non-disintegrating link belts or from several different types of ammunition boxes and containers ranging from small canvas bags holding twenty-five rounds to large boxes containing 250-round belts. Even larger containers are used with versions of the PK mounted on vehicles. The stock is made of wood and its distinctive skeleton shape is well-known to most troops.

The PKS version designed for use as a support weapon and for anti-aircraft defence. It does not have a bipod – a tripod mounting is used instead. The PKT is designed to be mounted on a vehicle and has a longer 28.4-inch barrel. It has no sights of its own, is aimed using the vehicle's sighting devices and is fired electrically by the vehicle's trigger. Kazakhstan has taken the PKT and put the manual features back onto it. The resulting PKD is essentially a PK with a longer barrel.

The current Russian production version of the PK – the PKM – has been lightened by removing the flutes from the barrel and making it from lighter, but stronger, steel. It comes in several versions. The PKMS uses a bipod which allows ammunition boxes to be secured to the right rear leg so that the gun and ammunition can be moved easily. The PKMSN is a PKMS with a bracket for Russian night-vision devices. And the PKMB is a PKM modified for use as a helicopter door gun. Later, a bracket for night-vision devices was added to the PKMB.

A newer version of the PK, called the 6P41 Pecheneg, has been seen carried by Russian troops in Chechnya. The PKM's light, quick-change barrel has been replaced by a heavy, fixed barrel tipped with a slightly different flash hider. The manufacturers say that the Pecheneg is 2.5 times more accurate than the PKM when fired from a bipod and 1.5 times more accurate when fired from a tripod.

L16A2 81-mm Mortar

The 81-mm mortar can fire high-explosive, smoke or illumination rounds 6,178 yards. It can be carried, but mortar detachments are normally vehicle-borne. It can fire up to fifteen rounds per minute.

The original 81-mm L16 mortar was developed during the late 1950s. Canada developed the base plate and sight unit, while the UK came up with the design of the barrel and bipod. The mortar entered service during the 1960s. The L16A2 was also used as the basis for the US Army and Marine Corps model M252. Over thirty-nine countries have purchased L16 series mortars.

The mortar is still being produced by BAe Systems and the Royal Ordnance Division in the UK, and by Watervliet Arsenals, as the 81-mm M252 mortar, in the US. Similar models are produced in Japan by Howa. Over 5,000 of these weapons have been produced.

L9A1 51-mm Light Mortar

The 51-mm Light Mortar is a platoon-level, indirect-fire weapon that can be carried and fired by one man. The mortar is used to fire smoke, illuminating and high-explosive rounds to a range of around 820 yards. A short-range insert allows the weapon to be used in close-quarter battles with accuracy. It can fire eight rounds a minute.

LAW 80

The Light Anti-Tank Weapon 80 is a portable, one-shot, disposable, anti-tank weapon used by the British Army. It comprises an extendable launch tube with an integral spotting rifle loaded with five rounds of 9-mm ammunition ballistically matched to the rocket.

To launch the rocket the protective caps are removed and launch tube is extended to the rear. The weapon is then armed in spotting rifle mode. Once the weapon is aimed, the firer moves a charge lever forward with his thumb. The rocket's propellant burns out before it leaves the launch tube, with the blast directed out of the rear of the launch tube. The rocket then speeds to the target, arming itself on the way. The warhead is a high-explosive, anti-tank, shaped charge and can penetrate 700 mm of armour.

M3A1 Grease Gun

The M3 sub-machine gun, also known as the Grease gun, was developed during the Second World War as a cheaper wartime alternative to the famous Thompson M1 and M1928 sub-machine guns. It was a simple weapon, made mostly from steel stampings. A fully automatic weapon, it was adopted by the US military in 1943, but problems were found with the cocking mechanism. These were solved in a modified version, the M3A1, in 1944. The M3A1 served with the US armed forces in Korea and Vietnam. US tank crews were issued with the M3A1 until the 1980s.

The retractable stock was made from steel wire and could be detached to be used as a cleaning rod and magazine loading tool. The hollow grip of the gun also contained a small oiler as the all-steel gun rusted easily when wet.

The M3A1 could be converted to use 9 x 19-mm Luger ammunition by replacing the barrel and bolt, and installing the magazine adaptor for British Sten magazines. A special version of the M3A1 featuring a long, integral silencer was produced for clandestine operations.

M72 66-mm LAW

The M72 Light Anti-Tank Weapon is a portable, one-shot, 66-mm, anti-tank weapon that replaced the bazooka as the US Army's primary anti-tank weapon after the Korean War.

It comprises a rocket packed inside a launcher that is made up of two tubes, one inside the other. While closed, the outer assembly acts as a watertight container for the rocket and firing mechanism. To fire it, the inner tube is telescoped out towards the rear. When fired, the propellant in the rocket motor burns completely before leaving the launcher. As the warhead emerges from the tubo, six fins spring out from the base to stabilize its flight. The launcher is then discarded.

The high-explosive anti-tank shell is activated on impact. The force of the main charge forces the copper liner into a directional jet that is capable of penetrating up to one foot of steel plate, two feet of reinforced concrete or six foot of soil.

After the Vietnam War, it was superseded by more powerful and sophisticated designs but is still being used in Iraq by the US Army and in Afghanistan by the Canadian Army. The British Army used a Norwegian version of the M72, which has now been replaced by LAW 80.

Mark 19 40-mm Grenade Launcher

The Mark 19 Grenade Launcher is an automatic, belt-fed grenade machine gun that first saw action during the Vietnam War and remains in service today. It can lob a 40-mm grenade up to 2,419 yards, though it is only accurate to about 1,640 yards. The nearest safe distance to launch the grenade is 82 yards. It can fire sixty 40-mm grenades a minute in rapid fire or forty rounds a minute in sustained fire.

The tripod- or vehicle-mounted weapon usually fires the high-explosive, dual-purpose M430 grenade. On impact, this will kill anyone within a radius of 5 yards, and wound those within 15 yards. It can also punch through 2 inches of armour with a direct hit, so it is a threat to most infantry fighting vehicles and armoured personnel carriers. Due to its low recoil and light weight, it has been adapted for use on small attack boats, fast attack vehicles such as the Humvee and Stryker military jeeps.

Originally used by the US Navy on its river patrol boats in Vietnam, it was adopted and improved upon by the US Army. It was used by Special Forces operating behind enemy lines in Iraq.

Pistolet Maszynowy Wz63 RAK

The Wz63 RAK is a Polish sub-machine gun used be reconaissance teams and anti-terrorist units. RAK is an acronym for *Rêczny Automat Komandosów* – "handheld automatic commando weapon".

It was designed in 1963 by Piotr Wilniewczyc and, at that

time, was one of the lightest sub-machine guns in the world. In effect it is an overgrown automatic pistol, using a slide instead of a moving bold, and can be fired singled-handed. This means that it is impossible to aim accurately in automatic fired. However, it is effective in self-defence at up to 164 yards. The PM-63 is no longer in production in Poland, but tens of thousands were made between 1963 and 1980 and the gun is still manufactured by Norinco of China.

Rheinmetall MG3 Machine Gun

The Rheinmetall MG3 is a German, air-cooled, belt-fed, general-purpose machine gun chambered for the 7.62 x 51-mm NATO cartridge, whose design can be traced back to the Second World War-era MG42 machine gun that fired the 7.92 x 57-mm Mauser round.

The first MG42 chambered in a standard NATO calibre went into service with the *Bundeswehr* in 1958 as the MG1. Soon after the machine gun was given a chrome-lined barrel and sights calibrated for the new round. This was known as the MG1A1 or MG42/58. It was further developed as the MG1A2, or MG42/59, which was adapted to use both the standard German continuous DM1 ammunition belt and the American M13 disintegrating belt. After further improvements in the weapon's bolt, muzzle device and bipod, the weapon became the MG1A3.

At the same time, the wartime MG42 machine gun was rechambered to take the standard 7.62-mm NATO round and became the MG2. In 1968, the MG2 was upgraded with an improved feeding mechanism, a new ammunition box and an anti-aircraft sight to become the MG3. Many of the parts of the MG3 and its variants are interchangeable with the original MG42. The MG3 has been adopted by the armed forces of over thirty countries.

RPD Light Machine Gun

The *Ruchnoy Pulemyot Degtyareva* – or "Degtyaryov light machine gun" – is a belt-fed weapon that was made in the former Soviet Union and in China. Using 100-round refillable belts, it can be fired from a prone position using the built-in bipod, or from the hip with the aid of a sling.

This Chinese version had minor modifications and was known as the Type 56 LMG. It was used by Communist forces in the Vietnam War. The RPD is still widely used by guerrilla armies around the world, notably the Tamil Tigers, and has been seen in the hands of private security contractors in Iraq.

Skorpion Vz.61

The Skorpion sub-machine gun development was initiated in the late 1950s as a lightweight personal-defence weapon that was more effective than a pistol, but no more obtrusive, for non-infantry units. The Scorpion was used by various Special Forces, because the selected cartridge – the 7.65 x 17-Browning/.32 ACP – can be easily silenced. It was officially adopted in 1961, under the designation of *Samopal Vzor* 1961 – "sub-machine gun model 1961" – or the SA Vz.61. This weapon was issued to various units in the Czechoslovak Army and was widely exported. A few Skorpions found their way into the hands of various terrorist groups, who also valued its small size and ease of silencing. It can also be easily fired single-handed like a pistol.

Sterling 9-mm L2A3 Sub-Machine Gun

The Sterling sub-machine gun was designed in 1942 by George Patchett. However the "Patchett machine carbine", made by the Sterling Engineering Company, was not adopted by the British Army until 1953, when it was designated the "9-mm Sterling sub-machine gun L2A1".

A modified version, known as L2A3 sub-machine gun, or Sterling Mk 4, was in use by the British Army until the early 1990s, when it was replaced by the L85A1 assault rifle. In all nearly 400,000 of Sterlings were made. In 1967, the British Army adopted a silenced version known as the L34A1, or Sterling Mrk 5, which is still in limited use with British Special Forces.

Sterling sub-machine guns were also exported to more than seventy countries.

US Ordnance 7.62-mm
M60 General-Purpose Machine Gun

The M60 is an air-cooled, belt-fed, automatic machine gun that fires at a maximum rate of fire of 550 rounds per minute. It can be fired from the shoulder, hip or under the arm, or it can be steadied on its built-in bipod or mounted on a tripod. It fires the standard NATO 7.62-mm round and the ammunition is fed into it from a hundred-round bandoleer containing a disintegrating metallic split-link belt. It has a quick-change barrel to prevent overheating.

The M60 has been the US Army's general-purpose machine gun since 1950. It is used as a general support crew-served weapon. It can fire M61 armour-piercing rounds, though the preferred combat ammunition mix is four M80 ball rounds to one M62 tracer.

The M60C is an electrically controlled, hydraulic-powered, aircraft version and the M60D was modified to use as a helicopter door-gun. The lightweight M60E3 replaced its heavier parent, but was itself replaced in the 1980s by the Belgian FN MAG-58, designated the M240, in general use. On 21 March 2001, USSOCOM approved the Mk 48 Mod 0 – a scaled-up version of FN's Minimi Light Machine Gun – as its new Lightweight 7.62-mm Machine Gun.

22

HANDGUNS

Beretta 9 x 19-mm Model 92 Pistol

The Beretta 92 is a series of semi-automatic pistols designed and manufactured by Beretta of Italy. Begun in 1972, only 5,000 of the original design were ever produced. But in difference calibres and configurations, variants are being made to this day.

The first, the 92S, was adopted by the Italian police and military units. Another, the 92SB, was designed for the US Air Force. In 1985, the Beretta 92SB-F was adopted as the standard sidearm of the United States military as the M9. Over 500,000 were made.

In 2005, the US Marine Corps placed an order with Beretta for 3,480 M9A1 pistols, a new variant with an accessory rail. The US Army were to have replaced their M9s with the XM8 compact carbine, but later that year the XM8 programme was suspended.

Browning High Power

After Browning sold his design for the M1911 to Colt, the French Army were looking for a new service pistol and the Belgian firm, Fabrique Nationale, commissioned him to come up with a design. However, he died before the pistol went into production and his design was completed by the Belgian designer Dieudonne Saive. It was known in France as the *Grand Rendement* – "high yield" – or the *Grande Puissance* – "high power".

Belgium was occupied by the Germans in the Second World War, FN's plant was taken over and the High Power was issued to the German armed forces as the Pistole 640(b) – "b" was for *belgisch*, or "Belgian". The High Power pistol was also produced in Canada for the Allies, by John Inglis and Company. The pistol was popular with covert operations groups such as the American Office of Strategic Services and the British SAS. It has been in continuous modification since it was first produced and variants are still in service today.

Colt .45 Model 1911A1 Automatic Pistol

The M1911 .45 cal, single-action, semi-automatic handgun – designed by John Browning and originally manufactured by Colt – was the standard-issue side arm for the United States armed forces from 1911 to 1985. Adopted by the US Army and Marine Corps, it saw action in the First World War. Experience in the Services led to some improvements and the modified M1911A1 was adopted in 1924. It was used throughout the Second World War, the Korean War and the Vietnam War. The design was widely copied. The US Marine Corps' Marine Expeditionary Unit's MEU(SOC) version is still in use today with the Marine Corps Special Operations Command. Because of the stopping power of the .45 cartridge and the superior handling of the weapon in close fighting, the M1911A1 is also used by Marine Force Recon, Los Angeles Police Department Special Weapons and Tactics, the FBI Hostage Rescue Team and Delta Force.

CZ-97B and CZ-100

The CZ-97B was a development of the famous Czech CZ-75 pistol, enlarged and reshaped to take a thicker magazine and bigger cartridge. Produced in the 1990s by the Czeska Zbroevka–Uhersky Brod arms factory, it was designed for the American market, where it has been picked up by police departments. In 1995, the company began producing a polymer-framed pistol, the CZ-100, that weighs just 24 ounces compared to the CZ-97B's 41 ounces.

Daewoo 9-mm K5 Pistol

In the 1990s, after extensive trials, the South Korean Army adopted the first domestically designed, 9-mm, semi-automatic pistol, the Daewoo K5 as its standard sidearm. A number of variants are exported.

It is a compact, lightweight pistol with an unconventional trigger mechanism said to be "fast action". This allows a cocked hammer to be pushed to its down position while still keeping the mainspring compressed. A light pull on the trigger causes the hammer to flick back.

FN Herstal 5.7-mm Five-seveN Pistol

The Five-seveN is a semi-automatic pistol manufactured by Fabrique Nationale de Herstal that uses the same 5.7 x 28 mm cartridge used in the P90 sub-machine gun. Although the 5.7-mm round is less that half the weight of a conventional 9-mm, FN claim that it can penetrate a Kevlar vest. Current users include Special Forces, counter-terrorist groups and SWAT teams.

In 2005, a United States government version, the Five-seveN USG, was produced with a square trigger guard, checkered grip and a larger, reversible magazine release.

Glock 17

The Austrian-made Glock 17 9 x 19-mm calibre pistol is the most widely used law-enforcement weapon worldwide and is in use in more than fifty countries. It is light and has an above-average magazine capacity of 17 cartridges. It is particularly popular among Special Forces because it is reliable even in extreme conditions such as the jungle, desert or Arctic.

Heckler & Koch 9-mm
P7M8 and P7M13 Pistols

After the terrorist attack at the 1972 Olympics, it was decided to equip the German police with a new pistol. The new weapon was to take the 9 x 19-mm Parabellum cartridge, weigh no more than 2.2 lb, have a barrel not exceeding 180 mm and a service life of 10,000 rounds. It should work equally well in either hand, be safe to carry with a loaded chamber, quick to draw and ready to fire instantaneously. After the resulting competition, the German police selected three different pistols: the Walther P5, Swiss SIG-Sauer P225, designated the P6, and the Heckler & Koch P7, officially designed the PSP or *Polizei Selbstlade Pistole* – "Police Self-Loading Pistol".

Production of the P7 started in 1979. Soon after, the pistol was adopted by the German Federal Police's counter-terrorism unit GSG 9 and the German Army's Special Forces. The pistol was also exported to several countries. The initial version had an eight-round magazine and was designated the P7M8. A later version taking a double-column 13-round magazine, the P7M13, was subsequently developed.

Heckler & Koch Mk23
Mod 0 SOCOM Pistol and USP

The Mk23 Mod 0 is an offensive handgun developed at the request of USSOCOM to compete with the Colt OHWS – Offensive Handgun Weapon System. It was selected over the Colt and went into production in 1991. It is powerful, reliable and accurate – capable of making a 2-inch target group at 50 yards. It comes with a silencer made by Knight's Armament Company and a laser sight developed by Insight Technology. Consequently operatives prefer to carry the smaller and lighter HK USP – Universal Self-loading Pistol – which shares most features of the Mk23 Mod 0 but is half the weight with a shorter barrel.

Heckler & Koch P11 7.62 Underwater Pistol

The Heckler & Koch P11 is a firearm made specifically to be used underwater. It has a cluster of five barrels that are turned electrically, powered by a battery in the grip.

As bullets do not travel well through water, each chamber is loaded with a 7.62-mm steel dart about 4 inches long. It is powerful and accurate enough to penetrate a diving mask at up to about 15 yards and can also inflict a deadly wound at that range, though in combat conditions underwater it is rare to see so far. Sights are also rudimentary. The trigger guard is very large so the weapon can be used when wearing diving gloves.

Out of the water, the P11 is effective at up to 32 yards and makes as much noise as a muffled 9-mm pistol. When all the barrels have been discharged, the gun is reloaded by replacing the entire barrel cluster, which can then be returned to Heckler & Koch for reloading.

A weapon was specially made for the German Bundeswehr *Kampfschwimmer* – "Combat Divers" – and remains classified. However, the P11 is thought to be in service with the British SAS, US Special Forces and the Dutch, Danish, Norwegian, Italian, French and Israeli navies.

IM Metal 9-mm HS2000 Pistol

The 9-mm HS2000 pistol was developed by the IM Metal company for the Croatian Army in the late 1990s. Production of the 9-mm HS2000 started in 1999, with the first pistols being delivered to the Croatian Army the same year. In the early 2000s the Springfield Armory Company of Genseo, Illinois, became the sole importer of HS2000 pistols in the US and began to offer an improved version of HS2000 as the Springfield XD – eXtreme Duty – pistol. Several American police departments began to issue these pistols or approve them for personal purchase by police officers – hence their interest to Special Forces. An earlier version, the HS95, is also in use.

IMI 9 x 19-mm Uzi Pistol

Uzi Pistol is a semi-automatic version of the Micro Uzi developed for export. Externally, it is distinguished by not having a stock or a recoil compensator. Israeli counter-terrorist units use the Para Micro Uzi. It has a side-mounted charging handle to make room for top- and bottom-mounted Picatinny rails and an angled pistol-grip to accommodate a 33-round Glock 18 magazine.

IMI Jericho 941 Self-Loading Pistol

During the early 1990s, Israel Military Industries developed a combat pistol, the Jericho 941. The design was based on the Italian Tanfoglio pistol, which is itself a clone of the Czechoslovak CZ-75. The model number 941 came from the two calibres initially available – the 9 x 19-mm Luger and the new .41AE. However, the .41AE cal has been dropped from the Jericho line and replaced by the more successful .40 S&W chambering and, later, by the .45ACP. Jericho pistols are used by Israeli security force and are widely exported.

MAB PA15 9-mm Pistol

The MAB PA15 pistol had been developed by Manufacture d'Armes Automatiques de Bayonne (MAB) in the late 1970s as the standard sid earm of the French Army. The production of the MAB PA15 was ended in the late 1980s, and has since been replaced in French service by the licence-built Beretta 92G pistol.

Makarova PM

The Makarov PM – or *Pistolet Makarova* – is a semi-automatic pistol designed in the late 1940s by Nikolai Fyodorovich Makarov. In 1951 it was chosen as the Soviet Union's standard military side arm because of its accuracy, killing power, ease of manufacture and simplicity – it had few moving parts. It remained in service with the Soviet military and police until the collapse of the Soviet Union in 1991, though variants remain in production in Russia and Bulgaria.

The most widely known variant, the Makarov PMM, was redesigned to take 9-mm Makarov High-Impulse cartridges with armour-piercing bullets.

SIG Sauer P226

The Schweizerische Industrie Gesellschaft-Sauer P226 is a full-sized service pistol originally chambered for a 9-mm Luger round. It was designed for the 1984 US trials as a replacement for the M1911A1. The Beretta 92SB-F won on cost, but the P226 performed so well that it was taken up by the US Navy and, when delivered to a higher specification, adopted by the SEALs.

In 2001, a new variant was taken up by the US Department of Homeland Security. The SIG Sauer P226 is also used by the British SAS.

Smith & Wesson M10 revolver

The Smith & Wesson M10 is one of the most successful revolvers of all times. It began in 1899, when S&W began to manufacture its "Hand Ejector" model in .38 Long Colt calibre. This was further developed by new versions in 1902 and 1915. In the 1920s, Smith & Wesson renamed the .38 Hand Ejector the Military and Police model. Then in 1958, after the introduction of a model numbering system, the Military and Police revolver became a model number 10.

During the twentieth century, it is estimated that over six million M10s were manufactured, including one million or so revolvers delivered to the US Government during the Second World War. A large number were also exported into Britain and Commonwealth countries.

The guns are popular with American police departments and were also used by the military, especially in the US Air Force and US Navy. The M10 was widely copied by manufacturers in France, Spain, France and elsewhere.

Steyr Special Purpose Pistol

The 9-mm Steyr SPP is a semi-auto-only version of the Steyr TMP – Tactical Machine Pistol. Under 12 inches long, the TMP has selective fire capability that in fully automatic mode has a cyclic rate of 900 rounds a minute. Available only to military, police and other official organizations, the TMP is finding favour among professionals in the field of VIP protection, given its compact size, high firepower and overall fine quality.

The SPP is slightly longer and weighs 3.1 lb with a fully loaded fifteen-round magazine in place.

Tsniitochmash 7.62-mm PSS Silent Pistol

The PSS or *Pistolet Sptsialnyj Samozaryadnyj* – "special self-loading pistol" – was developed for the Spetsnaz, Soviet Army's Special Forces, and the Soviet KGB for use on reconnaissance operations and assassinations. It uses a unique 7.62 x 42-mm necked round with an internal piston whose stem rests against the base of the bullet. When fired, the propellant pushes the piston forward, delivering enough force to project the bullet 50 yards or more. As it moves forward, the piston then seals the neck of the cartridge, preventing smoke, blast or noise from escaping the barrel. Adopted around 1983, it is still in use with elite Russian anti-terrorist teams.

Vanad P-93 Pistol

The Vanad P-83 first entered service in the late 1970s as a replacement for the P-64 in Polish service. Similar to the P-64, but generally using pressings, stampings and welding, it was cheaper and easier to produce. The P-93 is an updated version of the P-83 that is easier to use in two-handed shooting. It has a squared-off trigger guard front for the index finger of the supporting hand. The P-93 is also safer to carry, with a hammer safety, and has an adjustable high-contrast rear sight and high-contrast foresight.

Walther 7.65-mm Models PP and PPK Pistols

Produced in large numbers between 1929 and 1945, Walther PP pistols, along with the similar but smaller PPK, were widely used by the police and military in Hitler's Germany. After the Second World War, production of the PP and PPK pistols was resumed by Manurhin in France under licence. Later production was returned to the Walther factory in Germany and the pistols were used widely by police and many non-infantry officers in several European armies. The PP stands for *Polizeipistole* – "police pistol" – and the PPK for *Polizeipistole Kriminalmodell* – "police pistol detective model" – as it was easier to conceal in plain clothes. Mistakenly PPK is thought to be an acronym for *Polizeipistole Kurz* – "police pistol short". The Walther PPK is, of course, favoured by James Bond in the later Bond books.

The PPK/S is a high-bred sports model using the PPK's barrel and the PP's frame that was introduced after the 1968 US Gun Control Act excluded the PPK on account of its small size. Currently, Walther PP, PPK and PPK/S pistols are manufactured in the US by the Smith & Wesson Company under licence from Walther. Copies of the Walther PP were manufactured after the Second World War in East Germany, Hungary, Romania and Turkey.

Walther 9-mm Model P5 Pistol

The Walther P5 is a 9-mm semi-automatic pistol. It was developed from the Second World War-vintage Walther P38 pistol, and its P1 successor in 1979, when the German police asked for a new side arm incorporating modern safety features.

The British government bought 3,000 Walther P5 Compact pistols, a shorter and lighter version, in the 1980s for 14th Intelligence Company on active service in Northern Ireland. Designated Pistol L102A1, some have surfaced in the US collectors' market where they are erroneously called the "SAS Pistol". However, a short-barrelled version of the Walther P38, the P38K (for *Kurz* or "short") is in use by the *KSK* or *Kommando Spezialkräfte* – "Special Forces Command" – part of Germany's Special Forces modelled closely on the British SAS.

23

BAYONETS AND KNIVES

Eickhorn-Solingen Aircrew Survival Escape Knife

Advertised as the "ultimate escape tool", this knife has one laser-cut serrated edge and a second half-serrated edge. It is designed to work at temperatures from –40° to + 176° Fahrenheit. It has a black all-weather grip designed to work to military specification and each blade is individually serial numbered so they can be traced.

Eickhorn-Solingen KCB 77 Bayonets

The German Eickhorn-Solingen company produce a range of all-weather bayonets made from high-carbon steel that can be retro-fitted to all NATO weapons. The standard KCB 77 M10 is a bowie-type blade that is 6.9 inches long and weighs 10.76 ounces, though there are longer versions – and the KCB 77 M1 comes with a wire-cutter, screw and bottle-opener incorporated.

Eickhorn-Solingen Mk 3 Combat Knife

Eickhorn-Solingen Mk 3 is the standard NATO combat knife. It has a straight dagger blade 6.7 inches long. Like other

Eickhorn-Solingen knives, all parts are dull and non-reflective.
It weighs 6.3 ounces.

Eickhorn-Solingen USM 7
Bayonet with USM 8 A1 Scabbard

The Eickhorn-Solingen USM 7 Bayonet with a USM 8 A1
Scabbard is a standard equipment item in the US Army and in
many armed forces around the world.

With a relatively low weight, good balance, the USM 7, if
kept dry, is electrically insulated up to 500 volts. It is fungus-
resistant, NBC-resistant and de-contaminable. The catch can
easily be exchanged. The scabbard is made from polyester
which is resistant to fungus in tropical climates and is self-
draining to prevent any accumulation of water in the scabbard.
The ends are heat-cut and there are no metal pieces around the
opening to reduce noise. The bayonet weighs 10 ounces and has
a blade 6.6 inches long and less than an inch wide.

NRS Scouting Knife

Also known as the NRS-2, the Russian scouting knife is similar
to the Chinese Type 85 as it has a firearm concealed in the hilt,
although the Russian version only fires a single shot. In the
handle there is a short barrel and chamber which takes a single
7.62 x 42-mm SP-4 of the type used by the Tsniitochmash silent
pistol. This makes it virtually silent.

The gun is fired by reversing the knife in the hand as the
muzzle, in this case, is at the rear of the handle. The pistol is
aimed with a notched crosspiece that acts as a rudimentary
sight. A sliding safety catch is then released and a trigger bar set
into the handle fires the bullet. How practical the pistol is as a
weapon is debatable as the blade has to be pointed towards the
firer in use. The effective range is just 82 feet.

As a knife, though, it is a substantial tool. Its 6.4-inch blade
can sever steel rods up to a third of an inch in diameter. The
scabbard is insulated so the knife can be used to cut electrical
cables. A screwdriver is also incorporated.

Applegate-Fairburn Knife

This folding knife can be opened with one hand and locked open. Privately purchased by British Special Forces, it has a double-bevelled blade and sheath made from ballistic cloth. The covert version has a close length of 3.8 inches; open it is 8.3 inches. It weighs 3.9 ounces.

BCB Spec Plus and Survival 1201 Machetes

Bought privately by UK Special Forces, the Spec Plus machete has a high-grip, ribbed, moulded handle with finger guard and a 12.9-inch black-coated, single-edged, stainless-steel blade. It comes with a sheath and a lanyard.

The Survival 1201 machete is an altogether more sophisticated survival tool incorporating three cutting edges. There is one for heavy-duty chopping, a finer edge for stunning and a sharper edge for preparing food. The 15.7-inch blade is made from carbon steel 0.23 inches thick.

Fairburn-Sykes Fighting Knife

The Fairbairn-Sykes fighting knife was designed by William Ewart Fairbairn and Eric Anthony Sykes in the 1930s. It became famous during the Second World War when it was issued to British Commando units and the SAS, then taken up by Marine Raiders and the Office of Strategic Studies, who produced their own version. It continues to be made to this day.

The thin twin-edged dagger with a foil grip is often compared to a stiletto. But the stiletto is designed solely for stabbing, while the Fairbairn-Sykes fighting knife is also edged to cut, though it is still thin enough to slip between the ribs. It is also compared to the US Marine Corps Ka-Bar. However, the Ka-Bar is a multi-purpose combat tool, while the Fairbairn-Sykes fighting knife was designed exclusively for fighting.

According to Fairbairn: "The hilt should fit easily in your hand, and the blade should not be so heavy that it tends to drag the hilt from your fingers in a loose grip. It is essential that the blade has a sharp stabbing point and good cutting edges, because an artery torn through (as against a clean cut) tends to contract and stop the bleeding. If a main artery is cleanly severed, the wounded man will quickly lose consciousness and die."

The original design has a blade just 5.5 inches, but this was gradually increased to 6.5, then 7 inches. After the war the blade length was increased on 7.5 inches on the grounds that it might have to pass through a Soviet greatcoat. Fairbairn ran courses on how to use the knife in Britain and the US.

The Fairbairn-Sykes knife was in use throughout the Second World War, Korea and Vietnam, and dozens of companies started to make their own version. There are now more than 200 different makes based on the original Fairbairn-Sykes design. The US military has its own in the Gerber Mark II, adopted in 1966. Some two million of the original British version have been produced. The early ones are thought to be of better quality and are highly sought-after.

SOG RFB81 X-42 Recondo

In 1966, the MACV Recondo School was established to train Special Forces Units in long-range recon tactics and commando operations. Graduates capable of infiltrating enemy-controlled territory for long periods without being resupplied were called "Recondos" and were thought to exemplify courage and confidence. Their name was adopted for the X-42 knife by manufacturer SOG, who themselves borrowed their name from the Vietnam War-era Studies and Observation Group.

The 5.3-inch blade is made from BG-42 stainless steel, which is use to make high-speed ball bearings and jet-engine parts. It is strong and resistant to corrosion. The X-42 has a glass-reinforced Zytel handle designed to allow fluid movement from front to reverse gripping positions. It weighs 6.3 ounces.

SOG S37 SEAL Knife 2000

The SOG S37 US Navy SEAL Knife 2000 survived one of the most extensive test and evaluation programmes ever undertaken by the US government. This tactical knife was subjected to tests to evaluate its tip-breaking stress, blade-breaking limit, sharpness, edge retention, handle twist-off force, penetration, and gasoline and acetylene torch resistance. It was left immersed in salt water for two weeks, and used for chopping, hammering, prying and cutting six different types of rope and line, then subjected to intense hands-on competition in the field.

It has a 7-inch, partially serrated blade and weighs 12.6 ounces.

SOG Scuba/Demo SSD99

The original Scuba/Demo was the rarest of Special Forces knives and possibly the rarest military knife in existence. Only one is known to exist today. Originally, thirty-nine were made, thirty-eight of which were delivered to the Naval Advisory Detachment for missions along the North Vietnamese coastline. Of the thirty-eight issued, thirty-six were lost in operations and the other two were never seen again.

However, SOG have recreated the Scuba/Demo in the SSD99. It has a 7.25-inch steel blade that is just .230 inches thick. The blade is double-edged and has a unique fully serrated spine. It has a full tang that is surrounded by an epoxied, stacked-leather washer handle with a brass pommel. A brass cross-guard improves the balance. They are much sought-after. The first 250 were numbered.

Norinco .22 Type 85 Bayonet Pistol

A Chinese version of a Spetsnaz combination knife-pistol, the .22 Type 85 Bayonet Pistol has four barrels in the grip which fire standard .22 LR cartridges. There are two barrels on either side of the blade with the muzzles at the base. They are loaded by removing a cap at the rear of the handle. The hand guard incorporates a rotary catch that locks the trigger when the knife is used. Rotating anti-clockwise unlocks the trigger which then fires the barrels one at a time.

The pistol is held at arm's length. There is a sight incorporated in the hand guard and a notch at the rear of the handle. Projectiles can penetrate pine boards .335 inches thick at a range of 5.46 yards, but they cannot penetrate an aircraft's pressure bulkhead.

In one version, the blade can be folded for concealment. It only has three barrels and is chambered for .22 rimfire ammunition.

24

EXPLOSIVES AND RAPID-ENTRY EQUIPMENT

C4

C4, or composition 4, is a type of plastic explosive where the explosive chemicals are mixed with plastic binder. The binder coats the explosive materials, so they are less sensitive to shock and heat, making it relatively safe to handle the explosive. It also makes the explosive malleable, so you can mould it into different shapes.

The explosive component in C4 is cyclotrimethylene-trinitramine ($C_3H_6N_6O_6$), which is commonly called RDX – variously rapid demolition explosive, royal demolition explosive or research development explosive. When mixed with a binder and plasticizer it has the consistency of modelling clay. A third of a pound of the explosive was found in an abandoned suitcase in a Philadelphia bus terminal, enough to have levelled the building.

However, it is difficult to detonate and small amounts will burn without exploding. Indeed, soldiers in Vietnam used to burn C4 taken from Claymore mines to boil water or heat their C-rations. You can even fire a rifle bullet into it without setting it off. To do that, you need a detonator or a blasting cap which applies a powerful shock that triggers the RDX.

In the resulting chemical reaction, the RDX decays to release a large amount of hot gas – notably nitrogen and carbon oxides. These expand at about 26,400 feet per second, blasting everything around them. At this rate, it is impossible to outrun the explosion like they do in the movies. The explosion is essentially instantaneous and actually takes place in two phases. The initial blast moves outward so rapidly that it creates a vacuum at the centre. There is therefore a second blast as air rushes back inwards to equalize the pressure.

C4 is widely used in munitions such as the Claymore mine. It is also used for military demolition as it is relatively safe to carry on the battlefield and can be shaped easily to fulfil requirements. It has, unfortunately, also found favour with terrorists. The US is the major manufacturer of C4 and it tightly guards its supply. However, Iran has developed similar material and the UK manufactures is own version known as PE4.

Camlock PDE Vehicle System

Camlock Engineering Ltd of Hereford worked with the SAS to develop a system of platforms and assault ladders that fit on top of a Land Rover or any other heavy-duty four-by-four, such as a Range Rover, Mercedes G-Wagon or Toyota Land Cruiser. It is designed for Special Forces troops who are making a fast assault on an aircraft or building.

It has a rigid deck that can be fitted to the roof of the vehicle in seconds, and is designed to stay in place though any manner of manoeuvre. It has rails and grab handles, so the troopers can hang on as the vehicle accelerates, brakes or turns. There are a side ladder secured with heavy steel hooks to mount on the roof and a non-slip platform that fits over the bonnet for rapid dismounting. On top, the assault ladders are quickly adjustable, but lock easily into position making it simple to deploy to the entry point.

Claymore Mine

The M18A1 Claymore is a directional anti-personnel mine first used by the US military. It fires shrapnel in a 60-degree arc with a range of about 110 yards though it is designed to be most lethal at 55 yards. Its primary use is in ambushes and as an anti-infiltration device against enemy infantry.

The Claymore mine is renowned for the words "Front Toward Enemy" embossed on the outer surface of the curved case. Two pairs of scissor legs allow the mine to stand vertically. Otherwise it can be strapped to a post or tree and is aimed using a peep-sight. Inside there is a 1.5-lb block of C-4 explosive covered by a layer of epoxy resin containing around 700 $\frac{1}{8}$-inch diameter steel balls. When detonated, these are blasted out of the mine at a speed of 3,995 feet second. The mine is carried on a bandolier which has an instruction sheet attached to the inside. The mine can be detonated using either an electrical or non-electrical firing system. Usually it is set off using a M57 Firing Device known as a "clacker".

The mine can also be detonated using a short-timed fuse, usually as a way to deter a pursuer. It can also be set off by the enemy if it is armed with a M142 Multipurpose Firing Device, M5 Pressure Release Device or mousetrap, tripwires or infrared, acoustic or vibration sensors. However, this "uncontrolled" use of the M18A1 is banned under the 1996 treaty on anti-personnel mines.

The design of the Claymore dates back to the Second World War when German weapon designers discovered that when a sheet of explosive resting on a heavy backing surface detonates the blast develops in a single direction away from the backing plate.

During the Korean War, Canada developed the Phoenix landmine that projected a spray of 0.25-inch steel towards the enemy during mass attacks. Steel cubes were embedded in 5 lb of explosive but the mine was too large to be a practical infantry weapon and had a maximum effective range of only 20 to 30 yards.

In 1952 the Explosive Research Corporation further developed its concept and produced some 10,000 M18 Claymore mines. Some were used in Vietnam. Looking much like today's Claymore, though lacking the iconic "Front Toward Enemy", it stood on three folding spike legs on the bottom, blasting 0.25-inch steel cubes some 90 feet. A proposal to improve the mine was issued. A new version should weigh less than 3.5 lb and throw enough fragments of shrapnel 55 yards to achieve a

100 per cent strike rate on a man-sized 1.3 square feet target. The area covered by the fragment area should not be more than 8 feet high or 60 feet wide. The fragments should travel at more than 4,000 feet per second, delivering 58 lb – the energy required to produce lethal injury – to the target.

Initial experiments with hardened alloy ball bearings failed because the balls fractured into fragments that were neither aerodynamic nor large enough to be lethal. It was found that softer balls did not fragment and preformed aerodynamically; fixing them in a plastic matrix stopped blast from the explosive "leaking" around the shrapnel.

CN Gas

CN, or chloroacetophenone (C_8H_7ClO), commonly known as "tear gas", is supplied to paramilitary and police forces in a small pressurized aerosol. It is generally known by the proprietary name "Mace". Its use has widely been replaced by pepper spray or CS gas, although it is still used in combination with other agents.

Like CS gas, it irritates the mucous membranes of the eyes, nose, mouth and lungs, which can sometimes result in the temporary loss of balance and orientation. It can also produce longer-term effects such as dermatitis in those who are allergic to it.

CS Gas

CS gas, or 2-chlorobenzalmalononitrile ($C_{10}H_5ClN_2$) is issued to Special Forces for use in hostage or other urban situations. It was first made in 1928 by two Americans, Ben Corson and Roger Staughton, whose initials give the chemical its name. However it was developed as a weapon in England at the Ministry of Defence's laboratory at Porton Down in the 1950s and 1960s. It was first tested on animals with little effect as they were largely protected by fur and had only rudimentary tear ducts, but subsequently proved itself when used on British Army volunteers.

The compound is a solid at room temperature, though to be effective it has to be used as an aerosol. In civilian use, this causes problems, but in military use it can simply be vaporized by the hot gases from a thermal grenade.

Stronger than conventional tear gas, CS reacts with moisture on the skin, causing extreme irritation, and in the eyes, causing a burning sensation which activates the tear ducts. The sensation is so acute that the victim cannot help closing their eyes. Other reactions include the nose filling with mucus, a burning in the nose and throat areas, restricted breathing, and dizziness and disorientation. Concentrated doses can also induce uncontrollable coughing and vomiting. Those allergic to CS can develop dermatitis, but that is usually alleviated after a few months. However, it has been noted that people who are drunk, taking drugs or are mentally ill are unaffected by it. Soldiers are regularly exposed to it and can develop a certain tolerance.

The British first used CS gas in Cyprus in 1958, and it was widely used by the Americans in Vietnam to clear the Viet Cong out of their tunnel complexes. The British Army used it in Northern Ireland during the "Battle of Bogside" in 1969, and the British police used to quell riots in the Toxteth area of Liverpool in 1981. The military also use it to test their NBC suits. In the US, it was famously used in the Waco siege in 1993. Both British and American army recruits are exposed to CS during training.

Iraq successfully developed CS during the 1970s and Saddam Hussein used CS against the Kurds and against Iran during the Iran-Iraq War.

Door Rams and Rippers

Sigma Security Devices of Dover make the Enforcer door ram which is used by security services worldwide. The 35 lb steel ram has a heavy tube blocked at one end, mounted in a frame with two handles. Used by one man, it is swung against the lock and delivers an impact of over 3.5 tons. This can smash through even a reinforced door in seconds, breaking up to seven locks, bolts and chains with a single blow. The Enforcer is just 23 inches long and fits in a back-pack so that it can be deployed after climbing or abseiling to the entry point.

There is a smaller version known as the Firecracker, which

is just 18 inches long, and a heavier version, known as the Disrupter, that weighs 40 lb. The 55-inch Two-Man Enforcer weighing 72 lb can break through any door that opens inwards.

For doors that open outwards there is the Door Ripper. It has a blade that is driven into the gap between the door and the jamb and a racket mechanism that allows the blade to be worked behind the door to overcome resistance and improve leverage. One pull on the handle will break any bolt or lock. The Ripper is 31 inches long and weighs 13 lb.

The Hooligan Tool is designed to break open locks, grates, grilles, windows and such like. Some 42 inches long and weighing 14 lb, it has a straight, high-alloy, steel shaft with a claw at one end that can be used like a can opener to cut open vehicles and metal containers. Or it can be fitted with another type of claw that fits over locks and hasps, breaking them.

At the other end there is a flat "duckbill" wedge, that can be used to lever open windows or doors, and a sharp, tapered spike, that can be pushed behind locks and latches.

As an alternative to the Enforcer, assault teams use a hydraulic ram that can exert five tons of pressure. The device is clamped to the door and a valve released, taking down the door in thirty to forty seconds. It is virtually silent in operation.

A hydraulic version, known as the Blower, exerts 5 tons across the door frame and 11 tons of pressure on the door itself. The entire unit weighs just 60 lb.

Elsie

There is a minimal difference between the C3A1 and C3A2 anti-personnel mines, both of which are known as Elsie. Originally Canadian they were also manufactured in the UK and used by the British Army.

An Elsie mine is shaped like a short, stubby, black carrot. The small raised pressure plate on the top surface of the mine is covered with a pad of flock material that acts as camouflage. Pressure on this plate releases a retaining ball bearing, thus freeing a striker which is held under tension by a coiled spring. The striker flies upwards into the stab detonator, triggering the charge. This is small compared to other anti-personnel mines that contain a minimum of one ounce or high explosive. The Elsie contains just a third of an ounce of RDX explosive.

However, the Elsie is effective as it is the only anti-personnel mine which uses a shaped charge that drives the full force of detonation upwards, straight through the sole of the victim's foot, making a small, circular hole all the way through. The wound is debilitating, but rarely fatal. The Elsie is designed to disable its victims, not to kill them.

Elsie mines come with an aluminium ring to make them easy to locate using a metal detector. However, the ring can easily be removed making it a "minimal metal mine", hard to detect by conventional means. Due to the simplicity of the firing mechanism, the Elsie can be cleared using blast methods.

It is now being phased out under the Ottawa Treaty.

Hatton Round

The Hatton round or breaching cartridge is a shotgun shell designed to help speed an assault force through a locked door. Fired at a range of 4 to 6 inches, it is aimed between the jamb and the doorknob, and destroys the lock mechanism. Or it can be used on the hinges to knock the door down.

The 12-gauge round is designed to reduce the risk of ricochet. Weighing 1.75 ounces it is made of compressed zinc or lead powder bound with wax. This breaks up on impact, delivering the full force of the round to the target, thereby minimizing the risk of injury to anyone behind the door. These rounds will penetrate fire doors clad with metal plate on both sides, prison-cell doors, half-inch bulletproof glass and car tyres.

Lewes Bomb

The Lewes bomb was invented by Jock Lewes, second in command of the SAS in 1941. Using a delayed fuse, the charge was placed on enemy aircraft, the preferred location being where the wing met the fuselage as this was the best place to cause the most damage since aircraft often have their fuel cells in the wings.

It was developed because grenades and other explosive devices proved unreliable, and the only available bomb was too cumbersome to be carried by a paratrooper – initially, it was planned that the SAS would be deployed by parachute.

The bomb was a dual blast-incendiary device. It comprised a pound of Nobel 808 plastic explosive and a quarter pound of thermite mixed with a bit of engine oil. A 2-ounce dry guncotton primer, a detonator and a 30-second fuse were inserted. The fuse was usually ignited using a time pencil or pencil detonator, though pressure switches and release switches were also used.

M14 and M-16 Anti-Personnel Mines

The M14 is a non-metallic, blast-type AP mine whose main charge is one ounce of the explosive tetryl. The mine is cylindrical in shape, $2\frac{3}{16}$ inches in diameter and $1\frac{9}{16}$ inches high weighing approximately $3\frac{1}{2}$ lb. The M14 is designed to incapacitate, not to kill, as a wounded man on the battlefield ties up enemy resources. The original M14 mine has been modified by gluing a metal washer to the bottom to make it easier to detect and, consequently, to clear when the conflict is over.

The Americans developed the anti-personnel mine further in the 1960s with the M-16. It was developed as a "bounding mine" along the lines of the German Second World War S-mine, or *Schrapnellmine*, known among the Allies as the "Bouncing Betty" or "Jumping Jack", which jumped to approximately waist height before exploding into deadly fragments.

The latest version, the M-16A2, has a cylindrical, steel body that resembles a large tin can. A tubular, pronged M605 pressure/pull fuse is screwed into the top before the mine is armed and buried. A pressure of 7.7 lb on one of the three prongs or a pull of 3.3 lb on a tripwire sets off the mine. When tripped the mine bounds around five feet into the air and explodes, scattering fragments over a radius of 100 feet.

The mine can be spotted visually or located with a metal detector under most field conditions. Its effectiveness declines when left buried, however it is reckoned that 70 per cent will still remain functional for eight years buried in clay soil in temperate zones or up to twelve years in the tropics.

M61 (L2A2) Grenade

The M61 grenade is a fragmentation hand grenade used by the US Armed Forces since the Vietnam War. It weights 16 ounces and can be thrown 130 feet by the average soldier. The M61 contains 5.5 ounces of Composition B, a mixture of TNT and RDX explosive, around an M204A1 or M204A2 fuse.

The fragments are produced by a serrated wire coil inside the grenade's thin steel casing. When the grenade explodes, the coil breaks into sharp steel fragments that fly out at high speed, causing casualties up to 50 feet away, though its lethal radius is 16 feet. In Vietnam, these grenades gave their name to "fragging" as they were popularly thought to be used to dispose of unpopular officers.

Many nations have produced grenades of a similar design. The British have L2A2, the Russians the RGD-5, the Portuguese the M312, the South Africans the M26 and the Israelis the M26A2. Many millions of these grenades have been manufactured over the years. It is sometimes referred to as a "lemon" grenade, as it is shaped like a lemon.

P.W. Allen Explosive Wall Breaching

P.W. Allen have developed a purpose-built Explosive Wall Breaching system, which is a plastic shell with an oval frame which carries the explosives. This is surrounded by water. The device is placed against the wall and when fired the water traps the counter-blast and directs all the energy from the explosion forward, cutting a man-sized hole in the wall. The assault team can then pile through.

Protective Clothing

The Avon SF10 is the Special Forces variant of the standard S10 NBC Respirator, the protective gas mask currently in service with all branches of the British armed forces. It comprises a butyl rubber face-piece with two round scratch-resistant eyepieces and an adjustable rubber head-harness. Speech modules allow both direct speech and microphone communications, and there is a drinking straw and tap to allow the wearer to safely drink from a canteen in contaminated environments. This Special Forces version has tinted eye pieces to protect the user's eyes from the glare of flashbangs.

For assaults, troopers wear clothing made out of Nomex fire-resistant material – the same material used to make fire-suits for racing drivers. They also wear Blackhawk assault vests and belts which have plenty of pouches for spare ammunitions, flashbangs, CS-gas canisters, communications equipment, forced-entry tools and the like.

Russian PMN

The Russian PMN-1 and PMN-2 – both known as the Black Widow – are blast-type anti-personnel mines designed and manufactured in Russia. They are one of the most widely used and commonly found devices during demining operations. Both mines are cylindrical in shape and the size of a man's palm. They have a bakelite case with a black rubber pressure-plate and contain TNT explosive. Large numbers were found in Iraq in 2003.

The PMN-1 mine is particularly deadly because it contains half a pound of TNT, compared to the 1.8 ounces in a standard blast mine. While a normal mine is designed to take off a man's foot, the PMN-2 mines is designed to destroy his entire leg and injure the other one. The PMN-2 is almost as deadly, containing nearly a quarter of a pound of a mixture of TNT and RDX explosive.

PMN-3 mines have been used in Chechnya. These have anti-handling devices and a self-destruct incorporated. They can be dropped by helicopter and then armed by a pneumatic device. A self-destruct can be set to detonate in 30 minutes, one, two, four or eight hours.

Sting Grenades

Sting grenades have been developed alongside stun grenades. Their design is based on the fragmentation grenade, but instead of a metal casing which produces shrapnel, they are cased in two spheres of hard rubber. The explosive, primer and detonator are inside the smaller inner sphere and the space between that and the outer sphere is filled with tiny, hard rubber balls. When it is set off, the victim is hit by the blunt force of the projectiles. This winds and incapacitates him with, hopefully, no long-term deleterious effects. The subject is very often incapacitated, winded, or at the very least dislodged from cover. Some varieties are also loaded with CS gas.

The advantage over the flashbang is that there is no defence. A well-trained terrorist can mitigate some of the effects of a flashbang by closing his eyes and putting his fingers in his ears. And the victim does not have to be looking at the sting grenade for it to take its full effect. Sting grenades are also much more likely to cause a victim to fall or double up in pain, giving better lines of sight to unaffected targets in the area.

However, the effective range of a sting grenade is limited compared to a stun grenade and the determined terrorist can steel himself against its effects.

Stun Grenades

Stun grenades were developed for use in hostage situations by the British SAS, who call them flash-and-bang grenades, or "flashbangs". Officially designated NFDDs – Noise and Flash Diversionary Devices – they are used to disorientate and distract hostiles in a room, giving the entry team a few precious moments in which to enter and neutralize them. Typically, a stun grenade can incapacitate an enemy as a combat threat for up to a minute. Since its development in the late 1970s, the flashbang concept has been adopted by Special Forces and police forces around the world.

The stun grenade contains a mercury and magnesium powder which upon detonation creates a blinding flash, the equivalent to 300,000 candlepower. The flash of light momentarily activates all photosensitive cells in the retina, making normal vision impossible for approximately five seconds until the eye restores the retina to its normal state. Those who have witnessed flashbangs describe seeing a single frame for the five seconds, as if their vision had been "paused".

The 160 decibels of sound produced by the grenade not only shocks and stuns but is also loud enough to disrupt the balance function of anyone in range, causing severe dizziness. Modern stun grenades have evolved to detonate multiple times and can contain irritants such as CS or CN tear gas.

While the flashbang may knock out hostage-takers, members of the SAS assault force become gradually conditioned to the effects of flashbangs during training. Their equipment also protects them. Ear plugs protect the trooper's ears and the tinted eye pieces in SF-100 respirators protect the eyes against the flash, while the respirator itself guards against the effects of the smoke and gas released by the grenades.

The SAS used flashbangs when they assisted German GSG-9 Special Forces when they stormed a hijacked Lufthansa airliner at Mogadishu airport in 1977. As the GSG-9 team assaulted the plane, two SAS men hurled flashbangs towards the cockpit, causing confusion within. The SAS used stun-grenades during its breaking of the Iranian Embassy Siege in 1980 and again at Peterhead Prison.

The SBS also are also issued with flashbangs for use in their maritime counter-terrorist role. Naturally, their flashbangs are waterproofed.

The American version of flashbang is the XM84 Stun Grenade, which contains one-sixth of an ounce of a pyrotechnic metal-oxidant mixture of magnesium and ammonium perchlorate or potassium perchlorate. On detonation, this produces a blinding flash of six to eight million candela and a deafening blast of 170-180 dB. It is important that the fuse and body of the grenade body remain intact and do not fragment, harming the hostages, so the hexagonal steel body tube of the XM84 has holes down its sides to allow the light and sound out. Although there is no danger of injury from shrapnel, it is still possible to be burnt by the explosion or be injured by the concussive effect.

Recently, the Blank Firing Impact Grenade has been developed. This contains a mechanism to fire a blank cartridge when dropped at any angle onto a hard surface from a height of 3 feet or more. The advantage is that they are reusable and, when disarmed, are safe and easy to transport.

Surveillance Equipment

P.W. Allen produce a kit that comprises an endoscope with the appropriate drilling equipment. The scope is just one tenth of an inch in diameter – the size of a match head. It has an offset mirror giving a 55-degree field of view, but can be rotated to give an 85-degree view of the room under surveillance. The image can be viewed directly through an eyepiece, or remotely by connecting a video camera. If the room is in darkness, an infra-red camera can be used.

But pictures only tell half the story. A stainless-steel microphone one sixth of an inch in diameter can be inserted alongside. This is connected to a battery-powered amplifier.

The company also has under-door views that can be slipped through a gap of less than a quarter of an inch. Again it has a 55-degree field of view and can be adjusted to observe the entire room. It comes with a right-angle adaptor so the user can inspect the inner surface of the door to check for booby-traps or barricades.

Many front doors have peepholes that allow the person inside to see out, but prevent anyone outside looking in. However, there are devices like small telescopes that reverse the position. Otherwise a small low-light, purpose-built video camera can be clamped to the outside of the peephole. The angle of view depends on the optical characteristics of the peephole itself, though most surveillance units can be adjusted to give a good view on what is inside.

After the Columbine High School massacre in April 1999, America's National Institute of Justice funded the development of the K-9 camera, built into a dog's collar for hostage negotiations and rescues.

Wall-Breaching Cannon

BCB International have developed a wall-breaching cannon that also works on doors, ceiling, floors and upper-storey windows for forced entry. With a range of 10 feet up to 300 feet, it can also be used to clear barricades and road blocks, and stop moving vehicles.

As ammunition it uses a standard 44.5 lb drinking-water container. Fired at just 200 lb per square inch, this will blast a man-sized hole through a double-skinned concrete block wall. On impact, the filled plastic container loses most of its kinetic energy, so individuals on the opposite side of the breached wall are far less likely to be seriously injured than if a conventional explosive charge is used. In place of water, a standard plastic container can be filled with sand, gravel, concrete powder soil or any other "pourable" substance. This effectively increases the projectile's mass, momentum and penetrative capability.

The unit can be mounted on a vehicle or on wheels for one-man operation. At 350 lb, it can also be carried by two people. It can be recharged and reloaded in seconds.

25

CLOTHING AND KIT

Action ECW Boots

The Action Extreme Cold Weather Mukluk boot is rated down to –65° Fahrenheit. It has a half-inch removable felt insole and a plastic insole to improve circulation, and comes with a double-walled wool duffel sock. The boot can be used with snowshoes or skis and is waterproof up to six inches. It features a top "snow guard" lace to keep snow out.

Action also produce the ECW Thermo Boot with an outer sole of 100 per cent natural rubber with a Tractor tread that is self-cleaning and ensures good grip in all conditions. It has a third of an inch of Thermo insulation and a removable Thermo liner and insole. A polypropylene midsole also help prevent heat transfer to the ground.

Aktis Severe-Weather Gear

Arctic specialists buy the Arkis Severe-Weather jacket made in wind- and shower-resistant nylon. Inside it has low-bulk insulation material that can be removed in warmer conditions.

Altama Boots

Altama Footwear of Georgia make a range of boots used by the US armed forces. The 4155 Jungle Boot has a Ripple sole, rubber and cushion midsoles, and a removable lined inner sole. Their 4156 Desert has been supplied to the US Department of Defense for 30 years. It has seen action in Vietnam and the First Gulf War, and is in use in over seventy countries. The updated Altama 5850 Desert Boot has also been on active service in Vietnam and the Persian Gulf.

Altberg Mk II Desert Boots

Altberg Mk II Desert Boots are bought privately by UK Special Forces for desert operations. They are lightweight, with solid underfoot support and a light upper to minimize the retention of moisture.

Arctic Snow Camouflage Parka and Trousers

Military Logistics of Florida make white camouflage outfits with drawstrings at the waist and face for US Special Forces. They offer little in the way of protection against the weather and are designed to be worn over a wet-weather parka or Arctic attire.

The same company make desert night-camouflage parkas and trousers with liners. These are designed to be worn over regular clothes when it gets chilly in the desert at night.

Arktis 1724 Advanced Rig

British Special Forces are issued with this rig that carries four ammunition pouches, two first-aid field-dressing pouches, two slanted utility pouches and an internal zip pocket. The straps are padded with one fifth of an inch of closed cell foam to make is as comfortable as a vest, but with improved ventilation.

Arktis Marine Battle Vest

These Cordura battle vests can carry twelve magazines and are in use with Special Forces. They have two large utility pouches with a snow-lock on the water-bottle pouch. There are individual pouches for compass, tools, bayonet and FFD, and the ammo pouches have dividers. The clips can be closed using one finger.

Arktis Patrol Pack

The Arktis Patrol Pack is used by Special Forces worldwide. The 10-gallon (US) pack has snow-closures around the main compartment. Side zips attach Arktis or standard-issue PLC side pockets.

Armor of America TP-1E/TP-2E Vest

The TP-1E ballistic vest proved itself in combat with Naval Special Warfare in the Gulf. It can protect the wearer from lead-cored, steel-jacketed, 9-mm, sub-machine gun rounds. Special Operations personnel use the TP vest while scuba diving, climbing boarding nets, parachuting, abseiling and firing a multitude of weapons.

The tail extends down to protect the coccyx and a neck tab rises to the back of the helmet. The shoulder plates of the back armour are shaped so that the arms can be raised easily to fire a shoulder-mounted weapon or assist climbing. Four nylon tension bands also provide lower-back support.

The TP-1E is the Kevlar version of the jacket; the TP-2E uses Spectra, but offers the same level of protection.

Armor of America T-Series Armour

The T-panel ballistic vest is designed to protect paramilitary forces in jungle, desert or urban environments. It is resistant to water and mildew. Strong shoulder straps carry the weight of the front and back armoured plates, while wide belly bands keep them in place when running or climbing.

Armourshield Standard Body Armour

Over 100,000 Armourshield SBA units are in use worldwide. They are general-issue body armour, though they can be tailored to individual requirements. Coming in a variety of materials and camouflage patterns, they can be fitted with ceramic or composite plates for maximum protection.

Bates Enforcer Series Special-Ops Men's Amphibious Shoe EO2114

US maritime Special Forces wear quick-drying amphibious shoes made in synthetic materials by Bates of Michigan.

BCB Commando Socks

After the Falklands War, British Special Forces began buying BCB Commando Socks to keep their feet warm and dry, and prevent trench foot. Made from 60 per cent wool with a fully cushioned sole, the socks are designed to resist moisture and cold.

BCB Gloves

BCB International Ltd of Cardiff make a range of gloves that are non-standard issue but are widely used by the Special Forces. Their Combat Gloves are close-fitting and made in pliable leather so they can be worn when handling a weapon. Their linings are waterproof.

Their Arctic Gloves are made of Gore-tex with double-leather palms. They are waterproof and breathable. BCB's Arctic Mitts have an inner mitt of fleece and a waterproof lining.

BCB Goggles

BCB Goggles are not standard issue, but are bought by members of the UK Special Forces for use in desert, Arctic or maritime conditions. They are designed to protect the eyes from the sun, wind and dust, and are said to be 100 per cent resistant to ultra-violet.

BCB Jungle Boot

In use with UK Special Forces, the boot has a nylon and canvas upper, with leather toe and heel. They come in green and black.

Beaufort Mk 10 Immersion Suit

The SBS and aircrew are issued the Beaufort one-piece immersion suit. It has a urination tube and a diagonal zip to make it quicker to get in and out of.

Blackhawk Industries Commando Chest Harness

Blackhawk Industries of Virginia make a Commando Chest Harness for use by Special Forces. It has four pouches, with dividers, that can each hold three M-16 magazines, three AK-47 magazines or two M14 magazines. There is also a large utility or map pouch and the back is cushioned with quarter-inch closed-cell foam.

Blackhawk also make an abseiling or lifting Solar Harness that is used by US Special Forces.

Browning P302 Vest

The P302 can be worn under a shirt or uniform. It has either sixteen layers of protective Z2 fibre or twenty-two layers, depending on the level of protection required. It has a wide belt and Velcro closures. The P303 version comes with side protection; the P304 with dorsal and groin coverage. These vests are in use worldwide.

Divex Combat Polyurethane Drysuit

Several marine Special Forces around the world use the Divex Combat Drysuit. Its polyurethane material is welded so that it can withstand the rapid-entry shock when parachuting into water. The suit comes with hard-soled boots as standard and may be fitted with latex socks.

Divex Waterproof Bergens

The Individual Waterproof Bergen made by Divex Ltd is used by combat swimmers and is both watertight and airtight. The Special Operations version remains waterproof at any depth, provided air is pumped into it to equalize internal and external pressures. It has adjustable buoyancy control, an air cylinder, air supply hose and oral inflater.

DuPont Ranger Vest

DuPont developed a vest for the Rangers using Kevlar KM27 fibre, which is a little lighter that the standard Army-issue Personal Armor System Ground Troops (PASGT) while offering 25 per cent protection against shrapnel. The standard vest protects the wearer from bullets from a 9-mm or a 0.4 magnum. With optional chest plate it can take multiple hits by 7.62-mm rifle rounds.

Eagle Industries' Airborne Rucksack and Pack

US airborne forces use rucksacks and packs manufactured by Eagle Industries of Missouri. The A-111 has expandable cargo compartments and large pockets, and there is an attachment point for a lowering line and night-identification markings.

The company also has a Parachutist's Drop Bag designed to carry all necessary equipment and meet full certification for paratroopers. There is an Airborne Assault Pack "for more demanding operations" and the A-111 Medical Pack, which is frameless and lays out medical equipment for quick access.

The Eagle Load-Bearing Pack is designed for stealth operations, has two horizontal compression straps to prevent the load moving and a clean exterior to avoid the danger of snagging.

FBA Frogman Rucksack

The Frogman Rucksack was developed for use by Special Forces who must keep their equipment completely dry. It has a special pressure-control valve that allows the bag to be inflated to increase buoyancy or air to be forced out to decrease it.

Foil Force Fin

US Navy SEALs and other military divers use special split fins made by the American company Foil Force. Water is channelled through the split in the fin to drive the swimmer forward.

It is designed to reduce fatigue in the calves. The clean edges of the fin cut through the water, while wingtips that move independently allow divers to manoeuvre with small leg and foot movements.

Bumps known as Vortex Generators improve the water follow. The fin's upturned blades maximize thrust and the snap of the fins force the water through the splits for added acceleration. They come fitted with a parachute webbing strap and a ladder-lock buckle.

FSH RS-10T and G-9

The German company Fallschirm-Service Herbst make a range of parachutes for Special Forces. Its RS-10T is a steerable conical parachute that can be deployed from as low as 200 feet. The G-9 Tactical Ram-Air and Multi-Mission Parachute/Paraglider System is designed for HALO as well as HAHO operations.

The FSH G-9 has a span of 37 feet. It has eleven cells and can support up to 440 lb, though it has been tested up to 548 lb, at speeds of up to 175 knots. It has a forward speed of 15 to 25 knots and a glide ratio of between 4 and 6:1.

For HAHO operations it must be used in conjunction with a purpose-built Nightwing altimeter and Oxyjump High Altitude Breathing Equipment which can operate at up to 33,000 feet and down to −58° Fahrenheit must be used.

GB Combat Boots

UK Special Forces are issued with GB40 Desert Combat Boots, which are made in suede with a vulcanized-rubber sole, speed-lacing hooks and a deep-cleated tread. The GB37 has a heavy-duty nylon zip on the side of the leg, while the GB7 is a lightweight version.

GB Britton Ltd of Bristol also make the GB2 Combat Assault Boot in black leather, reinforced with steel.

Gentex EPS-21 Goggle System

Gentex EPS-21 Goggles are standard issue to the Israeli Defence Force and sought-after elsewhere. They are designed to protect the eyes against sun, wind, dust, laser light and ballistic fragmentation. Corrective lenses can be fitted and they can be used with a wide range of helmets and sighting devices.

Gentex HALO Lightweight Paratroop Helmet

The Gentex Corporation of Pennsylvania make a High Altitude Low Opening helmet to protect the head, eyes and face. It has facilities for built-in communications equipment and various oxygen masks.

Granqvist P1013 Cover Mitt

UK Special Forces use Granquist Cover Mitts in Arctic conditions. They are for use over fingered gloves and have a dotted inner surface for good grip.

Hawkmoor Sabre Patrol Pack

The Hawkmoor Sabre Patrol Pack is widely used by Special Forces. It allows the user to distribute the load more evenly, even when wearing other Personal Load Carrying Equipment or body armour. Hydrations systems can be incorporated.

The Sabre 30 Hydro has a capacity of 8–10.5 gallons US for use with a fast-fill hydration system. It has water-resistant zips and variable-capacity utility pouches.

The Victory is approximately a 6.5-gallon pack, expandable to 9 gallons, which is also designed to take a hydration system. These two small packs have been designed for patrols or quick-reaction teams where mobility and fast-fill hydration is more important than load-carrying capacity.

Hawkmoor Sabre Sack

Hawkmoor Ltd of Newton Abbot have developed the Sabre "load-bearing system" for Special Forces. Worn high on the back, it has a capacity of 21–34 gallons and detachable pockets.

Irvin-GQ LLP Mk 1 Low Level Parachute

The Irvin-GQ LLP Mk 1 Low Level Parachute is used with a static line and allows a fully equipped airborne soldier to make assault jumps from as low as 250 feet. It has a double-skirted canopy with internal rigging lines and there are extra inflation pockets around the hem of the canopy and inside it. These features ensure fast and consistent openings, quickly slow the rate of descent and damp any swinging movement.

The canopy disconnects easily from the harness once the parachutist is on the ground. The harness itself incorporates D-rings for the attachment of a reserve parachute and a bergen or weapon, together with an integral sling so that these can be dropped before the jumper hits the ground. The split-saddle harness is designed for comfort and maximum mobility once the soldier has landed.

Irvin-GQ LLRP Low-Level Reserve Parachute

The Irvin-GQ LLRP is a chest-mounted back-up parachute, cleared for drops as low as 250 feet. It has a conical canopy 20 feet in diameter. A kicker spring starts the initial deployment before a drogue takes over. However, rapid deployment at high speeds can cause problems, so a frangible line allows the drogue to break free. The canopy is then deployed by four small pockets around the apex of the canopy that normal keep the canopy aligned as its inflates.

The top vent of the canopy is closed by a breakable tie which stops the canopy losing pressure during the early stages of inflation during low-speed deployment. Once the canopy is fully inflated, it opens, stabilizing descent. "Skirt assist" lines attach the rigging lines to points inside the canopy so that there is no pull on the hem until the canopy is fully inflated. Again this allows the canopy to inflate more quickly, possibly saving the parachutist's life if the reserve has to be deployed at low altitude.

The reserve can be deployed even if the main chute is open to slow descent, or it can be used when the main chute has partially opened, or failed completely.

Irvin-GQ Low Level Parachute Assembly

The Irvin-GQ Low Level Parachute Assembly combines the pack and harness of the Mk 1 LLP and a 26.25-foot Low Level Conical Canopy. It can also be deployed on static line jumps from as low as 250 feet or at air speeds of up to 140 knots.

The highly developed conical canopy is fitted with air scoops to assist opening and its shape prevents it collapsing after it has opened. The design also makes it resistance to twisting the rigging. Any swing is damped by four vents, covered by mesh.

Irvin-GQ have also developed the XT-11 advanced tactical parachute system for the US Army to replace the T-10, which has been in use since the 1950s. The T-10 was designed to carry a gross weight of 250 lb, but modern soldiers carry more equipment. With kit, they can weigh as much as 400 lb. Standard jump heights have dropped to 500 feet and tactical transport aircraft now fly at between 130 and 150 knots. The XT-11 cuts the rate of descent by 25 per cent, giving a 40 per cent reduction in impact energy when they hit the ground.

LBA Paratroop Helmet

The LBA Paratroop Helmet meets European Standard 966, which limits the amount of force exerted on the head and neck on impact. It comes in individual combat style or as part of a Personal Armour System and is in use with airborne forces worldwide.

Military Logistics M-1944 Sun, Wind and Dust Goggles

M-1944 Goggles are standard issue in the US armed forces. They have a single-piece lens that is clear and neutral grey. Ballistic lenses can be purchased separately.

Military Logistics Magnesium Snowshoes

These snowshoes have a Magnesium Frame and are laced with steel cable that is coated with nylon. One-inch webbing with four buckles attaches the snowshoe to the wearer's boot.

Military Logistics also produce Men's Winter Socks for use with their mountain boots or mukluks. They are seamless knitted socks made of 25 per cent cotton and 75 per cent merino wool.

Mustang Rescue Swimming Drysuit

The US Navy use the Mustang tri-laminate nylon and butyl drysuit which was developed for surface swimmers. It weighs just 7 lb.

NO Aerospace Para Helmet

An alternative helmet used by UK airborne forces, the Aerospace Para Helmet, has been proven in combat. It offers protection from impact and bullets. With an energy-absorbing liner, it weighs just 2.4 lb.

PSP M31 Assault Vest

In use with several Special Forces units, the M31 has an armour-plated front and back. The front plate is mounted inside the vest to make room for two AK-47 magazine pockets.

Silverman's Bergens

Silverman Ltd of London make a range of bergens. The Marines' Arctic Bergen, issued to Special Forces, is water-resistant and has an external frame. The PLCE (Personal Load Carrying Equipment) Bergen is part of the Soldier '95 standard-issue that is also used by Special Forces. The waterproof bergen has an internal alloy frame and a waist belt. Its detachable side pouches can be used as a day-patrol pack. The SAS Para Bergen is specially designed for Special Forces. It has an external frame and is particularly hard-wearing.

Silverman's DPM Smocks

British airborne troops wear the Silverman Para Smock in a disruptive pattern camouflage material with knitted cuffs.

There is a Sniper version used by Special Forces and a SAS issue made of windproof gabardine DPM material.

SPP Paratrooper Conversion Kit for PASGT Combat Helmet

The US military issue a Paratrooper Conversion Kit for all Personal Armor System Ground Troops combat helmets. This consists of an extra retention strap, alongside the existing chinstrap for extra stability, and a foam neck pad for the rear. They can be added by loosening a single screw at the back of the helmet.

TechSpun Environmental Sock System

TechSpun Inc of Pennsylvania make Extreme Weather (EW) boot socks for use in temperatures from −40° to +120° Fahrenheit. They have a Coolmax inner sock and two reversed terry nap wool and polypropylene blend outer socks. They must be worn together for the system to work.

The Coolmax liner is designed to carry moisture away from the foot by capillary action in order to keep the foot dry and reduce the danger of infection. The outer sock provides the insulation and is designed for maximum wear.

TechSpun also make a lighter version, the All-Weather boot sock, to work in less severe conditions.

Typhoon Immersion Suit for Boating Operations

Several maritime Special Forces wear the Immersion Suit made by Typhoon Ltd of Cleveland. It can be worn over full battle-dress and boots.

WL Gore Boots with Gore-tex Membrane

WL Gore & Associates of Maryland make combat boots with a Gore-tex membrane that completely surrounds the foot. This makes the boot waterproof, while allowing sweat to escape.

WL Gore Intermediate Cold-Wet Gloves with Inserts

WL Gore make military gloves with a cowhide outer, but the inner lining exceeds the US military specification. They are waterproof, windproof and breathable.

WL Gore Lightweight Rainsuit

This consists of a parka and trousers that are designed to be stuffed into the pockets of other garments. They have reinforced elbows, shoulders, seat and knees, and have the added advantage of reducing the wearer's infra-red signature.

WL Gore Military Rain Suits

Part of Soldier '95 standard issue, the two-piece rain suit is made from Gore-tex, which keeps the rain out while allowing sweat to escape. It also reduces the risk of heat stress and hypothermia.

WL Gore Second Generation Extended Cold-Weather Clothing System

WL Gore's American sister company produce a parka and trousers with a Gore-tex membrane that are designed to be worn in the temperature range of –60° to –70° Fahrenheit. The trousers have patches on the seat and knees to resist abrasion. The parka has reinforced elbows and hook and loop closures on the wrists. Large cargo pockets have hand-warmer pockets behind them.

WL Gore Soldier '95 Gloves

These soldiers' gloves are standard issue to Special Forces and other British military personel. They are designed for dexterity when handling a weapon.

26

SURVIVAL EQUIPMENT

ACR L8-3 Personal Rescue Light

The ACR L8-3 Personal Rescue Light operates when it is immersed in water. The battery operates for eight hours and the light can be seen for more than a mile.

CamelBak Hydration Systems

Soldiers used to carry the water they needed in canteens, but Special Forces have adopted a new water-carrying system developed by CamelBak Products Inc of Petaluma, California. A 3.5-pint insulated flexible plastic water pouch is strapped to the trooper's back and a flexible tube runs over his shoulder so he can drink on the move. It is said that the system was the brainchild of a paramedic and cyclist who did not want to take his hands off the handlebars. So he got an old IV pouch, filled it with water, put it in a sock which he sewed to the back of his T-shirt and ran the line over his shoulder into his mouth.

The CamelBak also means that a trooper can drink without putting down his weapon – unscrewing the cap of a canteen takes two hands. The system holds up to three times as much as a canteen and soldiers in Afghanistan are advised to drink 12 pints of water per day. In those conditions, inevitably, the

CamelBak is being picked up by other branches of the service.

But CamelBak have moved on with the ThermoBak 3-Liter. As its name suggests, this keeps 5.2 pints of water cool for hours. It is fitted with D-ring attachment points to that it can be attached to a load-bearing vest, and Velcro straps to prevent it getting tangled with other equipment. There are quick-release straps to make it easily stowable and a built-in pocket accommodates CamelBak's Chemical Resistant Reservoir in case of an NBC attack. The patented Big Bite valve has no moving parts. You simply bite down on it and suck. The ThermoBak 3-Liter comes in olive drab, black or woodland camo.

The earlier system has been redesigned with a capacity of 6 pints and comes built into a day sack as the CamelBak Mule.

First Aid and Survival Kits

BCB International have a wide range of medical kits carried by Special Forces. There is the FA312 Extensive First Aid Kit, which has all the bandages and equipment needed to clean and dress a wound, while the FA096 Trauma Kit has syringes, burns equipment, catheters and saline solution.

The CK40 Air Crew Survival Go Pack Mk 4 was designed for the Royal Air Force and was used successfully in the First Gulf War. There are three sealed packs containing more than twenty pieces of essential medical kit. The whole lot weighs just 12 ounces and measures 8 x 5 x 2 inches.

Even smaller is the CK016 Military Survival Tin carried by individual members of the Special Forces. It measures 5 x 3 x 1 inches and weighs 7 ounces. There are twenty-seven items, each with multiple uses, stuffed into this tiny tin, and with the level of medical training Special Forces are given considerably improve a trooper's chances of survival in hostile conditions.

Finally there is the CK004 Ultimate Survival Pack. Weighing 12 ounces, it contains four water bags, water purification tablets, a nylon cord, a compass, a candle, a firelighter, fishing tackle, a knife, a single-edged blade, matches, a mirror, a sewing kit, a pair of folding scissors, six safety pins, a survival book, brass wire, cotton wool, eight Paracetamol tablets, twenty Piriton allergy tablets, potassium permanganate, a sachet of salt and camouflage cream. The container is 5 x 4 x 1 inches and can be used as a cooking pot.

Search and Rescue Beacons

Signature Industries of London, an offshoot of the BBC, have been making search and rescue beacons for more than forty years under the trade name SARBE – Search and Rescue BEacon. Their successful SARBE 5 dual-channel distress beacon was developed into the TACBE, or TACtical BEacon, a lightweight two-channel ground-to-air system that is also used in operations involving military swimmers.

Weighing around 9 ounces, it measures 5 x 3.5 x 1.5 inches. Using an aerial around 15 inches long, it transmits on distress frequencies in the UHF and VHF bands when a pin is pulled. It doubles as a simple voice transmitter, allowing the survivor on the ground to talk to aircraft overheard when they get close on one of two frequencies. It was used extensively during the First Gulf War.

The SARBE 6 Personal Locator Beacon is used by downed airmen. Once activated it works as an omni-directional distress beacon, operating continuously for twenty-four hours. It can also be used as a two-way voice channel to communicate with rescue aircraft.

The SARBE 7 is a lightweight compact version, while the SARBE 7 Plus activates on contact with water. It broadcasts a digitally synthesized voice saying: "Mayday, Mayday, man overboard", followed by an international distress signal.

The SARBE 8 incorporate GPS technology so that it had can broadcast its exact location. It can also be used as a voice channel and is partnered by a BE559 SARFIND unit that decodes its signal and displays the identity and position of each SARBE 8 it picks up. A stand-alone unit, it can be carried on an aircraft, boat, rescue vehicle or AWACS.

The latest unit is the SARBE 10 which is a Submarine Personal Locator Beacon. It works to a depth of over 820 feet.

ACR Electronics of Fort Lauderdale, Florida also make locator beacons and other identification equipment. The AN/ URT-33D is standard on US aircraft. It is a radio locator beacon that operates automatically on ejection.

In addition, they make the MS-2000 (M) range of distress

marker lights. The MS-2000 (M) H20 activates on contact with water. The Photofly is activated by a photocell, the Pilotlight is activated by water and a photocell, and the Doublefly is the stroke and incandescent version. They work underwater down to 50 feet, though a 200-foot diver's version is available, and a shield control whether it is visible from all directions or just one. In omni-directional mode only infra-red light is emitted; in uni-directional blue. The strobe flashes at a peak of 250,000 lumens, giving out 50 flashes a minute.

27

COMMUNICATIONS AND
NAVIGATION EQUIPMENT

Active Ear-Defender ED200K

US Special Forces use Active Ear-Defender ED2000K head-sets when making assaults. It allows whispered communication before entry, then protects the ears against the effects of stun grenades while allowing radio communication to continue. The electronics shut down during the explosion, limiting the level of sound that it will pass to a comfortable 90 dB. It will interface with other standard communications equipment.

Alinco DJ-X10 Scanning Receiver

The Alinco DJ-X10 Scanning Receiver has 1,200 memory channels and wideband coverage up to 2,000 MHz. The hand-held unit is fully programmable.

Caracel PRM 4740A Frequency Hopping
Hand-Held Transceiver

The manufacturers, Thales Communications of Crawley, Sussex, claim the Caracel was the first frequency-hopping hand-held transceiver to meet military specifications; it is thought to be used by US Special Forces. Messages are digitally encrypted and security codes can be erased at the flick of a switch.

CCS Ghost Series Transmitters

CCS Ghost Series Transmitters work both as a powerful radio mike and a tracking device. Shorter than a cigarette and as thin as a credit card, they fit inside the barrel of a pen. The WMTX 4200 is voice activated and the WMTX 4500 emits a tracking signal that can be picked up by a helicopter within a radius of one mile, while the WMTX 4700 MD has a "man-down" switch to alert the command post that urgent help is required.

Chinese Equipment

The Chinese Special Forces use a PSP-320 350 MHZ Hand-Held Transceiver and S9130 Mobile Radio, which is microprocessor controlled. This allows a number of channels to be scanned simultaneously.

Clansman

UK Special Forces use Clansman equipment that is fully integrate with Ptarmigan, the British Army's computer-controlled secure battlefield communications system. This provides voice, data, telegraph and fax communication via satellite, multi-channel relay and single-channel radio.

The TRA-967 VHF Manpack Transceiver, though designed to be carried, can also be used as fixed or vehicle station. It has 1,600 synthesizer-controlled channels, is powered by a 12-volt battery and is waterproof.

The PRC-349 VHF Hand-Held Transceiver was designed for personal communications at platoon-level via 400 channels on the battlefield. Weighing 3.3 lb and measuring 9.6 x 3.5 x 2 inches, it fits in a quick-release holster, a belt pouch or the pocket of a combat jacket.

The PRC-344 UHF Manpack Transceiver is used for ground-to-air communications between combat troops and ground-attack support aircraft. With 3,500 channels, it has a range of 100 miles and can be operated remotely from up to 2 miles.

The VRC-353 VHF Vehicle Radio was first developed by Marconi Space and Defence Systems in the 1970s. It transmits and receives voice and data via 1,860 channels, is rugged and waterproof, and weighs 55 lb.

Cougar-2000 Secure Radio

The Cougar-2000 uses scanning modes for the reception and transmission of messages, and the algorithms it uses for encryption have never been published, so the radio remains secure. The US Army and Navy also use the Cougarnet Communication System made by Thales Communications, a fully secure radio network operating over the entire FM band.

Davies Communications System

Davies Industrial Communications Ltd supplies specialist communications equipment to the UK Special Forces and other Special Forces worldwide. As part of the CT400 system, they produce two-way radios that are submersible to 25 feet and, as they are resistant to humidity, are often used in the jungle.

They have a range of communication harnesses that carry a radio, a push-to-talk switch, earphones and a microphone. This can be used with a respirator such as the SF-10. Using a Respirator Microphone Adaptor, it is attached to the external speech port of the respirator and does to impede its function.

The company also produce throat-microphones and covert communications system that are worn on the body.

Digital Global Listening Post

VASCON's Digital Global Listening Post (DIGLIPO) provides instant access to intelligence through public telephone lines, mobile and satellite phones. It can record fifteen channels at a time.

DSCS III

Defense Satellite Communications System is an old satellite communications system whose Phase III has been extended by the Service Life Enhancement Program. The DSCS programme began in 1966 and went into Phase III in 1982. There are currently nine satellites aloft – five primary and four in reserve. Five more are planned. They are in geosynchronous orbital positions 22,300 miles above the equator to provide coverage between 75° north and 75° south. The DSCS constellation provides communication services in each of the following five satellite areas: East Pacific (EPAC), West Atlantic (WLANT), East Atlantic (ELANT), Indian Ocean (IO), and West Pacific (WPAC).

EC-130 Commando Solo

The EC-130 Commando Solo is used by Air Force Special Operations Command. It is used to conduct psychological warfare operations, making civilian broadcast in the standard AM, FM, HF and TV frequencies, as well as taping into military communications bands. It can fly day and night, and is air refuellable. A typical mission consists of a flight at maximum height to broadcast propaganda to as wide an audience as possible. The target can be either military or civilian personnel. Secondary missions include command and control communications countermeasures and limited intelligence gathering.

These modified C-130 Hercules are also used to support disaster relief operations and perform communications jamming in the military spectrum. There is one oversized blade antenna under each wing, with a third extending forward from the vertical fin. A retractable wire antenna is released from the modified beavertail, with a second extending from the belly and held vertical by a 500 lb weight.

Elbit SC3 Sniper Control System

The Elbit SC3 Sniper Control System is deployed typically in a hostage situation or at any time when a number of snipers are covering a single incident. A camera unit is clipped onto the snipers' sights. Fitting takes approximately thirty seconds and does not effect the rifle's zeroing. This is connected to an image process and transmitter which relays what the snipers see through their sights back to a single controller, who can then assess the situation. It works over three miles in open country or half-a-mile in an urban environment.

Elite2000 XC

The Signalguard Elitle2000 XC encryptor is a lightweight unit that slides into a Motorola Microtac mobile phone for instant encryption during calls. Weighing less than 4 ounces it adds less than an inch to the thickness of the phone. Various levels of encryption can be selected and a global switch makes it internationally compatible. It also allows secure conference calls.

Harris Falcon II: AN/PRC-117F Multi-band, Multi-mission Radio

When the British Clansman communcations system became outdated, the Ministry of Defence set up the Bowman Future Combat Radio, but it soon ran into problems. So the Harris Corporation of Rochester, New York began shipping over their Harris Falcon II, already in use with US Forces. This was given the British designation AN/PRC-117F. It is a multi-band radio designed for ground-to-ground communications in combat situations, ground-to-air communications and satellite communications. Messages can be sent in clear or securely encrypted. It can be carried as amanpack, mounted on a vehicle or used as a base station. The AN/PRC-117F can act as a translator between otherwise incompatible radios and is readily ungradable.

Invisible Communications for Surveillance

The Collarset-II wireless earphone and concealed microphone, allowing the user to transmit and receive radio signals in total secrecy, is in use with the US Special Forces. The radio can be concealed in the user's arm using a shoulder harness. The microphone is then hidden under the user's clothes, near the collarbone, with a press-to-talk switch held in the hand or concealed on the belt or in a pocket. The earpiece is concealed in the ear and receives a signal by magnetic induction from the armpit unit. It has a battery life of up to 100 hours and a squelch circuit cuts out any electronic noise when no voice signal is on the channel.

KY-189 Intelligent Secure Handset

US Special Forces use the KY-189 Intelligent Secure Handset with the US Army's standard PRC-77 and VRC-12 radios, as well as other tactical sets, for high-security communication. The encryption algorithm provides over 100 million user-programmable security codes. The net resynchronizes with each use. It can be used with any set or network without affecting its range or efficiency.

LASH Headset

The LASH headset features a throat microphone with earpieces attached, leaving the mouth free for a respirator. The unit fits easily under a balaclava, flash hood or helmet. It is weather-proof and heat-resistant. Its press-to-talk switch is mounted on the chest and can be operated with heavy gloves. The LASH headset in compatible with the Active Ear-Defender ED200K.

LITE Headset

The LITE headset was developed for Special Forces assault teams and police SWAT units. It has two microphones – one boom mike positioned in front of the mouth and a throat mike for used when gas is deployed. The earphones have gaps around the edges to allow peripheral hearing, which can be vital in close-quarters combat. It has a chest-mounted press-to-talk switch and fits under a helmet. The LITE headset is also compatible with the Active Ear-Defender ED200K.

Magellan NAV 100M

During the First Gulf War, the SAS and other Special Forces found their way about using the Magellan NAV 1000M hand-held GPS receiver. Weighing just 1.9 lb and measuring 8 x 3.5 x 2, it fits easily into a pocket or pouch and is solidly built for specifically for military use. The display has three screens which show the status of the satellite, time and date, the elevation and the unit's current position, along with a FOM – figure of merit, or the estimated error of the fix. The lower the FOM is, the more accurate the fix. Powered by six AA batteries, the unit can store up to 500 way points.

Milstar

Milstar is the American joint force satellite communications network designed to provide global jam-resistant communications for the US military. Five satellites in low-inclination, geosynchronous orbits allow communications to be relayed between ground users and vehicles, ships, submarines and aircraft. Up to 10,000 users are able to access the system at any one time.

Each Milstar satellite serves as a smart switchboard in space that directs traffic from terminal to terminal anywhere on the Earth. Communications are also passed to other Milstar satellites via crosslinks. The crosslink signals use frequencies that are absorbed by the earth's atmosphere, so they cannot be eavesdropped on by ground stations. The satellite and ground station designs also incorporate advanced signal processing and encryption technology to deny access to downlinked signals to unauthorized users.

Satellite systems also include two nulling spot antennas that can identify and pinpoint the location of a jammer and electronically isolate its signal. This allows Milstar users to operate normally and at full capacity with no loss in signal quality or speed, despite any attempt by hostile forces to jam or intercept its signal.

Using Milstar the US Army, Navy, Marine Corps and Air Force can pass encrypted voice message, data, teletype or facsimile communications securely between themselves and each other. With modern communication equipment Special Forces also patch into the system.

Navstar Global Positioning System

The Navstar Global Positioning System was developed by the US Department of Defense for the military. It is a global navigation system that allows a receiver on the ground to triangulate between satellites and calculate exactly where they are. The system was restricted to the military until the shootdown of Korean Air Lines Flight 007 in 1983. The civilian airliner was shot down by Soviet jet interceptors when it strayed into Soviet airspace just west of Sakhalin island. The crew and 269 passengers, including US congressman Lawrence McDonald, were killed. The Soviet Union said that it did not know the aircraft was civilian and suggested it had entered Soviet airspace to test its military response capabilities. In response President Ronald Reagan issued a directive making the GPS system available free for civilian use to prevent such errors happening again.

Since then, GPS has become a widely used aid to navigation worldwide, and a useful tool for map-making, land surveying, commerce and scientific uses. GPS also provides a precise time reference used in many applications, including the scientific study of earthquakes, and synchronization of telecommunications networks. People even use SatNav in their cars. The system available to the public is relatively inaccurate compared to that encoded for the US military.

At any one time at least twenty-four Navstat satellites are in medium Earth orbit. They are managed by the US Air Force 50th Space Wing at a cost of around $750 million a year. The satellites transmit precise microwave signals, which enable a GPS receiver to determine its location, speed, direction and time.

The GPS receiver calculates its position by measuring the distance between itself and three or more GPS satellites. Each satellite has an atomic clock, and continually transmits messages containing the exact time and location of the satellite. The receiver uses its own clock to measure the reception time of each message, which gives the precise distance to each satellite as the signal travels at a fixed speed near the speed of light. Knowing the distance to at least three satellites, and their positions, the receiver computes its position. In practice, receivers typically do not have perfectly accurate clocks, but tracking four or more satellites allows them to compute both their location and the accurate time.

GPS provides two levels of service. The Standard Positioning Service is available to anyone with a GPS receiver, worldwide, free of charge. It is carried on the GPS L1 frequency, which contains a coarse acquisition code and a navigation data message. SPS provides a predictable positioning accuracy of 109 yards horizontally and 170 yards vertically, and the time to within 340 nanoseconds. This is what you have in your car.

The more accurate Precise Positioning Service used by the military is available worldwide on the GPS L1 and L2 frequencies to users authorized by the US P(Y) code. Military equipment capable of decrypting this provides a positioning accuracy of at least 24 yards horizontally and 30 yards vertically, and the time to within 200 nanoseconds. The encryption also acts as an anti-spoofing guard that shields the receiver from being fed false data.

PPS was designed primarily for US military use. However, it is also available to US federal government users and, on a limited basis, to non-federal government and civil users, both domestic and foreign. The British government would, for example, ask the US government for permission to use PPS for Special Forces missions. Naturally, on coalition operations in Iraq or Afghanistan, the US would hand over the encryption codes. Even during the Falklands War, the US government provided the British forces with covert assistance.

GPS has numerous military applications. In the dark or in unfamiliar territory, soldiers need to know where they are. It can be used to co-ordinate the movement of troops and supplies. Various weapons systems use GPS to track potential ground and air targets before they are flagged as hostile. These weapons systems pass GPS co-ordinates of targets to precision-guided munitions to allow them to engage the targets accurately. Military aircraft, particularly those used in air-to-ground roles, use GPS to find targets. For example, gun camera video from AH-1 Cobras in Iraq show GPS co-ordinates that can be looked up in Google Earth. Intercontinental ballistic missiles, cruise missiles and precision-guided munitions all use GPS in their guidance systems. Special Forces units assigned to target acquisition carry target designators equipped with GPS.

Artillery projectiles with embedded GPS receivers able to withstand forces of 12,000g have been developed for use in 155-

mm howitzers. Downed pilots can be located faster if they have a GPS receiver. Special Forces on reconnaissance mission use GPS to map enemy installations and track troop movements. It is also a vital tool when navigating behind enemy lines.

Nokia DA852 Patrol Message Terminal

Like their mobile phones, Nokia's military communications equipment is used worldwide. Their DA852 is a rugged, stand-alone computer terminal for sending and receiving data by radio. Transmission takes place in short bursts, so it is difficult to locate or jam.

Nokia M85050 Short Burst Message Terminal

The M85050 is a hand-held computer terminal for tactical communications by Special Forces units and is intended for use in hostile environments. Encrypted messages can be sent by radio, via satellite or down the telephone line.

Occasion Swimmer's Kit OSK-1

The OSK-1 provides Navy SEALs radio communications down to a depth of 66 feet. The radio, with antenna attached, is accommodated in soft, strap-on containers with waterproof zips. It operates with a single or double submersible headset, and a boom or throat mike. It can also be interfaced to an aircraft intercom for briefing.

OIP Head-Mounted Optical Projection System (HOPROS)

OIP's Head-Mounted Optical Projection System projects visual information before the wearer's eyes without blocking his normal vision and keeping his hands free. This means that technicians or doctors can be sent detailed instructions while they are performing delicate operations. Such equipment is useful on Special Operations where a Special Forces technician may be called on to disable complex machinery.

Phonito Wireless Earpiece

Phonak Communications produce a widely used wireless earpiece called the Phonito, which fits comfortably within the ear. It has a volume limiter to protect the ear from loud noises, and a squelch circuit that cuts out electronic noise when no voice is detected. It has a battery life of a hundred hours.

The company also produce the MicroEAR that fits in the ear and is thought to be the world's smallest radio receiver. Supplied pre-tuned to the user's communication channel, it has a range of about a mile.

PTAC Secure Terminal Rugged Data Terminal

Out in the field, the PTAC operates like a standard PC that can be configured to any specific tactical application by downloading the appropriate software. The keyboard and display have been modified for use under NBC, Arctic, low-light or hostile conditions. When the terminal is closed it can be carried in a pocket.

The unit is sealed so that it can survive immersion in water, driving rain, high humidity, and sand and dust. Its screen is armoured and its case reinforced. It can cope with high pressures down to 6 feet of water and low pressures when making a HAHO or HALO parachute jump.

Radio-Controlled Explosion Initiator

BDL Systems make a radio-controlled explosion initiator that is programmable so that users can programme their own security codes, preventing others using it.

Raytheon Systems

Raytheon also make radios used by Special Forces. The AN/PRC-119(V)1 SINCGARS Radio is operated by a sixteen-button keypad. Used for voice and data transmission, it can be used on a single-channel or in jam-resistant, frequency-hopping mode.

The AN/PRC-113(V) is a lightweight manpack designed to cope with a battlefield where a lot of radios are working in close proximity. It can also resist an electromagnetic pulse.

The AN/PSC-5D is a multi-band, multi-mission communication terminal that meets Department of Defense requirements for a lightweight, secure, network-capable, anti-jam radio system that can handle voice, data and images all in a single device. It weighs 11.5 lb without batteries and measures 3.3 x 10.6 x 13 inches.

Rockwell AN/PSC-11 SCAMP

Rockwell's AN/PSC-1 is a SCAMP – single channel anti-jam man-portable – radio. Via the Milstar satellite system, it provides worldwide, secure, jam-resistant, voice, data and imagery communications. It is also EMP protected.

Rockwell Collins PLGR "Plugger"

Rockwell's Precision Lightweight GPS Receiver has now been adopted by regular units as well as Special Forces. The AN/PSN-11 PLGR is a small hand-held device that incorporates selective availability/anti-spoofing and anti-jamming. It displays the longitude and latitude, along with grid references in the numerous different systems available. With enough memory for forty-nine maps, it can be used as a navigation aid. It is also compatible with night-vision goggles and can be installed in vehicles and aircraft.

Rockwell Collins PLGR II and VPLGR II

The PLGR II is an upgrade of the earlier version. It can be used underwater, and is thus favoured Special Forces. It also comes as a vehicle-mounted unit known as the VPLGR II. This is mounted on the dashboard and has a large display that can be read more easily when travelling over rough terrain.

Both versions can be loaded with Rockwell Collins' Gun Laying System and integrated with laser rangefinders and Leica range-finding binoculars.

Small Boat Intercom Set

US Navy SEALs uses the Small Boat Intercom Set to provide two-way communication between a crew of four. While two crew members can transmit at any one time, all four receive. This allows near normal conversation in the noisy environment of a speeding boat. Headsets are submersible.

Sonic Scrambler

Sonic Communications International's Sonic Scrambler is in use worldwide. It attaches to the handset of a regular phone, allowing secure calls to be made locally, nationally and internationally.

Tadiran HF-2000 HF Radio System

Tadiran Communications Ltd's secure digital radio communication systems for voice and data are used by the US Armed Forces and other Special Forces around the world. They have systems designed for the the individual fighting soldier through the squad and platoon up to the division and corps level.

The CNR-9000 is Tadiran Communications' latest multimode VHF/FM COMSEC/ECCM (communication security/ electronic counter-countermeasures – that is, anti-jamming) radio system for voice and data transmission. Half the size and weight of similar units, it can be carried by a man or mounted in a vehicle. It has menu-driven "man-machine interface" (MMI), high-speed data transmission, a communication controller utilizing MIL-STD (US military standard) protocols and GPS.

The older Tadiran Communications' HF-6000 radio system is still in use. Featuring digital squelch, auto-call and selective calling, it is available as a manpack or in various vehicle-mounted and fixed-station configurations. It is fully compatible with the widely used HF-2000 system.

The hand-held PRC-624 and PRC-710 radios provide voice and data COMSEC/ECCM. They have error detection and correction codes, together with automatic data rate adaptation to ensure error-free data communications at various data rates.

The GRC-2000 is an advanced line-of-sight, frequency hopping, multi-channel, radio relay with an optional automatic antenna positioner for rapid tactical deployment, while the GRC-400 is a fixed-frequency, multi-channel radio relay for high-speed communications.

Tadiran also make ruggedized computers for the battlefield. The Tacter-31 is a hand-held personal computer and digital messaging terminal designed to serve all combat echelons. It features an internal GPS receiver, giving the hand-held terminal navigation and mapping capabilities. It is in use with the US Marine Corps.

Thales Acoustics

Thales Acoustics also produce a range of radio accessories for covert use. The RA502 Inductive Earpiece picks up a signal from a combined inductive and microphone unit hidden under the user's collar or shirt. The transceiver itself is worn in a holster under the clothing. A cable runs down the sleeve to a push-to-talk switch held in the user's hand. In situations where the user cannot talk without compromising himself, he can tap out a pre-arranged code on the PTT switch.

Thales AN/PRC-148(V) (C)
Tactical Hand-Held Radio

The US Marine Corps use the Thales AN/PRC-148, which weighs less than two lb). Then in August 2000 US Special Operations Command put in a $15.7 million order for the upgraded AN/PRC-148(V) (C). The programme was called the Multiband Inter/Intra Team Radio, or MBITR, and the idea was to allow all the various US Special Forces units to communicate with each other. This could handle voice and data communications and integrate with all the latest systems; SINCGARS – Single Channel Ground and Airborne Radio System; Have Quci II – the latest frequency-hopping system; ANDVT – Advanced Narrowband Digital Voice Terminal; and Retransmit – a protocol for checking corrupted or lost data.

The Boomerang4

The Boomerang4 is a bug detector in use worldwide. It emits a low-power microwave signal and detects change caused by the transistors, diodes and other semiconductor devices used in clandestine listening equipment.

20-Metre Submersible Miniature
Secure Hand-Held Radio (MSHR)

The SEALs and air-sea rescue use the 20-Metre MSHR, which is submersible to 66 feet of salt water. The hand-held unit transmits voice and data, both in clear and encrypted, over a hundred channels.

VL5000 Counter-Surveillance Receiver

The VL5000 is used to sweep a room of bugs. It will locate bugs operating in AM and FM bands between 2 MHz and 1.5 GHz. LEDs illuminate in the presence of radio-frequency energy. The verifier then sweeps the room, recycling the sound picked up to a headset, while a signal-strength metre indicates the proximity of the transmitter.

Walker's Tactical Ear

Walker's Tactical Ear looks like a hearing aid mounted behind the ear. It amplifies ambient sounds nearly nine times, allowing the user to hear even the slightest noise during a stakeout. Sounds in the higher frequency range are preferentially amplified so that the user can make out muffled conversations, the noise of a foot on an abrasive surface or the click of a gun's safety catch. However, the ear is protected from loud noises with the earplug reducing high sound levels. It cuts out completely when a firearm is discharged.

Occupying only one ear, it leaves the other free to listen to radio communications. The Walker's Tactical Ear fits neatly behind the ear and weighs just one eighth of an ounce.

28

SURVEILLANCE AND
TARGET DESIGNATION EQUIPMENT

Surveillance

One of the advances in surveillance over recent years is the ability to see at night. There are two methods. One uses infrared, converting the heat given off by an object into a visual image in the eyepiece. In low-light conditions, an active night-vision device can illuminate the scene with infra-red radiation. This cannot be detected unless the enemy also has an infra-red night-vision device. The other, more popular, is a passive device that takes what little light there is – no night is completely black – and amplifies it using an intensifier tube. When a photon of light hits a detector plate, it gives off an electron. This electron is accelerated by a high-voltage electrical field. When it hits a second detector plate, a cascade of electrons is emitted. These are accelerated by a second field until they hit a phosphorescent screen, producing an enhanced image. Modern intensifiers can amplify light up to 50,000 times, which means that the light from one dim star can illuminate an entire field.

Leica Night-Vision Equipment

Leica of Switzerland have a range of night-vision equipment that is in general use by Special Forces. It includes monocular pocketscopes, night-vision goggles and night binoculars.

Northrop Grumman

Northrop Grumman produce night-vision goggles that were used by the SAS during the First Gulf War and, more recently, in operations in Afghanistan against al-Qaeda.

The company is one of the major suppliers of night-vision equipment to the US military and supply their devices using their latest Generation IV image-intensifier tubes to USSCOM as weapons sights and passive night goggles. These are particularly suited for use when driving vehicles or flying aircraft, especially helicopters. British helicopter crews inserting and extracting SAS and SBS teams during the Falklands War used them. It is said that a helicopter pilot practising with PNGs before the First Gulf War drove his souped-up sports car around the M25 that circles London at night with no lights. The police were stunned when a black-out vehicle shot passed them at something approaching 150 miles an hour.

OGVN6 Night-Vision Binoculars

Galileo Avionica SpA of Italy produce night-vision binoculars that are in use worldwide. They have brightness control that cuts the light amplification once brilliance exceeds a pre-set limit.

OIP Holographic Night-Vision Goggles

These lightweight Holographic Night-Vision Goggles are in use by NATO Special Forces units. They use Holographic Optical Elements to allow the wearer to see through the night-vision image to the real world beyond. This allows them to continue observing their surroundings even when flashes and flares are going off, and makes them suitable for Special Operations.

OIP Lightweight Universal Night-Observation System

LUNOS comes with a series of lenses so that the observer can get a close-up look a target or objective. It can be used as helmet-mounted night-vision goggles, or tripod-mounted night-vision binoculars.

P.W. Allen

Britain's P.W. Allen produce Nite-Watch that intensifies light 20,000 times, compared to 1,000 times with Generation I tubes. Their system weighs just 11 ounces, is water-resistant and gives 7,000 hours of continuous use.

It also forms the nucleus of the company's NVSK 1/00 Night-Vision Surveillance Kit which comes with a Sony Mini Digital Video Camera, a Canon EOS IV SLR Camera, mounts and adaptors for the cameras, zoom lens, a range finder, an infra-red illuminator, a cleaning kit, instruction manual and spare batteries, all in a waterproof case.

Simrad Night-Vision Goggles

Simrad of Norway supply their GN Night-Vision Goggles to Special Forces, which are are waterproof down to 32 feet. They also produce KDN Day/Night-Vision Binoculars that work in any lighting condition.

Thales Jay Night-Vision Goggles

Thales Optics of St Asaph produce Mono Night-Vision Goggles for general issue to UK troops. Hand-held or mounted on a face-mask or helmet, they produce a high-resolution image and can be worn with an NBC suit. There is an infra-red illuminator for close-order tasks and they can be used for weapon aiming with a target marker. The image intensifier automatically shuts down when the brightness exceeds a certain level.

The Special Force's version is the head-mounted Thales Jay Night-Vision Goggles, which use an updated intensifier tube and can be adapted for medium- or long-range surveillance with added lens systems.

UGO Day and Night Goggles

Thales Optronique of France produce binoculars that can be used during the day and at night. They can also be worn as goggles for night driving. Daytime magnification is x8; at night x4. The goggles weigh 1.6 lb.

Portaguard – Hand-Held
Microwave Radar Ground Surveillance System

There are other ways to tell what is going on during the hours of darkness. For example, when things move they make a distinctive sound. A cat moving through under-growth makes a different sound to a human or a vehicle. The Portaguard makes use of that fact. It can easily tell whether a target is an animal, a human or a vehicle. It can also identify types of movement behind windows, doors or walls. The unit's maximun range is 220 to 330 yards for humans, and 550 to 660 yards for vehicles. Output can be fed in to a PC and the unit can be operated remotely from three to five miles.

KillFlash

The art of surveillance is to see and not be seen. America's Tenebraex Corporation produces anti-reflective devices that prevent optics giving off a tell-tale glint on the battlefield. A cap comprising small honeycomb tubes fits over the lens, hiding reflections and cutting down glare from sources outside the field of vision inside the optic itself. They have versions that fit on binoculars, sights and night-vision devices.

Laser Rangefinders

As Special Forces are often used as forward observers they need to be able to measure the distance to a target and relay the information back to fire controllers or close-air support. Laser rangefinders allow them to do this with accuracy to within a few metres. The most common form of laser rangefinder operates by sending a pulse of laser light in a narrow beam towards the object and measuring the time it takes to be reflected off the target and returned to the sender. The pulse may be coded so the range-finder can be jammed. It is possible to use the Doppler effect to measure how fast the object is moving towards or away from the rangefinder.

OIP MLR30 and MLR40 Laser Rangefinder

These laser rangerfinders can be hand-held or mounted on a tripod. The MLR30 uses a neodymium-doped yttrium aluminium garnet laser, while the MLR40 uses an "eye-safe" version. They are small and lightweight and will range up to 12.5 miles, though the MLR40 comes in a 4.5-mile version. They calculate the range within seconds. Data can be fed into a computer or weapons-control system.

OIP Infa-Red Laser Target Pointer

Laser target pointers are designed for close combat at night. A laser attached to the barrel of a rifle or sub-machine gun sends out an invisible infra-red beam that can only be seen through night-vision goggles. A spot appears on the target at the exact point the bullet will hit. This means that the gun can be aimed without straining to look through the sights and the gun can be fired from the hip.

Rockwell Leica

Rockwell Leica Vector Rangefinder Binoculars – known as Viper in the US – have on-board processing to work out horizontal distances, height and angles, either between the user and the target or two remote objects. The body is protected by rubber and the device weighs 3.7 lb. However, to measure distances of greater than 2,200 yards the unit has to be mounted on a tripod. Mortar fire controllers and artillerymen usually need their target co-ordinates on a UTM grid. The conversion can be done with a Rockwell Collins PLGR with its built-in GPS receiver.

Leica also produce a pocket-size Pocket Laser Rangefinder known as the PLRF that weighs just 1.1 lb. Despite its small size, it can measure distances from 5.5 yards to 1.5 miles with an accuracy of 0.008 per cent.

Simrad Eye Safe Laser Rangefinder

Simrad's lightweight LE7 Eye Safe Laser Rangefinder measures ranges out to 6 miles. It can be hand-held or mounted on a support, and works at night when used with a Simrad image intensifier.

The upgraded Simrad LP10 has an integrated GPS, digital magnetic compass and high-resolution display. It has a magnification of x7 and weighs 5.5 lb.

Laser Target Designators

Special Forces operating behind enemy lines search out targets and "designate" them for destruction. On close-target reconnaissance missions, they locate enemy positions hidden from the air by camouflage, then call in an air strike. As the planes approach the CTR team "illuminate" the target with a laser designator so that the attack aircraft can see it, even though it may be invisible from the air. The designator sends out coded pulses of laser light, which are reflected from the target and unscrambled by detectors on board the plane. Usually infra-red light is used so that it will not readily be seen by the enemy. Laser-guided bombs, rocket and shells detect the pulsed laser light and home in on the target.

Litton GLTD II

The Litton GLTD II was developed to direct laser-guided munitions such as Copperhead artillery shells, Hellfire missiles and Paveway bombs onto their targets. It works out to three miles and also acts as a laser rangefinder out to 12.5 miles. Its telescope has a magnification of x10 and it can be used with night-vision equipment. The device weighs 12.6 lb and is in use in NATO countries.

Thales LF25 and LF28 Laser Target Designators

British Special Forces have been using the Thales LF25 Laser
Target Designator for some time. It weighs 17.5 lb and can be
carried by a single soldier. Set up on a small tripod, it has a
built-in x10 telescope to align the laser. An image intensifier or
thermal-imaging device can also be added so that it can be used
at night. The upgraded LF28 is now in use.

29

LAND TRANSPORT

Alvis Hägglunds BV 206 NS BVS
10 Armoured Personnel Carrier

Built in Sweden by Hägglunds, a subsidiary of the British company Alvis, the BV 206 is used both by the UK and US, along with many other countries. It has two tracked units connected by a steering unit. The BV 206 can climb a 45-degree slope on a hard surface, with a 40-degree side slope. On snow it can climb a 13.5-degree slope. The front unit will carry five to six men; the rear eleven. The unit is fully amphibious, driven by its tracks. Maximum speed on land is 32 miles an hour and in water 1.6 knots.

The updated version of the BV 206 is the BVS 10 trooper carrier, known as the Viking by the Royal Marines. It has a crew of four and carries ten. UK vehicles are armed with a roof-mounted 7.62-mm or 12.7-mm machine gun. It is still mobile even if one of the tracks is blown off by a mine. Banks of electrically operated smoke grenade launchers are carried as standard. The Viking can be transported by CH-53 and CH-47 helicopters as well as the C-130 Hercules.

Alvis Scarab

The Alvis Scarab is a new scout car based on the Mercedes Unimog engine and running gear. It can carry a crew of five and a full range of surveillance and communications equipment. Its armour protects against 7.62-mm fire, with protection against heavy-machine-gun fire across the front. It can also withstand the blast of a mine containing the equivalent of about 15 lb of TNT.

The patrol version has a one-man turret with a 7.62-mm or .50-calibre machine gun. The reconnaissance model has the Helio SWARM (Stabilized Weapons and Reconnaissance Mount) turret, developed with the French company Sagem. This has a 12.7-mm machine gun with a Sagem Iris thermal-imaging camera that can detect a target up to five miles away.

The sighting systems can be linked to the Sagem Tactis battlefield management system. It has the Sagem Sigma navigation system and GPS. The payload is 5,500 lb and top speed is 68 miles an hour.

Alvis Supacat

The Supacat has been with the British armed forces since the 1980s and has seen service in Iraq and Afghanistan. It is a fully automatic, 6 x 6, amphibious, airportable, all-terrain mobile platform. The Supacat III has a 1.9-litre turbo diesel engine that gives it a top speed of 40 miles an hour, and it can climb 45 and traverse 40.

The Alvis Supaca can act as a flexible weapons platform, mounting machine guns, grenade launchers and anti-tank systems. Alternatively it is used as a logistics vehicle with a payload of 1.7 US tons. It is steered by a central control column and, for added manoeuvrability, all the wheels on one side can be locked for a skid turn.

AM General HMMVW (Humvee)

The US Navy SEALs and other Special Forces now use Humvees for rapid land deployment. Since production began in 1985, more than 160,000 have been delivered to the US Army and the armies of more than thirty other nations. Four-wheel drive, independent suspension and 16 inches of ground clearance make them particularly suited to off-road conditions in Afghanistan and Iraq.

The one-ton Hummer can serve as a weapons platform, mounting 7.62-mm and .50-calibre machine guns, and the 40-mm Mark 19 grenade launcher. It can also carry a TOW anti-tank missile launcher. One Humvee can be slung under a UH-60A Blackhawk, two under a CH-53 Sea Stallion or a CH-47 Chinook. Three can fit in a C-130 Hercules transport plane, six in a C-141B Starlifter and fifteen in a C-5A Galaxy. They can also be parachute dropped from low altitude.

New versions have a 6.5-litre diesel engine, developing 160 hp, and a central tyre inflation system. The armoured version protects against 7.62-mm ball with under-body protection against anti-personnel and anti-tank mines. For use in the Middle East, they even have air conditioning.

Aquatrack Tracked 8000 kg Amphibious Vehicle

Made in Britain by Alvis Vickers Ltd, formerly GKN Defence, the Aquatrack will carry forty seated personnel or a payload of 8 tons. Powered by a single diesel engine with twin screws, it can make up to 7 knots an hour in rough water with waves up to 13 feet when fully laden. It can mount a beach in 10 feet of plunging surf and cope with soft sand, mud, frozen ground and harsh terrain.

Chenowth Light Strike Vehicle

The three-seater Chenowth LSV was used by both the UK and US Special Forces during the First Gulf War. Painted black, the US Navy SEALs climbed roadblocks and 8-foot berms to be dubbed by the grateful Kuwaitis "Ninja cars".

Chenowth LSV has a top speed of 80 miles an hour, 68 miles an hour off-road, and can climb a gradient of 75 per cent. It has an air-cooled engine for reliability in extreme weather. Armament includes two 7.62-mm machine guns mounted fore and aft, along with one 12.7-mm M2 machine gun or a 40-mm Mark 19 automatic grenade launcher. It can also carry a TOW 2 anti-tank missile launcher, a 30-mm ASP-30 cannon, an AT-4 anti-tank rocket launcher or a Stinger surface-to-air missile. Light armour can be added if required.

The new Advanced Light Strike Vehicle gives the main weapon station a 360-degree arc of fire. It is designed to carry a .50-calibre M2 machine gun and a Mark 9 automatic grenade launcher. With four-wheel drive and a souped-up diesel engine, it now provides a more stable platform for shoot-on-the-move manoeuvres.

Cobra Light Strike Vehicle (LSV)

The Cobra LSV is a highly mobile vehicle designed for reconnaissance missions and raids in hostile environments. Used for airborne operations, it can be slung under a Ch-47D, Puma or Sea King helicopter. It has also been para-dropped from a Hercules. A useful weapons platform is has a Universal Mount Interface that can carry a 7.62-mm and 12.7-mm machine guns, a 40-mm grenade launcher, a 30-mm ASP-30 cannon or six Milan anti-tank missiles and their launcher. A 51-mm or 60-mm mortar is sometimes carried for use dismounted.

FMC Amphibious Assault Vehicle

The AAV7A1, also known as the LVTP7 AAV, has a boat-shaped hull, tracks and six road wheels at the back. It is armed with a 12.7-mm M85 machine gun and one 40-mm Mark 19 machine gun with a rocket launcher. It can operate at sea for up to seven hours with a top speed of 7 knots. On land is can do 40 miles an hour and carries twenty-five men.

General Dynamics Advanced Amphibious Assault Vehicle

The AAAV is a tracked amphibious armoured personnel carrier with room designed to replace the AAV7A1. It has a crew of three, carriers eighteen and is armed with a 30-mm Mark 44 canon and one 7.62-mm M240 machine gun. It can travel at 25 knots at sea and at 45 miles an hour on land with a range, at sea, of 75 miles and 400 miles on land.

Land Rover Special Operations Vehicle

Based on the chassis of the Land Rover Defender XD 110, the Land Rover SOV is a updated version of the famous SAS "pinkie", and was introduced after the First Gulf War. It can be carried inside a CH-47, EH-101, slung under any medium-sized helicopter, or para-dropped from a Hercules. A 12.7-mm machine gun is pintle-mounted on the roll-bar. The front passenger has a 7.62-mm machine gun and it carries a Mark 19 40-mm grenade launcher.

It has a series of on-board racks that can be configured to carry all types of ammunition and stores. Mortars, rockets or anti-tank missiles are stowed on side racks and there are side bins to carry explosives or land mines.

The US Rangers bought sixty Land Rover SOVs, which they call RSOVs. They do not use it as an assault vehicle but rather as a fast-moving weapons carrier, communications vehicle or casualty transporter. In aggressive action, it can carry six fully armed Rangers and 8,000 lb of equipment.

LARC-5 Amphibious Cargo Carrier

US landing teams are resupplied by the 4 x 4 LARC-5. Weighing 5 tons, it can carry 4.4 tons of cargo or fifteen to twenty fully equipped men. The vehicle is propelled through the water by a three-blade propeller under the rear of the hull. It makes 7 knots in the water and 30 miles an hour on land.

LMC Over-Snow Vehicles

The Logan Manufacturing Company of Utah makes a series of over-snow vehicles that are used by the US Marine Corps and Special Forces.

The LMC 1200 carried ten men and a two-man crew. Although primarily designed to travel in snow, it can also be used in other marginal terrain such as swamps.

The LMC 1500 has a cargo area of 5.5 x 5.5 feet and can carry over a ton, while the LMC 1800 has a cargo platform of 32 square feet and carries 1.3 tons.

Over-Snow Strike/Support Vehicle

The OSV is a high-performance sledge that can carry 550 lb, including heavy machine guns and mortars that can be mounted on the front frame. It is also used for transporting casualties. The OSV floats and they can be connected together to form a pontoon.

Unimog

During the First Gulf War, the SAS used Mercedes Unimogs as a mother ship amid columns of eight or twelve Land Rovers. They carried supplies, ammunition, fuel, spares and NBC equipment, allowing the fighting columns to stay behind enemy lines for the duration of the war. The name Unimog derives from *Univeral-Motor-Gerät* – German for "universal power unit". The first was produced in 1951, but in 1955 Daimler-Benz developed it for military use.

In 1986, the US Army bought 2,460 Unimogs to use as engineer vehicles. The chassis has been used in the Scarab and the French Panhard armoured personnel carriers.

30

AIR TRANSPORT

Fixed Wing

Special Forces have to be deployed at lightning speed to all parts
of the globe. This is done by four principal transport planes.

C-5 Galaxy

USSCOM keep two gigantic US Air Force Lockheed C-5
Galaxys on standby at all times, ready to carry SEAL teams
and their Special Operations Craft to any trouble spot around
with world within forty-eight hours.

With a wingspan of 222.9 feet the C-5 is one of the largest
aircraft in the world and the largest transport plane in the US
Air Force inventory. It is 247.1 feet long and stands 65.1 feet
high. It can carry more than any other transport and can airlift
36 standard pallets and up to 81 troops simultaneously. The
Galaxy can also carry all of Special Forces' air-transportable
combat equipment. It can even transport such bulky items as
its 74-ton mobile scissors bridge to any theatre of combat
across the globe. Even carrying oversize cargo and loaded with
fuel for intercontinental flights, it can take off and land in
relatively short distances, and can operate from runways 6,000
feet long.

The cargo compartment is 143.75 long, 19 feet wide and 13.5 feet high. It has front and rear cargo openings, allowing ground crews to load and off-load the C-5 simultaneously, reducing the time it spends on the ground. The nose and aft doors open the full width and height of the cargo compartment with full-width drive-on ramps at each end to load two rows of vehicles. The huge plane has six sets of landing gear with a total of twenty-eight wheels to distribute the weight. The landing gear system also "kneels", allowing the parked aircraft to be lowered so that the cargo floor is at truck-bed height to make loading and unloading easier.

The Galaxy has the distinctive high T-tail, 25 wing sweep, and four TF39 turbofan engines mounted on pylons beneath the wings. These engines are rated at 43,000 lb of thrust each, and weigh 7,900 lb each. They have an air intake diameter of more than 8.5 feet in diameter. Each engine pod is nearly 27 feet long.

The plane has 12 internal wing tanks with a total capacity of 51,150 gallons of fuel – that's enough to fill 6½ regular-size railway tankers. A full fuel load weighs 332,500 lb. With a full cargo load of 270,000 lb a C-5 can fly 2,150 nautical miles, offload, and fly to a second base 500 nautical miles away from the original destination without aerial refuelling. Maximum range without aerial refuelling is 6,320 nautical miles. With aerial refuelling the aircraft's range is only limited by the endurance of its seven-man crew. It carries a pilot, a co-pilot, two flight engineers and three loadmasters.

The C-5A first went into service in June 1970. The last C-5B, including more than 100 additional system modifications to improve reliability and maintainability, joined the US Air Forces's airlift team in March 1989. However, a study in 1998 showed that 80 per cent of the C-5 airframe service life remained, so a programme was started to modernize its avionics. New CF-6 engines, pylons and auxiliary power units have been added and improvements have been made to the aircraft's skin and frame, flight controls, landing gear and the pressurization system. This modernization programme will increase the C-5 Galaxy's operational capability well into the twenty-first century.

The C-5A costs $152.8 million, the C-5B $179 million. There are 111 in service.

C-17 Globemaster III

The C-17 Globemaster III is the newest cargo aircraft in the airlift fleet of the US Air Force and the RAF. The C-17 is capable of rapid strategic delivery of Special Forces troops and their equipment to main operating bases or directly to forward bases in the deployment area. The aircraft can perform tactical airlift and airdrop missions, and evacuate casualties when required.

The Globemaster has a wingspan of 169 feet 10 inches, and is 174 feet long and 55 feet 1 inch high. The aircraft is powered by four, fully reversible F117-PW-100 engines – the military designation for the commercial Pratt & Whitney PW2040, currently used on the Boeing 757. Each engine is rated at 40,440 lb of thrust. The thrust reversers direct the flow of air upward and forward to avoid stirring up dust and debris that would then be sucked into the engine.

The aircraft has a crew of three – a pilot, co-pilot and loadmaster, which reduces the operating costs. The cargo compartment is 88 feet long, 18 feet wide and 12 feet 4 inches high. Cargo is loaded through a large aft door wide enough for military vehicles and palletized cargo. The C-17 can carry virtually all of the Special Force's air-transportable equipment.

Maximum payload capacity of the C-17 is 170,900 lb, and its maximum gross take-off weight is 585,000 lb. With a payload of 169,000 lb and an initial cruise altitude of 28,000 feet, the C-17 has a range of around 2,400 nautical miles with refuelling. Its cruise speed is approximately 450 knots (.76 Mach). The C-17 can carry 154 passengers and airdrop 102 paratroopers and equipment.

The design of the aircraft allows it to operate from small airfields. It can take off and land on runways as short as 3,500 feet and just 90 feet wide. Even on such narrow runways, the C-17 can turn around using a three-point star turn and its backing capability.

To cut costs, maximum use has been made of off-the-shelf and commercial equipment, including Air Force-standardized avionics and only twenty aircraft maintenance man-hours are required per flying hour.

The C-17 made its maiden flight on 15 September 1991. The first production model was delivered to Charleston Air Force Base, South Carolina, on 14 June 1993 and the first squadron of C-17s, the 17th Airlift Squadron, was declared operational on 17 January 1995. The US Air Force originally planned to buy 120 C-17s, with the last one being delivered in November 2004. However, the plan now is to buy 180. They cost $202.3 million each.

C-130 Hercules

The Lockheed C-130 Hercules is a four-engined turboprop cargo aircraft, the main tactical airlifter for many military forces worldwide, including Britain and America. As such it has been used to airlift Special Forces groups in to theatre and is regularly used to ferry troops to Iraq and Afghanistan. Over forty models and variants of the Hercules serve with more than fifty nations. In its AC-130 Spectre gunship version, armed with 40-mm, 105-mm cannons and a 25-mm Gatling gun that can fire 1,800 rounds a minute, it has been used to support Special Operations in southern Afghanistan.

In December 2006 the C-130 became the fourth aircraft to mark fifty years of continuous use with its first customer – the US Air Force. The first three planes to achieve that distinction were the English Electric Canberra in May 2001, B-52 Stratofortress in January 2005 and the Tupolev Tu-95 in January 2006.

Capable of short take-offs and landings from unprepared runways, the C-130 was originally designed as a transport plane for troops, cargo and medical evacuation. But soon its versatile airframe found uses in a variety of other roles – airborne assault, search and rescue, scientific research support, weather reconnaissance, aerial refuelling, aerial firefighting and, not least, as a gunship. The Hercules family has the longest continuous production run of any military aircraft.

During the Korean War of 1950–1953, Second World War-era transports such as the C-119 Flying Boxcar, C-47 Skytrain and C-46 Commandos were still being used but proved unsuitable for modern warfare. So on 2 February 1951, the US Air Force issued a General Operating Requirement for a new transport to all the major US aircraft manufacturers – Boeing, Douglas, Fairchild, Lockheed, Martin Company, Chase Aircraft, Airlifts Inc, North American and Northrop. The GOR specified that the new transport should be able to carry 92 passengers or 64 paratroopers 1,100 nautical miles, be able to take off and land using short, unprepared strips and be able to fly with one engine stopped.

Fairchild, North American, Martin and Northrop dropped out, but the other five companies came up with a total of nine designs – Douglas and Chase produced three each, Lockheed two, and Boeing and Airlifts Inc one apiece. In the end, the contest came down to the L-206, the lighter of Lockheed's two designs, and a four-turboprop from Douglas. There were genuine doubts about the design with Lockheed itself and the chief designer of the Lockheed plant in Burbank, California said that it would destroy the company. Nevertheless, the company signed a contract with the Air Force on 2 July 1951.

The first flight of the prototype was made on 23 August 1954 in Burbank when the plane made a 61-minute hop to Edwards Air Force Base. After two prototypes were completed, production was moved to the company's plant in Marietta, Georgia, where more than 2,000 C-130s have been built.

The initial production model, the C-130A, was powered by Allison T56 turboprops with three-blade propellers. Deliveries began in December 1956, continuing until the introduction of the C-130B model in 1959. Some A models were redesignated C-130D after being equipped with skis and rockets for jet-assisted takeoff. The newer C-130B had ailerons that give it more lift, uprated engines and four-bladed propellers that were standard until the late 1990s.

The extended-range C-130E model entered service in 1962. The increased range was achieved by under-wing fuel tanks carrying 1,360-gallon US fuel tanks, supplementing wing-mounted auxiliary fuel tanks, and more powerful Allison T-56-A-7A turboprops. The E model also featured structural improvements and upgraded avionics that gave it a higher gross weight.

The KC-130 tankers used for aerial refuelling were originally C-130Fs procured for the US Marine Corps in 1958. They are equipped with a removable 3,600-gallon US stainless-steel fuel tank carried inside the cargo compartment. The two wing-mounted hose and drogue aerial refuelling pods each transfer up to 300 gallons US a minute to two aircraft simultaneously.

The US Navy bought the strengthened C-130G, while the C-130H model has updated Allison T56-A-15 turboprops, a redesigned outer wing, updated avionics and other minor improvements. Later H models had a new, fatigue-life-improved centre wing that was retro-fitted to many earlier H-models. Deliveries began in 1964. An improved version was introduced in 1974 and production continued until 1996. The C-130H model remains in widespread use with the US Air Force and many foreign air forces.

Planes made between 1992 and 1996 were called the C-130H3 by the US Air Force. The three means that it is the third variation in design in the H series. Improvements included a partial glass cockpit with ADI and HSI instruments, an uprated APN-241 colour radar, night-vision-compatible instrument lighting and an improved electrical system.

The equivalent model for export to the UK is the C-130K, which the Royal Air Force call the Hercules C1. The C-130H-30, or Hercules C3, is a stretched version, produced by inserting a 100-inch section behind the cockpit and an 80-inch section at the rear of the fuselage. A single C-130K was purchased by the Met Office for use by its Meteorological Research Flight. This aircraft was heavily modified – most notably with a long red-and-white striped atmospheric probe on the nose. It was given the designation W2, to differentiate it from the ordinary C1 and named Snoopy. The C-130K is also used by the RAF Falcons parachute display teams for its jumps.

The HC-130N & P are long-range search and rescue variants used by the USAF Air Rescue Service. Equipped for deep deployment of para-rescue men, survival equipment and aerial refuelling of combat rescue helicopters, they are usually the on-scene command aircraft for combat search-and-rescue missions. Early versions were equipped with the Fulton surface-to-air recovery system, designed to pull a person off the ground using a wire strung from a helium balloon. The Fulton system was later removed when it proved safer and easier to refuel helicopters in flight. The film *The Perfect Storm* depicts a real-life search-and-rescue mission that involved aerial re-fuelling by a HC-130.

The C-130R and C-130T are US Navy and USMC models, both equipped with under-wing external fuel tanks. The C-130T is similar, but has numerous avionics improvements over the R model and is fully night-vision-system compatible. In both models, USMC aircraft are equipped with Allison T-56-A-16 engines. The USMC versions are designated KC-130R or KC-130T when equipped with under-wing re-fuelling pods and pylons.

The RC-130 is a reconnaissance version, used by the Islamic Republic of Iran Air Force. Lockheed also made a civilian version called the L-100.

In the 1970s Lockheed proposed a C-130 variant with tur-bofan engines rather than turboprops, but the US Air Force preferred the take-off performance of the existing aircraft. In the 1980s the C-130 was intended to be replaced by the Advanced Medium STOL (Short Take-off and Landing) Transport project, but the project was cancelled and the C-130 remained in production.

The C-130J Super Hercules is the newest version of the Hercules and the only model still produced, though many others are still in service. While remaining externally similar to the classic Hercules, it is a very different aircraft. It has new Rolls-Royce Allison AE2100 turboprops with six-bladed com-posite scimitar propellers, digital avionics with Head-Up Displays (HUDs) for each pilot and a reduced crew. It needs just pilots with no navigator or flight engineer. A C-130J-30 stretched version is also available. The first order for the C-130J came from the RAF, who ordered 25 aircraft. First deliveries of the C-130J, or Hercules C Mark 5, and C-130J-30, or Hercules C Mark 4, began in 1999.

The largest operator of the new model will be the USAF, who are ordering the aircraft in increasing numbers, although as of 2005 Congress announced C-130J acquisition would be dra-matically cut. Current operators of the C-130J are the USAF, United States Marine Corps with the KC-130J tanker, US Air National Guard, US Coast Guard, Royal Air Force, Royal Australian Air Force, Danish Air Force and the Italian Air Force. Total procurement of C-130J aircraft has reached 186 orders as of December 2006. More are to be bought by the Canadian, Indian and Norwegian air forces.

The Hercules holds the record for the largest and heaviest aircraft to land on an aircraft carrier. In October and November 1963, a USMC KC-130F, made 21 unarrested landings and take-offs on the USS *Forrestal* at a number of different weights. The pilot, Lieutenant James Flatley III, was awarded the Distinguished Flying Cross for his participation. The tests were highly successful, but the procedure was considered too risky for routine operations.

While the C-130 continues to be involved in cargo and resupply operations daily, it has been a part of some notable offensive operations. The MC-130 version carries the world's largest conventional bombs: the 15,000-lb BLU-82 "daisy cutter" and GBU-43/B Massive Ordnance Air Blast bomb. Daisy cutters were used during the Vietnam War to clear landing zones for helicopters and to eliminate minefields. They have recently been used against Taliban and al-Qaeda cave complexes in Afghanistan in an attempt to kill Osama bin Laden. The 18,700-lb GBU-43/B MOAB, first tested in 2003, is known of as the "mother of all bombs". At 8.2 and 10.5 tons US respectively the weight and size of these weapons make it impossible or impractical to load them on conventional bombers.

The MC-130 was also used in the 1976 raid on Entebbe when Israeli Special Forces staged a surprise assault on Entebbe Airport in Uganda to rescue 103 passengers of an airliner hijacked by Palestinian and German terrorists. A rescue force – comprising 200 soldiers, jeeps and a black Mercedes-Benz that resembled Ugandan Dictator Idi Amin's vehicle of state – was flown 2,160 nautical miles from Israel to Entebbe on-board five Israeli Air Force Hercules without mid-air refuelling. On their return, the planes refuelled in Nairobi, Kenya.

During the 1982 Falklands War, Argentine Air Force C-130s undertook highly dangerous, daily resupply flights to the Argentine garrison occupying the islands. Only one was lost during the war. Argentina also operated two KC-130s refuellers during the war, which refuelled the Skyhawk attack planes that sank the British frigate HMS *Antelope*. The British also used C-130s to support their logistical operations.

During the First Gulf War, the C-130 Hercules was used operationally by the US Air Force, US Navy and US Marines, and the air forces of Australia, New Zealand, Saudi Arabia, South Korea and the UK. In Afghanistan, the C-130 Hercules has been used operationally by Australia, Belgium, Canada, France, Italy, the Netherlands, New Zealand, Norway, South Korea, Spain, the UK and the US in support of the International Security Assistance Force. During the 2003 invasion of Iraq, the C-130 Hercules was used operationally by Australia, the UK and the US. After the initial invasion, the multinational force in Iraq used their C-130s to support their forces in Iraq. A C-130T aircraft, known as Fat Albert, is used as the support aircraft for the US Navy Blue Angels flight demonstration team.

The C-130 is generally regarded as a highly reliable aircraft. The Royal Air Force recorded an accident rate of about one aircraft loss per 250,000 flying hours over the last 40 years, making it one of the safest aircraft they operate – alongside Vickers VC10s and Lockheed Tristars with no flying losses. However, more than 15 per cent of the 2,350-plus production has been lost, including seventy by the US Air Force and the US Marine Corps while serving in the war in South-East Asia.

One of the specialist variants of the C-130 is the EC-130 Commando Solo, which is a modified Lockheed C-130 Hercules used to conduct psychological operations and civil affairs broadcast missions in the standard AM, FM, HF, TV and military communications bands. It is operated exclusively by the 193rd Special Operations Wing based in Middletown, Pennsylvania.

Missions are flown both day or night at maximum altitude for maximum coverage. The EC-130 is air-refuellable. Secondary missions include command and control communications countermeasures (C3CM) and limited intelligence gathering. The three variants are EC-130 ABCCC, EC-130E Commando Solo, and the EC-130J Commando Solo. In 2006, the EC-130E was retired from service, leaving the EC-130J.

The EC-130E Commando Solo entered service in 1978 as the EC-130E Coronet Solo with the Tactical Air Command (TAC). In 1983 the Coronet Solos mission was transferred to the Military Air Command (MAC) and redesignated the

EC-130E Volant Solo. With the formation of the US Air Force Special Operations Command, the mission was transferred to AFSOC and redesignated Commando Solo. In the early 1990s the aircraft were upgraded and designated Commando Solo II. The EC-130E variants were replaced with new EC-130J Commando Solo III aircraft beginning in 2003.

Highly specialized modifications have been made to the latest version, including enhanced navigation systems, self-protection equipment, and the capability to broadcast colour television on a multitude of worldwide standards throughout the TV VHF/UHF ranges.

Soon after the 193rd Special Operations Wing received its EC-130s, the unit participated in Operation Urgent Fury, acting as an airborne radio station to keep the people of Grenada and US Citizens on the island abreast of the US military action. Commando Solo was also used in Operation Just Cause, again broadcasting continuously throughout the initial phases of the operation to remove the regime of Manuel Noriega from Nicaragua. In 1994, Commando Solo was used to broadcast radio and television to the citizens and leaders of Haiti during Operation Uphold Democracy.

Other EC-130 variants include the ABCCC and Compass Call. The ABCCC is an Airborne Battlefield Command and Control Center used as an airborne command post, while the Compass Call is an airborne communications jamming platform. It was used extensively in the Gulf War to disrupt Iraqi communications at both the strategic and tactical levels. Air Force Special Operations Command use other variants: the MC-130E Combat Talon I, MC-130H Combat Talon II, MC-130W Combat Spear and the MC-130P Combat Shadow.

Finally there is the AC-130 gunship. The sole user of this heavily armed ground-attack plane is the US Air Force which has two versions in service – the AC-130H Spectre and AC-130U Spooky. The gunship squadrons are part of the Air Force Special Operations Command.

C-141 Starlifter

President John F. Kennedy's first official act after his inauguration was to order the development of an all-jet transport to extend the reach of the nation's military forces. Lockheed's C-141 StarLifter was the result. Soon after, President Kennedy began the Green Berets and the C-141 was one way that they could be transported into action in the far-flung theatres they were supposed to work in.

The C-141 Starlifter became the workhorse of Air Mobility Command. It could airlift combat troops and their equipment over long distances, airdrop men and machinery, resupply ground troops and extract the sick and wounded. The C-141 was the first jet aircraft designed to meet military standards as a troop and cargo carrier.

The original C-141A design was stretched to make the C-141B. This lengthened the plane by 23 feet 4 inches to 168 feet 4 inches. The height is 39 feet 3 inches and the wingspan is 160 feet, thereby stretching increased cargo capacity by about one-third, giving an extra 2,171 cubic feet. The C-141B was also given an in-flight refuelling capability.

The Starlifter carries a crew of six – a pilot, co-pilot, two loadmasters and two flight engineers). It has a top speed of 500 mph (Mach 0.66) and a ceiling of 41,000 feet. The maximum take-off weight is 323,100 lb. Empty, the plane weighs 144,492 lb.

It is powered by four Pratt & Whitney TF33-P-7 turbofan engines, each developing 20,250 lb of thrust. Its range is 2,500 miles (2,174 nautical miles) without refuelling. A universal air-refuelling receptacle on the C-141B transfers 23,592 gallons of fuel in about 26 minutes, allowing longer non-stop flights and fewer fuel stops during worldwide airlift missions. The C-141 force, nearing seven million flying hours, has a proven relia-bility and long-range capability. The aircraft cost $8.1 million in 1992.

The Starlifter has paratroop doors on each side and a rear loading ramp, which can also be used for paradrops. Air drops can be made from both low and high altitudes and it can airdrop equipment and supplies using the container-delivery system. The Starlifter was the first aircraft designed to be compatible with the 463L Material Handling System, which permits off-loading 68,000 lb of cargo, refuelling on the ground and reloading a full load in less than an hour.

The C-141 has an all-weather landing system, pressurized cabin and crew station. Its cargo compartment can easily be modified to perform around thirty different missions. About 200 troops or 155 fully equipped paratroops can sit in canvas side-facing seats, or 166 troops in rear-facing airline seats. Rollers in the aircraft floor allow quick and easy cargo pallet loading. A palletized lavatory and galley can be installed quickly to accommodate passengers, and when palletized cargo is not being carried, the rollers can be turned over to leave a smooth, flat surface for loading vehicles.

In its medical evacuation role, the Starlifter can carry about 103 litter patients, 113 ambulatory patients or a combination of the two. It provides rapid transfer of the sick and wounded from remote areas overseas to hospitals in the United States. The Air Force Reserve, through its associate units, provides 50 per cent of the Starlifter's airlift crews, 40 per cent of its maintenance capability and flies more than 30 per cent of Air Mobility Command's peacetime worldwide missions.

During the First Gulf War, a C-141 from the 437th Military Airlift Wing, Charleston Air Force Base, South Carolina, was the first American aircraft into Saudi Arabia, transporting an Airlift Control Element from the 438th Military Airlift Wing, McGuire Air Force Base, New Jersey. In the following year, the C-141 completed the most airlift missions – 7,047 out of 15,800 – supporting the Gulf War. It also carried more than 41,400 passengers and 139,600 tons of cargo.

The first C-141A, delivered to Tinker Air Force Base, Oklahoma, in October 1964, began squadron operations in April 1965. Soon, Starlifters made flights almost daily to South-East Asia, carrying troops, equipment and supplies, and returning patients to US hospitals. Several C-141s have been modified to carry the Minuteman intercontinental ballistic missile in its special container.

Some C-141s have been equipped with intraformation positioning sets that enable a flight of two to thirty-six aircraft to maintain formation regardless of visibility. The C-141 was the first jet transport to deploy US Army paratroopers to land on the Antarctic. A C-141 established a world record for heavy cargo drops of 70,195 lb

The first C-141B was received by the Air Force in December 1979 and conversion of 270 C-141s from A to B models was completed in 1982. Further C-141 modifications were made to preserve the remaining force by improving reliability and maintainability improvements, and capability improvements necessary for effective use through 2006.

Thirteen aircraft will receive additional SOLL II Special Operations (Low-Level II) upgrades under the Special Operations Forces Improvement programme. This gave the aircraft a low-level night-flying capability, enhanced navigation equipment and improved defensive countermeasures. These aircraft were operated by Air Mobility Command in conjunction with Air Force Special Operations Command.

During the 1990s sixty-three aircraft of the C-141 fleet underwent major modifications. They were given the All Weather Flight Control System (AWFCS) with a digital autopilot, advanced avionics display and the Ground Collision Avoidance System (GCAS). Other major improvements included Defensive Systems (DS) to protect against shoulder-fired SAM missiles, and GPS.

Rotary

Bell AH-1 HueyCobra/Super Cobra

The Super Cobra is an attack helicopter that gives ground support to Special Forces. It has two flight crew. Top speed is 222 knots and radius of action is 125 nautical miles. It has a M197 20-mm cannon in the nose turret and can carry Stinger missiles, TOW or Hellfire ATGWS, Maverick AGMS, 2.75-inch rocket pods and 12.7-mm machine gun or 20-mm cannon pods.

Bell UH-1 Iroquois/Bell 204/204/212

Popularly known as the Huey, the UH-1 is used to insert and extract Special Forces as well as give them ground support. With a crew of two it can carry up to fourteen passengers. Maximum speed is 128 knots and the range is 332 nautical miles. It has 7.6-mm, 12.7-mm machines guns or a 20-mm cannon mounted in the cabin. It also carries 12.7-mm or 20-mm cannon pods; or 2.75-inch, 68-mm, 71-mm or 81-mm rocket pods.

Bell/Boeing V-22 Osprey

The Osprey tilt-wing aircraft is distinctive due to its two rotors mounted on either end of stubby aircraft wings, which can be folded. It is used to support amphibious operations. It carries two pilots, a crew chief and 24 combat-laden troops. Top speed is 305 knots and it has a range of 515 nautical miles.

Boeing AH-64 Apache

The AH-64 Apache is also made in the UK by Westland under licence. It is an attack and reconnaissance helicopter and gives ground support to Special Forces. There are two pilots. Top speed is 197 knots and range is 220 nautical miles. It has a M230 30-mm Chain Gun mounted under the nose. It can also carry Mistral, Sidewinder, Starstreak or Stinger missiles, Hellfire ATGWS and 2.75-inch FFAR pods.

Boeing CH-47 Chinook

The Chinook has supported both British and American Special Forces in amphibious assaults. It has two pilots and a crew chief, and can carry up to 55 troops. Top speed is 154 knots and radius of action of 505 nautical miles. It carries two or three pintle-mounted 7.62-mm M134 Miniguns or 12.7-mm machine guns in the cabin. The Chinook is distinctive with its two rotor blades, fore and aft, and its fixed-wheel undercarriage.

EH 101 Merlin

The EH 101 is used to insert and extract Special Forces and can fly from ships and aircraft carriers in support of amphibious operations. It has a crew of two pilots and specialist mission crew, and can carry up to 45 troops. Top speed is 167 knots and research-and-rescue radius of action of 350 nautical miles. There is provision for a nose-mounted 12.7-mm machine gun and hardpoints for another four. It can also carry four torpedos, depth charges and a FFAR pod.

Puma

The French SA 330 Puma is used by British Special Forces as a medium-lift, tactical helicopter. It is made by Aerospatiale of France. Top speed is 158 knots and it has a range of 309 nautical miles. With a crew of two, it can carry sixteen to twenty passengers or 7,055 lb of externally slung cargo. Weapons include a Giat 20-mm cannon in a turret under the nose and hard points for four in the cabin. It is also fitted with pods for 57-mm or 70-mm rockets, or AAMS or ATGWS.

RAH-66 Comanche

Built by Boeing and Sikorsky, the Comanche is used to support Special Forces, as well as in a stealth and reconnaissance roll. It carries two pilots. Top speed is 175 knots and its radius of action is 150 nautical miles. It has a XM301 20-mm cannon in a nose turret and bays one either side that can each carry three weapons, including Stinger missiles, Hellfire ATGWS and 2.75-inch rocket pods.

Sikorsky S-70A/UH 60 Blackhawk

Used as battlefield support for Special Forces, the Black Hawk has a crew of three and carries eleven troops, 9,000 lb or an externally slung cargo. It has a maximum speed of 194 knots and a range of 1,200 nautical miles with external tanks. There is provision for two 7.62-mm Miniguns or 12.7-mm GECAL 50 machine guns in the fuselage doors. It can also carry Stinger missiles, Hellfire ATGWS, 2.75-inch FFAR pods, mine dispensers and ECM pods.

Westland HC Mk4 Sea King

The Sea King has regularly seen service deploying Special Forces. With two pilots, it can carry 28 troops or 8,000 lb of externally slung cargo. Top speed is 122 knots and range is 300 nautical miles. It has one door-mounted 7.62-mm machine gun and can carry Sea Eagle or Exocet ASMS, Sting Ray torpedoes and depth charges.

Westland WG.13 Lynx

Used for the insertion and extraction of maritime Special
Forces, the Lynx carries two crew and ten troops. Maximum
speed is 145 knots and its radius of action is 320 nautical miles.
It is armed with 7.62-mm or 12.7-mm door guns, and carries
Hellfire or TOW ATGWS, FFAR pods, or 7.62-mm or 12.7-
mm machine-gun pods.

Air Force Special Operations Command

AC-130H/U Spectre Gunship

Air Force Special Operations Command uses the AC-130 – the
gunship version of the C-130 – for close air support, air
interdiction and force protection. Close air support roles include supporting ground troops, escorting convoys and flying
urban operations. Air interdiction missions are conducted
against planned targets and targets of opportunity. Force protection missions include defending air bases and other military
facilities. They have a standard crew of 12–13 airmen, including
five officers – two pilots, a navigator, an electronic warfare
officer and a fire control officer. The enlisted men are a flight
engineer, electronics operators and aerial gunners.

The C-130 Hercules was selected to replace the AC-47
Gunship I (known as Spooky or Puff the Magic Dragon) during
the Vietnam War, due to its ability to carry more and heavier
weapons, and its better endurance.

In 1967, a USAF JC-130A was selected for conversion into the
prototype AC-130A gunship. The modifications were done that
year at Wright-Patterson Air Force Base, by the Aeronautical
Systems Division. A direct-view night-vision telescope was
installed in the forward door, an early forward-looking infrared
(FLIR) in the forward part of the left wheel well, and Gatling
guns mounted facing down and aft along the left side. The
analogue fire-control computer prototype was handcrafted by
RAF Wing Commander Tom Pinkerton at the USAF Avionics
Laboratory. Then flight testing of the prototype was performed
primarily at Eglin Air Force Base, followed by further testing
and modifications. By September 1967, the aircraft was certified

ready for combat testing and was flown to Nha Trang Air Base, South Vietnam for a 90-day test programme. Following its successes, a few more AC-130As were constructed using similar equipment and manufactured versions of the analogue computer. They were armed with 7.62-mm GAU-2/A miniguns and four 20-mm M61 Vulcan cannon.

The AC-130 Gunship first arrived in South Vietnam on 21 September 1967 under the Gunship II programme, and began combat operations over Laos and South Vietnam that year. By 30 October 1968, enough AC-130 Gunship IIs arrived to form a squadron. The 16th Special Operations Squadron (SOS), of the 8th Tactical Fighter Wing (TFW) were activated on that date at Ubon Air Base in Thailand.

In Vietnam, these heavily-armed aircraft incorporate side-firing weapons integrated with sophisticated sensors, navigation and fire-control systems to provide precision fire-power or area-saturation fire with its varied armament. The AC-130 can spend long periods flying over its target area at night and in adverse weather. The sensor suite consists of a television sensor, infra-red sensor, and radar. These sensors allow the gunship to visually or electronically identify friendly ground forces and targets in most weather conditions.

During the Vietnam era the AC-130 was sometimes equipped with a Magnetic Anomaly Detector (MAD), a highly sensitive passive device which picks up localized deviations in the Earth's magnetic field and is normally used to detect submerged submarines. The MAD array of the C-130 could detect the ignition coils of enemy trucks hidden under dense foliage, alerting the crew to their presence who then took appropriate action.

By December 1968 most AC-130s were flown under F-4 escort from the 479th Tactical Fighter Squadron, normally with three Phantoms per gunship. In late 1969, a new version of the AC-130 with the code name "Surprise Package" arrived. It had a solid-state, laser-illuminated, low-light-level TV with a companion YAG laser designator, an improved forward-looking infra-red (FLIR) sensor, video recording for TV and FLIR, inertial navigation, and a prototype digital fire-control computer. Surprise Package was equipped with the latest 20-mm Gatling guns and 40-mm Bofors cannon, but no 7.62-mm close support armament. Deployed to Ubon Air Base in 1970, the AC-130As were acquired under the "Pave Pronto" project. It was then that they picked up their squadron's call sign, Spectre.

Surprise Package served as a test bed for the avionic systems and armament for the AC-130E. It was given two 20-mm M61 Vulcan cannons, one 40-mm L60 Bofors cannon and one 105-mm M102 howitzer.

The first AC-130A loss of the war – "*The Arbitrator*" – occurred on 24 May 1969 while on armed reconnaissance over Southern Laos. Piloted by Lieutenant-Colonel W.H. Schwehm, the gunship was hit by 57-mm anti-aircraft fire while orbiting at over 6,000 feet. They made it back to Ubon Air Base. As they approached, Colonel Schwehm ordered his crewmen to bail out, while he attempted an emergency landing. As the damaged Spectre touched down, the right undercarriage collapsed and the gunship veered off the runway into an obstacle, catching fire. Neverthess eleven crewmen survived, though two were later killed in action.

The second AC-130A Spectre, named "War Lord", was lost on 22 April 1970 while "truck hunting" along the southern portion of the Ho Chi Minh trail, in Laos. The 16th SOS gunship was strafing the trucks when it was hit by 37-mm anti-aircraft shells and caught fire. Ten crewmen were listed as KIA. Staff Sergeant E. Fields was the only survivor.

On 25 March 1971, one of the first seven AC-130As deployed, known as "*First Lady*", was hit in the nose by anti-aircraft fire over the Ho Chi Minh Trail in Laos. The 37-mm anti-aircraft shell destroyed everything below the crew deck, but "*First Lady*" survived. In 1975, after the conclusion of US involvement in the hostilities in Indochina, it was transferred to the Air Force Reserve, where it served with the 711th Special Operations Squadron of the 19th Special Operations Wing. In 1980 the aircraft was upgraded from the original three-bladed propellers to the quieter four-bladed propellers and was eventually retired in late 1995. The retirement also marked an end to the Air Force Reserve flying the AC-130A. The aircraft now sits on display in the final Air Force Reserve configuration with grey paint, black markings and the four-bladed Hamilton Standard props at the USAF Armament Museum at Eglin AFB, Florida, USA.

Four more Spectres were lost in the Vietnam War. On 28 March 1972, Prometheus, piloted by Major Irving B. Ramsower of the 16th SOS, 8th TFW, was destroyed by a hit from a surface-to-air missile while truck hunting over the Ho Chi Minh Trail. There were no survivors. On 30 March 1972, the first AC-130E was lost while truck hunting along the Ho Chi Minh Trail. After confirming the destruction of three trucks, it was hit by 57-mm anti-aircraft fire and crashed near An Loc. The crew bailed out safely. The search and rescue mission that ensued turned out to be one of the largest in US history. Seven HH-53s Super Jolly Green Giants, eight A-1 Skyraiders, three C-130s, four EB-66s, six F-105 Thunderchiefs, fourteen NAIL FACs, three RAVENs belonging to the CIA, three Air America Helicopters, four more AC-130 Spectre Gunships and an F-4 Phantom were involved. The rescue formed the basis of the movie *Bat 21*, starring Gene Hackman.

On 18 June 1972, another 16th SOS AC-130A was operating some 25 miles south-west of Hué in South Vietnam, when a SA-7 SAM missile struck its number three engine, tearing off the wing. Three crewmen bailed out, but there were no other survivors.

The last Spectre lost in the Vietnam War was during the last days of America's involvement in the war, while B-52s were pounding North Vietnam in Operation Linebacker II. Nevertheless the Spectres continued their pursuit of trucks moving in convoy along the Ho Chi Minh Trail. On 21 December 1972, AC-130A pilot Captain Harry R. Lagerwall was attacking three trucks at nearly 8,000 feet, when he was struck by 37-mm anti-aircraft fire. His Spectre, Thor, exploded. Two crewmen managed to bail out safely but the other fourteen perished.

In Vietnam, AC-130 gunships destroyed more than 10,000 trucks and participated in many crucial close air support missions. During Operation Urgent Fury in Grenada in 1983, AC-130s suppressed enemy air-defence systems and attacked ground forces during the assault on Point Salines Airfield. The AC-130 aircrew earned the Lieutenant-General William H. Tunner Award for the mission.

AC-130s also had a principal role in Operation Just Cause in 1989 when they destroyed Panama Defense Force Headquarters and numerous command and control facilities. Aircrews earned the Mackay Trophy for the most meritorious flight of the year and another Tunner Award for their efforts.

During the First Gulf War, AC-130s provided close air support and force protection (air base defence) for ground forces, and battlefield interdiction. The primary interdiction targets were early warning/ground control intercept (EW/GCI) sites along the southern border of Iraq. The first gunship to enter the battle for Khafji helped stop a southbound Iraqi armoured column on 29 January 1991. One day later, three more gunships provided further aid to Marines participating in the operation. The gunships attacked Iraqi positions and columns moving south to reinforce their positions north of the city. Despite the threat of SAMs and increasing visibility during the early morning hours of 31 January 1991, one gunship opted to stay to continue to protect the Marines. A surface-to-air missile shot down the AC-130, call sign Spirit 03, killing all fourteen crewmen.

Employing technologies developed in the 1990s, the AC-130U is equipped with the AN/APQ-180, a synthetic aperture radar for long-range target detection and identification. The gunship's navigational devices include the inertial navigation systems and GPS. The AC-130U can attack two targets simultaneously. It also has twice the munitions capacity of the AC-130H and is armed with one 25-mm GAU-12/U Equalizer Gatling gun, one 40-mm L60 Bofors cannon and a 105-mm M102 howitzer or two 30-mm Bushmaster II cannon and one 105-mm M102 howitzer.

AC-130 gunships were used in Operations Restore Hope and United Shield in Somalia, in the NATO mission in Bosnia-Herzegovina, and the evacuation of American non-combatants from Albania in 1997. On 15 March 1994, over the Indian Ocean off the coast of Kenya, near the town of Malindi, an AC-130, then known as a Predator (but previously called both Bad Company and Widow Maker) was lost, along with the lives of eight crew members. Gunships were also part of the build-up of US forces in 1998 to try and convince Saddam Hussein to comply with UN weapons inspections. Gunships were deployed during the 2001 invasion of Afghanistan and the invasion of Iraq. In 2007, US Special Operations Forces used the AC-130 in attacks on suspected al-Qaeda militants in Somalia.

The AC-130H is produced at a cost of $132.4 million, and the AC-130U is produced at a cost of $190 million. Currently there are eight AC-130H and thirteen AC-130U aircraft in active duty service.

A programme has been started to upgrade the armament of existing AC-130s still in service by replacing the 25-mm GAU-12/U and 40-mm Bofors with two Mk 44 Bushmaster II 30-mm cannons. The 40-mm Bofors gun was becoming progressively more difficult to maintain and spare parts difficult to locate, while the 25-mm cannon lacks ammunition with an air-burst capability and suffers from too much scatter. Procuring the right types of ammunition for the 30-mm Bushmaster is much easier.

There are also plans to look into replacing the M102 howitzer with a breech-loading 120-mm mortar, and to give the AC-130 a stand-off capability using either the AGM-114 Hellfire missile, the Advanced Precision Kill Weapon System based on the Hydra 70 rocket, or the Viper Strike glide bomb.

MC-130E/H Combat Talon I and II, and MC-130w Combat Spear

The MC-130E Combat Talon I, MC-130H Combat Talon II and MC-130W Combat Spear are specifically modified to provide infiltration, exfiltration and resupply of Special Operations Forces, as well as psychological operations support and helicopter air refuelling. The Combat Talon I has served since the Vietnam War, including the American military campaigns in Grenada and Panama.

After the MC-130E was developed in the early 1960s, the Combat Talon I version was equipped with an electronic countermeasures suite and terrain-following radar, enabling it to avoid enemy radar and anti-aircraft weapons. It also featured a Fulton surface-to-air recovery system to extract personnel. In the Vietnam War, the aircraft was used to drop leaflets over North Vietnamese positions, and to insert Special Forces units into enemy territory.

The aircraft saw action again in Operation Eagle Claw in 1980, Operation Just Cause from December 1989 to January 1990, and Operation Desert Storm in 1991. The aircraft performed one-third of all airdrops during the First Gulf War, and participated heavily in psychological operations. Combat Talon I crews dropped several BLU-82 "daisy cutter" bombs and flew several leaflet-drop sorties in the war's opening stages, then converted to a search-and-rescue role as the conflict progressed.

After the failure of Operation Eagle Claw and the re-evaluation of the US's general poor management of Special Operation Forces after Vietnam, Special Operations Command was reorganized and, with it, Combat Talon II was developed.

The Combat Talon II became operational in the early 1990s, following the First Gulf War. It was originally designed to replace the Combat Talon I, but an increase in Special Operations meant that it went into service alongside it. The Combat Talon II has a stronger airframe and modifications to the rear and aft cargo doors. The electronics suite has been upgraded, and includes GPS, special radars for navigating in adverse weather and night-vision capability. These new technologies mean that the Combat Talon II can fly as low as 250 feet above the ground and make faster, more accurate airdrops. Increases in automation also reduced the aircrew by two.

The first combat deployment of a Combat Talon II was in 1996 when Special Operations units were deployed to Liberia to assist in the evacuation of 2,000 civilians from the US Embassy when the country was engulfed in civil war. The Combat Talon II performed the same role in Zaire in 1997.

The first MC-130W Combat Spear was delivered to Air Force Special Operations Command on 28 June 2006. It was developed from an updated C-130H to replace the Combat Talons lost since 1997, can carry out the same missions as the Combat Talon and has the added ability to air-to-air refuel Special Operations helicopters. The aircraft will eventually be based at AFSOC bases worldwide.

MC-130P Combat Shadow

The MC-130P Combat Shadow is a C-130 modified to fly clandestine or low visibility, low-level missions into politically sensitive or hostile territory to provide air refuelling for Special Operations helicopters. The MC-130P primarily flies its single-or multi-ship missions at night to reduce the risk of detection and interception. Secondary missions include the airdrop of small Special Operations teams, small bundles, and zodiac and combat rubber raiding craft. It can take off and land using night-vision goggles or approaches using tactical airborne radar. As well as providing aerial refuelling for helicopters, it can itself be refuelled in flight.

MC-130Ps used to be designated the HC-130N/P, but the "H" designation is a rescue-and-recovery mission code and did not accurately describe the aircraft's Special Operations role. So in February 1996, AFSOC's tanker fleet was redesignated MC-130Ps, adding the Combat Shadow to the role of other M-series Special Operations mission aircraft.

The HC-130P was similar to the HC-130N, the difference being that the HC-130P had the Fulton Surface-to-Air Recovery System fitted. However, a fatal accident in 1982, the only fatality in seventeen years of live pick-ups, damaged the credibility of the personnel pick-up system within the Special Operations community and the Fulton system gradually fell out of favour. By 1996 the 8th SOS was the only unit in the world that maintained crew proficiency in the use of the Fulton recovery system, and had been prepared to launch it if called upon since the late 1960s. Then with the increased availability of long-range, air-refuellable MH-53J Pave Low and MH-47E Chinook helicopters, and tightening budgets, AFSOC decided to drop the Fulton System in September 1996 and it was removed from the HC-130P.

Some HC-130P have been modified as dual tanker-transport with night-vision capability, head-up display, an infra-red missile warning system and forward-looking infra-red. It can drop parachutists in freefall and static line mode from the doors at a rate of ten every five seconds. The minimum safe height is 500 feet.

MC-130P Combat Shadows and MC-130E Combat Talon I aircraft have similar missions, but the Combat Talon Is have more instruments designed for covert operations. Both aircraft fly infiltration and exfiltration missions, airdropping or landing Special Forces teams and equipment in hostile territory. They also air refuel Special Operations helicopters and usually fly missions at night with aircrews using night-vision goggles. The

Combat Talon I, however, has an electronic countermeasures suite and terrain-following radar that enables it to fly extremely low, counter enemy radar and penetrate deep into hostile territory.

However in 2000, improvements were made to the MC-130P, modifying navigation, communications, threat-detection and countermeasures systems specifically for Special Operations. The fully modified Combat Shadow has a fully integrated inertial navigation and global positioning system, and night-vision, goggle-compatible interior and exterior lighting. It also has a forward-looking infrared radar, missile and radar warning receivers, chaff and flare dispensers and night-vision, goggle-compatible, heads-up display. In addition, it has satellite and data burst communications, and a refuelling capability.

The Combat Shadow can fly in the day against a reduced threat. However, crews normally fly night, low-level, air-refuelling and formation operations using night-vision goggles. To improve the chances of success, especially when flying near populated areas, crews use special tactics to avoid radar and weapons detection, flying with no external lighting and maintaining communications silence.

Originally ordered in 1963 and first flown in 1964, the HC-130s have served in many roles and missions. The aircraft was initially modified to conduct search and rescue missions, provide a command and control platform, refuel helicopters and carry supplemental fuel for extending range or air refuelling. In the Vietnam War they were used to refuel Jolly and Super Jolly Green Giant helicopters and, as an airborne command post, to direct rescue efforts. Four aircraft were modified to deploy 10,000-lb remotely piloted vehicles, and conduct search and rescue missions.

In 1986, the HC-130 fleet took on a Special Operations mission when they provided critical air refuelling to Army and Air Force helicopters during Operation Just Cause in Panama in 1989. They deployed to Saudi Arabia and Turkey in support of Desert Storm in 1990 to provide air refuelling of Special Operations forces helicopters over friendly and hostile territory, as well as taking part in psychological operations and leaflet drops.

Since the First Gulf War, the redesignated MC-130P has been involved in Operations Northern and Southern Watch, supporting efforts to keep Iraqi aircraft out of the no-fly zones. Although MC-130Ps left Southern Watch in 1993, they returned periodically to relieve Air Combat Command rescue forces. The aircraft also took part in Operation Deny Flight in Yugoslavia in 1993, and Operations Restore Democracy and Uphold Democracy in Haiti in 1994. The MC-130P has been involved in Operations Deliberate Force and Joint Endeavor in Bosnia since 1995. Additionally, the MC-130P took part in Operation Assured Response in 1996, providing air refuelling for the MH-53s shuttling evacuees between Liberia and the rear staging area.

In March 1997, the MC-130P was diverted from Italy to provide combat search and rescue during the evacuation of non-combatant Americans from Albania. Also in 1997, the MC-130P provided command and control and refuelling support during Operation Guardian Retrieval, the evacuation of Americans from Zaire. In July 1997, the aircraft provided aerial refuelling for MH-53Js when US forces prepared for possible evacuations of non-combatants from Cambodia. The aircraft also was part of Operation High Flight, the search to locate an American C-141 involved in a mid-air collision with another aircraft off the coast of Angola in September 1997.

During Operation Allied Force, a MC-130P Combat Shadow participated in a combat search and rescue mission for the pilot of a downed F-117A stealth fighter. For their efforts, the 67th Special Operations Squadron crew was named winner of the 1999 Brigadier-General Ross G. Hoyt Award. This award is presented annually by Air Mobility Command to the most outstanding air refuelling aircrew. The Combat Shadow crew took off en route to Bosnia-Herzegovina for a rendezvous with three rescue helicopters. Two were MH-53 Pave Lows, one from the 21st SOS and the other from the 20th SOS at Hurlburt Field, Florida. The third helicopter was a MH-60 Pave Hawk from the now deactivated 55th SOS at Hurlburt Field. The plan called for the rescue helicopters to refuel immediately before crossing the Serbian border to allow them to operate with full fuel tanks. Until needed, the MC-130P remained out of sight. After more than ninety minutes of orbiting close to the border, the call came from the helicopter crews for the desperately needed fuel that would enable them to continue the rescue mission. The refuelling took place at the unusually low altitude of 700 feet within three miles of the Serbian border. Afterwards, they waited for the second MC-130P to replace them before departing for badly needed fuel. Sustaining fuel was provided by rendezvousing with a KC-135 – a first for an MC-130P during a combat mission. The crew then flew to Tuzla Air Base in Bosnia-Herzegovina, where they picked up the downed pilot and transported him to Aviano Air Base.

In March 2000, Air Force MC-130P aircraft crew members used their flying time over Mozambique to take digital photos of flooded areas to help relief teams determine where supplies were needed. Initially this was a one-off operation for the US Army Corps of Engineers who wanted pictures of the flood damage to a dam. It then turned into daily photography requests from the Atlas Response Joint Task Force that co-ordinates the US military relief operation.

The HC-130P King deploys worldwide to provide combat search and rescue coverage for US and allied forces. Combat search and rescue missions include flying low-level, preferably at night, aided with night-vision goggles, to an objective area where aerial refuelling of a rescue helicopter is performed or para-rescuemen are deployed. The secondary mission of the HC-130P is peacetime search and rescue. HC-130P aircraft and crews are uniquely trained and equipped for search and rescue in all types of terrain including Arctic, mountain and maritime. Peacetime search and rescue missions may include searching for downed or missing aircraft, sinking or missing boats and ships, or missing persons. The HC-130P can deploy para-rescuemen to a survivor, escort a helicopter to a survivor, or airdrop survival equipment to a survivor. They have continued performing these roles in Iraq and Afghanistan.

MH-53J/M Pave Low III/IV

The Sikorsky HH-53 "Super Jolly Green Giant" is a USAF version of the CH-53 Sea Stallion helicopter for long-range Combat Search And Rescue (CSAR) helicopters. It was developed to replace the HH-3 "Jolly Green Giant". The HH-53s were later upgraded as the MH-53 Pave Low series. The US Air Force ordered HH-53B and HH-53C variants for Search and Rescue units, and developed the MH-53J Pave Low version for Special Operations missions, which now sees service with Air Force Special Operations Command.

The Pave Low's mission is low-level, long-range, undetected penetration into denied areas, day or night, in adverse weather, for infiltration, exfiltration and resupply of Special Operations forces. Pave Lows often work in conjunction with MC-130P Combat Shadow for navigation, communications and combat support, and with MC-130H Combat Talon for in-flight re-fuelling.

Although officially known as the Stallion, the large green air-frame of the HH-53B earned it the nickname "Super Jolly Green Giant". This name is a reference to the smaller HH-3E "Jolly Green Giant", a stretched variant of the H-3 Sea King, used in the Vietnam War for combat search-and-rescue operations.

The Sikorsky S-61R/HH-3E Jolly Green Giants were very successful as long-range combat search-and-rescue helicopters, and the US Air Force became interested in the more capable S-65 model. In 1966, they awarded a contract to Sikorsky for development of a minimum-change CSAR variant of the CH-53A.

Designated the HH-53B, it has a retractable in-flight refuel-ling probe on the right side of the nose and jettisonable external tanks, with a capacity of 650 gallons US, fitted to the sponsons and braced by struts attached to the fuselage. A rescue hoist capable of deploying a jungle penetrator with 250 feet of steel cable was fitted above the right passenger door. It has a Doppler navigation radar in the forward belly and 1,200 lb of armour. The HH-53B's armament includes three pintle-mounted, General Electric GAU-2B/A 7.62-mm, six-barrelled, Gatling-style miniguns, with one in a forward hatch on each side of the fuselage and one mounted on the tail ramp, with the gunner secured by a harness.

Early HH-53Bs featured T64-GE-3 turboshafts developing 3,080 shaft horsepower, but these engines were later upgraded to T64-GE-7 turboshafts with 3,925 shaft horsepower. They had a crew of five – a pilot, co-pilot, crew chief and two para-rescuemen.

While waiting for delivery of the HH-53Bs, the Air Force obtained two Marine CH-53As for evaluation and training. The first of eight HH-53Bs performed its initial flight on 15 March 1967, and the type was performing CSAR missions with the USAF Aerospace Rescue and Recovery Service in South-East Asia by the end of the year. The Air Force called the HH-53B the "Super Jolly". It was used for CSAR, covert combat operations and recovering re-entry capsules from photo-reconnaissance satellites.

The HH-53B was essentially an interim model, with production quickly moving on to the improved Air Force HH-53C CSAR variant. The most visible difference between the HH-53B and HH-53C was that the HH-53C dispensed with the fuel-tank bracing struts. Those flying the HH-53B found that the original tank was too big, so a smaller 450-gallon US tank was adopted in its place. More armour was added and a more comprehensive suite of radios to improved communications with C-130 tankers, attack aircraft supporting CSAR actions, and aircrews awaiting rescue on the ground. The HH-53C retained the upgraded HH-53B's more powerful T64-GE-7 engines.

A total of 44 HH-53Cs were built, with introduction to service in August 1968. Late in the war they were fitted with countermeasure pods to deal with heat-seeking missiles. Like the HH-53B, the HH-53C was also used for covert operations and recovering re-entry capsules and reconnaissance drones. A few were assigned to support the Apollo space programme, standing by to recover an Apollo capsule in case of a launch-pad abort. In the event, no such an accident ever happened.

In addition to the HH-53Cs, the Air Force obtained twenty CH-53Cs for more general transport work. The CH-53C was apparently very similar to the HH-53C, even retaining the rescue hoist, the most visible difference being that the CH-53C did not have an in-flight refuelling probe. Since CH-53Cs were used for covert operations, they were no doubt armed and armoured, just like HH-53Cs.

The Super Jollies made headlines in November 1970 in the unsuccessful Special Forces raid into North Vietnam to rescue prisoners-of-war from the Son Tay prison camp, as well as in the operation to rescue the crew of the freighter SS *Mayagüez* from Cambodian Khmer Rouge fighters in May 1975. The Air

Force lost seventeen Super Jollies in the war – three in accidents and fourteen in combat, including one that was shot down by a North Vietnamese MiG-21 while on a CSAR mission over Laos on 28 January 1970.

The HH-53B, HH-53C and CH-53C remained in Air Force service into the late 1980s. Super Jollies operating in front-line service were painted in various camouflage colour schemes, while those in rescue service in America were painted grey with a yellow tail band. Meanwhile a number of Super Jollies were converted into Pave Lows for Special-Operations missions.

While Super Jollies were excellent helicopters, they were more or less daylight and fair-weather machines. Aircrew were often downed at night or in bad weather. A limited night-flying and foul-weather sensor system based on a low-light-level TV imager called Pave Low was deployed to South-East Asia in 1969. It was combat-evaluated on a Super Jolly, but was found to be unreliable.

In 1975, a HH-53B was fitted with the much-improved Pave Low II system and redesignated YHH-53H. This proved much more satisfactory, so eight HH-53Cs were given a further improved systems fit and redesignated HH-53H Pave Low III, while the YHH-53H was also upgraded to this specification. All were delivered in 1979 and 1980. Two of the HH-53Hs were lost in training accidents in 1984, so two CH-53Cs were brought up to HH-53H standard as replacements.

The HH-53H retained the in-flight refuelling probe, external fuel tanks, rescue hoist and three-gun armament of the HH-53C – typically a Minigun on each side and a Browning 12.7-mm gun in the tail to provide more reach and a light anti-armour capability. The HH-53H also had a Texas Instruments AN/AAQ-10 forward-looking infra-red imager, AN/APQ-158 terrain-following radar, a Canadian Marconi Doppler-radar navigation system, a Litton or Honeywell inertial guidance system, a computerized moving-map display, a radar-warning receiver and chaff-flare dispensers. The FLIR and TFR were mounted on a distinctive "chin" mount.

The HH-53H could be fitted with twenty-seven seats for troops, or fourteen stretchers. The upgrades were done by the US Navy in Pensacola as the Navy handled high-level maintenance on Air Force S-65s. In 1986, the surviving

HH-53Hs were given an upgrade under the Constant Green programme, featuring incremental improvements such as a cockpit with blue-green lighting compatible with night-vision goggles. They were then reclassified as Special-Operations helicopters and consequently given a new designation of MH-53H.

The HH-53H proved successful and the Air Force modified it further with the MH-53J Pave Low III Enhanced configuration. The general configuration of the MH-53J is similar to that of the HH-53J, the major changes being the fitting of twin T64-GE-415 turboshafts developing 4,380 shaft horsepower and more armour, giving it a total armour weight of 1,000 lb. There were also some avionics upgrades, including the addition of a modern GPS satellite navigation receiver. Some 31 HH-53Bs, HH-53Cs and CH-53Cs were upgraded to the MH-53J configuration between 1986 and 1990. All the MH-53Hs were upgraded as well, so there was a total of forty-one MH-53Js.

The MH-53J Pave Low III heavy-lift helicopter is the largest, most powerful and technologically advanced transport helicopter in the US Air Force inventory. The terrain-following and terrain-avoidance radar, forward-looking infrared sensor, inertial navigation system with GPS, along with a projected map display, allow the crew to follow the contours of the land while avoiding obstacles, making it the perfect Special Operations vehicle for low-level penetration. Their main mission is to drop Special Forces behind enemy lines, supply them and pick them up after the job is done. They are also used for combat search-and-rescue missions. The MH-53J Pave Low III can transport thirty-eight troops at a time and sling up to 20,000 lb of cargo on its external hook. It has a top speed of 165 miles an hour and altitudes up to 16,000 feet.

The MH-53J evolved into the MH-53M Pave Low IV with the addition of Interactive Defensive Avionics System/Multi-Mission Advanced Tactical Terminal or IDAS/MATT. The system further improves the defensive capabilities of the Pave Low. It provides instant access to the total battlefield situation, through near real-time Electronic Order of Battle updates. It also provides a new level of detection avoidance with near real-time threat broadcasts over-the-horizon, so crews can avoid and defeat threats, and replan en route if needs be.

Army Special Operations Command

AH-6J Light Attack Helicopter

The AH-6J is a highly modified version of the McDonnell Douglas 530 series commercial helicopter in service with the 160th Special Operations Aviation Regiment. The unit provides aviation support to Army Special Operations Forces and other USSOCOM personnel.

Shortly after the failed hostage rescue mission in Iran, the Army formed a special aviation unit. The unit drew on some of the best aviators in the Army and immediately began an intensive training programme in low-level night operations. It formally became a battalion on 16 October 1981 and was designated the 160th Aviation Battalion, though it was popularly known as Task Force 160 because of the constant attachment and detachment of units to prepare for a wide variety of missions. Its focus on night operations resulted in the nickname, "The Night Stalkers". On 16 May 1990 the unit was reorganized, redesignated the 160th Special Operations Aviation Regiment (Airborne), and assigned to the US Army Special Operations Command.

Although all Army aviation units have an inherent capability to support special operations, the units of the 160th SOAR (Abn) have been specifically designated by the Secretary of Defense to be prepared, trained and task organized for special operations mission support. The 160th SOAR(Abn) organizes, trains, equips, validates, employs, sustains and maintains air assets for worldwide deployment and assignment to theatre CINCs for conducting direct action, special reconnaissance and other special operations.

The 160th SOAR(Abn) is based at Fort Campbell, Kentucky and is composed of four active-duty battalions and one forward deployed company. Its battalions include the Fort Campbell-based 1/160 which flies the AH-6, MH-6, MH-60K and MH-60L DAP; the Fort Campbell-based 2/160 which flies the MH-47E; and the Hunter Army Airfield, Savannah, Georgia-based 3/160 which flies the MH-60L and MH-47D. D/160 consists of five MH-60Ls assigned to the Southern Command.

The unit's AH-6Js are single-turbine engine, dual flight control, light-attack helicopters. They are primarily employed in close air support of ground troops, target destruction raids and armed escort of other aircraft. The AH-6J is normally flown by two pilots.

It can be deployed by any Air Force transport aircraft. A C-141 is capable of transporting up to six AH-6s and a C-130 can transport three AH-6s, with a rapid upload/offload capability. This means the AH-6s can offload, build up, and depart within fifteen minutes, or it can self-deploy provided there is refuel support at every 270 nautical miles.

AH-6Js have communications equipment capable of secure operations on UHF and VHF bands. SATCOM is also installed on some aircraft. They have forward-looking infra-red, and are armed with a variety of 7.62-mm miniguns, 70-mm rocket pods, .50-calibre machine guns, or Hellfire air-to-ground missiles as well as a 30-mm cannon and Stinger air-to-air missiles.

The 160th SOAR (Abn)'s AH-6s were developed by Boeing (McDonnell Douglas) – formerly Hughes – as the OH-6A which was used as a military scout during the Vietnam War. The Hughes OH-6A Cayuse was quite effective when teamed with the AH-1G Cobra attack helicopter as part of what were known as "Pink Teams". The OH-6A "Loach" would find targets by flying low, "trolling" for fire, and lead in a Cobra, or "Snake", to attack. The OH-6A could be armed with the M27 armament sub-system, the M134 six-barrel 7.62-mm minigun or the M129 40-mm grenade launcher on the XM8 armament sub-system.

Two "Little Bird" Special Operations versions of the OH-6A were developed. They were the AH-6C armed variant, and the MH-6B transport/utility version, which can carry up to six personnel for quick insertion and extraction missions. A previous version, the EH-6B, was used for command, control and radio relay. The AH-6 Little Bird Gun, a light-attack helicopter, has been tested and proven in combat. Armed with guns, Hellfire missiles, and 2.75-inch FFAR, it provides armed helicopter support to both ground and air Special Operations. These versions were all powered by a single Allison T-63 252 SHP engine.

MH-6J

The MH-6J is a single-engine, light-utility helicopter developed from the OH-6A alongside the AH-J and in service with the 160th SOAB (Abn). It has been modified to transport externally up to six combat troops and their equipment, and is capable of conducting overt and covert infiltrations, exfiltrations and combat assaults over a wide variety of terrain and environmental conditions. It is also used for command and control, and reconnaissance missions. Its small size allows it to be deployed rapidly in C-130, C-141, C-17 and C-5 transport aircraft.

The basic MH-6 configuration has the External Personnel System mounted on each side of the aircraft, giving a total of six external and two internal seating positions. The aircraft can be rapidly configured for Fastrope and STABO (Short Tactical Airborne Operation). Motorcycle racks can carry two bikes. Some MH-6s are equipped with Forward Looking Infrared Radar that provides an infra-red image of terrain features and airborne objects of interest. Images can be recorded for playback on a standard VHS video cassette recorder. The MH-6J also has a comprehensive range of communications – FM, UHF, VHF, Motorola Saber and SATCOM. All of them can be used securely.

The MH-6 can be deployed by any Air Force transport aircraft. A C-141 can carry six MH-6s and a C-130 three MH-6s, which can be offloaded and ready to fly within fifteen minutes. On self-deployment it needs to be refuelled every 270 nautical miles. Armed with a combination of guns and folding-fin aerial rockets, it can also provide support to Special Operations Forces on the ground.

MH-60 Blackhawk

The 160th SOAB (Abn) have a number of Blackhawks, specially adapted for Special Operations Mission – thereby earning them the "MH" designation.

The MH-60K Special Operations Utility Helicopter is a highly modified twin-engine utility helicopter based on the basic UH-60 airframe and developed specifically for Special

Forces. Modifications include aerial refuelling capability, an advanced suite of aircraft survivability equipment, and improved navigation systems, including multi-mode radar for pinpoint navigation in all environments and under the harshest conditions.

The MH-60L Special Operations Utility Helicopter is a highly modified version of the standard US Army Blackhawk, configured for special operations use. The helicopter's mission is insertion and extraction of Special Operations troops. It has an updated cockpit, additional avionics, precision navigation system, forward-looking infra-red, aircraft survivability equipment and external tanks. Older MH-60Ls can be adapted for attack missions by attaching dual weapons pylons to both sides of the fuselage to mount cannon, rockets or missiles. These can be supplemented by door-or port-mounting guns or launchers, limited mainly by the range, duration, cargo or number of troops needed to complete the mission. It is protected by radar- and missile-warning systems and IR jammers. The MH-60L is powered by two General Electric T700-GE-701C 1,843 shaft hp turboshaft engines.

The MH-60L Direct Action Penetrator is a MH-60L modified to mount a variety of offensive weapons systems. Its mission is to conduct attack helicopter operations utilizing area fire or precision-guided munitions and to conduct the armed infiltration or exfiltration of small units. It is capable of carrying out direct-action missions as an attack helicopter or it can be reconfigured for troop assault operations. In its direct-action role, the DAP would not normally be used as a primary transport for troops or supplies because of high gross weights.

The DAP is capable of conducting all missions during day, night or adverse weather conditions. It can provide armed escort for helicopter formations. Using team tactics, the DAP is able to provide suppression or close air support for formations and teams on the ground.

MH-47D/E Chinook

The 160th SOAR(Abn) also have their own versions of the Chinook modified for Special Operations missions. Designated MH-47, it conducts its overt and covert infiltrations, exfiltrations, air assault, resupply and sling operations over a wide range of environmental conditions. The aircraft can perform a variety of other missions including shipboard operations, platform operations, urban operations, water operations, parachute operations, FARP operations, casualty evacuation and combat search-and-rescue operations. The 160th SOAR (Abn) currently operates two models: the MH-47D Adverse Weather Cockpit, operated by 3/160; and the MH-47E, operated by 2/160.

The MH47 is capable of operating at night during marginal weather conditions. With the use of special-mission equipment and night-vision devices, the air crew can operate in hostile-mission environments over all types of terrain at low altitudes during periods of low visibility and low ambient lighting conditions with pinpoint navigation accuracy 30 seconds on target.

The MH-47E is a Special Operations heavy assault helicopter based on the CH-47 airframe, specifically designed and built for the Special Operations aviation mission. It has: an integrated avionics sub-system which combines a redundant avionics architecture with dual-mission processors, remote terminal units, multifunction displays and display generators, to improve combat survivability and mission reliability; an aerial refuelling probe for in-flight refuelling; an external rescue hoist; and two L714 turbine engines with Full Authority Digital Electronic Control which provides more power during hot/high environmental conditions. Two integral aircraft fuel tanks replace the internal auxiliary fuel tanks commonly carried on the MH-47D AWC, providing 2,068 US gallons of fuel with no reduction in cargo capacity.

The standard MH-47 is fitted with a full suite of communications equipment – FM, UHF (with HAVE QUICK II capability), VHF, HF, SATCOM and the Motorola Saber. The MH-47E is equipped with SINCGARS VHF-FM single channel ground and airborne radio system. The Automatic Target Hands-off System provides the capability of data-bursting pre-selected and formatted information to other equipped aircraft or ground stations. It has a navigation system consisting of a Mission Computer utilizing GPS/INS/Doppler navigation sources for pinpoint navigation.

Its fast-rope insertion and extraction system allows for the rapid insertion and extraction of personnel. From the rear ramp men can be inserted nine per rope at a time and extracted six per rope at the same time. Its internal rescue hoist uses the centre cargo hook and rescue hatch. It can carry 600 lb and has some 150 feet of useable cable. The external rescue hoist appears on the MH-47E only, works from the right front cabin door and carries 6,000 lb with 245 feet of useable cable.

Both the MH-47 D and E have forward-looking infrared. The MH-47E also has a map display generator that when used with the Data Transfer Module displays aeronautical charts, photos or digitized maps in the Plan and 3D modes of operation. For long-range missions the cargo compartment can be fitted with up to three ballistic-tolerant, self-sealing tanks. Each tank holds 780 US gallons of fuel and are refillable in flight.

MH-47s can be transported in a C-5 and two MH-47s fit in a C-17. However, once they arrive, it takes around eight hours to get them ready for service.

The MH-47 D and E are scheduled to be replaced by the MH-47G whose specialized mission equipment includes multi-mode radar that permits terrain following and terrain avoidance in all climatic conditions, a Common Avionics Architecture System-equipped cockpit that enhances joint operability and pilot situational awareness, the next generation of forward-looking infra-red, FLIRM-134 Gatling miniguns and M-240D machine guns for increased defensive firepower, and oversized main fuel tanks The Army has approved the purchase of sixty-one MH-47Gs which should all be in service by 2011.

31

SEA TRANSPORT

Surface

Boston Whaler Light Patrol Boats

Boston Whaler make Light Patrol Boats for US Special Operations Command. They have a crew of three and are armed with three 12.7-mm and one 7.62-mm machine guns. The hull is fibreglass and the twin 300-horsepower outboard engines give a top speed of 35 knots. Displacing 3.3 tons fully laden, they measure 25 x 8.6 x 1.5 feet and are air transportable.

Gemini

Gemini inflatables were first made in 1979 and have become a favourite among Special Forces. They were used to deliver the SAS and SBS during the Falklands War. They range in length from 9.6 feet to 17.4 feet. When air-dropped, the two middle chambers are left uninflated so the craft can be folded in half. Once in the water, a diver activates a high-pressure cylinder to inflate the compartments amidships.

Gemini inflatables are made form Hypalon 1670 DTEX fabric to military specification. The company also make RIBs.

High Speed Interceptor Craft

The SBS use two versions of the HSIC. Both are around 49 feet in length and are powered by two 750-hp diesel engines giving a top speed of over 55 knots. The FIC 145 has a conventional hull, while the VSV version has a wave-piercing hull that allows it to maintain high speeds in rough water.

Incat High Speed Logistics Craft

Made by Incat of Tasmania, the High Speed Logistics Craft is on trial with the US Special Operations Command. It has been modified by strengthening the foredeck to take a 564-square yard helicopter pad that can accommodate a CH-46 or a SH-60. A hydraulic ramp at the rear allows vehicles to be loaded. It has been fitted with military communications and will be used for the rapid deployment of Special Forces on a hostile shore.

Klepper Kayak

The SBS still use the old wooden-framed Klepper Kayak for silent approach on night-time operations. Built in Germany since the 1950s, the two-man canoe was used in the Falklands. It is 17.5 feet long and folds up so that it can be easily carried or concealed.

Mark V Class Special Operations Craft

The US Navy SEALs use the Mark V SOC made by Halter Marine Equitable Shipyard of New Orleans. It won a design competition in 1994 for a high-speed craft to insert and extract Navy SEAL teams and other Special Forces personnel. Its two 4,506-horsepower MTU 12V-396 TE94 diesels and two Kamewa waterjets give a top speed of 45 knots and a range of 515 miles at 35 knots.

Armaments include five Mk 46 mountings for twin 12.7-mm or 7.62-mm machine guns, one 40-mm Mk 19 grenade launcher and three Bushmaster 25-mm Mk 38s. It can also be equipped with the Singer missile. The aluminium hull measures 81.2 x

17.5 x 4.3 feet. The Mark V SOC has a full range of communications equipment, including SATCOM, GPS and IFF.

It has a crew of five and carries sixteen fully equipped SEALs. It is deployed with a Mobile Support Team to provide maintenance support during mission turnaround. Turnaround time is approximately twenty-four hours and the average mission lasts twelve hours. A Mark V SOC detachment and supporting equipment can deploy worldwide on two US Air Force Lockheed C-5 Galaxies within forty-eight hours of notification.

Patrol Coastal Class Ship

The US Navy Special Operations Command have its own fleet to undertake Special Operations on the high seas. Naval Special Warfare Command has fourteen Coastal Class patrol ships. Their missions include long-range SEAL insertions and extractions, and deploying tactical swimmers. They can launch and recover 12-yard RIBs and SEAL Delivery Vehicles.

Normally operating as two-boat detachments, they have a complement of four officers and twenty-four enlisted men. There is berthing for nine Special Forces men. Armaments include a Stinger station, a Mark 96 25-mm rapid-fire gun, a Mark 38 25-mm rapid-fire gun, four pintles supporting any combination of M60 machine guns, .50-calibre machine guns and Mark 19 grenade launchers. The ship carries the Mark 52 Mod 0 chaff decoy launch system and the crew carry small arms.

The boat measures 170 x 25 x 7.8 feet and displaces 328.5 tons fully loaded. Its four Paxman 3,350-hp diesels give a top speed of over 30 knots and a range of 3,000 nautical miles at 16 knots.

Rigid Inflatable Boats

The SEALs make beach assaults in RIBs made by USMI of New Orleans. Measuring 36.1 x 10.5 x 3 feet, they carry eight fully laden men along with a crew of three. The two 940-hp Caterpillar 3126 diesels and two Kamewa FF 280 waterjets give it a top speed of 33 knots and a range of 200 miles. Armaments include one 12.7-mm machine gun and one 7.62-mm machine gun, or a Mark 19 Mod 3 grenade launcher.

Rigid Raiding Craft and Rigid Inflatable Boat

The SBS also use the Mark 3 Rigid Raiding Craft, which is capable of eight combat-laden troops. It is 7.4 metres long and weighs 2.6 tons. Its single Yamaha 220-horsepower diesel engine gives a top speed of 40 knots, or 36 knots when fully laden.

They also use four types of RIBs – Halmatic Arctic 22 and 28, and Pacific 22 and 28. They are capable to top speeds between 26 and 35 knots when carrying between ten and fifteen combat-laden troops.

River Patrol Boat

Some 500 River Patrol Boats were built during the Vietnam War. A handful still serve with Navy Special Operations to this day. Introduced in 1966, the PBR was designed for the high-speed deployment of SEAL teams up rivers in South-East Asia. It is highly manoeuvrable in shallow, debris-filled waters and can make a 180 turn and reverse course in its own length at full throttle. The engine is quiet and it has a low radar profile. The reinforced fibre-glass hull is protected with ceramic armour around crew areas.

The boat weighs 8.75 tons and measures 32 x 11.6 x 2 feet. Its two 215-hp GM 6V53N diesel engines and two Jacuzzi 14Y water pumps give it a top speed of 24 knots. It is seaworthy to Sea State 3 and has a maximum range of 300 nautical miles at full speed.

Sewart Mini Armoured Troop Carriers

US maritime Special Forces use Mini Armoured Troop Carriers made by Sewart. With a crew of four, they have a large transport hold that can carry up to 16 SEALs on riverine or coastal operations. The aluminium hull has ceramic armour plates and it is armed with seven 12.7-mm machine guns. Displacing 14.8 tons fully laden, it measures 36 x 12.7 x 3.5 feet. The two 445-horsepower Detroit 6V-92TA diesel engines and two Jacuzzi 20YJ water jets give it a top speed of 33 knots. It has a low silhouette that makes it difficult to detect, and the engines are quiet.

Zodiac

Zodiac inflatables have a history that goes back to the end of the nineteenth century. Light, strong and easy to conceal, they are a natural choice for Special Forces, where they are known by their military designation CRRC – combat rubber raiding craft.

The SEALs and other Special Forces use the Zodiac F470, which can be dropped from a helicopter or transport plane. Some 15 feet 5 inches long, they can carry eight combat-loaded SEALs. Power by two 35-horsepower outboard motors or one 55-horsepower outboard, the F470 can make 20 knots, fully laden. However, in a rough sea, the craft is bouncy and a considerable number of men have been injured after being thrown about.

In 2002 Zodiac came up with that they said was a "bullet-proof" version of the F470, called the Armorflate. Soft armour-plate made from Simula ballistic material is folded on the inflatable tubes, taking up minimal space. It can be inflated and deployed in 40 seconds, giving protection to the boat, its occupants and the engine. Hard armour plate can also be inserted in pockets to give added protection.

In addition, Zodiac make rigid inflatable boats with aluminium hulls. They come with inboard and outboard motors and range in length from 15 feet to 33 feet. Powered by 300-horsepower outboard motors, they are used as fast commando boats. With inboard motors, they can be used to carry supplies, troops or divers and can be supplied with divers' doors. Both type of RIB can be air-dropped.

Hovercraft

Amphibious Special Forces sometimes deploy from hovercraft, known in military parlance as air-cushioned vehicles or air-cushioned landing craft. They were used for an adoptive landing on the Al Faw peninsular during the Second Gulf War and patrolled Iraq's inland waterways.

Griffon

The British company Griffon make a series of hovercraft that are in use around the world. The Royal Marines use the Griffon 2000 TDX(M) Light Hovercraft. With a crew of two, it can carry sixteen troops or two tons of cargo. It is armed with a 7.62-mm machine gun and has a top speed of 33 knots in waves less than 1.3 yards high.

Made of aluminium it displaces 6.8 tons with a full load and can be carried on a low loader, or an LCU landing craft.

The Griffon 8000 TD(M) Hovercraft is used by the Indian coast-guard to apprehend smugglers. The Griffon 1000TD is used by the Thai amphibious forces, while the British Hovercraft Corporation's Wellington (BH.7) Class Medium-Lift Hovercraft is in service with the Iranian amphibious forces.

Subsurface

Carleton Life Support S-10 Rebreather Diving Apparatus, Canada

Some NATO forces use the chest-mounted S-10 Rebreather diving set which was designed specifically for military and paramilitary use. It is a closed-circuit oxygen rebreather that can be used down to a depth of eight yards, though in specific circumstances it can be used at greater depths for short periods. Underwater endurance is four hours.

Divex

Britain's SBS use the Stealth Divex Rebreather which was designed specifically for Special Forces and Explosive Ordnance Disposal. It is a closed-circuit mixed-gas system that is controlled by a microprocessor mounted on the back. Closed-circuit rebreathing systems work by removing the CO_2 exhaled by means of a scrubber and injecting fresh oxygen to replace that being used up by the diver. With the Stealth system, a SBS man can dive to a depth of 390 feet, stay at 328 feet for up to twenty minutes, or operate in shallower waters for up to six hours.

The Special Forces' mixed gas system uses air to dilute the nitrox mixture for depths up to 177 feet. After that helium is added or a pure helium and oxygen mixture is used. The rebreather removes the danger of getting the "bends" and no decompression is needed. This considerably simplifies matters when swimmers are deployed from a submarine.

Other Special Forces use Divex's Oxymax 3 closed-circuit diving set, which allows the diver to work at 33 feet for up to three hours. It is non-magnetic and quiet.

Divex also produce a buoyancy jacket to go with the rebreather so the swimmer can adjust his buoyancy. They manufacture a combat swimmer's board with a built-in compass with luminescent marks to aid underwater navigation. A depth-gauge and clock can also be fitted. And the company's force fins are in use with Special Forces around the world.

The SBS also use Divex's Digicom Diver through Water Communications system. This allows a combat swimmer to communicate with other divers or with the mother ship with a range of at least 1.6 nautical miles, though tests have proved it effective at up to 2.4 nautical miles. It interfaces easily with the Divex Stealth Full Face Dual Mode Mask used with the rebreather and is also compatible with scuba gear.

Divex's Subtug Diver Propulsion Vehicle is a torpedo-shaped tow that can accommodate two divers. Its aluminium frame provides handholds for divers and fastening points for equipment. And for maritime counter-terrorist work, the company produces a range of special equipment for making rapid assaults on vessels. There is a plummet grapple that uses compressed air to fire an 8-mm climbing rope to a height of 21 yards, or a 6-mm rope to 32 yards. Wire-rope ladders with titanium hooks make scaling the side of ship easier. They can be put in place using carbon-fibre or aluminium poles up to 16.6 yards long.

Dry Deck Shelter

The General Dynamics Electric Boat Division of Northrop Grumman has developed a submarine Dry Deck Shelter for the US Navy SEALs, which is also being made available to the SBS. These are used to house Swimmer Delivery Vehicles or to deploy divers from the submarine. Watertight connections allow divers to enter the DDS while the submarine is underwater and leave to carry out their mission on their SDV or rubber inflatables.

The DDS can be transported by air and takes around twelve hours to fit. It has three compartments. The aft compartment carries the SDV and other divers' equipment. The middle compartment is a transfer chamber to prevent the inner compartment flooding. And the final chamber is used to treat injured divers.

Mk VIII Mod 1 SEAL Delivery Vehicle

Both the British SBS and the US Navy SEALs replaced their Mk VIII Mod 0 delivery vehicles with the Mod 1 in 1999. The new vehicle has a fully flooding crew compartment, a uniform hull shape and an enclosed propeller. And it has twice the range – 36 nautical miles at 9 knots. It can carry six fully equipped combat swimmers.

Northrop Grumman Advanced SEAL Delivery System

US Navy SEALs teams use the ASDS as a dry delivery system. With a crew of two, it can embark eight SEALs and is usually deployed off a hostile shore from a mother submarine. Powered by a 55-hp engine and four thrusters, it has a range of 125 nautical miles at 8 knots. It has an optical and a communications periscope, and a small sonar. The ASDS is 65 feet long and displaces 55 tons. It can be carried on C-5 or C-17 transport planes, or on the deck of a submarine.

SSK 96 Subskimmer Rigid Inflatable Boat

KSA (Underwater) Ltd of Alston make a rigid-hulled inflatable fitted with a two-stroke, three-cylinder 90-hp Yamaha outboard motor designed for the combat swimmer. It has a top speed of 25 knots, a range of 70 nautical miles and a payload of 1,322 lb.

Using an electrical propulsion unit, it can also operate underwater. Conversion takes a minute and a half. It can work underwater for over two hours and can be left parked on the sea floor for days.

PART FOUR
IN ACTION

THE FIRST GULF WAR
– OPERATION DESERT STORM

UK Special Forces

During the build-up to the First Gulf War, the Coalition commander General Norman Schwarzkopf felt he had little need to call in Special Forces. However, the commander of the British Forces, Lieutenant-General Peter de la Billiere, was a former commander of 22 SAS and he managed to convince Schwarzkopf that the very special skills of the British Special Forces would be useful.

Even so, no immediate role was seen for them as the Green Berets had already taken on the role of border reconnaissance. It was then proposed that the SAS and Delta Force be used to rescue the hundreds of foreign nationals being held hostage as part of Saddam Hussein's "human shield". By mid-November, Special Forces command had earmarked some men from the SAS, SBS and an RAF Special Forces section to join US units for the evacuation raids, although no formal plan had been approved. Helicopter insertion and extraction, and amphibious raids were all considered, but all meant that huge risks would have to be taken. In fact, any plan would have proved impractical as the hostages were held in various locations all over the country. However, suddenly on 6 December 1990, Saddam

Hussein released the hostages, saying they would no longer be needed.

The next plan was to use the SAS to create a diversion ahead of the main attack, destroying the Iraqi communications facilities. After being on standby for months, the SAS left for the Gulf shortly after Christmas 1990. Men from A, B and D Squadrons were sent to the Gulf, making this the largest deployment of the Regiment since the Second World War. Heavily armed desert fighting columns were formed to infiltrate Iraqi territory in order to carry out search and destroy missions. By destroying just about anything they could find, they aimed to force the Iraqis to deploy large forces to track them down. Each squadron was divided into two fighting columns and they underwent intensive training in the United Arab Emirates. Each column consisted of between eight and twelve type 110 Land Rovers, armed with a Browning .50-cal heavy machine gun. They also had GPMGs, American Mark 19 40-mm grenade launchers and Milan anti-tank missiles. With them would be a Mercedes short-wheelbase Unimog open truck that was used as the mother vehicle. It carried the bulk of the supplies – fuel, ammunition, NBC equipment and spare parts. These columns were effective at night, preferring to lie up in the day to avoid detection. All the SAS columns stayed inside Iraq for the full duration of the war.

When the air war began on 17 January, the Coalition air forces targeted the Iraqi command and control infrastructure. Saddam struck back with his Scuds, which evaded both air and satellite reconnaissance. He also fired them at Israeli cities, hoping to widen the war, so the priority quickly became tracking down Iraq's mobile Scud missile launchers.

Eight-man SAS patrols were dropped by helicopter far behind enemy lines. They set up static observation posts to survey the main supply routes for the movement of Scud launchers and call in air strikes to destroy them. As a result, Israel, which had been subjected to Scud attack, put on hold its threat to retaliate.

But the SAS men were ill-prepared for the conditions they faced. Standard-issue desert kit gave them little protection from the snow, sleet, rain and freezing night-time temperatures. It was winter in Iraq too and the men developed frostbite and hypothermia.

The desert units were resupplied by a temporary formation known as E Squadron. This was a resupply convoy, comprising ten Bedford 4-ton trucks and a heavily armed SAS Land Rover escort that met up with the fighting columns at a rendezvous point some 86 miles inside Iraq. The convoy left Saudi Arabia on 10 February and reached the RV at 1500 hours on the 12th. This was a huge operation. A large number of NCOs attended a mess meeting of warrant officers and sergeants called by the Regimental Sergeant Major. The vehicles were serviced or repaired, and prisoners handed over. The convoy returned to Saudi Arabia, reaching base on 17 February.

There was no amphibious role to assign to the SBS, but they wanted to get involved anyway. A line was drawn down the middle of Iraq. The SAS's area of operation was to the west and the SBS's to the east. As well as searching for mobile Scud launchers, the SBS had a special mission to perform. Their sector contained a mass of buried fibre-optic cable that provided Iraq with intelligence and front-line reports. The location of the main junction was just 32 miles from Baghdad.

On 22 January, with barely time for their usual work-up, thirty-six SBS embarked on two Chinook helicopters from No.7 Squadron's Special Forces Flight and flew into Iraq. The team carried 400 lb of explosives and was heavily armed. They were venturing into an area full of nomads and desert spies, close to Iraqi air and ground forces. As the helicopters landed, they disengaged their rotors but kept their engines running for a quick escape.

The SBS men quickly found the communications cables. Digging down, they pulled out a length to take back for analysis, then placed explosives along the exposed area. When the charge was detonated, it took out a 40-yard section of the cable. Within 90 minutes the SBS had destroyed what was left of the Iraqi communications grid with no casualties. The lieutenant leading the team grabbed one of the cable route markers and presented it to General Schwarzkopf on their return.

The most famous SAS patrol of the war had the callsign "Bravo Two Zero". On the evening of 22 January 1991, eight SAS men, loaded with equipment and supplies for an extended stay, were flown into Iraq by Chinook. As well as hunting down Scuds, they were tasked to observe the main westerly supply route and sever underground communications cables that ran between Baghdad and Jordan. Once on the ground, the patrol moved some 12 miles, where they found shelter in a small cave.

While there they discovered that their radio was not working and soon after made contact with the enemy. After a vicious firefight, the patrol was forced to withdraw and headed for the Syrian border some 75 miles to the west. On the way, the patrol suffered hypothermia and injury, and the men became separated. As a result, three died, one escaped and four were captured. The four who were captured endured weeks of beating and horrendous torture but at the end of the war they were released with the other PoWs and returned to the Regiment. The patrol was immortalized by two books: *Bravo Two Zero*, written by its sergeant-commander under the alias Andy McNab, and *The One That Got Away* by Chris Ryan, the patrol member who reached the Syrian border.

Other SAS units were not so unlucky. They engaged targets of opportunity and used laser designators to mark targets for air strikes, ensuring pinpoint accuracy. By the end of the war, they had helped take out numerous communications facilities and, it is estimated, destroy about a third of Iraq's Scud launchers.

Despite dangerous terrain, dreadful weather, radio problems, enemy action and intelligence, the Regiment lost only four soldiers. In recognition, members of the Regiment received fifty-five medals for gallantry and meritorious service and General Schwarzkopf gave the SAS his personal commendation.

The SBS kept a lower profile. However, at the end of the war they were chosen by General de la Billiere to reclaim the British Embassy in Kuwait. On 27 February 1991, they flew into Kuwait and set up a temporary base at Kuwait Airport. The SBS worked on the assumption that the embassy buildings might be booby-trapped or even harbour a suicide squad of Iraqi troops. They went in the next day. As two Chinooks hovered over the Embassy, the SBS team belayed down to the roof, threw stun grenades through the windows and blew down the famous front door designed by Edwin Lutyens.

It is thought that the SBS were involved in other operations during Desert Storm, but so far these have remained a secret.

While the British Special Forces had to shoehorn themselves in to Operation Desert Storm, the Americans had been there from the beginning. Iraq had invaded Kuwait on 2 August 1990. By 31 August 1990, the headquarters unit of the 5th Special Forces Group from Fort Campbell, Kentucky had moved to Saudi Arabia to began its initial mission to support the Saudi Arabian forces. The 1st Battalion, lead by Lieutenant-Colonel Jerry Thompson, followed. By 14 September, the 2nd Battalion under Lieutenant-Colonel "Ironman" Davis was in-country, followed by the 3rd Battalion under Lieutenant-Colonel Mike Shaw. The 1st Battalion was based on the east coast, near Dharan, and operated out of the King Fahad International Airport complex, while the 2nd and 3rd Battalions were stationed at King Khalid Military City.

The first task was to set up their Forward Operating Bases, arranging their living quarters and their operational, communications and support centres. They needed ranges and manoeuvre areas to acclimatize the troops and prepare them for combat. They had to develop defence and evacuation plans for the base. This presented a problem as the King Khalid Military City was isolated and there was a shortage of heavy weapons.

On 13 October 1990, Special Operations Team-A 505 under Captain Ken Takasaki was the first Special Forces unit into action when they deployed along the Saudi-Kuwait border with a Saudi Special Forces unit under Captain Prince Fahd, a graduate of the US Special Forces and Rangers course. They patrolled the border from the town of ArRuqi approximately 37 miles eastwards, setting up bases in border forts called *mazekahs*. The rest of the border was patrolled by US Special Forces and coalition units using Humvees armed with Mk 19 machines guns, night-vision devices and communications equipment. These units were the eyes and ears of the entire coalition force. The *mazekahs* also provided outposts where Iraqi deserters could surrender. Leaflets and loudspeakers were used to lure deserters over the border; they were then interrogated and provided invaluable intelligence.

The 5th Special Forces Group continued their border missions until 10 February 1991, where they were replaced by scouts and lead elements from regular units now in theatre. Even when Operation Desert Storm was underway, this border mission was no soft option. There were several firefights with the enemy and some close calls. On one occasion Captain Dan Kepper's detachment was forced to make a quick exit from its *mazekah* and flee in their Humvee under intense ground fire. They managed to escape without loss of life, though their vehicle was damaged. However, even this hasty retreat provided valuable intelligence on the tactics employed by the Iraqis.

US Special Forces played another vital role. They acted as liaison with the Arab members of the Coalition. Every Arab unit that went into action had Special Forces troops with them. Thanks to their language skills they were able to provide General Schwarzkopf with vital information about the Coalition forces ability and willingness to fight. Stationed on the brigade and battalion boundaries between Egyptian, Syrian and Saudi units, they played a valuable role in integrating units from different nations into a single force.

On 13 January, airborne intelligence discovered that Iraqi forces were moving up to the border and General Schwarzkopf ordered the US 1st Cavalry Division to move up to counter them. This meant moving through Syrian positions at night. The 2nd Battalion of the 5th Special Forces Group were called in to expedite their movement without the two Coalition partners mistakenly coming to blows – young American soldiers could easily have mistaken the Syrians for Iraqis, especially as they were both equipped with Soviet T-62 tanks.

Once Operation Desert Storm got underway, there were many other incidents where units of had to pass through the positions of different nations. Thanks to the Special Forces not one incident of fratricide was reported.

They also provided Arab troops with protective measures against the supposed threat from Saddam Hussein's chemical weapons, co-ordinated fire support and tactical operations. A Special Forces detachment was sent to the 35th Kuwaiti Armoured Brigade to train them in mine-clearing, Iraqi defensive tactics, aircraft and armoured vehicle identification, and tank-killing techniques. When the Kuwaitis received Yugoslav M-84 main battle tanks, Special Forces troops taught them how to operate and maintain them and, as the 35th Brigade led Joint Force Command, North into their homeland Special Forces soldiers went along as advisors.

The 2nd Battalion of 5th Special Forces Group turned their three line companies into four companies to divide themselves between Egyptian and Syrian armoured and commando divisions. In all they claim to have been responsible for the capture of 8,700 Iraqi prisoners of war.

General Schwarzkopf also sent US Special Operations teams deep into Iraq to look for Scuds once the air war started. These missions were extremely dangerous as the entire country was an armoured camp and even areas that looked empty on the map turned out to be heavily patrolled by Iraqi units sent out to capture downed flyers.

While the 2nd Battalion of the 5th Special Forces Group moved forward with their Egyptian and Arab units, the Battalion's main headquarters stayed behind in King Khalid Military City to collate incoming intelligence. During the Coalition offensive, the Special Forces detachment also co-ordinated close-area-support. The entire Arab force was dependent on US air cover and they needed English-speakers to call in air strikes.

Two Special Forces medical sergeants performed a combat amputation of an Egyptian soldier while under intense indirect fire. Another Special Forces soldier crawled into a minefield to drag a wounded Egyptian soldiers to safety under artillery fire. One Special Forces battalion commander with two of his officers made a close-quarters battle assault on an Iraqi command post, clearing the position. They later received awards for their valour.

Ahead of the main force were Special Forces on reconnaissance missions hundreds of miles deep into Iraq. These teams, support by the XVIII Airborne Corps and VII Corps, were placed near the highways to report any attempt by Republican Guard reserves to counter-attack or retreat. Special Reconnaissance units had been in training for this task since early October 1990 in flat areas outside the cities in Saudi Arabia that resembled Iraq. The teams worked on their patrolling techniques, immediate-action drills and reconnaissance procedures.

The construction of hide sites was a primary concern. Due to
the barren terrain the teams would be operating in, they would
have to rely on ground observation posts dug rapidly during the
hours of darkness. Problems soon became obvious. Where
would they put the dirt and sand they had excavated? What
could they cover the hide site with once it was almost finished?
What materials best camouflaged the viewing ports? But as they
conducted mock infiltrations and rehearsals, these problems
were gradually solved team-by-team.

US Special Reconnaissance teams also infiltrated by helicopter on Scud hunts in areas hundreds of miles from friendly
forces where they were surrounded by enemy troops. They
were ferried on MH-60s and MH-47s from the 3rd Battalion of
the Special Operations Aviation Regiment. Their pilots were
old hands at Special Operations flying. They came in at 20 feet
off the desert floor at 140 knots in the dead of night and dropped
the teams at isolated landing zones. Beforehand they had
poured over dozens of aerial reconnaissance photographs, looking for power lines, towns and areas where dogs and camels
might alert their owners.

After they had been set down the teams then had the problem
of finding somewhere to hide as daylight approached. In some
places there was not vegetation, hills or small folds in the
ground for miles. The ground was usually hard, covered with
just a dusting of sand. But where the ground was softer, along
the Euphrates River, for example, there were other problems.
Soft ground and water meant agriculture, and teams deployed
there found themselves surrounded by inquisitive farmers.

On 23 February, the day before the ground attack, eight
Special Forces teams flew into Iraq but they were unable to find
hide sites in the barren terrain and some were extracted; others
were captured. One MH-47 delivered two Special Forces A-
teams. One radioed for immediate extraction as the area where
they had landed was completely featureless and nothing like the
terrain they had prepared for. The other hung on for three days,
communicating via satellite.

Also on 23 February, three soldiers from Detachment A-532
of the 1st Battalion under Master Sergeant Jeffery Sims were
dropped off by a MH-60 from the 160th SOAR, having crossed
the border at 2100 hours. They landed at 2200 hours a position

north of the Euphrates River less than a hundred miles from Baghdad. The rest of the detachment would also infiltrate to a position 15 miles to the south. They would have less than five hours to prepare their hide sites. Unfortunately the helicopter landed in a ploughed field with furrows almost three feet deep and their boots sank into the loose earth. Although they were greeted by the sound of barking dogs, it seemed to alert no human interest. There was less than eight hours to go before XVIII Airborne Corps and VII Corps would cross the border.

By first light, Master Sergeant Sims and his men had hiked to their hide site and dug in. On their way, a 50-wagon railroad train had rolled close by their position, a fact that they communicated by satellite direct to the XVIII Airborne.

When the sun came up, the local people awoke, and farmers and sheep herders began walking around near the hide site. No one had expected so much foot traffic. One shepherd walked within a foot of the peephole, but took no notice and walked on. They had another close scrape when another sheep herder with a dog came dangerously close.

At around 1400 hours, their luck got worse. A small girl and a man who appeared to be her grandfather stopped in their tracks, staring in the direction of the hide site. The old man edged closer. Then the girl bolted towards the hide site. Slowly lifting the lid, she stared wide-eyed at the Green Berets inside. The three-men aimed their 9-mm pistols, armed with silencers, at the little girl's head and the old man began screaming. But the team had been compromised and shooting two civilians would serve no purpose.

Other shepherds were close by and the old man started yelling: "The Americans are here! The Americans are here!"

The Green Berets let the girl and the old man go and radioed for extraction. Then they ran to a ditch some 500 yards away where they intended to make a stand. Within thirty minutes, Iraqi troops began arriving by truck along the highway. The team began firing at the enemy soldiers, knocking them down one by one, their rifles set on single shot to preserve precious ammunition.

Two busloads of troops arrived while armed civilians began moving around their flanks. Several village men stood on an old masonry wall surrounding a stone house nearby, waving their hands towards Sims' position. The Green Berets picked one of them off as soldiers and villagers began creeping up the irrigation ditches, but the team hit several of them and they retreated. More buses carrying soldiers arrived. It was plain that the Green Berets could not hold them off for ever.

An hour and a half after they had been discovered, a F-16 Eagle roared overhead and, at Sims' direction, the plane dropped cluster bombs and thousand-pounders into ditches just 300 yards from Sims' position. Then a MH-60 flown by Chief Warrant Officer Randy Stephens and Chief Warrant Officer John Crisufulli arrived, having cross 240 nautical miles in broad daylight. Under an intense barrage of small-arms fire, Sims and his men dashed for the helicopter, got on without injury and the MH-60 whisked them back to Saudi. It was the only hot extraction in daylight carried out during Desert Storm.

Another Special Reconnaissance mission was led by Chief Warrant Officer Chad Balwanz, commander of Detachment A-525, whose eight-man team was inserted on a tributary of the Euphrates River. Their mission was to monitor traffic along Highway 8 from Baghdad to An-Nasiriyah. After infiltration they dug two hide sites but by morning the area was swamped by civilians, including throngs of small children playing nearby. At one point these children found themselves right on top of the hide sites and, meeting the Green Berets eyeball to eyeball, screamed and fled. The team had plainly been compromised.

They moved to a new position and at nightfall planned to move further south. Having established another temporary hide site, they carried out surveillance on the road for two hours but the children returned with adults, some of whom were carrying weapons. They were followed by four large trucks carrying Iraqi soldiers which came screeching down the road. More Iraqi soldiers appeared and Balwanz counted more than a hundred. He and his eight-man team managed to pick off some forty enemy soldiers in the next ten minutes, at which point a US Air Force F-16 came in to the attack and Balwanz was soon directing air strikes dangerously close to his own positions. Nevertheless they held out and, at 2000 hours, a MH-60 of the 160th SOAR managed to pull them out. Not one member of Balwanz's team was killed or wounded.

Between them, Master Sergeant Sims' Detachment A-532 and

Chief Warrant Officer Balwanz's Detachment A-525 accounted for an estimated 250 to 300 enemy dead and wounded.

Other Special Reconnaissance missions were not so dramatic. All the other teams infiltrated without any fuss, dug their hides and counted vehicles and soldiers. It was tedious work and they remained undiscovered.

US Special Forces conducted few direct-action missions during Desert Storm. Most were of a sensitive nature and details remain classified. General Schwarzkopf forbade the Special Forces sneaking into enemy territory before the air war started and rejected many proposed operations after the bombing started. The main objective of the few direct-action missions that were launched involved disrupting enemy communications. They joined British Special Forces in the operation to cut the fibre-optic cable that ran from Baghdad to south-west Iraq. According to an after-action report, this was "a totally successful operation in that the infiltration and exfiltration was perfect and no enemy activity was encountered".

Another direct-action mission followed a request by the two Army corps for soil samples so they could assess the capacity of the area to carry heavy traffic. The Central Intelligence Agency had warned General Schwarzkopf's generals that the tanks and trucks they wanted to send across southern Iraq for the "Hail Mary Play" would become bogged down in the sandy terrain.

General Schwarzkopf recognized that he was short of detailed intelligence on the weather and terrain in the region and allowed six-man Special Forces teams to be helicoptered covertly into Iraq to scoop up soil samples for analysis in Riyadh. The teams also carried camcorders and digital cameras that transmitted photographs back to headquarters. The soil samples showed that the ground was firm enough for tanks and the pictures gave commanders a close-up view of their intended battlefields.

US Special Forces were also tasked with search-and-rescue missions to recover downed pilots. The 2nd Battalion of the 5th Special Forces Group took it upon themselves to train for this role in September and October, and took over Combat Search and Rescue from the US Air Force, which did not have a tangible and effective programme.

As aircraft were needed for CSAR, Special Forces again called on the 160th SOAR for assistance as their MH-60

Blackhawks and MH-47 Chinooks were equipped for deep insertions. They began training together, developing new tactics and manoeuvres. Their plan was to infiltrate a rescue team and a Humvee up to 200 miles behind enemy lines, with the MH-47 setting down while the vehicle made the recovery.

Special Forces teams established a good rapport with the pilots of the 160th SOAR as they spent long hours practising rescuing downed airmen. They sawed down stretchers to fit on the MH-60s and procured communications devices for the Special Forces security teams.

When the air war began, CSAR units positioned themselves in forward operating bases. On 17 February, a US F-16 suffered engine failure 40 miles behind enemy lines and crashed. At 1815 hours the Airborne Warning and Control System (AWACS) aircraft in charge of the operation put out the call and within minutes two modified MH-60 Blackhawks from the 3/160th SOAR were in the air. They were equipped with night-vision devices and carried security teams from the 2nd Battalion of the 5th Special Forces Group armed with AT-4 hand-held rocket launchers and M-16/203 assault rifles. By 2000 hours, Chief Warrant Officer Thomas Montgomery located the pilot as enemy vehicles were closing in on him. Montgomery called AWACS for support, went down and picked up the pilot, Air Force Academy football star Captain "Spike" Thomas. As they made their escape Iraqis fired surface-to-air missiles at the retreating helicopter, but on-board jamming devices and emergency evasive action left the missiles far behind. Minutes later a F-16 was on station to take out the enemy vehicles. This was the only CSAR mission conducted at night using night-vision guidance.

The Special Forces did not have to carry out as many CSAR missions as they expected. Although it had been predicted that forty aircraft would be lost on the first night of the air war, in fact there were only three. The entire coalition lost just fifty-two aircraft during the entire war. Of the twenty-two pilots and crew who survived being shot down, fourteen were captured immediately, while eight evaded capture – two for more than twenty-four hours. Of the seven CSAR missions launched, three were successful. Nevertheless, knowing that the Special Forces were on hand to come to the rescue boosted the morale of the aircrew.

US Special Forces also played a key role in the liberation of Kuwait City. The plan was for the US Marines to hold their positions on the outskirts while a vanguard of Kuwaitis, Syrians, Egyptians and other Arab forces drove into the capital. This meant that the only American troops into the city in the first wave were the Green Berets with the Arab units. One of the Special Forces responsibilities was to see that the Kuwaitis did not retaliate against Iraqi prisoners for the atrocities that had been committed during the occupation – the Coalition did not want any atrocities of its own on its hands.

As the Allies entered the city, the Special Forces expanded their role beyond merely "advising" the Arab forces. With the help of Kuwaiti resistance fighters who had remained in the city during the occupation, Special Forces troops began clearing areas of booby traps and mines. Members of the resistance also guided Special Forces teams to key Iraqi headquarters buildings and torture facilities where they collected five truckloads of documents indicating violations of the Geneva Conventions.

With Special Forces teams accompanying Arab units who certainly overstepped the mark when it came to retaliation, the Special Forces came under criticism by the international press who had arrived by then. As a result they were withdrawn from the Arab units, but not before the Special Forces had help the Egyptians secure their embassy. US Special Forces also retook the US Embassy in Kuwait City.

At a press conference at the end of the war, General Schwarzkopf singled out Special Forces for special praise. This surprised his staff as he was known not to be a fan and had left half of the Special Forces commands back in the US.

"What you've done is never going to be made public and we can't make it public," he said solemnly, before adding, "but you kept Israel out of the war."

33

SOMALIA

The East African country of Somalia began to fall apart in January 1991, when long-time dictator Siad Barre was ousted by the United Somalia Congress led by Ali Mahdi Muhammad, who became President. However, this coalition quickly broke up into competing parties, the most powerful being the Somali National Movement under General Mohammed Farah Aidid.

In September 1991, fighting broke out in the capital Mogadishu, which quickly spread throughout the country. By the end of the year some 20,000 people had been killed or injured. The fighting led to famine with agriculture being brought to a halt and food aid being stolen and traded for guns. It is estimated 300,000 people died before a ceasefire was called in March 1992.

In July 1992, the United Nations sent fifty military observers to monitor the ceasefire. The following month humanitarian aid began. Under Operation Provide Relief, US Air Force C-130s airlifted in 48,000 tons of food and medical supplies, but the deteriorating security situation prevented the UN mission from delivering food to the starving Somalis. Relief flights were looted upon landing, food convoys were hijacked and aid workers assaulted.

In response to UN appeals, with only weeks left in office, President George Bush began Operation Restore Hope and sent 25,000 US troops into Somalia. On 9 December, the 1st

Marines land on the beach, and quickly secured the port and airport. After elements of the 2nd Battalion, 9th Marines had secured the routes to Baidoa, Balidogle and Kismayo, they were were reinforced by the 3rd Assault Amphibian Battalion and the US Army 10th Mountain Division.

In May 1993, the UN expanded their role in Somalia. Its stated aim was "nation building", a key part of which was the disarmament of the competing factions. During an inspection of a Somali weapons storage site in an area of Mogadishu controlled by General Aidid, twenty-four Pakistani soldiers were ambushed and massacred. It was widely reported that the bodies of the UN peacekeepers had been mutilated. Some were said to have been skinned. Admiral Jonathan Howe, a retired US Navy Admiral serving as the UN Secretary General's Special Representative in Somalia, offered a $25,000 reward for the arrest of Aidid. He also asked Washington to send in the Special Forces.

Meanwhile, US and UN troops began attacking various targets in Mogadishu associated with Aidid, including a radio station and ammunition depots. On 12 July, American Cobra helicopters attacked a house in south Mogadishu where a group of clan leaders were meeting, destroyed the building with TOW missiles and cannon fire and killed a number of Somalis. Four Western journalists who had gone to investigate were beaten to death by an angry mob.

On 8 August, four American military police were killed by a remotely detonated landmine set off by Somalis. Two weeks later, six more US soldiers were wounded in a similar attack. With the situation escalating out of control, on 26 August, US Army Task Force Ranger flew in to Mogadishu. Comprising 440 elite troops from Delta Force and the US Rangers, led by Major General William F. Garrison, they began pursuing Aidid and his top lieutenants with limited success.

On 3 October, a detachment of Task Force Ranger, with aviation support from the 160th Special Operations Aviation Regiment, tried to capture Aidid's foreign minister, Omar Salad Elmi, and his top political adviser, Mohamed Hassan Awale, who were in the Olympic Hotel in Mogadishu. The plan was to abseil from hovering MH-60 Black Hawk helicopters, capture the two men, bundle them onto a ground convoy and transport them back to the US compound. More Rangers, commanded by Captain Steele, were to be inserted by four helicopters to provide a secure perimeter around the building. In all, the assault force consisted of nineteen aircraft, twelve vehicles and 160 men.

Things began to go wrong from the beginning. The ground extraction convoy was supposed to reach the captive targets a few minutes after the beginning of the operation, but it was delayed by Somali citizens and local militia who had built barricades in the streets of Mogadishu with rocks and burning tires. One of the 5-ton trucks in the convoy was hit by a rocket-propelled grenade.

Meanwhile, other problems arose. Twenty-year-old US Army Ranger PFC Todd Blackburn fell while abseiling from a helicopter hovering 70 feet above the streets and suffered life-threatening injuries to his head and internal organs. Mede-vacked out to the Ranger's staging area, he survived, but minutes after his accident, a MH-60 Black Hawk helicopter, Super Six One, piloted by Chief Warrant Officer Cliff Wolcott, was shot down by a rocket-propelled grenade.

With communications between the assault team and the ground convoy having broken down, both groups just out of sight of one another for twenty minutes, each thinking the other was going to make contact first. While they waited, a second Black Hawk, Super Six Four, piloted by Chief Warrant Officer Michael Durant, was shot down.

By then the assault team had abandoned their mission and ninety of them headed for the first crash site to help survivors. When they reached it, they came under heavy fire from the militia. Air support was called in but, as a stiff breeze stirred up blinding brown clouds of dust, the Rangers found themselves trapped for the night. With a growing number of wounded needing shelter, they occupied several houses nearby, taking the occupants prisoner. The local militia commander, Colonel Sharif Hassan Giumale decided not to risk his men assaulting the houses and called for a mortar bombardment. He put in a request for 200 white-phosphorus bombs and six mobile 60-mm mortar crews, but when he heard that there were civilians in the houses he held fire.

At the second crash site, the injured crew were being me-naced by a mob. Two Delta Force snipers, Master Sergeant

Gary Gordon and Sergeant First Class Randy Shughart requested permission to go in and protect them. Their request was denied twice, but after the third request, they were inserted by helicopter.

Repeated attempts by the Somalis to mass forces and overrun the American positions were foiled by small-arms fire, and strafing and rocket attacks from US aircraft. No contingency plan had been drawn up before the operation, nor had coordination been arranged with the UN, significantly delaying the rescue of the beleaguered men. A relief convoy of men from the 2nd Battalion of the 14th US Infantry Regiment, 10th Mountain Division, aided by Malaysian and Pakistani UN forces, did not arrive until early the next morning. By that time, the second crash site had been overrun by the militia. Both snipers and three of the Black Hawk crewmen had been killed, and the helicopter's pilot, CW3 Durant, who was seriously injured in the crash, had been taken prisoner. Snipers Shughart and Gordon were posthumously awarded the Medal of Honor.

This action, now known as the First Battle of Mogadishu, was over by 0630 hours on 4 October, when the American forces were finally evacuated to the Pakistani base by the armoured convoy down the "Mogadishu Mile". In all, eighteen US soldiers were killed and another seventy-nine were injured. The Malaysian forces lost one soldier and had seven injured, while the Pakistanis suffered two injured. Casualties on the Somali side were heavy, with estimates on fatalities ranging from 500 to over 2,000 people. Militia casualties were initially reported as 700 killed and 1,000 wounded, but an eyewitness said there were fewer than sixty dead. It was inevitable that fighting in such a densely populated area of the city would result in substantial civilian casualties.

Two days later, a mortar round fell on the American compound, killing one US soldier, Sergeant First Class Matt Rierson, and injuring another twelve. On 7 October, the Americans abandoned the hunt for General Aidid and President Clinton announced that US troops would withdraw from Somalia and on 14 October, Mike Durant was released along with a Nigerian prisoner. The remaining American forces had withdrawn from Somalia by 25 March 1994 and on 1 August 1995

General Aidid died in hospital from a bullet wound received at the outbreak of fighting in Mogadishu.

Fighting continued in Somalia until, in December 2006, the Ethiopian Army went in to restore order. With them were some Special Operations forces in the US active duty and reserve military, including SEALs, Green Berets and other commando-style troops who perform covert missions behind enemy lines. Their job was to root out al-Qaida fighters who had used the disruption in Somalia as a haven.

34

AFGHANISTAN

On 11 September 2001, hijackers deliberately crashed two commercial airliners into the twin towers of the World Trade Center in New York. Another hit the Pentagon. A fourth, on its way to another target in Washington, crashed in rural Pennsylvania when the passengers fought back against the hijackers. In all some 3,000 people died. The perpetrators were affiliated to al-Qaeda, an Islamic terrorist group based in Afghanistan. It was led by Osama bin Laden, a Saudi Arabian millionaire who gleefully claimed responsibility for the 9/11 attacks. The US government repeatedly asked the Taliban, an Islamist group that ran Afghanistan at the time, to extradite bin Laden, but they refused. The US, with British support, then launched Operation Enduring Freedom as part of what President George W. Bush called his "war on terror". The British and Americans began bombing the terrorist training camps in Afghanistan and providing substantial logistical support to the North Alliance, a group of Afghan warlords opposed to the Taliban.

US Army Special Forces were deployed in northern Afghanistan on 19 October 2001 to serve as spotters for US bombing missions. That same day, in a tragic start to their Afghan ground campaign, Delta Force suffered twelve casualties when they were ambushed by Taliban troops using machine guns and rocket-propelled grenades. The Delta team had landed by helicopter at the summer retreat of Taliban leader Mullah Omar in the hills above Kandahar. According to Seymour Hersh of the *New Yorker*, several of those who participated in the raid called it a "total goat fuck", US military slang for "everything that could go wrong did go wrong".

Nevertheless between 5 and 10 November, Special Forces units played a key role in directing deadly US air-strikes on the Taliban front lines around Mazar and Taloquan using GPS co-ordinates and lasers. On 14 November, a Special Forces team was sent into Tarin Kot to protect Hamid Karzai, the man picked to become chairman of the Transitional Administration who later became President of Afghanistan, after he narrowly escaped capture by the Taliban in early November.

By mid-November several hundred elite troops led by 595 A-team had been inserted into the battlefields around Mazar and Kunduz working with Northern Alliance troops under General Abdul Rashid Dostum and Mohammad Atta. A team from the 5th Special Forces Group first met up with Dostum in October when its members were dropped by Chinook helicopter at his mountain redoubt. This became an embarrassment when the North Alliance began slaughtering prisoners in the Qala-i-Janghi prison fort in Mazar-i-Sharif. Nevertheless CNN later reported that Special Forces troops were seen taking an inaugural dip in Dostum's new indoor swimming pool.

From 15 November to 17 December, US Special Forces and British SAS teams were used extensively in the Tora Bora campaign, both as spotters and as groundassault units. Facing defeat and reluctant to fight fellow Muslims, al-Qaeda tried to negotiate a truce with a local militia commander on the pretext of giving them time to surrender their weapons. However, this seems to have been a ruse to allow al-Qaeda leaders, including Osama bin Laden, to escape. On 12 December, the fighting flared up again; this was thought to have been a rearguard buying time for the main force to escape through the White Mountains into the tribal areas of Pakistan. Once again, tribal forces backed by US Special Operations troops and allied air support attacked fortified al-Qaeda positions in caves and bunkers throughout the mountainous region. Twelve British SBS commandos accompanied the US Special Forces in the attack on the main cave complex at Tora Bora. By 17 December, the last defenders had been overrun and the area secured.

Other teams were inserted into the Kandahar area to the south near the Pakistani border and assaulted Mir Wais Hospital after remnants of the Taliban and al-Qaeda barricaded themselves in. Another team was assigned to protect Gul Agha Sherzai, who had regained his position as governor of Kandahar after the Taliban vacated the city on 7 December. Sherzai was dismissed as "warlord of the year" by Robert Fisk of the *Independent*.

With the demise of the Taliban as a fighting force holding territory, the role of the US Special Forces changed. They began interdiction and search-and-destroy missions, making commando-style raids, usually under the cover of night, upon villages suspected of harbouring members of al-Qaeda or the Taliban personnel. The Special Forces of other allied nations now got involved. A SEAL unit called Task Force K-Bar led by a Navy commodore that included German, Canadian, Danish and Norwegian Special Forces personnel, was involved in raids and surveillance in southern Afghanistan. The British SAS were involved in operations along the Kwaja Amran mountain range in Ghazni and the Hada Hills near Spin Boldak. They went in at night by helicopter, storming villages using stun grenades and grabbing suspects who were whisked away for interrogation.

In early March 2002, the US Special Forces Groups TF 11, TF Bowie, and TF Dagger, along with the Australian and New Zealand SAS, and the German KSK, led elements of the US 10th Mountain Division, 101st Airborne Division, British Royal Marines, Canada's 3rd Battalion, Princess Patricia's Canadian Light Infantry and the Afghan National Army in Operation Anaconda, an allied push to clear al-Qaeda and Taliban forces out of the Shahi-Kot Valley and Arma Mountains south-east of Zormat.

The operation began on 1 March when US Special Forces infiltrated the area and set up observation posts. Teams India and Juliet, taken primarily from Delta Force, were to take positions at the north and south ends of the Shahi-Kot Valley, where they could watch the approaches from Gardez. The third team, Mako 31, a SEAL unit, was tasked to set up an observation post on a feature known as the Finger where they could observe the TF Rakkasan – the 187th Airborne – landing zones. On their way, they saw a group of Afghan fighters with a Russian DShK machine gun in a position that would have allowed it to engage the Chinook helicopters bringing in the first wave of US troops. They made plans to destroy the emplacement at D –1 hour.

The following day US and Afghan forces begin to sweep the Shahi-Kot valley area to root out rebel forces regrouping there. At around midnight, the units of TF Hammer loaded into their vehicles and left their base in Gardez for the Shahi-Kot Valley. TF Hammer consisted of a large force of Afghan militia led by Zia Lodin and the Special Forces A-team Texas 14/ODA 594. The road was in poor condition and several soldiers were injured when their trucks overturned. It was then decided that the trucks should use their headlights, even though it would destroy any element of surprise.

Further down the road, a convoy led by Army Chief Warrant Officer Stanley L. Harriman of the 3rd Special Forces Group split from the main force and set out for its assigned observation point. An AC-130 aircraft, call sign Grim 31, providing fire support and reconnaissance for the assault, spotted Harriman's convoy. Due to a problem with the plane's inertial navigation system, the aircrew failed to identify the convoy as American, so Grim 31 engaged the column, killed CWO Harriman and wounded several US Special Forces and Afghan militia.

The main body of TF Hammer reached its start line around 0615 hours and waited for what they had been told would be an aerial bombardment lasting fifty-five minutes. In fact, only six bombs fell at which point a bomb got stuck in the launch bay of the next B-1B Lancer on its bomb run. While the third bomber waited for the B-1B to get permission to jettison the bomb and go round again, both planes and the two F-15E Strike Eagles received orders telling them to cease the bombardment. This order may have been the one telling Grim-31 to cease fire.

Already demoralized by the lack of air support, TF Hammer's trucks were raked with mortar fire that had been registered in advance on spots along the road. Plainly al-Qaeda had been expecting an attack. The Afghans suffered over forty casualties. TF Hammer's attack stalled even before they entered the valley, due to unexpectedly heavy small-arms and mortar fire. They also lacked close air support, which had been assigned to TF Anvil on the other side of the ridge.

At 0630 hours on 2 March, the first wave of Rakkasans and Mountain troops were landed by helicopter along the eastern and northern edges of the valley to await the fleeing fighters at their assigned blocking positions. However they came under fire almost immediately and were pinned down by heavy mortar fire throughout the day. Instead of the 150 to 200 fighters they had been expecting, they found there were between 500 and 1,000 dug in on the high ground surrounding the valley. The first wave had brought in just one 120-mm mortar with them, although they received fire support from the Apaches of the 3/ 101's aviation brigade. That night, after suffering twenty-eight killed, they were airlifted out.

It was not all bad news. Throughout the day, the Special Forces reconnaissance teams that had infiltrated into the area the previous day called in airstrikes from B-1, B-52, F-15 and F-16s, inflicting heavy casualties on hundreds of Taliban and al-Qaeda fighters. The Australian SAS provided in-depth operational intelligence and Signalman Martin "Jock" Wallace of the Australian SASR was awarded the Australian Medal for Gallantry for staying with a US company in a dry creek bed for twelve hours until they were evacuated.

The next evening, Lieutenant Colonel Blaber, commander of TF 11, was told that two SEAL teams commanded by Lieutenant Commander Vic Hyder were on their way to Gardez. The SEAL teams, Mako 21 and Mako 30, were to establish an observation point on the peak of Takur Ghar, which commanded the Shahi-Kot valley. They needed to be inserted by helicopter before dawn and it was proposed that they be dropped some 1,400 yards east of the peak.

They were supposed to have set off at 1123 hours on 3 March, but one of the Chinooks broke down. The delay meant that the SEALs would have to be dropped on the peak itself, otherwise they would not reach it by dawn. An AC-130 gunship reconnoitred the peak and saw no enemy activity, but was called away before the two Chinooks carrying the SEALs, Razor 03 and 04, arrived.

At around 0245 hours, Razor 03 landed on the peak and was

struck in the left side electrical compartment by a rocket-propelled grenade. As the stricken helicopter took off, Petty Officer First Class Neil Roberts fell out of the open ramp. Razor 03 tried to return and retrieve him, but the damage prevented proper control and the helicopter crash-landed some 4 miles away in the valley. When Razor 04 arrived at the LZ to drop off Mako 30, it came under fire immediately. Air Force combat controller Technical Sergeant John A. Chapman was hit and two SEALs were wounded. Mako 30 was forced off the peak due to its losses and called the Ranger quick-reaction force at Bagram Air Base for help.

The quick-reaction force consisted of nineteen Rangers, a tactical air control party and a three-man US Air Force special tactics team. It was carried by two Chinooks, Razor 01 and Razor 02 and led by Captain Nate Self. Due to difficulties with satellite communications, Razor 01 was directed to the hot landing zone on the peak by mistake. At around 0610 hours, Razor 01 reached the LZ and immediately came under attack. The right door minigunner, Sergeant Phillip Svitak, was killed by small arms fire, and a rocket-propelled grenade hit the helicopter, demolishing the right engine and forcing it to crash-land. As the quick-reaction force left the helicopter Sergeant Brad Crose, Specialist Marc Anderson and Private First Class Matt Commons, posthumously promoted to Corporal, were killed. The rest of the quick-reaction force and the surviving crew took cover in a hillock and a fierce firefight ensued.

Razor 02 had been diverted to Gardez as Razor 01 was landing on Takur Ghar so went with the rest of the quick-reaction force and Lieutenant Commander Hyder, arriving at 0625 hours. With the help of close air support, the small force was able to consolidate its position on the peak. Fortunately Australian SAS soldiers had infiltrated the day before and had remained undetected. They were able to co-ordinate multiple air strikes to prevent al-Qaeda from overrunning the downed aircraft.

They enemy counter-attacked at midday, mortally wounded Senior Airman Jason D. Cunningham. The wounded could not be medevacked out during daylight hours for fear of another downed helicopter, but finally, at around 2000 hours, the quick-reaction force and Mako 30 were rescued from the peak of Takur Ghar.

By 12 March, US and Afghan forces swept through the valley and cleared it of remaining rebel forces, and on 18 March Operation Anaconda was declared officially over. But that was not the end of the hunt for al-Qaeda and the Taliban. On 15 April 2002, Operation Mountain Lion began in the Gardez and Khost regions.

On 18 August, the Army Rangers and other coalition Special Forces joined the 82nd Airborne Division on Operation Mountain Sweep, mounting five combat air assault missions on the area around the villages of Dormat and Narizah, south of the cities of Khowst and Gardez. The troopers found an anti-aircraft artillery gun, two 82-mm mortars and ammunition, a recoilless rifle, rockets, rocket-propelled grenades, machine guns and thousands of rounds of small-arms ammunition, and detained ten people during the operation. But a week after the end of Operation Mountain Sweep reports surfaced in the *New York Times* that some US Special Forces commanders wanted to quit the futile search for bin Laden. Indeed Special Forces forward operating bases were regularly coming under attack. The base three miles north-east of Sarabagh was under more or less constant bombardment during March. By mid-May, six rocket attacks had reportedly been made at Orgun-e, Khost and Miran Shah.

A US Special Forces soldier was killed while on patrol in Paktia on 19 May 2002. On 17 June, a Special Forces patrol was fired-upon near Tarin Kot. The same day, another team of twenty US Special Forces troops and forty Afghan soldiers came under small arms fire near Shkin in the Birmal region of Paktika. On 22 June, a rocket landed near the US Special Forces in Khost. Before dawn on 3 September, four 107-mm rockets landed close to US Special Forces operating in south-eastern Afghanistan. Between 1100 hours on 15 September and the early morning of the 16th, at least ten rockets fell on the Khost bases where over 1,000 American troops were based.

The forty-six US Special Forces troopers guarding President Karzai did little better when, in early September 2002, ex-Taliban soldiers tried to assassinate him in Kandahar. They managed to wrestle one of the two attackers to the ground, but two innocent Afghans were killed in the fracas.

Eighteen months later, a CBS camera crew were given access

to the 19th Special Forces Group's base in the hostile Pesch Valley, an isolated place near the Pakistani border. Osama bin Laden had been seen in the valley a few months before, just before the unit entered the area.

By that time the Special Forces had dropped their aggressive role. Now they concentrated on make friends, though when they met with the local elders, they reminded them that they were still looking for bin Laden and that they would pay good money for him.

When the Special Forces had first arrived in the area, they had been rocketed every other day, but after five months, such attacks were only every two or three weeks. Green Berets medics helped local people who were sick or injured, and they began building schools. The aim, once again, was to win hearts and minds.

Although they maintained an artillery post on top of a nearby mountain, they were beginning to find that locals were helping turn in arms caches. As well as killing, winning hearts and minds is what the Green Berets are trained to do.

35

THE SECOND GULF WAR
– OPERATION IRAQI FREEDOM

During Operation Iraqi Freedom, the US, Britain and Australia put on the ground the largest Special Operations force since the Vietnam War. In northern Iraq particularly, there was a huge Special Operations presence. At the time of the invasion, as much as 80 per cent of the combat forces of the 53,000-strong US Special Operations Command – including Navy SEALs, Army Green Berets and Rangers, and Delta Force operatives – found themselves committed in Iraq and Afghanistan.

US Special Forces worked closely with Kurdish fighters in northern Iraq in their effort to bring down the regime. The SOF also helped bring in the 173rd Airborne Brigade, and marked and called in coalition air power on regime targets. Special Operations Forces were also responsible for attacking a number of specific targets such as airfields, sites for weapons of mass destruction, and command and control headquarters. In the south, special operations personnel gave aid to conventional forces and, in the cities, helped the anti-Ba'athist Shi'ia elements.

In the west, Special Forces undertook an "area denial mission" so that Saddam Hussein could not rain down Scud missiles on Israel as he had during the First Gulf War. UK Special Air Service units, backed by Royal Marines of 45 Commando, were in the vanguard of the free-wheeling war in the Iraqi western desert. Along with a squadron from Australia's Special Air Service Regiment and US Special Operations Forces, they set out to neutralize any Scud missile batteries threatening Israel. There was little opposition. One officer has called western Iraq a "Special Forces playground".

Even as the main forces went in, there were already hundreds of Special Forces in country. That figure rose rapidly as the glare of the international media turned on the main UK and US ground forces, allowing Special Forces units to conduct a shadowy war in the west and north. Unofficially, US and allied Special Forces were given freedom of action to operate anywhere inside Iraq.

On 21 March 2003, the day after the main force went in, Special Forces stormed two strategic airfields near the Jordanian border. From the second day of Operation Iraqi Freedom onwards, the Special Forces began using the two captured airfields as bases for long-range reconnaissance patrols. US Air Force Predator unmanned observation aircraft flew ahead, scouting for targets to be attacked. Special Forces then pushed eastwards across the desert towards Baghdad, backed by air support from UK Royal Air Force GR7 Harrier fighters flying from a forward air base in Jordan.

Over the next two weeks the Special Forces teams moved steadily towards the Euphrates valley. On 25 March, members of the US Army's 75th Ranger Regiment captured a third strategic airfield in a night-time parachute assault on 25 March. However, apart from these airfields and their small bases, which were guarded by UK Marines and US Rangers, the Special Forces teams were not trying to occupy ground. Instead they aimed to keep the small Iraqi garrisons in the region off-guard. Travellers on the road from Baghdad to the Jordanian border reported few signs of Western troops apart from the occasional vehicle checkpoint, suggesting they largely moved at night away from populated areas. However, on the night of 2 April 2003 – just two weeks after the beginning of the war and a week before Baghdad fell – they raided two presidential palaces near Baghdad.

On 31 March, Al Jazeera television showed UK equipment in the northern Iraqi city of Mosul, providing a brief glimpse into the SAS role in toppling Saddam Hussein's regime. Footage showed Iraqi civilians jubilantly driving a Land Rover through the streets of the city, then a quad-bike and a collection of weapons being displayed at an Iraqi military base. This included hand-held rocket launchers, 40-mm grenades, machine guns and specialized radio equipment, suggesting this was not from a conventional British Army unit. Iraqi television said the equipment was captured after an attempted helicopter landing. The location of the incident, far from the main UK operating area around Kuwait and Basra, immediately led to media speculation that the 22nd SAS Regiment was in some way involved. UK military spokesmen refused to comment.

UK officers would also provide little information about the operations UK Special Forces were undertaking in western Iraq. But the coalition commander General Tommy Franks publicly praised them, saying: "They have accomplished some wonderful things out there."

Coalition leaders were particularly pleased because no Scuds fired at Israel – a development that could have massively complicate allied war plans. Indeed no Scuds were even found. The main opposition to the Special Forces came from Iraqi commando units that were attempting to keep the main roads to Jordan and Syria open to allow key members of the regime to escape if Baghdad should fall.

The Battle of Debecka Pass

The most famous Special Forces action of the war was the Battle of Debecka Pass, which is sometimes referred to as the Alamo of the Iraq War. On 6 April 2003, twenty-six Green Beret Special Forces were given the task of securing a key crossroads near the town of Debecka in northern Iraq between the cities of Irbil and Kirkuk. If they succeeded, they would cut Highway 2, preventing the Iraqi Army moving north into Kurdistan, and allow friendly forces to take the crucial Kirkuk oilfields.

The battle was fought by two 3rd Special Forces Group A-teams who went through their final battle training in the pinelands of Fort Bragg, North Carolina, and Fort Pickett, Virginia from October to December 2002. The two teams specialized in deep reconnaissance. Their Ground Mobility Vehicles – souped-up Humvees equipped with .50-calibre heavy machine guns or Mark 19 automatic grenade launchers – enabled them to travel a thousand miles in ten days without any resupply. At Fort Pickett, the teams rehearsed how they would react if attacked by Iraqi armour. The GMVs' firepower, they knew, was not enough to see off a concerted attack by T-55 tanks, but knowing they were due to receive the Javelin, the Army's latest shoulder-held "fire and forget" anti-tank missile, the team leaders decided that, even if perilously outnumbered and faced with Iraqi tanks, they would not back down. ODA 391 even came up with a motto: "Ninety-one don't run."

On 8 March 2003, the two teams flew from Pope Air Force Base to Romania, and on 26 March, they infiltrated Iraq on an MC-130 Combat Talon, landing at As-Sulaymaniya some 60 miles east of Kirkuk.

Their first few days were spent fighting the Ansar Al-Islam militant Islamic group near Halabja. Then on 1 April, they moved to Irbil and on to a staging area where they linked up with ODA 044, a 10th Group A-team who were working with the Kurdish Peshmerga militia, known to the Green Berets as "the Pesh" or "Peshies".

On 4 April, they were given a new mission, code-named Northern Safari. Together with ODA 044 and their Peshmerga allies, the 3rd were to seize the Debecka intersection and hold it until they were relieved by the 173rd Airborne Brigade's artillery. The crossroads sat just to the west of a ridge line that formed the border dividing Kurdish-held Iraq from the rest of the country. The plan of attack was simple. Some 200 Peshmerga forces and a handful of ODA 044 troops would dash forward and seize the ridge line, while ODAs 391 and 392 would support them with fire from their GMVs. There was just one problem – there was no intelligence on Iraqi forces in the area.

As Captain Eric Wright, commander of ODA 391, put it: "No one knew what was on the ridge line or behind it."

This was because thick haze shrouded the ridge line and the valley beyond it, limiting visibility to less than two miles. The Green Berets quickly discovered that they were in for a fight. In the absence of aerial reconnaissance, they sought out human intelligence. Farmers who grazed their livestock on the ridge told the Green Berets that there were Iraqi forces on the ridge and beyond, and their positions were defended by minefields and trenches.

On 5 April, the 3rd sent two GMVs forward to reconnoitre the Iraqi positions on the ridge. From a position just behind a 12-foot berm east of the ridge line, they saw Iraqi soldiers.

"They were standing on top of their bunkers like everything was OK," said Sergeant First Class Scot Marlow, senior communications sergeant of ODA 392.

That night they called in a B-52 air-strike.

In the morning, only eighty of the expected 200 Peshmerga showed up and drove straight down the road towards the 12-foot dirt berm. They were stopped by a minefield and began picking their way through it, piling plastic Valmira anti-tank and anti-personnel mines alongside the road.

The Green Berets decided to outflank the berm and drive straight up the ridge line instead. However, CW2 Martin McKenna was keen to breach the berm anyway in case they had to make a hasty retreat. But there was no time as gunfire erupted from the other side of the berm and Captain Wright ordered them forward to support the Peshmerga. But catching up with them was difficult and ODA 391 hit a trench too deep and wide for the GMVs to cross. The Green Berets had to dismount and demolish a sandbagged fighting position on top to fill the trench.

The next obstacle was unexploded ordnance dropped by the B-52s the night before. Again the Green Berets had to dismount and go on foot to guide the GMVs through what was essentially a minefield about 700 yards deep.

South of the road, 392 had advanced up to the berm when they heard the Peshmerga's recoilless rifle firing somewhere up ahead. They also found themselves in another minefield. As the driver of the lead GMV tried to navigate a concertina wire barrier WO1 Robert Parker, 392's assistant detachment commander, leaned out of the door to look underneath.

"Stop!" he yelled. The driver slammed on the brakes and the GMV stopped with its wheels just 12 inches from the prongs of an anti-personnel mine.

By now, the fire had intensified and ODA 392 had decided to reverse down the flattened grass trail they had made on their way into the minefield back to the road.

By now the Peshmerga had taken the ridge. When the Green Berets caught up with them, they saw Iraqi trenches and fighting positions dug for armoured vehicles, along with two abandoned T-55 tanks. The two A-teams linked up with the Peshmerga and engaged the Iraqis in their bunkers. After a fierce firefight, they fought their way through to the crossroads, capturing about twenty Iraqi soldiers, one of whom was a major, who revealed that an Iraqi armoured unit had withdrawn to the south after the bombing, leaving him and his men behind.

There was no time to prepare defensive positions if attacked from the south so the 391 team leader decided it was a good time to follow McKenna's advice and blast a path through the berm where it crossed the road. This would allow them two withdraw quickly if necessary and would also clear the way for them to be resupplied.

The intersection did not offer the commanding view of the plains, so the Green Berets sent a team up to a small ridge known as Press Hill, from where they saw Iraqi vehicles approaching from the south. While half of 391 was busy collecting landmines to help blow the berm, the rest of the men found themselves in a firefight with Iraqi infantry. They tried to engage the vehicles with a .50-calibre machine gun but it proved ineffective against the fast moving trucks. The A-Teams then moved forward to a position designated the "Alamo" some 900 yards from the intersection, but found themselves dangerously exposed. As Iraqi air-defence cannon shells burst overhead, and incoming mortar and artillery rounds exploded around them, they watched transfixed as an armoured column bore down on their position.

It was then that they turned to their new Javelins. The first weapon was in the hands of Staff Sergeant Jason Brown, who had only fired one once before. Sitting cross-legged on a hillside and staring through the sights of the launcher, he did not that think he and his buddies stood a chance. But he knew that the Javelin missile system was his team's best hope for survival.

Although inexperienced, he thought that his best chance of hitting an armoured target through the haze blanketing the plain was to use the launcher's thermal sights to see through it. To do so he had to wait at least forty-five seconds before the launcher's cooling system would allow him to fire, whereas using the day sights he could have fired immediately.

As the seconds ticked away, he saw muzzle flashes and a few seconds later, rounds exploded on the hillside around him. The tanks were less than a mile away, but still the Javelin would not arm itself.

Finally Brown loosed off and his team's first Javelin fired in anger. The missile streaked low above the ground, slamming into an Iraqi troop truck about 3,200 yards away, the truck erupted in flames and the occupants scrambled out. The Green Berets mounted their GMVs and roared down the slope at about 70 miles an hour, firing at the fleeing Iraqis.

But it was far from a one-way fight. The Special Forces men at the crossroads were by now coming under mortar fire. USAF forward air controllers with the Green Berets identified two mortar tubes to the east near the town of Debecka and four GMVs set off to destroy them.

Back at the crossroads, seated on top of his GMV, ODA 391's junior engineer Staff Sergeant Bobby Farmer looked down the road and saw two white SUVs emerging from the haze to the west. They were driving slowly down the road toward the American positions with their lights blinking on and off. Special Forces Commander Frank Antenori, 391's senior NCO, told his men not to shoot – the troops in the vehicles might be trying to surrender.

Behind the grey metal forms Iraqi armoured personnel carriers began emerging from the mist. The American GMVs pulled off the road to the left and right to take up defensive positions. Worse was to come. As soon as the Iraqis in the APCs saw the Americans, the lead vehicle began pumping out smoke. Then through the smoke, a column of at least five T-55 tanks appeared. They were about a mile away and closing at about 40 miles an hour with their 100-mm main guns firing round after round of high-explosive.

Farmer banged on the roof of his GMV to alert his comrades. "Tanks!" he yelled.

When he heard this, Antenori jumped up on the roof of the vehicle.

"Holy shit!" he exclaimed.

Master Sergeant Kenneth Thompson and Sergeant Jeff Adamec grabbed Javelin launchers and jumped from the GMVs to begin the maddening test of nerves as they waited for the launchers to cool down.

Meanwhile the team attacking the mortars got the message that tanks were coming from the south and disengaged.

The Javelins were taking longer than normal to cool down, so the Green Berets pulled back 900 yards to the Alamo ridge line, along with the Peshmerga in an old overloaded truck.

Alerted to what was happening, Staff Sergeant Brown grabbed another Javelin and jumped on the bonnet of a GMV, while the US Air Force forward air controllers put out an urgent call for close-air support.

With the combined Special Forces and Peshmerga forced back on the Alamo, Brown's Javelin was ready fire. He squeezed the trigger. The missile shot out of the tube and slowed to almost a standstill before its booster kicked in. It arched up-wards, then came down like an arrow scoring a direct hit on the moving personnel carrier. Iraqi soldiers piled out of the burning vehicle and ran for cover in a field of tall wheat beside the road.

Sergeant Adamec and Staff Sergeant Eugene Zawojski, both armed with Javelins, joined Brown on the ridge, And together, they destroyed two trucks and two APCs within a couple of minutes. As Iraqi infantry poured out of the burning vehicles, Sergeant Farmer, Sergeant First Class Scot Marlow and Ser-geant First Class Van Hines rained .50-calibre fire and Mark 19 40-mm grenades on them.

The T-55s had taken cover in defilade positions on the far side of the road, making it impossible for the Javelins to get a lock onto their heat signatures. The Green Berets had already used up about half of their ammunition, but waves of Iraqis were coming on.

Then two US Navy F-14 Tomcats arrived to give close air support. They dropped 750-lb ordnance and Paveway II laser-guided smart bombs. The Iraqis responded with anti-aircraft fire and airburst shells began to explode some 300 yards in front of the Green Berets' position. An Iraqi artillery firing 152-mm high-explosive shells also began to find their range. When a smoke round nearly scored a direct hit, it was clear that the enemy artillery had accurately bracketed their position, so the Green Berets withdrew to Press Hill.

Despite this, some twelve Iraqi soldiers threw down their arms and attempted to surrender under a white flag. For moment it seemed that other Iraqi soldiers might join them, but two white trucks pulled up. Six Arabs in white robes – the uniform of Ba'ath Party enforcers – jumped out and began shooting the surrendering soldiers. An Air Force forward air controller called for an air strike on the white trucks, which were destroyed.

At 0720 hours Special Forces resupply vehicles arrived carrying ammunition and more Javelins, by which time they only had three missiles left. The Green Berets and their Peshmerga allies were now in a position to hold their own while the enemy was bombed for two hours until the Iraqi soldiers eventually abandoned their vehicles and fled the battlefield on foot.

For the next two days Iraqi artillery and multiple rocket launchers continued to fire upon the Special Forces positions. But the crossroads were secured and the Green Berets crossed to Kirkuk to secure oil facilities and prevent their destruction by Iraqi forces.

US Gallantry Awards

The SAS remain a highly secretive organization and members are never named, even when they are decorated. However, the US Special Forces are not so reticent. On 14 October 2005, a trio of Green Berets – two on active service and one retired – each received the Silver Star during a ceremony at Fort Carson, Colorado. Master Sergeant Robert Collins, Sergeant First Class Danny Hall and retired First Sergeant Cornelius Clark were recognized with the military's third highest valour award for their gallantry under enemy fire – Collins and Hall for their actions in Iraq early that year, and Clark for his heroism forty years earlier in Vietnam.

Collins and Hall, both of the 2nd Battalion, 10th Special Forces Group were deployed to Iraq earlier in 2005 in support of Operation Iraqi Freedom. During offensive operations in the Jazeera region in April, both men's aggressive actions in battle led to the defeat of attacking enemy forces and the survival of their Special Forces detachment, according to their Silver Star citations.

While searching for an anti-Iraqi forces training camp and weapons cache, Collins and Hall's joint Coalition element was engaged by a platoon-sized enemy force with mortars, rocket-propelled grenades, machine guns and grenades. After Collins personally directed close air support from F-16 aircraft armed with 500-lb bombs, Hall led a dismounted charge into small-arms fire and volleys of RPG.

Collins then led his element to engage the enemy, personally eliminating at least three enemy fighters. In addition to his combat role, Hall – a Special Forces medical sergeant – managed to set up a casualty collection point and a helicopter landing zone to medevac out his wounded troops.

Collins and Hall risked their lives again when, while their unit was pinned down by enemy fire, they ran through a hail of bullets to recover a critically wounded US soldier. They carried him to safety, administered first aid and saved his life.

Collins acknowledged the personal significance of his Silver Star, but said he felt that the award symbolized the heroism of his team during the battle.

"It's important, but it's representative of the efforts of the team, not just my individual effort," Collins said.

Sergeant Cornelius Clark's Silver Star was long overdue. At the end of his 1965 combat tour in Vietnam, while serving with the 5th Special Forces Group (Airborne), Clark had been awarded an Army Commendation Medal with valour device for his actions in defence of Camp Plei Me, according to his updated award citation.

Staff Sergeant (as he then was) Clark, serving as senior combat engineer for Operational Detachment Alpha 217, helped lead his team's defence of the camp during a week-long siege by the North Vietnamese Army. With Clark's tour finished, he could have been evacuated from the camp by helicopter on the sixth day of the siege but chose instead to stay two additional days with his team in the heavy fighting. Clark then personally led a dangerous mission outside the camp to recover badly-needed air-dropped supplies that had missed their mark.

Other members of Clark's former SF team, all of who had received Silver Stars for their own actions during the siege, had only recently discovered that Clark had received a lesser award. They had petitioned a congressman to get Clark's award upgraded to the Silver Star he so richly deserved. It is good to see such heroism rewarded. However, by their very nature, Special Forces units are secretive and the missions hush-hush. Much of what they do is classified and will remain so. But there can be no doubt that the ranks of the Special Forces are filled with numerous unsung heroes.

LIST OF ABBREVIATIONS

AAAV	Advanced Amphibious Assault Vehicle
AAV	Amphibious Assault Vehicle
AB	Ammunition Bearer
ABCCC	Airborne Battlefield Command and Control Center
AC	Active Component
ACLC	Air-Cushioned Landing Craft
ACV	Air-Cushioned Vehicles
ADA	Air Defence Artillery
AFSOC	Air Force Special Operations Command
AG	Assistant Gunner
AGES/AD	Air-to-Ground Engagement System/Air Defense
AGMS	Air-to-Ground Missile System
AIT	Advanced Individual Training
AK	Avtomat Kalashnikov
AM	Amplitude Modulated
AMOUT	Advanced Military Operations on Urban Terrain
ANDVT	Advanced Narrowband Digital Voice Terminal
ANG	Air National Guard
AOE	Army of Excellence
AP	Anti-Personnel
APC	Armoured Personnel Carrier
APFT	Army Physical Fitness Test
AR	Army Regulation
ARI	Army research Institute
ARNG	Army National Guard

ARTEP	Army Training and Evaluation Program
arty	Artillery
ASLV	Advanced Light Strike Vehicle
A-S	Anti-Spoofing
ASA(RDA)	Assistant Secretary of the Army (Research, Development and Acquisition)
ASDV	Advanced SEAL Delivery Vehicle
ASVAB	Armed Services Vocational Aptitude Battery
AT	Anti-Tank
ATGM	Anti-Tank Guided Missile
ATGWS	Anti-Tank Guided Weapon System
ATMP	All-Terrain Mobile Platform
ATSC	Army Training Support Centre
ATWESS	Anti-Tank Weapon Effects Signature Simulator
AWACS	Airborne Warning and Control System
AWFCS	All Weather Flight Control System
BAOR	British Army of the Rhine
BATT	British Army Training Teams
BDU	Battle Dress Uniform
BFIG	Blank Firing Impact Grenade
BILAT	Bilateral Training
blk	Blank
BMQ	Basic Mission Qualified
BMT	Basic Mission Trained
Bn	Battalion
BNCOC	Basic Non-Commissioned Officers' Course
CA	Civil Affairs
Cal	Calibre/Calibration
CALFEX	Combined Arms Live Firing Exercise
CAPEX	Capabilities Exercise
CAR	Carbine Automatic Rifle
CAT	Category
CCTS	Combat Crew Training Squadron
CG	Commanding General
CIA	Central Intelligence Agency
CIDG	Civil Irregular Defense Group
CMF	Career Management Field
COI	Coordinator of Intelligence
COMSEC	Communications Security
COP	Close Observation Platoon
CQB	Close-Quarters Battle
CQC	Close-Quarters Combat
CRD	Chemical Reconnaissance Detachment

CROWS	Common Remotely Operated Weapon System
CRRC	Combat Rubber Raiding Craft
CRT	Combat Readiness Training
CRW	Counter-Revolutionary Warfare
CS	Close Support/Combat Support
CSA	Chief of Staff of the Army
CSAR	Combat Search and Rescue
CSS	Combat Service Support
CTC	Combat Training Centre
CTIS	Central Tyre Inflation System
CTR	Close-Target Reconnaissance
CTT	Common Task Test
CUCV	Commercial Utility Cargo Vehicle
DA	Department of the Army
DAP	Defensive Armoured Penetration
DAV	Desert Attack Vehicle
DCSOPS	Deputy Chief of Staff for Operations and Plans
DDS	Dry Deck Shelter
det	Detachment
DFC	Distinguished Flying Cross
DG	Dhofar Gendarmerie
DMR	Designated Marksman Rifle
DODIC	Department of Defense Identification Code
DOR	Drop on Request
DPM	Disruptive Pattern Material
DPU	Diver Propulsion Unit
DPV	Desert Patrol Vehicle
DS	Directing Staff
DTWC	Diver Through Water Communication
ECCM	Electronic Counter-Countermeasures
ECW	Extreme Cold Weather
EDRE	Emergency Deployment Readiness Exercise
EFP	Explosive formed projectile
EMP	Electronic Magnetic Pulse
EOD	Explosive Ordnance Disposal
EVR	Emergency Rendezvous Point
EW	Extreme Weather
EXEVAL	External Evaluation
RAL	Fusil Automotique Léger or Light Automatic Rifle
FARP	Forward Arming and Refuelling Point
FARRP	Forward Area Rearm and Refuel Point
FAV	Fast Attack Vehicle
FDC	Fire Direction Centre

FFAR	Folding Fin Aerial Rocket
FIST	Fire Support Team
FLIR	Forward Looking Infra-Red
FM	Field Manual/Frequency Modulated
FMFLant	Fleet Marine Force Atlantic
FMLPac	Fleet Marine Force Pacific
FMQ	Fully Mission Capable
FO	Forward Observer
FOM	Figure of Merit
FORSCOM	US Army Forces Command
FRAG	Fragmentation
FSE	Fire Support Element
FTX	Field Training Exercise
GCAS	Ground Collision Avoidance System
GL	Grenade Launcher
GLS	Gun Laying System
GMG	Grenade Machine Gun
GOR	General Operating Requirement
GPMG	General Purpose Machine Gun
GPS	Global Positioning Satellite System
GSG9	*Grenz Schutz Gruppe 9*
gunwale	the upper edge of the sides of a boat or ship
H&K	Heckler and Koch
HAHO	High Altitude, High Opening
HAL	Helicopter Attack, Light
HALO	High Altitude, Low Opening
HB	Heavy Barrel
HE	High Explosive
HEDP	High Explosive Dual Purpose
HEPD	High Explosive, Point Detonating
HEAT(TPT)	High Explosive Anti-Tank (Target Practice Tracer)
HG	Hand Grenade
HHC	Headquarters and Headquarters Company
HMG	Heavy Machine Gun
HMMWV	High Mobility Multipurpose Wheeled Vehicles, a Humvee or Hummer
HOES	Holographic Optical Elements
HOPROS	Head-Mounted Optical Projection System
HQ	Headquarters
HQDA	Headquarters Department of the Army
HSIC	High Speed Interceptor Craft
HUD	Head-Up Display
IAD	Immediate Action Drills

IBS	Inflatable Boat, Small
ICBM	Inter-Continental Ballistic Missile
IDAS	Interactive Defensive Avionics System
IDN	Initial Distribution Number
IED	Improvised Explosive Device
IFF	Identification Friend or Foe
Illum	Illumination
INS	Inertial Guidance System
ISA	Intelligence Support Activity
JOTC	Joint Operations Training Centre
JRT	Joint Readiness Training
JRTC	Joint Readiness Training Centre
LAW	Light Anti-tank Weapon
LARC	Lighter, Amphibious Resupply, Cargo
lb	Pound(s)
LCU	Landing Craft, Utility
LDNN	Lien Doc Nguoi Nhia, South Vietnamese SEALs
LED	Light Emitting Diode
LES	Launch Environment Simulator
LFX	Live-Fire Exercise
LLLTV	Low-Light-Level TV
LLP	Low-Level Parachute
LLRP	Low-Level Reserve Parachute
LRDG	Long Range Desert Group
LRSD	Long-Range Surveillance Detachment
LSV	Light Strike Vehicle
LUNOS	Lightweight Universal Night-Observation System
LUP	Lying Up Position
m	Metre(s)
MAC	Military Airlift Command
MACOM	Major Army Command
MACV	Military Assistance Command, Vietnam
MAD	Magnetic Anomoly Detector
MARSOC	Marine Corps Forces Special Operations Command
MATT	Multi-Mission Advanced Tactical Terminal
MAWS(IR)	Missile Warning System (Infra-Red)
M&AW	Mountain and Arctic Warfare Cadre
MBITR	Multiband Inter/Intra Team Radio
METL	Mission-Essential Task List
MEU(SOC)	Marine Expeditionary Unit (Special Operations Capable)
MFC	Mortar Fire Controller
MG	Machine Gun

MICLIC	Mine Clearing Line Charge
MIL-STD	Military Standard
MILES	Multiple Integrated Laser Engagement System
ML	Mountain Leader
mm	Millimetre(s)
MMI	Man-Machine Interface
MOPP	Mission Oriented Protective Posture
MORTEP	Mortar Army Training and Evaluation Programme
MOS	Military Occupational Specialty
MOUT	Military Operations on Urban Terrain
MRE	Meals Ready to Eat
MSI	Military Ski Instructor
MTP	Mission Training Plan
MUTT	Military Utility Tactical Truck
MWMIK	Mobility Weapons Mounted Installation Kit
NATO	North Atlantic Treaty Organization
NBC	Nuclear, Biological and Chemical
NCO	Non-Commissioned Officer
NFDD	Noise and Flash Diversionary Device
NGB	National Guard Bureau
NSW	Naval Special Warfare
NTC	National Training Centre
NVA	North Vietnamese Army
NVG	Night Vision Goggles
OD(A)	Operational Detachment (A), an A-Team
ONR	Office of naval Research
OP	Observation Post
OSS	Office of Strategic Studies
OSV	Over-Snow Strike/Support Vehicle
OVD	Over-the-Beach
para	Parachute
PASGET	Personal Armour System Ground Troops
PBR	Patrol Boat, Riverine
PC	Patrol, Coastal
PCF	Patrol Craft, Fast
PDF	Panama Defence Forces
PLCE	Personal Load Carrying Equipment
PLGR	Precision Lightweight GPS Receiver
PLRF	Pocket Laser Rangefinder
PNG	Passive Night Goggles
PPS	Precise Positioning Service
PST	Physical Screening Test
PTF	Patrol Torpedo, Fast

PTT	Push To Talk
RAAWS	Ranger Anti-Armour-Antipersonnel Weapon System
RC	Reserve Component
RCLR	Recoilless Rifle
RDX	Rapid Demolition Explosive, Royal Demolition Explosive or Research Development Explosive (cyclotrimethylene-trinitramine)
REME	Royal Electrical and Mechanical Engineers
RIB	Rigid Inflatable Boat
RNG	Range, Ranger
RPG	Rocket-Propelled Grenade
RRC	Rigid Raider Craft
RRF	Ready Ready Force
RSOV	Ranger Special Operations Vehicle
RT	Reconnaissance Team
RTC	Regimental Training Circular
RTU	Return to Unit
RV	Rendezvous
RWR	Radar-Warning Receiver
SA	Selective Availability
SAAD	Small Arms Air Defence
SACO	Sino-American Cooperation Organization
SARBE	Search and Rescue Beacon
SAS	Special Air Service
SASR	Special Applications Scoped Rifle
SATA	Safety and Arming Test Aid
SAW	Squad Automatic Weapon
SAWC	Special Air Warfare Centre
SBS	Special Boat Section
SCAMP	Single Channel Anti-Jam Man-Portable
SCOBBS	School of Combined Operations, Beach and Boat Section
SCUBA	Self-Contained Underwater Breathing Apparatus
SDV	SEAL Delivery Vehicle
SDV	Swim Delivery Vehicle
SDVT	Swimmer Delivery Vehicle Team or SEAL Delivery Vehicle Team
SEAL	Sea, Air, Land
SERE	Survival, Evasion, Resistance and Escape
SFAS	Special Forces Assessment and Selection
SFD	Special Forces Detachment
SFOD-D	Special Forces Operational Detechment-Delta
SINCGARS	Single Channel Ground and Airborne Radio System

SLR	Self-Loading Rifle
SM	Soldier's Manual
SMG	Sub-Machine Gun
SMOTEC	Special Missions Operational Test and Evaluation Center
SO	Special Operations
SOAR	Special Operations Aviation Regiment
SOC	Special Operations Craft
SOCOM	Special Operations Command
SOF	Special Operations Force
SOG	Special Operations Group
SOPMOD	Special Operations Peculiar Modifications
SOS	Special Operations Squadron
SOT(A)	Support Operational Team (A)
SOV	Special Operations Vehicle
SOW	Special Operations Wing
SPARTAN	Special Proficiency at Rugged Training and Nation-building
SPAS	Special-Purpose Automatic Shotgun
SPIE	Special Procedures Insertion/Extraction
Sponson	Projection on the side of a ship, particularly a gun platform or buoyancy chamber
SPS	Standard Position Service
SPW	Special Purpose Weapon
SQT	SEAL Qualification Training
SRS	Special Raiding Squadron
SRTR	Short-Range Training Round
SRW	Small Raids Wing
STABO	Short Tactical Airborne Operation
STAR	Surface to Air Recovery
STLS	Stinger Training Launch Simulator
STOL	Short Take-off and Landing
STP	Soldier Training Publication
STRAC	Standards in Training Commission
SUSAT	Sight Unit, Small Arms, Trilux
SWARM	Stablized Weapons and Reconnaissance Mount
SWAT	Special Weapons Assault Team
SWCC	Special Warfare Combatant-craft Crewman
TAC	Tactical Air Command
TACAIROPS	Tactical Air Operations
TACBE	Tactical Beacon
TACP	Tactical Air Control Party
TADSS	Training Aids, Devices, Simulators and Simulations

TDFD	Time-Delayed Firing Device
TFR	Terrain-Following Radar
TFW	Tactical Fighter Wing
TNT	Trinitrotoluene
TOW	Tube-launched, Optically tracked, Wire-guided missile
TP	Training Projectile
TPT	Troop Proficiency Trainer/Target Practice Tracer
TRADOC	US Army Training and Doctrine Command
TRC	Training Readiness Condition
TSC	Training Support Centre
UDT	Underwater Demolition Team
UKSF	UK Special Forces
UMI	Universal Mount Interface
UNPFK	United Nations Partisan Forces, Korea
USAAF	United States Army Air Force
USAF	United States Air Force
USAFSOF	USAF Special Operations Force
USAR	US Army Reserve
USASOC	US Army Special Operations Command
USMC	US Marine Corps
USN	United States Navy
USSOCOM	United States Special Operations Command
UTM	Universal Transfer Mercator
UW	Unconventional Warfare
VCSA	Vice Chief of Staff of the Army
WMIK	Weapons Mounted Installation Kit
WP	White Phosphorus
WSP	White Star Parachute